THE NAVAL HISTORY OF
GREAT BRITAIN

VOLUME THE THIRD

ADMIRAL SIR HYDE PARKER, BART

FROM A PICTURE BY G. ROMNEY.

THE

NAVAL HISTORY

OF

GREAT BRITAIN

FROM THE DECLARATION OF WAR BY FRANCE
IN 1793
TO THE ACCESSION OF GEORGE IV.

BY

WILLIAM JAMES

*A NEW EDITION, WITH ADDITIONS AND NOTES
BRINGING THE WORK DOWN TO 1827*

VÉRITÉ SANS PEUR

IN SIX VOLUMES
VOL. III.

London
MACMILLAN AND CO., LIMITED
NEW YORK: THE MACMILLAN COMPANY
1902

Printed and bound by
Antony Rowe Ltd, Eastbourne

CONTENTS.

VOL. III.

1800 (*in continuation*).

1801.

1802.

1803.

1804.

[DIAGRAMS

DIAGRAMS.

BATTLE OF TRAFALGAR.

NAVAL HISTORY OF GREAT BRITAIN.

LIGHT SQUADRONS AND SINGLE SHIPS.

HAVING given an account of the first engagement fought between an American and a French frigate, we shall offer no apology for inserting in these pages an account of the second. On the 1st of February, at 7 h. 30 m. A.M., the United States 36-gun frigate Constellation, still commanded by Commodore Thomas Truxton,[1] being about five leagues to the westward of Basseterre-road, Guadaloupe, working to windward, discovered in the south-east quarter, standing south-west, the French 40-gun frigate Vengeance, Captain Sébastien-Louis-Marie Pichot.

The American commodore immediately went in chase; and M. Pichot ran from him, for the reason, as alleged afterwards by some of the French officers, that the Vengeance had her decks encumbered with hogsheads of sugar, which she had brought from Guadaloupe, and was carrying to Europe. Let that have been as it may, at 8 P.M. the Constellation got within hail of the Vengeance, and received a fire from her stern and quarter guns. In a little time the former, having gained a position on the French frigate's weather-quarter, opened a very destructive fire; and to which, from her position, the Constellation received a much less effective return than if she had run fairly alongside. The mutual cannonade continued, in this manner, until nearly 1 A.M. on the 2nd; when the Vengeance, owing to the damaged state of the Constellation's rigging and masts, particularly her mainmast, was enabled to range ahead out of gun-shot, and the battle ended.

The force of the Constellation, in guns, men, and size, has already been given.[2] The armament of the Vengeance, with the addition of four brass 36-pounder carronades, was the same as that of her sister-ship, the Résistance, captured in March, 1797;

[1] See vol. ii., p. 363.   [2] Ibid., p. 364.

and her complement may also be stated the same as the latter's, exclusive of about 60 passengers.

The loss sustained by the American frigate amounted to one officer and 13 seamen and marines killed, and two officers and 23 seamen and marines wounded : this would appear to be irrespective of the men lost overboard from the fall of the mainmast.   That of the Vengeance is represented, in the American accounts, at 150 in killed and wounded ; but, according to a published letter from one of her passengers, it amounted to only 20 men killed and 40 wounded.

The officer killed on board the Constellation was Mr. James Jervis, a young midshipman, who, with some of the men, fell overboard with the mainmast.   "It seems this young gentleman," says Commodore Truxton, "was apprised of the mast going in a few minutes, by an old seaman ; but he had already so much of the principle of an officer ingrafted on his mind, not to leave his quarters on any account, that he told the men, if the mast went, they must go with it; which shortly afterwards occurred, and only one man was saved."

Although, undoubtedly, the American frigate was the superior both in force and effectiveness, yet, had the Constellation made a prize of the Vengeance, no one can deny that it would have redounded to the honour of Commodore Truxton, and been a subject of fair triumph to so young a navy as that of the United States.   But, if it be true, as the French captain is represented to have stated, that the flag of the Vengeance came down three times during the contest, what was the Constellation about that she did not attempt to take possession?   It would seem that the Constellation, notwithstanding she was to windward, persisted in remaining at too great a distance from her antagonist to observe in the dark what the latter was doing.   According to Captain Pichot's account, indeed, the Vengeance lost all three masts by the Constellation's fire ; and yet Commodore Truxton, although so minute in his "Journal" as to tell us that, previous to the action, he got "the large trumpet in the lee gangway ready to speak" the French frigate, takes no notice of the loss of her masts.

The most extraordinary circumstance, however, remains to be told.   The Vengeance, M. Pichot declares, was compelled, owing to the inexperience of her crew, to remain stationary for three days, while jury-masts were erecting; and, during the whole of that time, the Constellation lay to windward, with her fore and

[1] See vol. ii., p. 91.

mizen masts still standing (her mainmast had fallen a few minutes after the firing had ceased), and yet did not bear down, or evince the least inclination to renew the engagement. The Constellation, soon afterwards, made sail for and anchored in Port Royal, Jamaica; and the Vengeance, no less happy than surprised at such an escape, steered for Curaçoa, where she arrived in a very shattered state.

No sooner did the commodore's account of his rencontre reach the United States than his fellow-citizens, particularly those of his own, or the federal party, set to work to bring to an issue on paper that which had been left undecided on the ocean. They pronounced and published the action as a victory; ate dinners, and drank themselves drunk in honour of it; and, when the commodore arrived in port, assailed him on all sides with addresses of congratulation, founded on assertions that the commodore's letter had never sanctioned, and from which, although not possessed perhaps of a very extraordinary share, his modesty must have recoiled.

We formerly mentioned, that the merchants of London presented the commodore with a piece of plate for having captured the Insurgente. Such was actually the spirit of party in the United States, that the democrats abused Commodore Truxton, calling him *Tory*, &c., for having accepted it. About the middle of the year 1800 the commodore was promoted to the command of the 44-gun frigate President; but the moment the democrats came into power, on March the 4th in the succeeding year, he was displaced, and, as a proof how liberal republics can be, was never afterwards put in command. The more moderate among the democrats, however, did at length relent a little; and Commodore Truxton got appointed (of all places for a commodore!) sheriff of Philadelphia; in which office he realized an independency.

On the 5th of February, at 6 A.M., the British 16-gun ship-sloop Fairy (armed similarly to Rattlesnake, vol. ii., p. 392), Captain Joshua Sydney Horton, and 18-gun brig-sloop, Harpy (same force as Racoon, vol. ii., p. 415), Captain Henry Bazely, weighed and set sail from St. Aubin's bay in the island of Jersey, with the wind a fresh breeze at north-west, to reconnoitre the port of St. Malo, and discover if a French frigate, which on the preceding evening had chased the 14-gun brig Seaflower, Lieutenant Murray, had got into that harbour. At 11 h. 30 m. A.M., Cape Frehel bearing south-east distant five or six miles, a large ship, evidently a frigate, was discovered in the south-south-west quarter, running down close alongshore to the westward, with a light breeze nearly aft, or from the south-south-east. This was the French 38-gun frigate Pallas, Captain Jacques Epron, from St. Malo bound to Brest, and the same, as it appears, that had chased the Seaflower.

At about 20 m. P.M., seeing no chance of bringing the Pallas to action while she remained so close under the land, Captain Horton tacked and stood off, in the hope that the frigate would follow the two sloops to an offing. This the Pallas immediately did; and at 1 P.M. an engagement, within pistol-shot, commenced between her and the Fairy and Harpy, the latter close astern of her companion. The action, during which the Harpy obtained several opportunities of raking the Pallas, continued until 3 P.M.; when the French frigate ceased firing, and made all sail to the northward and eastward, having the wind now from the south-west.

So great were the damages which the Fairy and Harpy had received in their rigging and sails, that it was not until 3 h. 15 m. P.M. that the sloops were in a condition to make sail in chase. About this time the Pallas, observing two sail nearly ahead, or in the north-east by north, hauled up to the northward and westward. Captain Horton immediately made the signal for the Harpy, who was the more advanced in the chase, to endeavour to gain the wind of the enemy. At 4 P.M. three sail, including the two already noticed as seen by the Pallas, were discovered by the two sloops. No doubt being entertained that the vessels approaching were friends, the Fairy made the signal for an enemy; which was repeated by the Harpy, both sloops firing guns every five minutes to enforce attention to it.

These ships, then working up from the northward with a light wind from the south-east by south, were the British 38-gun frigate Loire, Captain James Newman Newman, 20-gun ship Danaé, Captain Lord Proby, and 16-gun ship-sloop Railleur, Captain William James Turquand; and all of which had sailed from Plymouth on the 27th and 28th of January, purposely to intercept the Pallas and a corvette, expected to be on their way from St. Malo to Brest. At 4 h. 15 m. P.M. the Pallas bore away large; and, in order to deceive her new pursuers and distract their attention, hoisted English colours, and endeavoured to repeat the signal made by the Fairy and Harpy. At 4 h. 30 m. P.M. Roche Douvre bore from the Fairy north-north-east distant six or seven miles; and at 5 h. 30 m. P.M. the

Pallas bore west, and the Harpy west by south, the breeze now light from the south-east.

At 7 P.M. Captain Bazely received orders to go ahead, as far as signals were discernible between the two sloops, and make the private signal to the two ships, the Loire and Danaé, upon her lee bow. This was done, and subsequently the Fairy also made the private signal; but it was not answered by either the Loire, Danaé, or Railleur, which latter was considerably ahead and to windward of her two consorts. Notwithstanding this apparent remissness, Captain Horton was tolerably satisfied that the ships approaching were friends, and therefore stood on in chase of the Pallas. We may add to this, that Captain Newman also knew (although that is no excuse for not answering the private signal), that the two ships and brig in sight were the Pallas, Fairy, and Harpy; having learnt from Lord Proby, who had been detached for information to Jersey, upon what mission the two sloops had sailed.

At about 7 h. 45 m. P.M., observing ahead, and close under the Seven Islands, a ship approaching, which was the Railleur, the Pallas tacked; and at 8 P.M., while passing about three miles to windward of the Harpy, and at a still greater distance from the Loire, both on the opposite or larboard tack, was fired at, of course without effect, by the Loire. The latter and the Harpy then tacked in chase; and at about 9 P.M. the Loire spoke the Fairy, who had also just tacked, and whose commander informed Captain Newman of the name and force of the Pallas, at that time "about a gun-shot and a half" upon the Fairy's weather quarter. Whether owing to bad management, bad sailing, or disabled rigging from her previous action with the two sloops, the Pallas was gradually gained upon by the chasing ships, the Loire, Railleur, and Harpy especially.

At about 10 h. 30 m. P.M. the Loire had weathered her opponent so much as to be able to set her topgallant studding-sails, and at 11 P.M. arrived up with the Pallas. The Railleur, being ahead of the Loire, was directed to fire her broadside and drop astern. This the sloop did; and immediately afterwards, the nearest of the Seven Islands bearing south-west by south, distant about 750 yards, the Loire commenced a close action with the Pallas, who opened a spirited fire in return. In a little time a battery upon the island, of several guns and a howitzer, began a smart fire upon the British ships, and did considerable damage to the Loire. In this way the action continued between the French frigate and shore-battery on one side, and the

Loire, Railleur, Harpy, and Fairy on the other ; the combatants all on the starboard tack, with the wind, as before, blowing moderately from the south-east.

At about 1 h. 30 m. A.M. on the 6th, the Harpy fetched close under the stern of the Railleur, then engaging the Pallas with great gallantry, and poured her broadside into the French frigate's quarter. This was repeated with such destructive effect, as to induce some one on board the frigate (especially as a man had been shot while ascending the mizen-shrouds with a lantern to repeat the signal of surrender) to hail the brig with the exclamation, " Ne tirez pas encore, messieurs, nous sommes à vous." The Harpy then ceased her fire, as about the same time did the Loire, Railleur, and Fairy. The Loire and Harpy each lowered down a boat and sent her first-lieutenant (Edmund Rayner and James Watson) to take possession of the prize. Conceiving, from a bustle abaft on board the Railleur, that a man had fallen into the water, Lieutenant Watson yawed out of his course : in consequence of this, the Loire's boat reached the Pallas a few minutes before the Harpy's ; but the latter had the honour of conveying Captain Epron to the Loire.

The established complement of the Loire was 284 men and boys; but she had on board no more than 260, about 100 of whom had " volunteered " from the prison-ships, and ran from their quarters almost as soon as the action commenced. Of those 260 in crew, the Loire lost three seamen killed, and three midshipmen (Watkins Owen Pell, Francis William Eves, and John Allen Medway), 15 seamen, and one marine wounded. The Railleur, out of a complement of 76 men and boys, had one midshipman (William Prothers) and one gunner's mate killed, and three seamen and one marine wounded. The Fairy, out of a complement of 120 men and boys, had, in the day action, four seamen killed, her commander (slightly), purser (Mr. Hughes), and six seamen wounded, four of them badly ; but in the night action the Fairy had only one seaman wounded. The Harpy, out of a crew the same as the Fairy's, had one seaman killed and three wounded in her first action, but escaped without any casualty in her second ; making the total loss on the British side nine killed and 36 wounded.

The official letter of Captain Newman does not mention a word of any loss having been sustained by the Pallas : a very improper omission, as it leads to an inference that the enemy's frigate struck her colours without having lost a man in the action. That such was not the case is clear, as well from the state of the ship's hull, which was pierced by shot in several places, as from the state of her lower masts, all three of which, just before daylight on the 7th, went over her side in a squall.

Captain Newman states that the crew of the Pallas numbered 350; but the officers of the latter swore in the prize-court that they had 362 men when the action, meaning, we presume, that with the two sloops, commenced. Hence the 12 men constituting the difference between the two statements were, in all probability, killed in the preceding or day action. A greater loss than that must, we suppose, have been incurred in the night action, when the Loire's heavy broadsides came into play; but, for the reason already stated, we are unable to give the particulars.

Instead of exhibiting the usual comparative statement, we shall merely say that, unaided by any of her consorts, the Loire, mounting 46 guns (long 18 and 9 pounders, with 32-pounder carronades), was more than a match for the Pallas; and that the latter's defence was highly creditable to her officers and crew.

The Pallas was a remarkably handsome frigate of 1029 tons, and had never before been at sea. She was of course purchased by Government; and, under the name of Pique, long continued a favourite 36-gun frigate in the lists of the British navy.

For what, on one side at least, may be called a single-ship action, the details of the occurrences which led to the capture of the French frigate Pallas have given us considerable trouble, and are not yet drawn up to our entire satisfaction. Not, however, because there has been so little said or written on the subject, for few actions of the kind have given rise to so much discussion as the pages of the Naval Chronicle can testify; but owing to the obscure and contradictory statements which have been published, all resting upon authority equally respectable. At all events, no one can deny that the conduct of Captains Horton and Bazely was highly gallant and praiseworthy. Nor must the efforts of the Harpy be disparaged simply because she was an 18-gun sloop. The Harpy was armed in the same manner as the Pelican, that had rendered herself so famous in beating off the Médée; and the former's 32-pounder carronades, in the close and raking position in which they were frequently fired, did considerable mischief to the Pallas, as Captain Epron himself was candid enough to acknowledge.

Although, owing to some omission in Captain Newman's letter, a little delay occurred in doing justice to the claims of

Captain Bazely, that officer, as well as his brother commander Captain Horton, was at length promoted to post-rank.

On the 1st of March, in the middle of the night, the British 12-pounder 36-gun frigate Néréide, Captain Frederick Watkins, cruising off the Penmarcks, discovered to windward five ships and a schooner. As soon as she had made the necessary preparation for battle, the Néréide hauled up for the strangers; which, at daylight on the 2nd, were seen to be all armed vessels, and were then lying to, as if determined to have a contest with the British frigate. Nor will it be considered that the French commodore had formed a very rash resolve, when the force of his squadron is stated.

The largest ship was the Bellone, of Bordeaux, measuring 643 tons, and mounting 24 long 8-pounders on the main deck, and six brass 36-pounder carronades on the quarter-deck and forecastle; total 30 guns, with a complement of at least 220 men.[1] The three remaining ships, also from Bordeaux, were the Vengeance, of 18 long 8-pounders[2] and 174 men, Favorite, of 16 long 6-pounders and 120 men, and Huron, of 16 long 4-pounders and 87 men; and the schooner was the Tirailleuse, of 14 long 4-pounders and 80 men; making a total of 94 guns and 681 men.

Just as the Néréide arrived within gun-shot of these seemingly pugnacious privateersmen, their hearts failed them, and the four ships and schooner made all sail on different courses. The British frigate went in immediate chase, and continued the pursuit until night shut out the fugitives from her view. On the 2nd, however, at daylight, the Néréide regained a sight of one of the ships; and, after a 12 hours' chase and a run of 122 miles, captured the Vengeance.

On the 5th of March, at 8 A.M., in latitude 50° 2' north, longitude 14° 43' west, the British 18-pounder 36-gun frigate Phœbe, Captain Robert Barlow, was borne down upon, and fired at, by the French ship privateer Heureux, of 22 long brass 12-pounders and 220 men. The latter, as it appeared, mistook the Phœbe for an Indiaman, and did not discover her mistake until she had arrived within point-blank musket-shot. The Heureux then wore upon the Phœbe's weather-bow, and hauled to the wind on the same tack; hoping, by a well-directed fire, to disable the Phœbe's masts, rigging, and sails, and thereby effect her escape.

---

[1] In Captain Watkins's letter in the Gazette, 420; probably a typographical mistake.

[2] Ibid.; 12-pounders, but we know they were only 8-pounders.

The fire from the British frigate, however, was too powerful to be withstood by so comparatively inferior a foe, and the Heureux struck her colours.

The Phœbe had three seamen killed, or mortally wounded, and three slightly wounded; the Heureux, 18 men killed, and 25 wounded, most of whom lost limbs. The latter was a very complete flush-decked ship, coppered and copper-fastened, highly finished, and of large dimensions, measuring 598 tons. She was therefore readily purchased for the use of the British navy, and, under the same name, became classed as a 22-gun post-ship.

On the 15th of March the British 20-gun ship Danaé, Captain Lord Proby, while watching the French fleet in Brest, became lost to the service under the following discreditable circumstances. At 9 h. 30 m. P.M., Jackson, one of the captains of the foretop, and who had been secretary to Parker in the Nore mutiny, assisted by some prisoners and a part of the crew, rushed on the quarter-deck, knocked down the master, and cut him severely over the head. They then threw him down the main hatchway, and battened down the grating, placing over it the boats filled with shot. By this means the remainder of the crew were prevented from retaking the ship. When the mutiny broke out all the officers, except Lord Proby, the marine-officer, and the master, were in bed. On being informed by the marine-officer of what had happened, Lord Proby attempted to get up the after hatchway, but found it already guarded by nearly 20 men. One of them cut his lordship on the head; and no possibility existed of forcing the hatchway.

Lord Proby and the marine-officer then contrived to muster about ten cutlasses, four muskets, and some pocket-pistols. These were distributed among the most trustworthy of about 40 men; who, when the business commenced, were asleep in their hammocks. The hope then was that the mutineers would be forced to keep the sea; but the wind unfortunately changed, and they were enabled the next morning, the 16th, to fetch under Fort Conquête in Camaret bay, where they anchored the ship. Jackson then sent the jolly-boat on board the French 16-gun brig-corvette Colombe, at anchor in the bay; and which brig on the 14th, with a convoy under her charge, had been chased in by the Danaé herself. At 2 P.M. the first-lieutenant of the Colombe, accompanied by a detachment of soldiers, went on board the Danaé, and asked Lord Proby to whom he surrendered. His lordship replied, "To the French nation, but not to mutineers." Both vessels then steered for Brest, where they arrived on the 17th, after having been chased during several hours by the frigates Anson and Boadicea, Captains Philip Charles Durham and Richard Goodwin Keats; who, deceived by Jackson's hoisting the horary and numerical signals, supposed the Danaé to be in chase of an enemy. Lord Proby had, however, thrown out of the cabin-window and sunk, with lead attached to it, the box containing the private signals.

The officers of the Danaé were landed at Brest; but the ship's company, including the mutineers, were, to the astonishment and chagrin of the latter, marched to Dinan prison. Vice-admiral Bruix, together with the commandant of marines and all the other French officers at the port, behaved with great politeness and attention to Lord Proby and his officers; the whole of the former expressing their utter detestation of the conduct of the mutineers. Captain Louis-Léon Jacob, formerly of the 36-gun frigate Bellone, captured with the Hoche in the year 1798, nobly offered to give louis d'ors for all the bank of England notes of the officers. Several of the latter, soon afterwards, were permitted to return to England on their parole.

On the 20th of March, in the evening, as the British 12-pounder 32-gun frigate Mermaid, Captain Robert Dudley Oliver, and 16-gun brig-sloop Peterel (armed like the Fairy), Captain Francis William Austen, were cruising in the bay of Marseille, Captain Oliver directed the Peterel to keep close in-shore by way of deception, thereby to capture any vessels that might be running along the coast.

On the next morning some vessels of a convoy of 50 sail, from Cette bound to Toulon and Marseille, under the protection of an armed ship, brig, and xebec, were descried and chased, and two of them, a bark and bombard, both laden with wheat, captured. On the same afternoon, when near to Cape Couronne, the Peterel came to action with the three armed vessels; but which, after a short contest, observing the Mermaid, although at a great distance, beating up from to leeward, made sail to get away. The ship and xebec, one, the Cerf of 14 long brass 6-pounders and about 90 men, the other, the Lejoille (named after the captain of the Généreux), commanded by the commodore of the division, Captain (de vais.) Pierre-Paul Raccord, and mounting six long brass 6-pounders, and about 50 men, effected their escape by running on shore. The brig-corvette, which was the Ligurienne of 14 long 6-pounders and two 36-pounder carronades, all brass, and 104 men, Lieutenant Francois-Auguste

Pelabond, after sustaining the fire of the Peterel, in a running fight of an hour and a half's duration, within 250 yards, and sometimes half that distance only, of the shore, struck her colours ; at which time the Peterel was within six miles of the town of Marseille.

Although this service was performed under a heavy fire from a battery of four 24 or 18 pounders ; and although, for a few minutes of the time the sloop remained on a rock, which her stern had touched, the Peterel's damages were confined to a few shot-holes in her sails, and to the upsetting of four of her (12-pounder) carronades. Her first-lieutenant, gunner, and 30 men being absent in prizes, the Peterel had on board but 89 men and boys ; of whom she did not have a man hurt. The Ligurienne had her commander and one seaman killed, and one seaman and one marine wounded.

Admitting the active interference of the battery on shore to be a fair set-off to the mere appearance of the Mermaid to leeward, this affair was very creditable to the officers and crew of the Peterel. Lieutenant Pelabond, had he lived, would doubtless have expressed his sentiments on the premature flight of his two consorts. As it was, the conduct of Captain Raccord, although among the members of his court-martial we observe the fighting names of Bombart and Infernet, was pronounced " irreproachable." One thing we are bound to state : the Cerf is there described as " une demie-chebeck," and not as a ship-corvette. The vessel, whatever might have been her rig or force, was, we believe, totally wrecked ; but the Lejoille afterwards got off and reached Marseille.

The Ligurienne was a fine vessel of her class, well equipped with stores of all kinds, in excellent repair, and not two years old. She was built in a very peculiar manner, being fastened throughout with screw-bolts, so that she might be taken to pieces, and set up again, with ease ; and was originally intended, according to the account given by the prisoners, to follow Buonaparte to Egypt. Screw-bolts were not qualifications required in a British cruiser ; and therefore the Ligurienne being found unadapted in other respects, was not purchased into the service.

Before quitting Captain Austen, we shall relate another instance of his good conduct; and in which, without coming to actual blows, he performed an important, and not wholly imperilous service. On the 13th of August, at 10 A.M., as the Peterel, being then attached to the squadron of Sir Sidney Smith on the coast of Egypt, was standing in towards Alexandria with the wind at north-north-west, a ship of the line, totally dismasted, was perceived aground between Aboukir island and the fort or castle. The Peterel immediately hauled to the wind, and stood in the direction of the grounded vessel; which was a Turkish 80-gun ship, of remarkable beauty, commanded by Indjee-Bey.

At noon the Peterel anchored in four fathoms, about a mile and a half to the south-east of Aboukir island; and a number of djerms were seen to put off from the ships and pull towards the shore. At half-past noon three Turkish corvettes, that had come from the eastward, anchored about a mile outside of the Peterel. By this time the latter had hoisted out her pinnace; and in it was immediately despatched the master, Mr. John Thompson, with nine men, to endeavour to set the ship on fire, and prevent the French from obtaining any of the stores, guns, or ammunition.

The master was soon on board; and by 2 h. 30 m. P.M., he and his active party had completely set the ship in flames. In another hour Mr. Thompson returned to the Peterel, bringing with him 13 Greeks, all that remained of the 80-gun ship's crew; one part, with the commander, having surrendered to the French, and the other part having managed to escape to the three corvettes. To the nearest of these, not one of which, from an alleged dread of being fired at from the shore, would afford the slightest assistance in preventing the French from plundering the wreck, Captain Austen sent the 13 Greeks. As a proof that the captain's promptitude had been of use, the French had already got out of the ship one of the quarter-deck guns, and were taking measures, when the Peterel entered the bay, to remove the remainder. At 5 P.M. the Peterel weighed, and stood back to the westward; and, not long afterwards, the captain pacha testified his sense of the service Captain Austen had performed, by presenting him with a handsome sabre and rich pelisse.

On the 5th of April, in the afternoon, as a British squadron, composed of the 74-gun ships, Leviathan, Captain James Carpenter, bearing the flag of Rear-admiral John Thomas Duckworth, and Swiftsure, Captain Benjamin Hallowell, and the 18-pounder 36-gun frigate Emerald, Captain Thomas Moutray Waller, was cruising in the neighbourhood of the bay of Cadiz, 12 sail were discovered from the mast-head. Chase was given, and at 3 A.M. on the 6th, the Emerald crossed and captured a

Spanish ship, of 10 guns and 70 men, part of a convoy of 13 ships and brigs, which had sailed on the 3rd from Cadiz, bound to South America, under the protection of three frigates, two of which were the Carmen, Captain don Fraquin Porcel, and Florentina, Captain don Manuel Norates, both of the 34-gun or 12-pounder class.

At daybreak all the Spanish convoy had disappeared except a brig; and she was so near and the weather so calm, that the boats of the Leviathan and Emerald, under the orders of Lieutenant Charles March Gregory, second of the Leviathan, were detached in pursuit of her. After "a smart skirmish of forty minutes," but in which no loss appears to have been sustained on either side, the "Los-Anglese," or Barcelona, of 14 carriage-guns, six swivels, and 46 men, laden with bale goods, was captured by Lieutenant Gregory and his boat-party.

By the time this brig had been secured, three sail were seen, east, west, and south. The Swiftsure, being to leeward (the wind very light from the northward), was directed to chase south, and the Emerald, east; while the Leviathan herself steered to the westward. At noon the Emerald made the signal for six sail in the north-east. On this the Leviathan put about and stood after the Emerald, and at dusk saw nine sail from the mast-head.

It was at this time nearly calm; but at 11 P.M. a fresh breeze sprang up from the north-west. Profiting by it, the Leviathan and Emerald steered north, in the hope soon to cross the strangers. At midnight three sail were seen; and at 2 A.M. on the 7th, two of them were ascertained to be frigates, standing to the north-north-west, and close together. The British 74 and frigate now steered a parallel course, proportioning their sail to that of the strangers, in order to be ready to commence the attack just before daybreak, the rear-admiral judiciously considering, that a fire commenced in the dark might alarm the convoy and lead to their escape.

At dawn of day the Leviathan and Emerald bore down upon the Carmen and Florentina, who had evidently mistaken them for a part of their convoy. On being hailed by the Leviathan, the weathermost frigate crowded sail to get off; as did also her consort, then close upon her bow. A volley of musketry failing to induce the nearest frigate to strike, the Leviathan gave a yaw, and fired all her guns before the gangway, in the hope to bring down some of the frigate's masts and yards, but without effect. In a few minutes, however, the Emerald, having in a very spirited as well as judicious manner, closed with the leewardmost frigate, the two became so disabled in their sails and rigging, that after firing a few straggling and ineffectual shot, and just as the Leviathan had gained a position to discharge her broadside into both frigates, they hauled down their colours.

The Emerald immediately proceeded in chase of the third frigate, but, appearing to lose ground in the pursuit, was re-called and ordered to secure as many as she could of the convoy; four of the largest of which, before dark, fell into her hands. In the mean time the Leviathan lay by the two Spanish frigates, until they were in a state to make sail; which was not until two hours after the surrender. The 74 then stood after the remaining frigate; but the latter had by this time so increased her distance, that the Leviathan gave up the pursuit, and proceeded with her prizes to Gibraltar.

As a proof that the Carmen and Florentina had not struck their colours without making an honourable resistance, the first, out of a crew of 340, had one officer and 10 men killed, and 16 men wounded; the second, out of a crew of 314, one officer and 11 men killed, her captain, first-lieutenant, and 10 men wounded. Each frigate was laden with 500 quintals of quicksilver, for the use of the mines at Lima. The Carmen measured 908, and the Florentina 902 tons, and both were added to the British navy as 12-pounder 36-gun frigates.

On the 12th of April Captain Joseph Baker, of the 16-gun ship-sloop Calypso, being off Cape Tiberon, despatched the master, Mr. William Buckly, in the six-oared cutter, with 10 men, properly armed and provided, and a swivel in her bow, to cruise for two days under the cape, in order, if possible, to in-tercept some of the small craft that usually navigate within a mile of the shore. On the following day, the 13th, at 11 A.M., Mr. Buckly perceived, and immediately pulled towards, a schooner lying becalmed under the land. As the boat ap-proached within hail, the schooner desired her to keep off, and, finding the order not attended to, opened upon her a fire of musketry. Heedless of this, the British in the boat boarded, and—after a short but smart conflict on the deck—carried the French privateer-schooner Diligente, of six carriage-guns, 30 stands of arms, and 39 men actually on board. In this very gallant boat-attack, the British had only one man wounded; the French, seven, and those dangerously.

On the 21st of April, at 6h. 30m. A.M., the British hired-lugger Lark, of 14 guns (twelve 12-pounder carronades and two fours), and 50 men and boys, Lieutenant Thomas Henry Wilson, cruising off the Vlie passage into the Texel, discovered and chased a French cutter-privateer, which, after the exchange of a few broadsides, ran herself on shore; but, as the Lark was . unable to get near enough to destroy her, this privateer eventually got off and reached in safety the Texel road.

On the 25th, at 2 P.M., the Lark chased and soon came up with another French cutter-privateer, which, after engaging the lugger for some time, ran on shore upon the Vlie island. Here the cutter, which was the Imprenable, Captain Sparrow, of 12 long 3, and two long 8 pounders, and a crew of 60 men, defended herself pretty well for nearly an hour; at the end of which her men began escaping to the shore, under the cover of a party of troops estimated at about 100.

Seeing this, Lieutenant Wilson put off in the Lark's small boat, and directed the master, Mr. Thomas Geltins, to follow in the large boat. With his handful of men, and in the face of a smart fire of musketry from the shore, to which by this time all the French crew had escaped, Lieutenant Wilson boarded the Imprenable. Finding his endeavours to get the cutter afloat greatly impeded by the musketry from the troops, the lieutenant detached the master in the large boat to dislodge them from the sand-banks behind which they had taken shelter. This done, the British succeeded, without the slightest loss, in getting off the privateer, and carried her into Yarmouth roads. To add to the value of this gallant exploit, the Imprenable had been a great pest to British commerce in the North Sea.

On the 10th of June Rear-admiral Sir John Borlase Warren, cruising off the Penmarcks with the Renown and Defence 74s, Captains Thomas Eyles and Lord Henry Paulet, and Fisgard and Unicorn frigates, Captains Thomas Byam Martin and Philip Wilkinson, detached the boats of the squadron to attempt to cut out or destroy a convoy of brigs and chasse-marées lying at St. Croix, a small harbour within the Penmarck rocks, and known to be laden with wine and provisions for the Brest fleet.

In the evening the boats, eight in number, namely, two from the Renown, commanded by Lieutenant Henry Burke, two from the Fisgard, by Lieutenant William Dean, and Lieutenant of marines Mark A. Gerrard, two from the Defence, by Lieutenant Thomas Stamp, and two from the Unicorn, by Lieutenant William Price, assembled on board the Fisgard, then at anchor as near as possible to the shore. At 11 P.M., favoured by the darkness, Lieutenant Burke proceeded to execute the service intrusted to him. The freshness of the wind prevented the boats from reaching the enemy's anchorage until after daylight on the 11th; when, in opposition to a heavy battery, three armed vessels, and a constant fire of musketry from the shore, the British captured one gun-boat, Nochette, mounting two long 24-pounders, two chasse-marées, one of six, the other of 10 guns, and eight merchant-vessels. The remainder of the convoy, amounting to 20 sail, escaped capture by running upon the rocks.

This spirited little affair cost the British only three seamen and one marine wounded. Among the officers not already named, who distinguished themselves on the occasion, were acting Lieutenant Henry Jane of the Renown, master's mate John Fleming, and Lieutenant Killogrivoff, a volunteer from the Russian service.

On the night of the 23rd of June the same British squadron, with the exception of the Unicorn, having anchored off the Glénans, the boats, under the immediate direction of Captain Martin, proceeded to attack a French corvette mounting 28 guns, a brig of 18, lugger of 16, and cutter of 10 guns, lying at anchor, in company with several sail of merchant-vessels, in Quimper river. At daybreak on the 24th the boats arrived off the entrance of the river; and, for their protection in ascending it, two divisions of marines were landed, that on the right commanded by Lieutenant Henry Burke of the Renown, and that on the left by Lieutenant Mark A. Gerrard, of the Fisgard's marines. The boats, under Lieutenant Robert Yarker, in the mean time, pulled with all expedition to the attack, but soon found that the vessels had retired to an inaccessible distance up the river. Lieutenant Yarker then landed, and stormed, carried, and blew up, a battery mounted with two or three 24-pounders. Two other small forts, with their magazines, were also blown up by the British before they returned to their ships, and that without the occurrence of a single casualty.

Having received information that a French corvette, with a large convoy from Sable-d'Olonne bound to Brest, was lying within the island of Noirmoutier, Sir John on the 1st of July anchored in Bourneuf bay, with the intention of detaching the boats of his three ships against this force, consisting of the armed ship Therése, of 20 guns, a lugger of 12 guns, and a cutter and two schooners, each of six guns, moored within the sands at the bottom of the bay, in a strong position of defence, and under the protection of six batteries at the south-east end of Noirmoutier, besides flanking guns at every projecting point,

Having assembled on board the Fisgard, the boats pulled off in the evening, in three divisions, containing between them 192 officers, seamen, and marines, under the orders of Lieutenant Burke, assisted by Lieutenants of marines John Thompson and Charles Henry Ballinghall, of the Renown, Lieutenant William Dean, and lieutenants of marines Mark A. Gerard, of the Fisgard, and William Garrett and Hugh Hutton, of the Defence. At midnight the British in the boats boarded, and, after much resistance and loss on the part of the French, carried the ship and the three other armed vessels, together with 15 sail of merchantmen; all, as well as the armed vessels, laden with flour, corn, provisions, bale-goods, and ship-timber, for the fleet at Brest. Finding it impossible to bring off his prizes, Lieutenant Burke caused them to be effectually destroyed.

In high glee at having performed this essential service without any loss, the British now proceeded on their return; but unfortunately, in attempting to pass over the sand-banks, the boats took the ground, and in less than ten minutes, lay perfectly dry. In this helpless situation, Lieutenant Burke and his party became exposed to a continual fire from the forts on Noirmoutier island, and from about 400 French soldiers. Notwithstanding so formidable an opposition, the British commenced an attack upon some other vessels afloat near them, in the hope to secure one sufficiently large to carry them all off. This they accomplished, and, with great intrepidity and exertion, drew her upwards of two miles over the sands, until she floated; by which time the men were nearly up to their necks in water. It appears that 92 officers, seamen, and marines (several of them, including Lieutenants Burke, Thompson, and Ballinghall, wounded) were now taken prisoners; but that the remainder of the party, numbering in all 100, forced the French to retreat, and then got back to their ships by means of the boats they had taken. This was a very gallant, and, but for the latter half of it, would have been a very successful and important, boat-service.

On the 27th of June a British squadron, composed of the 12-pounder 32-gun frigate Andromeda, Captain Henry Inman, 28-gun frigate Nemesis, Captain Thomas Baker, one 20-gun ship, two ship-sloops, one bomb-vessel, and 11 fire-ships, gun-brigs, hired cutters, and luggers, assembled off Dunkerque, to attempt the destruction of the four French frigates, Poursuivante, of the 44-gun or 24-pounder class, Carmagnole, of the 40-gun, and Désirée and Incorruptible, of the 38-gun class; and which four frigates had long been blockaded in that port.

Contrary winds and a succession of unfavourable tides afforded no opportunity of making the attack until the 7th of July. On that evening the ship-sloop Dart (sister vessel to the Arrow already described[1]), Captain Patrick Campbell, followed by the Biter and Boxer gun-brigs, Lieutenants William Norman and Thomas Gilbert, and the four fire-ships Wasp, Captain John Edwards, Falcon, Captain Henry Samuel Butt, Comet, Captain Thomas Leef, and Rosario, Captain James Carthew, with the cutters and small-craft attending them, entered Dunkerque roads. At about midnight the Dart and her companions got sight of the French ships. Soon afterwards one of the latter hailed the Dart, and asked whence she came. The answer was, "De Bordeaux." The Frenchman then desired to know what convoy that was astern, meaning the gun-brigs and fire-ships. The reply was, "Je ne sais pas."

This conversation ended, the Dart continued to pass on un-molested, until she arrived alongside of the innermost frigate but one, when that frigate opened upon her a very heavy fire. This the Dart was enabled to return with 15 double-shotted 32-pounders, discharged in much quicker repetition than common, owing to the carronades being mounted on the non-recoil prin-ciple. The Dart then ranged on, and boarded the innermost frigate, the Désirée, by running her bowsprit between the latter's foremast and forestay, having previously let go a stern-anchor to check her own way. The first-lieutenant, James M'Dermeit, at the head of a division of seamen and marines, immediately boarded the French frigate on the forecastle, carrying all before him, but not without being badly wounded in the arm. He then hailed the Dart, to say he had possession of the ship; but as he feared the crew would rally, and he was wounded, he requested that an officer might be sent to take charge. Having cut her stern-cable, the Dart had just swung alongside the Désirée; on whose quarter Lieutenant William Isaac Pearce instantly leaped with a second division of men. This officer completely repulsed the French crew, who were rallying at the after hatchway. Lieutenant Pearce then cut the frigate's cables, got the Désirée under sail, and steered her over the banks that could not have been passed half an hour later in the tide.

In this dashing enterprise, which was concluded in about 15 minutes, the Dart had only one seaman killed, her first-lieu-tenant, already named, one master's mate (James Hall), and

---

[1] See vol. ii., p. 388; but the Dart appears to have mounted two additional car-ronades on her quarter-deck or 30 in all.

nine seamen and marines wounded; while the loss sustained by the Désirée, a fine new frigate of 1015 tons, was supposed to have amounted to full 100 in killed and wounded together, including nearly the whole of the officers present. The established complement of the Désirée was from 300 to 350 men; but it does not appear that the frigate had all her crew on board. The exact number that was on board we are, however, unable to state; especially as, from some unexplained cause, no head-money certificates were signed, or at least recorded.

The four fire-ships were admirably conducted, and not abandoned by their officers until completely in flames: on board the Comet, indeed, the captain and one seaman were wounded by the explosion. By alacrity, however, in cutting their cables, during which they were exposed to the fire, within pistol-shot of the Dart, and of the gun-brigs Biter and Boxer, the three remaining French frigates escaped before the wind, and ran out of the road to a short distance down the channel that passes within the Braak sand. One of them here got on shore, but at daylight on the 8th got off; and all three ships subsequently regained their anchorage.

During the attack the hired 14-gun cutter Kent, Lieutenant Robert Baron Cooban, found employment for some French gun-boats that would otherwise have annoyed the attacking vessels. In this cannonade the Kent had one seaman wounded; and the 12-gun hired cutter Ann, Lieutenant Robert Young, and the gun-brig Biter, Lieutenant Samuel Norman, had each one seaman, and the latter her commander, wounded, in the service which they were respectively rendering. The better to direct the enterprise, Captain Inman, with 30 volunteers from the Andromeda, had embarked on board the hired lugger Vigilant, Mr. William Dean, master, and proceeded with the other vessels into Dunkerque roads. Captain Inman, very humanely, sent the prisoners, many of whom were dreadfully mangled, to Dunkerque on their parole. For this he received the thanks of Commodore Castagnier. If *all* the prisoners were thus sent away, the reason is explained why there were no head-money certificates.

For his skill and gallantry in laying on board and capturing the Désirée, Captain Campbell was advanced to post-rank, and appointed to the 20-gun ship Ariadne: in point of rank, certainly a step forward, but from the Dart to the Ariadne nearly two steps backwards, as respected the relative force and effectiveness of the two vessels. As the least reward that could be bestowed upon an officer who had behaved so gallantly and suffered so severely, Lieutenant M'Dermeit was promoted to the rank of commander; and we should, we confess, have been gratified at seeing Lieutenant Pearce among the newly made commanders of the year.

We sincerely hope that those careful gentlemen, the established pilots, got their deserts, for having pusillanimously abandoned the charge of their ships when their services were most required. We wish we knew their names, in order to hand them down with becoming infamy. Fortunately the master of the Ann cutter, Mr. Henry Moor, was competent to take charge of the Dart; and Mr. James Wheatland, mate of the Ann, also volunteered his services. These, with some men obtained out of smugglers, enabled Captain Campbell to send a pilot to each gun-brig and fire-vessel.

The Désirée was afterwards added to the British navy as a 36-gun frigate, and Captain Inman, very deservedly, was appointed to commission her. One mistake we are bound to rectify; it is as to the French gun-force of the Désirée, as well as of one of the other frigates in her company. In his letter to Captain Inman, Captain Campbell states the main-deck guns of both the Désirée and Incorruptible to have been " 24-pounders;" and every one of our contemporaries, relying on such good authority, have assigned the Désirée guns of that caliber. But this French frigate, in fact, was armed the same as No. 6 in the table at p. 59 of the first volume, except in having two 8-pounders more, and two carronades fewer than the number there specified.

In the latter end of July, while the 14-gun cutter Viper, commanded by acting Lieutenant Jeremiah Coghlan, and attached to Sir Edward Pellew's squadron, was watching Port-Louis, it occurred to the former young officer, that he might succeed in boarding one of the cutters or gun-vessels, which were constantly moving about the entrance of that harbour. His first step was to request of Sir Edward Pellew a ten-oared cutter, with 12 volunteers. Having obtained the boat and men, Mr. Coghlan, on the night of the 26th, placed in her a midshipman of the Viper, Mr. Silas Hiscutt Paddon, and six seamen, making with himself a total of 20. With this ten-oared cutter, a boat from the Viper, and another from the Amethyst frigate, Mr. Coghlan set out to board a French gun-brig, mounting three long 24, and four 6 pounders, full of men, moored with springs on her cables, lying in a naval port of difficult access, within pistol-shot of three batteries, surrounded by several armed small craft, and not a mile from a French 74 and two frigates.

Undismayed by such formidable appearances, regardless of the early discovery of his approach, as evinced by the gun-brig's crew being at quarters, or even of the lost aid of the two other boats, which in spite of all the endeavours of their respective crews could not keep pace with the cutter,—in the very teeth of all these obstacles, Mr. Coghlan and his handful of men boarded the gun-brig on the quarter. Owing to the extreme darkness of the night, the leader of this resolute band jumped into a trawl-net hung up to dry. In this helpless situation Mr. Coghlan was pierced through the left thigh with a pike; several of his men were also hurt; and the whole were forced back into the boat.

Unchecked in ardour, the British hauled their boat farther ahead; and again boarding the gun-brig, maintained against 87 men, 16 of whom were soldiers, an obstinate conflict, during which many of the British were knocked overboard, and the whole, a second time, beat back to their boat. Notwithstanding this, however, the assailants returned to the charge with un-abated courage; and after killing six men, and wounding 20, among whom was every officer belonging to her, Mr. Coghlan and his truly gallant comrades carried the Cerbère. His own loss on this splendid occasion was one man killed, and eight wounded, himself in two places, and Mr. Paddon in six. With the aid of the two other boats, the British towed out their prize, under a heavy but ineffectual fire from the batteries.

The language of Sir Edward Pellew, in his letter to Earl St. Vincent, describing the affair, is so very energetic and appro-priate, that we cannot do better than transcribe his words : " I trust I shall stand excused by your lordship for so minute a de-scription, produced by my admiration of that courage, which, hand to hand, gave victory to a handful of brave fellows over four times their number, and of that skill which formed, con-ducted, and effected so daring an enterprise." The officers and men of Sir Edward's squadron, to mark their sense of such dis-tinguished bravery, gave up the Cerbère as a prize to the con-querors ; and Earl St. Vincent was so much pleased with Mr. Coghlan's intrepidity, that he presented him with a handsome sword. Moreover, the young man obtained, what his aspiring mind valued above all other gifts, a confirmation of his rank as lieutenant ; and that, although he had not quite served the time which the regulations of the navy required, and which had never been dispensed with, we believe, previous to this gallant affair.

On the 4th of August, soon after daylight, the British 64-gun ship Belliqueux, Captain Rowley Bulteel, being off the coast of Brazil with a fleet of outward-bound Indiamen under her protection, discovered four sail in the north-west or leeward quarter, steering about north by east. These were the French 40-gun frigate Concorde, Commodore Jean-François Landolphe, 36-gun frigates Médée, Captain Jean-Daniel Coudin, and Franchise, Captain Pierre Jurien, and a captured American schooner fitted out as a tender. This squadron had sailed from Rochefort on the 6th of March, 1799; and, after committing serious depredations upon the coast of Africa, had refitted at Rio de la Plata.

At 7 A.M., hoping to pick up a prize or two, the French commodore hauled his wind, tacked, and stood towards the convoy; which, to facilitate the junction, bore down. At noon, when a nearer approach brought into full view the China ships with their two tiers of ports and warlike appearance, the French ships bore up under a press of sail, and by signal separated.

The Belliqueux immediately steered for the Concorde as the largest ship; and at 5 h. 30 m. P.M., after a partial firing of about ten minutes' duration, by which no one on either side appears to have been hurt, compelled the French commodore, with a crew, as asserted, of 444 men, to haul down his colours. In the mean time four of the Indiamen, the Exeter, Captain Henry Meriton, Bombay Castle, Captain John Hamilton, Coutts, Captain Robert Torin, and Neptune, Captain Nathaniel Spens, all 1200-ton ships, had been ordered by signal to proceed in chase: the first two, of the Médée, and the other two, of the Franchise.

According to Captain Bulteel's letter in the Gazette, the Médée, with a crew of 315 men, was captured at 7 P.M. by the Bombay Castle and Exeter; but the following somewhat different, and, we must add, not very consistent account, appears in the work of a contemporary: "The chase was long, and at midnight Captain Meriton, of the Exeter, found himself coming very fast up with the enemy, while the Bombay Castle, another Indiaman, commanded by Captain Hamilton, was still very far astern. The position was critical, and the British officer, with great presence of mind, formed his determination; running alongside of the Frenchman with all his ports up, he commanded him to surrender to a superior force; with this order, supposiug himself under the guns of a ship of the line, the

French captain instantly complied. Meriton gave him no time
for deliberation, but sent an officer and brought him on board,
and he delivered his sword to the English captain, in due form,
on the quarter-deck. The Bombay Castle was still at a great
distance, but on her coming up, the prisoners were quickly
taken out and divided. By this time the French captain began
to recover from his surprise, and looking very attentively at the
little guns on the quarter-deck, asked Captain Meriton what
ship it was to which he had surrendered. Meriton drily
answered, ' To a merchant-ship :' the indignant Frenchman
begged to be allowed to return with his people to the frigate
and fight the battle again."[1]

The remaining French frigate, the Franchise, by throwing
overboard a part of her guns, together with her anchors, boats,
and booms, and by the timely approach of night, effected her
escape; as did also the armed schooner. Owing to the late
period at which the Concorde and Médée (both of which were
armed precisely according to the establishment of their respective
classes, already so frequently adverted to) arrived in a port of
England, and to the turn which affairs had then taken, neither
frigate was purchased for the use of the British navy.

On the 20th of August, at 8 h. 30 m. A.M., the British 38-gun
frigate Seine, Captain David Milne, cruising in the Mona passage with the wind easterly and very light, saw, right ahead,
standing to the northward on the starboard tack, the French
frigate Vengeance, Captain Pichot (the Constellation's late antagonist), not many days from Curaçoa, bound to France. The
Seine immediately made all sail in chase. At 10 A.M., the wind
having come more northerly, so as to prevent the Vengeance
from weathering Cape Raphaél on the St. Domingo shore, the
French ship tacked, and steered south-south-east under all sail.
At noon, or soon after, the wind shifted back to the eastward,
but was still very light; and both ships continued under a crowd
of canvas. At 4 P.M., the Vengeance began firing her stern-
chasers. At 11 h. 30 m. P.M., the Seine, having gained so in
the chase as to be close on her opponent's quarter, fired several
broadsides at her; but the Vengeance still stood on, firing in
return all the guns she could bring to bear. This greatly
damaged the rigging and sails of the Seine, and compelled her,
at about midnight, to drop astern.

The remainder of the night was occupied in reeving fresh
rigging, and preparing to renew the combat; each ship carrying

[1] Brenton, vol. iii., p. 341.

every sail she could set. On the 21st, at 7 h. 30 m. A.M., the Seine got again within gun-shot, and at 8 A.M. close alongside, of the Vengeance. The action now recommenced, and continued, with unabated fury, until 10 h. 30 m. A.M.; when the Vengeance, having lost her foremast, mizenmast, and maintopmast, all of which had fallen in-board, and being terribly shattered in her hull, surrendered. This was made known by an officer, who hailed the Seine from the end of the French ship's bowsprit.

The Seine lost none of her masts, but had her mainmast badly wounded, and received several shot in her remaining masts and hull. Her loss, out of a complement of 281 men and boys, amounted to her second-lieutenant (George Milne) and 12 seamen killed, and one lieutenant of marines (Archibald Macdonald), her master (Andrew Barclay), captain's clerk (Mr. Horne), 22 seamen, three marines, and one boy wounded. The loss of the Vengeance, Captain Milne merely says, "has been very great." As 291 were the number of prisoners received out of her, and 326, according to the deposition of her officers in the prize-court, the number of persons on board when the action commenced, we may fairly set down the killed at 35; and the wounded, if in the usual proportion, were probably about 70 or 80.

The Seine, late the French frigate of that name taken by the Jason and Pique in June, 1798,[1] carried two long nines and eight 32-pounder carronades more than the establishment of her class.[2] The force of the Vengeance has already, on more than one occasion, been referred to.[3] Captain Milne calls the eights of the Vengeance twelves; but no French frigate, not even the Forte of 1401, nor the Egyptienne of 1430 tons, mounted a heavier caliber than 8-pounders on the quarter-deck and forecastle. Moreover the Vengeance, as Captain Milne admits, was a sister-vessel to the Résistance; and the latter, as has already been shown, carried 8-pounders.[4] In calling the 36-pounder carronades 42s, Captain Milne has only erred as other captains have done; but, in adding, "The weight of metal I have mentioned in French pounds," he has given the French a caliber they never possessed. With respect to "shifting guns on the main and quarter decks," it appears, that the Vengeance had every broadside port already filled. But even admitting that the

---

[1] See vol. ii., p. 248.
[2] For which see letter Z in the small table at p. 101 of the first volume.
[3] See vol. i., p. 380, and vol. ii., p. 90.
[4] See vol. ii., p. 92.

Vengeance fought a gun on one broadside which she transported
from the other, the Seine did the same; as appears from the
following extract of a letter from Sir David Milne to Sir Robert
Sepping, one of the surveyors of the navy. "In La S——e I
had the quarter-galleries formed into ports, and in action that
ship fought a gun there, by transporting it on (from) the other
side."[1] Having, as we hope, cleared up these points, we can,
with more confidence, present the following as the

Comparative Force of the Combatants.

		Seine.	Vengeance.
Broadside-guns. . . . . { No.		24	26
{ lbs.		434	498
Crew . . . . No.		281	326
Size . . . . tons		1146	1180

Considering the inferiority in effectiveness between the French
and the English ship's eight carronades to have been compensated by the former's tier of swivels along the gangway, we may
pronounce this to have been as pretty a frigate-match as any
fought during the war.   There is on the face of the statement,
undoubtedly, a numerical superiority in favour of the French
ship, but far too slight for a British ship to notice; above all,
not such as to justify the captor in saying, "Your lordship will
perceive the Vengeance is superior in size, guns, and number of
men to his majesty's ship I have the honour to command." It is
sufficient to say, that this was an action which, both in the conduct and the result, did great credit to Captain Milne, his officers,
and ship's company; and, let us be just in adding, it was one,
also, in which M. Pichot, on finding that to run would not avail
him, made a manful resistance, surrendering only when his ship
was reduced to an unmanageable hulk.

As soon as the prisoners were removed and the wreck of the
masts cleared, the Seine, taking her prize in tow, proceeded with
her to Jamaica.   On the 25th, in the morning, the mainmast of
the Vengeance, having been badly wounded, fell over the side.
On the 27th in the evening, the two ships, the prize with nine
feet water in the hold, anchored in the harbour of Port Royal.
Shortly afterwards, as was fully his due, Lieutenant Edward
Chetham, first of the Seine, was promoted to the rank of commander.

The Vengeance was purchased for the use of the British navy,
and became classed with the frigate that had captured her; but

1 Sir Robert Sepping's Letter to Lord Melville upon Circular Sterns, p. 13.

owing to her damaged state and the heavy cost of repairs at Jamaica, the ship never again quitted port. As the exaggerated account given of the size of the Vengeance, namely, that she was as large as a British 64, tended greatly to mislead the public as to the merits of the action which had led to her capture, we beg to be allowed to digress a little, to show how the mistake arose.

When a captured vessel is purchased by government, it is at so much a ton, according to the age and condition of the prize. Hence the ship's measurement must be taken before the sum can be fixed. In the case of the Vengeance, the master-ship-wright, shipwright's assistant, and boatswain, belonging to Port Royal yard, took her dimensions and computed her tonnage, but in such a way that they made the sister-ship of one that was 1182, measure 1370 tons. As the Vengeance was prevented from coming home to be properly measured, no way remains to prove the erroneous calculation of the dockyard officers, but by analogy. For instance, in the year 1803 the same officers measured, among many other ships, the French prize-frigates Clorinde, Surveillante, Vertu, and Créole, and the 74-gun ship Duquesne. The following little table will show that, in their way of performing the task, the Port Royal dockyard officers could not have made a ship of 1180 tons measure less than 1370 :—

		Tons.			Tons.
Clorinde, measured at Jamaica		1375	Measured in England	. .	1161
Surveillante,	,,	1235	,,	. .	1094
Vertu,	,,	1245	,,	. .	1073
Duquesne,	,,	2151	,,	. .	1903
Créole,	,,	1267	{ Foundered on her way home, but was known to be similar in size to Vertu . . }		1073
Vengeance,		1370	{ Actual measurement of Résistance, afterwards Fisgard }		1182

Consequently, the average rate per ton, at which these six French ships were purchased, being 10l. 10s. for the Clorinde, 12l. 10s. for the Surveillante and Duquesne, 7l. for the Vertu, 8l. 10s. for the Créole, and 6l. 5s. for the Vengeance, government paid 11,137l. 10s. more than they had agreed to give.

On the 29th of August, while the British squadron, already mentioned as under the command of Sir John Borlase Warren in the 74-gun ship Renown, was, with several transports in company, proceeding along the coast of Spain to its ulterior destination, a large French ship-privateer, alarmed by the appearance of so formidable a force, was seen to run into Vigo, and to anchor at a spot near the narrows of Redondela, and close to some batteries. In the evening a division of boats, 20 in number, from the ships of the squadron, placed under the orders of Lieutenant Henry Burke of the Renown, proceeded to attack the privateer ; which was the Guêpe, mounting 18 long 8-pounders, and manned with 161 men.

At about 40 minutes past midnight the boats got alongside of the ship, the crew of which had previously cheered, to show that they were prepared. Notwithstanding this, and that the Guêpe's commander, Citizen Dupan, had laid over the hatches to keep his men to their quarters, the British resolutely boarded, and in 15 minutes carried the vessel; with the loss of three seamen and one marine killed, three lieutenants, 12 seamen, and five marines wounded, and one seaman missing, probably drowned.

Among the wounded officers was the gallant leader of the party, Lieutenant Burke, an officer who had previously distinguished. himself on more than one similar occasion; and who, immediately after this additional proof of his gallantry, obtained the rank of commander. The two other wounded Lieutenants were John Henry Holmes and Joseph (misnamed in the Gazette James) Nourse, both of the Courageux. The loss on board the Guêpe, as a proof how obstinately she had been defended, amounted to 25 men killed and 40 wounded, including among the mortally wounded her brave commander. This formidable French privateer had been fitted out at Bordeaux, and was stored and provisioned, in the most complete manner, for a four months' cruise.

On the 3rd of September, at about 8 P.M., eight boats from the 74-gun ship Minotaur, Captain Thomas Louis, and armed en flûte (late 12-pounder 32-gun) frigate Niger, Captain James Hillyar, placed under the orders of the latter, assisted by Lieutenants Charles Marsh Schomberg, and Thomas Warrand, Midshipmen James Lowry, and Richard Standish Haly, and Lieutenant of marines John Jewell, proceeded to cut out or destroy two Spanish armed ships, or corvettes, at anchor in Barcelona roads ; one, the Concepcion. alias Esmeralda, the other, the Paz, each described as mounting 22 long 12 and 8 pounders, and laden with stores, reported, but which did not prove to be the case, for the relief of Malta.

At the time these eight boats were detached upon the service, one of them was boarding a Swedish galliot bound into the port:

and, to join this boat and give directions to her commander, Captain Hillyar pulled, in the first instance, for the galliot. On arriving alongside the latter, the British boats hooked on, and they and the Swedish galliot of course stood together towards the mole of Barcelona.

Having approached within about three-quarters of a mile of the nearest battery, and being reminded, by two shots which passed over the galliot, that it was time to retire from under the shelter of a neutral vessel, Captain Hillyar and his party pulled away towards the object of attack. Shortly afterwards the outermost of the two Spanish armed ships, the Esmeralda, discharged her broadside at the boats, but without effect, her shot falling short. Pushing on with their accustomed alacrity, the British were alongside the Esmeralda before the ship could reload her guns. This was at 9 P.M.; and in a few minutes afterwards, but not without a smart struggle, Captain Hillyar and his party boarded and carried the Esmeralda.

The announcement of this victory, by the cheers of the British, was the signal for the Spaniards in the other ship to cut their cable, and endeavour to run close under the battery at the mole-head; but the ship canting the wrong way, and the British being alert in their movements, the Paz, before 10 P.M., in spite of a heavy fire from four strong batteries, 10 gun-boats, two schooners, each armed with two long 36-pounders, and a fort upon Mount Ioni which threw shells, shared the fate of her consort. At about 11 P.M. the two prize-ships, and the boats that had taken them, covered as they stood to the offing by two men-of-war, were brought off in safety; with a loss to the British of only two seamen and one marine killed, the Minotaur's master, Mr. Reid and four seamen wounded. On board the Paz, one seaman was killed and four wounded; and on board the Esmeralda, two seamen were killed, and 17 wounded.

Each of the captured ships is represented to have measured about 400 tons, and to have been laden with provisions and stores supposed for Batavia. Besides which they were to have taken on board between them 300 Batavian troops from the island of Majorca. Admitting the crew (for no number is stated in the gazette letter) to have amounted only to 50 men, we have a ship of 400 tons, carrying, besides a cargo of provisions, 200 men, and mounted with " 22 brass guns, 12 and 9 pounders." We must therefore be permitted to consider, that the guns of the Esmeralda were only 8 and 6 pounders; and that even the majority of the guns were of the lesser caliber. Still the exploit, performed as it was in the very teeth of a force both afloat and ashore so very superior, reflected the highest honour upon the victorious party.

It is true that some altercation took place between the courts of Spain and Sweden relative to the alleged seizure of the galliot to surprise the ships; but it led to nothing except, for a while, to mislead public opinion as to the merits of the case. A contemporary states that the capture of the Paz and Esmeralda, "led to the promotion of Captain Hillyar and Lieutenant Schomberg."[1] If so, the operation as regards Captain Hillyar at least, was rather a tardy one; for he was not, we find, made post until February, 1804, rather more than six months after the senior lieutenant who had served under him at Barcelona attained the same rank.

On the 10th of September, as the British privateer-brig, Rover, of Liverpool, Nova-Scotia, armed with 14 long 4-pounders and 54 men and boys, under the command of Captain Godfrey, was cruising near Cape Blanco on the Spanish Main, the Spanish schooner Santa-Ritta, mounitng 10 long 6-pounders and two English 12-pounder carronades, with about 85 men, and accompanied by three gun-boats also under Spanish colours, and which, as well as the schooner, had the day before been equipped by the governor of Puerto-Caballo, on purpose to capture the Rover, came out from near the land to fulfil their orders. The light breeze which had been blowing having died away, the schooner and two of the gun-boats, by the aid of a number of oars, gained fast upon the brig; keeping up as they advanced a steady fire from their bow-guns, which the Rover returned with two guns pointed from her stern, and, as her opponents drew near, with her small-arms also.

Apprised, by their motions, that the schooner intended to board on the starboard quarter, and the two gun-boats (the third appeared to keep aloof) on the opposite bow and quarter, the Rover suffered them to advance until they got within about 15 yards of her: she then manned her oars on the larboard side, and, pulling quickly round, brought her starboard broadside to bear right athwart the schooner's bow; upon whose decks, then filled with men ready for boarding, the brig poured a whole broadside of round and grape. Immediately after this, her active crew passed over to the guns on the opposite side, and raked the two gun-boats in a similar manner. The Rover then commenced a close action with the Santa-Ritta, and continued

[1] Brenton, vol. iii., p. 24.

it for an hour and a half; when finding her opponent's fire grow slack, the Rover, by the aid of a light air of wind, backed her head-sails, and brought her stern in contact with the schooner's side. The British crew then rushed on board of, and with scarcely a show of opposition carried, the Santa-Ritta. The two gun-boats, seeing the fate of their consort, sheered off, apparently in a very shattered state.

Notwithstanding this long and hard-fought action, the Rover had not a man hurt; while, on board the Santa-Ritta, every officer, except the commander of a detachment of 25 soldiers, was killed; the whole of the killed, as found on the deck, amounted to 14, and the wounded to 17. The prisoners, including the latter, numbered 71. These, being too many to be kept on board, were all, except eight, landed; the Rover's captain having previously taken from them the usual obligation not to serve again until exchanged. This was an achievement that did great honour to Captain Godfrey, his officers, and crew; and proved how well the hardy sons of British America could emulate their brother-tars of the parent country.

On the 8th of October, at 8 A.M., the British schooner Gipsy (tender to the 74-gun ship Leviathan, Captain James Carpenter, bearing the flag of Rear-admiral Duckworth), of 10 long 4-pounders and 42 men, commanded by Lieutenant Coryndon Boger, cruising off the north end of Guadeloupe, chased and soon overtook an armed sloop; which, on the schooner's firing a shot at her, hoisted French colours and began cannonading in return. During one hour and a half the two vessels continued warmly engaged at close quarters; when the Gipsy, receiving great annoyance from the musketry of her opponent, hauled a little further off. Here the Gipsy kept up a sharp fire with round and grape shot, and at 10 h. 30 m. A.M. compelled the sloop, which was the Quidproquo, of eight guns, 4 and 8 pounders, and 98 men, commanded by M. Tourpie, represented to have been formerly a capitaine de vaisseau, to strike her colours. Eighty of the 98 men were Guadeloupe chasseurs; and it was to save his people from their powerful musketry that the Gipsy's commander, with so much judgment, had hauled off to a long-gun range.

The Gipsy had three seamen killed, and nine, including Lieutenant Boger, wounded; the Quidproquo, her captain and four seamen killed, and 11 wounded. Although upon a small scale this action was not the less creditable to those who, by their skill and bravery, had brought it to a successful termination.

On the 9th of October the honourable East India Company's ship Kent, of 26 guns (20 long 12, and six long 6 pounders), commanded by Captain Robert Rivington, being off the Sand-heads, on her way from England to Bengal, fell in with the French ship-privateer Confiance, of 20 or 22 long 8-pounders, commanded by M. Surcouff, a very able and experienced officer. An action immediately ensued, and was maintained with great bravery by the Indiaman, for one hour and 47 minutes; during which the two vessels were frequently foul of each other. At length the Kent was carried by boarding; her crew, besides their inferior numbers, being very ill-supplied with weapons of defence, while the assailants were all armed with sabres, pikes, and pistols. After having given decided proofs of his bravery, Captain Rivington received, at the moment of boarding, a musket-shot through his head.

Besides the loss of her captain, the Kent had 13 men killed, including four or five of her passengers, and 44 men wounded, including also several passengers. The loss on board the Con-fiance does not appear to have been recorded. It is, indeed, to be regretted, that on these interesting occasions some capable person does not take the pains to collect and publish the parti-culars. Many highly creditable actions between merchant-ships and enemy's privateers are either given to the public with such marks of doubt that an historian is fearful of admitting them into his pages; or they are so summarily stated, that the account, when the most is made of it, amounts to little more than that one vessel was captured by another.

The Confiance was a ship of 490 tons, and had, it is said, a complement of 250 men. The Kent was a new ship, of 820 tons, and had probably about 90 or 100 men in crew, exclusive of 38 male and three female passengers. Seven or eight of those passengers had been taken from the Queen Indiaman, when she was consumed by fire at St. Salvador. So long and manful a resistance with such limited means, was very honourable to the officers, crew, and passengers of the Kent. In the following month M. Surcouff arrived with his prize at the Isle of France.

We may remark, in passing, what an advantage the Kent would have derived, had she mounted on her quarter-deck and forecastle a tier of 18 or 24-pounder carronades, instead of long sixes. A few discharges of grape from the former would pro-bably have induced the Confiance to keep at long-shot, and then the Kent's 12-pounders, well plied, would either have captured or repulsed her.

Having already recorded two actions fought between American and French ships of war, we will here give a brief account of the third ; the last, indeed, of any consequence which occurred during the short interruption in the amicable relations of the two countries. On the 12th of October, in latitude 22° 50′ north, longitude 51° west, the United States 32-gun frigate Boston[1] (of the same long-gun force, we believe, as D in the table at p. 101 of the first volume, with 12 carronades, 32-pounders, in addition), Captain Little, fell in with the French ship-corvette Berceau, of 22 long eights and two English 12-pounder carronades, Lieutenant Louis-André Senes. An action ensued, and continued with mutual spirit, for two hours ; when the Berceau, having had her masts reduced to a tottering state, and being dreadfully shattered in hull, struck her colours to the Boston ; whose masts, rigging, and sails were also considerably wounded and cut.

Out of a crew of about 320 men and boys, the Boston lost her purser and 11 seamen and marines killed or mortally wounded, and eight others wounded who recovered. The precise loss of the Berceau does not appear in Captain Little's letter. We are only enabled to state, that, out of a crew of about 200, exclusive of 30 passengers, it was very considerable in both killed and wounded ; and that among the former was her captain. We may add, also, that the fore and main masts of the Berceau fell over the side soon after her surrender.

Who can read of a two hours' resistance under such a disparity of force as, without the aid of a comparative statement, it is clear must have existed between these two ships, without being surprised that no account of this action is to be found in any French publication ? Is it, then, French victories only that French ears can listen to, or French patriotism record ? Too true it is. The most insignificant triumph is puffed up to the skies, while an unsuccessful action, no matter how resolutely and ably fought, is passed over in silence. This will never make a navy. Much credit is due to the American captain for his candour (not the less estimable for its rarity on his side of the Atlantic[2]) in publicly acknowledging, that " the captain of the Berceau fought his ship gallantly, so long as she was in a situation capable of being defended." Captors, did they but know their true interest, always gain by such acts of fairness. The public places a greater reliance upon their remaining state-

[1] [The force of the Boston seems a little overstated. In James's ' Naval Occurrences ' her size is given as 790 tons and 42 guns.—H. Y. POWELL.]

[2] The Boston writers, for instance, in their account of this very action, declared that the two ships were " of nearly equal force."

ments; and, after all, is there not more honour in conquering a brave than a cowardly enemy?

As soon as she had cleared away the wreck of the Berceau's masts, and properly secured her own, the Boston took her prize in tow, and on the 14th of November anchored with her in Nantucket road. A treaty of peace had, since the 30th of September. been signed at Paris between France and America; and the Berceau, after being thoroughly repaired and refitted, was restored to the French government.

On the 27th of October, late in the evening, the boats of the British 38-gun frigate Phaëton, Captain James Nicholl Morris, placed under the orders of her first-lieutenant, Francis Beaufort, supported by Lieutenant George Huish, lieutenant of marines, Duncan Campbell, and midshipmen Augustus Barrington Hamilton and Anthony Collings Stanton, proceeded to attack the Spanish national polacre-ship San-Josef, mounting two long 24-pounders in the bow, two long brass 18-pounders for stern-chasers, and four 12 and six 4 pounders, all brass, on her sides, having on board 34 seamen (out of a crew of 49, a boat's crew being absent) and 22 soldiers or marines, and lying moored under the protection of five guns mounted upon the fortress of Fuengirola, near Malaga.

The launch, with an 18-pounder carronade in her, not being able to keep up with the barge and two cutters, Lieutenant Beaufort was proceeding with only the latter, when he was unexpectedly fired at by a French privateer-schooner, which had entered unseen in the night, and lay in a position to flank the ship. The three boats, however, still advanced; and on the 28th, at 5 A.M., in the face of an obstinate resistance of musketry and sabres, boarded, carried, and brought off the polacre.

In this gallant affair one seaman was killed alongside. Lieutenant Beaufort was first wounded in the head, and afterwards received several slugs through his left arm and in his body; Lieutenant Campbell received several slight sabre-wounds; and Mr. Hamilton was shot through the thigh while in the boat; notwithstanding which he gallantly boarded with the rest. A seaman also was wounded; making the loss, on the part of the British, one killed and four wounded. Of the San-Josef's crew, six men were found badly, and 13 slightly, wounded.

Being a fine fast-sailing little vessel, the San-Josef was immediately commissioned as a British sloop-of-war under the name of Calpé, the ancient name of Gibraltar. It would have

gratified us to be able to state that the officer, who as the con-
ductor of the enterprise had so gallantly and effectively co-
operated, as well as so seriously suffered, in capturing the
vessel, an officer "in whom" says Captain Morris, "I have
ever found a most capable and zealous assistant," had been
appointed to command her. But Vice-admiral Lord Keith,
the Mediterranean commander-in-chief, chose to appoint to the
Calpé an officer who, whatever may have been his merit in other
respects, was both junior to Lieutenant Beaufort, and an utter
stranger to the transaction at Fuengirola.

Among the few vessels in the British navy to which the non-
recoil principle of mounting the carronade had been extended,
was the Milbrook, a schooner of 148 tons, whose sixteen
18-pounders were so fitted, and whose commander, Lieutenant
Matthew Smith, put such confidence in the plan, that he ventured, as we shall presently show, to attack a ship mounting
double his number of guns. The carronades of the Arrow and
Dart sloops were also fitted upon the non-recoil principle; and
it is related of the latter of these vessels, that, when the British
troops landed in Holland, in August, 1797, she fired one of her
forecastle 32-pounders 68 times without breaking the breeching,
or injuring the carriage, or even the paint that covered, or the
pitch in the seams of it. The Eling schooner, armed with
18-pounders, is represented to have fired, on the same occasion,
400 round shot from her aftermost carronade, without doing the
slightest injury on board, or even breaking a single pane of glass
in the cabin skylight.

All this, if true (and the statement is officially founded),
would appear to refute most of the objections made to non-
recoil guns: that they destroy the upperworks, break the
breechings, dismount themselves, and expose the men, who are
obliged to load outside the bulwarks, to the enemy's fire. The
last is certainly a very serious objection, and one, we believe,
which yet keeps its ground. But we must not, in digressing,
forget Lieutenant Smith and his exploit.

On the 13th of November, early in the morning, the Milbrook, then lying becalmed off the bar of Oporto, descried a
French ship wearing a pendant, and, to all appearance, a frigate
of 36 guns. Having under his protection two brigs of a Newfoundland convoy, and observing several other vessels in the
offing, which, if as he conjectured English merchantmen, were
equally an object of desire to the Frenchmen, Lieutenant Smith
got out his sweeps, and pulled towards the enemy. At 8 A.M.

the schooner received a broadside from the ship, which was the celebrated French privateer Bellone, of Bordeaux. Before the Bellone could bring her second broadside to bear the Milbrook had fired three broadsides, and by the time the former had fired her third the schooner had discharged eleven broadsides. Such was the rapidity of firing where no time was lost by running out the guns.

The carronades of the Milbrook were seemingly fired with as much precision as quickness; for the Bellone from broadsides fell to single guns, and showed, by her sails and rigging, how much she had been cut up by the schooner's shot. At about 10 A.M. the ship's colours came down; and Lieutenant Smith used immediate endeavours to take possession of her. Not having a rope left wherewith to hoist out a boat, he launched one over the gunwale; but, having been pierced with shot in various directions, the boat soon filled with water. At this time the Milbrook, having had 10 of her guns disabled, her masts, yards, sails, and rigging wounded and shot through, and all her sweeps cut to pieces, lay quite unmanageable, with her broadside to the Bellone's stern. In a little while a light breeze sprang up, and the Bellone, hoisting all the canvas she could set, sought safety in flight.

Out of the 47 men of her crew, the Milbrook had eight seamen and one marine severely, and her master (Thomas Fletcher, but who would not quit the deck), surgeon's mate (I. Parster), and one seaman, slightly wounded. The loss sustained by the Bellone, as rumoured at Vigo, into which port she was compelled to put, amounted, out of a crew probably of 250 or 260 men, to 20 killed, her first and second captains and 45 men wounded.

The guns of the Bellone, as has already been stated, consisted of 24 long French 8-pounders and six or eight brass 36-pounder carronades. The ship, therefore, was almost quadruply superior to the Milbrook; and Lieutenant Smith, by his gallantry and seamanlike conduct, not only preserved from capture a valuable convoy, but added, in no slight degree, to the naval renown of his country. This became appreciated in the proper quarter, and Lieutenant Smith was promoted to the rank of commander. Also the English factory at Oporto, to evince their sense of the service performed by the Milbrook, voted Lieutenant Smith their thanks, accompanied by a piece of plate of 50l. value.

There was another British schooner, armed much in the same manner as the Milbrook, and cruising on the same station, whose commander, although not afforded an opportunity of repulsing a ship like the Bellone, distinguished himself greatly by his activity in capturing privateers, and in protecting British convoys from their depredations. The serviceable and far from inglorious career of the Netley, Lieutenant Francis Godolphin Bond, began in the months of November and December of the preceding year; and, on one occasion in particular, Lieutenant Bond captured a Spanish privateer, with more men in her than he had on board as a crew.

We shall pass over several cases in which the Netley captured Spanish privateers and retook their prizes, to relate one instance of decided gallantry on the part of her commander and crew. On the 7th of November in the present year, being off the rock of Lisbon, Lieutenant Bond received information that a Spanish privateer-schooner was lurking in the neighbourhood, and that the vessels of the Newfoundland convoy, being dispersed, were daily expected to approach the Tagus. Having, in the evening, stood in close to the shore, the Netley, after dark, discovered the above privateer, and a brig-prize which she had that morning made, at anchor. Despatching her boat to take possession of the brig, the Netley gallantly ran on board of, and, dropping her anchor, carried, without the discharge of a shot or the loss of a man, the Spanish privateer San-Miguel, *alias* l'Alerta, of nine guns, described as 18 and 6 pounders, and 65 men. With these her two prizes, the Netley, on the 8th, anchored in the Tagus.

On the 17th of November the British 74-gun ship Captain, Captain Sir Richard John Strachan, 32-gun frigate Magicienne, Captain William Ogilvy, and hired armed cutter Nile, Lieutenant George Argles, and lugger Soworrow, Lieutenant James Nicholson, cruising off the entrance of the Morbihan, to intercept a French convoy, discovered the French 20-gun ship-corvette Réolaise, the commodore of a convoy, endeavouring to get under the protection of the batteries. The Nile, by her skilful management, prevented the corvette from reaching the north shore; and the latter, upon the Magicienne's approach, ran into Port-Navalo; where she took the ground, and struck her colours.

Captain Ogilvy immediately despatched the boats of the Magicienne, under the orders of Lieutenants George Skottowe and the Honourable Edward Rodney, to endeavour to board and bring off or destroy the corvette; but the Réolaise rehoisting her colours, and making sail, fired upon the boats and ran

further into the port.   On seeing this the Magicienne recalled
her boats.   Lieutenant Rodney, however, being determined not
to return empty-handed, gallantly captured, with his single
boat, a merchant-vessel from under one of the batteries.

Being resolved to attempt the destruction of the corvette, Sir
Richard sent the boats of his little squadron, under the orders
of Lieutenant William Hennah, assisted by Lieutenants Charles
Clyde and Richard William Clarke (the latter of the Marlborough, a portion of whose men were also present), and also, we
believe, by the two lieutenants already named of the Magicienne.
The enterprise, thus intrusted to Lieutenant Hennah, was conducted with great judgment and gallantry ; and, notwithstanding a heavy fire from the shore on all sides, the Réolaise was
boarded and destroyed.   To add to the value of this exploit, it
was performed with no greater loss to the British than one seaman killed and seven wounded.

On the 7th of December the Nile cutter, while cruising off
the mouth of the river Vilaine in Quiberon bay, discovered a
convoy of 15 or 16 vessels coming round the point of Croisic ;
but, having just before detached the Lurcher cutter, Lieutenant
Robert Forbes, to cruise off the Morbihan, Lieutenant Argles,
instead of going in chase, permitted the French vessels to
approach nearer to the point of St. Gildas, in order to have the
assistance of his consort in overtaking and capturing them.

In the evening the Nile stood out from the shore and made
the necessary signals to the Lurcher, who, being to windward,
turned all the vessels and they made for the Vilaine.   At 8 P.M.,
just as the battery on Pointe Saint Jacques was hailing her, the
Nile captured one small vessel, and manning her, sent her alongshore ; by which means, before 4 A.M. on the 8th, five more
vessels were taken.   The whole coast was by this time alarmed,
and the battery of Notre Dame at the entrance of the river
Peners kept up so brisk a fire as to send three shot through the
last vessel boarded ; but the British, notwithstanding, brought
her off with only one man slightly scratched by a splinter.   The
Lurcher, in the meanwhile, had succeeded in taking three more
of the convoy, making nine in the whole.   This enterprise
reflects great credit upon the commanders and crews of the two
cutters ; and shows what serious annoyance may be done to an
enemy, even by such small vessels as the Nile and Lurcher,
when under the guidance of an active and intelligent officer.

On the 10th of December, the British armed brig Admiral
Pasley, of 16 guns, 14 of them 12-pounder carronades, with 40

men and boys, commanded by Lieutenant Charles I. Nevin, being off Ceuta on her passage from England to Gibraltar with despatches, was attacked in a calm by two Spanish gun-vessels of the largest class. After an engagement of an hour and a half, during the greater part of which the gun-vessels kept entirely out of range of the Admiral Pasley's paltry carronades, while the former, with their heavy long guns were cutting the brig to pieces, the Admiral Pasley, having previously thrown overboard her despatches, hauled down her colours.

As a proof that the Admiral Pasley had not been given away, her loss amounted to three seamen killed, her commander (in three places), master (Mr. Gibbs, badly), and eight seamen wounded. The captors carried their prize first to Ceuta, and afterwards to Algesiras. Here we have an example showing, in the clearest manner, the unfairness of pronouncing upon the merits of an action until its particulars are known. Fortunately for the Admiral Pasley's commander, the court-martial that sat upon him took cognizance of all the circumstances; and, although captured in a 16-gun brig by two Spanish gun-boats, Lieutenant Nevin was honourably and deservedly acquitted.

Colonial Expeditions.—West Indies.

On the 11th of September, while the British 12-pounder 36-gun frigate Néréide, Captain Frederick Watkins, was cruising off the port of Amsterdam, in the island of Curaçoa, the Dutch inhabitants of the latter, tired out with the enormities of the band of 1500 republican ruffians that were in possession of the west part of the island, sent off a deputation to claim the protection of England. On the 13th the capitulation surrendering the island to his Britannic majesty, was signed in form, by the governor, Johan Rudolph Lausser, on the one part, and by Captain Watkins, of the Néréide, on the other. The vessels, large and small, lying in the harbour of Amsterdam, numbered 44; but no ships-of-war were among them.

In one of his despatches announcing this event, Captain Watkins speaks of the "activity and spirited conduct" of Lieutenant Michael Fitton,[1] commanding the Active schooner, then in company with the Néréide. Among the many occasions which called forth that eulogium, one, although it did not end decisively, may merit a place here. The Active was a schooner of about 80 tons, tender to the Abergavenny 54, the flag-ship at

1 See vol. ii., p. 398.

Jamaica, and carried eight 12-pounder carronades, with a crew of about 45 men and boys. The service upon which the Active had been ordered by Captain Watkins, was to watch the mouth of the harbour of Amsterdam, while the Néréide cruised in the offing. This the schooner continued to do for several days, standing in frequently so near, as to be just out of range of the long 18s and 24s on Fort Fiscadera, and in full view of five or six French privateers lying moored close to the walls of it, and one of which was the Quidproquo, already mentioned as captured by the Gispy.[1] Upon these privateers Lieutenant Fitton looked with a longing eye, till he could resist no longer. Observing that, at a certain hour every day, the officers went on shore at the fort to dine; and aware that, owing to his daily practice of standing across and across without molesting them, the privateersmen or garrison paid very little attention to the Active's manœuvres, Lieutenant Fitton resolved to afford them an unexpected treat. Having seen the boats pass as usual, and being in perfect readiness, the Active stood close in, and bringing her broadside to bear, opened the contents of it right into the sterns of the cluster of privateers.

Instantly all was bustle on board the latter and in the fort, and the boats, in their hurry back, became also exposed to a destructive fire from the schooner; some of whose 12-pounder shot, so well and closely directed as they were, could not have fallen harmless even in the fort itself. The instant he saw the guns of the latter in motion (and the people in charge of them appeared not very brisk), Lieutenant Fitton crowded sail away, in such a direction, however, as to expose no wider mark to the enemy than the Active's stern. This, as he anticipated, the artillerists at the fort failed to hit; although some of the shot pierced the schooner's sails, and a few others fell near enough to dash the spray on board. As the smallest of the five or six privateers had, undoubtedly, a larger number of men than the Active, any attempt by her to cut them out would have been madness in her commander. Probably the privateers were of opinion that the Néréide, who with her boats might easily have executed the service, would shortly make the attempt; for, in a few days afterwards, they took advantage of a clear coast, and made sail, each laden with a cargo of plunder. Nor was Lieutenant Fitton in a situation to intercept any one of these mischievous freebooters, the Active having sailed for Jamaica with the captain of the Néréide's despatches.

[1] See p. 30.

STATE OF THE BRITISH NAVY.

THE abstract of the British navy, for the commencement of the present year,[1] shows a considerable increase in its line-of-battle total; but the number of line-cruisers in commission remains the same as in the last abstract, and the lowèr totals exhibit, in reference to the latter, a very slight improvement in their numbers. As the one cause of this, the " Captured " column, owing chiefly to the reduced state of the Dutch, and the blockaded state of the French and Spanish navies, does not amount to half what it did in the preceding year.[2]

A very slight diminution occurs in the wrecked and foundered cases of the British navy in the year 1800; and the accidental losses of that year, including the melancholy loss by fire, ended the lives of upwards of 1300 British officers, seamen, and marines. All four of the foundered vessels belonged to the sloop-classes, and three of them had been French privateers. The number of cruisers employed in watching the enemy's ports, the boldness and perseverance with which their commanders performed that arduous duty, and the frequent gales of wind which occurred during the winter months of the year, render eleven wrecked cases, out of so many ships as were then at sea, no extraordinary number.[3]

The carronade still maintained, and more than maintained, its ground. On the 21st of February, 1800, an admiralty-order had issued, directing that in future all ships of 24 and 20 guns should be fitted on the main deck for 32-pounder carronades, in lieu of the long nines they had hitherto carried. This was giving

[1] See Appendix, Annual abstract, No. 9,   [2] See Appendix, No. 1.   [3] Ibid., No. 2.

the ships a great increase of force, without the necessity of detaching so many men to the guns; a 9-pounder long gun requiring seven men to fight it, but a 32-pounder carronade only six. Hence a greater number remained to handle the small-arms, and, a very important duty in action, to attend to the rigging and sails, and to work the ship in a proper manner. A few active seamen, promptly sent to repair a shroud or stay, will frequently save a mast; and a manœuvre, the success of which may decide the fate of a battle, often depends upon alacrity in splicing the old, or in reeving the new running-rigging.

The number of commissioned officers and masters, belonging to the British navy at the commencement of the year 1801, including among the flag-officers all that were promoted on the 1st of January, in consequence of the union of Great Britain and Ireland, as established by act of parliament on that day, was,—

Admirals	46
Vice-admirals	39
Rear-admirals	59
„ superannuated 29.	
Post-captains	516
„ superannuated 18.	
Commanders, or sloop-captains	391
Lieutenants	2135
„ retired, with rank of commanders 48	
Masters	517

and the number of seamen and marines, voted for the service of that year, was 120,000 for the first three lunar months, and 135,000 for the remaining ten.[1]

Although no Dutch navy existed capable of giving alarm to the British, Holland's northern neighbours, with Russia at their head, confederated together, to force England, either by diplomacy or war, to abandon a long recognised right, that of searching the ships of neutrals for contraband of war. This sudden uproar in the north arose out of a circumstance, of which we will here present a summary.

On the 25th of July, 1800, at 6 P.M., a British squadron, of three frigates, the Arrow sloop, and a lugger, fell in with the Danish 40-gun 18-pounder frigate Freya, Captain Krabbe, having under her convoy two ships, two brigs, and two galliots. Captain Thomas Baker, of the 28-gun frigate Nemesis, the

1 See Appendix, No. 3.

senior British officer, hailed the Freya, to say he should send
his boat on board the convoy. Captain Krabbe replied that,
if such an attempt were made, he would fire into the boat. Both
threats were put into execution ; and an action ensued, which,
with so decided a superiority against her, ended of course in the
Freya's submission. This affair, unhappily, did not pass off
without loss. The Nemesis and Arrow had each two seamen
killed and several wounded. The Freya had also two men
killed and five wounded, two of the latter badly. The English
vessels, accompanied by the Danish frigate and her convoy,
then proceeded to, and anchored in, the Downs; where the
Freya, by the order of Vice-admiral Skeffington Lutwidge, the
commander-in-chief on that station, still kept flying the Danish
ensign and pendant.

As, besides this fracas, a somewhat similar circumstance had
occurred in the Mediterranean, the British government lost no
time in despatching Lord Whitworth to the court of Denmark,
to place the business on an amicable footing. To give additional weight to his lordship's arguments, he was accompanied
by a squadron of four sail of the line (to which six more were
afterwards added), three 50-gun ships, and several frigates and
smaller vessels, under Vice-admiral Archibald Dickson, in the
74-gun ship Monarch. On the 29th of August Lord Whitworth
terminated the negotiation with the Danish minister, Count
Bernstorff; and a convention was mutually signed, agreeing that
the Freya and convoy should be repaired at English expense,
and then released; that the right of the British to search convoys should be discussed at a future day in London; that Danish
vessels should only sail under convoy in the Mediterranean, to
protect them from the Algerines, and should be searchable as
formerly ; and that the convention should be ratified by the two
courts in three weeks.

Russia, although the ally of England, took offence at the
attack upon the Freya, and particularly at the passage through
the Sound of a British squadron. The first overt act of the
Emperor Paul's displeasure, was to sequester all British property in his dominions; the next, was to place his army and
navy upon a war-establishment. On the 22nd of September,
however, about three weeks after it had been ordered, the seques-
tration was taken off. But on the 5th of November, the news
of the capture of Malta having excited fresh anger in the breast
of the emperor, an embargo was again laid on all the British
shipping in the ports of Russia amounting, at this time, to

about 200 sail. This was followed, in December, by a convention between Russia and Sweden, agreeing to the re-establishment of an armed neutrality between those powers. Denmark also, at the instigation of the first of these powers, and of Prussia, was induced to join the confederacy.

The menacing attitude thus assumed by the three principal northern powers requiring to be met in a corresponding way by England, the latter, on the 12th of March, despatched from Yarmouth roads, under the command of Admiral Sir Hyde Parker, in the London 98, with Vice-admiral Lord Nelson in the St. George 98, as his second, a fleet of 15, afterwards augmented to 18, sail of the line, with as many frigates, sloops, bombs, fire-ships, and smaller vessels, as made the whole amount to about 53 sail: on board a division of which fleet had embarked, the 49th regiment under Colonel Isaac Brock, two companies of the rifle-corps, and a detachment of artillery, the whole under the command of Colonel Stewart.

The nominal or paper force of the three powers against which this fleet was destined to act, was Russia 82, Denmark 23, and Sweden 18 sail of the line, besides, between them all, about 89 frigates, corvettes, and brigs, and nearly twice the number of armed small-craft. But Russia, even as late as October in the present year, did not possess more than 61 sail of the line; of which number 31 were in commission in the Baltic, and the remainder in the Mediterranean and Black seas. Those 31 ships were divided between Petersburg, Archangel, Cronstadt, and Revel. Perhaps the effective number, or that which might be brought to act as a fleet, did not exceed 20 sail of the line; and these were badly equipped, ill-appointed, and worse manned. The Swedes, at one time, had 11 sail of the line at Carlscrona ready for sea, and, by all accounts, in tolerably fighting trim. The Danish fleet at Copenhagen consisted, in the middle of March, of 10 sail of the line ready for sea, exclusive of about the same number in an unserviceable state.

This makes 41 Russian, Swedish, and Danish effective ships of the line, instead of 88, the number stated by several writers to have been afloat in this quarter. It must have been a very happy combination of circumstances that could have assembled in one spot 25 of those 41 sail of the line; and against that 25, made up, as the number would be, of three different nations, all mere novices in naval tactics, 18, or, with a Nelson to command them, 15 British sail of the line, were more than a match. Without this explanation, it might seem the height of rashness

in the British government to send to the Baltic so apparently
small a force.

In the hope that Denmark, in spite of her hostile demonstrations, would prefer negotiation to war, the Honourable Nicholas
Vansittart, with full powers to treat, had, about a fortnight
previous to the sailing of the fleet, departed for Copenhagen
in the 32-gun frigate Blanche, Captain Graham Eden Hamond.
Adverse winds kept the British fleet from reaching the Naze of
Norway until the 18th; and still heavier gales, during the two
succeeding days, scattered the vessels, especially the small-
craft, in all directions. To collect these, the admiral, on the
21st, anchored at the entrance of the Sound, within sight of
Koll point on the Swedish shore. Some of the smaller vessels
were unable to rejoin; and the Blazer gun-brig was driven
under the Swedish fort of Warberg, and there captured. In the
height of the bad weather the 74-gun ship Russel parted company, by signal, to take the Tickler gun-brig in tow; and,
during the dark and hazy night that ensued, was only saved
from being wrecked herself, by the great exertions of her officers
and crew.

On the 23rd the Blanche returned to the fleet, having on board,
with Mr. Vansittart, Mr. Drummond, the British chargé d'affaires
at Copenhagen; and from the Danish government, instead of a
reply of conciliation, came, as was to be expected, one of open
defiance. Much valuable time had thus been lost, and the
Danes were taking advantage of it in strengthening their means
of defence; the formidable appearance of which had already
excited the surprise of the British envoy.

The pilots, who, not having to share the honours, felt it to be
their interest to magnify the dangers of the expedition, occasioned
a few more days to be dissipated in inactivity. In the course of
these Admiral Parker sent a flag of truce to the governor of
Elsineur, to inquire if he meant to oppose the passage of the
fleet through the Sound. Governor Stricker replied, that the
guns of Cronenburg castle would certainly be fired at any British
ships-of-war that approached. At length, at 6 A.M. on the 30th,
the British fleet got under way, and, with a fine breeze at north-
north-west, proceeded into the Sound, in line ahead; the van
division commanded by Lord Nelson in the Elephant 74, into
which ship, as a lighter and more active one than the St.
George, he had, the preceding day, shifted his flag; the centre
division, by the commander-in-chief; and the rear division, by
Rear-admiral Graves. At 7 A.M. the batteries at Elsineur com-

menced firing at the Monarch, who was the leading ship, and at the other ships, as they passed in succession. The distance, however, was so great, that not a shot struck the ships; nor did any but the van-ships fire in return, and these only two or three broadsides. The seven bomb-vessels, however, threw shells; 200 of which were stated to have fallen in Cronenburg and Helsingen, and, among other damages, to have killed two, and wounded 15 men. The bursting of a 24-pounder on board the Isis, whereby seven men were killed and wounded, was the only casualty that attended the British in their passage through the Sound.

As the strait at Elsineur is less than three miles across, a mid-channel passage would undoubtedly have exposed the ships to a fire from Cronenburg castle on the one side, and from the Swedish city of Helsinburg on the other; but the latter, the batteries of which, instead of being a subject of dread as the pilots had given out, mounted only eight guns of a light caliber, did not make even a show of opposition. On observing this, the British inclined to the Swedish shore, passing within less than a mile of it; and thus avoided a fire which, as coming from nearly 100 pieces of cannon, could not fail to have been highly destructive.

About noon, or soon after, the fleet anchored at some distance above the island of Huën, which is about 15 miles from the city of Copenhagen. The commander-in-chief, Vice-admiral Lord Nelson, and Rear-admiral Graves, accompanied by Captain Domett, and the commanding officer of the troops, then proceeded, in the Lark lugger, to reconnoitre the enemy's defences. They were soon ascertained to be of the most formidable description. This led, in the evening, to a council of war: at which, as usual, much was urged to forego, or at least delay the attack; but Lord Nelson prevailed, and offered, with 10 sail of the line and all the small-craft, to carry the business through in a proper manner.

Admiral Parker, to his credit, cheerfully accepted the offer, and granted to his enterprising second two sail of the line more than he had asked; that is, two 50-gun ships, which in these northern parts are considered as of the line, partly because of their light draught of water as two-decked ships, and partly because a similar description of vessel is usually to be found in the opposite line. The detachment thus intrusted to Vice-admiral Lord Nelson, by the time the whole had joined, consisted of the

Gun-ship.

	Elephant . . .	{	Vice-admiral (b.) Lord Nelson, K.B. Captain Thomas Foley.
	Defiance . . .	{	Rear-admiral (w.) Thomas Graves. Captain Richard Retalick.
74	Edgar	,,	George Murray.
	Monarch	,,	James Robert Mosse.
	Bellona	,,	Sir Thos. Boulden Thompson.
	Ganges	,,	Thos. Francis Fremantle.
	Russel	,,	William Cuming.
64	Agamemnon . . .	,,	Robert Devereux Fancourt.
	Ardent	,,	Thomas Bertie.
	Polyphemus . . .	,,	John Lawford.
54	Glatton	,,	William Bligh.
50	Isis	,,	James Walker.

Gun-frig.

38	Amazon	,,	Henry Riou.
36	Désirée	,,	Henry Inman.
	Blanche	,,	Graham Eden Hamond.
32	Alcmène	,,	Samuel Sutton.
24	Jamaica	,,	Jonas Rose.
Sh.-slps.	Arrow	,,	William Bolton.
	Dart	,,	John Ferris Devonshire.
Br.-slps.	Cruiser	,,	James Brisbane.
	Harpy	,,	William Birchall.

Bomb-vessels, Discovery, Explosion, Hecla, Sulphur, Terror, Volcano, and Zebra.

Fire-ships, Otter and Zephyr.

Gun-brigs, Cutters, &c.

The force at Copenhagen was not the only obstacle to be surmounted; the approach to it was by a channel extremely intricate, and little known. To increase the difficulty of navigating it, the Danes very judiciously had removed or misplaced the buoys. On the same night, therefore, on which Sir Hyde had come to the happy decision of intrusting the affair to Lord Nelson, the latter, accompanied among others by Captain Brisbane of the Cruiser, proceeded in his boat to ascertain and rebuoy the outer channel, a narrow passage lying between the island of Saltholm and the Middle Ground. This was a very difficult, as well as a very fatiguing duty, and the vice-admiral rejoiced greatly when he had accomplished it. An attack from the northward was at first meditated : but a second examination of the Danish position on the 31st, and a favourable change of wind determined the vice-admiral to commence his operations from the southward.

On the morning of the 1st of April the British fleet weighed, and shortly afterwards re-anchored off the north-western extremity of the Middle Ground, a shoal which extends along the

whole sea-front of the city of Copenhagen, leaving an intervening channel of deep water, called the Konig-Stiefe, or King's
Channel, about three-quarters of a mile wide ; and in which
channel, close to the town, the Danes had moored their block-
ships, radeaus, prames, and gun-vessels. The distance of the
anchorage from the city of Copenhagen was about six miles.
In the course of the forenoon, Lord Nelson, embarking on board
the Amazon with some chosen friends, reconnoitred for the last
time the position he was about to attack ; and soon after his
return at 1 P.M., the signal to weigh appeared at the Elephant's
masthead—a signal, which was received by the different ships'
companies with a shout that must have been heard at a considerable distance. Immediately afterwards the vice-admiral's
squadron, amounting in the whole to 36 sail of square-rigged
vessels, got under way and set sail, in two divisions, with a light
but favourable wind, leaving Admiral Parker at anchor with
the

Gun-ship.			
	London . . .	{	Admiral (b.) Sir Hyde Parker.
98			Captain William Domett.
			,, Robert Waller Otway.
	St. George . . .		,. Thos. Masterman Hardy.
	Warrior		,, Charles Tyler.
74	Defence		,, Lord Henry Paulet.
	Saturn		,, Robert Lambert.
	Ramillies		,, Jas. William Taylor Dixon.
64	Raisonable . . .		,, John Dilkes.
	Veteran		,, Arch. Collingw. Dickson.

The ships of Lord Nelson's detachment, preceded by the
Amazon, entered the Upper Channel ; coasting along the edge
of the right-hand shoal or Middle Ground, until they had reached
and partly rounded its southern extremity. Here, off Draco
point, at about 8 P.M., just as it grew dark, the detachment
anchored ; the north-westernmost British ship being then distant about two miles from the southernmost ship of the Danish
line.

The same north-westerly wind, which had blown so fair passing along the outer channel, was now as foul for advancing by
the inner one. This, however, occasioned no delay ; for in so
difficult a navigation, daylight was as fully indispensable as a
fair wind. Part of this night, as many others had been, was
passed in active service. Captain Hardy proceeded in a small
boat to examine the channel between the British anchorage and
the Danish line, and actually approached near enough to sound
round the first ship of the latter ; using a pole, lest the noise of

throwing the lead should lead to a discovery. On his return, at about 11 P.M., Captain Hardy went on board the Elephant, and reported the depth of water up to the Danish line. This assurance of the practicability of the channel was gratifying news to Lord Nelson, and prevented him from sleeping during the remainder of the night.

We will now endeavour to give a description of the formidable force, which was to be the object of the morning's attack. It consisted of two-decked ships, chiefly old and in a dismantled state, frigates, prames, and radeaus, mounting altogether 628 guns, as particularized in the following table :—

Denomination.[1]	Name.	Description of Vessel.	Guns.						Men.[3]
			36[2] pds.	24 pds.	18 pds.	12 pds.	8 pds.	Tot	
B.S.	Provesteen . .	An old three-decker cut down, dismantled, and condemned	28	28	.	.	.	56	No 515
,,	Wagner . . .	An old two-decker; quarter-deck cut down, and condemned	.	48	.	.	.	48	361
Pr.	Rensburg . .	A prame for the transport of cavalry, with masts and sails	.	20	.	.	.	20	216
,,	Nyburg . . .	Ditto ditto	.	20	.	.	.	20	209
B.S.	Jutland . . .	An old two-decker condemned; without poop or masts	.	24	.	24	.	48	396
Rad.	Suersishen . .	Square floating battery, with masts	.	.	20	.	.	20	117
B.S.	Cronburg . .	An old condemned frigate; cut down and dismantled	.	22	.	.	.	22	196
Rad.	Hajen	A square battery like the Suersishen	.	.	20	.	.	20	155
B.S.	Dannebrog . .	An old condemned two-decker, cut down and dismantled	.	24	.	24	14	62	336
Sm.-ves.	Elwen	A small repeating vessel, rigged	.	6	.	.	.	6	80
Rad.	Grenier's-float	Old and without masts . . .	.	24	.	.	.	24	120
Pr.	Aggerstans . .	An old cav. transport, without masts	.	20	.	.	.	20	213
Gun-ship 74	Zealand . . .	A two-decker condemned and unrigged	.	30	30	.	14	74	529
B.S.	Charl.-Amelia	A condemned Indiaman . . .	.	26	.	.	.	26	225
Rad.	Sohesten . . .	A square battery like the Suersishen	.	18	.	.	.	18	126
Gun-ship 60	Hoistein . . .	A two-decker, newly repaired	.	24	.	24	12	60	400
B.S.	Indosforethen.	An old condemned two-decker, cut down and dismantled	.	26	.	26	12	64	390
Frigate	Hielpern . . .	A good completely rigged ship or frigate	20	.	.	.	.	20	265
		Total . .	48	360	70	98	52	628	4849

[1] B.S. stands for *block-ship*, Pr. for *prame*, and Rad. for *radeau*.
[2] For the mode of equalizing the Danish and English calibers, see vol. i., p. 46.
[3] Believed to be exclusive of soldiers and artillerymen.

These 18 vessels were moored in a line from a mile to a mile and a half in extent; flanked at the north end, or that nearest the town, by two artificial or pile-formed islands, called the Trekroner batteries, one of thirty 24, the other of thirty-eight 36-pounders, with furnaces for heating shot; and both of which batteries were commanded by the two two-decked block-ships Mars and Elephanten.

The entrance into the harbour and docks, which latter lie in the heart of the city, was protected by a chain thrown across it; also by some batteries on the northern shore, and particularly by the Trekroner or Crown batteries already described. In addition to this, the two 74-gun ships Dannemark and Trekroner, a 40-gun frigate, two 18-gun brigs, and several armed xebecs, with furnaces for heating shot, lay moored in advantageous positions off the harbour's mouth. Along the shore of Amag[1] island, a little to the southward of the floating line of defence, were several gun and mortar batteries; thus making the whole line of defence, in front of Copenhagen, cover an extent of between three and four miles. The Danish naval commanding officer was Commodore Olfert Fischer, who had his broad pendant on board the Dannebrog 62; nor was there a want of men, both skilful and brave, to work the Danish guns either afloat or on shore. One spirit, indeed, seemed to animate all Denmark, and that was to repel the invaders by every possible means.

The day of the 2nd of April opened, as the British had hoped it would, with a favourable or south-easterly wind. The signal for all captains on board the flag-ship was hoisted almost as soon as it could be seen; and at 8 A.M. the several captains were made acquainted with the stations assigned them. As circumstances, which will be mentioned in their place, prevented the plan's being strictly followed, it may suffice to state, that all the line-of-battle ships were to anchor by the stern abreast of the different vessels composing the enemy's line, and for which purpose they had already prepared themselves with cables out of their stern-ports. The Amazon, Blanche, Alcmène, Arrow, and Dart, with the two fire-ships, placed under the immediate directions of Captain Riou, were to co-operate in the attack upon the ships stationed at the harbour's mouth, and to act otherwise as circumstances might require. The bomb-vessels were to station themselves outside the British line, so as to throw their shells over it; and the Jamaica, with the brigs and gun-vessels, was to take a position for raking the southern ex-

[1] Spelt Amak by Southey, and other authors.

tremity of the Danish line. A similar station was assigned to
the Désirée. It was also intended that the 49th regiment under
Colonel Stewart, and 500 seamen, under Captain Fremantle of
the Ganges, should storm the principal of the Trekroner batteries, the instant that the cannonade from the ships had
silenced its fire.

At 9 A.M. the pilots and several of the masters were ordered
on board the Elephant. Their hesitation and indecision, about
the bearings of the shoal and the line of deep water, might well
provoke a more patient man than Lord Nelson. At 9 h. 30 m.
A.M., however, the signal was made to weigh in succession. The
Edgar led. The Agamemnon was to have followed; but, having
anchored rather outside, than off, the end of the great shoal, she
could not weather it, and was obliged again to bring up, in six
fathoms water. Here the current was so strong against her,
that, although the ship afterwards re-weighed, and continued
for a long time to warp with the stream and kedge anchors, the
Agamemnon was compelled a second time to bring up, nearly in
the spot from which she had last weighed. In the mean time
the Polyphemus, by signal, had followed the Edgar; and the
Isis steered after the former. Owing to the unskifulness or
unsteadiness of her master, Mr. Alexander Briarly, who had
undertaken the office of pilot, the Bellona, in spite of a fair
wind and ample room, hugged the Middle Ground too closely,
and grounded abreast of, and about 450 yards distant from, the
rear of the Danish line. Following closely, the Russel also
grounded, with her jib-boom almost over the Bellona's taffrail.

In compliance with the wish of the pilots, each ship had been
ordered to pass her leader on the starboard side, from a supposition that the water shoaled on the larboard shore; whereas
Captain Hardy had proved, that the water kept deepening all
the way to the enemy's line. The Elephant was next to the
Russel; and Lord Nelson, as soon as he perceived the state of
that ship and the Bellona, ordered the helm to be put a-starboard, and passed to the westward, or along the larboard beam,
of those ships; as, very fortunately, did all the ships astern of
the Elephant.

At the same moment that Lord Nelson's detachment weighed,
Admiral Parker's eight ships did the same; and the latter took
up a new position somewhat nearer to the mouth of the harbour,
but still at too great a distance to do more than menace the
north wing of defence. A nearer approach, indeed, with both
wind and current against the ships, was impracticable; in suf-

ficient time, at least, to render any active service in the engagement.

At 10 A.M. the cannonade commenced ; and, for nearly half an hour, the principal British ships engaged were the Polyphemus, Isis, Edgar, Ardent, and Monarch. At about 11 h. 30 m. A.M. the Glatton, Elephant, Ganges, and Defiance got to their stations ; as did several of the frigates and smaller vessels, and the action became general. The Désirée was of great service in raking the Provesteen, and drawing off a part of her heavy fire from the Polyphemus and Isis ; particularly from the latter, who bore the brunt of it, as her heavy loss will presently show. Owing to the strength of the current, the Jamaica, with the gun-vessels, could not get near enough to be of any service in the action ; nor were the bomb-vessels able to execute much. The absence of the Russel, Bellona, and Agamemnon occasioned several of the British ships to have a greater share of the enemy's fire than had been allotted to them, or than they were well able to bear. Among the many sufferers on this account was the Amazon, who, with the four other ships intrusted to Captain Riou, had most gallantly taken a position (the three frigates in particular) right against the Trekronen batteries.

At the end of a three hours' cannonade, few, if any, of the Danish block-ships, prames, or rideaus had ceased firing ; nor could the contest be said to have taken on either side a decisive turn. It was at this time that, in consequence, as is understood, of the pressing solicitations of the captain of the fleet, founded upon information received a full hour before that signals of distress were at the mast-heads of two British line-of-battle ships (the Bellona and Russel), and the signal of inability on board a third (the Agamemnon), coupled with the imperfect view which the London's distance from the scene of action enabled Sir Hyde himself to take of the relative condition of the parties in it ; observing also the zig-zag course and necessarily slow progress of the Defence, Ramillies, and Veteran, which had been detached as a reinforcement to the vice-admiral, the commander-in-chief was persuaded to throw out the signal for discontinuing the engagement.[1]

The manner in which Lord Nelson received this signal is very

---

[1] It is but common justice towards Sir Hyde Parker to state, that he made the signal " to discontinue the action," in order that Lord Nelson might withdraw from the contest, if, owing to the different ships unable to reach their station, some being *a-ground*, he felt his force insufficient to maintain the attack ; for it was evident that Sir Hyde's division could not proffer the least assistance : the signal was made with a generous intention, and Mr. Southey has added a note similar to this in his second edition of his Life of Nelson.—ED.

forcibly depictured in a popular biographical work. "About this time," says Mr. Southey, "the signal-lieutenant called out that No. 39 (the signal for discontinuing the action) was thrown out by the commander-in-chief. He continued to walk the deck, and appeared to take no notice of it. The signal-officer met him at the next turn, and asked if he should repeat it. 'No,' he replied, 'acknowledge it.' Presently he called after him to know if the signal for close action was still hoisted; and, being answered in the affirmative, said, 'Mind you keep it so.' He now paced the deck, moving the stump of his lost arm in a manner which always indicated great emotion. 'Do you know,' said he to Mr. Fergusson, 'what is shown on board the commander-in-chief? Number 39!' Mr. Fergusson asked him what that meant. 'Why, to leave off action.' Then, shrugging up his shoulders, he repeated the words—'Leave off action? Now d—n me if I do! You know, Foley,' turning to the captain, 'I have only one eye,—I have a right to be blind sometimes;' —and then putting the glass to his blind eye, in that mood of mind which sports with bitterness, he exclaimed, 'I really do not see the signal.' Presently he exclaimed, 'D—n the signal! keep mine for closer battle flying! That's the way I answer such signals. Nail mine to the mast.'" [2]

Thus, the signal to discontinue the action was answered only, not repeated, on board the Elephant; and, although the Defiance repeated it, Rear-admiral Graves would not suffer the signal to be hoisted anywhere but at the lee maintopsail yard-arm, and still kept No. 16, the signal for close action, flying at the maintopgallantmast head. The frigates and sloops now hauled off from the Trekroner batteries, and by doing so were probably saved from destruction. It was while unavoidably presenting her stern to those batteries that the Amazon had her gallant captain shot in two, and sustained the principal part of her loss.

At 1 h. 30 m. P.M. the fire of the Danes slackened; and, at a little before 2 P.M., it ceased along nearly the whole of the line astern of the Zealand. Some of the prames and light vessels had also gone adrift; but few if any of the vessels whose flags had been struck would suffer themselves to be taken possession of. They fired at the boats as the latter approached, and the batteries on Amag island aided them in this irregular warfare. "This arose," says Mr. Southey, "from the nature of the action; the crews were continually reinforced from the shore:

[1] Southey's Life of Nelson, vol. ii., p. 124.

and fresh men coming on board did not inquire whether the flag had been struck, or, perhaps, did not heed it; many, or most of them, never having been engaged in war before, knowing nothing, therefore, of its laws, and thinking only of defending their country to the last extremity."

At all events it greatly, and very naturally, irritated Lord Nelson; who at one time had thoughts of sending in the fireships to burn the surrendered vessels. As a preliminary measure, however, his lordship wrote the celebrated letter to the Crown Prince of Denmark, wherein he says: " Vice-admiral Lord Nelson has been commanded to spare Denmark when she no longer resists. The line of defence which covered her shores has struck to the British flag; but, if the firing is continued on the part of Denmark, he must set on fire all the prizes that he has taken, without having the power of saving the men who have so nobly defended them. The brave Danes are the brothers and should never be the enemies of the English." A wafer was then given him, but he ordered a candle to be brought from the cockpit, and sealed the letter with wax, affixing a larger seal than he ordinarily used. " This," said his lordship, " is no time to appear hurried and informal."

This letter was carried on shore, with a flag of truce, by Captain Sir Frederick Thesiger (a young commander acting as one of Lord Nelson's aides-de-camp), who found the crown prince at the sallyport. In the mean time the destructive cannonade, still kept up by the Defiance, Monarch, and Ganges, and the near approach of the Defence and Ramillies (the Veteran far astern), silenced the fire of the Indosforethen, Holstein, and the ships next to them in the Danish line. But the great Trekroner, having had nothing but frigates and sloops opposed to it, and that only for a time, was comparatively uninjured. This battery therefore continued its fire; and, as about 1500 men had been thrown into it from the shore, was considered too strong to be stormed. It was now deemed an advisable measure to withdraw the fleet out of the intricate channel while the wind continued fair; and preparations were making for that purpose, when the Danish Adjutant-general Lindolm came bearing a flag of truce: upon sight of which the Trekroner ceased firing; and the action, after having continued five hours, during four of which it had been warmly contested, was brought to a close.

The message from the crown prince was to inquire the particular object of Lord Nelson's note. The latter replied, in

writing, that humanity was the object; that he consented to
stay hostilities; that the wounded Danes should be taken on
shore; and that he should take his prisoners out of the vessels,
and burn or carry off his prizes as he should think fit: his lordship concluded with a hope that the victory he had gained
would lead to a reconciliation between the two countries. Sir
Frederick Thesiger, who had returned with the Danish adjutant-general, was again sent with the reply; and the latter
was referred to the commander-in-chief for a final adjustment of
the terms.

The opportunity afforded by this delay, the London being
nearly four miles distant, was not lost by Lord Nelson; and the
leading British ships, all of which were much crippled in their
rigging and sails, weighed or slipped in succession. The
Monarch led the way, and touched upon the shoal; but the
Ganges, taking her amidships, pushed her over it. The Glatton,
drawing less water, passed clear; but the Defiance and Elephant
grounded about a mile from the Trekroner; and, in spite of the
exertions of their active crews, there remained fixed for many
hours. The Désirée, also, at the opposite end of the line,
having gone to assist the Bellona, became fast on the same
shoal as the latter. The Bellona, however, was soon got afloat
by resources of her own. An experienced quartermaster, observing the Isis in the act of slipping, suggested to the first-
lieutenant that, if a boat were sent to pick up that ship's cable,
they might haul off by it. The hint was taken, and the Bellona
quickly freed herself from the shoal.

Soon after the Elephant had grounded, Lord Nelson quitted
her, and followed the Danish adjutant-general to the London.
While the conference is holding, we will proceed to show, as
well as we are able, at what expense England had brought
Denmark to so subdued a tone. Taking the ships in the order
in which they stand in a list at a subsequent page, the Désirée
had one lieutenant (Andrew King) and three seamen wounded;
the Russel, five seamen and one marine wounded; the Bellona,
nine seamen and two private marines killed, and her captain (leg
amputated), two lieutenants (Thomas Southey and Thomas
Wilks), one master's mate (James Emmerton), four midshipmen
(John Anderson, Edward Daubenny, William Sitford, and William Figg), 48 seamen, 10 private marines, one captain (Alexander Sharp), and five privates of foot wounded: the greater
part of this loss, unfortunately, arose from the bursting of two
of her lower-deck guns, owing, as is understood, to their having

been overcharged. The Polyphemus had one midshipman
(James Bell), four seamen, and one marine killed, and her boatswain (Edward Burr), 20 seamen, and four marines wounded;
the Isis, her master (Daniel Lamond), two midshipmen (George
M'Kinlay and Thomas Ram), 22 seamen, one lieutenant (Henry
Long) and four privates of marines, one lieutenant and two
privates of foot killed, and one lieutenant (Richard Cormack),
three midshipmen (Reuben Pain, Simon Frazer, and Charles
Jones), 69 seamen, 13 privates of marines, and two privates of
foot wounded; the Edgar, her first-lieutenant (Edmund Johnson), 24 seamen, one lieutenant (Benjamin Spencer) and two
privates of marines, and three privates of foot killed, and two
lieutenants (Joshua Johnson and William Goldfinch), five midshipmen (Thomas Gahagan, William Whimper, John James
Ridge, Peter Procter, William Domett), 79 seamen, 17 privates
of marines, and eight privates of foot wounded; the Ardent,
one midshipman (George Hoare), and 29 seamen and marines
killed, and 64 seamen and marines wounded; the Glatton, one
pilot and 17 seamen and marines killed, one lieutenant (William
Tindall) one master's mate (Robert Thompson), one midshipman (John Williams), and 34 seamen and marines wounded;
the Elephant, one master's mate (Henry Yaulden), four seamen,
three privates of marines, one captain and one private of foot
killed, and two midshipmen (Robert Gill and Hugh Mitchel),
eight seamen, one private of marines, and two privates of foot
wounded; the Ganges, her master (Robert Stewart) and five
seamen killed, one pilot wounded, and one seaman missing; the
Monarch, her captain, 35 seamen, 12 privates of marines, and
eight privates of foot killed, one lieutenant (William Minchin),
her boatswain (William Joy), five midshipmen (Henry Swimmer,
William John Bowes, Thomas Harlowe, George Morgan, and
Philip le Vesconte), 101 seamen, one lieutenant (James Marrie)
and 34 privates of marines, and one lieutenant and 20 privates
of foot wounded; the Defiance, one lieutenant (George Gray),
one pilot, 17 seamen, three privates of marines, and two privates
of foot killed, her boatswain, one midshipman (James Galla-
way), one captain's clerk, one pilot, 35 seamen, five privates of
marines, and seven privates of foot wounded; the Amazon, her
captain, one midshipman (Honourable George Tucket), one
captain's clerk (Joseph Rose), 10 seamen, and one marine
killed, two masters' mates (James Harry and Philip Horn),
16 seamen, and five marines wounded; the Blanche, six seamen
and one marine killed, and seven seamen and two marines

wounded ; the Alcmène, five seamen killed, and one lieutenant (Henry Baker), her boatswain (Charles Church), one master's mate (George Augustus Spearing), one pilot, 12 seamen, one lieutenant and two privates of marines wounded ; and the Dart, her first-lieutenant (Richard Edward Sandys) and two seamen killed, and one seaman wounded : making, including among the killed the one missing in the Ganges, a total of 255 killed and 688 wounded.

Thus say the official returns ; but it would appear that these take no notice of the slightly wounded. As one instance, the Ardent, besides her 64 in the returns, had 40 wounded who were able to go to quarters. The whole of the slightly wounded, according to the testimony of officers in the fleet, would have swelled the wounded total to at least 950, and the total of killed and wounded to upwards of 1200. More than half of the wounded enumerated in the returns are also represented to have died of their wounds. If this be correct, the loss may be stated thus : killed and mortally wounded, 350; recoverably and slightly wounded, 850.

Even the smallest in amount of the two returns of loss here given could only have resulted from good and steady firing ; and, truly, the British ships displayed the marks of it in their hulls, lower shrouds, and lower masts, rather than, as on most occasions, in their upper masts, running rigging, and sails. The Glatton, indeed, had her foretopmast shot away ; but it does not appear that any other ship's topmast, or even topgallantmast, came down during the action. Most of the ships had a part of their guns rendered useless. Of the Ardent's main deck 42-pounder carronades, more than half were disabled ; as were seven of the Glatton's 32, and two of her 68-pounders. It has already been stated, that a part of the Bellona's heavy loss arose from the bursting of two of her guns : a similar accident, it is believed, occurred a second time (see p. 45) on board the Isis. Both of these ships were very old, the one having been built in 1760, and the other in 1774 ; and their guns were probably the same originally established upon them.

The damages sustained by the Danish ships, or floating-hulks, may be summed up by stating, that the greater part of them were literally knocked to pieces. To this condition they would undoubtedly have been reduced, in much less time than four hours, the duration of the general cannonade, had the pilots permitted the British ships to take a closer position to their Danish opponents, than from 300 to 400 yards ; in which case the heavy carronades of the Glatton and Ardent would have produced their full effect. With respect to the Danish loss, we are unable to particularize it. Commodore Fischer reckoned his killed and wounded, according to the lowest estimate, at between 1600 and 1800 men, including 270 lost by the Dannebrog alone. In the British accounts, the Danish alleged loss by shot is mixed up with the loss by prisoners taken; and the whole is made to amount to about 6000 men.

The following table, besides showing how the Danish vessels were disposed of, places the British ships, from the Polyphemus downwards, in the order in which they anchored; nor does the station of each of the latter, in reference to her opponent or opponents in the Danish line, materially vary from what it really was. A column for the official numerical loss, and another, to the best of our ability, for the surviving first-lieutenant, of each British ship engaged, have also been added:—

DANISH.	How disposed of.	BRITISH.	Loss. K.	Loss. W.	First-Lieutenants.
		Désirée	..	4	Andrew King.
		Russel	..	6	Samuel Bateman.
		Bellona . .	11	72	John Delafons.
Provesteen .	Taken and burnt, having been forsaken when	Polyphemus .	6	25	Edward Hodder.
Wagner . . .	the guns were useless.	Isis	33	88	Robert Tinkler.
Rensburg . . .	Driven on the shoals, and burnt by the British.				
Nyburg	Escaped; afterwards sank.	Edgar	31	111	Joshua Johnson.
Jutland . . .					
Suersishen . .	Taken and burnt by the				
Cronburg . .	British.	Ardent . . .	30	64	Andrew Mott.
Hajen					
Dannebrog . . .	Caught fire, and blew up after the action.				
Elwen . . .	Escaped.	Glatton . . .	18	37	Rob. Brown Tom.
Grenier's-float					
Aggerstans . .	Ditto, and afterwards sank.	Elephant . .	10	13	Wm. Wilkinson.
Zealand	Driven under the Trekroner battery, and taken; afterwards burnt.				
Charl.-Amelia	Taken, and afterwards	Ganges . . .	7	1	William Morce.
Sohesten . .	burnt.				
Holstein	Ditto; put in sailing condition and carried away.	Monarch . . .	56	164	John Yelland.
Indosforethen .	Ditto, and afterwards burnt.				
Hielpern . . .	Escaped.	Defiance . . .	24	51	David Mudie.
		Amazon . . .	14	23	Jos. Ore Masefield.
		Blanche . . .	7	9	Thos. M'Culloch.
		Alcmène . .	5	19	Rt. Wal. Dunlop.
		Dart	3	1	Richard Hawkes.
			253	688	

Although, as, without reckoning the two prames which sank in shoal water while escaping and were probably recovered, the British had captured or destroyed 13 out of the 18 floating-batteries that formed the Danish line to the southward of the Trekroner islands, the victory was to them; yet the Danes, viewing Lord Nelson's message to the crown prince as the first overture to a cessation of hostilities, solaced themselves with the belief, that the affair, at the most, could only be considered as a drawn battle. Whatever name the contest went by, it fully succeeded, as we shall presently have to show, in attaining the object for which it had been commenced.

No nation could behave better, no men could fight more bravely, than did the Danes on this occasion; but Commodore Fischer, nevertheless, was a little in error in regard to his report to the crown prince. That account states, that the British line, reckoning from the Defiance, did not stretch further northward than the Zealand, and therefore did not engage more than two-thirds of the Danish line of defence; while the Trekroner battery, and the block-ships Elephanten and Mars, with the frigate Hielpern, did not come at all into action. This is disproved by the single fact, that the Defiance had her mainmast, mizenmast, and bowsprit badly wounded by the very first broadside fired from the Trekoner battery. Not only, then, was the latter engaged, but the Defiance must have been stationed nearly abreast of it, to have suffered as she did. It will be creditable to Captain-lieutenant Lillenshield to suppose, that it was the fire of the Defiance, and not the want of an antagonist, which drove his ship, the 36-pounder frigate Hielpern, out of the line. As to the Elephanten and Mars, they properly belonged to the north wing of defence; and many of their heavy shot, no doubt, fell among the frigates and sloops, appointed, owing to the unavoidable absence of more able ships, to act against this formidable quarter of the Danish position.

Commodore Fischer assures his countrymen, that the British had two ships to his one, and therefore were doubly superior in force. Let us, without being over-minute, submit this assertion to proof. Dismissing from the calculation the whole of the Danish north wing, and the frigates and sloops opposed to it; also the bomb-vessels (for they really were useless), the two ships aground,[1] the Quintus redoubt and five adjacent batteries on

[1] These were only partially effective. Although abreast of the Polyphemus, the Russel, lying obliquely, or with her stern to the westward, was enabled to fire athwart the bows of that ship; while the Bellona, with her six aftmost guns on each deck, fired astern of the Isis, and with her six foremost ones (leaving the two midship guns on each deck unemployed), ahead of her. Doubtless many shot from both grounded ships struck the Polyphemus and Isis.

Amag island, and the Jamaica and the little fry with her, we have five 74-gun ships, two 64s, one 54, one 50, and one 36-gun frigate to oppose to the 18 block-ships, prames, radeaus, and other vessels which have already been named. Taking the Danish guns from the Danish accounts, we submit the following statement as not materially incorrect :—

British.				*Danish.*			
Long guns.		No.	No.	Long guns.		No.	No.
32-pounders	. .	140		36-pounders	. .	48	
24 ,,	. .	74		24 ,,	. .	360	
18 ,,	. .	192		18 ,,	. .	70	
12 ,,	. .	22		12 ,,	. .	98	
9 ,,	. .	114		8 ,,	. .	52	
6 ,,	. .	6				——	628
		——	548	Carronades.			
Carronades.							•
68 ,,	. .	28		None apparently.			
42 ,,	. .	26					
32 ,,	. .	54					
24 ,,	. .	8					
18 ,,	. .	36					
		——	152				
	Total	700			Total	628	

This, although something less than a "two-to-one" superiority, is sufficient to entitle Commodore Fischer, and the brave officers and men under his command, to great credit for the obstinate defence they made. As an instance of individual courage and devotion on the part of the Danes, and of most noble feeling on the part of Lord Nelson, we transcribe from the pages of a respectable periodical work the following anecdote : "During the repast (at the palace) Lord Nelson spoke in raptures of the bravery of the Danes, and particularly requested the prince to introduce him to a very young officer, whom he described as having performed wonders during the battle, by attacking his own ship immediately under her lower guns. It proved to be the gallant young Welmoes, a stripling of seventeen. The British hero embraced him with the enthusiasm of a brother, and delicately intimated to the prince that he ought to make him an admiral; to which the prince very happily replied, 'If, my lord, I were to make all my brave officers admirals, I should have no captains or lieutenants in my service.' This heroic youth had volunteered the command of a prame, which is a sort of raft, carrying six small cannon, and manned with 24 men, who pushed off from the shore, and in the fury of the battle placed themselves under the stern of Lord Nelson's ship, which they most successfully attacked, in such a manner that, although they were below the reach of the stern-chasers, the British marines made terrible slaughter amongst them: 20 of these gallant men fell by their bullets, but their young commander continued knee-deep in dead at his post, until the truce was announced."[1]

Having taken some notice of the Danish accounts of this battle, we must not behave so disrespectfully as to neglect bestowing a word or two upon the English accounts. According to the misplaced "Note," which we formerly quoted from Admiral Ekins's work,[2] Lord Nelson attributed the grounding of the Bellona and Russel to his not having ordered his ships, in so intricate and shallow a navigation, to cut instead of to weigh. It is certainly the first time we ever heard that the Vice-admiral was in this respect to blame: but we are convinced that, of all other men, Lord Nelson was the most likely to acknowledge an error, if he thought he had committed one.

Although Admiral Ekins has not considered it necessary to give any account of the Copenhagen affair, another contemporary has entered into it with rather more than his usual conciseness. Captain Brenton has also given a "Plan of the battle;" but, as is often the case, the engraved and the letter-press descriptions do not correspond. One important instance will suffice:—The Bellona and Russel are placed in the plan, within a ship's length or so of their actual stations; but the letter-press tells us, that those ships were "much exposed to the fire of the Crown batteries;"[3] which Crown batteries, as rightly laid down in the same plan, are to the northward of the northern extremity of the Danish line, or perhaps about two miles and a half from the nearest of the two grounded ships, the Bellona. The fact is, neither ship received or could receive a shot from the Trekroner, although they both received several from the Wagner and Provesteen; and a Danish 36-pound shot, from one of the batteries on Amag island, went through the centre of the Bellona's mainmast.

In almost all the published unofficial accounts, a misstatement also occurs respecting the Agamemnon. Lord Nelson in his letter says: "The Agamemnon could not weather the shoal of the middle, and was obliged to anchor;"[4] but Captain Brenton

[1] Naval Chronicle, vol. xiv., p. 398.
[2] See vol. ii., p. 203.
[3] Brenton, vol. ii., p. 545.
[4] Ibid., p. 203.

tells us, that "the Agamemnon grounded on the starboard quarter of the Bellona," and Mr. Southey (but who, by-the-by, is very poor authority in naval matters) declares that she was "immovably aground."[1]

The night of the 2nd of April was employed by the British in bringing out their shattered prizes, and in floating their grounded ships. By the morning of the 3rd the whole of the latter, except the Désirée were got off. During the five days that the negotiation was pending, all the prizes, except the 60-gun ship Holstein, were set on fire and destroyed. The generality of these were not worth carrying away; but Sir Hyde's reason for extending the order to the Zealand, a much larger and finer ship than the Holstein, is not very clear.

On the 9th, after some altercation as to the duration of the armistice, one was agreed upon for 14 weeks; and Denmark engaged to suspend all proceedings under the treaty of armed neutrality which she had entered into with Sweden and Russia. The prisoners, also, were to be sent on shore, and accounted for in case hostilities should be renewed. Moreover the British fleet had permission to provide itself, at Copenhagen and elsewhere along the coast, with all things requisite for the health and comfort of the seamen.

On the 12th, having despatched home the Holstein, Monarch, and Isis, with the wounded men, Admiral Parker sailed from Copenhagen road with the remainder of the fleet, except the St. George and one or two frigates, and directed his course along the difficult channel of the Grounds, between the islands of Amag and Saltholm. This was both a tedious and a dangerous navigation, as most of the men-of-war had to tranship their guns into merchant-vessels; and even then, several of the former got on shore. The whole of the ships at length extricated themselves; and, to the astonishment of Danes, Swedes, Russians, and Prussians, entered the Baltic by this route.

The British admiral's first object was to attack the Russian squadron at Revel, before the breaking up of the frost should enable it to effect a junction with the Swedish squadron at Carlscrona; but, in his way thither, hearing that a Swedish squadron, reported at nine sail of the line, was at sea, Sir Hyde steered for the northern extremity of the island of Bornholm. The Swedish admiral, however, whose force consisted of only six sail of the line, conceiving himself no match for a British admiral with 16, sought refuge behind the forts of Carlscrona.

---

[1] Southey's Life of Nelson, vol. ii., p. 118.

Here a negotiation was opened between Sir Hyde Parker and the Swedish Vice-admiral Cronstadt; which, on the 22nd, ended in an agreement by his Swedish majesty to treat for the accommodation of all existing differences.

By this time Lord Nelson had joined the admiral, and had his flag again flying on board the Elephant. How he had got thither merits to be related. On the 18th the St. George, having removed her guns to an American vessel, and, by the excellent management of Mr. Briarly, of the Bellona, whose local experience was very great, succeeded in passing the Grounds, was ready to follow Sir Hyde; but a contrary wind detained her. On the following evening Lord Nelson received intelligence from the admiral, of the Swedish fleet's having been seen by one of his look-out frigates. Instantly he quitted the St. George, and, embarking in a six-oared cutter, with Mr. Briarly, set off to join the admiral, although the latter was at a distance of 24 miles, in the very teeth of the wind and current. "The moment he received the account," says Mr. Briarly, "he ordered a boat to be manned, and, without even waiting for a boat-cloak (though you must suppose the weather pretty sharp here at this season of the year), and having to row about 24 miles with the wind and current against him, jumped into her, and ordered me to go with him, I having been on board that ship (the St. George) to remain till she had got over the Grounds. All I had ever seen or heard of him could not half so clearly prove to me the singular and unbounded zeal of this truly great man. His anxiety in the boat for nearly six hours, lest the fleet should have sailed before he got on board one of them, and lest we should not catch the Swedish squadron, is beyond all conception. I will quote some expressions in his own words. It was extremely cold, and I wished him to put on a great coat of mine which was in the boat: 'No, I am not cold; my anxiety for my country will keep me warm. Do you think the fleet has sailed?' 'I should suppose not, my lord.'—'If they have, we will follow them to Carlscrona in the boat, by God!'" The distance to which place, Mr. Briarly goes on to state, was about 50 leagues. At midnight, Lord Nelson reached the Elephant; and Mr. Briarly returned to the St. George, to conduct her to Kioge bay.

On the 23rd a lugger joined the fleet, then not far from Carlscrona on its way to the gulf of Finland, with despatches from Count Van der Paklen, the Russian ambassador at Copenhagen, containing overtures of a pacific nature from Alexander I., who now, by the decease of the Czar Paul, had become invested with the imperial sceptre. This induced Sir Hyde to return with the fleet to Kioge bay; where, on the 5th of May, he was found by a vessel that brought despatches recalling him from the com mand. Shortly afterwards Admiral Parker sailed for England in the Blanche, leaving the command of the fleet to Vice-admiral Lord Nelson. Almost the first signal made by the new commander-in-chief was, to hoist in all the launches and prepare to weigh. On the 7th the fleet, by the addition of the St. George now augmented to 17 sail of the line, a 54 and a 50 gun ship, besides a few frigates and smaller vessels, set sail from Kioge bay. On the 8th, after having by a flag of truce informed Vice-admiral Cronstadt, that although Sir Hyde Parker had consented not to interrupt the Swedish navigation, he should act against the Swedish fleet if he found it at sea, Lord Nelson left Captain Murray, with the Edgar, Russel, Saturn, Agamemnon, Ardent, Raisonable, Glatton, and a frigate to cruise off Carlscrona; while, with the remaining 11 sail of the line, one frigate, and two brig-sloops, the vice-admiral hastened to the gulf of Finland.

On the 14th Lord Nelson anchored in Revel roads; but no Russian squadron was in that quarter. The bay had been clear of firm ice since the 29th of April, at which time Sir Hyde Parker, with the fleet, was lying inactive at Kioge: and the Russians had subsequently sawed through the ice in the mole, and on the 3rd had sailed for Cronstadt. A communication with the shore now took place; and the Emperor Alexander repeated his friendly intentions, but expressed surprise at the appearance of the British admiral at Revel. On the 17th the latter quitted the road; and on the 19th the Russians and Swedes took off the embargo that had been laid on British vessels in their ports. Thus were the amicable relations between England and those two powers once more restored.

On the 6th of June, after having been at anchor some days off Rostock, Lord Nelson retired to Kioge bay, and on the 13th received the sanction of the admiralty to an application which, on account of the bad state of his health, he had made to return to England. On the 17th or 18th Vice-admiral Sir Charles Morice Pole, in the 32-gun frigate Æolus, arrived to take the command; and on the 19th Lord Nelson quitted the Baltic in the Kite brig. Vice-admiral Pole remained on the station until the latter end of July; when, there being no longer any occasion for so powerful a fleet in the Baltic, he was ordered home. Although his command had been short and pacific,

Vice-admiral Pole found means to increase the high opinion that his predecessor had gained for the British navy in these inland seas, by carrying safely through the intricate channel of the Great Belt, against an adverse wind, a fleet of line-of-battle ships, two of which were three-deckers.

For the successful result of the Copenhagen battle, and the gallantry displayed in it by Lord Nelson and his associates, the thanks of both houses of parliament were voted to the admirals, captains, officers, and men of Sir Hyde Parker's fleet. Owing to some political considerations, having reference, we believe, to the ties that existed between the crowned heads of England and Denmark, the only mark of royal approbation bestowed upon the conquerors was the investment of Rear-admiral Graves with the order of the bath. This infraction of the usual custom did not, however, extend to the promotion of the junior class of officers, all the lieutenants of the ships engaged, and perhaps a few others, being made commanders, and Captains Devonshire, Brisbane, and Birchall, post-captains.

British and French Fleets.

The continental war having ceased, by a treaty of peace concluded at Luneville on the 9th of February between France and the Emperor of Germany, the first-consul began more seriously than ever to entertain hopes of being able to plant his victorious legions upon British ground. "Tous les moyens propres à entretenir la haine de la nation contre la Grande-Bretagne fut employés avec activité et avec succès. Les autorités, les orateurs du gouvernement, les écrivains publicistes, rivalisèrent de zèle pour prêcher cette espèce de croisade contre l'éternelle ennemie de la France."[1]

The port of Boulogne was to be the central rendezvous of the grand flotilla; and on the 12th of July Buonaparte issued an order for the assemblage there of nine divisions of gun-vessels, and of the same number of battalions of troops, besides several detachments of artillery to serve the guns on board the flotilla. Of which flotilla Rear-admiral René-Madeleine La Touch-Tréville was appointed the commander-in-chief, with directions to exercise the troops in ship-working, in firing the guns, in boarding, and in getting in and out of the vessels.

These preparations, exaggerated as they were by the French journals, spread no slight degree of alarm on the shores of

[1] Victoires et Conquêtes, tome xiv., p. 18.

England, and caused corresponding preparations, in the defensive way, to be made by the British government. Among other measures taken to calm the public mind, was the appointment of Vice-admiral Lord Nelson to the chief command of the defence constructing and collecting along the coast from Orfordness to Beachy Head.

On the 30th of July the vice-admiral hoisted his flag on board the 18-pounder 32-gun frigate Medusa, Captain John Gore, at anchor in the Downs; and on the 3rd of August, having under his charge about 30 vessels, great and small, Lord Nelson, by orders from the admiralty, of which Earl St. Vincent was now at the head, stood across to Boulogne; the port whence, as already stated, the main attempt was to be made, and which the French, informed by their secret intelligence that an attack would be made, had recently been fortifying with great care.

On the 4th the English bomb-vessels threw their shells amidst the French flotilla, consisting of 24 brigs, lugger-rigged flats, and a schooner, moored in a line in front of the town. The effect of the bombardment was, by the English account, the sinking of three flats and a brig, and the driving of several others on shore; but the French declare that only two gunboats were slightly damaged, and that not a man was hurt on board the flotilla. Nor did the British sustain any greater loss than one captain of artillery and two seamen wounded by the bursting of a French shell.

On the night of the 15th of August, Lord Nelson despatched the armed boats of his squadron, formed into four divisions, under the respective commands of Captains Philip Somerville, Edward Thornborough Parker, Isaac Cotgrave, and Robert Jones, and accompanied by a division of mortar-boats, under Captain John Conn, to attempt to bring off the French flotilla, which had been much strengthened since the last attack. At about 11 h. 30 m. P.M. the boats put off from the Medusa, in the most perfect order; but the darkness of the night, co-operating with the tide and half-tide, separated the divisions.

The first division, under Captain Somerville, on getting near to the shore, was carried by the current considerably to the eastward of Boulogne bay. Finding it impracticable to reach the French flotilla in the order prescribed, Captain Somerville ordered the boats to cast each other off and make the best of their way. By this means, at a little before the dawn of day on the 16th, some of the leading boats got up to and attacked a brig lying close to the pier-head; and, after a sharp contest, carried the vessel, but were prevented from towing her off, owing to her being secured with a chain, and owing to a heavy fire of musketry and grape-shot, opened as well from the shore as from three luggers and a second brig, lying within half pistol-shot of the first. Thus compelled to abandon their prize, and the daylight putting a stop to further operations, the boats of the first division pushed out of the bay. The persevering efforts of the officers and men of this division had cost them dearly; their loss amounting to one master's mate (Alexander Rutherford), 14 seamen, and three marines killed, four lieutenants (Thomas Oliver, Francis Dickenson, Jeremiah Skelton, and William Basset), one captain of marines (George Young), one master's mate (Francis Burney), one midshipman (Samuel Spratley), 29 seamen, and 19 marines wounded; total, 18 killed and 55 wounded.

The second division, under Captain Parker, was more successful than the first in meeting less obstacles from the current, and at about half an hour past midnight got to the scene of action. One subdivision of the boats, led by the captain, immediately ran alongside of a large brig, the Etna, moored off the Mole head, wearing the broad pendant of Commodore Etienne Pévrieux. Nothing could exceed the impetuosity of the attack; but a very strong netting, traced up to the brig's lower yards, baffled all the endeavours of the British to board, and an instantaneous discharge of her great guns and small-arms, the latter from about 200 soldiers stationed on the gunwale, knocked back into their boats nearly the whole of the assailants. The second subdivision, under Lieutenant Williams, carried a lugger, but, in attacking a brig, the Volcan, met with a repulse, and was obliged to retire with the other subdivision. The loss sustained by the British in the two subdivisions proved with what obstinacy the contest had been maintained. It amounted to two midshipmen (William Gore and William Bristow), 15 seamen, and four marines killed, Captain Parker himself (mortally), two lieutenants (Charles Pelly and Frederick Langford), one master (William Kirby), one midshipman (the Honourable Anthony Maitland), Mr. Richard Wilkinson, commander of the Greyhound revenue cutter, 30 seamen, and six marines wounded; total, 21 killed and 42 wounded.

The third division, under Captain Cotgrave, displayed the same gallantry, and experienced nearly the same opposition as the two others had done; and was equally compelled to retire without effecting the object. The loss of this division amounted

to one midshipman (Mr. Berry) and four seamen killed, one
gunner, 23 seamen, and five marines wounded; total, five killed
and 29 wounded.　The fourth division of boats, under Captain
Jones, not being able, owing to the rapidity of the tide, to get to
the westward of any part of the enemy's line, put back to the
squadron.

The French say they captured four of the English boats, and
ran down several others; and that their loss amounted to only
10 men killed and 30 wounded: whereas that of the British
amounted altogether to 44 killed and 126 wounded.　Of course
the French boasted, and certainly not without reason, of the
successful opposition they had made to the persevering assaults
of the British.

The appellation of gun-brig, and of flat or raft, convey, without some explanation, a very imperfect idea of the description of
vessels of which the Boulogne flotilla was composed.　The brigs
were vessels of from 200 to 250 tons, armed with from four to
eight heavy long guns, generally 24 and 18 pounders, and in
some instances 36-pounders.　The account of a comparatively
small lugger-flat, taken at Hâvre in the early part of the present
year, may suffice for the generality of those at Boulogne.　This
flat drew but three and a half feet water, had very stout bulwarks, and carried 30 men in crew, besides 150 soldiers; she
was armed with one 13-inch mortar, one long 24-pounder, and
four swivels, and had also abundance of small-arms.

This was the last affair with the invasion-flotilla, except a
spirited little boat-attack performed in the neighbourhood of
Etaples.　On the 20th of August, in the evening, as the British
24-gun ship Jamaica, Captain Jonas Rose, accompanied by four
or five brig-sloops and gun-vessels, lay at anchor off the above-
named French port, a large fire was seen, and a heavy cannonade
heard in the south-south-east.　Captain Rose immediately got
under way with his little squadron, and at 10 P.M., while running
down to the spot, spoke Captain George Sarradine, of the brig-
sloop Hound.　From the latter Captain Rose learnt that the
light proceeded from a cargo of pitch and tar belonging to a
vessel wrecked some time before, and which the boats of the
Hound and of the Mallard gun-vessel had set on fire; that
six flat-boats had come out from St. Valery to attack the
British, but had been driven on shore and then lay upon the
beach.

Being resolved to attempt the capture or destruction of these
French boats, Captain Rose, on the morning of the 21st, de-

spatched upon that service the boats of the Jamaica, Gannet, and Hound sloops, and Tigress and Mallard gun-vessels, under the orders of Lieutenants James Agassiz and Henry Le Vesconte. The squadron at the same time stood in to cover the boats from the fire of the military and of five field-pieces, posted behind some sand-hills on the beach. In spite of this opposition, the British succeeded in bringing off three of the French boats, and would have brought off the others had they not been scuttled; they were, however, damaged as much as the time would admit. The loss of the British on this occasion amounted to no more than one seaman killed, and one midshipman (Thomas Hamblin), and three seamen wounded. The captured flats were each about 45 feet long and 18 or 20 broad, and mounted one brass 8-inch howitzer.

After his repeated promises to send supplies and reinforcements to the army he had left in Egypt, Buonaparte must have felt sorely aggrieved that almost all his endeavours to do so had been frustrated by the vigilance of British cruisers: even the offer of large rewards to the equippers of merchant vessels or privateers that should first reach a port of Egypt with provisions and military stores, served only to augment the number and enhance the value of Lord Keith's prizes.

Hitherto the efforts to relieve the Egyptian army had been confined to such frigates and smaller vessels as might be able to escape from Toulon or some other French Mediterranean port; but, no sooner did the first-consul learn the real destination of the army under General Abercromby, than he contemplated the forwarding of a reinforcement upon a grander scale. That reinforcement was to consist of seven two-deckers, the *élite* of the Brest fleet, having on board 5000 troops under the command of General Sahuguet.

The officer intrusted with the charge of this secret and hazardous mission was one of the ablest at this time belonging to the republic, Rear-admiral Ganteaume: and the following were the ships of which this squadron was composed:—

Gun-ship.

80	Indivisible . .	{ Rear-admiral Honoré Ganteaume. { Captain Antoine-Louis Gourdon.
	Indomptable . .	. Commodore —— Moncousu.
	Formidable . .	. Captain Joseph Allary.
74	Desaix . . .	. Commodore Jean-Anne Christy-Pallière.
	Constitution . .	. Captain Gilbert-Amable Faure.
	Jean-Bart . . .	,, François-Jacques Meynne.
	Dix-Août . . .	,, Jacques Bergeret.

Gun-frigate.
40   Créole   .   .   .   . Captain Pierre-Paul Gourrege.
36   Bravoure .   .   .   .   ,,   Louis-Auguste Dordelin.
Lugger, Vautour.

On the 7th of January this squadron sailed from Brest, and anchored in the road of Bertheaume; and about the same time, in order to draw the attention of the British cruisers in a different direction, the French ships at anchor in the minor ports of the Channel and bay of Biscay made demonstrations of putting to sea. In the hope to profit by this ruse, Rear-admiral Ganteaume, on the 8th, got under way, and stood through the passage du Raz; but here, contrary to his expectation, he was discovered and chased by a division of the Channel fleet under the command of Vice-admiral Sir Henry Harvey. This obliged the French admiral to regain the coast; and he soon afterwards came to an anchor at the mouth of the river Vilaine. Thence, in order that the British might be led to suppose he had no other object in view than the other French squadrons in motion at this time, M. Ganteaume subsequently departed, steering for the road of Brest; where he anchored, as if the service he had been detached upon was executed.

Here lay the French admiral, waiting for a northerly gale of wind, to blow the British blockading force off the coast. On the 23rd a storm arose, favourable alike in direction and violence; and late on that night the squadron of M. Ganteaume weighed and put to sea. The only safe passage under such circumstances, that of the Iroise, was now entirely free from British cruisers; but such was the violence of the gale that, besides carrying away the topmasts of several of the ships, it separated the Indivisible and Créole from the rest of the squadron.

On the 27th of January, at 9 P.M., Cape Finisterre bearing east half-north distant 25 leagues, the British 12-pounder 36-gun frigate Concorde, Captain Robert Barton, while steering to the eastward, discovered by the light of the moon seven large ships, about two miles to windward, under easy sail, standing to the westward. These were the Indomptable, Formidable, Desaix, Constitution, Jean-Bart, Dix-Août, and Bravoure, under the orders of Commodore Moncousu.

One of the 74s and the frigate immediately bore up in chase; whereupon the Concorde, casting off a Swedish ship she had in tow, made sail ahead. In a little time the line-of-battle ship, hauling up again, steered to rejoin her squadron; while the

Bravoure continued bearing away in chase of the Concorde. As soon as she had reached what was considered to be a distance of about six miles from the French squadron, the Concorde hove to, and, by the usual mode of signalling, presently convinced herself that the ship in chase of her was not a friend.

After a mutual hail, an order to strike to a French frigate, and a volley of musketry, the Bravoure ranged up on the Concorde's lee side, and gave and returned a heavy fire; until, passing on, she shot so far ahead as to bring the Concorde on her larboard quarter. In this position the latter kept her opponent warmly and closely engaged for about half an hour; when the fire of the Bravoure ceased, and almost at the same instant one of her boats and some other wreck fell from her stern and larboard quarter. Captain Barton now concluded that his antagonist, having discontinued the action, had surrendered; but presently the Bravoure was observed making sail, and soon stood away before the wind. The damaged state of the Concorde's running rigging delayed her in chasing; and, at 3 A.M. on the 28th she lost sight of the Bravoure. At daylight, however, the Concorde again discovered the French frigate; but the appearance of the latter's squadron to windward compelled Captain Barton, not only to relinquish the pursuit of the Bravoure, but to attend to the safety of the Concorde.

The latter's loss in the action, out of a crew on board of not more than 224 men and boys, amounted to four men killed and 19 wounded, one of them mortally. The loss on board the Bravoure, out of a complement of about 320 men and boys, is officially stated to have been 10 men killed, including her third lieutenant and pilot, and 24 wounded, including her captain, who had the misfortune to have half his hand carried away by a grape-shot.

The guns of the Concorde have already appeared; but owing to the bursting of one of her 28[1] main-deck 12-pounders on the 10th of the preceding August, whereby nine men were killed and five badly wounded, and another 12-pounder was disabled, the frigate mounted on the present occasion but 40 guns. The Bravoure appears to have mounted 42 guns, two more than the establishment of her class, on account of having, like the Concorde herself previous to her accident, 28 twelves on the main-deck. In point of force, therefore, the Concorde and Bravoure

[1] See vol. i., p. 223. We omitted to mention, that the Concorde differed from her class in mounting 28, instead of 26 guns on the main deck; but the total of her guns is there correctly stated at 42.

were tolerably well matched; but, in practical gunnery, the relative execution shows that, if the two combatants had been left to themselves, the British frigate, without some extraordinary chance in her opponent's favour, must have come off the conqueror.

A writer in the French work so frequently quoted by us declares, that the two frigates did meet by themselves, but that Captain Dordelin, by closing with the intention to board "frightened away Captain Barton," "effraya le capitaine ennemi."[1] The latter assertion appears to be founded upon a statement, although not quite so forcibly expressed, in the despatch of Rear-admiral Ganteaume; but who, be it understood, is merely reciting the report made to him by Commodore Moncousu, as the substance of the information received by the latter from Captain Dordelin himself. It is Captain Dordelin, therefore, who vaunts of his own prowess; who declares that he compelled the Concorde to run away, that her guns were 18-pounders, and that he heard "groans and cries" proceeding from her after the discharge of his first broadside. Crediting the statement, M. Ganteaume strongly urges the minister of marine to promote M. Dordelin from a capitaine de frégate to a capitaine de vaisseaux; but the first-consul appears to have seen further into the business than M. Ganteaume, and did not promote the Bravoure's captain to that rank until two years and eight months (September 24, 1803) had elapsed since the date of the action upon the merits of which M. Dordelin founded his pretensions.

After this exploit by one of his squadron, Commodore Moncousu pursued his way towards the Straits; and on the 30th, off Cape Spartel, the first appointed rendezvous, effected his junction with Rear-admiral Ganteaume; who, on the preceding evening, after a long chase, had captured the British ship-sloop, or fireship, Incendiary, Captain Richard Dalling Dunn. Imitating the example of some British admirals and captains, M. Ganteaume described his prize as "of," when he should have said, "pierced for," 28 guns. The Incendiary, we believe, mounted only sixteen 18-pounder carronades; but the Spitfire and one or two others of the Incendiary's class, were established with 24 guns, for which, by opening their main-deck ports, they had ample room.

After destroying his prize, Rear-admiral Ganteaume stood towards the Straits; and, on the morning of the 9th of February,

1 Victoires et Conquêtes, tome xiv., p. 151.

passed through them into the Mediterranean under a press of sail. The only sea-going ship at this time at Gibraltar, the 12-pounder 32-gun frigate Success, Captain Shuldham Peard, immediately weighed and steered after the French squadron. Having no doubt that M. Ganteaume's destination was Egypt, Captain Peard intended, if he could, to pass him on the passage, and apprise Lord Keith of his expected arrival. On the 10th, in the morning, the Success came up with the French ships off Cape de Gata, where the second rendezvous had been appointed, and passed them in the night. During the whole of the 11th and 12th, owing chiefly to light and variable winds, the French squadron kept sight of the Success. Soon after dark the wind began to blow fresh from the southward; and, as the Success went occasionally at the rate of nine knots an hour, Captain Peard flattered himself that he should see no more of his pursuers. At daylight on the 13th, however, the leading French ships were close up with the British frigate. Finding escape impossible, Captain Peard, with great judgment, put back to the westward, not only to retard the French admiral in his progress, but to expose him to the risk of meeting any British force that might have been detached in pursuit. At noon the wind fell; and at 3 P.M., after two or three of the line-of-battle ships had got within musket-shot and opened their fire, the Success hauled down her flag.

Learning from his prisoners, among whom were the officers and crew of the Sprightly cutter, Lieutenant Robert Jump, captured and scuttled on the 10th, that Admiral Lord Keith, and Rear-admiral Sir Richard Bickerton were already, where they did not arrive until more than a fortnight afterwards, upon the coast of Egypt with a great force, and that Rear-admiral Sir John Borlase Warren, with a force about equal to his own, might be hourly expected in pursuit from the westward, Rear-admiral Ganteaume steered for the gulf of Lyons, and on the 19th anchored with his squadron in the road of Toulon. After a captivity of only five days, during which every attention was paid to their comfort by Rear-admiral Ganteaume and those about him, all the British officers and men were permitted to depart in a Cartel for Port-Mahon; where, on the morning of the 26th, they safely arrived.

It is now time to see what steps had been taken, in consequence of the escape of this French squadron from Brest, by the commander-in-chief of the Channel fleet, Admiral Earl St. Vincent. On the 3rd of February the Concorde anchored at

Plymouth with the account of her engagement with the Bravoure; and, in a day or two afterwards, Rear-admiral Sir Robert
Calder, with seven sail of the line, two frigates, and a brig, was
detached from the Channel fleet in pursuit of M. Ganteaume;
not, however, to the Mediterranean, but, owing to a lack of
information on the subject, to the West Indies.

Nothing can afford a stronger proof of the national confidence,
as well as fairness, in naval warfare, than the sending in pursuit
of an enemy's squadron a British squadron of the same numerical
force; but we cannot help asking, what was the use of selecting
six of the fastest two-deckers from the Channel fleet, when the
flag-officer in command of them was to take his passage in a
three-decker? The question of force offers no obstacle, for
both the Cæsar and the Malta were fully equal to the Prince of
Wales. The total number of three-deckers possessed by France
at this time was six; and of these two only were in a serviceable state; whereas England had actually at sea 18 three-
deckers, 13 of which, at this very time, were cruising off Brest.
The superior accommodations of a three-decker have, we know,
been alleged as a reason for retaining so many of them in the
service, especially to carry flags; but, in a fighting ship, the
comfort of the commanding officer, whether admiral or captain,
ought always to be a secondary consideration.

The only British force, in a situation to molest Rear-admiral
Ganteaume, was the squadron of Rear-admiral Sir John Borlase
Warren, composed of the 80-gun ship Gibraltar, Captain William Hancock Kelly, 74-gun ships Renown (flag), Captain John
Chambers White, Dragon, Captain John Aylmer, Généreux, Captain Manley Dixon, and Hector, Captain John Elphinstone,
64-gun ship Haerlem, with only a portion of her lower-deck guns
on board, Captain George Burlton, and two or three frigates
and smaller vessels.

It was on the 8th of February, while cruising off Cadiz with
a part of this squadron, that the rear-admiral received the first
intelligence of the squadron of M. Ganteaume. Sir John immediately steered for Gibraltar; and, arriving there on the morning of the 10th, learnt that the French squadron had, 24 hours
before, passed into the Mediterranean. On the 13th Sir John,
with his squadron, quitted Gibraltar, and steered for Minorca,
having previously despatched two frigates to reconnoitre the
ports of Carthagena and Toulon; and on the 20th he anchored
in the harbour of Port-Mahon. On the 24th, having thoroughly
refitted his squadron, Sir John sailed on a cruise; but

experiencing during the same night a heavy gale of wind, was obliged to put back with several of his ships damaged, and on the 27th re-anchored at Mahon.

On the 4th of March the rear-admiral again set sail, but with only five of his squadron, having left the Généreux behind, as some protection in the event of an expected attack upon Minorca by the Spaniards and French. On the 7th Sir John spoke two vessels, who informed him that the King of Naples had concluded an armistice with General Murat. Upon this intelligence the rear-admiral steered for Palermo, to protect the British interests in Sicily, as well as to effect a junction with the 74-gun ship Alexander, Captain Alexander John Ball, and 64 Athénien, Captain Sir Thomas Livingstone. On the 18th, when off the island of Maritimo, the Athénien joined; as on the 22nd, off the small island of Calita, did the Alexander.

With his force thus augmented to seven sail of the line, including two 64s, Sir John stood back towards Toulon, to blockade M. Ganteaume in the road; but on the 25th the brig-sloop Salamine, Captain Thomas Briggs, joined from Captain Dixon at Mahon, bringing information that the French admiral, with seven sail of the line, three frigates, and three merchant-vessels, had on the morning of the 19th again put to sea. No sooner, in fact, did the first-consul receive the mortifying account, as well of the arrival of M. Ganteaume at Toulon before his mission had been fulfilled, as of the capture of the frigate Africaine, on her way to the coast of Egypt, than he despatched from Paris his aide-de-camp, Gérard Lacuée, with orders that Rear-admiral Ganteaume should sail immediately for Alexandria; and that, should he find the port blockaded by a superior force, he was to disembark the troops at any practicable spot to the westward of Alexandria, between Tripoli and Cape Rasat. With this object in view, Rear-admiral Ganteaume accordingly sailed, but on the same night experienced so heavy a gale of wind, that one of his line-of-battle ships lost her main-mast and put back, some of the other ships were greatly damaged, and one of the merchant-vessels, having also parted company, was fallen in with and captured by the British frigate Minerva.

On the 25th at daybreak, when about 14 leagues south-west of the island of Toro, Sir John Warren obtained a distant sight of M. Ganteaume's weatherbeaten squadron, counted by the Mercury at 10 sail, being three short of its original number. Chase was immediately given; and, before evening, some of the

British ships had gained upon the enemy; but the slow sailing
of the Gibraltar and Athénien induced the rear-admiral to order
the remainder of the squadron to shorten sail, and at dark, or
soon afterwards, every French ship disappeared.   Nor was
the enemy again seen; as, while Sir John was hastening to the
southward and eastward, M. Ganteaume had stood back to the
northward, and shortly afterwards re-anchored in Toulon.

Buonaparte sent orders to M. Ganteaume to make a third
attempt to reach Egypt. Accordingly, on the 27th of April,
the persevering French admiral again set sail with his seven
line-of-battle ships and two frigates, besides one corvette and
two store-ships. Finding, when at Leghorn, into which port he
had put by the way, to co-operate in the siege of Porto-Ferrajo,
that the Formidable, Indomptable, and Desaix, as well as the
frigate Créole, were too short-manned to proceed on the voyage,
Rear-admiral Ganteaume ordered them back to Toulon; and,
with four two-deckers, one frigate, one corvette, and four store-
ships, stood away for the Straits of Messina. These he passed
on the 25th of May; and on the 5th of June, while on his way
to the coast of Egypt from off Brindisi, where he had expected
to be joined by three Neapolitan frigates, M. Ganteaume fell in
with and chased, but could not overtake, the British 18-pounder
36-gun frigate Pique, Captain James Young.

On the 7th, being only about 70 leagues to the westward of
Alexandria, the French admiral detached the corvette Héliopolis
to reconnoitre the Egyptian coast, and ascertain the exact situation of the hostile fleet. On the 9th, at daylight, the Héliopolis
arrived close off Alexandria; and, after a distant chase by the
Kent and Hector 74s and Cruelle cutter, succeeded in entering
the port. The fact is that, in consequence of the information
brought to Lord Keith by the Pique on the evening of the 7th,
the British squadron, on the morning of the 8th, made sail to
the westward, in search of the hourly-expected French squadron.
So that, when the Héliopolis arrived in sight of Alexandria, the
chief part of the blockading force was abreast of the Arab's
tower, or about four leagues to the westward.

The non-return of the Héliopolis leaving scarcely a doubt that
she had been captured by the British fleet, Rear-admiral Ganteaume, conformably to his instructions, searched to the westward of Alexandria for a convenient spot to disembark the
troops, and found it as he conceived, at a small town situated
about 180 leagues to the eastward of Tripoli, and a dependence
upon that regency; with which, as well as with the regency of

Tunis, Buonaparte had just concluded a treaty. Having come to an anchor off Bengazi, the squadron began making preparations to land the troops; but, so spirited and effectual was the opposition of the inhabitants, that the attempt was found impracticable. Just at this moment the squadron of Lord Keith, or some of the advanced ships belonging to it, hove in sight to the eastward. The French admiral immediately cut his cables, and crowded sail from the coast; leaving two of his store-ships, which could not keep up with him, to be captured by the British 28-gun frigate Vestal, and one or two smaller vessels, then far ahead of their companions.

On the 24th, at 3 h. 30 m. A.M., Cape Derna on the coast of Barbary bearing south-west, distant about seven leagues, the British 74-gun ship Swiftsure, Captain Benjamin Hallowell, then, with the wind at north-west, steering towards the island of Malta, to reinforce the squadron under Rear-admiral Sir John Borlase Warren, discovered the squadron of M. Ganteaume hull-down to leeward. From previous information Captain Hallowell concluded that the ships were those of M. Ganteaume, and made all sail to escape. At 5 h. 30 m. the Jean-Bart and Constitution, by signal from the admiral, tacked and stood on until they fetched into the Swiftsure's wake. At 8 A.M. the remaining three French ships, having fore-reached considerably, tacked also, until they arrived upon the lee quarter of the Swiftsure, when they tacked again.

Such was the very superior sailing of the French ships, that by 2 P.M. the Indivisible, Dix-Août, and Créole had arrived nearly within gun-shot. Observing that the ships astern were also fast coming up, Captain Hallowell determined to bear down and engage the three nearest, in the hope to disable one of them, and effect his escape to leeward. Accordingly, at 3 P.M., the Swiftsure bore down under all sail, steering to pass astern of the rearmost of the three French ships; whereupon all of the latter tacked and stood towards her. In half an hour the Indivisible and Dix-Août, standing on in close order, opened their fire within half gun-shot, and, by their superior rate of sailing, baffled every effort of the Swiftsure to get to leeward. In this way the action was maintained until 4 h. 37 m. P.M.; when, the Constitution and Jean-Bart being within gun-shot on the Swiftsure's starboard quarter, and closing fast, the Indivisible almost on board of her on the larboard bow, and the Dix-Août as near on the larboard quarter, the British ship struck her colours.

The masts, yards, rigging, and sails of the Swiftsure were completely cut to pieces; but, it having been the principal object of the French to dismantle the ship, her loss, out of a crew at quarters, owing to 59 being sick and 86 of her best men having been taken from her by Lord Keith, of not more than 450 men and boys, amounted to only two men killed, and one lieutenant (Lewis Davis) and seven men wounded, two of them mortally. That the Swiftsure did not act quite so tenderly towards her antagonists, appears by the French admiral's return of loss; according to which, the Indivisible had four men killed and wounded, and the Dix-Août six men killed and 23 wounded. M. Ganteaume manned his prize by detachments from the ships of his squadron; and, after labouring at her for six days, in the most favourable weather (a tolerable proof of the state to which she had been reduced), succeeded in placing her in a condition to accompany him to Toulon; where, on the 22nd of July, the squadron safely arrived.

In his public letter, Captain Hallowell, much to his credit, as well as to the credit of his captors, speaks in the highest terms of the treatment which himself, his officers, and men experienced from the officers of M. Ganteaume's squadron, and from the French admiral in particular. On the other hand M. Ganteaume's report of the conduct of the Swiftsure's captain has called forth the following panegyric from a French naval writer : " Le capitaine Hallowell, se défendit avec opiniâtreté, et n'amena son pavillon que lorsqu'il se vit en danger de couler bas." [1] It is almost unnecessary to state that Captain Hallowell and the late officers and crew of the Swiftsure, on their return to England, were most honourably acquitted for the loss of their ship.

Having, by a treaty concluded on the 28th of March, upon his own terms, got Naples to cede to him Porto-Longone, and the whole of the Neapolitan part of the isle of Elba, the first consul of France determined to possess himself of the remaining or Tuscan portion of the island, including the strong fortress of Porto-Ferrajo, but the garrison of which did not exceed 400 men.

On the 2nd of May General Tharreau, with about 1500 men, disembarked at Porto-Longone from the opposite port of Piombino; and, after vainly summoning, and as vainly trying to corrupt, Carlo de Fisson, the Tuscan governor, the French general commenced his investment of the place. The only British force off the port at this time were two frigates, the

[1] Victoires et Conquêtes, tome xiv., p. 157.

Phœnix and Mermaid, under the orders of Captain Lawrence William Halsted, of the former. But these soon afterwards departed on some other service, and the harbour of Porto-Ferrajo was blockaded by the French 28-gun frigate Badine, and subsequently by the following French squadron :—

Gun-frigate.
38	Carrère	.	.	.	.	. Captain Claude-Pascal Morel-Beaulieu.
36	Bravoure	.	.	.	.	,, Louis-Auguste Dordelin.
32	Succès	.	.	.	.	,, Jac.-Fr.-Ignace Bretel, *senior officer.*

Towards the latter end of July, to render still more critical the state of the small garrison of Porto-Ferrajo, General Watrin. at the head of 5000 men, landed on the island to supersede General Th'arreau in the command; and, in pursuance of the orders he had received from General Murat in Tuscany, the newly-arrived French general began the most active preparations for reducing the fortress.

On the 1st of August Rear-admiral Sir John Warren, with the Renown and squadron, arrived off the island, and, chasing the Bravoure and Succès into Leghorn, raised the blockade of Porto-Ferrajo.

On the 3rd, at 2 h. 30 m. P.M., the British 18-pounder 36-gun frigate Phœnix, Captain Lawrence William Halsted, 18-pounder 40-gun frigate Pomone, Captain Edward Leveson Gower, and 12-pounder 32-gun frigate Pearl, Captain Samuel James Ballard, cruising off the west side of the island of Elba, discovered the Carrère, on her passage from Porto-Ercole to Porto-Longone, with 300 barrels of powder on board, and a convoy of small vessels in charge laden with ordnance-stores and provisions.

At 8 h. 10 m. P.M., after the interchange of a few shot from bow and stern chasers, and a resistance alongside of about 10 minutes' duration, the Carrère hauled down her colours to the Pomone, the only British ship near enough to open a fire. Out of her complement of about 320 men and boys, the Pomone lost her boatswain (Thomas Cook) and one quartermaster killed, and one lieutenant of marines (Charles Douglas, loss of a leg) and one seaman mortally, and two other seamen slightly wounded. The loss on board the Carrère is not stated in Captain Halsted's letter; but, according to the French account, it was tolerably severe. The whole of the convoy appear to have escaped, and one or two of the vessels to have got into Longone.

The Carrère was a fine Venetian-built frigate of 1013 tons, and mounted the same guns as those assigned to her class, in the small table at p. 59, vol. i., except that she had only two.

carronades, and therefore but 40 guns in all, and that her 8-pounders were brass. Her complement, as deposed to by her officers, was 352. The Carrère became added to the British navy as an 18-pounder 36-gun frigate, but her reign as a cruising ship was a short one.

Finding, towards the end of August, that the Phœnix was at anchor alone off Piombino, a port on the main land of Tuscany, distant about seven miles from the north-east extremity of Elba, General Watrin sent orders to Captain Bretel at anchor in Leghorn mole, to get under way with his two frigates, and endeavour to capture the British frigate. Accordingly, on the evening of the 31st, the Succès and Bravoure put to sea upon that service.

On the 2nd of September, very early in the morning, these two frigates, just as they were about to enter the Piombino channel, fell in with and chased the British 38-gun frigate Minerve, Captain George Cockburn; who, at 6 h. 30 m., made the signal for an enemy to the Phœnix, then at anchor in the south-east in company with the Pomone, who had rejoined two days before. The two last-named frigates, getting quickly under way, bore up in chase under all sail; and at 9 A.M. descried the Succès and Bravoure to the northward, steering back towards Leghorn, pursued by the Minerve.

At about 10 h. 30 m. A.M., finding herself dropping astern of her consort, the Succès ran aground on the shore of Vada; and, upon receiving a shot from the Minerve in passing, hauled down her colours without firing a single gun in return. While the Minerve stood on in chase of the Bravoure, the Pomone took possession of the Succès, or, as now again entitled to be called, the Success. The wind, shifting to the northward, frustrated every attempt of the Bravoure to reach Leghorn; and the French frigate, after missing stays, and vainly attempting to wear, got on shore under the Antignano battery, about four miles to the southward of the mole. Here the three masts of the Bravoure soon went by the board, and the ship became totally lost. Owing to the height of the surf and the approach of night, and to the enemy on shore firing upon the boats, Lieutenant William Kelly, first of the Minerve, who had been sent to board the Bravoure, was not able to bring away more than a few prisoners.

By the exertions of Lieutenant Charles Thompson of the Phœnix, and the officers and men under his orders, the Success was at length got afloat without receiving any material injury, and was restored to her rank in the British navy. This capture of one, and destruction of a second French frigate, was performed without any loss on the part of the British. A contemporary, with his accustomed inaccuracy in regard to the force of ships, calls the Bravoure an "18-pound frigate,"[1] although Captain Halsted, in his letter to Sir John Warren, expressly states that the Bravoure mounted "twenty-eight 12-pounders on the main deck, with 283 men." In adding that the Bravoure was "of 46 guns," Captain Halsted must of course have adopted the report of Captain Cockburn; but, according to a document now before us, the Bravoure was pierced, exclusive of two pairs of bow-chase ports, for no more than 40 guns; although by filling every port on her main deck, we have elsewhere assigned her 42.[2]

Shortly after these French frigates, hitherto so annoying to the garrison of Porto-Ferrajo, had thus been disposed of, Lieutenant-colonel George Airey, whom General Fox had recently sent to supersede Captain Gordon in the command of the few British troops in the fortress, applied to Rear-admiral Sir John Warren, who had arrived off Porto-Ferrajo on the 12th of September, for a detachment of marines and seamen from the squadron, to assist in an attack upon some of the French batteries, those especially which shut up the port. This was acceded to, and arrangements were forthwith made for an active co-operation on the part of the squadron, which consisted of the Renown, Gibraltar, Dragon, Alexander, Généreux, Stately, of the line, Pomone and Pearl frigates, and brig-sloop Vincejo.

On the 13th, at daybreak, the Dragon and Généreux, for the purpose of creating a diversion, opened a fire upon a round tower at Marciana; and on the 14th, a little before daylight, 449 marines and 240 seamen, commanded by Captain George Long of the Vincejo, along with a party of Tuscans, peasants, pioneers, &c., amounting in the whole to about 1000 men, were landed in two divisions under the personal direction of Captain John Chambers White, of the Renown. The attack was made, and several of the French batteries were destroyed, and 55 prisoners, including three captains and two subalterns, brought off; but, the force being found insufficient to complete the whole business, the allied detachment was compelled to retire with a loss altogether of 32 killed, 61 wounded, and 105 missing. Of this number the navy lost a very large proportion; namely, Captain Long, while gallantly leading on his men to storm a

---

[1] Brenton, vol. iii., p. 50.   [2] See p. 70.

narrow bridge, two seamen, and 12 marines killed, one officer, 17 seamen, and 20 marines wounded, and one officer, 12 seamen, and 64 marines missing; total loss to the navy, 15 killed, 33 wounded, and 77 missing.

By the aid of a well-penned despatch, General Watrin makes this repulse of the allied British and Tuscans, cover the troops of the republic with glory. He augments the assailants to 3000 men, and their loss to 1200, exclusive of 200 prisoners, and declares that his batteries wholly dismasted a frigate, and sank seven of the British boats. But, in spite of all these strong incentives to success on the part of his troops, the French general could make no impression upon Porto-Ferrajo; of which Lieutenant-colonel Airey, notwithstanding he lost the aid of Sir John Warren and his squadron on the 22nd of September, continued to maintain possession until the treaty of Amiens relieved him from his charge. The important operations of this year upon the coast of Egypt now demand our attention.

In our account of the last year's proceedings of the British and Spanish fleets, we noticed the assemblage at Gibraltar of a powerful naval and military force under the respective commands of Admiral Lord Keith and General Sir Ralph Abercromby.[1] On the 31st of January, after having stopped a short time at Minorca and at Malta, the bulk of the British force, intended to act against the French in Lower Egypt, anchored in the fine harbour of Marmorice on the coast of Karamania, in Asia Minor. The fleet here assembled consisted of full-armed line-of-battle ships, frigates, and sloops, reduced 64s, 50s, 44s, and frigates, in number from 60 to 70 sail, including the following squadron:—

Gun-ship.		
80 Foudroyant	. .	Admiral (b.) Lord Keith, K.B.
		Captain Philip Beaver.
		,, William Young.
	Kent	Rear-admiral (w.) Sir R. Bickerton, Bart.
		Captain William Hope.
	Ajax	,, Hon. Alex. Inglis Cochrane.
74	Minotaur	,, Thomas Louis.
	Northumberland . .	,, George Martin.
	Tigre	,, Sir William Sidney Smith.
	Swiftsure	,, Benjamin Hallowell.

As soon as news reached him that this powerful British armament had assembled at the island of Malta, Buonaparte could no longer be in doubt respecting its destination. We have already shown what efforts were made to get a squadron to

[1] See vol. ii., p. 451.

Egypt from Brest.   The port of Toulon also lent its aid ; but, as no sea-going line-of-battle ships were now there, it could only be by frigates.   Two of these, the Egyptienne and Justice, each having on board a quantity of troops and munitions of war, anchored on the 3rd of February in the old or western port of Alexandria.   The number of French troops at this time in Upper and Lower Egypt, founded upon the returns published in the Moniteur, consisted of nearly 21,000 fighting men.   Here were also about 900 sick, about 1000 sailors, 400 or 500 Greek auxiliaries, and perhaps 1000 or 1200 persons in civil employment ; and the commander-in-chief of the whole was, as already mentioned (see vol. ii., p. 450), General Abdallah-Jacques Menou, a man very unfit for the station, and not at all liked by the army.

After a considerable delay, arising from a twofold cause, the tardiness of the Turks and the badness of the weather, the British and Turkish men-of-war and transports, having on board in the whole about 16,000 men, set sail from Marmorice, and on the 1st, with the exception of the Turkish division consisting of several gun-boats and kaicks, which in a westerly gale had bore up for Marcie, Cyprus, and other neighbouring ports, arrived in sight of the minarets of Alexandria.

Just as Lord Keith and his fleet gained a sight of Alexandria, the French frigate Régénérée, with 200 troops and a company of artillery on board, besides a quantity of military stores, slipped into the western port.   This frigate, in company with the Africaine, had sailed from Rochefort on the 13th of February, and since parted from her consort, of whose fate we shall hereafter have to give some account.   A contemporary states that the Régénérée kept company with the British fleet during a whole day, answering every signal that was made ; but we doubt the assertion, no mention being made of it in the French accounts. On the night of the 1st, or morning of the 2nd, the brig-corvette Lodi also got into Alexandria from Toulon.

On the same day the British fleet brought up in Aboukir bay. Too much of that day elapsed, however, before all the ships could get to an anchorage, to accomplish the disembarkation previously to the approach of night ; and a succession of strong northerly gales, attended by a heavy swell, then set in, and lasted until the evening of the 7th.   Preparations were instantly commenced ; and at 2 A.M. on the 8th the troops began embarking in the boats, the total number of which was upwards of 320. At 3 A.M. the signal was made for the boats to rendezvous near the brig-sloop Mondovi, Captain John Stewart, at anchor about

a gun-shot from the shore; but such was the extent of the anchorage occupied by so numerous a fleet, and so great the distance of many of the ships from any one given point, that it was
not until 9 A.M. that the signal could be made for the boats to
advance towards the shore.

This was then accomplished, under the direction of Captain
Cochrane of the Ajax, assisted by Captain James Stevenson of
the Europa, George Scott of the Stately, John Larmour of the
Diadem, Charles Apthorp of the Druid, and John Morrison of
the Thisbe, and by the several agents for transports present in
the fleet. The right flank of the boat-flotilla was protected by
the armed cutter Cruelle, Lieutenant David M'Gie, and gun-
vessels Dangéreuse and Janizary; and the left by the armed
cutter Entreprenante, schooner Malta, and gun-vessel Negresse,
besides two armed launches, one on each flank, in place of the
Turkish gun-boats, which, as already mentioned, had parted
from the fleet. The launches, containing the field-artillery as
well as a detachment of seamen to co-operate with the army,
moved under the direction of their commanding officer, Captain
Sir William Sidney Smith, assisted by Captains Peter Ribouleau
of the Astræa, Daniel Oliver Guion of the Eurus, John G. Saville
of the Experiment, John Burn of the Blonde, and James Hillyar
of the Niger. The bomb-vessels Tartarus and Fury, Captains
Thomas Hand and Richard Curry, were advantageously posted
for throwing shot and shells at the enemy, and the sloops Peterel,
Cameleon, and Minorca, Captains Charles Inglis, Edward
O'Bryen, and George Miller, were moored as near as possible to
the beach, with their broadsides sprung towards it.

The force which the French were enabled to bring to the spot,
to oppose the disembarkation of the British troops and seamen,
in number just 7000 men, consisted of the whole garrison of
Alexandria (except the invalids and seamen), amounting, according to the French accounts, to 1500 infantry and 180 cavalry,
exclusive of several detachments from Rosetta and elsewhere,
numbering altogether at least 2500 men. These French troops
were under the command of General Friant; who, with great
judgment, had stationed a part of his men, with 15 pieces of
heavy artillery, upon an almost inaccessible hill, which commanded the whole space of disembarkation, and others, with
field-pieces and mortars, in the different excellent positions
which the ground afforded.

No sooner did the boats arrive near to the shore than a heavy
fire of grape-shot and musketry from behind the sand-hills

seemed to threaten them with destruction, while the castle of
Aboukir on their right flank maintained a constant and harassing discharge of large shots and shells; but the ardour of the
British officers and men was not to be damped. No moment of
hesitation intervened. The beach was arrived at, and a footing
obtained; the troops advanced, and the enemy was forced to
relinquish all the advantageous positions he had held. The
boats returned without delay for the second division; and, before
the evening of the 9th, the whole army, with a proportion of
stores and provisions, was landed.

A detachment of 1000 seamen, placed under the orders of
Captain Sir William Sidney Smith, formed part of the landed
force. The duty of these was to drag the cannon up the heights;
a service they performed with their usual alacrity and perseverance, and in which, and in disembarking the army, they sustained a loss of 22 seamen killed, three lieutenants (John Bray,
George Thomas, and Francis Collins), one master's mate (Richard
Ogleby), three midshipmen (John Finchley, John Donellan, and
Edward Robinson, the latter mortally), and 63 seamen wounded,
and three seamen missing. The loss sustained by the army, on
the same occasion, amounted to four officers, four sergeants, 94
rank and file killed, 26 officers, 34 sergeants, five drummers,
450 rank and file wounded, and one officer, one sergeant, one
drummer, 32 rank and file missing; making a grand total of 124
killed, 585 wounded, and 38 missing. The loss sustained by the
French, when they were driven from the hill, is stated by them
at 400 in killed and badly wounded; but it was believed to have
exceeded that amount: they left behind them eight pieces of
artillery, one of which was a 24-pounder, besides a great number
of horses.

On the 12th the British army moved forward, and came in
sight of the French army; which, having been reinforced by a
body of 4400 troops under General Lanusse, including upwards
of 1000 cavalry commanded by General Bron, now amounted to
about 7000 men. The French were formed upon an advantageous ridge, having their right on the canal of Alexandria, and
their left towards the sea. On the following day, the 13th, a
battle was fought, in which the detachment of seamen under Sir
Sidney Smith, and of marines under Lieutenant-colonel Walter
Smith, emulated the brave troops with whom they were associated. The British gun-boats on the lake of Aboukir, commanded by Captains Frederick Lewis Maitland and James
Hillyar, were also particularly useful in annoying the right flank

of the French army. At length, after a sharp struggle, the French were repulsed at all quarters, with the loss, as admitted by themselves, of 750 killed and badly wounded; and the British took up a position at the village of Bedah, distant about a league from the town of Alexandria, having on their right the sea, on their left the canal of Alexandria (then dry) and Lake Madieh, and in front a sandy plain.

The loss sustained by the British in this last encounter was, on the part of the navy, one midshipman (Mr. Wright) and five seamen killed, and 19 seamen wounded; on the part of the marines, two lieutenants (Paul Hussey and John Linzee Spea), and 22 rank and file killed, one major (William Minto), one captain (Robert Torkington), two lieutenants (Richard Parry[1] and George Peebles), two sergeants, two drummers, 27 rank and file wounded; and on the part of the army, six officers, six sergeants, one drummer, 143 rank and file, 21 horses killed, 66 officers, one quartermaster, 61 sergeants, seven drummers, 946 rank and file, five horses wounded, and one rank and file missing: grand total, 186 killed, 1135 wounded, and one missing.

On the 18th of March the castle of Aboukir, mounted with ten guns and two heavy mortars, and garrisoned, the French say, with 300 men under chef de bataillon Vinache, after a bombardment of two days, surrendered on honourable terms to a detachment of the army under Colonel Dalhousie. Whatever may have become of the rest of the garrison, the prisoners taken did not amount to more than 150 officers and men.

On the same day, in an affair of patroles between the cavalry of the two armies, the British sustained a loss of one quartermaster, seven rank and file, and 18 horses killed, one officer, six rank and file, and 12 horses wounded, and one quartermaster, 12 rank and file, and seven horses missing. On the same day, also, a Turkish squadron, of two 74s, four frigates and corvettes, and a few smaller vessels, anchored in Aboukir bay. It was likewise on the same day that Generals Friant and Lanusse despatched a vessel to France, with information of the actual state of the French army: and the commander was directed to look out on his passage for the squadron of M. Ganteaume, whose intended arrival the Régénérée had announced, and to inform him of the position of the British fleet. This despatch-vessel appears to have arrived safe at Toulon; but, for the rea-

---

[1] This gallant officer is the same mentioned in the cutting out of the Mundovi. His wounds might have entitled him to a pension, but the liberality of government was asleep on this occasion.

sons elsewhere stated, she did not, in her way thither, meet M. Ganteaume.

· Although it was on the 4th of March that General Menou had become officially apprised of the arrival of the British expedition in the bay of Aboukir, he did not, it appears, set out from the head-quarters at Cairo until the 11th, nor arrive at the camp under the eastern walls of Alexandria before the evening of the 18th. The reinforcement he brought with him augmented the French force at Alexandria, according to the Moniteur, to 14,000 men, exclusive of cavalry, artillery, and guides; but the French historians say, to only 9730 men, including 1380 cavalry, with 46 pieces of cannon. The effective force of the British army at Bedah is represented not to have exceeded 10,000 men, including only 300 cavalry, with, according to the French, 12 pieces of movable artillery, and 30 pieces in the different redoubts thrown up to protect the encampment. This is taking the numbers, except in the case of the British artillery, which we believe to be overrated, as each party has represented his own to be; but, according to the statement on the opposite side, the British force was 16,000, or the whole that had been landed, and the French force between 11,000 and 12,000, an amount considerably less than is admitted by the Moniteur.

On the 21st, at about an hour before daylight, the French attacked the British with great impetuosity ; but, after an obstinate and sanguinary contest, were repulsed, with a loss estimated by themselves at 800 killed, 200 wounded (a small proportion), and 400 prisoners ; but other accounts represent the French loss on this day, in killed, wounded, and prisoners, at nearly 3000 men. Among the killed were Generals Lanusse, Roize, ano Baudot, and, among the wounded, General Destaing, and several other distinguished officers.

The loss on the part of the British was also unusually severe . it amounted to 10 officers, nine sergeants, 224 rank and file, and two horses killed, 60 officers, 48 sergeants, three drummers, 1082 rank and file, and three horses (a sufficient proof of the small quantity of cavalry present) wounded, and three officers, three sergeants, and 28 rank and file missing. Among the mortally wounded was the commander-in-chief, by a musket-shot at the upper part of the thigh ; and among the remaining wounded were Major-general Moore and Brigadier-general Hope, both in the head, but not dangerously.

The marines, having been appointed to the duty of Aboukir castle and its vicinity, were not present in this action ; but the seamen, under their gallant leader, Captain Sir Sidney Smith, shared in it, and sustained a loss of one master's mate (Mr. Krebs) and three seamen killed, Sir Sidney himself, but not badly, Lieutenant Lewis Davis of the Swiftsure, and 48 seamen wounded; making the grand total of the British loss in the Battle of Canopus, as the French have named it, amount to 247 killed, 1243 wounded, and 34 missing.

General Sir Ralph Abercromby, at his own request, was conveyed on board the Foudroyant, where he breathed his last on the 28th of March, leaving as his successor in the command of the British army, Major-general John Hely Hutchinson, who thus feelingly and eloquently expresses himself on the subject of General Abercromby's death: " Were it permitted for a soldier to regret any one who has fallen in the service of his country, I might be excused for lamenting him more than any other person ; but it is some consolation to those who tenderly loved him, that as his life was honourable, so was his death glorious. His memory will be recorded in the annals of his country, will be sacred to every British soldier, and embalmed in the recollection of a grateful posterity."

On the 26th a second Ottoman squadron arrived, having on board about 5000 Turks and Albanians. This made the Turkish force at anchor in the bay of Aboukir, including the Sultan-Selim three-decker, of 110 guns, amount to six sail of the line, and eight frigates and corvettes; all tolerably fine vessels, but in bad hands. On or about the 3rd of April the Turkish troops were landed, and shortly afterwards, with a division of 800 British troops and eight pieces of cannon under Colonel Spencer, were sent to attack the town and castle of Rosetta, which commands the western branch of the Nile. After a fatiguing march across the desert, the allied troops succeeded, with little or no opposition from the few French troops, apparently not more than 800, there stationed, in gaining possession of this important post which, besides giving to the British the unmolested navigation of the Nile, enabled them to open a communication with the friendly inhabitants of the Delta, and thus obtain supplies of provisions for the numerous mouths they had to feed.

On the 16th, at 11 h. 30 m. A.M., the castle of Jullien, situated on the banks of the Nile, and defended by 15 pieces of cannon, four armed djerms moored under its walls, and a garrison of nearly 400 men, part of the troops which had retired from Rosetta, was attacked, on the side of the Nile, by a division of British and Turkish gun-boats, commanded by Captain Richard

Curry of the bomb-vessel Fury, and on the land-side by the British division of Colonel Spencer's corps, including the principal part of the artillery. Two other divisions, it appears, were sent against the tower of Abou-Mandhour and the village of Gehdid. These were soon reduced; but it took until the 19th, at 6 A.M., before the castle of Jullien surrendered. This the garrison, numbering 368 men, did upon honourable terms, after a brave defence, in which they lost about 40 men in killed and wounded.

In the pocket of General Roize, left dead on the field of battle at Canopus, was found a letter from General Menou at Cairo, expressing a fear that the British had, or would, cut the canal of Alexandria, and thus let the waters of the Mediterranean, or those more immediately of Lake Madieh, into the basin of the ancient Lake Mareotis, which for ages past had been dry, except that a considerable portion of it, at certain seasons especially, was impassable owing to the swampy nature of its bed. The hint was taken, and on the 15th of April the cut was made; but, although the first rush of water, from its volume, and impetuosity, was awfully grand, some time elapsed before the whole area of the lake became covered. As soon as that was accomplished, the troops under General Menou, shut up in Alexandria, and numbering, according to the French accounts, 6000 men, became separated from the 4000 under General Lagrange, intrenched at El-Aft, and the 5000 under General Belliard, in garrison at Cairo. If to these numbers, short as they are of the returns published in the Moniteur, be added, the loss known to have been already sustained, together with the several detachments in Upper Egypt, particularly the garrisons of Salalieh, Belbeis, Suez, Lesbeh, and Bourlos, our previous enumeration of the French force spread over this country will not be considered immoderately estimated.

On the 26th of April, having left Major-general Coote in command of the army before Alexandria, Major-general Hutchinson arrived at Rosetta, to press in person the operations against the French in the interior of the country. On the 5th of May, Major-general Hutchinson, with the combined British and Turks, in number about 8000, marched along the banks of the Nile, towards the position of General Lagrange at El-Aft, accompanied on the river by a division of British and Turkish gun-boats, under the command, since the occupation of Rosetta and the expected arrival of Rear-admiral Ganteaume upon the coast (when Sir Sidney Smith returned to the Tigre), of Captain James

Stevenson, assisted by Captain John Morrison, Richard Curry, and James Hillyar.

On the 7th, having previously destroyed their gun-vessels with all the provisions and stores on board of them, the French abandoned El-Aft and retreated towards Rahmanieh. On the same evening the allied troops entered El-Aft, and on the 9th advanced to Rahmanieh, where General Lagrange had taken post, with an apparent intention of making a stout resistance. At 10 A.M., Captain Curry, with four flats and three armed launches, commenced an attack upon the French forts at Rahmanieh, and continued in action with them until 4 P.M., when his division was relieved by the Turkish gun-boats. In this creditable affair the navy sustained a loss of Lieutenant Hobbes and three seamen killed and seven seamen wounded. During the same night the French general retreated towards Cairo, leaving in the fort his sick and wounded, about 110 in number, under the command of chef de brigade Lacroix. A detachment of 50 cavalry from Alexandria were taken at the same time that Rahmanieh surrendered. The possession of this important post effectually cut off all communication between Alexandria and the interior of Egypt; and in gaining it the allied forces suffered no greater loss than one drummer, four rank and file, and 10 horses killed, and four officers, one sergeant, one drummer, 18 rank and file, and 18 horses wounded.

Continuing their march towards the capital of Egypt, which General Lagrange with his division had entered on the 13th, the allied forces, on the 14th, fell in with and captured a French armed vessel and 16 djerms, conveying wine, spirits, clothing, about 5000l. sterling in specie, some heavy pieces of ordnance, and about 150 troops, from Cairo to Rahmanieh. Having entered the Nile by the canal of Menouf, which joins the Damietta and Rosetta branches, the French commanding officer knew nothing of the retreat of General Lagrange, and the surrender of Rahmanieh. On the 17th a division of cavalry and infantry under Brigadier-general Doyle, from previous information furnished by the Arabs, intercepted a body of 550 camels escorted by 560 French under the command of chef de brigade Cavalier, going from Alexandria, which they had quitted on the 14th, towards the province of Bahireh, to procure provision, of which the garrison of Alexandria were now in great want. Finding himself likely to be overpowered, M. Cavalier very properly quitted his sluggish charge, and with his troops took to the desert. Here the French officer was overtaken by a party of British cavalry, and surrendered upon honourable terms.

On the same day on which this surrender took place, the small garrison, about 200, of the fort of Lesbeh, on the Damietta branch of the Nile, invested on the land-side by a Turkish force, and near the Bogaz of Damietta by a flotilla of British gun-boats, abandoned the post and retired upon Bourlos. This post the two garrisons, numbering together about 700 men, also evacuated, and embarked on board five small vessels in the hope to be able to reach the new or north-eastern port of Alexandria. Four of these vessels were captured and carried into Aboukir bay; but the fifth, after being chased in vain by a Turkish cor-vette, succeeded in reaching the coast of Italy.

Owing to delays from various causes, among others perhaps the non-arrival of more than about 300 of the troops expected to join from the borders of the Red Sea, the allied British and Turkish forces marching towards Cairo, which is distant about 164 miles from Rosetta, did not until the 20th of June arrive at Embabeh, a village distant a mile and a half from the fortress of Giseh, on the banks of the Nile directly opposite to Cairo, and in which fortress General Belliard had stationed a garrison. On the 22nd, while preparations were making to besiege Cairo and its different forts by the allied forces (of which a numerous army under the grand vizier now formed a part), General Belliard sent a flag of truce to Lieutenant-general [1] Hutchinson, offering to capitulate upon honourable terms. These were soon settled and drawn up, and on the 27th, were signed by the respective parties. By the terms of the treaty the French troops, of which there were, in effective men, 8000, besides 1000 sick, and about half as many in a convalescent state, were to be conveyed to a port of France.

Before we descend the Nile to bring the campaign to a con-clusion, some account must be given of the British and native troops from Bombay, amountng to about 6000, which, according to the original plan of proceeding, were to have co-operated with those disembarked on the shores of the Mediterranean.

On the 21st of April the British 50-gun ship Leopard, Captain Thomas Surridge, bearing the flag of Rear-admiral John Blankett, anchored in the road of Suez, with two or three frigates and sloops, and about the same number of transports. On the 22nd, at daybreak, an officer and a party of the 86th regiment landed from the Leopard, and took possession of the

[1] Promoted some time before, but we are uncertain when.

town of Suez, which the French garrison had previously evacuated. At 8 A.M. the British union jack was hoisted at the flag-
staff on shore. In a day or two afterwards the transports disembarked their troops ; and on the 14th of May Lieutenant-
colonel Lloyd, of the 86th regiment landed from the Leopard.
On the 6th of June, everything being in readiness, Lieutenant-
colonel Lloyd, with his detachment numbering about 320 men,
set out to march across the desert to Cairo, a distance by the
regular route, of about 60 miles, but by the route intended to be
taken, in order to avoid meeting a superior force of the enemy,
somewhat more. On the occasion of the departure of the British
detachment upon this hazardous service, the Leopard fired a
salute of 11 guns.

On the 13th the Leopard and vessels in her company sailed
from Suez, and on the 15th anchored in the Bay of Kosseïr ;
where were lying the 50-gun ship Romney, Captain Sir Home
Riggs Popham, and 12-pounder 36-gun frigate Sensible (armed
en flûte, we believe), Captain Robert Sauce, with several transports. These, since the 9th, had landed Major-general Baird,
with the second division of the Bombay troops : the first division
under Lieutenant-colonel Murray, had arrived and disembarked
since the 14th of May.[1] Some time between the 10th and 15th
of June the two divisions set off upon their march across the
desert, by the valley of Kuittah, and on the 30th arrived at Kéné,
or Kenneh, on the banks of the Nile; but, owing to the difficulty of procuring boats to descend that river, Major-general
Baird did not effect his junction with Lieutenant-general Hutchinson until several days after the surrender of Cairo, Lieutenant-
colonel Lloyd had joined since the 11th or 12th ; but his journey
had been a most painful and distressing one, 23 of his detachment, including three officers, having perished in the desert
with thirst.

The last division of the French troops taken prisoners at Cairo
and at other places, the whole of which amounted to nearly
13,500 men, having, by the 10th of August, sailed from the bay
of Aboukir, and Lieutenant-general Hutchinson having arrived
from Cairo at his head-quarters before Alexandria, immediate
measures were taken to reduce that remaining stronghold of

[1] A contemporary has made a sad jum-
ble of the proceedings of the British
squadron in the Red Sea. According to
Captain Brenton (vol. iii., p. 78), Rear-
admiral Blankett died as soon as he was
joined by Sir Home Popham, and Captain
Surridge thereupon "left the direction of
the naval forces under the able management " of the latter. So far from this
having been the case, the Rear-admiral
died on the 14th of July, when the Leopard
and Romney, sailing in company, were
about to cast anchor in Mocha road on
their return to Bombay.

the French in Egypt, and thus accomplish the ultimate object of the expedition.

On the night of the 16th about 5000 troops, under Major general Coote, embarked on Lake Mareotis, in the boats of the men-of-war and transports, and in a quantity of djerms which had been assembled for the purpose, and, escorted by the flotilla of gun-vessels still under the orders of Captain Stevenson, proceeded to a position to the westward of the town of Alexandria. Early on the morning of the 17th the detachment disembarked with a slight opposition; previous to which the French had set fire to their flotilla of 18 gun-boats, which had been stationed opposite to Pompey's pillar, under the protection of a battery of three long 18-pounders. The slight opposition experienced by the British is acknowledged by the French to have been mainly owing to the spirited demonstration which Captain Sir Sidney Smith, with some sloops-of-war and armed boats, made upon the town of Alexandria from the sea.

On the night of the 18th a combined military and naval attack was made upon the small fortified island of Marabou, which protects the entrance to the western or great harbour of Alexandria. The naval force consisted of the armed launches of the squadron, under the command of Captain Cochrane of the Ajax. Finding it in vain to hold out longer, the commandant of Marabou, chef de brigade Etienne, capitulated on the 21st; and on the same evening Captain Cochrane, with the ship-sloops Cynthia and Bonne-Citoyenne, brig-sloops Port-Mahon and Victorieuse, and three Turkish corvettes, entered the harbour: soon after which, to prevent the further progress of the British to the eastward, the French sank several merchant-vessels, having previously moved their two 64s, frigates, and corvettes, from Cape Figuiers close up to the town at the extremity of the harbour.

On the morning of the 26th four batteries on each side of the town were opened against the intrenched camp of the French; and on the 27th, in the evening, being thus pressed on all sides, General Menou sent an aide-de-camp to Lieutenant-general Hutchinson to request a three days' armistice, in order to give time to prepare a capitulation. This was acceded to; and on the 2nd of September Alexandria surrendered. By the terms of the treaty the garrison, consisting of upwards of 8000 soldiers, and 1300 sailors, were to be conveyed to France at British expense, as had already been the case with the garrison of Cairo.

This concluding operation of the campaign was effected after a loss to the British army, in the four or five skirmishes which had immediately preceded it, of only 13 rank and file killed, and six officers, four sergeants, one drummer, and 113 rank and file wounded, and to the British navy, in the attack upon Marabou, of one midshipman (Mr. Hull of the Ajax) and one seaman killed and two seamen wounded; thus making the general loss on the part of the British in the Egyptian campaign, as far as it has been officially reported, 330 killed, 1872 wounded, and 39 missing. That of the French, commencing at the disembarkation of the British troops in Aboukir bay, may be stated at from 3000 to 4000 men in killed alone; an amount, great as it may appear, considerably below what some of the English writers have declared it to have been.

The French ships-of-war found in the old or western harbour were the Causse 64, the frigates Egyptienne, Justice, and Régénérée, and two small ex-Venetian frigates, of whose names we are uncertain. The Dubois appears to have been broken up. The Héliopolis was probably one of the ex-Turkish corvettes restored to the captain pacha; and the Lodi, since the middle of May, had been despatched to France with General Reynier, sent home by General Menou. This remarkably fine brig, in spite of the numerous British cruisers at that time in the Mediterranean, accomplished her passage in safety, arriving on the 28th of June at the port of Nice.

In the division of the ships between the British and Turkish naval commanders-in-chief, the latter received the Causse, Justice, and one of the Venetian frigates; and the former, the Egyptienne, Régénérée, and the other Venetian frigate. What became of the latter frigate we are unable to say; but the Régénérée, a ship of 902 tons, and a very fast sailer, was added to the British navy as a 12-pounder 36-gun frigate, by the name of Alexandria. The Egyptienne was also added to the British navy, by her own name; and, from her size and qualifications, claims a more particular notice.

Of the two new ships of the line which Buonaparte, in his letter to the Directory of April, 1798,[1] contemplated to have ready by the ensuing September, one, as already stated, was the Spartiate, just ready to be, if not actually launched. The other ship either had already been, or then was, so altered in her construction, that, instead of becoming a 74 of about 1700 tons French, or 1900 English, she was launched on the 18th of July,

[1] See vol. ii., p. 125.

1799, as a frigate of 1430 tons English. This had been done, by throwing in her stem and stern until they were perpendicular, and proportionably contracting the breadth of her frame. The ship, thus reduced in length and breadth, was pierced for 15 guns of a side on the main deck, and 10 on the quarter-deck and forecastle, or 50 guns in the whole. But, when ready to be fitted for sea, the foremost main-deck port was found too much in the bend of the bow to admit a gun: hence the Egyptienne (as, considering her first destination, the ship was appropriately named) received on board 28, instead of 30, long 24-pounders for her main deck, 12 long 8-pounders and two 36-pounder brass carronades for the quarter-deck, and four long 8-pounders and two 36-pounder brass carronades for the forecastle; total 48 guns, with a complement, as alleged, of 400, but, we rather think, of 450 men and boys.

Conformably to this arrangement of her guns, the Egyptienne, when, about six months after her capture, the British admiralty ordered her to be armed, was established with 28 long 24-pounders on the main deck, 12 carronades, 24-pounders, and two long 9-pounders on the quarter-deck, and four carronades and two long guns of the same two calibers on the forecastle, total 48 guns; with a complement, upon the prevalent economical scale of the British navy, of 330 men and boys. A contemporary, whose mistakes respecting the armaments of ships, English as well as foreign, we are almost tired of correcting, says thus of the frigate in question: " The Egyptienne, a frigate of sixteen hundred tons, taken at Alexandria, in Egypt, in 1800, carried on her main deck sixteen long thirty-two pounders on each side, and on her quarter-deck and forecastle sixteen forty-two pound carronades, and four long twelve-pounders."[1] ·

As we have done on most other occasions, so we must here, give some account of the honours and rewards bestowed upon the conquerors. The thanks of parliament were voted to both commanders-in-chief. Lieutenant-general Hutchinson was made, and no one can say undeservedly, first a knight of the bath, and then a peer of Great Britain; and Lord Keith was raised from a peer of Ireland to a peer of Great Britain: not certainly for any active exertions in bringing the campaign to a close, nor, we presume, for doing what any clever agent for transports might have done as well, disembarking the troops; but as the head of the naval part of the expedition, without the aid of which, it is clear, the campaign itself could not have been undertaken.

[1] Brenton, vol. i., p. 43.

We are unable to state what officers of the navy gained steps
in rank; but undoubtedly those serving on shore with the army,
and on board the flotilla upon the Nile and the neighbouring
lakes, well merited the promotion they may have obtained.   The
following is the handsome manner in which the commander-in-
chief of the army speaks of their exertions: "The labour and
fatigue of the navy have been continued and excessive; it has not
been of one day or of one week, but for months together.   In the
bay of Aboukir, on the new inundation, and on the Nile, for 160
miles, they have been employed without intermission, and have
submitted to many privations with a cheerfulness and patience
highly creditable to them and advantageous to the public
service."

We cannot dismiss the Egyptian campaign without observing,
that all the benefit derived from its successful termination, the
removal of the French army from Egypt, might have been attained 18 months before, had Lord Keith not refused to ratify the
treaty entered into by Sir Sidney Smith.   What blood and treasure would then have been saved! Treasure, indeed, could it but
be known how the British government was defrauded by jobbers,
contractors, and agents of one sort or the other.   At all events,
the infraction of the treaty of El-Arich, how much soever others
may have suffered by it, eventually benefited him, whose consent alone had been wanting to carry that treaty into effect. We
now gladly quit the shores of Egypt and its military warfare, to
resume our narrative of naval operations; and, in particular, to
give some account of the proceedings of the French and their
allies the Spaniards at the opposite extremity of the Mediterranean.

British and Franco-Spanish Fleets.

Very soon after the conclusion of the treaty of Luneville, the
first consul of France began using every means in his power to
detach from England the few powers that were on friendly
terms with her.   With Naples Buonaparte succeeded; but,
although by the intrigues of his brother Lucien with the famous
Godoy, the Prince of Peace, Spain was induced, on the 27th of
February, 1801, to declare war against her neighbour, and although a powerful French army had crossed the Bidassoa,
Portugal remained firm.   The subsequent irruption of a Spanish
army into the province of Alentejo, however, altered the tone of
the prince regent; and on the 6th of June, at Badajos, the
latter concluded a treaty of peace with Spain, and agreed, not

only to cede to her the conquered province of Alentejo, but to expel the English from the ports of Portugal. The effect produced upon Buonaparte by this separate concession to Spain, and the measures taken by England to prevent either France or Spain from reaping any solid advantage from their sinister attempts upon her ancient ally, we shall advert to hereafter.

Some time in the month of March, by his secret and corrupt influence at the court of Madrid, Buonaparte got King Charles to make over to France, either by sale or hire, six sail of the line lying in the port of Cadiz; and which ships were to be there manned by French crews, and then, as was understood, to co-operate with a Spanish naval force, in entering the Tagus and sacking Lisbon. This was a plan which, as far as respected the British property in the port, a French admiral, of whom honourable mention has already been made in these pages, recommended as a feasible enterprise for the Brest fleet, when it put to sea in the beginning of the year 1795. "I propose," says M. Kerguelin, "to conduct the fleet of the republic to Lisbon, to anchor in front of the capital, within musket shot of the city and the palace of the king; to send ahead of the fleet a frigate with a flag of truce, announcing that the fleet of the republic comes not to do harm to the Portuguese, although the allies and slaves of England, but to require that all the British storehouses and ships be forthwith delivered up, under a penalty of having the city rased to its foundation. This enterprise would gain for France 200 millions, in cash or British merchandise; England would receive a terrible shock, which would produce bankruptcies and a general consternation; our fleet, without being buffeted about the sea,[1] would return to Brest, loaded with riches and covered with glory; and France would once more astonish Europe with a new triumph.[2]

We formerly noticed the return to Toulon from Leghorn of three ships of Rear-admiral Ganteaume's squadron, on account of the paucity of hands to work them.[3] These three ships, the Indomptable and Formidable, of 80 guns, Captains Moncousu and Lalonde, and Desaix, of 74 guns, Captain Christy-Pallière, along with the ex-Venetian 38-gun frigate Muiron, Captain Jules-François Martinencq, were placed under the orders of Rear-admiral Durand-Linois, with directions to proceed to Cadiz, and there effect a junction with Rear-admiral Dumanoir-le-

[1] Alluding to the storm from which the Brest fleet suffered so much in January, 1795. See vol, i., p. 262.

[2] For the original, see Appendix, No. 4.
[3] See p. 73.

Pelley and his six newly-made French sail of the line. These nine ships, with a Spanish squadron of six more under Vice-admiral Don Juan Joaquin de Moreno, were then, as a case more urgent than that of despoiling Lisbon, to carry a reinforcement to Egypt; not, we believe, wholly from Toulon, but principally from the Neapolitan ports of Ancona, Manfredonia, Brindisi, and Otranto; at which several ports there were assembled, in the month of June, as many as 32,000 French troops.

On the 13th of June, Rear-admiral Linois, with his squadron of three sail of the line and one frigate, having on board a small detachment of troops, under Brigadier-general Devaux, put to sea from the road of Toulon, bound to Cadiz; off which port, by the last advices, were cruising two British 74s only, and occasionally but one. On the next day the French admiral chased away some British frigates, left cruising in the gulf of Lyons by Rear-admiral Sir John Borlase Warren; who, with the Renown and squadron, was then about to enter the harbour of Valetta, island of Malta, to revictual, preparatory to his pursuit of M. Ganteaume, of whom he had just received intelligence. Delayed by head winds, M. Linois was not able, until towards the end of the month, to double Cape de Gata.

On the 1st of July the French ships, then working against a strong west-north-west wind, were seen from Gibraltar; where the only British vessel of war at anchor was the 14-gun polacre-sloop Calpé, Captain the Honourable George Heneage Lawrence Dundas. On the 2nd M. Linois captured a small British brig employed as a packet to Minorca; and on the 3rd, when more than two thirds through the Straits, the French admiral was so fortunate as to capture, but not until she had resorted to every manœuvre to escape which her skilful commander could devise, the 14-gun brig-sloop Speedy, Captain Lord Cochrane. Learning now that Cadiz was blockaded by a superior force, Rear-admiral Linois, with his squadron and prizes, bore up for Algeziras. On the 4th, at about 10 A.M., he rounded Cabrita point in sight of the Calpé at her anchorage, and at 5 P.M. came to with his ships in front of the town of Algeziras, still in full view of the British at the rock.

At this time the British squadron stationed off Cadiz consisted of the

Gun-ship.

80 Cæsar . . . . { Rear-admiral (b.) Sir James Saumarez.
                  { Captain Jahleel Brenton.

Gun-ship.

74 {
Pompée . . . . Captain Charles Sterling.
Spencer . . . . ,, Henry D'Esterre Darby.
Venerable . . . . ,, Samuel Hood.
Superb . . . . ,, Richard Goodwin Keats.
Hannibal . . . . ,, Solomon Ferris.
Audacious . . . ,, Shuldham Peard.
}

Frigate Thames, and *brig* Pasley.

On the 5th of July, at 2 A.M., Lieutenant Richard Janvarin, who had been despatched from Gibraltar by Captain Dundas of the Calpé, joined the Cæsar in a boat, and informed Sir James of the appearance off the rock of the squadron of M. Linois, endeavouring to get to the westward. The British squadron in Cadiz bay consisted now of only six sail of the line, the Superb having, since the 1st of the month, been detached to watch the entrance of the Guadalquivir, a river about 18 miles to the northward.

Sir James and the ships with him immediately tacked off shore. At daylight another despatch vesssl from Gibraltar boarded the Thames, with intelligence of the French squadron's having put into Algeziras. The frigate was immediately despatched by the Rear-admiral to recal the Superb, then in the north by east with her topgallants just above the horizon, and direct Captain Keats to follow the squadron to Algeziras. At 8. A.M. the Cæsar made the signal to prepare for battle, and for anchoring by the stern; and immediately afterwards bore away for the gut, with a moderate breeze from the northward and westward. In the mean time the Superb, to whom at about 5 h. 15 m. A.M. the Thames had made the signal of recal, lay nearly becalmed, in company with the Pasley brig.

Towards 10 A.M, the squadron also became becalmed; but, having got into the strength of the current, the ships continued drifting so fast to the eastward, as very soon to be entirely out of sight of the Superb, Thames, and Pasley.

At about 4 P.M. a light air sprang up from the west-north-west; and the Cæsar and squadron recently joined by the Plymouth lugger from Gibraltar, took immediate advantage of it. At 9 P.M. the weather again fell calm, and continued so until 3 A.M. on the 6th. A light breeze then sprang up from the same quarter as before, and the ships crowded sail through the Straits. Owing to the local experience of Captain Hood, it had been arranged that the Venerable should lead to the attack; but it was not, we believe, intended that any of the ships should anchor, unless, from a sudden fall in the wind, or any other circumstances, compelled to do so. At 4 A.M., the ships then standing on in line ahead thus, Venerable, Pompée, Audacious, Cæsar, Spencer, and Hannibal, Cape Tariffa bore from the Pompée north-east distant three miles.   At 7 A.M. the Venerable, opening Cabrita point, made the signal for seeing the French ships, which were then warping further in shore, to get completely under the protection of the batteries that defended the road.   The signal was immediately made by the Cæsar, to engage the enemy on arriving up with him in succession.

Of the defensive means possessed by the French admiral, we will now endeavour to give a description. The road of Algeziras is open and shallow, with sunken rocks in different parts of it. Upon a point of the coast, at the distance of rather more than a mile and a half south-east of the town, stands Fort Santa-Garcia ; and, about the third of a mile from the town, in the same direction, another tower or fort.   Directly in front of the point on which this latter tower stands, and at the distance from it of rather more than a quarter of a mile, is a small island, named Isla-Verda, upon which is a battery mounting seven long 24-pounders.   About three-quarters of a mile, or rather less, to the northward of the town, stands the battery of San-Iago, mounting five long 18-pounders, and close to the northern extremity of this battery, near the water's edge, is the tower of Almirante, but in what manner mounted we are unable to say. There are also several forts on the northern shore of Gibraltar bay, but at too great a distance to afford any protection to the road of Algeziras, except perhaps by throwing shells.   The road, however, is admirably protected by the flanking fire of the San-Iago and the island batteries.   There were also, at this time in the road, 14 heavy gun-boats ; a description of force peculiarly advantageous, where an enemy is likely to be baffled by light and variable winds, and perplexed with an intricate and dangerous navigation.

In a road thus defended by nature and art, M. Linois moored his three ships in line ahead thus: the Formidable abreast, or nearly abreast, of the San-Iago battery, the Desaix about 500 yards astern and to the southward of the flag-ship, and the Indomptable about the same distance astern of the Desaix. The Muiron took her station a little within and to the northward of Isla-Verda.   Three of the gun-boats were anchored about a quarter of a mile to the south-west of the last-named island ; four others between Fort San-Iago and the Formidable, and the remaining seven off a point of land about half a mile to the northward of the tower of Almirante.

At about 7 h. 50 m. A.M., just as the Pompée with a fresh breeze had shortened sail and hauled round Cabrita, the battery at the point fired several shot at her, but without effect. At 8 A.M. the Venerable lay becalmed at a considerable distance on the starboard bow of the Pompée; and in a few minutes afterwards that ship and the Audacious, who was on the Pompée's starboard quarter, passed the Venerable to windward. At this time the Cæsar and two remaining ships were upwards of three miles astern using every endeavour to get up.

Hauling close up for the tower of Santa-Garcia and the island battery, the Pompée, at 8 h. 30 m., received the fire of the Muiron, and successively of the Indomptable, Desaix, and Formidable. It now falling calm, the Pompée fired a broadside at each of the two latter ships; and at 8 h. 45 m. dropped her anchor so close to the Formidable's starboard bow that the latter's buoy was on the Pompée's off or starboard side. As soon as she had clewed up her sails, and tautened her springs, the Pompée opened a heavy fire upon the Formidable; but who very soon, by warps from the shore, increased her distance.

At about 8 h. 50 m. the Audacious, and in five minutes afterwards the Venerable, baffled also by the want of wind, dropped their anchors; the one abreast of the Indomptable, but not so near as her captain wished, and the other, from unavoidable causes, at a still greater distance from the quarter of the Formidable. A furious cannonade now ensued between these three British ships, and the four French ships, gun-boats, and batteries. In less than half an hour from its commencement, and when the Formidable, for some cause or other, had suspended, not to say ceased, her fire, the Pompée, owing to the strength of the current, swang with her head towards her opponent's broadside. In this situation, the Pompée could only ply her starboard guns at the batteries of San-Iago and Almirante, and at the gun-boats moored in front of them; all of which kept up in return a very destructive fire.

At about 9 h. 15 m. A.M. the Cæsar got up; and, as she made the signal for the ships to anchor in the best manner for mutual support, dropped her anchor ahead of the Audacious. After sending a spring on board of the Venerable, which ship was on her starboard quarter, the Cæsar opened her heavy broadside upon the Desaix. The Hannibal, about five minutes afterwards, got also into action, anchoring within hail of the Cæsar, and rather upon her starboard bow. The Spencer, baffled as much as any of her companions and to leeward of the whole of them.

could not get much nearer than was sufficient to expose her to the heavy fire of the Spanish batteries, from which, towards the latter part of the action especially, hot shot, as well as shells, were thrown.

At a few minutes past 10 A.M. the Hannibal was hailed by the Cæsar, but no person on board the former appears to have heard distinctly what was said. Soon afterwards a boat with an officer came on board the Venerable, bearing the rear-admiral's orders, that Captain Ferris should "go and rake the French admiral;" no doubt with the intention of supporting the Pompée, who just at that time was in a very critical situation.

Cutting her cable and casting herself by the spring, the Hannibal immediately made sail to the northward with what wind there was, still blowing from the west-north-west. Having stood, in the direction of Rio Palmenos, into a quarter less six, the Hannibal tacked for the Formidable ; but about 11 A.M., just as she had arrived abreast of the tower of Almirante, and was in the act of hauling more closely in shore, to cross the hawse of the French ship, nearly within hail of whom she then was, the Hannibal took the ground. In this distressing situation, the Hannibal with as many of her foremast guns as would bear, opened a fire upon the Formidable, and directed the remainder, with evident effect, upon the tower of Almirante, battery of San-Iago, and gun-boats. The ship appearing to swing a little, an effort was made, by letting go an anchor and heaving a strain upon it, to get her afloat, but without effect. With some difficulty, owing to the signal-halliards having been shot away, the Hannibal apprised the admiral of her situation; and shortly afterwards one boat came from the Cæsar and another from the Venerable. Finding that no assistance could be afforded by them, Captain Ferris sent back the Venerable's boat, and sent the Cæsar's officers and men in one of the Hannibal's cutters, their pinnace having been sunk alongside by a shot.

The light westerly breeze, by which the Hannibal had so gallantly steered to her present unfortunate situation, appears to have been very partial, as the other British ships all the while lay nearly becalmed. Soon after the Hannibal had grounded, however, a light breeze sprang up from the north-east. Hoping by this means to get further from the reach of the British ships, some of whom were observed preparing to take advantage of it and approach nearer, M. Linois threw out the signal for his ships to cut and run themselves on shore, " de couper les câbles pour s'échouer."[1] The French ships did so ; but, the wind suddenly falling, they were a long time in wearing. The Formidable brought up again with her larboard broadside to the enemy ; but the Desaix grounded upon a shoal directly in front of the town, and the Indomptable upon one to the north-east of Isla Verda, with her larboard bow presented to the sea.

Desirous to take advantage of this state of the French ships, as well as of the breeze which had just sprung up, the Cæsar, making the signal for the squadron to do the same, cut her cables ; and, wearing round the Audacious and Venerable, soon brought her broadside to bear upon the Indomptable ; into whose bows, with her foretopsail to the mast, the Cæsar poured several destructive fires. At a little before noon the Audacious, having likewise cut, passed between the Cæsar and Indomptable ; and shortly afterwards the latter's foretopmast came down. The Venerable and Spencer, in compliance with the signal, cut their cables, and strove their utmost, but with little effect on account of the calm that immediately ensued, to co-operate in the attack upon the southernmost French ships and island battery. The Venerable, indeed, had her mizentopmast shot away just as she was in the act of wearing. The Pompée after remaining nearly an hour without being able, on account of her position, to bring a gun to bear, had also cut, and was now being towed out of action by the boats of the squadron.

Scarcely had the Audacious, in her new station, brought her broadside to bear with effect, ere the calm frustrated her intentions ; and that ship and the Cæsar, without the power of returning a shot, lay exposed to a heavy fire from the guns of the island battery. To add to their perilous state, both ships were drifting upon the reef that was near it. Again, a fine breeze raised the hopes of the British ; but no sooner had the ships prepared to take advantage of it. than it again died away.

Frustrated thus, as much by the unfavourable state of the weather as by the serious opposition experienced from the enemy's batteries and shipping, and being prevented, by the destruction of most of the boats and the absence of the remainder in towing the Pompée, to storm the island, as had been intended, with the marines of the squadron, Sir James Saumarez, at 1 h. 35 m. P.M. (by the Cæsar's log, but at 1 h. 20 m. by the log of the Audacious), discontinued the action. The Cæsar and Audacious then cut their cables and springs, and, profiting by a light breeze

---

[1] Victoires et Conquêtes, tome xiv., p. 160.

which had just sprung up from the shore, made sail on the starboard tack, in company with the Venerable and Spencer; leaving, and being compelled to leave, the dismasted and shattered Hannibal as a trophy in the hands of the enemy.

As this action is one in which the want of a diagram is particularly felt, we have done the best in our power to supply the deficiency. The coast, the soundings, and the positions of the French ships, and of the Hannibal when aground, are taken from a French chart; and the positions of the British ships, except that of the Spencer, which we have marked at hazard, are taken from the British logs; as far, at least, as they afford any information on the subject.

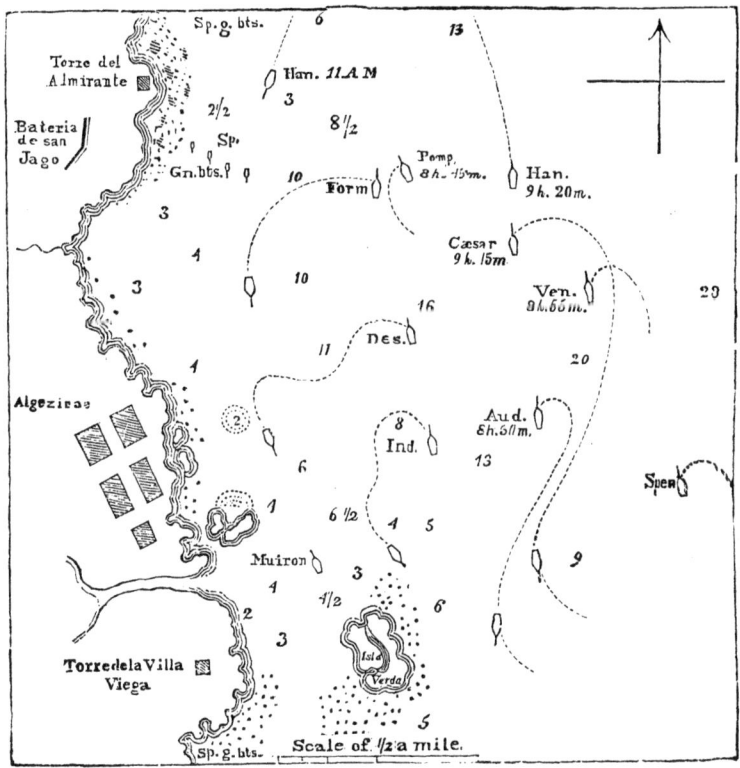

As soon as the unequal contest, which the Hannibal was now alone sustaining with the French and Spaniards, had inflicted upon her a serious loss in killed and wounded, had disabled the

greater part of the guns that would bear, and had shot away her
fore and main masts, Captain Ferris ordered the firing to cease,
and the officers and men to shelter themselves in the lower part
of the ship. In a little while afterwards, or at about 2 P.M., the
Hannibal's colours were hauled down, and were presently rehoisted union downwards; whether by the British, because the
battery and gun-boats still continued their fire, or by the French,
who had come on board to take possession, in order to decoy the
Calpé, then approaching from Gibraltar, we are not prepared to
say : at all events Captain Dundas, deceived by the signal, sent
his boats, with a laudable promptitude, to save the Hannibal's
people. The boats were detained by the French; and, after firing
several broadsides at the enemy's shipping and batteries, the
Calpé returned to Gibraltar.

The loss and damage sustained generally by the British
squadron were very serious. The Cæsar had her master (William Grave), six seamen, and two marines killed, her boatswain
(George William Forster,) 17 seamen, one boy, and six marines
wounded, and one master's mate (Richard Best) and seven seamen missing; probably drowned in one of her boats. The mainmast had been shot through in five places, and all her other
masts and yards were more or less injured: several shot had
also entered her hull. Her two barges, large cutter, launch,
and jollyboat, had been cut to pieces; and her small cutter or
pinnace, as already stated, had been sunk as it lay alongside the
Hannibal. The Pompée had her master (Robert Roxburgh),
one midshipman (Mr. Steward), 10 seamen, and three marines
killed, three lieutenants (Richard Cheeseman, Arthur Stapledon,
and Thomas Innes), two master's mates (Messrs. Curry and
Hillier), one midshipman (I. Hibberd), 53 seamen, and 10
marines wounded. In point of damages, the Pompée was even
in a much worse state than the Cæsar, not having a mast, yard,
spar, shroud, rope, or sail, but which was more or less injured
by the enemy's shot: had it not been, indeed, for the aid of
several small craft and boats from Gibraltar, the Pompée would
probably have shared the fate of the Hannibal. The Spencer
had one first-class volunteer (R. Spencer) and five seamen
killed, one midshipman (Joseph Chatterton), 23 seamen, and
three marines wounded. Her principal damages were confined
to her rigging and sails. The Venerable had one midshipman
(William Gibbons) and seven seamen killed, two midshipmen
(Silvester Austin and Martin Collins), 20 seamen, and three
marines wounded. The Hannibal had her captain's clerk

(David Lindsey), 68 seamen, one lieutenant of marines (James D. Williams), and five private marines killed, one lieutenant (John Turner), her master (John Wood), one midshipman (William Dudgeon), 44 seamen, one lieutenant of marines (George Dunford), and 14 private marines wounded, and six seamen missing, who had probably gone overboard with one of the masts. The Audacious had eight seamen killed, and one lieutenant of marines (Robert I. W. Day), 25 seamen, and six private marines wounded: her damages were not material. This makes the total loss in the British squadron, 121 killed, 240 wounded, and 14 missing.

The loss incurred by the French and Spaniards amounted, according to their own published accounts, on the part of the latter, to 11 men killed, exclusive of several wounded, and on the part of the former, to 306 killed, including the captains, Moncousu and Lalonde, besides 280, or rather, if the Madrid Gazette account is to be relied on, nearly 500 wounded. The French ships suffered considerably in their masts and hulls; and five Spanish gun-boats were sunk, and two materially damaged. The forts, also, received considerable injury from the fire of the British ships. How then would it have been, had the weather permitted the latter to bestow that fire with full effect?

One would suppose it difficult to raise a doubt as to the gallantry, whatever may have been thought of the prudence, of the attack upon Algeziras; yet the French, in their version of the affair, made it appear one of the most brilliant exploits which their navy had ever performed. It was no less than that " three French sail of the line and a frigate were attacked by six English sail of the line and a frigate; that the English were completely beaten, and took refuge in Gibraltar, leaving in the possession of the French the Hannibal, of 74 guns; and that another ship of the line struck, but was afterwards towed off by a great number of English gun-boats."

Fortunately for the cause of truth, the Spaniards, as well as the French, had a little self-love to gratify. "The action," says the Madrid Gazette-Extraordinary, "was very obstinate and bloody on both sides; and likewise on the part of our batteries, which decided the fate of the day." And, in another place: "The fire of our batteries was so hot and well supported, that the enemy suffered most from them; and particularly, it is to that of San-Iago we owe the capture of the English ship; for, her bold manœuvre, of attempting to pass between the French rear-admiral's ship, the Formidable, and the shore, made her take the ground; and, notwithstanding the utmost exertion to get her afloat, it was found impossible to move her: then the fire from the battery very soon dismasted her, and compelled her to strike."

We must, however, do the French the credit to state, that it was their soldiers and artillerymen, disembarked from the ships, that occasioned the Spanish batteries to be so admirably served as they were towards the middle and latter part of the action. With respect to the supposed striking of the Pompée, it may be explained by the fact, as noted down in that ship's log, that her colours were shot away, but they were quickly rehoisted. We might be disposed to remark upon the ostentatious manner in which the victory of "three unaided French ships of the line over six British" was announced at the Paris theatres, but that we should perhaps be reminded of what had occurred, nearly two years before, upon an occasion of much less importance, at one of the principal theatres of London.

Being aware of the relationship which subsisted between a contemporary and the distinguished officer who was the flag-captain of Sir James Saumarez in this action, we naturally turned to our contemporary's account, in the expectation of seeing that account so fully and accurately drawn up, as to afford some ground for the assertion, that none but a naval officer can write a naval history. For such we take to be the meaning of the following passage in Captain Brenton's Preface: "Other writers on the subject, not having the advantage of professional knowledge, have fallen into errors natural enough to them, but which prove their incompetency to the task they had undertaken. It has indeed been the misfortune of our service, that its history has generally been written by men who, however qualified by classical education, have wanted those indispensable requisites which can only be acquired by professional habits, local knowledge, and constant attention: hence it has arisen that many important events connected with the navy have been improperly stated," &c.[1]

This writer informs us, that the Venerable "was directed by the admiral to anchor between the batteries of Algeziras and Green Island."[2] Had the "local knowledge" of Captain Hood been of a par with our contemporary's, the Venerable would have bought experience at a dear rate; but, according to the letter of Sir James Saumarez, although Captain Hood was to

---

[1] Brenton, vol. i., p. vii.   [2] Ibid., vol. iii., p. 33.

lead the squadron, " it was not intended he should anchor " at all, much less anchor where there was less water than his ship drew ; nor, as far as we can learn, was any signal to anchor made until the Cæsar herself was compelled to bring up. The latter ship is represented to have anchored " immediately " after the Audacious ; whereas there was an interval of at least 25 minutes. The French, indeed, describe the attacking force as composed of two divisions of three ships each ; and so far they are right.

As to the plate given to illustrate the action, it is so full of mistakes, and, in many parts, so totally at variance with the letter-press, that we shall pass it by as unworthy of any further remark. We cannot, however, leave unnoticed the statement, that, " at about twelve o'clock, Captain Ferris hauled down his colours and surrendered ;" nor the charge against the Hannibal's captain, conveyed in these words : " Nothing could exceed the decision and intrepidity of Captain Ferris, although the result of his manœuvre was unfortunate : it is, however, due to Sir James Saumarez to state, that the squadron did not withdraw from action until the Hannibal had surrendered. A contrary assertion is made in the narrative of Captain Ferris ; an unaccountable error, proving that the most correct officers may sometimes be deceived, and the more to be lamented in this instance, as bearing the sanction of an official document." [1]

Our complaint against Captain Ferris is, that his account of the time, which intervened between the " ships driving out of the bay " and the surrender of the Hannibal, is not very clearly expressed. The captain might with propriety have stated, that the Hannibal did not strike her colours until nearly half an hour after Sir James Saumarez, from unavoidable causes undoubtedly, had discontinued the action and made sail for Gibraltar. Such was the fact. Not a word is there to contradict it either in the rear-admiral's official letter, or in the Cæsar's log ; but there is ample proof in confirmation of it, as we will now proceed to show. No time whatever, beyond the day of the month, and that only by inference, appears in the letter of Sir James Saumarez ; but the log of the Cæsar says : " At 12 h. 30 m. made signal for Hannibal being aground ;" that is, about half an hour according to our contemporary, after the Hannibal had " surrendered." " At 1 h. 35 m.," says the flag-ship's log, " action ceased ;" which, be it observed, is even fifteen minutes later than the log of the Audacious dates the same incident : whereas the

---

[1] Brenton, vol. iii., p. 35.

" Narrative " of Captain Ferris fixes the time of the Hannibal's
surrender at " nearly two o'clock."

A French account now before us also says : " L'Annibal,
échoué près du Formidable, essuyant en même temps le feu de
la batterie Saint-Jacques et celui du vaisseau françois, amena
son pavillon à deux heures du soir." [1] Of the four logs we have
been able to get a sight of, the only one which notices the surrender of the Hannibal is the Venerable's. That says : " At two,
observed the Hannibal cease firing and hoist the colours reversed."   But there is another witness to the truth of Captain
Ferris's statement. The Calpé in her log says : " At half-past
one, the Hannibal grounded under a very heavy battery, and
was much shattered. At 4, she hauled her colours down, which
the enemy kept again flying. Sent boats to save the people,
which were all detained. Standing off and on, ships and forts
firing on us. Half-past 6 bore up for the bay, and found the
squadron at anchor, and the Cæsar and Pompée in the mole."
The mistake in the Calpé's absolute time is of little consequence,
provided the relative time corresponds ; and that it does tolerably well. It is clear, also, that the squadron had all anchored
at Gibraltar when the Calpé returned, and the Cæsar and Pompée had even gone into the mole. So much, therefore, for the
assertion of Captain Brenton, that " the squadron did not withdraw from action until the Hannibal had surrendered ;" as well
as for the " unaccountable error " of Captain Ferris in having,
in a manner the least offensive that can well be imagined, stated
the contrary.

On the following morning, the 7th, Captain Brenton of the
Cæsar, was despatched with a flag of truce, to endeavour to
negotiate the exchange of Captain Ferris, his officers and men.
After some correspondence between Sir James and the French
admiral, the latter permitted Captain Ferris, with all his officers
and wounded men, to depart on their parole ; and granted the
same privilege to Captain Lord Cochrane and the officers of the
Speedy brig.

Thus it stands in the first edition of this work, and so we yet
believe the fact to be ; but the brother of the officer who carried
the message, says thus : " Sir James Saumarez sent his captain
over to Algeziras with a flag of truce to the French admiral
proposing an exchange of prisoners, which M. Linois declined,
alleging that it was not in his power to consent to such a
measure, without first receiving the sanction of the minister of

[1] Victoires et Conquêtes, tome xiv., p. 161.

marine at Paris, to whom he had despatched a courier immediately after the termination of the action."[1]   At all events both Captain Ferris and Lord Cochrane, with their respective officers, the sole object, we believe of Captain Jahleel Brenton's mission, were in England in the month of August.

It would be almost superfluous to state the result of the court-martial which was afterwards held upon Captain Ferris, and the late officers and ship's company of the Hannibal.   The court, of which Rear-admiral Holloway was president, sat on board the Gladiator, in Portsmouth harbour, on the 1st of September.   After the most honourable acquittal that a brave man could desire, Captain Ferris had his sword returned to him by the president, with the following address : " Captain Ferris, I have great pleasure in returning this sword to you, as I feel assured, if ever you have occasion to unsheath it again, it will be used with the same gallantry which you so nobly displayed in defending his majesty's ship Hannibal."

We formerly mentioned the transfer by Spain to France, for immediate employment, of six ships of the line at anchor in Cadiz harbour.[2]   On the 13th of June, in the morning, the two French 40-gun frigates Libre and Indienne, after a few hours' chase by the 74-gun ships Venerable and Superb, the only British force then off the port, anchored in the road of Cadiz from Brest, having on board Rear-admiral Dumanoir-le-Pelley, Commodore Le Ray, and a number of other officers, as well as of seamen, for the Franco-Spanish ships equipping in the port. The remainder of the crews, not already arrived by these and other conveyances, were daily expected from Brest, Lorient, and Rochefort.

The first step taken by Rear-admiral Linois, after getting his grounded ships and prize afloat, and which, notwithstanding the belief of Sir James Saumarez, that " the whole were rendered entirely unserviceable," he soon did, was to send an express overland to Admirals Massaredo and Dumanoir at Cadiz, imploring them to come or send a squadron to his assistance, before the British could get their ships repaired for renewing the attack; adding, in his second despatch to the Spanish commander-in-chief: " I have just received advice that the enemy intends burning us at our anchorage : it is in your power to save for the republic three fine ships of the line and a frigate, by merely ordering the Cadiz squadron to come and seek us."

Even these urgent calls would in all probability have failed in

[1] Brenton, vol. iii., p. 36.   [2] See p. 96.

their effect, had not Rear-admiral Dumanoir been on the spot to unite his solicitations with those of Rear-admiral Linois. Thus pressed, Admiral Massaredo, on the afternoon of the 8th, ordered Vice-admiral Don Juan Joaquin de Moreno, with five Spanish and one Franco-Spanish sail of the line, three frigates, and a lugger, to anchor in the outer road ready for a start by the land-wind of the next morning. This movement was seen by the Superb, then with the Thames and Pasley cruising off the port.

How these vessels happened to be here, when the Superb had been ordered to follow the squadron to Algeziras, may require some explanation. About three hours after the latter ship, still lying nearly becalmed, had lost sight of the rearmost of the ships with Sir James, an American vessel from the Mediterranean gave information that she had seen a French squadron of three sail of the line come out of Algeziras bay, and had left the ships well towards the African shore, standing out of the Straits, Inclining to think that the French admiral, if met by Sir James, as the American master had no doubt would be the case, would run direct for the Mediterranean ; considering that, by the delay which had unavoidably happened, the Superb had lost all chance of joining the admiral in time to be of any service ; and having not the slightest apprehension of the result of a contest at sea between three French and six British sail of the line, Captain Keats judged it to be the wisest plan to return off Cadiz, and, with his 74, frigate, and brig, watch the motions of the immeasurably superior force at anchor in that port.

On the 9th, at daylight, the Franco-Spanish squadron put to sea, all except the Saint-Antoine 74, which either got aground, or, not being able to fetch out, came again to an anchor. The remaining five sail of the line, three frigates and a lugger, made sail towards the Gut, preceded by the Superb, Thames, and Pasley. Early in the afternoon the brig came crowding into Gibraltar with the signal for an enemy flying ; and at 3 P.M., while the Spanish squadron was hauling round Cabrita point, the Superb and Thames, by signal from the Cæsar, came to an anchor in Gibraltar bay. Shortly afterwards the squadron from Cadiz was seen from the rock to cast anchor in the road of Algeziras. On the next morning the San Antonio, or, as her recent change of ownership entitled her to be called, Saint-Antoine, anchored with Rear-admiral Moreno's squadron.

That the object of this reinforcement was to conduct in safety to Cadiz the squadron of M. Linois was well known at the rock ; and nothing could surpass the exertions of the British officers

and men to get their damaged ships ready for sea. The Pompée
was in too bad a state to leave any hopes that she could be got
ready in time : her men, therefore, were turned over to assist in
the repairs of the other ships. "The Cæsar," says Captain
Edward Brenton, "lay in the mole, in so shattered a state, that
the admiral gave her up also ; and, hoisting his flag on board
the Audacious, expressed his intention of distributing her men
to the effective ships. Captain (Jahleel) Brenton requested that
his people might remain on board as long as possible, and, addressing them, stated the admiral's intentions in case the ship
could not be got ready : they answered, with three cheers, 'All
hands to work day and night, till she is ready.' The captain
ordered them to work all day, and watch and watch all night ;
by these means they accomplished what has, probably, never
been exceeded. On the 8th they warped her into the mole and
shipped the lower masts ; on the 9th they got their new mainmast in. On the the 11th the enemy showed symptoms of sailing,
which only increased, if possible, the energies of the seamen
On Sunday the 12th, at dawn of day, the enemy loosed sails ;
the Cæsar still refitting in the mole, receiving powder, shot, and
other stores, and preparing to haul out.

"At noon the enemy began to move ; the wind was fresh
from the eastward, and as they cleared the bay, they took up
stations off Cabrita point, which appeared to be the rendezvous,
on which they were to form their line of battle. At one o'clock
the enemy's squadron was nearly all under way ; the Spanish
ships Real-Carlos and Hermenegildo, of 112 guns each, off
Cabrita point : the Cæsar was warping out of the mole. The
day was clear ; the whole population of the rock came out to
witness the scene ; the line-wall, mole-head, and batteries were
crowded from the dockyard to the ragged-staff ; the Cæsar's
band playing, 'Come cheer up my lads, 'tis to glory we steer ;'
the military band of the garrison answering with 'Britons strike
home.' The effect of this scene it is difficult to describe : Englishmen were proud of their country ; and foreigners, who beheld
the scene, wished to be Englishmen. So general was the enthusiasm among our gallant countrymen, that even the wounded
men begged to be taken on board, to share in the honours of the
approaching conflict."[1]

At 3 P.M., just as, in her way out of the mole she passed
under the stern of the Audacious, the Cæsar rehoisted the flag
of Sir James Saumarez, and made the signal for the squadron

1 Brenton, vol. iii., p. 39.

to weigh and prepare for battle. This was promptly done; and the squadron consisting of the Cæsar, Venerable, Superb, Spencer, and Audacious of the line, 12-pounder 32-gun frigate Thames, Captain Askew Paffard Holles, 14-gun polacre-sloop Calpé, Captain the Honourable George Heneage Laurence Dundas, hired armed brig Louisa, and Portuguese frigate, Carlotta, Captain Crawfurd Duncan.

As soon as they had got from under the lee of the rock, the British ships formed in line ahead on the larboard tack, with the wind from the eastward. At 7 P.M. they wore together, and stood on the starboard tack under easy sail, watching the combined squadron, which, at about 7 h. 45 m. P.M., cleared Cabrita point; except the Hannibal, who, having only topmasts for lower masts, still remained astern, in spite of all the efforts of the Indienne frigate by whom she was in tow. The frigate and her charge eventually returned to Algeziras, leaving the following as the force of the combined squadron :—

Spanish.

Gun-ship.

112 { Real-Carlos .   .   . Captain Don J. Esquerra.
     { Hermenegildo .   .   •   ,, Don J. Emparran.
96   San-Fernando .   .   .   ,, Don J. Malina.
80   Argonauta   .   .   .   ,, Don J. Harrera.
74   San-Augustin .   .   .   ,, Don R. Jopete.

Frigate, Sabina.

French.

Gun-ship.

80 { Formidable   .   .   . Captain Amable-Gilles Troude.
    { Indomptable .   .   .   ,,   —— ——
74 { Saint-Antoine   .   . Commodore Julien Le Ray.
    { Desaix   .   .   .   .   ,,   Jean-Anne Christy-Pallière.

Frigates, Libre and Muiron ; *lugger* Vautour.

It appears that it is the invariable custom for a Spanish admiral, when in the presence of the enemy, to shift his flag from a line-of-battle ship to a frigate.[1] Accordingly, while the squadron was lying to off Cabrita point, Vice-admiral Moreno shifted his flag from the Real-Carlos to the Sabina ; and by the Spanish admiral's desire, but with much reluctance on his part, Rear-admiral Linois quitted the Formidable and repaired on board the same frigate.

At 8 P.M., or a little after, the British squadron bore away in chase ; and, at about 8 h. 40 m., Sir James hailed the Superb, who was close astern of the Cæsar, and directed Captain Keats

---

[1] Victoires et Conquêtes, tome xiv., p. 164.

to make sail ahead, and attack the sternmost of the enemy's ships, none of which were then visible. In an instant all sail was set upon the Superb; and, passing the Cæsar, she regained a sight of the hostile squadron. At 10 P.M. the wind freshened, and the Cæsar and Venerable were then the only ships of her own squadron seen by the Superb. At 11 P.M. the Superb had so increased her distance, that the Cæsar was full three miles astern, and the Venerable no longer visible. At 11 h. 20 m. P.M., observing a Spanish three-decker, the Real-Carlos, about a point before her larboard beam, and a three and a two decker, the San-Hermenegildo and Saint-Antoine, in a range with and on the larboard side of the former, the Superb shortened sail: and, when about 300 or 350 yards from the Real-Carlos, opened a fire upon her from her larboard guns. At the third broadside the Real-Carlos, whose foretopmast had just been shot away, was observed to be on fire. The Superb instantly ceased engaging the Spanish ship; and the latter continued her course before the wind. Shortly afterwards the Real-Carlos came suddenly to the wind, and then dropped astern in evident confusion, she and her two nearest companions firing their guns in all directions.

The total destruction of her first opponent being now no longer doubtful, the Superb again made sail, and at 11 h. 50 m. P.M. came up with and brought to action the Saint-Antoine. After a contest of about 30 minutes, part of which was close and fought upon a wind, the French 74 ceased firing, and hailed repeatedly that she surrendered. Shortly afterwards the Cæsar and Venerable came up in succession, and, deceived by the Saint-Antoine's broad pendant, which, owing to the halliards having been shot away and got entangled amongst the rigging, still remained flying, fired into her; as did also the Spencer and Thames. In a few minutes the discovery was made that the Saint-Antoine had already surrendered, and the firing at her ceased.

At about 15 minutes past midnight the Real-Carlos blew up, but not until she had fallen on board of, and set in a similar blaze, the San-Hermenegildo, who, having in the dark mistaken the Real-Carlos for a foe, had been engaging her; and who, in another quarter of an hour, exploded also. Thus, melancholy to relate, out of 2000 men composing the united crews of these Spanish first-rates, two officers and 36 men that got on board the Superb, and 262 who were fortunate enough to reach the Saint-Antoine and some of the other ships of their squadron,[1] were all that escaped destruction.

[1] Victoires et Conquêtes, tome xiv., p. 166.

The loss on board the Superb, in her action with the Saint-Antoine (for in her short one with the Real-Carlos, she does not appear to have sustained any), amounted to one lieutenant (Edmund Waller) and 14 seamen and marines wounded, most of them severely.   The Saint-Antoine, in crew and supernumeraries, had on board 730 men, of whom about 200, including those saved from one of the two three-deckers, were Spaniards.   The loss on board the Saint-Antoine, except that Commodore Le Ray was wounded. has not been enumerated; but from the half an hour's close cannonade of so well disciplined a ship as the Superb, it must have been very severe.[1] The latter, accompanied by the Carlotta, Calpé, and Louisa, remained with the Saint-Antoine, while the rest of the squadron stood on in chase.

During the latter part of the night it came on to blow very hard; and on the 13th, at 4 A.M., the only ships in company with the Cæsar were, the Spencer far astern, the Venerable and Thames ahead, and the French 80-gun ship Formidable, at some distance from and upon the lee bow of the latter, standing towards the shoals of Conil, with a light air from off the land. Sail was immediately made by the Cæsar and her three consorts; but the easterly wind soon afterwards failing, the Venerable and Thames, who were nearer in shore, were the only ships in a situation to chase with any prospect of success; and, as the Formidable had only jury topmasts, they came up with her fast. At 5[2] A.M. the French ship hoisted her colours, and at 5 h. 15 m. commenced firing her stern-chase guns at the Venerable; but the latter, for fear of retarding her progress, did not fire in return until 5 or 6 minutes afterwards, when the light and baffling airs threw the two ships broadside-to, within musket-shot of each other.

At 5 h. 30 m. the Venerable's mizen topmast was shot away; and at 5 h. 45 m. the Thames, by signal, hauled up and poured a raking broadside into the Formidable; who fired from her stern-chasers in return, but without effect.   At 6 h. 45 m., by which time the French 80 and British 74 had gradually approximated to a pistol-shot distance, the mainmast of the latter came down by the board.   Her standing and running rigging being also cut to pieces, the Venerable fell from alongside her

---

[1] Although when first fitted (1825), carrying 24-pounders on her main deck, the Superb mounted only 18-pounders in her action with the Saint-Antoine, her previous commander, Captain John Sutton, from an idea that the ship was crank, having induced the admiralty to issue an order for the exchange. [The Superb was built in 1798. She could not have been in 1825, as James published his first edition in 1823!—H. Y. POWELL.]

[2] Misprinted "seven" in the Gazette.

opponent. Profiting by the circumstance, the Formidable continued to stand on; but owing to the almost calm state of the weather, increased her distance so slowly, as to give considerable annoyance to the Venerable by the fire from her stern-chasers. At 7 h. 50 m. A.M. the Venerable's foremast fell over her side, and almost at the same instant the ship herself, driven by the strength of the current, struck upon the rocky shoals off San-Pedro, situated about 12 miles to the southward of Cadiz. Having thus effectually rid herself of this her principal opponent, the Formidable continued her course to the northward, under all the sail she could spread, in the hope to reach Cadiz before the enemy's two remaining line-of-battle ships in sight, the nearest of which, the Cæsar, was still at a considerable distance, could approach within gun-shot. At 8 A.M., just as the mizenmast of the Venerable had shared the fate of the other masts, the gig of the Cæsar, with Captain Brenton on board, reached the ship (over which the stern-chase shot of the Formidable were still flying), with discretionary orders to Captain Hood, to withdraw his crew and destroy the Venerable, should the combined squadron, which appeared so inclined, evince an intention of attacking her; and the Thames had been ordered to close for the purpose of receiving the people. Captain Hood, however, requested the rear-admiral to depend upon his exertions to save the Venerable, notwithstanding her critical and almost hopeless situation. Just as the Cæsar's boat had quitted the Venerable on her return, the appearance of the Audacious and Superb to the southward induced the Spanish admiral to haul up for Cadiz, where he and his ships were soon safely moored.

In her smart encounter with a ship so decidedly superior to her in force as the Formidable, the Venerable had her master (John Williams), 15 seamen, and two marines killed, one lieutenant (Thomas Church), her boatswain (John Snell), two midshipmen (George Massey and Charles Pardoe), 73 seamen, and 10 marines wounded. The Thames does not appear to have had a man hurt: and we do not believe that any of the Formidable's shot even struck her. The loss sustained by the Formidable herself, according to her captain's official report, amounted to 20 men killed, or mortally wounded, but the remaining wounded M. Troude has seemingly omitted to enumerate. The Sabina frigate had also one man killed and five wounded; but whether from the fire of the British ships, or of two unfortunate three-deckers that blew up, it is difficult to ascertain.

The British had now leisure to devote the whole of their attention to the only remaining object, the safety of the Venerable. Fortunately for her gallant officers and crew, the weather continued calm; and at 2 P.M., by the assistance of the Thames who had anchored near, and of the boats of the Cæsar and Spencer, the Venerable was hove into deep water. The Thames then took the dismasted 74 in tow, and stood with her towards the flag-ship in the offing. At 6 P.M. the Venerable cast off the Thames, and was taken in tow by the Spencer, who made sail with her towards the Gut. Having cleared away the wreck of her masts, the Venerable now got up a main topgallantmast for a foremast, the driver-boom for a mainmast, and a studdingsail-boom for a mizenmast. Soon after dark a maintopgallant-sail was set for a foresail, and before daylight on the 14th a mizentopsail for a mainsail. So that by 8 A.M., the Venerable had made herself sufficiently manageable to cast off the ship of the line that was towing her, and take again to the frigate. Even this state of comparative seaworthiness had not been accomplished without great exertions on the part of her officers and crew; yet a contemporary states that, at sunset on the preceding day, which was little more than five hours after she lay a dismasted hulk upon the rocks, the Venerable was "in such efficient order as to be fit for action had an enemy appeared."[1]

For the service rendered to the country, by the prompt and effective manner in which the combined squadron under Vice-admiral Moreno and Rear-admiral Linois was chased and attacked by the British squadron under Rear-admiral Sir James Saumarez, the latter, with the captains, officers, and crews of the ships under his orders, received the thanks of parliament; and Sir James himself, for his conspicuous gallantry in going in pursuit of a force so decidedly superior, was created a knight of the bath, with a pension of 1200l. per annum. The first-lieutenant of the Cæsar, Philip Dumaresq, was made a commander. The first-lieutenant of the Superb and Venerable, the two ships that bore the brunt of the action, were Samuel Jackson and James Lillicrap; and they also received that step in rank which was so justly their due.

The Saint-Antoine, which, on account of the miserable fate of the two Spanish three-deckers, was the only trophy carried off by the British, became afterwards added to the navy of her captors; but being an old 74 of only 1700 tons, the ship

[1] Brenton, vol. iii., p. 42.

never quitted Portsmouth after she arrived there. By way of perpetuating an acknowledged error in the official letter of Captain Keats to Sir James Saumarez, the Saint-Antoine, both in Steel's lists and in the navy-office books, continued, and in the latter still continues to be called the San-Antonio.

Although from a desire to be impartial we invariably, if in our power, consult the accounts on both sides of the question, and are frequently enabled to extract, even on the subject of British naval history, much useful information from an account drawn up by a Frenchman or Spaniard, the best French account we can find of the proceedings of the combined squadron under Vice-admiral Moreno and Rear-admiral Linois is so amusingly extravagant, that, if only as a relief to the dry matter-of-fact detail of these pages, we are induced to subjoin a translated extract: "At 4 o'clock in the morning, he (Captain Troude) perceived in his wake four vessels which he knew were enemies: they were, in fact, a part of the English squadron: the Cæsar, commanded by Admiral Saumarez, the Venerable, Superb,[1] and frigate Thames. The brave Troude prepared for action, and strengthened his lower batteries by men from those of the quarter-deck and forecastle. He was soon overtaken by the Venerable and Thames: the first discharged her broadside into his larboard quarter, and the Formidable bore up to close this adversary: a most spirited combat ensued, yard-arm and yard-arm; and frequently at no greater distance than the spunge of the gun. The French captain ordered three round-shot to be put into each gun. The Thames cannonaded him astern, but the latter's stern-chasers replied to her fire. The two other enemy's ships (now comes the inventive part of the story) successively arrived up; and, not being able to double the Formidable to windward, they took their stations upon her larboard quarter. One of the first broadsides of the French ship carried away the Venerable's mizentopmast, and soon afterwards her mainmast: the English vessel bore up; but Troude followed her in this movement to rake her astern, at the same time that he cannonaded the Cæsar, who, finding herself close ahead of the Venerable, could not return the fire: not a French shot was lost. In this position the Venerable lost her foremast. Troude now directed the whole of his fire at the Cæsar, whom he closed as much as possible. After an engagement of half an hour, although the English ship, being able to carry more sail, ran past the Formidable and obliged the latter to manoeuvre to keep

---

[1] The Spencer is here meant.

alongside of her opponent, the Cæsar abandoned the. combat, bore up in confusion, hauled on board her larboard tacks, and joined the Venerable, to whom the Thames was affording succour. It remained still to fight the Superb, who was on the larboard bow of the French ship; but the English ship bore up, passed under the lee of the Formidable out of gun-shot, and rejoined the other vessels. At 7 o'clock in the morning Captain Troude was master of the field of battle. He got upon deck the remainder of the shot, sufficient still for another hour's action; refreshed his gallant crew, who had so well seconded him, and repaired his rigging; his sails were in tatters, the land-wind had ceased, and he found himself becalmed, within gun-shot of the English squadron, the boats of which were occupied in giving assistance to the Venerable. This ship had now lost her mizenmast, and the current drove her upon the coast. At 10 o'clock, the wind having freshened, the Thames attempted to take the Venerable in tow; but not being able to get her afloat, she was wrecked between the Isle of Léon and the point of San-Roche."[1]

The French government believed, or affected to believe, all this fanfaronade, and therefore could do no less than reward the Formidable's commanding officer. This was done forthwith; and, from a very young capitaine de frégate, M. Amable-Gilles Troude was promoted to a capitaine de vaisseau, by commission dated on the 14th of July, 1801, the very day on which, with the aid of his pen, if not of his sword, he had added so greatly to his own and his country's renown.

Light Squadrons and Single Ships.

On the 3rd of January, the British 38-gun frigate Melpomène, Captain Sir Charles Hamilton, being off the bar of Sénégal, the latter resolved, with the concurrence of Lieutenant-colonel Frazer, the commandant of the garrison of Gorée, to attempt to carry by surprise a French 18-gun brig-corvette and an armed schooner at anchor within it; in order, by their means, as vessels of a less draught of water than the frigate, to get possession of the battery that commanded the entrance to the river, and eventually of the settlement itself.

Accordingly, at 9 h. 30 m. P.M., five boats, containing 55 volunteers from the Melpomène, five from the crew of a trans-

---

[1] For the original extract, see Appendix No. 5.

port in company, and Lieutenant Christie and 35 men from the African corps, being 96 in all, placed under the orders of Lieutenant Thomas Dick, assisted by Lieutenant William Palmer, and by Lieutenant William Vyvian of the marines, quitted the Melpomène upon the service intrusted to them. Having passed in safety the heavy surf on the bar with the flood-tide, also the battery at the point, without being discovered, the boats, at 11 h. 15 m., arrived within a few yards of the brig; when the latter, by a single discharge of her two bow-guns, killed Lieutenant Palmer and seven men, and sank two of the best boats. Notwithstanding this, the three remaining boats pulled alongside of, boarded, and, after a 20 minutes' severe contest, carried, the French brig-corvette Sénégal, of 18 long 8 and 12 pounders (the latter carronades probably) and about 60 men, commanded by Citizen Renou.

In the mean time the schooner had cut her cable, and run for protection nearer the battery; the fire from which, and from some musketry on the southern bank of the river, frustrated every attempt upon the former, although Lieutenant Dick had turned the guns of the brig against her. Having effected as much as he could, Lieutenant Dick cut the cables of the brig, and made sail with her down the river; but, owing to the ebb tide's having made, and no one on board being acquainted with the navigation across the bar, the Sénégal grounded. After several vain attempts to get off the prize, Lieutenant Dick and his party quitted her; and, with the three boats, succeeded in making his way to the ship, across a tremendous surf, and under a heavy fire of grape-shot and musketry from the adjoining batteries. The brig afterwards sank up to her gunwales, in the quicksand on which she had grounded. The loss sustained by the British in this spirited, although but partially successful affair, amounted to one lieutenant (William Palmer), one lieutenant of marines (William Vyvian), one midshipman (Robert Main), six seamen, one marine, and one corporal of the African corps killed, one master's mate (John Hendric,) one surgeon's mate (Robert Darling), 10 seamen, one corporal and four privates of marines, and Lieutenant Christie of the African corps wounded; total, 11 killed and 18 wounded.

On the 6th of January the British 26-gun frigate Mercury, Captain Thomas Rogers, cruising in the gulf of Lyons, fell in with a convoy of about 20 sail of vessels, bound from Cette to Marseilles, under the escort of two or three French gun-boats. The weather being nearly calm, Captain Rogers despatched his boats (but how commanded does not appear in the gazette-letter) to attack the convoy; 15 of which, including two ships and four brigs, and all deeply laden with brandy, sugar, corn, wine, oil, and other merchandise, were brought off with very little resistance and no loss, the gun-boats having all fled upon the Mercury's approach.

On the 20th, the island of Sardinia bearing east-south-east distant 40 leagues, and the wind blowing fresh, the Mercury fell in with, and after a nine hours' chase captured, without loss or resistance, the French 20-gun ship-corvette Sans-Pareille, of 18 brass 8-pounders and two brass 36-pounder carronades, and (the London Gazette says, "fifteen," but the French captain's deposition in the prize-court) 155 men, commanded by Lieutenant Gabriel Renaud, from Toulon the day preceding, bound to Alexandria, with a full cargo of shot, arms, medicines, and supplies of every kind, for the French army. Although described as quite a new vessel, and well-found with stores of every description, the prize does not appear to have been added to the British navy.

On the 15th of January, while the 20-gun ship Daphne, Captain Richard Matson, 18-gun ship-sloops Cyane and Hornet, Captains Henry Matson and James Nash, and schooner-tender Garland, were at an anchor in the harbour of the Saintes, a convoy of French coasters, in charge of an armed schooner, was observed standing across towards Vieux Fort, island of Guadeloupe. At midnight the Garland schooner, accompanied by two boats from each of the three ships, under the command of Lieutenants Kenneth Mackenzie and Francis Peachey, was despatched to attempt the capture or destruction of the convoy. The whole of the vessels, however, except one, succeeded in getting under the guns of Basse-terre. That one, having anchored near Vieux Fort, was boarded and brought off under a heavy but apparently harmless cannonade.

On the 17th in the afternoon, the French schooner Eclair, of four long 4-pounders, twenty $1\frac{1}{2}$ pounder brass swivels, and 45 men, the escort of the convoy in question was observed to put into Trois-Rivières, and anchor under the protection of one principal battery and two smaller flanking ones. Lieutenants Mackenzie and Peachey volunteered to attempt cutting her out. For this purpose the first-named officer, with 25 seamen and marines, went on board the Garland; and at 5 A.M. on the 18th, which was as early as the breeze would permit, the Cyane, tender, and boats stood across to Trois-Rivières. On arriving at the anchorage, the Garland ran the Eclair on board, and Lieutenants Mackenzie and Peachey, with 30 men, boarded and carried the French schooner in the face of the batteries.

This gallant exploit was not performed wholly without loss, the British having had one seaman and one marine killed, and a sergeant of marines and two seamen wounded. In defending herself, which she appears to have done in a very manful way, the Eclair lost one seaman killed, two drowned, and her captain, first and second lieutenants, and six men wounded. The schooner had recently sailed from Rochefort; and, although mounting only four guns, was pierced for, and, being 145 tons, was well able to carry, 12 guns, the number she afterwards mounted in the British service.

Late in the month of December, 1800, the British 8-gun schooner Active, Acting-lieutenant Michael Fitton, having returned to Port Royal from a long cruise, needed a thorough repair. To employ to advantage the intervening time, Captain Henry Vansittart, of the Abergavenny 54, of which ship the Active was the tender, allowed Lieutenant Fitton to transfer himself and crew to one of the Active's prizes, the late Spanish privateer N.-S. de los Dolores; a felucca of about 50 tons, mounting one long 12-pounder on a traversing carriage, with a screw to raise it from the hold when wanted for use. Having embarked on board of her, and stowed as well as he could his 44 officers and men, Lieutenant Fitton, early in January, 1801, sailed out on a cruise upon the Spanish Main.

In her way along the coast, for every part of which her commander was a pilot, the tender, whose rig and appearance were an admirable decoy, destroyed two or three enemy's small craft; such as, although not worth sending in, were precisely the kind of vessels which had recently been committing such serious depredations on West India commerce. It may be observed here, that small, swift-sailing, armed vessels, properly commanded and appointed, are the only description of cruisers which can operate with effect against the hordes of tiny, but well-manned, and, to a merchant-vessel, formidable privateers, that usually swarm in the West India seas. The Active herself had perhaps captured or destroyed more of these marauders than any frigate upon the station; and it need not be urged at what a comparatively trifling expense.

A succession of stormy weather, and the leaky state of the felucca's deck, by which chiefly 22 of the men had been made sick, induced her commander to steer for, and take possession of, a small key near Point Canoe on the Spanish Main. Here Lieutenant Fitton errected a tent, landed his men and stores, and, after making the best disposition his means would admit to resist an attack, examined the state of his vessel. The main beam, on which the gun rested, was found to be badly sprung. This was irreparable. The vessel's rigging was decayed, and he had no cordage; her sails were split and torn, and he had neither canvas, nor even sail-twine. Being, however, a man of resources, Lieutenant Fitton reduced and altered the shape of the sails, the seamen using for twine what they unravelled from the remnant pieces. He then rigged the tender as a lugger, and re-embarked his men, gun, and the few stores he had left.

In this ineffective state, the tender bore up for Carthagena; her commander intending to coast down the Main to Porto-Bello, in the hope of being able to capture or cut out some vessel that might answer to carry his crew and himself to Jamaica. On the 23rd of January, early in the morning, as the tender was hauling round Cape Rosario, a schooner was discovered, to which she immediately gave chase. The schooner, which was the Spanish garda-costa Santa-Maria, of six (pierced for 10) long 6-pounders, 10 swivels, and 60 men, commanded by Don Josef Coréi, a few hours only from Carthagena, bore down to reconnoitre the lugger. The latter having her gun below, and as many of her men hid from view as the want of a barricade would permit, the garda-costa readily approached within gunshot. Although he could have no wish to contend with so powerful an adversary, Lieutenant Fitton could not resist the opportunity of showing how well his men could handle their 12-pounder. It was soon raised up, and was discharged repeatedly, in quick succession, with evident effect.

After about 30 minutes' mutual firing with cannon and musketry, the Santa-Maria sheered off, and directed her course for the isle of Varus, evidently with an intent to run on shore. Her persevering though one gun opponent stuck close to her, plying her well with shot, great and small; but the tender was unable, as her commander wished, to grapple the schooner, because the latter kept the weather-gage. At length the Santa-Maria grounded; and Lieutenant Fitton, aware that, if the schooner landed her men in the bushes, no attempt of his people would avail, eased off the lugger's sheets, and ran her also on shore, about 10 yards from the Santa-Maria. The musketry of the latter as she heeled over greatly annoying the tender's men, who had no barricades to shelter them, Lieutenant Fitton leaped overboard ; and, with his sword in his mouth, followed by the greater part of his crew similarly armed, swam to, boarded, and after a stout resistance carried, the Spanish schooner.

In this splendid little affair, the tender lost two seamen killed and five wounded : and of her small crew, numbering originally but 45, many were too sick to attend their quarters. Four or five, also, who were in the sick-list, heedless alike of the doctor's injunctions and their own feeble state, had, when the boarding call was made, sprung over the side with their comrades; and one or two of them nearly perished, in consequence of their inability to struggle with the waves. The loss on board the Santa-Maria, as acknowledged by her officers, amounted to five men killed and nine wounded, including her commander, who, poor fellow, had both his hands carried away by a grape-shot.

It took some hours ere the tender, with the help of the prize's anchors and cables (her own having parted in a gale four days before), was again got afloat; and, before that could be effected, the 12-pounder, then in a disabled state, was obliged to be thrown overboard. The Spanish inhabitants having collected along and opened a fire from the shore, and the prize having grounded too fast to be got off, Lieutenant Fitton set the Santa-Maria on fire ; but not until he had taken out of her what was most wanted for his own vessel, and had landed as well the living of her crew, for whom, being without a 'tween-decks, he had no room, as—from a respect to the scruples even of an enemy—the five that were dead. Having thus destroyed a Spanish garda-costa of very superior force, the Abergavenny's tender sailed back to Jamaica, and on the fourth day reached Black River with scarcely a gallon of water on board.

On the 26th of January, at 8 A.M., in latitude 45° north, longitude 12° west, the British 12-pounder 36-gun frigate Oiseau, Captain Samuel Hood Linzee, fell in with and chased the French 36-gun frigate Dédaigneuse, bound from Cayenne to Rochefort with despatches. The Oiseau continued the pursuit alone until noon on the 27th ; when, Cape Finisterre in sight, the British 18-pounder 36-gun frigates Sirius and Amethyst, Captains Richard King and John Cooke, joined in the chase. But so well did the Dédaigneuse maintain her advantage, that it was not until 2 A.M. on the 28th, that the Sirius and Oiseau got near enough to receive a fire from her stern-chasers.

After a running fight of 45 minutes, and a loss of "several" men killed and 17 wounded, among the latter her captain (not named in the official letter) and fifth-lieutenant, the French frigate, when about two miles from the shore near Cape Belem, hauled down her colours. The only British ship struck by the shot of the Dédaigneuse was the Sirius ; and she did not have a man hurt, but had her rigging and sails a trifle damaged, and her mainyard and bowsprit slightly wounded. The Dédaigneuse, a fine little frigate of 897 tons, was afterwards added to the British navy under the same name as a 12-pounder 36.

On the 29th of January, at noon, the British 24-gun ship Bordelais, Captain Thomas Manby, while cruising to windward of Barbadoes, discovered, in chase of her to windward, two men-of-war brigs and a schooner. The Bordelais immediately short-ened sail to comply with their wishes ; and, at sunset, the French national brigs, Curieux, of 18 long 8-pounders and 168 men, Captain Georges Radelet, and Mutine, of 16 long 6-pounders and 156 men, and the schooner Espérance, of six 4-pounders and 52 men, got within gun-shot. At 6 P.M., having wore round, the Bordelais was enabled to bring the Curieux to action, at about 10 yards' distance. Scarcely had the Bordelais opened her heavy metal upon the Curieux, than the latter's two consorts aban-doned her. When it was known that the Bordelais was a ship of 625 tons, mounting twenty-two 32-pounder carronades and 2 long nines, with a complement of 195 men, the surprise will be great that the Curieux alone should, for 30 minutes, sustain an action with her ; and that, too, at a distance so favourable to a carronade-battery.

On being taken possession of after having hailed that she had struck, the Curieux's deck was found, as might indeed be ex-pected, strewed from end to end with the dying and the dead. The captain had had both his legs shot off, and survived but a few hours ; and the brig's killed and wounded, in the whole, amounted to about 50. The Bordelais, on the other hand, escaped with only one man killed, and seven wounded ; includ-ing among the latter Lieutenant Robert Barrie, who did not quit his quarters, Master's Mate James Jones, and Midshipman John Lions.

It was not in the killed and wounded only that the French brig afforded proofs of the obstinacy of her resistance : her hull had been so pierced with shot, that, in about half an hour after she was taken possession of, the Curieux was found to be sinking. Already had 120 prisoners been received from her ; and every exertion was now made to save the wounded. So zealous were Lieutenant Archibald Montgomery and his 20 men in performing this service, that, at 8 P.M. the vessel foundered under them, close alongside of the Bordelais. The floating wreck buoyed up all those brave men except two midshipmen, Messrs. Spence and Auckland, and five seamen; who consequently perished, with the whole, if not the greater part, of the brig's wounded.

Nothing could exceed the gallantry of Captain Radelet, unless it was the pusillanimity of his two brother-officers, Captains Raybaun and Haymond; and whose vessels, on account of the three hours' delay which had taken place in endeavouring to save the crew of the prize, in shifting the prisoners, and in reparing the Bordelais' rigging and sails, effected their escape. These two French brigs and schooner had been fitted out by Victor Hugues at Cayenne, principally to intercept the outward-bound West India fleet. It is but fair to mention, that a French " Etat général de la Marine," of 1803, does not contain the names of the two gentlemen represented to have been the commanders of the Mutine and Espérance. The probability therefore is, that they were not officers belonging to the French navy.

On the 18th of February, at about 2 P.M., latitude 28° 24' south, and longitude 18° 17' west, the British 18-gun brig-sloop Penguin (sixteen 32-pounder carronades and two long-sixes), Captain Robert Mansel, standing to the south-east with a fresh breeze at north, discovered in the west-north-west three warlike-looking ships apparently in chase of her. At 2 h. 45 m., finding the private signal not answered, the brig, having previously shortened sail, cleared for action, to be ready to receive the leading ship; which had edged away towards her, and, showing 12 ports of a side, appeared to be a corvette of at least 20 guns, while her two consorts, apparently armed merchantmen, and either her convoy or prizes, kept their wind.

At 3 h. 45 m. the corvette, as if not liking the Penguin's appearance, tacked and rejoined her consorts; whereupon the Penguin tacked also and stood after them. At 5 h. 10 m. P.M. the Penguin arrived nearly within gun-shot of the sternmost ship, when the corvette, firing a shot, hoisted French colours, as did the others. All three ships then formed in line, and bore down for the brig's larboard quarter. The Penguin again tacked to close, and presently afterwards received and returned the fire of the three ships as they passed in succession. Being desirous to obtain the weather-gage, the Penguin stood on; and at 6 h. 15 m. P.M., having got into the wake of the French ships, the brig a third time tacked.

Immediately on this the corvette hauled to windward, and her two friends or prizes astern bore away and steered different courses : one of these ships, however, soon afterwards hauled up again as close as she could lie.   In a few minutes the Penguin arrived nearly abreast and to leeward of this ship ; when the latter, relying upon her weight and size, steered for the British brig's beam, with the intention of running her down. Two or three heavy and well-directed broadsides from the Penguin, poured in just as the ship approached near, caused the latter to let fly her top-gallant sheets, and haul down the French flag.

Scorning to stay to take possession of so unworthy an antagonist, when a ship more than equal to herself remained to be subdued, the Penguin stood on close hauled, and at about 7 h. 25 m. observed the corvette upon her larboard and weather quarter.   In five minutes afterwards, just as the brig was about to recommence the engagement, her foretopmast came down ; and, to add to the misfortune, it fell over on the larboard side, and temporarily disabled the fore-yard.   Seeing the unmanageable state of her opponent, the French corvette, at 7 h. 45 m., bore close down ; and a spirited action ensued, during which, until towards the latter part when the Penguin managed to get her starboard broadside to bear, the brig's foretopgallant-sail and rigging frequently caught fire from the explosion of her guns.   Notwithstanding this, the Penguin maintained the contest with so much vigour and effect, that, at 8 h. 30 m., the French ship sheered off and hauled to the wind on the larboard tack.

After several attempts to wear in pursuit, the Penguin found it impracticable ; and the corvette and her two consorts were presently out of sight.   Although the action had lasted so long, the very high firing of the corvette, some of whose missiles were iron bars from eight inches to a foot long, occasioned the Penguin's principal damages to be in her rigging and sails ; and, from the same cause, the brig's loss amounted to only one man killed and a few wounded.   Having in the course of the night repaired her rigging and got up another topmast, the Penguin, at daylight on the 19th, again saw her three opponents, and chased them into the island of Teneriffe.

For the sake of Captain Mansel, and the officers and crew of the Penguin, we regret not to have succeeded in discovering the name and other particulars of the ship, which they had so gallantly fought and so fairly beaten.   If the vessel was a

national corvette, she probably was one of those which Buonaparte had sent to Cayenne or the Seychelles with banished persons; but, supposing the ship to have been a privateer, her
evident size and force, and the knowledge that some of the
French privateers, cruising at this particular period, were a
match for a British 28-gun frigate, will prevent that from
operating as the slightest disparagement, to the Penguin's action.

On the 19th of February, at 4 P.M., the British 18-pounder
36-gun frigate Phœbe, Captain Robert Barlow, being about two
leagues to the eastward of Gibraltar, beating up for that port
with a light breeze at west, discovered on the African shore,
nearly abreast of the fortress of Ceuta, a strange ship under a
press of sail, steering directly up the Mediterranean. The
Phœbe, having her head to the northward, immediately tacked
and stood for the stranger; who, however, made no alteration in
her course. At 7 h. 30 m. P.M. the Phœbe, by her superiority
of sailing, closed the stranger upon the larboard quarter; and
the latter, finding an action inevitable, shortened sail. Having
done the same, and being unable from the darkness to discern
her colours, the Phœbe fired a shot over the strange ship, to
induce her to bring to. Almost immediately afterwards the
French 40-gun frigate Africaine, Commodore Saulnier, with 400
troops, six brass field-pieces, several thousand stands of arms,
and a great quantity of ammunition (but not "implements of
agriculture," as erroneously stated in the official letter), which
she had embarked at Rochefort (and, having sailed with and
since parted from the 36-gun frigate Régénérée, similarly
freighted, was conveying to Egypt), altered her course to port:
and, as soon as she could bring her broadside to bear, discharged it at the Phœbe, but with little or no effect.

Having altered her course so as to keep parallel with her
opponent, and got quite near to her, the Phœbe poured in a
well-directed, and, as it proved, most destructive broadside.
The two ships with their heads to the northward, then continued the engagement within pistol-shot distance, until 9 h.
30 m. P.M.; when the Africaine being nearly unrigged, having
five feet water in the hold, her decks literally encumbered with
dead, and the greater part of her guns dismounted, struck her
colours. Her masts were all badly wounded, and, had there
been any swell, would have fallen over her side. The Phœbe's
masts were also much injured, and chiefly owed their stability
to the smoothness of the sea. Her rigging and sails, too, were
scarcely in better plight than those of the Africaine.

Although her net complement, including 18 boys, was 261, the Phœbe had sailed from Cork seven men short, and since manned and sent to Gibraltar, one recaptured brig with seven, and one detained brig with eight men; so that her crew on board was reduced to 239. Of this number the Phœbe had only one seaman killed, and her first-lieutenant (John Wentworth Holland), master (Thomas Griffiths), and 10 seamen wounded.

The loss on board the Africaine was truly dreadful. The total number of persons on board of her were 715; of which number 315 composed the ship's regular crew, and the 400 were troops and artificers of various descriptions. Of her 715 in crew and supernumeraries, the Africaine had Commodore Saulnier, one brigadier-general, two captains in the army, eight petty-officers, three surgeons (actually killed in the cockpit, while dressing the wounded!) and 185 seamen, marines, artillerymen, troops, and artificers killed, and one general of division (Desforneaux), one general of battalion, one general of cavalry, one aide-de-camp, one major of battalion, her first-lieutenant, or capitaine de frégate (Jean-Jacques Magendie, in the head), five other lieutenants, two volunteers, two lieutenants of grenadiers, one lieutenant of foot, three petty officers, and 125 seamen, marines, artillerymen, troops and artificers wounded; making a total of 200 killed, and 143 wounded, the greater part of them mortally. A return to this effect, signed by Captain Magendie, was delivered to Captain Barlow; but the former stated in the return, that it probably fell short of the real loss sustained, especially in killed.

The force of the Phœbe, whose guns were in number 44, has already appeared.[1] That of the Africaine consisted, according to the return signed by Captain Magendie and subjoined to the official letter, of 26 long 18-pounders on the main deck and 18 long 8-pounders[2] on the quarter-deck and forecastle: total 44 guns also. If her eight 32-pounder carronades gave the Phœbe a slight preponderance in broadside weight of metal, the decided superiority in number of men, even of her regular crew, gave the Africaine a still greater advantage in that very essential point; an advantage which would have been in the proportion of nearly three to one, could the whole of the Africaine's crew and supernumeraries, in the event of boarding for instance, have been in a situation to act. But, as a combat to be decided by great guns only, an allowance is requisite, and a considerable

[1] See vol. ii., p. 104.
[2] Misprinted in the London Gazette " 18 de 9," instead of " 18 de 8."

one too, for that which a mere confrontation of figures can never explain, the lumbered state of the French ship's decks; an inconvenience which the troops themselves, by their valour, their mistaken valour, contributed to increase. Although their musketry could be of little or no avail in the dark, yet, upon the same erroneous principle that so augmented the loss among the soldiers on board one of the British ships at Copenhagen, they considered it as a point of honour to remain on deck and be mowed down by scores.

Circumstanced as he was, Commodore Saulnier acted as wisely in endeavouring to avoid a contest, as, when it actually began, did the officers, ship's company, soldiers, and all that were on board the Africaine, heroically, in defending their ship until she was reduced to a sinking state, and they to half their original number; all by the heavy, the searching, the irresistible broadsides of the Phœbe.

With ships so damaged in masts and rigging, and with so many prisoners on board, Captain Barlow had still a most anxious duty to perform. To increase the difficulties of his situation, the westerly breeze freshened. For four days the Phœbe and her prize persevered in working to windward; but on the fifth day, having made very slow progress and feeling for the sufferings of the wounded, Captain Barlow bore up for Minorca. On arriving off the south end of Majorca, the two frigates got becalmed; and it was not until a fortnight after the action, that the Phœbe and Africaine dropped their anchors in the harbour of Port-Mahon.

For his gallantry and good conduct in capturing the Africaine, Captain Barlow was most deservedly rewarded with the honour of knighthood; and the Phœbe's first-lieutenant, already named, was as justly promoted to the rank of commander. Her second and third lieutenants were Frederick Bedford and Edmund Heywood, and her lieutenant of marines, Thomas Weaver; of all whom, as well as of his officers and crew generally, Captain Barlow in his official letter speaks in the highest terms.

The Africaine, a fine new frigate of 1059 tons, was of course purchased for the use of the British navy; and, having the ports for the requisite number of guns on the main deck, became classed as a 38-gun frigate. Probably because there was an Africa already in the British service, the name of the Africaine was changed to Amelia; under which name the Phœbe's prize long continued to be an active cruiser.

On the 22nd of March, while the British 12-pounder 32-gun

frigates Andromache, Captain Israel Pellew, and Cleopatra, Captain Robert Lawrie, were cruising of Punta de Mulas, on the north-east coast of the island of Cuba, a convoy of 25 Spanish vessels, known to be richly laden, were seen at an anchor in the bay of Levita, protected by three armed galleys, or gun-vessels, armed with long 24 and 18 pounders. The two captains considering it practicable to capture or destroy this convoy by the aid of their boats, the latter under the command of Captain Lawrie himself, at about 9 h. 30 m. P.M., proceeded to execute the service.

Soon after midnight the boats arrived within gun-shot of the galleys, and were received, quite unexpectedly, with a heavy and destructive fire of grape, langridge, and musketry. In spite of this opposition, the British gallantly pushed on, and boarded several of the vessels; but from the heavy loss they sustained, could only bring off one of the galleys. That loss consisted of the first-lieutenant of the Andromache (Joseph Taylor), one master's mate (William M'Cuin), one midshipman (William Winchester, both of the Cleopatra), and six seamen killed, and 12 seamen wounded. Some of the boats had also been sunk by the enemy's shot. The loss among the Spaniards on board the captured gun-vessel was nine killed and several wounded.

On the 3rd of April, at daybreak, the British 18-pounder 36-gun frigate Trent, Captain Sir Edward Hamilton, while lying at an anchor among the rocks off the isles of Bréhat, discovered a ship, with French colours flying, under the protection of an armed cutter and lugger, making sail with the flood from the anchorage of Bréhat towards Plampoul. The boats of the frigate, under the orders of Lieutenant George Chamberlayne, assisted by Lieutenants Robert Scallon and John Bellamy, lieutenant of marines, Walter Tait, and Mr. Thomas Hoskins; the master, instantly proceeded to endeavour to secure the ship.

With the seeming intention of defending what proved to be a prize recently made, the French sent many boats from the shore; and these, assisted by the lugger, took the ship in tow. The intrepid advance of the Trent's boats, however, caused the shore-boats and lugger to cast off the ship, and prepare to defend themselves. A sharp conflict now ensued; at the end of which the French lugger and boats, although protected by five batteries, were subdued and chased upon the rocks. Shortly afterwards the ship was boarded by the first-lieutenant and the lieutenant of marines; which latter, however, lost his right leg on the occasion. This, with two seamen killed, appears to have

been the extent of the loss on the British side. The ship proved
to be an English merchant-vessel; but, as the French had all
quitted her and taken the crew with them, no particulars could
be obtained. Two men were found dead upon her decks, and
several are supposed to have been drowned in attempting to
escape from the British when they boarded.

On the 19th of April, at 8 h. 30 m. A.M., the British 38-gun
frigate Sibylle, Captain Charles Adam, observing signals flying
on St. Anne's island, one of the Seychelles, hoisted French
colours; and at 9 A.M., having rounded the island, discovered
in Mahé roads, close in shore, a frigate with her foremast out,
accompanied by several small craft. The Sibylle immediately
backed her main topsail, cleared for action, and got springs on
the anchors: she then filled, and set the foresail. At 10 A.M.
the French 36-gun frigate Chiffonne, Captain Pierre Guieysse,
fired a shot and hoisted her colours. At 10 h. 15 m. A.M.,
having passed through a winding and intricate channel formed
by various dangerous shoals, and discoverable only by the change
of colour in the water as seen by a man stationed at the mast-
head, the Sibylle anchored within about 200 yards of the French
frigate; not being able to get nearer, on account of a shoal that
lay on the Chiffonne's larboard or outermost bow.

At 10 h. 25 m. A.M., having dropped her best bower under foot,
so as to bring her best broadside to bear, and substituted English
for French colours, the Sibylle opened her fire, receiving in
return a fire from the Chiffonne, as well as from a battery
erected in a raking position on the neighbouring shore. The
cannonade continued with tolerable spirit until 10 h. 42 m. A.M.,
when the Chiffonne struck her flag, cut her cable, and drifted
upon a reef. While an officer and party went to take possession.
the Sibylle veered away her cable, so that her broadside might
bear upon the battery, which still continued its fire. No sooner,
however, did a lieutenant and a few of the Sibylle's men land
upon the beach, than the battery also struck its colours.

At the surrender of the frigate, a great number of her crew
took to the boats and escaped on shore; and the men at the
battery also escaped. The latter was found to consist of four of
the frigate's forecastle guns, mounted on a plank platform, defended by fascines, and provided with a furnace for heating shot.
The Sibylle's force in guns and men has already appeared.[1] Of
the latter, she had only two seamen killed, and one midshipman
slightly wounded. The Chiffonne appears to have been armed

---

[1] See vol. ii., p. 366.

the same as the generality of French 36-gun frigates, and had a complement of 296 men; of whom the Sibylle's fire killed 23, and wounded 30. About 100, including those stationed in the battery, escaped: the remainder were made prisoners.

Although the Chiffonne was certainly no match for the Sibylle, the dangerous circumstances under which she had been approached and attacked entitle the officers and crew of the British frigate to a considerable share of credit. The Chiffonne with 32 banished Frenchmen on board, had sailed from Nantes on the 14th of April, 1800, and had since, agreeably to her orders, landed them upon the Seychelles. The prize was a fine frigate of 945 tons, and was afterwards purchased for the use of the British navy ; in which, under her French name, she classed as a 12-pounder 36.

The British 14-gun brig-sloop Speedy, Captain Lord Cochrane, during one of her cruises in the Mediterranean, had so annoyed the Spaniards by cutting up their coasting trade, that the government despatched armed vessels in pursuit of her from several ports. Early in April one of the seekers of the British brig, the 32-gun xebec Gamo, by means of closed or hanging ports, decoyed the Speedy within hail, and then, drawing them up, discovered her heavy battery. Against a vessel that appeared to mount 36 guns, and to be numerously manned, the Speedy, whose 14 guns were only 4-pounders, resolved not to risk an engagement until she had tried the effect of a ruse. To escape was out of the question, as the xebec sailed two feet to the Speedy's one. The Speedy therefore passed for a Danish brig of war, and, in addition to the colours at her gaff-end, exhibited on the gangway a man dressed in a Danish officer's uniform ; who also, in the short interchange of hailing that ensued, conversed in Danish, or, which was the same thing, in what passed for Danish.

Not quite satisfied as to the national character of the Speedy, the Gamo sent her boat with an officer. The latter, before he well got alongside, was informed, kindly informed, that the brig had lately quitted one of the Barbary ports ; and he was at the same time reminded, of what he well knew, that a visit would undoubtedly subject the Spanish ship-of-war to a long quarantine. This was enough ; and, after a few mutual salutations and wavings of the hand, the two vessels parted company ; one glad at having escaped the plague, the other equally glad, one might suppose, at having escaped capture. The truth is, however, that the Speedy's officers and crew were all impatience to combat their superior foe ; and Lord Cochrane promised them, if ever he met her again, as he had no doubt he should, to give full scope to their wishes.

On the 6th of May, at daylight, being close off Barcelona, the Speedy descried a sail standing towards her. Chase was given ; but, owing to light winds, it was nearly 9 A.M. before the two vessels got within mutual gun-shot. The Speedy soon discovered that the armed xebec approaching her was her old friend the Gamo. Being then close under the latter's lee, the former tacked and commenced the action. The Speedy's fire was promptly returned by her opponent, who, in a little while, attempted to board ; but, the instant she heard the command given, the brig sheered off. The attempt was again made, and again frustrated. At length, after a 45 minutes' cannonade, in which the Speedy, with all her manœuvring, could not evade the heavy broadsides of the Gamo, and had sustained, in consequence, a loss of three seamen killed and five wounded, Lord Cochrane determined to board. With this intent the Speedy ran close alongside the Gamo ; and the crew of the British vessel, headed by their gallant commander, made a simultaneous rush from every part of her upon the decks of the Spaniard. For about 10 minutes the contest was desperate, especially in the waist ; but the impetuosity of the assault was irresistible : the Spanish colours were struck, and the Gamo became the prize of the Speedy.

The Speedy's gun-force has already been stated at 14 long 4-pounders. Her number of men and boys at the commencement of the action was 54. Of these the brig lost, in the boarding-attack, only one seaman killed, her first-lieutenant, Richard William Parker (severely, both by musketry and the sword), her boatswain and one seaman wounded ; making, with her loss by the cannonade, three killed and eight wounded. The Gamo mounted 22 long Spanish 12-pounders on the main deck, with eight long eights and two "heavy carronades," probably 24-pounders, on the quarter-deck and forecastle. Her crew amounted to 274 officers, seamen, boys, and supernumeraries, and 45 marines, total 319 ; of which number she had her commander, Don Francisco de Torris, the boatswain, and 13 men killed, and 41 men wounded.

The Gamo's was a force which was enough to alarm, and, in abler hands, might easily have subdued, such a vessel as the Speedy. A crew of 280 or 300 was the lowest number of men that a ship, of the evident force and size of the Gamo, could be

supposed to have on board; and yet Lord Cochrane, at the head
of about 40 men, and, deducting the boys, the helmsman (who
was Mr. James Guthrie, the surgeon), the eight killed and
wounded, and one or two others, leaped into the midst of them.
He and his 40 brave followers, among whom were Lieutenant
Parker, midshipman the Honourable Archibald Cochrane, and
the boatswain, found 319, or, allowing for some previous loss
and for six or eight boys, 300 armed men to struggle with. But
the British broadsword fell too heavily to be resisted ; and the
Spaniards were compelled to yield to the chivalric valour of their
opponents.[1] Accustomed as is the British navy to execute
deeds of daring, Lord Cochrane's achievement has hitherto found
in these pages but three compeers, the Surprise and Hermione,
the Dart and Désirée, and the Viper and Cerbère ; to which let
us now add, as the next in chronological order, the Speedy and
Gamo.

With so many prisoners in his charge, Lord Cochrane had
still an arduous duty to perform, but his judgment and presence
of mind overcame every difficulty; and, in the course of a few
days, the Speedy brig and her lofty prize were safe at anchor in
the harbour of Port-Mahon. For the gallantry he had so successfully displayed in capturing the Gamo, Lord Cochrane, as
soon as the account reached England, was promoted to post-rank ;
and the Speedy's only lieutenant, Richard William Parker, was
also, we believe, made a commander.

On the 9th of June, in the morning, the British 18-gun brig-
sloop, Kangaroo, Captain George Christopher Pulling, and 14-gun
brig-sloop Speedy, Captain Lord Cochrane, discovered a Spanish
convoy, lying at an anchor under the battery of Oropeso, a small
seaport of Old Castile. The armed vessels protecting it consisted of a xebec of 20 guns, and three gun-boats, and the battery
was a large square tower, which appeared to mount 12 guns.
The two commanders resolved, at once, to attack this force
with their brigs. Accordingly, at noon, the Kangaroo and
Speedy came to an anchor, within half-gun shot of the enemy,
and a brisk cannonade ensued ; but which, by 2 P.M., had con-

---

[1] During the action, and after Lord
Cochrane had boarded the Gamo, he practised another ruse. The crew of the
Speedy being nearly overpowered by the
great superiority in point of numbers of
her adversary, were once on the point of
giving way; Lord Cochrane, with the
greatest coolness, hailed the Speedy,
ordering fifty more men to be sent on
board, although, at the time, his vessel
did not contain more than three. The
expected reinforcement to their adver-
saries cooled the little courage remaining
in the Gamo's crew, and having already
experienced the bold daring of the first
fifty men, they were by no means
anxious to cope with fifty more, and
consequently surrendered.—ED.

siderably decreased on the port of the vessels and battery. Encouraged, however, by a felucca of 12 guns and two gun-boats that came to their assistance, the Spaniards recommenced firing, and by 3 h. 30 m. P.M., had their 20-gun xebec and two of their gun-boats sunk by the fire of the two brigs: in a little while another of the gun-boats shared the same fate. The tower and the remaining three gun-boats continued to annoy the brigs with their shot, until about 6 h. 30 m., when the fire of the tower slackened. The Kangaroo soon afterwards cutting her cable to get to a nearer position, the gun-boats fled; and, by 7 P.M., the tower was completely silenced.

The Kangaroo and Speedy continued until midnight to be annoyed by a heavy fire of musketry from the shore; but, in the mean time, the boats of the two brigs, under the orders of Lieutenant Thomas Foulerton, first of the Kangaroo, assisted by Lieutenant Benjamin Warburton, of the Speedy, and by midshipmen the Hon. Archibald Cochrane, William Dean, and Thomas Taylor, had succeeded in bringing out three brigs laden with wine, rice, and bread. On the return of the boats from this service, Lord Cochrane himself, with his wonted zeal, took them under his command, and went in-shore again, in the hope of bringing away more, but found all the remainder either sunk or driven on the beach. It was fortunate for the tower, that the ammunition of the two brigs was by this time expended, or the two enterprising captains would have razed it to its foundation; as indeed, only the day previous, they had the adjacent tower of Almanara, mounting two brass 4-pounders.

The loss of the British, in the attack upon this Spanish convoy, consisted of one midshipman (Thomas Taylor), killed by a musket-shot in one of the boats, and two lieutenants (Thomas Foulerton and Thomas Brown Thompson), seven seamen, and one marine wounded; all belonging to the Kangaroo, although, as Captain Pulling handsomely acknowledges, the Speedy, from situation and distance, was equally exposed to the enemy's fire. At the demolition of the tower of Almanara, however, the Speedy did not wholly escape, Lord Cochrane himself having received a bruise, and been a little singed; as were also two of his men.

The British 28-gun frigate Mercury, Captain Thomas Rogers, having on the 25th of May, while cruising in the Adriatic, captured a small vessel just out of Ancona, received intelligence that the late British bomb-vessel Bulldog, which about three months before, under the command of Captain Barrington

Dacres, had entered the port unapprised of its being in possession of the French, was lying in the mole, laden with supplies
for the French army in Egypt, and ready for sea. Captain
Rogers immediately made sail for Ancona, with the determination of attempting to cut out the Bulldog; and soon after dark
the same evening, the Mercury anchored off the mole. At
10 h. 30 m. P.M. the boats of the latter, under the orders of
Lieutenant William Mather, quitted the frigate : and, at about
midnight, surprised and carried the Bulldog, without even
having been hailed by the sentinels on the mole, to which,
while the ship was riding with three cables ahead, her stern
had been secured by the two ends of a bower cable. The seamen presently cut all the cables, and the boats began to tow
away their prize; but the alarm had now spread, and the
British became exposed to a heavy fire of cannon and musketry
from the mole.

As there was a favourable light breeze, and the sails were set,
the Bulldog, in rather less than an hour, got without the reach
of the batteries. Unfortunately, however, the wind died away
to a perfect calm, and the current carried the prize along the
coast close to the shore; from which a crowd of boats, some of
them gun-boats, came out to attack her. Having the hatch-
ways to guard, to prevent the French crew from rising, and
being without a sufficient force to resist the gun-boats, which
were fast approaching, and had already several times raked the
ship, Lieutenant Mather reluctantly abandoned his prize; but
not until he had made three ineffectual attempts to set her on
fire.

The loss of the British on this occasion amounted to one
seaman and one marine killed, and four seamen wounded. That
of the French on board the Bulldog is stated to have been 20
in killed, wounded, and drowned. As soon as she descried the
prize standing out of the mole, the Mercury weighed and steered
towards her; but the calm so retarded the progress of the
frigate, that the Bulldog was towed back to her former station
at the mole long before the Mercury could get near her. The
Bulldog afterwards succeeded in putting to sea, but was taken
on her passage to Egypt by the 24-gun ship Champion, Captain
Lord William Stuart.

On the 23rd of June, in the morning, the British 18-gun brig-
sloop Corso, Captain William Ricketts, chased among the rocks
in the small islands of Tremiti, lying in the gulf of Venice, and
inhabited by a few renegadoes only, a pirate tartan, the Tigre,

of eight 6 and 12 pounders, and a crew of 60 French and Italians. Upon the appearance of the Mercury soon afterwards, the pirate landed the greater part of her crew; who, with a 4-pounder and musketry, posted themselves upon a hill to defend their vessel, which lay aground close to them with hawsers fast to the shore.

Being resolved to make an effort to stop the further career of this band of robbers, Captain Rogers despatched upon that service the boats of the frigate and brig, under the orders of Lieutenant William Mather, assisted by Lieutenant Wilson of the marines. Notwithstanding that they were exposed to a smart fire of cannon and musketry, both from the vessel and the hill, the boats gallantly rowed in; and while Lieutenant Mather with the seamen boarded the Tigre, Lieutenant Wilson with the marines landed to drive away the banditti from the hill: the Mercury and Corso at the same time overawed the pirates by occasionally firing such of their guns as would bear. The marines succeeded in their object without the loss of a man, and took several prisoners; and the seamen, with equal good fortune, hove the tartan off the rocks and brought her out, together with a quantity of plunder, consisting of bales of cotton and other goods, which the Tigre had taken from vessels of different nations.

In the summer of this year, the three British frigates, Doris, Captain Charles Brisbane, Beaulieu, Captain Stephen Pointz, and Uranie, Captain George Henry Gage, by the orders of Admiral Cornwallis, who since the 21st of the preceding February had succeedeed Earl St. Vincent (appointed first lord of the admiralty) as commander-in-chief of the Channel fleet, were stationed off the point of St. Mathieu, to watch the motions of the French and Spanish fleets in Brest harbour. In the month of July, while the above frigate-squadron was lying at anchor about three miles to the south-south-east of St. Mathieu's lighthouse, and in full view of the combined fleet, the French 20-gun ship-corvette Chevrette was discovered also at an anchor, under some batteries in Camaret bay; a position in which the French considered their vessel almost as secure as if she was in the road of Brest. It will, nevertheless, not be thought surprising that the British resolved to attempt cutting her out. Accordingly, on the night of the 20th, the boats of the Beaulieu and Doris (the Uranie not then present) manned entirely by volunteers, and placed under the orders of Lieutenant Woodley Losack, of the Ville-de-Paris, purposely sent by the admiral to take the

command, proceeded on the enterprise; but the boats not pulling
alike, and the leading ones being too zealous to slacken their
efforts, the detachment separated. In consequence of this accident some of the boats returned; while the remainder, having
reached the entrance of Camaret bay, where they expected to
be joined by their companions, lay upon their oars until daybreak on the 21st. The service being one that required darkness for its success, the boats now pulled back to their ships;
but the mischief was done; they had been discovered from the
Chevrette and the shore, and so much of the plan as contemplated a surprise was defeated.

As a proof of this, on the same morning, the Chevrette got
under way, and, after running about a mile and a half further
up the bay, moored herself close under some heavy batteries,
one in particular upon a point of land off her larboard and inner
bow. The corvette then took on board a body of soldiers, sufficient to augment her number of men to 339, had the arms and
ammunition brought upon deck, and loaded her guns almost up
to their muzzles with grape-shot. The batteries, also, prepared
themselves; temporary redoubts were thrown up upon the adjacent points, and a gun-vessel, armed with two long 36-pounders,
was moored as a guard-boat at the entrance of the bay. Having
thus profited by the discovery of the morning, the Chevrette
displayed in defiance a large French ensign above an English
one. This was plainly seen by the three frigates, and served
but to inspire their crews with increased ardour to engage, and
with redoubled determination to reverse the position of the
flags.

At about 9 h. 30 m. P.M. the boats of the three frigates,
joined by the barge and pinnance of the Robust 74, numbering
15 in the whole, and containing between them about 280 officers
and men, still under the command of Lieutenant Losack, proceeded a second time to attempt the daring service of cutting
out the Chevrette. Shortly afterwards Lieutenant Losack, with
his own and five other boats, proceeded in chase of a boat from
the shore, supposed to be a look-out boat belonging to the Chevrette, and therefore proper to be secured. The remainder of the
boats, as they had been ordered, lay upon their oars or pulled
gently, awaiting their commanding officer's return. Lieutenant
Losack not returning so soon as expected, the next officer in
command, Lieutenant Keith Maxwell, of the Beaulieu, considering that the boats had at least six miles to pull, and that the
night was already far advanced, resolved, notwithstanding that

the force was reduced to more than a third, or to less than 180 men, to proceed without him. He did so; and gave orders that, while one party was engaged in disarming the enemy's crew on deck, the smartest topmen of the Beaulieu should fight their way aloft, and cut loose the sails with their sabres; and that others, who were named, should cut the cable: and he appointed one of the ablest seamen in the boats, Henry Wallis, quartermaster of the Beaulieu, to take charge of the corvette's helm. Many other suitable arrangements were made; and the nine boats, in high glee, hastened to the attack.

At about 1 A.M. on the 22nd the boats came in sight of the Chevrette; who, after hailing, opened a heavy fire of musketry and grape upon the assailants. This was presently seconded by a fire of musketry from the shore. In the face of all this, however, the British pulled undauntedly towards the ship. The Beaulieu's boats under the command of Lieutenant Maxwell, assisted by Lieutenant James Pasley, and Lieutenant of marines James Sinclair, boarded the vessel on the starboard bow and quarter; the Uranie's, under Lieutenant Martin Neville, one of the Robust's, under midshipman Robert Warren, and one of the Doris's, under Lieutenant Walter Burke, on the larboard bow. The attempt to board was most obstinately resisted by the Frenchmen, armed with fire-arms, sabres, tomahawks, and pikes; and who, in their turn, boarded the boats. Notwithstanding this formidable opposition, and that, in their attempts to overcome it, the British had lost all their fire-arms, the latter, with their swords only, effected the boarding. Those who had been ordered to go aloft, fought their way to their respective stations; and, although some were killed, and others desperately wounded, the remainder gained the corvette's yards. Here the seamen found the footropes strapped up; but surmounting every obstacle, the intrepid fellows quickly performed the service upon which they had been ordered. Thus in less than three minutes after the ship had been boarded, and in the midst of a conflict against numbers more than trebly superior, down came the Chevrette's three topsails and courses. The cable, in the mean time, having been cut outside, and a light breeze having sprung up from the land, the ship began drifting out of the bay.

No sooner did the Frenchmen see the sails fall, and their ship under way, than some of them leaped overboard; while others dropped their arms, and sprang down the hatchways. The British thereupon got possession of the quarter-deck and forecastle; which, although but five minutes had elapsed since the assault had commenced, were nearly covered with dead bodies. Those of the corvette's crew, that had fled below, still maintained a smart fire of musketry from the main deck and up the hatchways, but were at length overpowered and compelled to submit. In her way out, during a short interval of calm, the Chevrette became exposed to a heavy fire of round and grape from the batteries: but a light breeze from the north-east soon drove the ship out of gun-shot. It was at about this time that the six boats under Lieutenant Losack joined company; and Lieutenant Maxwell, of course, was superseded in the command.

The British had one lieutenant of marines (James Sinclair), one midshipman (Robert Warren), seven seamen, and two marines killed, two lieutenants (Martin Neville and Walter Burke, the latter mortally), one master's mate (William Phillips), three midshipmen (Edward Crofton, Edward Byrn, and Robert Finnis), 42 seamen, and nine marines wounded, and one marine drowned in the Beaulieu's barge, which was sunk by the enemy's shot; total, 11 killed, 57 wounded, and one drowned or missing. The loss sustained by the Chevrette was far heavier. The corvette had her captain, two lieutenants, three midshipmen, one lieutenant of troops, and 85 seamen and troops killed, one lieutenant, four midshipmen, and 57 seamen and troops wounded; total, 92 killed and 62 wounded.

It is such daring feats as these that ennoble the character of the British navy; and long will be remembered, long held up as an example for imitation, the cutting out of the Chevrette. A few of the many instances which this enterprise afforded, of individual heroism, have already been recorded in the pages of a naval periodical work. We have selected the following:

Lieutenant Sinclair, of the marines, was killed in the act of defending Mr. Crofton, midshipman of the Doris, who in his efforts to get on board the corvette was wounded in two places. Mr. John Brown, boatswain of the Beaulieu, after forcing his way into the Chevrette's quarter-gallery, found the door planked up, and so securely barricadoed, that all his efforts to force it were ineffectual. Through the crevices in the planks he discovered a number of men sitting on the cabin deck, armed with pikes and pistols; and with the fire of the latter was frequently annoyed while attempting to burst in. He next tried the quarter, and after an obstinate resistance gained the taffrail. The officer who commanded the party was at this time fighting his way up a little farther forward. For an instant, while looking round to see where he should make his push, Brown stood exposed a mark to the enemy's fire; when, waving his cutlass, he cried, "Make a lane there:" he gallantly dashed among them, and fought his way forward till he reached his proper station, the forecastle; which the men, animated by his example, soon cleared of the enemy. Here Mr. Brown remained during the rest of the contest, not only repulsing the French in their frequent attempts to retake his post, but attending to the orders from the quarter-deck, and assisting in casting the ship and making sail, with as much coolness as if he had been on board the Beaulieu.

Henry Wallis, who, as already stated, had been appointed to take charge of the corvette's helm, fought his way to the wheel; and, although severely wounded in the contest and bleeding, this brave seaman steadily remained at his post, steering the Chevrette until beyond the reach of the batteries. Wallis had been seven years in the Beaulieu, and was ever among the foremost in a service of danger. "If a man had fallen overboard he was always fortunately in the way, and either in the boat or the water: during the time he belonged to the ship nearly a dozen men were indebted to him for their lives, which he had saved by plunging overboard, sometimes even in a gale of wind, at the utmost hazard of his own."[1]

The Chevrette, when attacked, was bound with a cargo of stores to Sénégal, and thence to the island of Guadeloupe: she was a similar ship to the Bonne-Citoyenne; but owing, we believe, to the probable successful termination of the pending negotiation between the two countries, more than to anything else, the Chevrette was not purchased for the use of the British navy. Lieutenant Losack, on account of some misunderstanding respecting the actual commanding officer at the cutting out of the corvette, was promoted to the rank of commander. On the 9th of August, however, upon some facts coming to his knowledge, Admiral Cornwallis ordered a court of inquiry to be held on board the Mars. The result was, that Lieutenant Keith Maxwell received from the admiralty immediate promotion to a commander's rank, and from the public at large that share of credit which, had it not been for the official investigation of his claims, he might never have obtained.

On the 27th of July, at 1 A.M., in latitude 43° 34' north, and longitude 11° 42' west, the British 18-pounder 36-gun frigate

[1] Naval Chronicle, vol. vii., pp. 216, 217.

Immortalité, Captain Henry Hotham, fell in with an enemy's cruiser of a very extraordinary appearance, a ship with four masts, which the former immediately chased, and at 7 h. 30 m. A.M., the 38-gun frigate, Arethusa, Captain Thomas Wolley, in sight, captured. The prize proved to be the Invention, French privateer, nine days from Bordeaux, on her first cruise, having only been launched since the beginning of the month.

The Invention had been designed by her commander, M. Thibaut, and was peculiar in more respects than her masts, her length being 147 feet, with only 27 feet in breadth of beam. Her force consisted of 24 long 6-pounders on a single deck, and two 12-pounder carronades, either on her poop or topgallant forecastle, with a crew of 210 men and boys. Her four masts were nearly at equal distances apart, the first and third of the same height, the second stouter and higher, and the fourth much smaller. She had four topgallant yards rigged aloft, and was accounted a good sea-boat and sailer.

On the 10th of August, while the British 12-pounder 32-gun frigate Unicorn, Captain Charles Wemyss, and 16-gun brig-sloop Atalante, Captain Anselm John Griffiths, were cruising in Quiberon bay, the six-oared cutter of the latter, with eight men commanded by Mr. Francis Smith, midshipman, in the face of a brisk discharge of grape and canister from the French national lugger Eveillé, mounting two long 4-pounders, and four large swivels, and of a cross-fire from two small batteries on the shore, pulled up towards, boarded, and carried the vessel, the French crew deserting her at the moment and escaping to the shore, which was only a musket-shot distant. To add to the value of this very gallant little exploit, it was achieved without a single casualty.

On the night of the 20th of August Captain Thomas Byam Martin, cruising off Corunna with the frigates Fisgard, Diamond, and Boadicea, sent Lieutenant Philip Pipon, with the boats of the squadron, to attack the Spanish vessels in the port. The boats immediately pulled for and entered the harbour; and Lieutenant Pipon and his party succeeded in boarding and carrying the Neptuno, a new ship pierced for 20 guns, belonging to his catholic majesty, a gun-boat mounting one long Spanish 24-pounder, and a merchant ship; all moored within the strong batteries that protect the port, and lying so near to them that the sentinels on the ramparts challenged the boats' crews, and opened upon them a heavy fire. Notwithstanding this opposition, the British officers and men, with their accustomed coolness and perseverance, proceeded to execute the remainder of their task, and brought all three vessels safe out of the harbour without sustaining the slightest loss. For his gallantry and address on this occasion, Lieutenant Pipon, early in the following year, was promoted to the rank of commander.

On the 2nd of September, at 11 h. 30 m. A.M., the ritish 18-gun ship-sloop Victor (sixteen 32-pounder carronades and two sixes), Captain George Ralph Collier, being off the Seychelle islands, discovered and chased a strange man-of-war brig. At 5 h. 30 m. P.M., proving the better sailer going off the wind, the Victor was enabled to bring to close action the French brig-corvette Flêche, of 18 long 8-pounders, commanded by Lieutenant Jean Baptiste Bonnavie. The latter's 8-pounders being no match for the former's 32-pounder carronades, the Flêche, after receiving and returning two broadsides, hauled her wind and endeavoured to escape. Having had her driver topping-lift, maintopmast-stay, and her principal braces on the starboard side shot away, the Victor was unable to wear quick enough to check the progress of her opponent; who, by the time the two vessels tacked, at 7 P.M., was half a mile to windward: and, even when the Victor had repaired her rigging, the Flêche convinced her that, in sailing by the wind, the advantage was the reverse of what it had been when going before it.

In the little interchange of firing which had ensued, the Victor had a master's mate and one seaman slightly wounded; with, besides damaged rigging and sails, one shot through the foremast, and a few in the hull. The Victor continued to pursue the Flêche, and during the night was frequently within gunshot; but the latter would not allow the British vessel a second time to close. The chase continued all day of the 4th. At sunset the Flêche was four or five miles to windward of the Victor, and, by daylight on the 5th, was no longer to be seen.

Judging, from the course which the brig was steering when first seen, that her destination was the Seychelle islands, Captain Collier pushed for them; and, at 3 h. 30 m. P.M., the Victor descried her late opponent standing in for the anchorage of Mahé. The Victor proceeded under easy sail till 7 P.M., which was just as it grew dark, and then anchored in 11 fathoms. The ship not having a pilot, and no one on board being acquainted with the channel, the master, Mr. James Crawford, though ill of a fever, volunteered to sound it. Accordingly, in the course of the night, a boat, in which Mr. James Middleton, the master's mate who had been wounded, also embarked as a volunteer, proceeding on the service; and, not-withstanding they were repreatedly fired at by a boat from the French brig, these officers would not desist until they had completely performed the duty upon which they had been detached.

Daylight on the 6th showed the Flêche lying at the mouth of the basin or inner harbour, with springs on her cables, and a red flag at her fore topgallantmast-head, the signal of defiance, as afterwards understood. It was not merely the strength of their position, or the difficulty of approaching it, that had actuated the French officers to hoist this foolish signal: the Flêche now mounted the whole of her guns; which had not, it appears, been the case in the skirmish of the 2nd. Soon after daylight the Victor weighed and made sail towards the channel; the narrowness and intricacy of which, added to the unfavour-able state of the wind, compelled her to use warps and her stay-sails only.

So fine an opportunity was taken due advantage of by the Flêche, and the Victor became exposed to a raking fire, until, shoaling her water, the latter, at about 9 P.M., came to with the best bower. The British sloop soon recommenced warping, and continued it until 11 h. 45 m. P.M.; when, letting go the small bower with two springs, the Victor brought her broadside to bear, and instantly commenced firing. Between the two vessels an incessant cannonade was maintained until 2 h. 20 m. A.M. on the 7th, when the Flêche was discovered to be sinking. In a few minutes afterwards the latter cut her cable, cast round, and grounded at the bow on a coral reef. An officer and party were sent from the Victor to board her; and immediately the French crew commenced setting fire to their vessel. Another party from the sloop quickly followed the first; and the British then took possession and struck the colours of the French brig. Scarcely, however, had they succeeded in extinguishing the flames, than the Flêche fell on her larboard bilge into deeper water, and sank.

Out of her 120 men and boys, the Victor, in this second, and, for the present, decisive affair, had not a man hurt. This was rather extraordinary, as several shot had struck her hull, some between wind and water, and her rigging and boats had also been a good deal cut. The loss on the part of the Flêche, out of an alleged complement of 145 (including four lieutenants, besides her commanding officer), from the number of dead and wounded reported to have been found on her forecastle, was supposed to be very severe; but Captain Bonnavie acknowledged to having had only four men killed: the wounded he did not enumerate.

Like the Chiffonne, the Flêche had brought from Nantes, about four months back, and since deposited on one of the Seychelle islands, 35 banished Frenchmen. Some of her men had been left sick at the Isle of Bourbon; but, to compensate for their loss, 20 of the late Chiffonne's crew had assisted in serving the guns. Had the action been carried on wholly at close quarters, the heavy metal of the Victor would certainly have rendered her too powerful to be an equal match for the Flêche; but, in that respect, the French brig had managed to give herself the advantage by keeping her adversary at long-shot. Great credit was therefore due to the officers and crew of the Victor, for their gallantry, skill, and perseverance; but the Flêche was not eventually lost, the French having afterwards weighed, and, we believe, refitted her.

On the 31st of July, in the evening, the British 18-gun brig-sloop Sylph, Captain Charles Dashwood, cruising off Santander, or San-Andero, on the north coast of Spain, with a light air from the southward, chased an armed schooner standing to the north-east; but, before there was a possibility of arriving up with her, a large frigate, then judged to be Spanish, but afterwards believed to be French, was descried under the land advancing towards the brig, and to which frigate the schooner fled for refuge.

Finding it impracticable to gain the wind of the strange frigate, whose hull, at sunset, was clearly discernible, the Sylph shortened sail, hove to, and prepared for battle. At 11 P.M. the frigate arrived within half gun-shot; when, having in the usual manner ascertained the ship's hostile character, the brig opened her fire. Soon afterwards the frigate approached within hail, and a spirited cannonade was kept up for one hour and 20 minutes; when, having had her sails and almost all her running rigging cut to pieces, and one carronade dismounted, and having received several shot between wind and water, the Sylph edged away to repair her damages. Perceiving, however, that the frigate either was unable or unwilling to make sail in pursuit, the Sylph, as soon as she was out of gun-shot, hove to.

On the 1st of August, at daybreak, the Sylph discovered her late opponent, with her foreyard upon deck, about seven miles off in the north-west, which was now to windward, the wind having shifted to that quarter in a squall during the night.

Seeing the frigate in this apparently disabled state, the Sylph made sail in chase; but, on account of a severe wound in her mainmast and a rising sea, the brig was obliged, instead of tacking, to wear, which retarded her progress. While the Sylph was thus slowly advancing, the frigate swayed up her foreyard, wore, and made all sail for the land, but still without hoisting any colours. As the brig's mainmast was every moment expected to go over the side, as she was then making a foot and a half of water per hour from shot-hole leaks, and as the stranger was evidently a frigate of 14 guns of a side on her main deck, Captain Dashwood felt it to be his duty to wear and stand to the northward; having already sustained a loss, by the preceding night's action, of one seaman killed, and one midshipman (Lionel Carey) and eight seamen wounded, three of them dangerously.

Before we submit any remarks upon the alleged name and force of the Sylph's antagonist in this to her very creditable action, we will relate another contest in which, about a month afterwards, the brig was engaged almost in the same spot.

The damages the Sylph had received rendering her return to port indispensable, Captain Dashwood was directed by Admiral Cornwallis, under whose orders he was cruising, to proceed to Plymouth. Having here undergone a complete refit, the Sylph sailed to rejoin the commander-in-chief off Ushant, and by the latter was ordered to resume her station off the north coast of Spain. On the 28th of September, in the afternoon, Cape Pinas bearing south distant 42 leagues, the Sylph chased a ship in the north-west; and, although before sunset the discovery was made that the stranger was a French frigate of the same apparent force as the one which the brig had formerly engaged upon this coast, Captain Dashwood gallantly resolved to do his utmost to bring her to action.

Being desirous, as before, to gain the wind of an antagonist so decidedly superior, the Sylph made all sail for that purpose; and the French frigate seemed equally determined to frustrate the attempt. At 7 h. 30 m. P.M., however, after various manœuvres, during which the two vessels crossed each other three times, and exchanged, at a very short distance, as many heavy broadsides, the Sylph obtained a station within pistol-shot upon the frigate's weather bow. A severe conflict now ensued, and continued without intermission for two hours and five minutes, when the frigate wore and made sail on the opposite tack; leaving the Sylph with her standing and running rigging cut to pieces, and maintopmast badly wounded, but, on account of the skilful

manner in which the brig was manœuvred, and the unskilful
manner in which the frigate's guns (admitting them to have
been such as supposed) were fought, with so trifling a loss as
one person slightly wounded, Mr. Lionel Carey, who had been
wounded in the former action.

The following is the concluding passage of Captain Dashwood's letter to Admiral Cornwallis on the subject of this
second action : " Having received certain information since my
return to this station, that the ship, which the Sylph was engaged with some time since, was the French frigate l'Artémise,
of 44 guns and 350 men ; so I can with equal truth pronounce
this to be the same, from the many corresponding observations
which I made. She had then 20 men killed and 40 wounded,
and was obliged to return to St. Andero to refit ; and from the
disordered state which she was in when making off, I have the
strongest reason to suppose she has now met with a similar fate,
particularly as a number of lights and men were seen hanging
over her bows, from which I infer she must have received considerable damage ; and I think there is every probability of some
of his majesty's frigates falling in with her, as I unluckily parted
with the Immortalité a few hours before." Some additional
information is contained in the following note to a passage of
this letter : " The French journals of that period also stated, that
the captain was tried by a court-martial, and condemned to be
shot, for his conduct on that occasion ; which sentence Buonaparte approved, and ordered to be carried into execution."[1]

We wish it were in our power to adduce some stronger evidence than that contained in the two extracts above given, as to
the identity of the ship twice so gallantly engaged by the Sylph.
The old Artémise, it will be recollected, was blown up at the
battle of the Nile :[2] consequently this must have been a new
ship of that name ; and, as the French had very wisely discontinued building any more 12-pounder frigates, the Artémise of
1801 must have been a 40-gun frigate carrying 18-pounders, and
mounting in the whole at least 44 guns. Had the improbability
that such a ship would retreat from an 18-gun brig, or, in an
action of more than two hours' continuance, do no more execution than cut away a few ropes, send a shot through a topmast,
and slightly wound one man, struck the compiler from the
" French journals " as forcibly as it has us, he would have
quoted the passage entire, and have given a name and a date to
the journal which contained so important an admission in favour

1 Marshall, vol. ii., p. 456.   2 See vol. ii., p. 193.

of the Sylph's commander and crew.   Even the name of the
French captain " condemned to be shot " is not given : and not
only have we been unable to discover in the Moniteur, or in any
other French paper, a single paragraph calculated to throw light
upon the subject, but, out of the many lists of French frigates
occasionally before us, we have no recollection of the name of
the Artémise until it occurs in an English account of her destruction in September, 1808.

On returning to Plymouth after his first action, Captain
Dashwood wrote an official account of it to Admiral Cornwallis,
and appears to have made an immediate application to the first
lord of the admiralty for a post-commission ; to which application the following, as we think, very sensible reply was transmitted by Earl St. Vincent: " I have read your official letter
with all the attention such a recital merits ; but until the board
receive official information of the force, and the nation to which
the vessel belongs, which the Sylph was engaged with, an adequate judgment cannot be formed of the merits of the action."[1]
The circumstances, stated in the official account of the second
rencontre, very properly removed all doubt as to the ship engaged having been very superior in force to the Sylph ; and on
the 2nd of the following November Captain Dashwood, " for his
meritorious conduct in the above actions," was promoted to post-
rank.   The first-lieutenant of the Sylph, upon both these highly
creditable occasions, was Samuel Burgess ; but who, although
highly commended by Captain Dashwood in each of his letters,
remained a lieutenant for 15 years longer.

On the 13th of September, in the afternoon, the British 18-gun
ship-sloop, Lark, Acting-commander Lieutenant James Johnstone, being close off the island of Cuba, fell in with and chased
the Spanish privateer-schooner Esperanza, of one long 8 and two
4 pounders, and 45 men ; which for shelter, ran within the
Portillo reefs.   Lieutenant Johnstone immediately despatched
the Lark's yawl and cutter, with 16 men in each, under the
orders of Lieutenant James Pasley, assisted by Mr. M'Cloud,
midshipman, to attempt to cut her out. At about 10 h. 30 m. P.M.
the two boats found the privateer at anchor, waiting the attack ;
and, on their near approach, received a fire from her that severely
wounded several of the men.   In spite of this, however, the
British boarded, and, after a short but severe contest, carried
the schooner.   In this well-conducted and gallant boat-attack,
the British sustained a loss of one seaman killed, Mr. M'Cloud,

[1] Marshall, vol. ii., p. 454.

and 12 seamen wounded; within two of half the party. The loss on board the Esperanza was represented to have been 21 killed and six wounded; including, among the former, the captain, Josef Callie, and all his officers. Considering the unquestionable gallantry of this enterprise, we regret to see the name of James Pasley in the list of lieutenants of the present day.

On the 21st of July, soon after daylight, the island of Cabrera bearing north-east distant six or seven leagues, the British hired brig Pasley, mounting fourteen 12-pounder carronades and two long sixes, with a crew of 54 men and boys, commanded by Lieutenant William Wooldridge, fell in with a Spanish man-of-war xebec, of 22 guns; which at 7 A.M. hailed the Pasley and desired her to send her boat on board. The reply to this was a broadside within pistol-shot distance; and the Pasley continued to engage her superior opponent until 8 h. 15 m.; when the xebec ceased her fire, and taking advantage of the calm which had followed the heavy firing, pulled away with her sweeps. The Pasley used her sweeps, but the xebec having more sweeps and more men out-pulled the British brig, and before night reached the island of Ivica. In this very creditable affair to the Pasley, the latter had one seaman killed and two wounded.

In a few months afterwards an opportunity occurred in which Lieutenant Wooldridge was more successful. On the 28th of October, Cape de Gata bearing west-north-west distant 20 leagues, the Pasley fell in with and was chased by the Spanish privateer polacre-ship Virgen-del-Rosario, of 10 guns (pierced for 20), eight of them long 12, and two long 24 pounders, with a crew of 94 men. Being to windward, the Rosario soon neared the Pasley, and an animated engagement commenced. After the action had continued about an hour, the Pasley, having had her gaff and most of the stays and main rigging shot away, found her opponent's guns, upon the whole, much too heavy. As the readiest mode to reduce this inequality, the Pasley ran athwart the hawse of the Rosario, and lashed the latter's bowsprit to her own capstan. The British crew in an instant were on the Spanish ship's decks; and, after a sanguinary hand-to-hand struggle of about 15 minutes' duration, carried the Rosario.

The Pasley's loss amounted to her gunner, Mr. James Pooke, and two seamen killed, her commander (shot through the left shoulder), master (Ambrose Lions, mortally), first mate (George Davie), and five seamen wounded. The loss on board the privateer was very severe: it consisted of her first and second captains, second lieutenant, two prize-masters, the gunner, and 15 seamen killed, and 13 officers and seamen wounded. Considering the great disparity of force between the two vessels, this must be pronounced a very gallant affair on the part of the Pasley; and the judgment, promptitude, and valour displayed by Lieutenant Wooldridge on the occasion, gained him not only the just applause of his superiors, but that to which he had an equal claim, the rank of commander.

Colonial Expeditions.—West Indies.

The rupture between England and Denmark and Sweden was soon followed by the seizure of the colonies of the latter by the former. On the 20th of March the Swedish island of St. Bartholomew surrendered by capitulation to a British naval and military force, under Rear-admiral John Thomas Duckworth and Lieutenant-general Trigge. On the 24th the Swedish island of St. Martin; on the 29th the Danish islands of St. Thomas, St. John, and their dependencies; and on the 31st the Danish island of Santa Cruz, all accepted the same terms as St. Bartholomew. On the 16th of April the French garrison evacuated the Dutch island of St. Eustatia; which, with the island of Saba, was taken possession of by the 20-gun ship Arab, Captain John Perkins, and a small detachment of troops under Colonel Blunt, of the third regiment of Buffs.

Coast of Africa.

As soon as the British government became apprised of that article in the treaty of Badajos, by which Portugal agreed to exclude British shipping from her ports, a force was sent to occupy the island of Madeira. On the 23rd of July a squadron anchored in the bay of Funchal, and a detachment of troops under Colonel Clinton landed and took possession, without re sistance, of the two forts which commanded the anchorage.

These prompt measures, on the part of England, induced the prince regent to use his most strenuous endeavours to prevent the first consul of France, who would not acknowledge himself a party to the treaty with Spain, from overrunning Portugal with the powerful army which, under General Leclerc, Buonaparte's brother-in-law, was already upon the frontiers. Before, however, matters became ripe enough for action, England and France had commenced the negotiations which ended in the treaty of Amiens; and, on the 29th of September, a treaty of peace was signed at Madrid between France and Portugal; by the fourth article of which the latter ceded to France all that part of Portuguese Guiana (nearly equal in extent to the whole of French Guiana), which extends to the Carapanatuba, a river that flows into the Amazon at some distance above Fort Macussa.

East Indies.

On the 21st of June the Dutch island of Ternate, after an obstinate resistance of 52 days, surrendered by capitulation to the military and naval forces of the honourable East India Company, under the respective commands of Colonel Burr and Captain Hayes.

Upon the same principle, we believe, that induced them to occupy the island of Madeira, the British government placed garrisons in all the colonies or factories of Portugal, in the East Indies, except Macao.

Peace between England and France.

On the 1st of October was signed in London, by Lord Hawkesbury, the secretary of state for foreign affairs on the part of Great Britain, and by citizen Louis-Guillaume Otto, commissary for the exchange of French prisoners in England, on the part of France, preliminary articles of peace between the two nations. On the 10th, the ratifications were duly exchanged; and, on the 12th, his Britannic Majesty issued a proclamation, ordering a cessation of arms by sea and land. According to the preliminary articles, five months from the date of the exchange of ratifications was the longest period during which hostilities could legally exist in the most distant part of the globe.

In consequence of the proclamation, the British blockading squadrons retired from the opposite coast; at which time, however, the French ports were all alive. In them ships were getting ready, and troops embarking, for an expedition to St. Domingo, where the blacks were in open rebellion against the whites. The Dutch and Spanish ports began also to exhibit an unusual activity. England, therefore, with a becoming forecast, delayed awhile disarming her ships.

As any treaty of peace to which England is a party is necessarily made up, in a great degree, of colonial cessions, this appears the proper head of the work under which to offer the few remarks we have to make on the subject. And, although the definitive treaty between all the belligerents was not finally concluded until the 25th of March, 1802, at Amiens, we shall at once state what change it effected, more particularly in the colonial propriety of the different powers.

Let us first briefly advert to the stipulations which affected the European territory of the several belligerents. France got back the small islands of Saint-Marcouf. Portugal was to remain as before the war, except as to the province which, by the treaty of Badajos, she had ceded to Spain.[1] The republic of the Seven Islands was acknowledged. Egypt and the other territories of the Sublime Porte were to be retained in their integrity as before the war. For this article there would have been no occasion, had the British government known, as well as Buonaparte did, the issue of the Egyptian campaign. The islands of Malta, Goza, and Comino were to be restored to the order of St. John of Jerusalem as before the war; and the British troops were to evacuate those islands within three months after the exchange of the ratification. The French troops were to evacuate Naples and the Roman territory; and the British troops, in like manner, were to evacuate Porto-Ferrajo, as well as all the islands and forts which they might occupy in the Mediterranean or Adriatic. The colonies now demand our attention.

North America.

England had taken from France the valuable fishery islands of Saint-Pierre and Miquelon; but France, by the treaty of Amiens, got them restored to her.

West Indies.

England had taken from Holland all her possessions except Dutch Guiana, and gave them all back to her. From Spain she had taken Trinidad; and Buonaparte, as a declared punishment to Spain for having made peace with Portugal without his privity, allowed England to retain that fine island. Portugal so far benefited by the treaty of Amiens, that the boundary line between the two Guianas was brought much nearer to its ancient limit than it was by the treaty which her fears had just before induced her to sign with France at Madrid. Denmark had lost, but now regained her three islands. Sweden, also, got back

[1] See p. 96.

St. Bartholomew. France had lost all her sugar islands but Guadeloupe and its dependencies, and got them all restored to her.

Coast of Africa.

Holland had lost the Cape of Good Hope, but got that important settlement restored to her. To Portugal, Madeira was of course restored ; and France got back Gorée.

East Indies.

Holland had lost Malacca and the islands of Amboyna, Banda, and Ternate; also Trincomalé and the remaining Dutch settlements in the island of Ceylon. The latter were retained by Great Britain; but all the former were restored to Holland. Spain's East Indian territories had remained unmolested; and such of Portugal's as had been recently garrisoned were restored. Denmark still held Tranquebar. France had lost Pondicherry, Chandernagore, and other settlements up the Ganges; also Foul-Point on the island of Madagascar. The whole of these were restored to her by the treaty of Amiens.

Whatever grounds politicians might have for auguring, from the terms of this solemn compact, a short-lived peace, certain it is, that the activity which reigned on the ocean, an activity much greater than any which had been witnessed during the last two or three years of the war, gave to the treaty the air of a truce, or suspension of arms, in which each of the belligerents, some of whom signed it for no other purpose, was striving to gain an advantageous position, in order, when the tocsin should again sound, to be ready for the recommencement of hostilities. French, Dutch, and Spanish fleets were preparing to put to sea ; and English fleets, to follow them and watch their motions : who, then, could doubt that, although the wax upon the seals of the treaty concluding the last had scarcely cooled, a new war was on the eve of bursting forth ?

STATE OF THE BRITISH NAVY.

THE difference in the totals, between the abstract for this year[1] and that for the last, is too slight to need any observation. The casualty-list of the French navy contains few important losses.[2] That of the Spanish navy, with the exception of the Gamo, is filled with the issue of one unfortunate rencontre.[3] The Dutch navy, having lain quietly in port, ran no risk of suffering any diminution in its numbers. The loss sustained by the Danish navy was of trifling amount; and, considered in a national point of view, was far overbalanced by the renown which the Danes acquired on the occasion.[4] The British casualty-list is distinguishable from any that have preceded it, except that connected with Abstract No. 3, for the number of its captures; among which, as a very rare occurrence, appear two line-of-battle ships.[5]

The number of commissioned officers and masters, belonging to the British navy at the commencement of the year 1802, was,

Admirals	45
Vice-admirals	38
Rear-admirals	55
,, superannuated 30	
Post-captains	544
,, superannuated 15	
Commanders, or sloop-captains . . .	406
Lieutenants	2322
,, retired as commanders 50	
Masters	540

and the number of seamen and marines voted for the service of the year, was, 130,000 for the first five lunar months, 88,000

---

[1] See Appendix, Annual Abstract, No. 10.
[2] See Appendix, No. 6.
[3] Ibid., No. 7.
[4] Ibid., No. 8.
[5] Ibid., No. 9.

for one lunar month, and 70,000 for the remaining seven lunar months.[1]

Although, in reference to the abstract immediately preceding it, the abstract for 1802 offers nothing worthy of remark, yet, as coming the next in succession after the close of a war, it contains a variety of matter for consideration. The first circumstance that strikes a reader conversant with the subject is, the important variation between the numerical grand-totals, both line and general of Abstract No. 10, and of the " Statement and Distribution of the Naval British Force," as given in Steel's list for February, 1802. The Abstract's line-total, with the addition of the two ships remarked upon in the asterisk note belonging to it, is 191, Steel's 198 ; the Abstract's general total, with the addition just noticed, 783, Steel's 803. Of Steel's line-of-battle number, nine will be found in class q, and one in class u ; thus reducing it to 188. But Steel has anticipated the breaking up of the Warspite 74, Captivity and Eagle 64's, and Panther 60 ; which again augments his number to 192. If from the latter be deducted the Prince Edward, a ship he classes as a 60 instead of a 50, we have 191, which, with the correction in the note already referred to, is the precise number in the Abstract. Having thus explained the difference that exists between the line-total in the Abstract, and that in Steel's February list, we shall have very little difficulty in approximating the two under-line totals ; one of which is 592, the other 603. If we deduct from the latter, four fire-vessels, four river-barges, and four or five transport-tenders and other small craft, which, for reasons already given, are excluded from the former,[2] the numbers will be equal.

A test yet remains, more authoritative than Steel, the official list or register of the British navy for the 1st of January, 1802. There the line-total is 180, the under-line total 665, and the grand-total 845. It seldom happens that the official register takes any notice of the *armées en flûte*, or reduced ships : consequently, they remain, list after list, among their full-armed class-mates. If, then, we deduct, as was done in the comparison with Steel, the nine ships at q, and the one at u, we bring the official line-total to 170. Four line-of-battle ships appear among the official " ship-rigged sloops ;"[3] two among the " prison-

---

[1] See Appendix, No. 10.
[2] See Note e* to Abstract No. 3, at vol. i., p. 455.

[3] Sandwich, San-Ysidro, Royal Oak, and Prudent; all of which had been prison-ships.

ships ;"[1] one among the "hospital-ships ;"[2] seven among the "receiving-ships ;"[3] and there were seven others which, although in service, some of them since 1800, were not registered at the date of the abstract.[4] Here, at once, is the number required. With respect to the under-line totals, we have merely to deduct from the 665, the 67 "hoys, lighters, and transports," and the 10 "hulks," and we have 588, a number which is four below the abstract number. This trifling difference is to be found, if we could stay to trace it, among the small craft, several of which are included in the abstract, and not registered in the official list; while others, as fire-vessels, river-barges, "barge-magazine," "latteen-settee," &c., that assist to swell the latter, are not to be found in the former.

Having thus established the general correctness of the numerical totals of Abstract No. 10, and through it, we hope, of its nine tabular predecessors, we will, after premising that, should any doubt arise respecting the proper classification of a ship, a reference to the notes (which, in fact, are the key to the abstracts) may clear up the point, proceed to draw a slight comparison between the first and last abstracts, the two between which an eight years' war had intervened. In doing this we shall confine ourselves to the line-totals, and even then, to the cruising totals only. According to the latter, the numerical increase is 13 ships; but the most decided improvement is discoverable in the relative tonnages. For instance, the 113 ships in No. 1 measured upon an average 1645 tons; while in the 126 ships in No. 10 measure 1740 tons. The accession of the five ships at B, C, and G, and of 26 out of the 30 at K, L, and M, have chiefly contributed to this important augmentation.

The number of line-of-battle ships, added to the British navy from the navies of foreign powers, were, French 27, Dutch 17, Spanish 5, and Danish 1; total 50 :[5] a number that, besides being considerably short of what Steel and other writers have recorded, contains a larger proportion of ineffective ships than they allow, as the following statement will show :—

[1] Sultan and Captivity.
[2] Union, afterwards Sussex
[3] Royal William, Cambridge, Grafton, Chichester Yarmouth, Medway, and Rippon.
[4] Athénien, Nassau (late Holstein), De-Ruyter, Guelderland, Leyden, Texel (late Cerberus), and Utrecht.
[5] See Appendix, No. 10.

	FOREIGN BUILT.	
	Cruisers.	Stationary Harbour-Ships, &c.
	No.	No.
In Abstract No. 10 . . , ...	23	18
„ No. 1	3	2
Remaining, of ships captured in the war of 1793 . .	20	16
Reduced by the " Converted " column	5	..
Captured, &c.	5	..
Sold, or taken to pieces	..	4
Whole of the ships of the line captured in the war of 1793	30	20

The line-of-battle loss, which the British navy sustained in the same war, amounts to 20 ships; of which no fewer than three-fourths were wrecked and accidentally burnt.[1]

It is usual, at the termination of a war, to exhibit, by a few figures, the relative gains and losses of the parties that had been engaged in it. Accordingly, in December, 1801, a cabinet minister laid before the British parliament a statement express-ing that, when the war commenced, the British navy consisted of 135, and, when it ended, of 202 ships of the line. But for the concurrent testimony of several reporters, one might sup-pose the former number to contain a typographical error, in the transposition of the 3 and 5. We have shown, in its proper place, the accuracy of the number 153, which appears in the line column of the first Annual Abstract;[2] and have just done the same, in the fullest manner, respecting the number 191, in Abstract No. 10.[3] The number, which comes nearest to the minister's number, is to be found in Steel's list for November, 1801 : it wants but two of the amount. Admitting the minister to have collected 200 of his 202 line of-battle ships from Steel's list (it is evident he did not get them from the official list), whence did he obtain the number 35, for the whole of the line-of-battle ships possessed by France at the close of the year 1801 ? At the commencement of the year 1803, we shall show, in the clearest manner, that this number scarcely covers half of the line-of-battle ships which must have belonged to France at the peace of Amiens ; and it already has appeared that, instead

---

[1] See Appendix, No. 11.
[2] See Note * to that Abstract, and the same note to Abstract No. 2, vol. i., p. 453.

[3] See Note * to that Abstract, in the Appendix of this volume.

of 202 ships of the line, 126, or, including those building, 148,[1] was the proper number to be confronted with the French number.

America and the Barbary States.

Although this was a year of peace between England and the other great powers, there were still some naval operations of a warlike character going on, a summary of which may serve, if to do no more, to keep alive the interest in such matters until, by the general clash of arms throughout Europe, the annalist is again called upon to record events of magnitude and importance.

It is too well known to be creditable to them, that the formidable christian powers of Europe have long paid a tribute, either in specie or kind, to the regencies of Algiers, Tripoli, and Tunis, to induce these merciless freebooters to abstain from molesting the commerce of the former ; from making prizes of their vessels and slaves of their people. The United States of America, having a considerable Mediterranean commerce at stake, found it wise to follow the example of the older and richer states of Europe. It is difficult to say how much this sop to the three-headed monster annually cost the American republic; but, in articles of merchandise, timber, cannon, cordage, money, and now and then a frigate or corvette armed and equipped for war, we should consider that the United States did not pay less to the three regencies than from 100,000 to 150,000 dollars per annum.

In the month of October, 1800, the United States 32-gun frigate George Washington, Captain William Bainbridge, was lying at an anchor in the road of Algiers. The dey considered this as a fine opportunity to get the presents, which he, as well as the heads of the other regencies, annually made to the grand seignior, conveyed to Constantinople. The demand for the American frigate to be sent upon this mission was formally made, and reluctantly complied with. Laden with presents to the amount of a million and a half of dollars, encumbered with 100 Turks as passengers, and degraded by carrying the flag of Algiers at her maintopgallantmast-head, the George Washington sailed for and arrived at Constantinople. Having there disembarked her live and dead lumber, the American frigate sailed upon her return, and on the 21st of January 1801, re-anchored at Algiers.

[1] See Note * to that Abstract, in the Appendix of this volume.

The disgraceful use to which an American frigate had thus been put "deeply affected," to use the words of Mr. President Jefferson, "the sensibility, not only of the president, but of the people of the United States." The "indignity" was certainly calculated to do all this; but we cannot anywhere discover that the Washington was sent "by force" upon her extraordinary and humiliating mission. We think that both Captain Bainbridge and the American consul, Mr. Richard O'Brien, made out but a poor case to substantiate that fact.

Whatever feelings the submission of these gentlemen may have excited in their own country, its effect was a very natural one in Algiers and the two neighbouring regencies: they became more loud and exorbitant than ever in their demands for money and presents. Algiers, however, was partially appeased by the seasonable arrival of a ship from America with the arrears of the subsidy due to her. But, jealous of the favours shown to the Dey of Algiers, the Bashaw of Tripoli became very outrageous. In some of his conferences with the American consul, the bashaw says: "There is no nation I wish to be at peace with more than yours; but all nations pay me, and so must the Americans."—"Compliments, although acceptable, are of very little value; and the heads of the Barbary States know their friends by the value of the presents that they receive from them." To give a practical proof of his estimation of compliments, the Bashaw of Tripoli, on the 14th of May, 1801, caused the flagstaff of the United States in front of the consul's house to be cut down; the customary mode, with these summary gentlemen, of promulgating a declaration of war.

Not to be behindhand with his two brother spoliators to the westward, the Bey of Tunis made use of a somewhat ludicrous pretext for levying a contribution upon his "friends." On the night of the 18th of June a fire broke out in the palace, and in its progress consumed 50,000 stands of arms. On the 20th the American consul, Mr. William Eaton, having been summoned to the Bey's presence, was told that his government must supply 10,000 stands of arms. "I have," says the Bey, "proportioned my loss among my friends, and this falls to you to furnish. Tell your government to send them without delay." The consul made a very proper reply; and upon the whole conducted himself with becoming, and, as the result proved, successful firmness.

Expecting from the tenour of the consular communications from Algiers, Tripoli, and Tunis that a rupture with one or more of them would shortly take place, the government of the United States, since the latter end of May, had despatched to the Mediterranean a squadron of three frigates and a sloop or two, just half the force then in commission, under the orders of Commodore Dale; which squadron also carried out presents to a tolerably large amount, for such of the regencies as yet remained at peace.

On the 2nd of July Commodore Dale, with the 44-gun frigates President and Philadelphia, 32-gun frigate Essex, and the brig-sloop Enterprise, anchored in the bay of Gibraltar; where were also lying, having come in to get a supply of water, a Tripolitan ship-of-war, with the high-admiral's flag on board, carrying 26 guns, 9 and 6 pounders, and 260 men, and a brig of 16 guns, 6-pounders, and 160 men. The commanders of these vessels, who were now performing quarantine, pretended not to know that their government had declared war against the United States; but Commodore Dale became assured of the fact from a communication with the shore. He soon afterwards made sail for the coast of Barbary, and in the course of the month showed his squadron off Algiers, Tunis, and Tripoli in succession. The two first of these regencies appear to have lowered their tone a little on this rather unexpected visit. With Tripoli, however, no arrangement was effected, and the war went on. After remaining off Tripoli about 18 days, Commodore Dale stood along the coast to the westward as far as the island of Pidussa, then steered for Malta to get a supply of water; and on the 16th came to an anchor in the harbour of Valetta.

On the 1st of August the United States schooner Enterprise, of 14 long 6-pounders and 90 men, commanded by Lieutenant Andrew Sterrett, being on her way to join Commodore Dale at Malta, and not far from that island, fell in with a Tripolitan polacre-ship, of 14 guns (probably 4-pounders, and it is doubtful if some were not swivels) and 80 men, commanded by Rais-Mahomet Sous. An action immediately commenced within pistol-shot, and continued for nearly two hours, when the Tripolitan colours were either shot away or struck. Elated with their victory, the American crew gave three cheers, and quitted their guns. In an instant the corsair rehoisted her flag, and renewed the action with redoubled vigour, the Tripolitans brandishing their sabres, and seeming desirous to board the Enterprise. The crew of the latter, however, having flown back to their guns, poured into their opponent so destructive a fire, that the barbarians unequivocally hauled down their colours. Lieutenant

Sterrett now ordered the corsair under his lee quarter, and kept his men at their guns. But the Tripolitan vessel, the instant she got to the station to which she had been ordered, poured another broadside into the Enterprise, and, hoisting the red or bloody flag, made an attempt to board. The Americans were now most justly incensed against the Mahomedans; and the Enterprise, obtaining a raking position, brought down the corsair's mizenmast, and well riddled her hull. Seeing what was now likely to be his fate, the Tripolitan captain implored for quarter; and bending in a supplicating manner over the waist-barricade of his vessel, threw his colours into the sea, as the surest indication of his sincerity. The Enterprise immediately ceased her fire; and thus ended an action which had lasted just three hours.

As a proof no less of the utter incompetency of the Tripolitans as men-of-war's men, as of the skill to which the Americans had already arrived in the use of their guns, the Enterprise did not have a man hurt, and received very little damage in hull or rigging; while the corsair was greatly shattered in her hull and two remaining masts, and sustained, out of her 80 men in crew, a loss of 20 killed and 30 wounded, including among the latter her captain and first-lieutenant.

Agreeably to the instructions he had received, Lieutenant Sterrett ordered the guns, swords, pistols, and ammunition of his prize to be thrown overboard, and both her masts to be cut away by the board. A spar was then raised to serve for a mast, and an old tattered sail hung to it as a flag. In this condition the corsair was sent to Tripoli; and it is related that, on her arrival there, the bashaw marked his indignation by ordering the wounded captain to be paraded through the streets mounted upon an ass, and then to receive 500 bastinadoes. This was a fine reward, certainly, for having held out, against a very superior antagonist, until nearly two-thirds of his crew were killed or disabled.

On the 21st of August Commodore Dale put to sea from Malta with his squadron, and on the 30th captured a Greek ship from Smyrna bound to Tripoli, having on board one officer and 20 soldiers, 14 merchants, and some women and children, all Tripolitans. Considering this a good opportunity to negotiate an exchange with the bey for some Americans whom his cruisers had taken, the commodore proceeded straight to Tripoli; and, arriving off the port on the 3rd of September, sent on shore a message to that effect. The bey said he would not give one

American for all the soldiers; that only eight of the merchants were his subjects; and that he cared very little about any of them. He at length, however, agreed to give three Americans for the 21 soldiers, and three more for the eight merchants. With this the American commodore was obliged to be satisfied. Soon afterwards, finding his crew getting very sickly and his provisions very short, Commodore Dale raised the blockade of Tripoli, and steered for Gibraltar. During the winter months the American squadron visited Tripoli only occasionally. In March, 1802, having had all their arrears of presents paid up, the regencies of Algiers and Tunis became satisfied with the United States. Nothing, however, during the whole of this year appears to have been done against Tripoli, although the cruisers of that regency were capturing American vessels where-ever they could find them.

French Expedition to St. Domingo.

We have already noticed the bustle of preparation going on in the continental ports, just when a treaty of peace had apparently set fleets and armies to at least a temporary rest. An expedition to the island of St. Domingo was the plan in agitation. Previously to any account of occurrences on the shores of that ill-fated island, we will bestow a glance upon the changes which the preceding two or three years had effected in a colony that, when France owned it, was the most profitable of any in the West Indies.

Buonaparte, as soon as he had got himself placed at the head of the French government, sent out to St. Domingo an arrêté, containing the programme of a constitution for the government of the island; and, by way of gilding the pill, he appointed the celebrated black General Toussaint-Louverture, commander-in-chief of the colonial army; of which, owing to the unhealthy state of the island and the impossibility of sending out reinforcements, a very small portion were natives of France. Before the close of the year 1799 Toussaint possessed himself of the Spanish part of the island, including the city of Santo Domingo. Shortly afterwards this gifted negro drew up, and finally got adopted, the plan of a colonial constitution, in which he named himself governor of the island and president for life, with the right of appointing his successor. Toussaint probably would not have ventured to take so bold a step, had he been aware that the war was so near its close: he knew that, while it continued, he should have the protection of the English; and that the ships of the latter would prevent those of France from transporting any troops to recapture the island, or from otherwise molesting him in his possession.

As soon as the negotiation between France and England had assumed a favourable appearance, the ex-proprietors of estates in St. Domingo, strengthened by the whole body of French merchants, who keenly felt the loss of so fair a portion of their trade, applied to the first consul to send out an army and retake the island. The nation at large seemed to have but one feeling on the subject; and Buonaparte, in despite, as he had himself declared, of his better judgment,[1] gave orders to equip an expedition suitable to the magnitude of the undertaking. The army was to be composed of 21,200 men, under General Leclerc; and the fleet to convey them to the Antilles was to consist of 33 sail of the line, and nearly an equal number of frigates, ship and brig corvettes, and flûte-transports, under the command of Vice-admiral Villaret-Joyeuse.

On the 14th of December, 1801, after a long delay by contrary winds, a fleet composed of 10 French sail of the line, under the commander-in-chief, and of five Spanish, under Vice-admiral Gravina, accompanied by six frigates, four corvettes and smaller vessels, and two transports, containing altogether 7000 men, set sail from the road of Brest. On the morning of the 17th, off Belle-Isle, one French sail of the line, one frigate, one corvette, and one flûte, with 900 men on board, joined from Lorient; and a squadron from Rochefort, under Rear-admiral La Touche-Tréville, consisting of six sail of the line, six frigates, two corvettes, and two despatch-vessels, and having on board 3000 men, was expected to join, but did not until the combined fleet, on the 29th of January, 1802, reached Cape Samana on the island of its destination. One 74, the Duquesne, and one frigate, the Cornélie, having on board 700 men between them, had parted company; which left 10,500 as the number of men to be disembarked from the first division of the fleet.

The following were the dispositions for landing the troops; 1000, under General Kerverseau, at Santo-Domingo; 3000, under General Boudet, at Port-au-Prince; 2500, under General Rochambeau, in Mancenille bay, to attack Fort-Dauphin, and, on carrying it, to proceed to the mole St. Nicolas, there to be joined by 4000 men under General Hardy. While the ships were proceeding to their assigned points of debarkation, two

---

[1] See O'Meara's Napoléon in Exile, vol. ii., p. 199.

other French squadrons arrived at the rendezvous : one from Toulon, of four sail of the line and one frigate, under Rear-admiral Ganteaume, with 2300 men; the other from Cadiz, of three sail of the line and three frigates, under Rear-admiral Linois, with 1500 men on board. In the mean time, the 10,500 troops that had arrived in the first division, partly by intrigue and partly by force, had effected their landing.

It is foreign to these pages to enter upon the details of the military operations which, after a brave and protracted resistance on the part of the indigenes, led to their dispersion or surrender ; but even this did not take place until the remaining 6900 of the 21,200 French troops ordered upon the expedition arrived at the island. The black chief, who had exhibited so many traits of moderation and generalship, after capitulating and being allowed to return to his home, was suddenly arrested and conveyed on board the Héros 74, lying off Gonaïves. On being brought on board the French ship, this extraordinary man is said to have uttered these words. "En me renversant, on n'a abattu que le tronc de l'arbre de la liberté des noirs, il repoussera par les racines parcequ'elles sont profondes et nombreuses."

Having been thus illegally dragged on board the Héros, Toussaint was most inhumanly, and contrary to all the assurances held out to him by General Leclerc, transported to France, to end his days in a prison. He was shut up in Fort de Joux, and died six months afterwards in rather a mysterious way. On this subject the following appears in a work of considerable notoriety : "I mentioned Toussaint-Louverture, and observed that, amongst other calumnies, some of his (Buonaparte's) enemies had asserted that he had caused him to be put to death privately in prison. 'It does not deserve an answer,' replied Napoléon; 'what possible interest could I have in putting a negro to death after he had arrived in France ? Had he died in St. Domingo, then indeed something might have been suspected, but, after he had safely landed in France, what object could have been in view ?' "[1]

Whatever, in reality, was the mode by which Toussaint ended his days, the act of forcibly withdrawing him from St. Domingo, after he had honourably capitulated, proved in the end as impolitic as it was cruel. Several enterprising black chiefs still remained on the island : Clerveaux, Christophe, Paul-Louverture (nephew to Toussaint), and Dessalines ; and who, with the whole of their countrymen, were exasperated at the treachery which

[1] O'Meara's Napoléon in Exile, vol. ii., p. 198.

had deprived them of their gallant leader. Part of the French troops were sent away to aid in subduing the revolted negroes at Guadeloupe; and, among the remainder, as the summer advanced, the yellow fever made dreadful ravages.

About the middle of August accounts reached St. Domingo, of the success of the French at Guadeloupe, and that slavery, in all its horrors, had been re-established in the colony. This news spread like wildfire among the negroes at the first-named island, and operating upon minds already smarting under their own wrongs, determined them to revolt. The first eruption broke out about the middle of September. The death of General Leclerc of the fever, on the 2nd of November,[1] conferred on General Rochambeau the command of the French forces on the island; but all the efforts of these, ably directed as they were, and although strengthened by the arrival, on the 5th of April, 1803, of a reinforcement of 2000 troops of the line, could not, it is believed, have preserved the colony to France, even if the war between the latter power and England had not, as it just then had, broken out afresh. That war and its mass of interesting details now claim our attention.

---

[1] His body, after being embalmed, was conveyed to France on board the (late British) Swiftsure 74.

WAR OF 1803.

SCARCELY had the embers of the bonfires, lit up in celebration of the peace of Amiens, grown cold on the ground, ere the two principal parties to the treaty became again involved in war. Although the formal declaration, the act of England herself in this instance, did not issue until toward the middle of the year, each nation, with well-grounded forebodings of what was to happen, began her preparations at its commencement. So much of those preparations as relate to naval concerns fall properly within the scope of this work; and, as usual, we shall begin with the abstract, or tabular statement, of the British navy for the current year.[1]

Between that abstract and the preceding one a difference occurs, as well in one or more of the principal heads as in the arrangement of the lower part of the Table. A desire to improve the remaining abstracts of the series has suggested the alteration, and the necessary explanations on the subject will be found in the notes which accompany the present year's abstract.

A state of peace having filled the period between this abstract and the last, no "Captured" column appears; and the "Built, Purchased, and Wrecked" columns exhibit an unusual paucity of numbers.[2] The decrease observable in many of the totals arises, partly from the alterations above alluded to, but, in a much greater degree, from the multiplicity of vessels sold or taken to pieces since the termination of the war. One fact is remarkable: the total of line-of-battle ships employable for sea-service falls short by two of the corresponding total in the abstract for 1793. So that, during a period of 10 years, eight of them in war, the British navy had slightly decreased in ships of the line. If

1 See Appendix, Annual Abstract, No. 11.   2 See Appendix, No. 12.

statesmen and historians have asserted otherwise, it has been because they drew their comparisons between the wrong totals. An increase of 11 certainly appears among the permanent harbour-service ships, but it is the sea-service cruisers which constitute the effective strength of a navy.

The number of commissioned officers and masters belonging to the British navy at the commencement of the year, was,

Admirals		45
Vice-admirals		36
Rear-admirals		51
,, superannuated 26		
Post-captains		668
,, superannuated 13		
Commanders, or sloop-captains . . .		413
,, superannuated 49		
Lieutenants		2480
Masters		529

And the number of seamen and marines voted for the service of 1803 was, 50,000 for the first two, 60,000 for the next four, and 100,000 for the remaining seven lunar months of it.[1]

The King of England's message to parliament on the 8th of March, in the impression it made upon the public mind, was nearly tantamount to a declaration of war; and preparations for carrying it on with vigour were immediately commenced in all the dockyards of the empire. The state of the British navy, as it stood on the 1st of January, has already appeared in its proper place. To the 32 line-of-battle cruisers, then in commission, were added, before the 1st of May, 20 additional ones; and, by the 1st of the following month, the number of ships of the line in commission was augmented to 60, besides a proportionate number of 50-gun ships, frigates, sloops, and smaller vessels, all either at sea or fitting for sea. A great many vessels of every class, including a large proportion of line-of-battle ships, were repairing; and several frigates, sloops, and schooners were ordered to be constructed with all possible despatch.

The first consul of France was not, on his part, inactive. In the month of March he gave orders that the port of Flushing should be got ready to receive and equip a squadron, to be called the "Squadron of the North," and which was to consist of ten 74-gun ships from Dutch models. This was probably, because they draw less water, in proportion to their rate, than the ships of other nations. The ships thus ordered were imme-

[1] See Appendix, No. 13.

diately to be laid down, part in Flushing and Ostende, and.the remainder in ports of France. Gun-vessels and flat-bottomed boats were also to be constructed at every convenient spot along the shores of the Scheldt, the Weser, and the Elbe ; and a quantity of ship-timber, hemp, and other naval stores, to the value of 20,000,000 of francs, was ordered to be immediately purchased in Holland. In testimony, also, of his love for the naval service, Buonaparte, since the 25th of January, 1802, had made his brother Jérôme an enseigne de vaisseau.

In the road of Brest were lying four ships of the line : nine others were in the docks, repairing and nearly ready ; and these were ordered to be expedited by all possible means. Three were on the stocks, nearly finished ; and five lay in the inner harbour, waiting their turns to be docked ; making a total of 21 serviceable line-of-battle ships in the port of Brest. There were also lying up in the harbour six or eight old and worn-out ships, including the Invincible and Terrible three-deckers.

In the port of Lorient were three ships on the stocks, expected to be launched in November ; and two additional ones were ordered to be laid down. At St. Malo a 74 was ordered to be built ; and at Nantes four frigates, exclusive of two Dutch-built 74s, intended for the Scheldt squadron. At Bordeaux another of the latter was ordered to be built. At Rochefort three line-of-battle ships were building, and nearly ready : three others were now ordered. At Toulon there were eight ships of the line afloat, two on the stocks nearly finished, and two others about to be commenced. At Marseilles the last of the 10 Dutch-built 74s for the Scheldt squadron was ordered to be laid down. At Genoa a 74-gun ship and frigate were immediately to be put in hand, from draughts prepared at Brest.[1] There were also nine French line-of-battle ships at, or coming from, the island of St. Domingo, and one, the Marengo, on her road to the East Indies ; making a total of 66 ships, including 47 afloat, or soon expected to be so.[2]

If it were not quite clear, from the very nature of these formidable preparations, thus carried on in the midst of peace, that a renewal of the war with England was contemplated, no doubt could exist, on a perusal of the instructions which, since early in February, Buonaparte had drawn up for the guidance of General Decaen. On the 6th of March this officer sailed from Brest, in

[1] Précis des Evénemens Militaires, &c., par M le Comte Mathieu Dumas, Lieu-tenant-Général des Armées du Roi. A Paris, 1822 ; tome xi., p. 189.
[2] See p. 158 ; also Appendix, No. 14.

the Marengo 74, for the French settlements in India, of which
he had been appointed governor-general; and whither the Marengo, and the frigates Atalante, Belle-Poule, and Sémillante,
and transports Côte-d'Or and Marie-Françoise, were carrying,
for the alleged purpose of taking possession of Pondicherry
agreeably to the third article of the treaty of Amiens, about
1350 troops.

It appears by one or two paragraphs in the document alluded
to,[1] that the first consul did not anticipate an actual rupture
before the month of September. War was, however, declared by
England, virtually on the 16th of May, when letters of marque
and general reprisals were ordered, and formally in two days
afterwards; and, had the declaration bore date in the preceding
February, no one acquainted with the avowed intentions of
Buonaparte could say it had issued a day too early. Simul-
taneously with the order for reprisals against French ships,
issued one for detaining ships belonging to the Batavian republic, Holland being to all intents and purposes a province of
France.

Convinced that the peace of the world is generally held by a
thread, which the caprice of a minister may almost at any time
break, we shall not puzzle ourselves, or the reader, with endeavouring to investigate the causes of the war which commenced
in the year 1803, but shall plunge at once into the details of its
operations; such operations at least as lie within our province,
those in which the navies of the several belligerents take a part.

On the 17th of May, at 7 P.M., Admiral the Honourable
William Cornwallis, in whose able hands the command of the
Channel fleet still remained, having his flag on board the Dreadnought 98, sailed from Cawsand bay, with a fleet of 10 sail of
the line and frigates, to cruise off Ushant and watch the motions
of the French ships in Brest harbour, five or six only of which
were in a state to put to sea. Of the remaining 21 ships of the
line which the port contained, some were fitting, others repairing, and three were still upon the stocks, but on the eve of being
launched. Could, therefore, a greater force than 10 sail of the
line have been sent to cruise off Brest, it would, in the divided
state of the French navy, have been wholly unnecessary.

Owing to the very reduced state of the Batavian navy, which,
including three or four ships in the ports of Spain, now consisted
of not more than seven sail of the line and a few frigates in a
serviceable state, three British ships were all that were required

[1] For the original of which see Appendix, No. 15

in the North Sea. Four or five others were in the Irish Channel ; about an equal number cruised to the southward of Brest ; and, of those remaining in Plymouth and Portsmouth, upwards of 20 were fitting for sea, as fast as the dearth of seamen, and unfortunate want of stores, would admit.

Although the watchfulness of Admiral Cornwallis, who, on the 9th of July, shifted his flag from the Dreadnought to the 112 gun-ship Ville-de-Paris, precluded any addition to the Brest fleet from without the port, two fine ships joined it from within. Both were launched on the same day, the 15th of August ; one the Cassard 74, the other, the celebrated three-decker on hand since the year 1794, and which, under such highly-wrought feelings, was then ordered to be named the Vengeur, to commemorate the supposed martyrdom of the 74 of that name, captured and sunk in Lord Howe's action.[1]

The summer passed, and the year nearly closed, without any material change in the relative positions of the Brest and Channel fleets. On Christmas day, however, the strong south-west gales, which, with short intermissions had blown for some weeks, increased to so alarming a height, that the blockading ships, one and all, were compelled to retire from the French coast, and seek safety in Plymouth and other British ports. At this time lay in the outer road of Brest, ready for sea, the Vengeur three-decker, bearing the flag of Vice-admiral Laurent-Jean-François Truguet, an 80, with Rear-admiral Ganteaume's flag, and six 74s, attended by about an equal number of frigates and corvettes, but they made no attempt to sail.

Before the end of the year there were several other of the continental ports opening into the ocean, which, besides Brest, contained French ships of the line, and in sufficient number when united to excite some attention. At Rochefort had recently arrived, along with some frigates, two of the nine sail of the line, already mentioned as at, or coming from, the island of St. Domingo when the war broke out. In Ferrol and Corunna were lying five other of those line-of-battle ships, and a sixth ship (making the eighth in the whole), the Aigle 74, had put into Cadiz. To guard all these ports, except the last, was a part of the duty of the commander-in-chief of the Channel fleet ; and, as soon as practicable, they were watched by British squadrons corresponding in force with the French squadrons within them.

Although a single gun-boat is not of a force to excite alarm, several scores of such vessels, united in a fleet, are sufficiently

[1] See vol. i., p. 193.

formidable to call for the fullest attention of an enemy. With this view the British government, very soon after war was declared, stationed cruisers, commanded by active and experienced officers, in front of all those ports along the Channel frontier of France, from Ostende to Cape La Hougue, and thence to Granville, at which divisions of gun-vessels were known to be constructing or fitting out. Buonaparte's plan, for the employment of this apparently insignificant description of force in the invasion of England, was not matured until the ensuing year; but, in the mean time, considerable activity prevailed among the different entrepots along the above line of coast. On most occasions, when any of the flotilla ventured from under the protection of their batteries, they were met, and either captured or driven back, by the blockading force; and were sometimes attacked with success, even when moored, as they considered, beyond the reach of British enterprise. We mean now to embody the most interesting of the skirmishes that ensued, during the present year, between British cruisers and the French invasion-flotilla.

On the 14th of June, in the morning, the British 18-pounder 36-gun frigate Immortalité, Captain Edward William Campbell Rich Owen, and 18-gun brig-sloops Cruiser and Jalouse, Captain John Hancock and Christopher Strachey, chased the two French gun-vessels, Inabordable schooner and Commode brig, each carrying one 18, and three 24 pounder long guns, on shore upon the east part of Cape Blanc-Nez. As soon as the flood-tide made, the Cruiser and Jalouse stood in, and, anchoring with springs, commenced engaging the batteries under which the gun-vessels had grounded. At the end of an hour's mutual cannonade the batteries were silenced; and, in the face of a heavy fire of musketry from the cliffs, by which Mr. Charles Adams, master's mate of the Jalouse, the only person hurt, was badly wounded, the boats of the three British vessels boarded and brought off the French brig and schooner.

On the 1st of August a French armed lugger, which the British 38-gun frigate Hydra, Captain George Mundy, had prevented from entering the port of Hâvre, having hauled close to the beach about two miles to the westward of the river Touque, Captain Mundy despatched the Hydra's boats, under the orders of Lieutenant Francis M'Mahon Tracy assisted by Messrs. John Barclay and George French, midshipmen, to endeavour to bring off or destroy her. On the near approach of the boats the crew of the lugger, which was the Favori, of four carriage-guns,

commanded by a lieutenant de vaisseau, abandoned her and
retreated to the shore; where, in concert with a party of military,
they posted themselves behind some sand-banks that lay abreast
and within musket-shot of their vessel. From this position the
French soldiers and sailors kept up a constant fire upon the
people in the boats and on board the Favori; and received a
return from the British marines, until the lugger, by the exertions
of the prize-master and his men, had gained a safe distance from
the shore. One seaman killed was the extent of the loss on the
British side.

On the 14th of September, at 8 A.M., the Immortalité frigate,
in company with the bomb-vessels, Perseus, Captain John
Methuist, and Explosion, Captain Robert Paul, commenced an
attack upon the batteries that protect the town of Dieppe, also
on 17 gun-vessels building in the port. The firing was continued on both sides until 11 h. 30 m. A.M.; when the lee-tide
making strong, and the town having taken fire badly in one
place, and slightly in two others, the frigate and bomb-vessels
weighed, and proceeded off St. Valery cn Caux, where six gun-
boats were constructing. At 3 P.M. the British opened a fire
upon that place, and continued it for an hour, apparently with
some effect: Captain Owen then retired, with the loss of one
man missing and five men wounded.

On the 13th of September, in the evening, the British
18-pounder 32-gun frigate Cerberus, Captain William Selby,
bearing the flag of Rear-admrial Sir James Saumarez, anchored
as close to the town of Granville as the tide would admit,
having only 16 feet under her keel at low water. In company
with the Cerberus were the sloops-of-war, Charwell and Kite,
Captains Philip Dumaresq and Philip Pipon, Ealing schooner,
Lieutenant William Archbold, and "Cartaret" cutter, with
whose commander's name we are unacquainted. As soon as the
bomb-vessels Sulphur and Terror, Captains Daniel M'Leod and
George Nicholas Hardinge, which were hourly expected, should
arrive, it was intended to bombard the port of Granville, in the
hope to destroy some of the numerous gun-boats lying within
the pier.

At 11 P.M. the Terror came up; but, having as well as the
Cerberus grounded at low water, it was not until 2 A.M. on the
14th, that Captain Hardinge could get to the station assigned
him. Being then judiciously placed by her commander, the
Terror commenced throwing shells from her two mortars, and
received an immediate return from the gun and mortar batteries

on the heights near the town, also from some guns mounted upon
the pier, and several gun-vessels stationed at the entrance of the
harbour. The fire was kept up until after 5 A.M.; when the
Terror was recalled, and, weighing, re-anchored at a greater
distance from the town, with a loss of only two men wounded
by splinters.

Shortly afterwards the Sulphur bomb, whose bad sailing had
prevented her from beating up, arrived and anchored in company
with the Cerberus and squadron. In the evening both bomb-
vessels threw a few shells; but the tide prevented them from
getting near enough to produce much effect.

On the 15th, in the morning, all the ships were enabled to
take capital positions; and soon after 5 A.M. the bombardment recommenced with great spirit, and continued until 10 h. 30 m. A.M.;
when the falling tide rendered it necessary for the British ships
to withdraw from the attack. Although 22 gun-vessels, which
had hauled out of the pier and formed themselves in a regular
line, had united with the batteries around the port in replying to
the fire of the British, no loss and very little damage was sustained by the latter.

Shortly after getting under sail to remove into deeper water,
the Cerberus grounded upon one of the sand-banks. Nine of the
French gunboats, perceiving the situation of the British frigate,
attempted to annoy her, and began a heavy cannonade, but were
eventually compelled, by the fire of the Charwell, Kite, bomb-
vessels, and cutters, to retire for shelter into the harbour. After
remaining aground about three hours, the Cerberus floated with
the rising tide. The attack upon the French town and gun-
vessels then ceased; nor was it known that any material effect
had been produced by it.

On the 27th of September, in the evening, a division of sloops,
bombs, and smaller vessels, under the orders of Captain Samuel
Jackson of the 16-gun ship-sloop Autumn, anchored off Calais,
the bomb-vessels to the north-east of the town, and the remainder of the squadron abreast of the town and pier-head
battery. The French immediately opened a fire from all directions, and the first shell fell within a ship's length of the Autumn
and burst under water. The vessels being at this time so close
to each other as to be in danger from the enemy's shells, Captain
Jackson directed them to weigh and re-anchor in more open
order, while he remained with the Autumn in her original
station. In this way the bombardment continued for several
hours, with some apparent damage to the east end of the town,

but with none whatever to the British squadron. At length a gale from the north-east obliged the ships to weigh and stand off; and thus the action ended.

On the next day, the 28th, a division of gun-boats, taking advantage of the absence of the British squadron, quitted Calais for Boulogne; and, although chased and fired at by the 36-gun frigate Leda, Captain Robert Honyman, they arrived in safety at their destination. On the 29th, a second division, 25 in number, attempted to do the same; and, after a three hours' cannonade by the Leda, the whole, except the two which ran on shore and were bilged upon the rocks, succeeded in reaching the anchorage off the pier of Boulogne; forming, with those already there, a force of 55 sail.

On the 31st of October, at 9 A.M., while the Leda frigate, in company with the Lark and Harpy sloops-of-war, were off Etaples, working towards the shore against a strong east-south-east wind, a large gun-brig, said to be of 12 long 24-pounders, with six schooners and sloops under her convoy, was observed coming out of the port. Captain Honyman immediately signalled the Harpy and Lark to make sail in chase. About this time, however, the British hired cutter, Admiral Mitchell, of 12 carronades, 12-pounders, and 35 men and boys, commanded by Lieutenant Alexander Shippard, being close off Boulogne, the port to which the vessels were steering, gallantly stood after them; and, at 10 A.M., brought the gun-brig to action, close under the batteries of Portet. At the end of a two hours and a half's engagement, the cutter drove the gun-brig and one of the sloops on shore.

The Admiral Mitchell's mast and cross-jack yard were wounded in several places, by a shell which fell on board, and her sails and rigging were a good deal cut by grape: the cutter had also one carronade dismounted, and was hulled in several places. Fortunately, however, her loss did not amount to more than two men badly, and two slightly wounded. The strong land-wind having entirely prevented the small British squadron in the offing from acting, this affair was highly creditable to Lieutenant Shippard, and the officers and crew of the Admiral Mitchell. Our attention is now called to the Mediterranean.

The British naval force upon that station, at the breaking out of the war, consisted of 10 sail of the line, under the command of Rear-admiral Sir Richard Bickerton, in the Kent 74. The probability that this extensive and important station would soon become the scene of very active operations, led to the appointment of Vice-admiral Lord Nelson to the chief command.   His lordship, accordingly, on the 18th of May, hoisted his flag on board his old ship the Victory, in Portsmouth harbour.   On the 20th, at 5 P.M., accompanied by the 18-pounder 32-gun frigate Amphion, Captain Thomas Masterman Hardy, the Victory sailed from Spithead, bound, in the first instance, to the fleet off Brest, to ascertain if her assistance would be required by Admiral Cornwallis ; in which event she was to remain with the latter, and the vice-admiral was to proceed to his station in the frigate.

On the 22nd, at 4 P.M., the two ships arrived off the island of Ushant, the appointed rendezvous ; but a severe gale of wind had blown the British fleet from its station.   After a vain search for the admiral, both at the rendezvous and nearer to Brest, Lord Nelson, at 7 h. 30 m. P.M. on the 23rd, shifted his flag to the Amphion, and at 8 P.M., made sail, with a fair wind, leaving the Victory to follow, in case her services should be dispensed with by the commander-in-chief of the Channel fleet.

On the 25th, in the morning, the wind shifted from north-west to south-west, and blew fresh.   The foul wind, with a heavy sea, continued until the night of the 30th, when a light air sprang up from the northward.   With the aid of this, the Amphion, on the morning of the 3rd of June, entered the Straits, and at 9 h. 30 m. P.M. anchored in the bay of Gibraltar.   On the 4th, at 4 A.M., the Amphion weighed and made sail.   On the 15th, the frigate reached Malta ; quitted it on the 17th, at 3 A.M., and on the 25th, arrived off Naples, where his lordship expected to find the squadron.   Sir Richard had, however, since the 4th, sailed for Toulon ; and thither the Amphion immediately bent her course. A succession of calms and light winds made it the 8th of July ere Lord Nelson could reach his old cruising-ground, where he found Sir Richard, with the

Gun ship.
80	Gibraltar	Captain George Frederick Ryves.

74	Kent	{ Rear-admiral (w.) Sir Richard Bickerton, Bart.
		{ Captain Edward O'Bryen.
	Donegal	,, Sir Richard John Strachan, Bart.
	Superb	,, Richard Goodwin Keats.
	Belleisle	,, John Whitby.
	Renown	,, John Chambers White.

| 64 | Monmouth . . . | ,, George Hart. |
| | Agincourt . . . | ,, Charles Marsh Schomberg. |

Frigates, Active, Phœbe, and (now) Amphion.

The French line-of-battle force in Toulon consisted of seven ships, nearly ready for sea, under Vice-admiral René-Madeleine La Touche-Tréville, two repairing in the arsenal, and five on the stocks. The ships afloat were the 80s Formidable and Indomptable, and 74s Atlas, Berwick (late British), Intrépide, Mont Blanc, and Scipion ; the two in dock were the late British ships Hannibal, now Annibal, and Swiftsure ; and those on the stocks, were the 80s Bucentaure and Neptune, and 74s Borée, Phaëton, and Pluton, the two 80s and the last-named 74 nearly ready for launching.

At this time nearly the whole of the Mediterranean coast was subject, more or less, to the sway of France. In Barcelona and other Spanish ports, French cruisers were allowed to carry in and sell their prizes, while to a British vessel admittance was prohibited by an order of the government. Genoa was as much France as Toulon, and in her dockyard was constructing a French 74, to be named after her, the Génois. Tuscany was gradually becoming French ; and so was Sardinia, although under the mask of a rigid neutrality. Except Naples, every state in the two Sicilies was obedient to the nod of Buonaparte ; who had set his emissaries at work in the Morea, to excite the Greeks to an insurrection against the Turks, in the hope, by taking part with the latter, to obtain Egypt as the price of, what could not fail to be, a successful interference.

Expecting, probably, that the Victory would not be detained by Admiral Cornwallis, Lord Nelson continued on board the Amphion, in preference to removing to a larger ship. Within forty hours after the Amphion had, as already stated, separated from the Victory, the latter fell in with the Channel fleet, and, after a stay of scarcely two hours, was permitted to proceed on her passage to the Mediterranean. On the 28th of May, in latitude 45° 40' north, longitude 6° 10' west, Captain Sutton was fortunate enough to fall in with and capture the French 32-gun frigate Embuscade (late British Ambuscade[1]), Captain Jean-Baptiste-Alexis Fradin, 30 days from Cape-François, bound to Rochefort, with not the whole of her guns mounted, and with a crew of only 187 men.

On the 12th of June, in the evening, the Victory anchored in Gibraltar, and departed thence on the afternoon of the 15th. On the 9th of July, she anchored in the harbour of Valetta, island of Malta, and quitted it on the 11th ; and on the 30th, at about 4 P.M., a few leagues to the westward of Cape Sicie, the Victory joined the Mediterranean squadron, then consisting of the Gib-

[1] See vol. ii. p. 273. The Ambuscade was restored to her rank in the British Navy.

raltar, Belleisle, Donegal, Renown, and Monmouth, with the three frigates, Active, Phœbe, and Amphion. On the same evening, Lord Nelson shifted his flag to the Victory, taking Captain George Murray as his first captain, and Captain Hardy as his second, the latter being succeeded in the command of the Amphion by Captain Sutton, late of the Victory. The station off Cape Sicie had been chosen by the vice-admiral on two accounts; one, should Spain, as was not thought unlikely, suddenly ally herself to France, to prevent the junction of a Spanish fleet from the westward; the other, to be sufficiently to windward to be able, if the usual north-easterly gale should shift to north-north-west, or north-north-east, to take shelter under the Hyères islands, or under Cape San Sebastian.

Early in the month of August the 80-gun ship Canopus, Rear-admiral George Campbell, Captain John Conn, joined the British squadron; and on the 15th of the month the fine 80-gun ship Neptune was launched at Toulon. This, in a little while, augmented the French force in the road to eight sail of the line; while Lord Nelson, having detached the Canopus and Monmouth, was still left with only six, the Victory, Belleisle, Kent, Renown, Superb, and Triumph; the latter recently arrived, and commanded by Captain Sir Robert Barlow. A French writer, alluding to the British naval force in the Mediterranean at this time, says: " L'amiral Nelson croisait avec dix-huit vaisseaux et un nombre correspondant de frégates."[1] This must have explained to the satisfaction of the French people why their admiral, with only eight sail of the line, made no effort to capture or drive away the blockading force.

His ships being short of water, Lord Nelson, on the 24th of October, steered for a newly discovered anchorage among the Magdalena islands, on the north coast of Sardinia; leaving, to watch the French force in Toulon, the frigates Seahorse and Narcissus. On the 31st, at 6 P.M., after a seven days' anxious struggle with adverse gales and currents, dark nights and a rocky and most intricate passage, the whole squadron anchored, without an accident, in Agincourt sound, under the Sardinian shore; a noble harbour formed by an indented bay in the latter, and defended to the northward by the small islands of St. Estevan, Spargiotou, Magdalena, and Cibrera.

This being an anchorage, which, according to the declaration of Lord Nelson, was one of the finest harbours he had ever seen, we feel bound to state how Captain Ryves happened to make

---

[1] Précis des Evènemens, tome x., p. 55.

the important discovery. Some time in the year 1802 the 64-gun ship Agincourt, then commanded by Captain Ryves, was detached by Sir Richard Bickerton, to proceed to the Magdalena islands, and, if possible, prevent the French taking possession of them, as, according to intelligence recently received, they were about to do, notwithstanding the treaty of Amiens. At this period there did not exist a chart of those islands ; nor was it known that any ship-of-war had ever anchored among them : the Agincourt herself, indeed, was nearly lost in doing so. No Frenchmen appearing, Captain Ryves spent the week he was directed to remain there, in making a survey of the islands : which he performed alone, there not being a single person on board able to assist him. In May, 1803, Captain Ryves was promoted to the Gibraltar, and Lord Nelson, we believe, named the anchorage Agincourt sound.

On the 9th of November, having obtained a supply of water and fresh beef for the squadron, Lord Nelson got under way and sailed from the Magdalena islands ; but, owing to a continuance of foul weather, he did not arrive off Toulon until the 23rd. Here the British admiral found the French squadron in the outer road, to all appearance, just as he had left it a month previous. On the 24th the Excellent 74, Captain Frank Sotheron, joined the squadron from England.

The continuance of gales of wind, with a heavy sea from the north-west to north-east, and a belief that Spain had at length settled her neutrality, induced Lord Nelson to take his winter station off Cape San-Sebastian, keeping frigates off Toulon, to apprise him of the least movement on the part of the French ships. Of the weak and ill-provided state of several of his ships, Lord Nelson, in his letters to the admiralty, complained very bitterly, and as it appears, not without reason. " The Superb," says his lordship, " is in a very weak state, but Keats is so superior to any difficulties, that I hear but little from her. The Kent is gone to Malta, fit only for a summer passage. Every bit of twice-laid stuff belonging to the Canopus is condemned, and all the running rigging in the fleet, except the Victory's. We have fitted the Excellent with new main and mizen rigging : it was shameful for the dockyard (Portsmouth) to send a ship to sea with such rigging."

The severity of the weather, coupled with the inefficient state of his squadron, compelled the British admiral, about the 12th of December, to enter the bay of Palma, where the ships remained until the want of water sent them, on the 21st, a second time to Agincourt sound. In this commodious harbour, Lord Nelson and his squadron lay at anchor at the close of the year ; the port of Toulon, and the force within it, being carefully watched by Captain Ross Donnelly, of the Narcissus, with another frigate or two in company.

Light Squadrons and Single Ships.

On the 18th of May the British 18-pounder 36-gun frigate Doris, Captain Richard Henry Pearson, cruising off Ushant, fell in with and chased the French national lugger Affronteur, of 14 long eights and 92 men, commanded by Lieutenant Morce-André Dutoya. Gaining fast upon the lugger the Doris fired a shot wide of her, to induce her to shorten sail, but without effect. To a second shot, discharged this time at her, the lugger fired a shot in return, and actually maintained a running fight with the frigate, until the latter ran close alongside. Nor did the Affronteur even then give up the contest, until her captain and eight of her men were killed, and 14 wounded, one of them mortally. The Doris received some slight damage in the hull and rigging, and had one man wounded, by the fire of her puny but resolute antagonist.

It is hard to draw the line between a resistance that is prudential, and one which is, as this has been pronounced, "fraught with temerity." Had the lugger shot away the frigate's fore-topmast, and thereby effected her escape, all would have united in praising the skill and bravery of M. Dutoya and his people. Had the Affronteur surrendered at the first fire, few would have admitted that her officers and men deserved to belong to a national cruiser, even of her small class. At all events, in a service where so much is to be effected by undauntedness, it is safer to praise the extreme of that quality, than not to censure an over-cautious discretion.

The capture of the Affronteur, it will be observed, took place on the very day on which the declaratian of war issued from St. James's. This, with the capture of two merchant-vessels on the same or the following day, was made a subject of serious complaint against England. " Contre le droit des gens, mais suivant un usage trop commun de la part de l'Angleterre, les hostilités précédèrent la déclaration de guerre. On croyait encore à Paris les négociations en activité lorsqu'on y apprit, par une dépêche télégraphique du préfet maritime de Brest, que les Anglais s'étaient emparés de deux bâtimens marchands dans la baie d'Audierne; le même jour, ou le lendemain, ils attaquèrent les bâtimens de guerre français."[1] The fact is, so far from the negotiation being "in activity," Lord Whitworth had obtained his passports since the 12th of the month, and General Andreossi had applied for his a week earlier. Moreover, it was only on the 25th of May that General Mortier, from his head-quarters at Coërveden, summoned the Hanoverian electorate to surrender to his army.

On the 28th of May the French 36-gun frigate Franchise, still commanded by Captain Jurien, but with 10 of her guns in the hold, and a reduced complement of 187 men, was captured by the 74-gun ship Minotaur, Captain John Charles Moore Mansfield, and two other 74s, which had chased from the Channel fleet. The prize was 35 days from Port-au-Prince, bound to Brest. Being a tolerably fine frigate of 898 tons, the Franchise was added to the British navy, by the same name, as a 12-pounder 36.

On the 25th of June, in latitude 47° 10' north, longitude 20° west, the British 24-pounder 40-gun frigate Endymion, Captain the Honourable Charles Paget, fell in with, and after a chase of eight hours, captured, the French ship-corvette Bacchante, of 18 long 12-pounders and 200 men, commanded by Lieutenant François-Louis Kerimel; and who persisted so long in his endeavours to escape, that the Endymion's chase-guns killed his first-lieutenant and seven seamen, and wounded nine others.

When fallen in with, the Bacchante was on her way to Brest from St. Domingo, whither she had sailed with despatches about three months previous. The prize was a remarkably fine corvette of 642 tons, and became added to the British navy, under her French name, as a post-ship.

On the 27th of June, at night, three boats belonging to the British 38-gun frigate Loire, Captain Frederick Lewis Maitland, cruising off the Isle of Bas, was despatched, under the orders of Lieutenants Francis Temple and James Bowen, assisted among others by Midshipman Philip Henry Bridges, to attack the French 10-gun brig Venteux, Lieutenant Gilles-François Montfort, lying close under the batteries of the island. Owing to the heavy rowing of one of the boats, two only could get up. These, in the most gallant manner, boarded, and after a severe conflict of 10 minutes carried, the French brig; whose 10 guns consisted of four long 18-pounders, and six 36-pounder brass carronades. The Venteux was perfectly prepared for the attack,

---

[1] Victoires et Conquêtes, tome xvi., p. 2.

and had her deck covered with men. Of these she lost her second officer and two seamen killed, her commander, with her four remaining officers, and eight seamen, wounded. The British loss amounted to the boatswain (Mr. M'Gwier), four seamen, and one marine wounded, two of the seamen dangerously.

Even without reckoning the force of the batteries, the capture, by two boats' crews, of a brig armed and manned like the Venteux, was a truly gallant exploit; and Lieutenant Temple, the leader of the party, well merited the promotion which he in consequence obtained. Mr. Bridges, also, of whose conduct on the occasion Lieutenant Temple spoke in the highest terms, was made a lieutenant.

On the 28th of June, as a British squadron, composed of the 74-gun ships Cumberland, Captain Henry William Bayntun, Goliath, Captain Charles Brisbane, and Hercule, acting captain Lieutenant John B. Hills, was cruising off Cape Nicholas Mole, two strange sail were discovered in shore. These were the French 24-pounder 44-gun frigate Poursuivante, Commodore Jean-Baptiste-Phillibert Willaumez, and 16-gun ship-corvette Mignonne, Captain Jean-Pierre Bargeau, neither of them fully armed or manned, two days from Cayes, bound to the Cape on their way to France.

The Goliath by signal went in chase of the Mignonne; and, carrying up the breeze while the latter lay becalmed close under the land, overtook and captured the corvette after the exchange of a few harmless shot. The Mignonne had landed six of her 16 long 12-pounders (described as 18-pounders in the official letter), and had on board a crew of only 80 men and boys. The prize, a remarkably fast-sailing ship,[1] was afterwards added to the British navy under her French name; but, getting aground soon after she was commissioned, the Mignonne was obliged to be laid in the mud in Port Royal harbour, Jamaica.

When the Goliath's signal was made to chase the Mignonne, the Cumberland made the Hercule's to endeavour to cut off the Poursuivante. The Hercule made sail in very light and baffling winds, and appears to have brought to to fire her broadside long before there was any occasion. Owing to this the Poursuivante, untouched by a shot, gained considerably in the chase, although the Hercule was evidently the faster sailer. Subsequently the Hercule filled and got within gun-shot, and a smart action ensued; but the British 74, owing perhaps to a dread of shoal

---

[1] The Jamaica measurement of the Mignonne was 642 tons, but 500 was probably nearer the mark. See p. 26.

water, managed so badly that the French frigate effected her escape into Cape Nicholas Mole.

The Hercule was a good deal damaged in her rigging and sails, and had a few men wounded, but none killed. A French account erroneously states, that the Hercule had 40 men killed and wounded, including among the former her captain. Captain Ferris, in fact, was at Jamaica, and the first-lieutenant, as we have stated, was the acting commander. The Poursuivante had her masts, rigging, sails, and hull very much cut up, and lost six men killed and 15 wounded. Great credit was due to Captain Willaumez, his officers and crew, for the skill and spirit which they evinced upon the occasion. The Poursuivante, we believe, eventually reached Rochefort; but, as far as our researches go, this powerful frigate never afterwards went to sea. Having been built in a Dutch port, and that as long ago as the year 1794 or 1795, the Poursuivante, in all probability, was found to be rotten and unserviceable.

On the 30th of June, soon after daylight, as the Cumberland and Vanguard 74s, Captains Henry William Bayntun and James Walker, were cruising between Jean-Rabel and Cape Nicholas Mole, a large ship was discovered steering down towards the last-named port. The two 74s immediately went in chase, and soon arrived up, the Vanguard on the starboard beam, and the Cumberland on the larboard bow, of the French 40-gun frigate Créole, Captain Jean-Marie-Pierre Lebastard.

After receiving a few shot from the Vanguard, and firing one in return, the Créole hauled down her colours. The frigate had quitted Cape-François the preceding day, and had on board General Morgan, the second in command at the island, and his staff, together with 530 troops, but only 150 seamen. Being a fine large frigate, the Créole was added in her own name to the 38-gun class of the British navy; but, owing in a great degree to the insufficient manner in which she was repaired at Port Royal dockyard, the Créole, commanded by Captain Austin Bissell, foundered on her passage to England, and had it not been for the presence of other ships, would have consigned her officers and crew to a watery grave.

On the 2nd of July the British 38-gun frigate Minerve, Captain Jahleel Brenton, grounded and was captured at the entrance of the harbour of Cherbourg. The circumstances under which this happened have been so fully detailed by Captain Brenton's brother, that we cannot do better than transcribe our contemporary's account.

" In the evening the Minerve, running close in with Cherbourg in a thick fog, mistook Fort de la Liberté for Pélée; and a number of vessels being seen to the eastward, the pilot assured the captain he might run amongst them without hesitation. The helm was accordingly put up for the purpose, when just as the ship was about to open her fire she grounded, and the fog at the same time dispersing, discovered her to be in a very perilous situation. She was on the western Cone Head, about six furlongs from Fort de la Liberté, of 70 guns and 15 mortars; and one mile from the isle of Pélée, of 100 guns, and 25 mortars, from both of which a fire almost immediately opened. This happened about nine o'clock in the evening. Captain Brenton, aware that strong and decided measures were necessary, and that the launch of a frigate was not calculated to carry out a bower anchor, immediately despatched his boats armed, to cut out a vessel from under the batteries, of sufficient capacity for the purpose; whilst the launch, with her carronade, should be employed in diverting the fire of two gun-brigs, lying in such a position ahead of the Minerve, as to annoy her greatly by a raking fire. The yawl, being the first boat in the water, was sent under the orders of the Honourable Lieutenant William Walpole, and the other boats were directed to follow as soon as ready; but the gallant officer, to whom the enterprise was intrusted, found his own boat sufficient. He proceeded under a heavy fire of round, grape, and musketry, and from her position close to the batteries, cut out a lugger of 50 tons, laden with stone for the works, and towed her off to the ship. Before the bower anchor could be placed in this vessel, it was necessary to clear her of her cargo, and that this might be done, without adding to the shoal on which the ship lay, she was veered astern by the ebb-tide to the length of a hawser. Unfortunately, the moon shone with great brightness. The enemy's fire became very galling: the more so as no return could be made but from the two forecastle guns, those of the main deck having been all run close forward for the purpose of lightening the ship abaft, where she hung. At 11 p.m. the lugger, being cleared, was brought under the larboard cathead, to receive the small bower anchor, and during this operation, was so frequently struck by the gun-brigs, as to keep a carpenter constantly employed in stopping the shot-holes. By midnight all was ready; a kedge anchor had been previously laid out for the purpose of warping the lugger, but the moment the hawser became taut, it was shot away. Everything now depended upon the boats, which were sent to take the lugger in tow, and succeeded, under a severe fire, in gaining their object, and the anchor was let go in a proper position. At three o'clock in the morning, the wind had entirely subsided, and the captain, almost hopeless of being able to save the ship, contemplated the probable necessity of being obliged to abandon her. With this view he caused the wounded men to be brought up and put into the lugger, destroyed his private signals, and prepared fires in the store-rooms, to be lighted at the last extremity. A fine breeze, however, springing up from the land, as the tide rose, revived the hope of saving the ship, and the wounded men were returned to the cockpit. The lugger's masts were soon after shot away by the guns of the batteries, over the gangway of the Minerve. At four the cap-stan was manned, and many of the crew were killed and wounded as they hove at the bars. At five the ship floated, under the most heartfelt cheers of the crew. It was considered as a certainty, that in the course of two or three minutes they would be out of gun-shot of the batteries, and consequently out of danger ; but this pleasing prospect soon vanished. The wind again declined into a perfect calm, and the last drain of the flood-tide carried the now helpless ship into the harbour, and laid her upon a broken cone. In this situation she remained until the top of high water, when she surrendered, after sustain-ing the fire of the enemy for 10 hours, and having 11 men killed and 16 wounded.

"Such was the state of her masts that, had there been a moderate breeze, they must have gone by the board. She was lightened in the course of the day by the French, and got off. The capture of so fine a frigate at the commencement of the war, occasioned great triumph, and was announced in the theatre at Brussels by Buonaparte in person ; who, addressing the au-dience, stated the circumstance in the following terms : ' La guerre vient de commencer sous les plus heureuse auspices, une superbe frégate de l'ennemi vient de se rendre à deux de nos chaloupes canonnières.' The ship was called the ' Canonnière,' in order to support this despicable falsehood.

"Captain Brenton was detained a prisoner in France for two years and a half ; many of his officers and men died in captivity. The greater part, suffering a barbarous imprisonment of eleven years, were not released till the tyrant was defeated on the plains of Leipsic, in 1814. A British sailor, who had both his legs shot off while the Minerve lay under the fire of the bat-teries, was carried to the cockpit. Waiting for his turn to be dressed, he heard the cheers of the crew on deck, and eagerly demanded what they meant. Being told the ship was off the shoal, and would soon be clear of the forts ; ' Then d—n **the** legs!' exclaimed the poor fellow, and taking his knife from his pocket, he cut the remaining muscles which attached them to him, and joined in the cheers with the rest of his comrades. When the ship was taken he was placed in the boat to be conveyed to the hospital ; but determined not to outlive the loss of liberty, he slacked his tourniquets and bled to death." [1]

To this account we have only to add, that, among the gun-vessels which attacked the Minerve in her defenceless situation, were the two brigs Chiffon and Terrible, each armed with eight or ten heavy long guns. They, in fact, were the " chaloupes cannonières " alluded to in the French accounts. In capturing the Minerve, the French got back one of their own frigates ; and they represent her, truly, we believe, to have mounted, including fourteen 32-pounder carronades and six nines on the quarter-deck, and forecastle, 48 guns.

In the month of January, 1806, and not before, Captain Brenton was released from his captivity in exchange for Captain Infernet, of the Intrépide, taken at the battle of Trafalgar. At a court-martial subsequently held at Portsmouth, Captain Brenton, his officers, and surviving ship's company were not only most honourably acquitted for the loss of the Minerve, but highly praised for their gallant defence of her.

On the 4th of July, in the evening, the British 38-gun frigate Naiad, Captain James Wallis, sent her boats, under the orders of Lieutenant William Dean, assisted by Lieutenant John Louis, Lieutenant of marines Robert Irwin, and Messrs. Gordon Glenny, and Stewart, midshipmen, to cut out from among the rocks and shoals of the Saintes near Brest the French national schooner Providence, of two guns and 22 men and boys, Lieutenant Martres Préville, on her way from the foundry near Nantes to Brest, laden with heavy cannon, 36, 24, and 18 pounders and some choice ship-timber. Notwithstanding all the difficulties they had to encounter in the rapidity of the tide and the number of rocks and shoals with which the French schooner was surrounded and protected, the British boats brought her safely off, without the occurrence of the slightest accident.

On the afternoon of the 24th of July a heavy squall from

---

[1] Brenton, vol. iii., p. 213.

the land induced the two French 74s in Cape François, the Duquesne, Commodore Pierre-Maurice-Julien Querangal, and Duguay-Trouin, Captain Claude Touffet, accompanied by the 40-gun frigate Guerrière, Captain Louis-Alexis Beaudouin, to put to sea, in the hope to be able to effect their escape to Europe. On clearing the harbour, the two 74s hauled to the westward, but not unseen by a part of the British blockading squadron; which then consisted of the four 74-gun ships Belle-rophon, Commodore John Loring, and Elephant, Theseus, and Vanguard, Captains George Dundas, John Bligh, and James Walker.

At about 9 P.M., when darkness favoured the manœuvre, the French ships separated, the Duguay-Trouin tacking to the east-ward, while the Duquesne continued her course alongshore to the westward. The Elephant being the weathermost of the chasing ships, was ordered to tack after the Duguay-Trouin; while the commodore, in the Bellerophon, accompanied by the 18-pounder 32-gun frigates Æolus and Tartar, Captains Andrew Fitzherbert Evans and John Perkins, pursued the Duquesne. At about midnight the Theseus and Vanguard joined in the chase. On the 25th, at 7 A.M., the Theseus was detached in conse-quence of a heavy firing being heard to the eastward. At 8 A.M. a brigade battery opened a fire upon the Duquesne, which she returned. The Vanguard and Tartar, towards noon, were fast coming up with the French ship; and at about 3 h. 30 m. P.M., after an exchange of several shot from bow and stern chasers, the Duquesne struck her colours. It appears that the French ship sustained no loss; nor did the British loss amount to more than one man killed and one wounded on board the Vanguard. The prize, a fine 74 of 1901 tons, was afterwards added to the British navy under her French name; but being, in the following year, carelessly run aground on Morant Keys, went to England only to be broken up.

The Elephant was not so fortunate as to make a prize of her chase. At daylight, when off Cape Picolet, Captain Dundas saw the Duguay-Trouin about a mile from him, and immediately wore in pursuit. At 6 A.M. the French 74 opened a fire from her stern chasers, and hulled the British ship two or three times. Soon afterwards the Elephant gained a position upon the star-board quarter of the Duguay-Trouin, and there fired into her several distant broadsides. About this time the British 18-gun ship-sloop Snake, Captain William Roberts, made herself known in the north-west quarter; but the appearance of the

Guerrière frigate to windward, or some other unexplained cause, prevented the Elephant from maintaining her position. The consequence was, that both the Duguay-Trouin and the Guerrière effected their escape. The Elephant had a few shot in her hull, and one in her bowsprit, and sustained some slight damage in her rigging and sails; but it does not appear that a single man on board of her was hurt.

The French 74 and frigate steered straight for Europe, and reached latitude 46° 40' north, longitude 11° 16' west, without any occurrence worth notice. On the 29th of August, in the afternoon when as near as that to the port to which they were bound, Ferrol, they fell in with the British 38-gun frigate Boadicea, Captain John Maitland. The latter immediately made sail in chase, and before dark ascertained that the strangers were enemies. On the 31st, at daybreak, the weather being foggy, the strange ships were not discernible. At 1 h. 30 m. P.M., however, the fog having dispersed, and the wind shifted from west to east-north-east, the Duguay-Trouin and Guerrière again made their appearance, and were now so near as fully to discover that the largest and weathermost ship was a French 74.

This would have justified Captain Maitland in discontinuing the pursuit, except perhaps to watch the enemy's motions and endeavour to ascertain his route. Being aware, however, that French ships, ships, singly and in small divisions, were coming from the island of St. Domingo; and that they were mostly armed en flûte, and manned with a very sickly, as well as numerically inferior crew, Captain Maitland resolved to have some stronger proof that the two ships to leeward were not of that description. Accordingly the Boadicea stood on; and at 2 P.M., when passing at the distance of about a quarter of a mile, exchanged broadsides with the Duguay-Trouin. The fire from the latter, although ineffectual, indicated that the ship was fully armed; and the Boadicea found it necessary to make all sail to escape from her opponents so decidedly superior to her. The Duguay-Trouin and Guerrière, who was considerably to leeward of her consort, immediately wore round in pursuit of the British frigate; but finding, at 2 h. 50 m. P.M., that the Boadicea was gaining ground, the French 74 and frigate gave over the chase and hauled to the south-east.

It is stated, in a contemporary work, that the Boadicea brought down the Duguay-Trouin's foretopsail-yard, and sent several shot between wind and water; and that according to the testimony of a prisoner on board the 74, the latter was compelled to keep her pumps incessantly going for three days.[1] With respect to the fall of the topsail-yard, no notice is taken of it in the Boadicea's log; and the alleged damage to the hull of the Duguay-Trouin rests upon very questionable authority.

On the 2nd of September the latter ship and her consort arrived off Cape Prior. Here they fell in with a British squadron, under Commodore Sir Edward Pellew. The only ship of this squadron, in a situation to chase with any effect, was the Culloden 74, Captain Barrington Dacres; and at about 11 h. 50 m. A.M. the latter commenced action with the Duguay-Trouin and Guerrière, both of whom were well to windward. The French 74, being the weathermost ship, got first into Corunna, the forts of which fired at the Culloden as she approached. With the frigate the latter kept up a running fight until 2 h. 30 m. P.M.; when, being almost in the jaws of the port, the British 74 was obliged to haul off. The Culloden had four men wounded ; and the Guerrière, according to the French accounts, six men killed and 15 wounded, including among the latter her captain and first-lieutenant. The frigate's masts and rigging were also much cut.

On the 11th of July, in the forenoon, as the British 18-gun brig-sloop Racoon (16 carronades, 18-pounders, and two long sixes[2]), Captain Austen Bissell, was working between the islands of Guanda and St. Domingo, she observed, and immediately bore up for, a French brig-corvette, lying at anchor in Leogane roads. The latter which was our old acquaintance the Lodi, now reduced in force to 10 guns, 6-pounders, and 61 men, and commanded by Lieutenant Pierre-Isaac Taupier, placed springs on her cables, and prepared to repel the attack of the British vessel. At 3 h. 15 m. P.M., having anchored, with a spring on her cable, within 30 yards of the Lodi, the Racoon commenced the action. After a mutual cannonade of 30 minutes' duration, the French brig cut her cables, and began to make off; whereupon the Racoon cut also, and, following closely, compelled her opponent, at the end of ten minutes more, to strike her colours. The Lodi was nearly unrigged by the Racoon's well-directed fire, and sustained a loss of one man killed and 14 wounded. The Racoon had only one person wounded, master's mate Thomas Gill, whose left arm was carried away by a round shot.

On the 17th of August, at 1 P.M., the Racoon, cruising off

---

[1] Marshall, vol. i. p. 845.

[2] The Racoon's carronades had originally been 32-pounders (see vol. ii., p. 415); but on March 3, 1800, these were ordered to be exchanged for 24s ; and, on September 14, 1802, the latter were again exchanged for 18s. On this subject see vol. i., p. 456, note Y*.

San-Jago in the island of Cuba, in company with a prize-schooner, observed an armed brig coming alongshore ; and who, soon afterwards, hauled her wind to speak a schooner which had been avoiding the Racoon since morning. At 3 P.M. the strange brig and schooner bore up together, under all sail, with a strong breeze. Captain Bissell stood off until certain of fetching them, and then made sail in shore. At 4 h. 15 m. P.M. the brig hoisted French colours, and fired a gun, still keeping within half a mile of the shore, under a press of sail. At 4 h. 20 m. P.M. she fired her broadside at the Racoon, and attempted to cross the latter's hawse ; but the Racoon although going eight knots through the water, put her helm hard a-port, and fired her broadside, which, as the two vessels were nearly on board of each other, brought down the French brig's studding-sails, top-sails, &c. The latter then luffed up, ran on shore in a small rocky bay, and struck her colours. To avoid a similar fate, the Racoon hove in stays, and, on wearing round, discovered the breakers nearly under her stern. In about half an hour the French brig rehoisted her colours, and was repeatedly fired upon, in passing, by the Racoon. Towards sunset the former's mainmast went overboard, and the vessel fell on her beam-ends. As the French brig had landed boats full of armed men, and lined the shore, and the Racoon was 44 men short of complement, including her two lieutenants, Captain Bissell felt himself obliged to refuse the application of the master, Mr. John Thompson, to go, with a few picked men, and endeavour to burn the vessel. By morning the latter had lost her remaining mast, and lay a perfect wreck full of water.

On this occasion the Racoon sustained neither loss nor damage. As to the name and force of his opponent, Captain Bissell says : " I have since learned her name is La Mutine, national brig, carrying 18 long 18-pounders, and was full of men from Port-au-Paix, bound to St.-Jago." Such a force for a brig has not been met with. The guns, if 18-pounders, must have been carronades ; or, as is more probable, were long eights or sixes.

On the 13th of October, in the afternoon, the Racoon, still commanded by the same enterprising officer, while cruising off Cumberland harbour in the island of Cuba, observed several vessels to windward coming close alongshore, all of which, before sunset, hauled in towards the harbour. Having heard of the evacuation of Port-au-Prince, Captain Bissell anchored in a small bay, in the expectation of seeing those vessels pass him in the night. Daylight on the 14th discovered eight or nine sail, a few miles to windward, nearly becalmed. The Racoon instantly weighed, with a fine land wind, and proceeded in chase. At 6 h. 30 m. A.M. a brig, a schooner, and a cutter, all apparently full of men, hoisted French colours, and fired guns to windward. The brig attempted to get in-shore of the Racoon, and her two consorts, with the assistance of their sweeps and boats, endeavoured to join her. The land breeze, however, carried the Racoon within gun-shot of the brig; which, after receiving one or two broadsides, struck, and proved to be the Petite-Fille, French national gun-brig, having on board 180 troops, including about 50 officers of all ranks.

Scarcely had the Racoon sent an officer and a small party of men to secure her prize, than the schooner and cutter, having got nearly within gun-shot, commenced firing. Calms and baffling winds prevented the Racoon from getting nearer until 10 A.M., when the sea-breeze set in. At 11 A.M. the two vessels bore up together, evidently with a determination to board the Racoon, the cutter steering for her bows, and the schooner hauling out to pass astern. The British brig shortened sail to receive her two opponents, but kept herself under sufficient command to counteract their design. When the assailants had arrived within pistol-shot, the Racoon fired a broadside at the cutter, who speedily returned it with long guns and musketry. The Racoon then wore round and fired her opposite broadside into the schooner; and so, alternately, maintaining a running fight, and preventing either from boarding. This mode of engaging lasted more than an hour, both schooner and cutter keeping up an incessant fire of musketry; nor was it until she had been literally beaten to a wreck, and had lost many men in killed, that the cutter struck her colours. She proved to be the Amelie, a national vessel, carrying four carriage-guns, with swivels, and upwards of 70 troops.

Having taken possession of the cutter, the Racoon crowded sail after the schooner, the Jeune-Adèle, carrying six small guns and 80 troops; and which vessel, on being approached within gun-shot and fired at, surrendered without further resistance. Standing in-shore to rejoin her first prize, the Racoon soon discovered that the Frenchmen on board, while the latter was engaging the cutter and schooner, had overpowered the prize-crew, and run the brig on shore among the rocks. Captain Bissell, however, got back his officer and men. The loss on board the cutter and schooner was about 40 in killed and wounded; that of the Racoon was only one person wounded, Mr. Thompson, the master, who in the early part of the action had received a violent contusion, which completely disabled him.

On the 14th of August, when in latitude 48° north, longitude 16° west, on her homeward voyage, the British East-India Company's ship Lord Nelson, Captain Robert Spottiswood, of 26 guns (20 long 18 and six long 12 pounders), and 102 men in crew, exclusive of passengers, was fallen in with by the French ship-privateer Bellone, of 34 guns, including 24 long eights on her main deck, and 260 men. An action ensued, and lasted an hour and a half, when the privateer succeeded in carrying her opponent by boarding, but not until the Bellone had been once repulsed, and the Indiaman sustained a loss of five men killed and 31 wounded. Placing an officer and 41 men in charge of the Lord Nelson, the Bellone proceeded with her towards Corunna. On the 20th a British frigate chased the two ships, and would have retaken the Indiaman, had not the Bellone, trusting to her great sailing powers, led away the former. The Lord Nelson, now alone, was attacked on the 23rd by an English cutter-privateer, of fourteen 6-pounders ; and the latter, highly to the credit of her officers and crew, maintained a two hours' action before she was beaten off.

On the 25th, at 1 P.M., in latitude 46° north, longitude 12° west, the British 18-gun brig-sloop Seagull (sixteen 24-pounder carronades and two sixes), Captain Henry Burke, discovered to leeward and chased the Lord Nelson. At 5 P.M. the latter hoisted French colours, and fired a gun. At 7 P.M the Seagull having got within gun-shot, an action commenced ; which continued, with very slight intermission, until 6 A.M. on the 26th ; when the brig, having received two shot between wind and water, had her masts and rigging much wounded and cut up, and her foreyard shot away in the slings, hauled off to refit. At 8 h. 30 m., just as the Seagull, having replaced her damaged rigging, was about to renew the action, a British squadron, of four sail of the line, under Captain Sir Edward Pellew, in the 80-gun ship Tonnant, hove in sight. By noon, or a little after, the Colossus, the advanced ship of Sir Edward's squadron, overtook and recaptured the Lord Nelson. In her two actions, particularly in that with the Seagull, the Indiaman had received considerable damage in hull, masts, and rigging : her loss by the brig's fire has not been recorded. The loss sustained by the Seagull amounted to two seamen killed, and seven seamen and one marine wounded.

On the 9th of September, at daylight, the British hired cutter

Sheerness, of eight 4-pounders and 30 men and boys, commanded by Lieutenant Henry Rowed, having the look-out on the French fleet in Brest harbour, observed, close in-shore, two chasse-marées stealing towards the port. Sending a boat, with seven men and the mate, to cut off one, the Sheerness herself proceeded in chase of the other, then nearly five miles distant, and close under a battery about nine miles to the eastward of Bec du Raz. At 10 A.M. it fell calm, and the only mode of pursuing the enemy was by a small boat suspended at the stern of the Sheerness, and which with difficulty would contain five men. Lieutenant Rowed acquainted the crew with his determination to proceed in this boat, and called for four volunteers to accompany him. Immediately John Marks the boatswain, and three others, came forward; and the boat with her five hands put off from the cutter, in chase of the chasse-marée, then about four miles off, and, by the aid of her sweeps, nearing the shore very fast.

After the boat had pulled for two hours, the chasse-marée was seen to run on shore under the above-mentioned battery, which stood within a stone's throw of the beach. Notwithstanding this, and that there were 30 French soldiers drawn up on the beach to protect the vessel, Lieutenant Rowed continued his pursuit; and, as he and his four followers laid the French chasse-marée on board on one side, her crew deserted her from the other. It was then that the soldiers opened a heavy fire of musketry upon the British, who had just commenced cutting the cable, and were using other means to get the vessel afloat. In order that the French soldiers might not see how to point their pieces, the British seamen, although there was not a breath of wind, hoisted the foresail; but of which the halliards, almost at the same moment, were shot away. Fortunately for the enterprising crew now on board the chasse-marée, the tide was flowing and aided their exertions: the vessel got off, and the boat commenced towing her from the shore. Fortunately, also, not a man of the five was hurt, although, as afterwards counted, 49 musket-balls, intended for them, had lodged in the side and the two masts of the chasse-marée.

Scarcely had the prize been towed a third of a mile, when a French boat, containing an officer and nine men, armed with muskets, and who had pulled up in the wake of the vessel unobserved by the boat ahead of her, suddenly made her appearance alongside. In an instant, and without waiting for any orders, John Marks, the boatswain, dropping his oar, and neglecting to take any kind of weapon in his hand, leaped from the boat on board the chasse-marée ; and, running to the side close off which the French boat lay, stood, in a menacing attitude, unarmed as he was, for at least half a minute, until his four companions, with a supply of muskets and ammunition, and who could only quit their ticklish boat one at a time, got to his assistance. If not astonishment at the sight, it must have been a generous impulse, that prevented the Frenchmen from shooting or sabring the brave boatswain ; for they were, it seems, near enough to the vessel's side, to have done even the latter. Seeing that Lieutenant Rowed and his four men were determined to defend their prize, the French boat, after a feeble attempt to get possession, sheered off, the soldiers in her keeping up, for a short time, as they receded from the vessel, an ineffectual fire of musketry. The battery also opened a fire upon the chasse-marée as she was towing off; but it proved equally harmless with that from the soldiers, both on the beach and in the boat.

The capture of two unarmed chasse-marées (for the mate had taken his prize without any difficulty) would, indeed, be a trifling occurrence, were it not for the circumstances under which one of them had been boarded and brought off ; circumstances that ennoble the act, and rank it above many which are blazoned in the Gazette, and yield to the parties both praise and promotion. The navy-list shows, that Lieutenant Rowed gained no step in his profession : indeed it was not, as the same document proves, until nearly ten years afterwards, that he was made a commander. As to the boatswain, he, it appears, on account of the very station he filled, and, by every account so well filled, was, according to the etiquette of the service, excluded from the reward of promotion. It was only, therefore, from the Patriotic Fund at Lloyd's that he could receive some testimony of the high opinion entertained of his services. Lieutenant Rowed himself made the application, founding it on the inability of the admiralty, without violating precedent, to provide for the " poor fellow ; and who," adds his commander, and where was there a better judge ? " exclusive of his bravery, is a very good character." The committee, it is believed, presented Mr. Marks with a handsome sum of money. Acts like this of Lieutenant Rowed and his four men (the names of all of whom we would record, did we know them) deserve to be made public, if only for the example they hold out, not of adequate reward certainly, but of the impunity which often accompanies the most hazardous attacks. Let him, therefore, who is disposed to calculate the chances of personal risk that may attend the enterprise in which he is called upon to embark, reflect upon the 49 musket-balls which were aimed at, and yet missed, Lieutenant Rowed and the four gallant fellows who were on board of this captured French chasse-marée.

On the 20th of September, at 5 P.M., the British hired-cutter Princess Augusta, of eight 4-pounders and 26 men, commanded by Lieutenant Isaac William Scott, being off the Texel, saw two schooners in the south-west, bearing down under British colours. The cutter, however, suspected them to be enemies, and cleared for action. At 6 h. 30 m. P.M. the schooner hauled down the English and hoisted Dutch colours. The largest, which was the Union, Lieutenant St. Faust, mounting 12 guns, and stated to have had on board 70 men, hailed from to-windward, and then opened her broadside, which killed the cutter's gunner and boat-swain, and mortally wounded Lieutenant Scott. The cutter was not slow in returning the fire, and successfully repulsed several attempts to board. Meanwhile the other schooner, the Wraak, Lieutenant Doudet, mounting eight guns, and manned with about 50 men, had ranged up under the cutter's lee, and now poured in her broadside. This schooner also made a vain attempt to board. After an hour's engagement, during which the large schooner's bowsprit was several times over the cutter's stern, the latter beat off both her opponents, with the additional loss of two seamen wounded, making a total loss of three, including her commander, killed, and two wounded.

In his dying moments, Lieutenant Scott recommended the master to fight the cutter bravely, and desired him to tell the admiral (Lord Keith) that he had done his duty. The lieutenant certainly had done so in a manner that became a British officer; and Mr. Joseph Thomas, the master, fully acted up to his com-mander's injunctions: he, and the few hands about him, fought their vessel heroically, and by so doing brought her off in safety. The same Dutch newspaper from which we have extracted the names of the two schooners, states, that the carpenter of the Wraak was killed, and her first-lieutenant and several of her men badly wounded.

On the 9th of October, in the evening, the British 16-gun brig-sloop Atalante, Captain Joseph Ore Masefield, chased and drove on shore off the mouth of the river Pennerf, near St. Guildas, two French ketches and one brig. The wind blowing directly off shore, Captain Masefield conceived it practicable to cut the vessels out; and accordingly, soon after dark, the six-oared cutter under Lieutenant John Hawkins, and the five-oared cutter under Mr. Richard Burstal, the master, were despatched upon that service, the Atalante standing in, as close as the shoals would permit, to protect them.

At 9 h. 30 m. P.M. the two boats reached the French vessels, when Lieutenant Hawkins, with his boat, boarded and took possession cf the in-shore vessel, then fast aground within 120 yards of the beach ; but the British could not succeed in getting her afloat, owing to a heavy fire of musketry from a number of troops drawn up on the beach, assisted by two field-pieces and a party of troops, which had previously embarked from the shore on board of the other two vessels. Thus frustrated in his plan, the lieutenant cut the cable of the vessel, and then abandoned her to go to the assistance of his coadjutor in the other boat.

In the mean time Mr. Burstal, with a sergeant of marines and five other men, in defiance of a party of 10 soldiers armed with muskets and bayonets, had boarded and carried the French brig; but not until the former had killed six of the soldiers, hove two overboard, and drove the remainder, with the brig's crew, down her hatchway. Finding that this vessel, besides being light and of no value, was also fast aground upon a ridge of rocks, Lieutenant Hawkins, who had now joined his companion, contented himself with cutting the brig's cable; not thinking proper, from motives of humanity, to set the vessel on fire, as several people were heard below, supposed to be wounded. In this very dashing little exploit, Mr. Burstal's boat, in boarding the French brig, had one man killed and two wounded, the only loss sustained by the British.

On the 26th of October the British 18-gun ship-sloop Osprey, Captain George Younghusband, being off Trinidad, saw and chased a suspicious sail under the land. On arriving within four miles of the stranger the Osprey found herself becalmed, and at the same time discovered, from the number of sweeps rowed by her, that the vessel was a privateer. The Osprey's further progress being checked by the calm, Captain Younghusband despatched three boats, under the command of Lieutenant Robert Henderson, in the cutter, to attempt the capture of the schooner. The unequal speed of the boats being greatly in favour of the cutter, Lieutenant Henderson, apprehensive that if he waited for his companions the privateer would escape, continued to pull ahead, and at length, with his 17 seamen, in the bravest manner, under a heavy fire from the guns and musketry of the vessel, boarded and captured the French privateer-schooner Ressource, mounting four 4-pounders, with a crew of 43 men, of whom two were killed and 12 wounded. On board the cutter, Lieutenant Henderson and four seamen were wounded, one of the latter dangerously.

On the 27th of October the British 16-gun ship-sloop Merlin, Captain Edward Pelham Brenton, and 14-gun schooner Milbrook, Lieutenant Mauritius Adolphus Newton De Starck, discovered the French lugger-privateer Sept-Frères, of two carriage-guns and 30 men, commanded by Captain Pollet, endeavouring to get into Calais. Captain Brenton immediately despatched in pursuit of her the boats of the Merlin, under the orders of Lieutenant Henry Clement Thompson, who had already lost an arm in the service. Finding her retreat effectually cut off by the British boats, the lugger ran herself on shore about half a mile to the westward of Gravelines. In the evening the Milbrook stood in, and anchored within musket-shot of the Sept-Frères; and, in the face of a heavy fire opened upon the schooner and the boats by some field-pieces brought down to the beach, the British totally destroyed the French lugger, without incurring any loss, although the Milbrook was several times struck by shot.

On the 3rd of November, while the 18-pounder 36-gun frigate Blanche, Captain Zachary Mudge, was lying at an anchor off the entrance of Mancenille bay, island of St. Domingo, the French cutter Albion, armed with two 4-pounders, six swivels, and 20 muskets, and manned with 43 officers and men, was discovered lying close to the guns of Monte-Christi, waiting to carry her cargo, consisting of 52 bullocks, to the relief of the garrison of Cape-François. As the cutter, notwithstanding her proximity to the fort, which mounted four long 24-pounders and three field-pieces, appeared to be assailable, Captain Mudge, on the same day, despatched the launch, barge, and two cutters, with 63 officers and men, under the command of Lieutenant William Braithwaite, to attempt cutting her out. The boats returned unsuccessful, not owing to any lack of zeal in officers or men, but to their having proceeded to the attack in open day, with the sea-breeze blowing right into the bay. The battery, in consequence, had begun early to fire at the boats, and soon convined Lieutenant Braithwaite that, should he even succeed in capturing the cutter, it would, in the state of the wind, be impossible to get her from the shore without a great sacrifice of lives.

With more judgment, a night attack was determined upon, and Lieutenant Edward Nicolls, of the marines, volunteered, with one boat, to attempt cutting out the vessel. His offer was accepted; and on the evening of the 4th the red cutter, with 13 men, including himself, pushed off from the frigate. A doubt respecting the sufficiency of the force, or some other cause, induced Captain Mudge to order the barge, with 22 men, under the orders of Lieutenant the Honourable Warwick Lake, first of the Blanche, to follow the red cutter and supersede Lieutenant Nicolls in the command. The second boat joined the first, and, as soon as the two arrived abreast of the French cutter, Lieutenant Nicolls hailed Lieutenant Lake, and pointed her out to him; but the latter professed to disbelieve that the vessel in sight was the Albion: he considered that she lay on the opposite or north-east side of the bay, and with the barge proceeded in that direction; leaving the red cutter to watch the motions of the vessel, which Lieutenant Nicolls still maintained was the Albion, the object of their joint search.

It was now 2 h. 30 m. A.M. on the 5th, and the land wind was blowing fresh out of the bay. An hour or two more, and the day would begin to dawn, and the breeze to slacken, perhaps wholly to subside. The men in the boat were few, but their hearts were stout. In short the red cutter commenced pulling, cautiously and silently, towards the French vessel; the crew of which, expecting a second attack, had made preparations to meet it. As soon as the boat arrived within pistol-shot, the cutter hailed. Replying to the hail with three hearty cheers, the boat rapidly advanced, receiving in quick succession two volleys of musketry. The first passed over the heads of the British; but the second severely wounded the coxswain, the man at the bow-oar, and a marine. Before the French cutter could fire a third time, Lieutenant Nicolls, at the head of his little party, sprang on board of her. The French captain was at his post, and discharged his pistol at Lieutenant Nicolls just as the latter was within a yard of him. The ball passed round the rim of the lieutenant's belly, and, escaping through his side, lodged in the fleshy part of his right arm. Almost at the same moment a ball, either from the pistol of Lieutenant Nicolls, or from the musket of a marine standing near him, killed the French captain. After this the resistance was trifling; and the surviving officers and men of the French cutter were presently driven below and subdued, with the loss, besides their captain killed, of five men wounded, one of them mortally.

As yet, not a shot had been fired from the battery, although it was distant scarcely 100 yards from the cutter. Judging that the best way to keep the battery quiet would be to maintain the appearance of the Albion's being still in French possession, and able to repulse her assailants, Lieutenant Nicolls ordered the marines of his party to continue firing their muskets: the seamen, meanwhile, busied themselves in getting the vessel under sail. A spring having been run out from the cutter's quarter to her cable, and the jib cleared, the cable was cut, and the jib hoisted to cast her. At this moment the barge came alongside, and Lieutenant Lake took command of the prize. Scarcely had he done so, and the musketry by his orders been discontinued, when the battery opened a fire of round and grape, which killed two of the Blanche's people. However, the breeze being fair, and blowing moderately strong, the captured cutter, with two boats towing her, soon ran out of gun-shot, and without incurring any further loss, joined the frigate in the offing.

Cutting out an armed vessel is usually a desperate service, and the prize seldom repays the loss which is sustained in capturing her. The spirit engendered by such acts is, however, of the noblest, and, in a national point of view, of the most useful kind: its emulative influence spreads from man to man, and from ship to ship, until the ardour for engaging in services of danger, services, the repeated success of which has stamped a lasting character upon the British navy, requires more frequently to be checked than to be incited. An attack by boats upon an armed sailing-vessel, as respects the first foot-hold upon her deck especially, may be likened to the "forlorn hope" of a besieging army; great is the peril, and great ought to be the reward. So the reward usually is, if the affair be represented in its true colours to the proper authority. The same officer, who, when about to transmit to his government the account of an engagement between his ship and another, fears saying too much, lest he should be chargeable with egotism, when, in the routine of his duty, he has to write about an act performed exclusively by his subordinates, enters minutely into the merits of the case, points out those who distinguished themselves, and separates, as well as he is able, the actual combatants from such as, by accident or otherwise, did not partake of the danger; well knowing that, without this act of justice on his part, promotion, honours, and other rewards may light upon the undeserving, while he who fought and bled, he who both planned and achieved the enterprise, may find himself passed over and neglected.

The captain of the Blanche had a fine opportunity, without detracting from the bravery of one party, to state the good fortune (call it nothing else) of the other. Here follows his letter to the admiralty : "Having gained intelligence that there was a large coppered cutter full of bullocks for the Cape, lying close under the guns of Monte-Christi (four 24-pounders and three field-pieces), notwithstanding her situation, I was convinced we could bring her off; and at 2 this morning she was masterly and gallantly attacked by Lieutenant Lake, in the cutter, and Lieutenant Nichols of the marines, in the barge, who cut her out. She is ninety-two tons burthen, coppered close-up and fastened, with two 4-pounders, six swivels, and twenty muskets. This affair cost me two men killed, and two wounded."

The misstatements in this letter, now that the correct details are confronted with them, discover their importance ; and it cannot be doubted that Captain Mudge had a favourite whom he was determined to serve, no matter at whose expense. How came he not to name Lieutenant Nicolls among the wounded? It was not a scratch of his finger nor a graze of his shin, but a hole on each side of his body and a ball in his arm, that sent him bleeding to the Blanche's cockpit. Who would expect that, of the "two" men wounded, one was a commissioned officer? In every case, except this, the rank, if not the name, of the officer is stated in the official letter ; and, in some letters, the smallest boy in the ship, if he has been wounded ever so slightly, may find his name in the returns. The name of Lieutenant "Nichols," however, as the commanding officer of one of the boats (not of "the barge"), entitled him, in the estimation of the committee at Lloyd's, to a second best claim upon their bounty ; so that, when the Patriotic Fund presented Lieutenant Lake, "for his gallantry," with a sword valued at 50l., they gave Lieutenant Nicolls one valued at 30l. Another quarter, equally deceived, promoted one officer, but, until a subsequent explanation at least, paid no attention to the claims of the other.

Between the two attacks upon the Albion, another boat-party from the Blanche captured, in a very gallant manner, a vessel of superior force. On the 4th, in the morning, the launch, armed with a 12-pounder carronade, and manned with 28 men, under the command of Mr. John Smith, master's mate, attacked, and, after an obstinate conflict of 10 minutes, boarded and carried, as she was coming out of the Caracol passage, a French schooner, mounting one long 8-pounder on a pivot, and manned with 30 men, of whom one was killed and five were wounded. The launch had one man killed and two wounded. The prize was a beautiful ballahou-schooner, and had on board a considerable quantity of dollars.

In his official letter, announcing the capture of this schooner Captain Mudge says: "She is one of the finest vessels of her class I ever saw, and is fit for his majesty's service;" and, to show how ready he was, in some cases, to atone for his apparent neglect of a young officer, Captain Mudge in a postscript adds: "I have omitted mentioning the Honourable Frederick Berkley; but the only apology I can make is saying he behaved nobly, and was much to be envied."

A day or two after the affair of Mr. Smith, midshipman Edward Henry a'Court, with a marine and seven seamen, was despatched from the Blanche in the red cutter, to collect sand for the use of the ship. Although it had been ordered that youngsters, sent upon services of this kind, lest their pugnacious spirit should lead them into danger, were not to be allowed arms, the men in the boat, before they pushed off from the frigate, contrived to smuggle five or six muskets through the ports. It so happened that, in the dusk of evening, the boat fell in with a schooner, nearly becalmed. The midshipman and his little party of sanders unhesitatingly pulled towards her; and, as she had the appearance of a privateer, and might open a cannonade upon them, Mr. a'Court judiciously kept in her wake. Just as the boat had approached the stern of the schooner, a fire of musketry from the latter mortally wounded one man, and badly wounded another, of the boat-party. Mr. a'Court, nevertheless, pulled straight up alongside, and, with the assistance of his five remaining hands, boarded and carried a French schooner, bound to Cape François, having among her passengers a detachment of between 30 and 40 soldiers, commanded by a colonel, who had fought, bled, and distinguished himself at the battle of Arcole. His wound was a fractured skull, and, upon the piece of plate that covered the denuded part, and which extended over a great portion of one side of his head, was engraven, in large characters, the word "Arcole."

When asked how he could surrender to so insignificant a force, the French colonel, with a shrug replied, that it was all owing to "le mal de mer;" and that, had he been on shore, the case would have been otherwise. Let that have been as it may, the conduct of young a'Court evinced unparalleled gallantry, a considerable degree of judgment, and certainly both the officer and men in the boat deserved to have their names recorded for the bravery they had displayed.

No public mention was made by Captain Mudge of this affair, which is, we think, entitled to the publicity and the praise which we have endeavoured to render to a young, enterprising, and gallant officer.

On the 14th of November, while the British 74-gun ship Blenheim, Captain Thomas Graves, lay at anchor off the Diamond Rock, island of Martinique, intelligence reached her that the French privateer-schooner Harmonie, a vessel the most destructive to commerce of any in the Caribbean sea, had just put into the harbour of Marin in the bay of Sainte-Anne. The Blenheim immediately weighed, but, having a strong sea-breeze and lee-current to contend with, did not, until the morning of the 16th, arrive abreast of Marin. Having reconnoitred the harbour, the battery on each side of it, and that situated above the town, Captain Graves resolved to detach 60 seamen under Lieutenants Thomas Cole and Thomas Furber, and 60 marines under Lieutenants George Beatty and Walter S. Boyd, to attempt cutting out the privateer. The seamen in their boats were to attack the latter, while the marines were to endeavour to surprise, or in any event to storm, Fort Dunkirk, a battery of nine guns, situated on the starboard side of the harbour, and the possession of which was necessary, to prevent the island militia from rendezvousing on Marin point, whence they could have much annoyed the British boats on their return.

Just as the party was about to proceed, the British 14-gun brig-sloop Drake, Captain William Ferris, accompanied by the hired armed cutters Swift, joined the Blenheim. Captain Ferris, having volunteered, was permitted to take the command of the expedition, and to add 14 of the Drake's seamen to the 60 from the Blenheim, making a total of 134 seamen and marines, officers included. All things being prepared, the boats with the seamen, towed by the Drake, and those with the marines, by the Swift, at 11 P.M., proceeded off the mouth of Marin harbour, about three miles from the entrance to which the privateer lay. By judiciously timing their departure from the ship, both parties arrived at the same instant at their respective destinations. The marines surprised the fort, took 15 prisoners, dismounted and spiked the guns, among which were six 24-pounders, destroyed the carriages and blew up the magazines; but Lieutenant Beatty humanely spared the barracks, as, had they been set on fire, a large and ripe field of canes adjoining would inevitably have been destroyed.

The boats with the seamen passed the battery on the larboard side of the harbour undiscovered, but the privateer was upon her guard, and commenced a heavy fire on the British; who, nevertheless, in the most prompt and gallant manner, boarded, and in a few minutes carried her. The seamen had one of their number killed and five wounded; the marines, although fired upon by two sentinels, had no one hurt. The Harmonie, mount- ing eight carriage-guns, with a complement of 66 men, had two of the latter killed and 14 wounded. The boats accompanied by their prize, repassed the larboard fort, within musket-shot, but were so fortunate as to escape without further loss. In the conduct of this enterprise, much judgment as well as gallantry was evinced; without which, from the many obstacles opposed to success, the result might not have been so favourable.

On the night of the 10th of December the British 18-pounder 36-gun frigate Shannon, Captain Edward Leveson Gower, in company with the 16-gun ship-sloop Merlin, Captain Edward Pelham Brenton, while standing across from Cape la Hève to Cape la Hougue, in a gale of wind from the south-south-west, was taken under the lee bow by the flood-tide, and carried up towards the river Isigny; "and, when the captain supposed himself to the northward of Cape Barfleur, he had that light- house bearing about north." [1] The night was extremely dark and tempestuous, and the Shannon, about 8 P.M., struck the ground. The Merlin just then got a glimpse of the land in a flash of lightning, and instantly wore from it under her foresail and close-reefed maintopsail. The Shannon, a fine new frigate of 881 tons (sister vessel to the Tribune), just launched, was totally wrecked: her officers and crew, fortunately, were all saved, but made prisoners by the French.

On the 16th, at 11 h. 30 m. A.M., Barfleur lighthouse bearing north half-west distant four leagues, the Merlin discovered her late consort the Shannon on shore under the batteries of Tatihou island. At 5 P.M., having approached quite near to the wreck, Captain Brenton despatched two boats manned and armed, under the orders of Lieutenants John Sheridan and Henry Clement Thompson, to endeavour to set fire to and destroy the frigate: a service which these officers effectually executed, with- out the loss of a man, although exposed to a heavy fire from the

1 Brenton, vol. iii., p. 302.

French batteries. About three years and three months after the loss of the Shannon, her late captain and officers, having returned to their country, were honourably acquitted of all blame by the sentence of a court-martial.

Colonial Expeditions.—West Indies.

A renewal of the war brings us again to the round of successful operations against the colonies of the weaker maritime powers. On the 21st of June, at 11 A.M., Commodore Samuel Hood, with the 74-gun ships Centaur and Courageux, Captains Bendall Robert Littlehales and Benjamin Hallowell, and some smaller vessels, having on board a detachment of the British army under Lieutenant-general Grinfield, anchored in Choc-bay, Sainte-Lucie, for the purpose of reducing the island. Before 5 P.M., by the able disposition of Captain Hallowell, the whole of the troops were disembarked in good order. At 5 h. 30 m. P.M. the French outworks were driven in, and the town of Castries taken. The commandant of Morne-Fortunée, the principal fortress of the island, was then summoned to surrender. Brigadier-general Noguès refusing to do so, the works were stormed at 4 A.M. on the 22nd, and at 4 h. 30 m. were carried, with a loss to the British army of 20 officers and men killed, and 110 wounded. What was the exact strength of the garrison, or the loss which the French sustained in resisting the assault, does not appear by the official despatches; but it is stated, to the credit of the British, considering the custom on such occasions, that not a Frenchman was hurt after possession of the place had been obtained.

On the third day after effecting this capture, the Centaur, accompanied by some smaller vessels containing a division of the troops, sailed from Sainte-Lucie to attack Tobago. On the 31st the expedition arrived off the island, and on the same day the troops, covered by a heavy fire from the ships-of-war, landed without loss. So rapid and so decisive were the movements of the British, that in the evening General Berthier commanding at Fort Scarborough proposed a capitulation; which, by half-past four the following morning, was acceded to, and the island of Tobago again became a colony of Great Britain.

Previously to the end of September the Dutch colonies of Demerara, Essequibo, and Berbice had only changed masters, with equal facility, and happily without bloodshed. In the river Demerara was captured the Batavian 14-gun corvette Hippomenes.

About the middle of June, which was almost immediately after the intelligence of the recommencement of hostilities reached the island of Jamacia, a squadron of ships sailed from Port Royal, to cruise in the neighbourhood of St. Domingo, and co-operate with the Black insurgents in freeing the island of the small remnant of French whom the scurvy and the yellow fever had yet spared, and who still retained possession of the line of posts on the sea-coast. Hitherto their ships had enabled the French to hold and provision these; but the British ships soon drove away or captured the former, and effectually shut up the ports against all succours and supplies from Europe or elsewhere.

By the end of October the only ports remaining in the hands of the French, in what was formerly the French part of the island of St. Domingo, were Cape-François and the mole of St. Nicholas. At the latter port General Noailles commanded, at the former General Rochambeau. Cape-François, besides being blockaded at sea by the British, was invested on land by the insurgents; and the French garrison had the additional misfortune of being reduced to a state bordering on famine.

Thus situated, General Rochambeau, on the 17th of November, proposed to Commodore John Loring, the commanding officer of the British blockading force, to evacuate the Cape, provided he and his garrison were suffered to go to France on board one or more of the ships-of-war in port. Such terms were of course rejected. The general then concluded a treaty with Dessalines, by which, in 10 days from the 20th of November, he was to evacuate the Cape and its dependencies, and to be allowed, himself, and his troops, and their baggage, to retire on board the French ships lying in the harbour. By the fifth day General Rochambeau had embarked his garrison, and hoped to escape the English squadron; but the latter was too vigilant to afford the former even an opportunity of making the attempt. On the 30th, the day on which the truce expired, the Negroes hoisted their colours upon all the forts, and began to prepare for sinking the French ships with red-hot shot, should they any longer delay their departure. To know the reason of this delay, Captain Loring had sent in Captain Bligh with a flag of truce; when, at a meeting between him and Captain Barré, the French naval commanding officer, a rough sketch of a capitulation was drawn up and signed, and General Dessalines was induced to allow the French ships, with colours hoisted, to sail out of the harbour. They were then, after firing each a broadside in return to a shot discharged athwart their bows by one of the British ships, to haul down the French colours and surrender.

The 40-gun frigate Surveillante, accompanied by some smaller vessels, came out in this manner, and was taken possession of by the British; but the Clorinde, another 40-gun frigate, in her way out grounded upon the rocks under Fort St. Joseph at the entrance of the harbour, and beat off her rudder. The frigate, in short, was in so desperate a situation, that the British boats, which had been detached to assist the French ships in getting out of the mole, were returning to the squadron, upon a supposition that no efforts of theirs could save the Clorinde. The ship, which was thus abandoned to her fate, had on board, besides a small crew of from 150 to 200 men, General Lapoype and 700 French troops, together with several of the officers' wives, their women-servants, and children; in all full 900 souls.

Among the boats of the squadron employed upon the service just mentioned, was the launch of the Hercule, manned with from 30 to 40 hands, under the command of Acting-lieutenant Nisbet Josiah Willoughby. From slow-pulling, or from some other unexplained cause, retarded in her progress, the launch was among the rearmost of those boats. Anxious to rescue so many persons as were evidently on board the Clorinde, from the certain death that awaited them, either by perishing in the ship or by being massacred, as was the execrable practice, on the shore; feeling it to be almost a stigma upon the character of the British navy not to make an effort to save human beings, political enemies especially, so critically circumstanced, Lieutenant Willoughby took upon himself the whole responsibility, and put back with his launch towards the grounded ship.

Finding, as he approached the Clorinde, that her side was crowded with men ready to spring into the first boat which came alongside, and knowing that his people, as well as those who entered the launch from the ship, would fall an immediate sacrifice, the lieutenant searched for, and with difficulty procured, a small punt. In this he embarked, directing the launch to lay off, and was soon on board the frigate; which he found heeling much and beating heavily. Despairing now of saving the ship, Lieutenant Willoughby yet resolved to put in practice every resource to save her numerous crew. As the most feasible plan which suggested itself, the lieutenant represented to General Lapoype that, as by the terms of the capitulation the French vessels of war were to haul down their colours when outside the harbour, it would not be a greater sacrifice of national honour, considering the situation of the Clorinde, if he did so imme- diately, and gave the frigate up to him. Lieutenant Willoughby would then, he said, hoist English colours, wait upon General Dessalines, and demand, not only that the British flag should be respected, but that, if assistance could not be procured from the shore, and the Clorinde should be lost in the night then fast approaching, the crew and passengers should be con- sidered as prisoners to the British, and be protected until the commanding officer of the squadron had it in his power to send for them.

General Lapoype readily assenting to the terms proposed, the French flag was hauled down, and replaced by the British flag ; and Lieutenant Willoughby immediately hailed the Haytian officer in command of Fort St. Joseph, and expressed a wish to wait upon General Dessalines. Permission was granted, and Lieutenant Willoughby, after experiencing some difficulty in landing, obtained an interview with the Haytian general, who not only received the British lieutenant with great urbanity, but promised all that he requested. · With the assistance thus ob- tained, and that of two or three more boats which had just joined from the squadron, and favoured by a sudden fall in the wind, Lieutenant Willoughby succeeded in heaving the Clorinde off the rocks. Thus "to the uncommon exertions and pro- fessional abilities," as Rear-admiral Duckworth happily expresses it, of Acting-lieutenant Willoughby, was owing the preservation of more than 900 people's lives, and the acquisition to the British navy of a frigate which, with her late consort, the Surveillante, continued, for many years afterwards, to be one of the finest ships of the 38-gun class.

Having now no French force to blockade at Cape-François, Commodore Loring bore up for the mole of St. Nicolas, to treat with M. Noailles, the French general in command there. On the 2nd of December a proposition to that effect was made ; but the general declined acceding to the terms, alleging that he had provisions for five months, and would not surrender until the last extremity. The Bellerophon and squadron then pro- ceeded with the prizes and prisoners to Jamaica. On the very night on which the blockade of the Mole was raised, General Noailles, having previously made his arrangements, sailed out of the port, with his garrison contained in seven small vessels, and arrived in safety at the island of Cuba. Among the French " Victoires et Conquêtes," recorded in a work bearing that title.

is an extraordinary one performed by M. Noailles on his short voyage to Cuba. It seems that " une corvette anglaise " crossed the path of his brig (on what day or night is not stated), and hailed her, to know if General Noailles was on board. The French brig concealed her numerous crew, and, hoisting English colours, declared that she also had been sent to intercept the general and his garrison. The two vessels then steered in company ; and, in the night, General Noailles, at the head of 30 grenadiers, leaped on board of, and after a short resistance carried, the " corvette anglaise." The conqueror proceeded with his prize to Havana, and died shortly afterwards of the wounds he had received in the action. Notwithstanding the grave manner in which this story is told, the British navy lost no " corvette," or even 4-gun schooner, by capture in these seas, in the year 1803.

Thus, by the departure of the last European garrison from the French part of the island of St. Domingo, were the negroes, after a long and sanguinary struggle, freed from their invaders. A part of the latter had previously escaped to the Spanish part of the island ; and Generals Kerverseau and Ferrand, with a few troops, still occupied the cities of Santo-Domingo and San-Jago. According to a French writer, France, by her expedition to this island, lost 20 general officers and upwards of 40,000 men.[1] This amount must include colonial troops, and some reinforcements which we have not been able to enumerate.

East Indies.

It has already been stated that, on the 6th of March, a small French squadron, consisting of one 74, three frigates, and two transports, with a French governor-general and about 1350 troops on board, sailed from the road of Brest, bound to the East Indies, for the alleged purpose of taking possession of Pondicherry, ceded to France by the treaty of Amiens.[2] On the 28th of April, in a violent gale of wind, the Belle-Poule parted company from the squadron : and, although she called at Madagascar, this fast-sailing frigate anchored in Pondicherry road on the 16th of June, being the 102nd day from her quitting Brest.

The Belle-Poule brought out a French colonel, appointed lieutenant-governor under M. Decaen ; and who now, in pursuance of his instructions, called upon the commanding officers of the different factories to restore the settlement agreeably to

---

[1] Victoires et Conquêtes, tome xiv., p. 330.   [2] See p. 169.

the article in the treaty. Owing to the want of orders, or to the informality of the application, the latter declined giving up their charge; and thus matters remained, when, on the 5th of July, Vice-admiral Peter Rainier, with the 50-gun ship Centurion, Captain John Sprat Rainier, 74-gun ship Tremendous, Captain John Osborn, 64-gun ships Trident and Lancaster, Captains Thomas Surridge and William Fothergill, 44 en-flûte Sheerness, frigates Concorde, Dédaigneuse, and Fox, and ship-sloop Victor, from Bombay, partly in consequence of information from England representing that the peace was not very secure, anchored in the road of Cuddalore, situated about 20 miles to the south-west of Pondicherry. Consequently, when, on the morning of the 11th of July, Rear-admiral Linois, with the Marengo 74, and Atalante and Sémillante frigates, joined the Belle-Poule, Pondicherry and its dependencies still remained in the hands of the British.

Aware that his own and General Decaen's mission to the East had an object in view covertly inimical to British interests, the French admiral could well have dispensed with the presence of a British squadron; and yet no sooner had he anchored than he found himself overlooked by one, consisting of three sail of the line, a 50, and four or five smaller vessels. Two of the squadron, the Trident and Victor, at this time lay at anchor in Pondicherry road; and the remainder, including the flag-ship, in the road of Cuddalore. As soon as he observed the French squadron come to anchor, the British admiral got under way, and advanced nearer; and, on being joined by the Trident and Victor, who had weighed since noon, re-anchored at 7 P.M. about midway between Cuddalore and Pondicherry roads. On the 12th, at 10 A.M., the French transport brig Marie-Françoise joined Admiral Linois, and at 6 P.M. the brig-corvette Bélier, with despatches from France. This vessel had quitted Brest ten days later than the Marengo, and, it was understood, brought out the substance of the king of England's message to his parliament of March 8; with directions to M. Linois to repair instantly to the Isle of France, there to get his ships, already armed and manned on a war establishment, refitted and provisioned, and expect every day to receive an order to commence hostilities against the English. This appears to have been the substance of these despatches, but their full contents have not transpired. The instructions put into the hands of M. Decaen when he sailed from France, and which appear to have been drawn up by Napoleon himself, afford indubitable proofs of his bad faith towards England, particularly as regarded her Indian possessions.[1]

It was not many hours before the arrival of the Bélier, that Captain Joseph-Marie Vrignaud, of the Marengo, accompanied by the French admiral's nephew, had paid a visit to Vice-admiral Rainier, for the purpose of inviting the latter to break-fast on the following morning with M. Linois. The invitation was accepted, and the 16-gun ship-sloop Rattlesnake, which had just joined the squadron, was ordered to be ready to convey Vice admiral Rainier to the anchorage of the Marengo and her consorts. But, whether it was owing to the peremptory nature of his orders, or that he feared their warlike tenour might escape, and he and his ships be detained by the British admiral, the French admiral at midnight, unseen and unheard, slipped his cables, and, with the transport-brig Marie-Françoise, put to sea under all sail.

At daydawn on the 13th, to the surprise of the British, no-thing was to be seen of M. Linois and his ships, either in the road, where he had left his anchors, and even the longboats of his ships fast at their grapnels, or, as far as the eye could stretch, in the offing. In the course of the morning the principal part of the British squadron got under way and set sail for Madras; but the admiral, with the Centurion and one or two of the smaller ships, remained at the anchorage. On the same even-ing the French transport ship Côte-d'Or, with 326 troops on board, anchored in Pondicherry road; and, at noon, the Cen-turion and Concorde got under way and anchored close to her.

On the 15th, at daybreak, the Belle-Poule, who had sepa-rated from her squadron and since been to Madras, appeared off the road, in company with the Terpsichore frigate. The latter cast anchor; but the Belle-Poule, after making some signals to the transport, stood away to sea. At 11 P.M. the Côte-d'Or weighed and dropped out of the road, and in half an hour the Terpsichore was under all sail in chase of her. On the 16th, at daylight, the Terpsichore hailed the transport, and ordered her to return, but the French ship refused. On this the frigate fired a few shot, when the Côte-d'Or hauled down her colours, and quietly accompanied the Terpsichore back to the anchorage. On the 24th, in the forenoon, the French transport was allowed to sail, attended by the British frigate Dédaigneuse, to see that she went nowhere else but to her alleged destination, the Isle of France. On the same day, at 8 P.M., Vice-admiral Rainier

[1] See p. 169, and Appendix, No. 15.

weighed and steered for Madras, where he arrived on the following morning. Shortly afterwards the Dédaigneuse also arrived,
having seen the French transport as far on her way to the Isle
of France as the latitude of 1° 50′ north.

The message of the 8th of March, considered everywhere as
the signal of the approach of war between England and France,
reached Madras on or about the 5th of July. It is probable
that the intelligence was communicated to Admiral Rainier by
the Terpsichore. At all events, in a week or two after the
admiral's arrival at Madras, the British ships began taking on
board their war-stores. It was not, however, until the 3rd of
September that the king's message of the 16th of May, which
was tantamount to a declaration of war, reached that settlement ;
nor until the 13th of September, that the news of the actual
commencement of war arrived at Fort William. The intelligence had been received at Bombay on the 21st of August ;
where, two days afterwards, arrived the board of admiralty's
directions for the conduct to be pursued by Vice-admiral Rainier,
and which could not well have reached him at Madras earlier
than the first week in September.

Rear-admiral Linois, with his squadron, arrived at the Isle of
France on the 16th of August ; and, about the latter end of the
succeeding month, the French 20-gun corvette Berceau, it is
believed, brought out the news of the war. On the 8th of
October (why he deferred sailing till then does not appear) the
French admiral, having detached the Atalante on a special mission to Mascat, a Portuguese settlement in Arabia-Felix, put to
sea with the Marengo, Belle-Poule, Sémillante, and Berceau.
The ships retained on board a portion of the troops they had
brought from France, and with which they were now proceeding to reinforce the garrisons of the Isle of Réunion, or Bourbon,
and of the city of Batavia, the capital of Java.

In the early part of his voyage M. Linois had the good fortune to fall in with and capture several richly-laden English
ships; and, on making Sumatra, he resolved to pay a visit to
the road of Bencoolen, a British settlement upon that island.
A pilot belonging to the port, mistaking the Marengo for, what
by her colours she appeared, an English man-of-war, went off
to her, and anchored the French squadron just out of range of
a battery which commanded the road. Meanwhile the merchant-
vessels, having discovered the true character of the strange
ships, had cut or slipped and proceeded to Sellabar, a small
port about two leagues to the southward of Bencoolen. They

were soon followed by the Sémillante and Berceau, but not in time to prevent six of the vessels from being burnt, and two others run on shore, by their crews. The French burnt the two vessels that were aground, also three warehouses filled with spice, rice, and opium, and carried off a ship and two brigs, richly laden; but not with entire impunity, as the Sémillante had two men killed by a shot from the shore. Having performed this exploit, the French set sail, and on or about the 10th of December anchored in the road of Batavia

BRITISH AND FRENCH FLEETS.

BETWEEN the second abstract of the present and the same of the preceding war,[1] there appears, in the "Sea-service Commission" column, a diminution of no fewer than 10 line-of-battle ships. This arose chiefly out of the extensive plan of reform, projected by the first lord of the admiralty, and since put in practice with all the vigour and perseverance which characterised the proceedings of the gallant earl. Many old and useful officers, and a vast number of artificers, had been discharged from the king's dockyards; the customary supplies of timber, and other important articles of naval stores, had been omitted to be kept up; and some articles, including a large portion of hemp, had actually been sold out of the service. A deficiency of workmen and of materials produced, of course, a suspension in the routine of dockyard business. New ships could not be built; nor—and a very serious misfortune it was—could old ones be repaired. Many of the ships in commission, too, having been merely patched up, were scarcely in a state to keep the sea.[2]

On the other hand, much fraud and peculation was put a stop to; many thousands of pounds were saved to the country; and, if some suffered who had done no wrong, others gained who had long had their rights withheld. In short, Earl St. Vincent, by his measures for reforming the civil branches of the British navy, did much temporary evil, but he also did much permanent good.

A reference to the proper lists will give the names of the purchased enemy's line-of-battle ships and frigates,[3] also of the British ships captured or otherwise lost during the year 1803.[4]

[1] See Appendix, Annual Abstracts, Nos. 12 and 2.
[2] See p. 179.
[3] See Appendix, No. 16.
[4] See Appendix, No. 17

Anything further deserving notice in No. 12 Abstract will be found in the notes belonging to it.

The number of commissioned officers and masters, belonging to the British navy at the commencement of the year, was,

Admirals	41
Vice-admirals	32
Rear-admirals	50
,, superannuated 23	
Post-captains	673
,, superannuated 11	
Commanders, or sloop-captains . . .	409
,, superannuated 48	
Lieutenants	2457
Masters	541

And the number of seamen and marines, voted for the year 1804, was 100,000.[1]

As soon as the commerce of France began to suffer from the viligance and activity of British cruisers, the war acquired among the French, those especially who were engaged in trade and resident along the coasts of the Channel, a truly national character. The conduct of some of the king's ships, in firing upon small towns and defenceless places upon the French coast, excited in the inhabitants a strong feeling of indignation; and some of the London journals betrayed a very ill taste when they extolled such exploits. It was this hostile spirit against the English that induced the first consul, amidst his many plans for a vigorous prosecution of the war, to prefer that plan which had for its basis a descent upon the island that held him at defiance; as if resolved, by a single campaign, to verify the assertion which he had publicly made, that England, unsupported, could not withstand the power of France.

To assemble an army deemed sufficient for the purpose, even though it should amount to 160,000 men, was not very difficult in a country that could boast of a population of thirty millions; nor, with so much manual strength at command, and such high-wrought zeal in the cause, was the construction of 2000 prames, gun-vessels, and flat-bottomed boats, to contain that army, an inexecutable task. But some doubt existed, even in France, about the practicability of getting this formidable armament across the 20 or 30 miles of sea, which so provokingly flowed betwixt it and its destined shore. However, as it was with the reflecting, and not with the labouring, class of society, that any

[1] See Appendix, No. 18.

such doubt existed, the work of preparation still went on, and that with all the enthusiasm for which the French are so celebrated. Almost every department in the state voted a ship of the line, each of the larger villages a frigate, and every commune gave its prame, gun-vessel, flat-bottomed boat, or péniche. Vessels for the flotilla were constructing, not only in the great naval ports and in the small harbours along the coast, but upon the banks of every river that contained more than three feet of water; no matter whether that river emptied itself directly into the ocean, or first united its waters with those of the Seine, the Loire, the Garonne, or the Rhine. Even Paris became for a time a maritime arsenal: two slips were erected there, and many vessels of the smaller kind were launched from them. A due share of attention was also bestowed upon vessels of a more warlike class. At Anvers, or Antwerp, on the river Scheldt, for the first time during a great many years, the keels of ships of the line were laid down. The dockyards of Brest, Lorient, Rochefort, and Toulon also displayed the new-laid keels of several ships of force and magnitude.

Our attention must now be directed to what is going on at the first of the four last-named ports. At the close of the preceding year, the port of Brest was left, owing to the extreme severity of the weather, without a blockading force. Before, however, the new year was many days old, a favourable change enabled Admiral Cornwallis to regain his station off Ushant, and to assemble, by the 12th of January, 13 of his ships. Three or four more subsequently joined. Such had been the exertions in Brest harbour during the winter months, that, by the latter end of April, 17 sail of the line, including two three-deckers, lay at anchor in the road, ready for sea.

The first day of the following month gave birth to a set of directions, framed by Napoleon himself, for the improvement of his fleet in Brest water. He begins by complaining, that the enemy should be permitted, with a small number of vessels, to blockade so considerable a fleet as the one at anchor in that port. He orders that the ships shall get under way every day, as well to exercise the crews, as to harass the British, and favour the passage of the flotilla coming from Audierne; that 200 soldiers shall be placed on board each ship of the line; and who, besides being exercised at the guns and about the rigging and sails, are to row in the ship's launch. Premiums are to be given to those who excel in these matters; and nothing that can excite the emulation of either soldiers or sailors appears to have been overlooked. Every ship of the line is to be provided with a quantity of 36-pound shells for her lower battery, and the men are to be taught how to fire them off with effect. The captains are ordered not to quit their vessels to go on shore, and even the commander-in-chief is not allowed to lodge elsewhere than on board his ship.[1]

About ten days after the date of Napoleon's directions to the minister of marine, Vice-admiral Decrès, two sail of the line from the inner harbour joined themselves to the 17 already at anchor in the road. It does not appear, however, that any movement of consequence took place among the ships ; either because the first consul's attention was too much engrossed by the new dignity he was about to assume, or that he required the presence of the fleet to assist in giving *éclat* to the imposing ceremony, which, on the 14th of that same month of May, made him Emperor of France.

Even after the bustle of this business was over, the Brest ships remained at their moorings until the 25th of July, when, encouraged by a fine wind at east-north-east and a thick fog, the advanced squadron, of five sail of the line and two or three frigates, got under way, and stood for the passage du Raz. A sudden return of clear weather, however, enabled the British look-out cutter to discover and make a signal of the circumstance. Immediately Rear-admiral Sir Thomas Graves, commanding the in-shore squadron, proceeded in chase ; but the French ships, in the mean time, had hauled to the wind, and were working back to Brest road. No second attempt to escape, of which the British outside were aware, was made during the remainder of the year ; although, as will presently appear, an expedition of the utmost consequence had been designed to quit Brest before the end of November.

The number of ships of the line at this time ready for sea in Brest road was 22, exclusive of the Océan three-decker, repairing in the docks, but expected soon to be afloat, the shipwrights having been ordered to work at her by torchlight. This fleet was now under the command of Vice-admiral Ganteaume. A curious circumstance had led to the expulsion of this officer's predecessor. When, in the month of May, the officers of the Brest fleet were called upon to put their signatures to a note for conferring the imperial dignity upon Napoleon, Vice-admiral Truguet, true to his republican principles, refused to sign the paper. He wrote to Buonaparte, assigning his reason ; and, to

[1] Précis des Evènemens, tome xi., p. 195.

show his readiness to perform his duty against the enemies of
the nation, made use of the following laconic expression : " Un
mot, et l'armée est à la voile." Napoleon, feeling himself personally offended, removed the admiral from his command,
dismissed him from being a member of the council of state, and
ordered his name to be struck out of the list of the legion of
honour.

The directions given by Napoleon to his minister of marine
were, that the Brest fleet of 23 (the Océan included) sail of the
line, under Vice-admiral Ganteaume, with from 30,000 to 40,000
troops on board, under General Augereau, should quit port at
the first opportunity that might occur in the month of November, proceed to Lough-Swilly bay in the north of Ireland, and
there disembark the men. Should any difficulty arise, the coast
of Scotland was to receive the troops. Vice-admiral Ganteaume
was then to call off the Texel, and, bringing away with him the
seven Dutch sail of the line and transports with 2500 troops on
board in that harbour, make his appearance before Boulogne.
The 30 sail of the line, by this means assembled, added to the
20 sail under M. Villeneuve approaching from off Rochefort,
would, it was considered, be sufficient to cover the grand flotilla,
and enable it to fulfil the ultimate object of all the expeditions
on foot, a disembarkation of its host of troops on the shores of
England ; and which, it was at last discovered, could not be
accomplished without the powerful aid of the larger vessels.
The year 1804, however, was not destined to witness the attempt,
much less the execution, of this gigantic, and, in the opinion of
most persons, impracticable undertaking.

Before we proceed, as is now our intention, to narrate the
different engagements which, during the present year, ensued
between the British cruisers and the French flotilla, prepared
or preparing for the invasion of England, some account of the
vessels of that flotilla, and of the ports in which they were
assembling, will free the subject from much of the obscurity
that must otherwise attend it. The armed vessels of the
flotilla were divided into five or six classes. It will suffice to
describe the prame, and the gun-vessel, or canonnière. The
prame was a remarkably strong-built vessel, measuring in her
extreme length about 110 French feet, and 25 in breadth, and
drawing from seven to eight feet of water. She was rigged as
a ship, and carried 12 long 24-pounders, with a crew of 38 sailors,
and upwards of 100 soldiers, the majority of them, from daily
practice, as useful on shipboard as the sailors themselves.

Of these prames, or corvettes, 20, each with stalls for 50 horses, were ordered to be constructed; but the number was afterwards greatly augmented.

The first-class gun-vessels, rigged as brigs, were usually armed with three long 24-pounders and an 8-inch mortar, and the second class, with one 24-pounder forward, and a field-piece abaft; some rigged as schooners, and some as luggers. Of these two classes between 600 and 700 were constructed; and, of a smaller and lighter class called "péniches" (rigged chiefly as schuyts), about 400. The gun-vessels, as well as the prames, were afterwards increased in number; so that the armed vessels of the flotilla amounted to 1339, and the transports to 954; total 2293 vessels. The naval commander-in-chief of this numerous flotilla was Vice-admiral Eustache Bruix, having as an assistant, on account of ill health, Rear-admiral Jean-Raimond Lacrosse, a brave and intelligent officer, and the same, it will be recollected, who commanded the Droits-de-l'Homme at the time of her loss.

The ports of reunion for the flotilla were seven: Ostende, Dunkerque, Calais, Ambleteuse, Vimereux, Boulogne, and Etaples. Boulogne, as being situated directly in front of, and only about 12 leagues distant from, the low land between Dover cliff and Hastings point, was made the main depôt, or capital. Until the grand project of invasion was thought of, Boulogne possessed a worthless harbour, formed by the estuary of the little river Laine, and nearly dry at low water, with only one quay. In a short time both banks of the river were lined with quays; moles were constructed, a capacious basin dug, and a bridge thrown across the river. By means of a dam the waters were confined, and the vessels kept afloat; and, to prevent any annoyance on the part of the British, immense batteries were erected at all the commanding points. As a still further protection against a bombardment, a strong line of heavy gun-vessels was moored across the road; which, by nature, was difficult of approach, on account of the numerous shoals and sand-banks in its vicinity. Vimereux, situated about a league to the north-east of Boulogne, was actually formed into a port expressly to receive the flotilla; and the harbour of Ambleteuse was deepened and enlarged, to answer the same purpose. A glance at the chart of this coast will show how difficult the whole of these ports are of access on account of the sands. No vessel, indeed, beyond a gun-brig in size, can approach near enough to do any execution. The tides, too, which cross each other in an extraordinary manner, are very serious obstacles in the way of a bombarding force.

Corresponding exertions were making on the opposite side of the Channel. An immense number of small vessels, armed each with one or two heavy long guns, were stationed at the Nore and at all the most assailable parts of the English coast; as were also several large armed ships, mounted with heavy carronades, and which ships, although not in a state to go to sea, answered perfectly well for floating-batteries. Mortella towers were also erected along the coast; and an immense army, composed of regulars, militia, and volunteers, were ready, on the first summons, to rush to the point of danger. In mid-channel and along the French coast, British cruisers were constantly on the watch, ready to blaze away upon the vessels of the flotilla the instant they showed themselves outside the sands and batteries by which they were protected. The commander-in-chief on the Downs station, Admiral Lord Keith, had this important service under his immediate direction; and several enterprising officers had the command of flying squadrons, that cruised close along the French coast.

On the 20th of February, in the morning, the British hired cutter Active, of six small guns and about 30 men and boys, commanded by Lieutenant John Williams, being off Gravelines, discovered, within three-quarters of a mile of the shore, 16 sail of French gun-boats and transports running from Ostende towards Boulogne. In spite of the great disparity of force, Lieutenant Williams gallantly gave chase; at 10 h. 30 m. A.M. commenced a running fight with the flotilla; and at 11 A.M. compelled the outermost vessel, a horse-transport, to haul down her colours. The delay in taking possession of the Jeune-Isabelle enabled the other vessels to get under the protection of the batteries, before the Active could again make sail in pursuit.

On the 8th of May, at daybreak, the British 18-gun brig-sloop Vincejo, Captain John Wesley Wright (18-pounder carronades, with a crew on board of 51 effective men and the extraordinary number of 24 boys), having been becalmed close to the mouth of the river Morbihan, coast of France, was carried by the ebb-tide, in less than an hour, so near to the Teigneuse rock, that she was forced to anchor to avoid running upon it. Having sounded, the brig weighed and warped herself into the fair channel, still baffled in her manœuvres by a calm and a strong tide directly against her. While in this situation, sweeping with all her strength to get clear of the coast, a flotilla of 17 armed vessels was rowing towards her from the Morbihan;

consisting of six brigs, first-class gun-vessels, with three guns, one 24 and two 18 pounders, and from 60 to 80 men each; six luggers, second-class gun-vessels, two guns, 18-pounders, with from 40 to 50 men each; five luggers, third-class gun-vessels, one brass 36-pounder carronade throwing shells, and from 20 to 30 men each; total, 35 guns (of which 30 were long 18 and 24 pounders), and from 700 to 800 men, commanded by Lieutenant Laurent Tourneur.

By 8 h. 30 m. A.M., having advanced within extreme range, the gun-vessels began to open their fire. They continued gaining rapidly upon the brig until 9 h. 30 m.; when they had approached so near that the Vincejo was obliged to sweep her broadside to and engage, under the additional disadvantage that her few men were fatigued by hard labour at the oar, and divided during the action between the larboard guns and the starboard sweeps. The Vincejo maintained this unequal contest for nearly two hours, and that within grape and hailing distance. The brig's hull, masts, yards, and rigging had at length received great damage: three guns were disabled; and, owing to the booms having fallen upon the main deck (the brig having a quarter-deck like the Port Mahon), and the loss, out of her small effective crew, of two men killed and 12 wounded, including Captain Wright himself, in the groin (but who would not quit the deck), the fire was reduced to one gun in about five minutes. Thus situated, the Vincejo had no alternative but to strike her colours.

The loss sustained by the flotilla could never be ascertained; but, from the marks of blood on board the brig to which the prisoners were first carried, and the evident damage done to several of the vessels, not a doubt was entertained as to its severity. A highly exaggerated account of this action appears in a French work, in which the little Vincejo, described as " une forte corvette," is associated with " un lougre anglaise," and the French force is reduced to " quatre canonnières."[1]

The subsequent mysterious death of Captain Wright in the Temple at Paris struck all Europe with horror. Although the affair is still involved in doubt, it is but justice to state, that Napoleon has strenuously denied having offered any violence to the person of this gallant British officer.[2] Among the papers discovered at Captain Wright's death, and restored by the

---

[1] Victoires et Conquêtes, tome xvi., p. 33.

[2] See O'Meara's Napoléon in Exile, vol. i. pp. 340, 449; and vol. ii., pp. 24, 182, 215.

present French government to Sir Sidney Smith, under whose
auspices, it will be recollected, Captain Wright, when a lieutenant of the Tigre, had greatly distinguished himself, was a
narrative of the circumstances of the Vincejo's capture, drawn
up for the needless purpose of justifying her officers and crew
from the charge of pusillanimity advanced by the hireling press
of France. To show how differently the actual antagonists of
the British brig thought of her behaviour in the action, we have
only to subjoin the speech of Lieutenant Tourneur upon receiving Captain Wright's sword: " Monsieur, vous avez noblement
défendu l'honneur de votre nation, et la réputation de votre
marine. Nous aimons et estimons les braves, et l'on vous
traitera, vous et votre équipage, avec tous les égards possibles."

Having, like a ship-sloop, a detached quarter-deck and forecastle with barricades and port-holes, and being, on account of the
smallness of her ports and the spaces between them, pierced for
10 guns of a side on the main deck, the Vincejo appeared to be
a much more formidable vessel than she really was. In point of
size, being only 277 tons, she was not much larger than a French
gun-brig, and, in point of armament, not nearly so effective. All
this was made known to the commanding officer of the French
gun-boats, by two deserters from the brig a few days before her
capture. The surprise is, that a vessel, so poorly armed and
manned as the Vincejo, should have been sent alone to cruise
in waters where she was so likely to be assailed by a tenfold
superior force. Captain Wright, it appears, made frequent
complaints of this nature to Admiral Lord Keith; but the latter
took an effectual way of silencing them,—he menaced the enterprising young officer with his displeasure.[1]

The following portion of Captain Wright's narrative will show,
as well the effect produced upon his mind by the statements circulated in France to his disadvantage, as the species of daring
service in which he had employed the Vincejo for some weeks
previous to her capture—a capture of the importance of which
the French government were so fully sensible, that they promoted Lieutenant Tourneur on the spot to a capitaine de
frégate.

"Had it ever occurred to me," says Captain Wright, " that
blame could in any manner attach to my conduct, under the
closest scrutiny of a court composed of my brother officers,
famed for the severity of their criticism on all that concerns the
honour of the country and the reputation of the navy, and who

[1] Naval Chronicle, vol. xxxv., p. 450.

are at least as good judges as the enemy, of the risks that a
brave and enterprising officer ought reasonably to run in performing the king's service; I confess that I should more readily
have anticipated a charge of temerity than a censure of pusillanimity. If with, I may fairly assert, as ill-manned a ship as
ever sailed from England, a station was maintained singly, with
very little interval, for three months, without a pilot, within the
enemy's islands, in the mouth of their rivers, in the presence of
an extremely superior force continually in motion; if his convoys, attended by this force, were as often chased, forced out of
their course, and obliged to take shelter in ports they were not
destined for; if that very weak and inefficient ship's company
was, in that time, by unremitting attention and exertion, brought
to such a state of discipline as gave me sufficient confidence to
wait for, and chase into her own ports, an enemy's ship, in all
respects greatly superior to the brig I commanded; if lying-to a
whole day in the enemy's road at the mouth of a river, bidding
defiance to two brigs, each of nearly equal force with the Vincejo, a schooner, and 50 sail of armed gun-boats, brigs, and
luggers, all under way, and occasionally laying their heads off
the land, but keeping close to their batteries; if, after having got
ashore in the mouth of a river, within grape-range of the batteries, I had—I may well be permitted to say—the audacity to
unrig the Vincejo, get her guns out, and haul her high and dry
into an enemy's port in a small island, between Belle-Isle and
the Main, within four miles of the continent, to examine her
keel and repair her damage, making preparations in the mean
time to fight a land battle, in case of a very probable attack,
protected only by the presence of a frigate for a day or two; if
taking and running on shore several of the enemy's vessels under
the batteries, in sight of the above force; if unreeving and
reeving double all my running rigging that was susceptible of it,
and almost entirely rigging my ship anew, as much to increase
my mechanical purchases, to supply the deficiency of hands in
working her, as promptly to make sailors of my landmen and
boys, with whatever circumstances may be added to this cata-
logue, from my public account of the action, and the testimony
of my immediate captors, be proofs of want of energy, bravery,
intelligence, and seamanship, it must be acknowledged that I
ought to take my place among arrant cowards and incorrigible
lubbers."[1]

Owing to the great preparations making in Flushing,

[1] Naval Chronicle, vol. xxxv., p. 445.

Helvoet, and Ostende, these ports were narrowly watched by a force placed under the orders of Commodore Sir William Sidney Smith, in the 50-gun ship Antelope; whose accustomed anchorage was near the north-east extremity of the Schonevelde channel, about six leagues west-north-west, or thereabouts, of Flushing, and rather more than the same distance, in nearly a south-south-west direction, from Ostende. The following was the plan adopted for a quick communication of intelligence. One vessel took her station within view of distant signals (flags as large as ensigns, expressing their import, not by colour, but by number and position) from the commodore's ship; and the vessel or vessels close off the enemy's port, on having anything important to communicate, stretched out to the offing until their signals were seen and answered by the intermediate cruiser, and then resumed their station or otherwise, as circumstances might require.

On the 15th of May the British force stationed close off the port of Ostende consisted of the 18-gun brig-sloop Cruiser, Captain John Hancock, and 16-gun ship-sloop Rattler, Captain Francis Mason; who kept up a communication with the squadron cruising off Calais, by means of three or four gun-brigs, under the orders of Lieutenant Patrick Manderston, of the Minx. On the evening of this day 22 one-masted gun-vessels and one schooner were seen to haul out of the harbour of Ostende, and to take up an anchorage to the westward of the lighthouse, within the sand. Captain Hancock immediately made the signal of recal to the four gun-brigs, then standing to the westward, and despatched the hired armed-cutter Stag, Lieutenant William Patfull, with the intelligence to the commodore. Having done this, Captain Hancock, as soon as it grew dark, got under way with his two sloops; and, the better to prevent the escape of the division of gun-boats outside, which were commanded by Capitaine de frégate Bernard-Isidore Lambour, re-anchored within long range of the batteries at the pier-head.

On the 16th, at daybreak, the four British gun-brigs, being still in sight, when again recalled; but, as on the preceding evening, they did not see or understand the signal. At 9 h. 30 m A.M. the Rattler, who lay a little to the eastward of the Cruiser, made the signal, first for five sail, and then for a fleet, in the east-south-east. This was a strong division of the Gallo-Batavian or Flushing flotilla, which had sailed from its anchorage in the Inner Wieling at daybreak on that morning, under the command of Rear-admiral Ver-Huell, bound to Ostende, and consisted of the two ship-rigged prames (12 long 24-pounders each) Ville-d'Anvers, bearing the admiral's flag, Lieutenant André Dutaillis, and Ville-d'Aix, Captain François-Jacques Meynne, 19 schooners, and 47 schuyts, in all 68 sail; mounting between them upwards of 100 long 36, 24, and 18 pounders, besides lighter pieces on the side, brass carronades, and mortars, and carrying a body of between 4000 and 5000 troops.

At 10 A.M., which was as early as the tide served, the two sloops got under way and began working towards the enemy. At about 11 A.M. the wind shifted to the south-west; which, while it favoured the two sloops, headed the flotilla, then nearly abreast of Blanckenberghe, and induced the Dutch admiral to bear up and put back towards Flushing. At about noon Sir Sidney Smith's squadron, consisting, besides the Antelope, of the 36-gun frigate Penelope, Captain William Robert Brough-ton, and 32-gun frigate Aimable, Captain William Bolton, hove in sight of the two sloops; and which squadron had weighed from the Schonevelde since between 10 and 11 A.M., in conse-quence of an announcement by one of the in-shore ships, that the Gallo-Batavian flotilla was making sail from the Inner Wieling.

At about 1 h. 30 m. P.M. the Cruiser came up with, fired at, and compelled to strike, one of the rearmost vessels, a schuyt mounting one long 36-pounder, and carrying five Dutch seamen and 25 French troops. Making the signal for the Rattler to take possession, the British brig continued to stand on, in the hope to close with one of the prames. Feeling himself, as the French accounts state, somewhat nettled at having one of his vessels captured by a force so comparatively insignificant, Admiral Ver-Huell, took advantage of a slight change of wind in his favour, and stood back towards Ostende with all his re-maining flotilla except eight schuyts, which continued their route towards the Inner Wieling. At about 1 h. 45 m. P.M., the Ville-d'Anvers fired a shot at the Cruiser, which passed over her, and fell close under the bows of the Rattler. Shortly afterwards, the wind shifting six points, both sloops fell off in their course, and found themselves nearly abreast of the lead-ing prame, and upon the lee beam of the flotilla, then crowding sail to get in-shore. At a few minutes before 2 P.M., the Ville-d'Anvers commenced a heavy fire upon the Cruiser and Rattler, and several of the schooners and schuyts also opened their fire. In a short time the two sloops were in the midst

of the flotilla, engaging on both sides, and frequently assailed
by shot and shells from the batteries of Blanckenberghe. Notwithstanding all this the Cruiser and Rattler gallantly drove
on shore the Ville-d'Anvers prame, and four of the schooners.

At 3 h. 45 m. P.M. the Aimable arrived up with, and opened
her fire upon, a portion of the flotilla close under the batteries
of Blanckenberghe. At about 4 h. 30 m. P.M. the Penelope
and Antelope also got into action, and, by their heavy fire, drove
several other schooners and schuyts on shore. At 7 P.M. the
Aimable found herself near to the grounded prame, and received
from her a very destructive fire; several artillerymen from the
shore having got on board the Ville-d'Anvers, and replaced her
crew, most of whom had fled upon her first grounding: at which
time, too, her colours were either hauled down or shot away.
At about 7 h. 45 m. P.M., the tide having fallen and left the
British ships in little more water than they drew, the Antelope
made the signal to discontinue the engagement; and the
squadron drew off into deeper water. The Gallo-Batavian
flotilla, or what remained of it, took this opportunity of getting
into the basin of Ostende; whither they were accompanied by
the division of French gun-vessels which, by the orders of Rear-
admiral Charles Magon, the commanding officer of the Ostende
flotilla, had on the preceding evening, as already stated, anchored to the westward of the lighthouse, and which had subsequently gone to the assistance of Rear-admiral Ver-Huell.

The loss on the part of the British, compared with the vigour
and duration of the firing, was of no great amount. The Cruiser
had one seaman killed, and her captain's clerk (George Ellis)
and three seamen wounded; the Rattler, two seamen killed and
three wounded; the Aimable, one master's mate (Mr. Christie),
one midshipman (Mr. Johnson), four seamen, and one boy
killed, and one lieutenant (William Mather), her purser (William Shadwell), one midshipman (Mr. Conner), and 11 seamen
wounded; total, 13 killed and 32 wounded. Besides having
her rigging and sails a good deal cut, the Cruiser received two
large shot between wind and water. The Rattler suffered also
in her rigging and sails; and the Aimable, in addition to her
damages aloft, was struck in several parts of her hull. The acknowledged loss, on the Gallo-Batavian flotilla amounted to 18
killed and 60 wounded, 29 of the latter and four of the former
on board the two prames.

From the sketch here given it now appears that the Cruiser
and Rattler, unsupported by any other ships, most gallantly

attacked, and after a two hours' action very nearly discomfited, this formidable Gallo-Batavian flotilla. Unfortunately the public letter of Commodore Sir Sidney Smith, although it admits that "Captains Hancock and Mason bore the brunt of the attack, and continued it for six hours against a great superiority of fire," was calculated to convey an impression, the letter in fact expressly states, that the Antelope, Penelope, and Aimable participated in the action from its commencement. Sir Sidney says: "The signal was made to the Cruiser and Rattler for an enemy in the E.S.E. to call their attention from Ostend; the squadron weighed," &c. But, in reality, neither of the sloops was in sight of the Antelope for a full hour after she and her companions had weighed; nor does the log of the Antelope mention their names until the following entry occurs: "At 2, observed the Rattler and Cruiser commence firing on the enemy's flotilla." The log of the Aimable refers to the first appearance of the two sloops in nearly the same manner: "At 2, Cruiser and Rattler brought the enemy to action," &c. And how could the commodore well have descried the two sloops earlier than the commencement of the afternoon, when the Antelope had been at anchor full six leagues (some accounts say nine) from their anchorage; at such a distance, in fact, that it took the Stag, from 9 P.M. on the 15th to 5 h. 30 m. A.M. on the 16th, before her commander could deliver his despatches to Sir Sidney? Moreover, the first signal of any kind, noticed in the log of the Antelope, is one made at 4 P.M., "to engage the enemy." Whereas, in proof that much had been effected two hours before he was in a situation to make that signal, Sir Sydney in his letter says: "Since 2 o'clock (a little earlier than was the case) the sternmost prame struck her colours and ran on shore."

But there is a more disinterested testimony in favour of the claims of the Cruiser and Rattler than is to be found in the logs of any of the British ships. The French minister of marine, Vice-admiral Decrès, under date of May 20, 1804, gives as the substance of the report of Rear-admiral Ver-Huell, that an English frigate and corvette, or, in other words, that an English frigate-built and brig-rigged corvette, who were very near, manœuvred to cut off two of the gun-boats and a transport, &c. "The action during two hours," proceeds the account, "was extremely warm: the two enemy's vessels were disabled and retreated." The rear-admiral goes on to state, that the port of Ostende being left open, he steered towards it; but that Commodore Sir Sydney Smith, "having assembled his squadron, attacked the flotilla within three leagues of Ostende," &c. As this translation is at complete variance, in some material points, with that which appears in the work of a contemporary, we will here add the original passages, or so much of them as is necessary : " Une frégate et une *corvette* anglaise,[1] qui étaient fort près, manœuvrèrent." &c.   "Le combat, pendant deux heures, fut extrêmement chaud, les deux bâtimens ennemis furent *désemparés* et firent chasses."[2]   "Le Commodore Sidney Smith, ayant pu réunir sa croisière, joignit la flotille gallo-batave à trois lieues d'Ostende."

From the above extracts, it is evident that Rear-admiral Ver-Huell considered that he was attacked, and engaged for two hours, by the Cruiser and Rattler, before the Antelope, or any other ship of Sir Sydney's squadron, fired a shot at him ; and thus, like an honest man, did he report the fact to the official organ of his government. But the appearance of Sir Sydney Smith's official letter, in the columns of the Moniteur, made M. Decrès condemn the haste he had used in publishing the report of the Dutch admiral. Instead of the attack having been made by two sloops, or, taking the literal translation, by one frigate and one sloop, it was here confessedly made by one 50-gun ship, three frigates, two sloops, and two cutters. Accordingly M. Dumas, and all the other French historians, reject their own official account as too tame and inglorious, and prefer incorporating in their pages the official account of their enemy. This is particularly the case in one work, which, on most other occasions, would scorn to glean its materials from any source that was not decidedly French.[3] We regret that we were so far misled by Sir Sydney's letter, as, in the former edition of this work, to have contributed to mislead the public respecting the real merits of the engagement off Boulogne in May, 1804.

On the 17th, at daybreak, the four gun-brigs, commanded by Lieutenant Manderston, having joined, were sent in, under the direction of Captain Hancock, to see what could be done with the French prame Ville-d'Anvers, aground to the eastward of Ostende. The gun-brigs opened their fire, but received from the numerous train of horse and other artillery assembled along the beach, as well as from the heavy mortars and pieces of cannon mounted upon the heights, so heavy a fire in return, that they were obliged to desist and haul off. No loss appears to have

[1] An English frigate and a *cutter*.— Brenton, vol. iii., p. 244.   [2] The two vessels of the enemy were *dismasted* and sheered off.—Ib., p. 245.
[3] Précis des Evènemens, tome xi., p. 19.

been sustained by the gun-brigs ; but the Minx was struck by a
large shot in the hounds of her mainmast. On the morning of
the 19th the 16-gun ship-sloops Galgo, Captain Michael Dodd,
and Inspector, Captain Edward James Mitchell, co-operated
with the gun-brigs in a second attack upon the grounded prame ;
but, protected by the powerful batteries on shore, the Ville-
d'Anvers floated with the rising tide and got safe into Ostende.
Five of the eight grounded schooners and schuyts were also
floated into the basin.

Hâvre, owing to its central position on the French Channel-
coast, was made a temporary depôt for the vessels of the flotilla
constructed to the westward, or in the Seine and the rivers flowing into it.   As soon as a sufficient number was assembled, they
were to be convoyed, by prames and gun-brigs, to the grand en-
trepôt at Boulogne.   In the month of July a British squadron,
composed chiefly of sloops, bombs, and small craft, under the
orders of Captain Robert Dudley Oliver, in the 38-gun frigate
Melpomène, was stationed off Hâvre, to reconnoitre and harass
the port, and prevent, as well the vessels of the flotilla inside
from escaping, as those on the outside from joining.   On the
23rd the bomb-vessels bombarded the town, set it on fire, and
compelled several of the vessels to retire behind the pier and up
the river. The mortar-batteries on shore opened a fire in return,
which, although continued for some time, inflicted very little
damage, and no loss on the British vessels. On the 1st of August
a second attack was made, attended with nearly a similar result.

On the 19th of July, in the afternoon, the wind, setting in
strong from the north-north-east, made so much sea, that the
French flotilla in the road of Boulogne became very uneasy. At
about 8 P.M., the leewardmost brigs began to get under way,
and work to windward, while some of the luggers ran down
apparently for Etaples, leaving in the road at anchor 45 brigs
and 43 luggers. The British frigate Immortalité, Captain Owen,
with the 38-gun frigate Leda, Captain Robert Honyman, and
several small vessels, was then at anchor about eight leagues to
the westward of the town of Boulogne.   The commodore
immediately directed the 18-gun brig-sloop Harpy, Captain
Edmund Heywood, and the gun-brigs Bloodhound and Archer,
Lieutenants Henry Richardson and John Price, to run in and
open their fire upon such of the enemy's vessels as attempted
to stand off from the land. The 16-gun ship-sloop Autumn,
Captain Samuel Jackson, was at this time getting under way,
and lost no time in giving her support to the Harpy and her two

consorts; all four vessels maintaining an occasional fire during the whole weather tide.

At daylight on the 20th there were 19 brigs and eight luggers only remaining in the bay; and at about 6 A.M. these began to slip singly, and run to the southward for the port of Etaples, or Saint-Valery-sur-Somme, the Autumn and three brigs being then too far to leeward to give them any interruption. As soon as the tide permitted, the Immortalité and Leda weighed and stood in close to Boulogne, when it was perceived that a brig, a lugger, and several large boats, were stranded on the beach west of the harbour. The crews of the vessels were endeavouring to save from them what they could, but the tide most probably completed their destruction. Three other French brigs and a lugger were on the rocks near the village of Portet, totally destroyed. A brig and two luggers remained at anchor close to the rocks, with signals flying; the brig had lost her topmasts, topsails, and lower yards, and one of the luggers the head of her mainmast: besides which the sea was making a perfect breach over them.

In the French version of the affair no mention is made of the presence of the British. All is ascribed to the fury of the gale, which did, indeed, occasion sufficient havoc among the numerous craft. The exact number of gun-vessels that foundered, or were stranded, is not stated; but the account acknowledges, that upwards of 400 soldiers and sailors were ingulfed with the former, and that a great many perished with the latter. The emperor was a spectator of the scene, and if we are to credit the French writers, evinced much sensibility on the occasion. " L'empereur, arrivé de la veille à Boulogne, fut temoins de ces désastres ; il se montra encore plus affligé que furieux; la sensibilité chez lui parut bien supérieure au dépit, et l'orgueil de son caractère ceda à la bonté de son cœur."[1] Napoleon, no doubt, was taught a lesson by the disaster: he saw that the shots and shells of British ships were not all he had to fear in getting his immense armada across the English Channel.

Boulogne being, as already mentioned, the head-quarters of the grand armament preparing for the invasion of England, occupied a due share of the latter's attention. The British squadron, which cruised off Boulogne in August, consisted of from 15 to 20 vessels, under the command of Rear-admiral Louis in the 50-gun ship Leopard. The main body usually lay at anchor, in 15 fathoms water, about 10 miles north-west of the port; and a detached or flying division, of five or six vessels,

[1] Victoires et Conquêtes, tome xvi., p. 138.

under the command of Captain Owen, in the frigate Immortalité, generally cruised just out of shell-range of the enemy's batteries, anchoring occasionally, as the state of the tide rendered necessary. It should here be observed, that, in addition to the batteries, masked as well as open, all along the edge of the cliff, there were seven or eight forts erected on the sands at low water; where also lay ready several mortar-beds, over which the tide flowed, and to which the mortars were brought as soon as it left them dry.

On the 25th of August there were lying in the road of Boulogne, moored in line, 146 French gun-vessels, 62 of them brigs, or first-class gun-vessels, the remainder chiefly luggers. Of these gun-vessels, 45 composed the Hâvre division, which, under Capitaine de vaisseau François-Henri-Eugène Daugier, had since the 16th entered the road. On the same 25th an unusual degree of bustle and activity prevailed in the port, on account of the presence of the French emperor, who had just done presiding at the grand ceremony of distributing to the troops the cross of the legion of honour. This imposing spectacle took place on the 16th of August, the anniversary of the day on which "Saint Napoléon" had usurped in the French calendar the place of "Saint Roch." Upwards of 80,000 men, taken chiefly from the camps of Boulogne and Montreuil, were present on the occasion.

To amuse the French emperor, probably, Admiral Bruix, at about 1 h. 45 m. P.M., ordered a division of gun-vessels, under Capitaine de vaisseau Julien le Ray, to weigh, and, with the north-easterly wind then blowing, work up towards Pointe-Bombe; near to which lay the British gun-brig Bruiser, Lieutenant Thomas Smithies, or, as the French writers have it, "une grande corvette anglaise à trois mâts,"[1] watching their manœuvres. In a short time a firing commenced between the parties, and soon brought to the spot the Immortalité; who, at 2 h. 30 m. P.M. opened her broadside upon the gun-vessels, and received in return a heavy fire from the batteries, one shot from which struck her under the main chains, but did no material injury. It now became necessary to haul further from the shore; and the Immortalité, having done so, lay-to about three miles off the port.

[1] One would hardly suppose this possible, but it is no less true; and, as a proof what strange optics the writer was blessed with, he could not discover a single brig in the British squadron: "Leurs forces se composaient," he says, "de deux vaisseaux de ligne," (meaning a 50 and a frigate,) "deux frégates de quarante-quatre, de sept corvettes de guerre à trois mâts, de deux lougres, et d'un cutter."—*Précis des Evènemens*, tome xi., p. 45.

Early on the morning of the 26th the Archer and Blood-hound, commanded as before,[1] fired at some luggers coming round Cape Grinez, but who kept too close to the shore to be molested. Towards the afternoon a second division of gun-vessels, under Capitaine de vaisseau Etienne Pevrieux, and two sections of Prussian mortar-vessels, got under way, and, when joined to Captain Le Ray's division, which was still manœuvring between Vimereux and Ambleteuse, formed a total of 60 brigs, and upwards of 30 luggers. The French emperor himself, it appears, was at this time in the road in his barge, attended by Marshals Soult and Mortier, and Admiral Bruix. At 4 p.m. the Immortalité, followed by the Harpy, still commanded by Captain Heywood, gun-brig Adder, Lieutenant George Wood, and hired armed-cutter Constitution, commanded by Lieutenant J. S. A. Dennis, made sail towards the flotilla, and in a quarter of an hour afterwards opened her fire; as did the vessels astern of her. The gun-vessels, however, kept near the shore, pur-posely to draw the British within reach of the batteries. There was no withstanding the temptation, and the Immortalité and her three companions tacked and stood in, within three-quarters of a mile of the batteries, which kept up an incessant fire.

As if that were not enough to preserve the gun-vessels from capture, the greater part of those in the road weighed and pro-ceeded to their assistance. "Presque tous les bâtimens qui se trouvaient en rade prirent part à ce combat, selon leur position, et furent soutenus par le feu des batteries de la côte, quand l'ennemi tenta de s'en approcher. Les mortiers à grande portée lui firent beaucoup de mal, &c."[2]

At about 5 p.m., while the Constitution with her 12-pounder carronades was engaging, in the most gallant manner, a heavy gun-brig and two lugger-rigged yachts, painted with white bottoms and green sides, and richly gilt, a 13-inch shell fell on board between the companion and skylight, passed through the deck, stove a skuttle-butt, and went through the cutter's bottom. The hole being too large to be stopped, and the vessel filling fast, a signal of distress was hoisted. In a few minutes the boats of the squadron were alongside, and the whole of the crew were saved. A shell also fell on board the Harpy, and, after killing one of her seamen, lodged in a beam on the main deck, without doing further harm. The reason given for its not exploding is a very extraordinary one. According to several English accounts, the fusee was actually extinguished by the

---

[1] See p. 227.   Précis des Evènemens, tome xi., p. 47.

blood of the poor man through whose body the shell had just passed. The Immortalité was twice struck by shot in the hull, and had four men slightly wounded. This frigate and her division, to which the Bruiser gun-brig, commanded as before, had since joined herself, now hauled off out of gun-shot. Some of the French vessels were compelled to run on shore on account of the shot-holes in their hulls ; and such of the remainder as the batteries had not permitted to be materially damaged, bore up for the road of Boulogne. On the two succeeding days some slight skirmishes also took place, but nothing decisive could be effected on account of the French batteries ; nor was any injury done to the British vessels beyond a wound in the Bruiser's bowsprit.

It is singular that the same French writer, who tells us of the immense advantage which a host of these gun-vessels derived from the gun and mortar batteries along the coast, should cite the engagement or skirmish of the 26th of August, as "une des plus fortes épreuves de l'effet réciproque du feu des petits bâti-mens de flotille opposés à une ligne de vaisseaux et frégates d'un rang très-supérieur." [1] The writer should have stopped until a case occurred where a score or so of these gun-vessels, having got beyond the reach of their protectors, suddenly found themselves, in a fine commanding breeze, close to leeward of a single British frigate, of the Immortalité for instance. How many of them, does he think, would escape capture or destruction? None, provided the frigate stayed not to pick up the drowning crews of those she crushed by her stem, or sank by her broadsides ; and provided those vessels that hauled down their flags to save themselves from the fate of their companions did not treacherously rehoist them, because the frigate was too much occupied to send a boat to take possession. None knew this better than Napoleon. The affair of the 26th of August, of which he had unintentionally been an eye-witness, convinced him. He did not say so, it is true : it was not his policy. Within the short space of little more than five weeks, the French emperor had witnessed, both what the Channel gales and the Channel cruisers would do with his flotilla, if it fell in the way of either.

Towards the latter end of the summer a plan was submitted to, and received the sanction of the British government, for destroying such vessels of the invasion-flotilla as should moor in any of the open roads along the French Channel-coast. This

---

[1] Précis des Evènemens, tome xi., p. 45.

desirable object was to be attained chiefly by means of a novel, or, rather, of a revived species of fire-vessel of a very peculiar description. It consisted of a coffer of about 21 feet long, and three and a quarter broad, resembling in appearance a log of mahogany, except that its extremities were formed like a wedge. Its covering was of thick plank, lined with lead, calked and tarred. Outside this was a coat of canvas, paid over with hot pitch. The vessel weighed, when filled (done of course before the covering is wholly put on), about two tons. The contents consisted, besides the apparatus, of as much ballast as would just keep the upper surface of the deck of the coffer even with the water's edge. Amidst a quantity of powder (about 40 barrels) and other inflammable matter, was a piece of clockwork, the main spring of which, on the withdrawing of a peg placed on the outside, would, in a given time (from six to ten minutes), draw the trigger of a lock, and explode the vessel. This " catamaran," as it was called, had no mast, and was to be towed to the spot of its operation. On the opposite end to that to which the tow-rope was fixed was a line, with a sort of grappling-iron at its extremity, kept afloat by pieces of cork, and intended to hook itself to the cable of the object of destruction, and swing the coffer alongside.

The appearance of about 150 vessels, moored in a double line outside the pier of Boulogne, offered a fit opportunity for trying the effect of these much-vaunted machines. Accordingly on the 1st of October, in the morning, Admiral Lord Keith, in the Monarch 74, with three 64s, two 50s, and several frigates, sloops, bombs, gun-brigs, cutters, and fire-vessels, anchored about five miles from the French line off Boulogne. In the course of the day, the Monarch, accompanied by three frigates and some smaller vessels, weighed, and re-anchored just out of gun-shot of the French batteries and flotilla. This movement, coupled with the information previously furnished by spies, left no doubt in the minds of the French as to the nature of the attack that was about to ensue. Every defensive preparation had already been made by Rear-admiral Lacrosse, whose flag was flying on board the Ville-de-Mayence prame, stationed in the centre of the line. Towards evening the French admiral despatched several gun-boats and armed launches to a distance outside, that they might be ready as well to give notice by signal of the enemy's approach, as, if possible, to grapple and tow away the fire-vessels. On shore the batteries were all ready, and bodies of troops, with numerous field-pieces, were stationed along the coast.

On the 2nd of October, at about 9 h. 15 m. P.M., the four fire-vessels, Amity, Devonshire, Peggy, and Providence, towed by armed launches, proceeded upon the service assigned them. In less than a quarter of an hour their approach was signalled by the French videttes; who, as soon as they found that the fire they opened was not returned, suspected the nature of the vessels which, with a strong tide and fair wind, were fast driving towards them. A scuffle now ensued between the French gunboats and the English launches ; and the latter, having towed their charges to a proper distance, and ignited the fusees, left the tide to perform the rest, and rowed back to their ships. As the fire-vessels approached the left of the French line, a heavy cannonade commenced with a view of sinking them, but it failed in its effect. The Providence, entering among the gunboats, exploded at 10 h. 15 m., between No. 149 and No. 142, stationed in the second line, wounding two men on board the latter vessel. The explosion was awfully loud, and created considerable alarm, as well along the French line, as among the spectators on shore ; but no more mischief appears to have been done than has just been stated.

In another 20 minutes the Peggy, passing through a vacant space left purposely for her, exploded in the rear of the line, with an effect as slight as the first, merely wounding an officer and two men. A third fire-vessel, the Devonshire, exploded at about 1 A.M. on the 3rd, wounding two men only. The fourth, which was the Amity, pointed to the admiral's prame ; but the Ville-de-Mayence, slacking her cables, let the enemy drift harmlessly by. This vessel, at her explosion, appears to have effected even less than her three companions.

Four or five of the catamarans also exploded, the last at about 3 h. 30 m. A.M.; but only one, and that by an unexpected occurrence, appears to have caused any destruction to the French. A British boat, having just done towing a catamaran, was, the French say, abandoned by her crew, but left with a sail up. If so, it must have been as a ruse, and the English must have transported themselves to another boat, as the enemy's gun-vessel was approaching. Lord Keith's letter containing not a word of details, the French accounts are all to which we have to trust. A heavily-armed launch, or péniche (No. 267), approached this vacant boat, into which 27 French soldiers and sailors instantly leaped. Scarcely had the latter made off with their prize, before the péniche ran foul of the catamaran, and was instantly blown into the air, with the loss of all her remaining crew, consisting of her commander and 13 soldiers and sailors. Those left in the captured boat gained the port of Vimereux. This made the French loss amount, altogether, to 14 killed and seven wounded. The British had not a man hurt.

Many were the anathemas hurled against England for the barbarity of this attack by catamaran, but surely without reason. Had she not a right to crush, in the ports of its formation if she could, the flotilla which, it was publicly declared, had for its sole object the conveyance of troops for a descent upon her shores? What is there, compared with explosion-vessels and fire-ships, peculiarly gentle in the employment of red-hot balls, and grape and langridge shot; or, indeed, in any of the missiles or weapons with which war is usually waged? That the catamaran affair was a silly project was asserted with more reason than that it was a cruel or an illegal one. It was a complete failure, and, like every failure of the kind, conferred additional strength upon that which it was intended to destroy. Under an idea, for instance, that the British would improve their plans, and make a second attempt at burning the flotilla, " une chaîne de barrage " was constructed, which completely sheltered the line of gun-boats at Boulogne from explosion-vessels of every description.

On the 8th of October, a division of French lugger-rigged gun-vessels being perceived from the road of Jersey, creeping along the coast of Normandy from the southward, the British 18-gun ship-sloop Albacore, Captain Major Jacob Henniker, slipped and made sail, followed by a gun-brig and cutter; but who, missing the sloop in the haze, returned to the anchorage. Towards evening the Albacore, being near the Grosnez de Flamanville, compelled five of the luggers to anchor close to the surf, under the corner of a battery to the southward of Grosnez. The wind being dead on shore and a lee tide making, the Albacore lay off until the 9th, at 10 A.M.; when, with the assistance of the weather tide, Captain Henniker stood in, under a heavy fire from the battery and gun-vessels. At 11 A.M. the Albacore anchored, with springs, close to the gun-vessels, and within about 200 yards of the surf: the sloop then opened her fire, and continued it until all five vessels were driven on shore, and lay broadside-to in a heavy surf, which broke with great violence over them. Their men, in great numbers, landed upon the beach; and some were seen bearing the wounded in their arms. Having, owing to the strength of the wind, dragged her anchor, the Albacore, at the falling of the tide, slipped and hauled off, without any loss, but with her hull struck in several places, her main and maintop masts shot through, and her rigging of every kind much cut.

On the 23rd of October, at 4 P.M., a division of the French flotilla, consisting of two prames, one with a commodore's broad pendant, and 18 armed schuyts, put to sea from Ostende, and steered to the westward, just as the Cruiser, Captain Hancock, accompanied by the gun-brigs Blazer, Lieutenant John Hinton, Conflict, Lieutenant Charles C. Ormsby, Tigress, Lieutenant Edward Greensword, and Escort, Lieutenant Joseph Gulston Garland, and hired armed cutters Admiral Mitchell and Griffin, Lieutenants Richard Williams and James Dillon, was standing in to reconnoitre the port. Chase was given, and the headmost prame, at 5h. 18 m. P.M., was brought to action by the Cruiser and her consorts. The mutual cannonade continued until 6 h. 35 m. P.M.; when the prame's fire, which had been confined to musketry for the last half hour, entirely ceased. As, however, the tide was rapidly falling, darkness coming on, and no person on board was acquainted with the shoals to the westward of Ostende, the Cruiser, then in less than three fathoms water, hauled off and anchored.

Meantime, in her eagerness to close with the prame, the Conflict gun-brig had grounded; and, although the brig was in two fathoms water, the prame steered safe in-shore of her. As soon as the prame had passed out of gun-shot, Lieutenant Ormsby commenced lightening his vessel, in the hope to get her off. His endeavours proving fruitless, the lieutenant and his men quitted the Conflict, and pulled for the Cruiser, whose lights were then in view. An attempt to bring away the gun-brig was afterwards made by the Griffin and Admiral Mitchell cutters, manned, in addition to their own crews, by the whole of the Conflict's crew, and by 10 seamen and half the marines belonging to the Cruiser. But the Conflict was found to be high and dry on the beach, and in complete possession of the enemy; the fire from whose howitzers and field-pieces, besides greatly damaging the Griffin in her advance, killed one and wounded seven of the party, including Acting-lieutenant Abraham Garland of the Cruiser most severely, having lost his right leg very high up. Two seamen had also been wounded in the previous cannonade.

On the 8th of December, in the evening, an attempt was made, under the direction of Captain Sir Home Popham, of the 50-gun ship Antelope, by means of the Susannah explosion-vessel and two carcasses, or catamarans, to destroy Fort Rouge, the advanced pile-battery at the entrance of the harbour of

Calais; but, if the French accounts are to be credited, little or no damage was effected by the single explosion—that of the Susannah—which took place. One carcass could not be fixed; and the other, when fixed, would not go off. On the British side not a man was hurt; and it appears that the same good fortune attended the persons on shore. We must now quit, for a while, gun-boats and catamarans to attend to the operations of fleets of line-of-battle ships.

Among the advantages which the British government had contemplated by retaining possession of the island of Malta, its proximity to Toulon was not the least important; and yet Lord Nelson often emphatically declared, that he would as soon the news of the sailing of the Toulon fleet reached him at St. Helen's as at Malta. In proof of the force of that impression upon Lord Nelson's mind, the Mediterranean fleet had not once entered Valetta harbour since he had taken the command, the vice-admiral invariably, when he was compelled to seek a port, steering for Agincourt sound; where, on the last day of the preceding year, we left him and his fleet at anchor.[1] Lord Nelson readily admitted, however, that the island of Malta was an important out-work to Egypt, and, through the latter to India; and that England, by possessing it, acquired a decided influence in the Levant and over the whole of southern Italy.

On the 4th of January, leaving the 38-gun frigate Amazon, Captain William Parker, and some smaller vessels, to aid the Sardinians, in the event of an expected invasion from the neighbouring island of Corsica, the vice-admiral, with the remainder of his fleet, weighed and put to sea. On the 9th Captain Keats in the Superb was detached, to settle some dispute with the Dey of Algiers; and, to give weight to the negotiation, Lord Nelson himself, on the 17th, made his appearance off the Barbary coast. The Superb having rejoined on the following day, the fleet stood back to Sardinia, and on the 27th, at 5 P.M., again dropped anchor in Agincourt sound.

Between February 1st and 8th the fleet cruised in the neighbourhood of the French coast, and then anchored near the island of Cabrera. On the 19th Lord Nelson again put to sea, and remained out until the 25th of March; having on the 15th been joined by the 100-gun ship Royal Sovereign, Captain Pulteney Malcolm, from England. Weighing again on the 3rd of April, the fleet passed between the island of Elba and Cape Corse, and on the 9th, in the morning, took a station about

[1] See p. 179.

midway between the capes Sicie and Sepet. On the same afternoon the French batteries at the latter place fired several shot
at the Amazon, while taking possession of a prize-brig in-shore;
and three French frigates came out of Toulon, and stood
towards her. On this the 74-gun ship Donegal, Captain Sir
Richard John Strachan, and 38-gun frigate Active, Captain
Richard Hussey Moubray, closed the Amazon; whereupon,
at 6 h. 30 m. P.M., the French ships, including four others that
had just rounded Cape Sepet, tacked and put back.

On the 10th of May the Leviathan 74, Captain Henry William Bayntun, accompanied by three bomb-vessels, joined the
fleet, which, on the day following, anchored among the Magdalena islands. On the 14th the Gibraltar rejoined from Naples,
and on the 19th the British fleet weighed and steered for
Toulon. By this time the French fleet had also received an
accession of force : the 80-gun ship Bucentaure had been
launched, and, with seven other line-of-battle ships, lay in the
outer road ready for sea. A few other ships were in nearly the
same state of readiness in the inner road ; and the whole were
still under the command of Vice-admiral la Touche-Tréville,
who had now the new 80 for his flag-ship.

On the 24th of May, in the forenoon, as the Canopus, Donegal,
and Amazon, having been detached from the fleet, then out of
sight in the offing, were standing upon the larboard tack, with
a light air from the south-west, close to the eastward of Cape
Sepet, for the purpose of reconnoitring the fleet in Toulon, a
French line-of-battle ship and frigate were observed under sail
between the capes Sepet and Brun, which form the entrance to
the harbour. At half-past noon, when about three miles from
the shore, the Amazon, Donegal, and Canopus tacked in succession. No sooner had the Canopus put about, than several
French gun-boats swept from under Cape Sepet, and, profiting
by the calm state of the weather, opened a distant fire upon
her and the Amazon. The Canopus, in return, discharged
a few of her lower-deck guns, and stood on to the south-east
by east, with the wind, now a moderate breeze, from west-
north-west.

On hearing the firing, two French ships of the line and two
frigates had slipped their cables and made sail, to assist the
line-of-battle ship and frigate already outside. At 2 h. 30 m
P.M., two more sail of the line slipped, and followed the others ;
making now five sail of the line and three frigates that were in
chase of the reconnoitring ships. Shortly afterwards the

French van-frigate, being on the weather-quarter of the Cano-pus, opened a fire upon her and the Donegal, which these ships immediately returned. With so superior a force it was in vain to contend, and Rear-admiral Campbell directed his little division to make sail. At 3 h. 30 m. P.M., finding pursuit use-less, the French ships tacked and stood back to their port; and at 9 h 30 m. P.M., and not before, the Canopus and her two companions joined the Victory and the fleet.[1]

On the 13th of June, in the afternoon, two strange ships having been signalled as under sail off the east end of the island of Porquerolles, Lord Nelson, who, with the in-shore or lee division, consisting of the Victory, Canopus, Belleisle, Donegal, and Excellent, lay off the Hyères, while Sir Richard Bickerton, with the weather-division, also of five sail of the line, cruised about 20 leagues from the land, ordered the frigates Amazon and Phœbe, the latter commanded by Captain the Honourable Thomas Bladen Capel, to proceed in chase. Light winds made it noon on the following day, the 14th, before the two frigates reached the entrance of the Grande-Passe; and soon afterwards, it being signalled that the strangers were frigates, and known that batteries were near them, Lord Nelson directed the Excel-lent to lend her aid to the Amazon and Phœbe. At 5 P.M. the two French frigates, Incorruptible and Sirène, and 18-gun brig-corvette Furet, were seen at anchor under the castle of Porque-rolles. At 5 h. 30 m. P.M. one of the forts fired at the Phœbe, but the shot did not reach her. In another quarter of an hour both British frigates having cleared for action, anchored with springs on their cables, just out of gun-shot of the northmost fort. Scarcely had the frigates done this, than the whole French fleet in Toulon road was discovered getting under way. The Amazon and Phœbe immediately reweighed, and stood out to sea. The Excellent, having also been recalled by signal, put about and rejoined her division; which, since 4 h. 30 m., had bore up, with the wind at west-south-west, under all sail, for the Grande-Passe.

At 5 P.M., or soon after, the Victory and the ships with her, observing the French admiral coming out of Toulon with eight sail of the line and four frigates, shortened sail and hauled to the wind, in line of battle, on the starboard tack. At 8 P.M. Cape Sicie bore from the Victory north-west by west distant

---

[1] The authors of the quarto " Life of Nelson," by confounding this sortie with another that occurred three weeks after-wards, have entangled themselves and their readers in a labyrinth of mistakes. See Clarke and M'Arthur's Book, vol. ii., pp. 366-7.

seven leagues; and at 1 h. 30 m. A.M. on the 15th, having wore and tacked several times, the lee division hove to. At 3 h. 45 m. A.M. Lord Nelson again made sail, and at noon was only 11 miles to the westward of the north-west end of Porquerolles. At 5 P.M. the Amazon and Phœbe joined the vice-admiral; at which time the French fleet, counted at 14 sail of ships, was standing off and on between Cape Sepet and the last-named island. At 6 P.M. the lee division again hove to for a short time. At 7 P.M. the Incorruptible, Sirène, and Furet joined their fleet; which, having effected the apparent object of the sally, now stood back into port, and was followed, until well inside of Sepet, by Lord Nelson and his division.

This would have passed off as an occurrence of no moment, had not M. La Touche-Tréville thought proper to make it the subject of an official communication to his government. He admits having sent the two frigates and a brig-corvette to cruise in the bay of Hyères, as well as that he sailed out, with the whole of his fleet, to prevent their retreat from being cut off by a line-of-battle ship and two frigates detached by Lord Nelson. He states truly, that the latter, upon this, recalled his detached ships, but most untruly, that the British admiral "ran away."

What Lord Nelson thought of the French admiral's exploit may be gathered from a letter which, on the 18th of June, he wrote to Sir John Acton: " Mons. La Touche came out on the 14th. I was off the Hyères with five ships; he had eight of the line and six frigates. In the evening he stood under Sepet again, and, I believe I may call it, we chased him into Toulon the morning of the 15th. I am satisfied he meant nothing beyond a gasconade; but am confident, when he is ordered for any service, that he will risk falling in with us, and the event of a battle, to try and accomplish his orders."[1] It was not until some weeks after the date of this letter that Lord Nelson saw a copy of the official one of M. La Touche.[2] The statement of the French admiral gave his lordship much more concern than it ought to have done; so much, indeed, that he transmitted a copy of the Victory's log to the admiralty. It was sufficient for M. La Touche that his assertion, taken in a larger sense than he had probably anticipated, that of having chased the British admiral with all the latter's 10 sail of the line present, gained credence in a quarter which immediately promoted him from

---

[1] Clarke and M'Arthur, vol. ii., p. 372.
[2] For a transcript of the original letter, see Appendix, No. 19.

" un grand officier de la légion d'honneur," to " un grand officier de l'empire," and conferred upon him, also, the lucrative appointment of " inspecteur des côtes de la Méditerranée."

Napoleon's letter, apprising M. La Touche-Tréville of the manner in which he had rewarded his gallantry, is dated at Malmaison, the 2nd of July, and contains some important directions relative to the proceedings of the Toulon fleet. The vice-admiral is informed, that two battalions of picked troops of the line, consisting of 800 men each, have received orders to embark on board his ships, presumed to be 10 of the line, ready for sea in the road. If seamen are wanted, the corvettes are to be disarmed, and pressgangs sent to the port of Marseilles. The orders about the employment of shells for the 36-pounders in the Brest fleet are here repeated, with an assurance that, if fired at a distance of not more than 200 or 300 toises, they will produce a much greater effect upon the hull of a ship than cannon-balls.[1]

M. La Touche-Tréville is then directed, after having, if possible, deceived Lord Nelson as to his destination, to put to sea, pass the Straits, sail wide of Ferrol to avoid being seen by the blockading squadron, and arrive off Rochefort; where he is to be joined by the six sail of the line, including the new ship Achille then expected to be ready, in that port. With his 16 sail of the line and 11 frigates, the vice-admiral is then to proceed off Boulogne, either doubling Ireland, or otherwise, as circumstances may warrant. The Brest fleet, composed of 23 sail of the line, with a strong body of troops on board, is in the mean time to draw off the attention of Admiral Cornwallis, and to oblige him to keep close to the coast of Bretagne, to be ready to intercept it on its supposed route to the westward. The further destination of M. La Touche-Tréville is left to be communicated to him when he arrives in the neighbourhood of Boulogne; which, Napoleon conjectures, will be in the course of September, admitting the fleet to have sailed from Toulon, as he trusts it will, about the 28th of July.

For 16 or 17 days previous to the day last mentioned, a succession of heavy gales of wind had rendered it very difficult for Lord Nelson to keep his station; especially as scarcely more than half his ships were in a seaworthy state.[2] On the 19th of July the Ambuscade frigate, with eight sail of transports, joining from England, Lord Nelson wore and stood for the gulf of Palma, with the double object of unloading the transports and

---

[1] Précis des Evènemens, tome xi., p. 198.   [2] See p. 212.

of sheltering the fleet. The station off Toulon, in the mean time, was left in charge of Captain William Hargood, of the Belleisle, having in company the Fisgard and Niger frigates, the Acheron bomb-vessel, and two transports.

On the 2nd of August, when the violence of the wind had driven these ships out of sight of the shore, five French sail of the line and six frigates, under the orders of Rear-admiral Dumanoir-le-Pelley, in the Formidable 80, sailed out of Toulon, for the sole purpose, as alleged, of practising manœuvres. The division cruised within six or seven leagues of the port until the 5th, when the Belleisle and her consorts making their appearance, were telegraphed by the signal-posts on Cape Sepet as six sail of the line, "six vaisseaux ennemis ;" and the Neptune, of 80 guns, "pour rendre la partie égale," went out and joined M. Dumanoir: so states the letter which M. La Touche-Tréville thought it worth while to send to his government on so important an occasion.

On the 6th the French squadron returned to Toulon, and the Belleisle and her five highly-honoured companions approached near enough to count seven of the ships standing into the harbour. On the 8th, in the evening, the Belleisle reconnoitred the port, and observed 10 sail of the line, six frigates, and one brig, at anchor in the road. On the same day Lord Nelson, with his fleet, anchored in a bay in the island of Pulla; where, he had been informed, excellent fresh water could easily be procured. "A very fine watering-place," says his lordship in his diary, "found by Captain Hillyar, about five miles to the westward of Porto-Torres, with the springs about 200 yards from the beach, where 40 casks may be filled at the same time."

On the 10th the Vice-admiral[1] weighed and put to sea ; but, having by a severe gale of wind been blown under Cape San-Sebastian, was not able, until the 26th, to reconnoitre Toulon. In the outer harbour the Victory counted 20 ship-rigged vessels, including 10 sail of the line ; and in the inner harbour, fitting, one sail of the line and one frigate.

On the 18th of August, in the night, Vice-admiral La Touche-Tréville died on board the Bucentaure ;[2] and the command of the fleet, until a successor should be appointed by Buonaparte, devolved upon Admiral Dumanoir-le-Pelley, whose flag, as

---

[1] Since the first of the month, Lord Nelson had changed his flag from blue to white, as Sir Richard Bickerton had from white to red.

[2] "The French papers say he died in consequence of walking so often up to the signal-post upon Sepet to watch us."— *Letter of Lord Nelson, in Clarke and McArthur, vol. ii., p. 387.*

already stated, was flying on board the 80-gun ship Formidable. The British fleet outside of Toulon, although the Conqueror, Spencer, and Tigre had joined, still consisted of only 10 sail of the line, the Gibraltar, Kent, and Triumph having parted company. Even had Lord Nelson's force been less, or the blockade of the port actually raised, the French rear-admiral, as will presently appear, had received no orders to quit port.

In a letter from Napoleon to his minister of marine at Brest, of date September 29, are contained directions that Vice-admiral Villeneuve, then appointed to the command of, and supposed to have already joined, the Toulon fleet, should quit the road, if possible, before the 21st of October, having previously received on board about 6500 troops under General Lauriston. The fleet, stated to consist of 11 ships of the line and seven or eight frigates, was to sail out of the Mediterranean, call for the Aigle at Cadiz, detach two of its fastest sailers, along with four frigates and two brigs, having on board 1800 troops, to relieve Sénégal, retake Gorée, ravage the British settlements on the coast of Africa, and capture the island of St. Helena, wanted as a depôt for the French cruisers and their prizes in that quarter of the globe; while, with 10 sail of the line and frigates, and the remainder of the troops, M. Villeneuve was to steer for Cayenne. Having there taken on board the celebrated General Victor Hugues, the French admiral was to proceed off Surinam, and effect a junction with a squadron of five sail of the line and four frigates, under Rear-admiral Missiessy, M. Villeneuve's successor at Rochefort, and who, it was supposed, would already have fulfilled the first part of his mission. This was, with 3500 men under General Legrange, to proceed to Martinique and Guadaloupe; and, after leaving 1000 men at each of those islands, to attempt, with the remaining 1500, the capture of the island of Dominique, and, if possible, of Sainte-Lucie. Having garrisoned the captured islands, Rear-admiral Missiessy was to proceed off Surinam, and await the arrival of Admiral Villeneuve; who, with his force now augmented to 15 sail of the line, seven or eight frigates, and full 5000 men, was to possess himself of Surinam, and the other Dutch colonies in this quarter. That done, the French admiral was to place under contribution all the British West India islands, enter the different roadsteds, and capture or burn the vessels lying there; leaving in the Antilles, purposely to harass British commerce, the greater part of his corvettes, of which as many as possible were to quit Toulon with the expedition. He was, next, to leave 1200 men with General Ferrand at the city of Santo-Do-mingo, raise the blockade of Ferrol, and, taking out the five ships in that port, appear off Rochefort with 20 sail of the line. Here Vice-admiral Villeneuve would receive directions at what point he was to join Vice-admiral Ganteaume and his 30 sail of the line,[1] in order to fulfil the ultimate object in view, the descent upon England.

Napoleon, it appears, had wavered in his choice of an admiral for the Toulon command between MM. Bruix, Villeneuve, and Rosily. Owing to this or to some other delay, Vice-admiral Villeneuve did not hoist his flag on board the Bucentaure until the 6th of November, a few days anterior to which Lord Nelson had returned to his station from Agincourt sound; whither, since the 18th of the preceding month, the want of wood, water, and provisions had driven the British fleet. On the night of the 14th of November Lord Nelson received intelligence of the seizure of the Spanish frigates, and had, in consequence, a part of his attention directed to a squadron of five or six sail of the line at anchor in Carthagena. On the 25th of December the Swiftsure joined Lord Nelson; and on the 31st, in the evening, the British fleet, owing to the absence of the Superb, reduced again to 10 sail of the line, besides two frigates and a bomb-vessel, cruised about six leagues to the southward and eastward of Cape San-Sebastian. The French fleet in the outer road of Toulon, now increased to 11 sail of the line and seven or eight frigates, had since the 12th of the month been embarking the troops allotted for the intended expedition, and was ready for a start the moment a fair wind and a clear offing should afford the opportunity.

By the Swiftsure, or some small vessel that joined on the same day, Lord Nelson received despatches from the admiralty, respecting the conduct he was to pursue towards the Spaniards. The despatches were dated September 19, and directed him to take such measures of precaution only, as might be necessary for opposing or counteracting any hostile attempts of the Spaniards against the British dominions or trade. He was, however, not to suffer any act of hostility or aggression, with the exception of detaining Spanish ships with treasure on board, to be committed by his fleet until he received further orders, or had obtained positive information from unquestionable authority of hostilities having been committed by the Spaniards against the English. Additional directions, dated September 25, ordered

[1] See p. 216.

the captains and commanders of the Mediterranean fleet to keep a vigilant look-out, and to detain Spanish ships or vessels laden with military stores. On November 25, lest any misapprehension might arise, further instructions were sent out not to detain, in the first instance, any ship belonging to his catholic majesty, sailing from a port of Spain, but to require the commander to return directly to the port whence he came ; and, only in the event of his refusing to comply with such requisition, was the admiral to detain and send the vessel to Gibraltar or England : he was further directed not to detain any homeward-bound Spanish ship-of-war, unless she should have treasure on board, nor merchant-ships of that nation, however laden, on any account whatever.

Light Squadrons and Single Ships.

At the distance of rather less than a mile from the south-west end of the island of Martinique, or Pointe du Diamant, and about six miles south-east from the entrance to the harbour or bay of Fort Royal, stands the roche du Diamant, or Diamond rock, in latitude 14° 24' north, longitude 61° 6' west. In height, as measured by a quadrant, it is 600 feet ; in circumference rather less than a mile ; and " in form very much resembling a round haystack." The south side of the rock is inaccessible, it being a flat steep, like a wall, but sloping a little towards the top. The east and the south-west sides are also inaccessible ; the first has an overhanging cave about 300 yards high, and the other several caves of great magnitude. The west side, where breakers run into the sea, affords the only landing. But even this landing is not at all times practicable, on account of the surf; and a person, when he has landed, has to creep through crannies, and over dangerous steeps, until he reaches the north-west side, where the eye is suddenly relieved by a sloping grove of wild fig-trees.

In the latter end of the year 1803 the British 74-gun ship Centaur, Captain Murray Maxwell, bearing the broad pendant of Commodore Samuel Hood, was cruising off Fort Royal bay, to watch the port and intercept the vessels bound in or out of it. Finding that, as the Diamond had deep water all round, many vessels escaped capture by running inside of it, Captain Hood determined to take possession of and fortify the rock ; and make it a sort of depôt, or stationary ship of war, whence boats could be detached to harass the enemy's trade. A landing was effected ;

and in the course of the month of January, 1804, with incredible difficulty, five of the Centaur's guns, three long 24 and two 18 pounders, were mounted in different parts of this stupendous rock. The mode of getting them from the ship to an eminence so much higher than her mast-heads was characteristic and ingenious: a cable was made fast by one end to the ship and by the other to the rock, along which passed a traveller, or running loop; to this was suspended the cannon, or whatever else it was desirous to remove, and which, by means of suitable tackles, was dragged up the acclivity of the cable to the summit of the rock. "Were you to see," says a writer, who was on the spot, "how, along a dire, and, I had almost said, a perpendicular acclivity, the sailors are hanging in clusters, hauling up a four-and-twenty pounder by hawsers, you would wonder; they appear like mice hauling a little sausage: scarcely can we hear the governor on the top of the rock directing them with his trumpet, the Centaur lying close under it, like a cocoa-shell, to which the hawsers are affixed."[1]

One of the 24-pounders, fitted upon a circular carriage, commanded the landing place, and would reach in an eastern direction nearly across the bay of Marin. Another was mounted upon the north-east side, and the third 24 about midway up the rock. Upon the summit, which commands an immense distance, were mounted the two 18-pounders. As soon as these guns were all mounted, and a sufficient quantity of powder and shot for their use was brought from the Centaur, Lieutenant James Wilkes Maurice, of that ship, with the rank of commander, and a crew of 120 men and boys, for whom a four months' supply of provisions and water had also been landed, hoisted his pendant *on board* the British "sloop of war"[2] Diamond-rock.

On the evening of the 3rd of February four boats, containing 60 seamen and 12 marines, under the orders of Lieutenant Robert Carthew Reynolds, of the Centaur, then at her old station off the Diamond, were detached to attempt the capture of the French brig-corvette Curieux, Capitaine de frégate Joseph-Marie-Emmanuel Cordier, of 16 long 6-pounders and (supposed to have been about 100, but with only, as admitted) 70 men, lying at anchor close under Fort Edouard at the entrance of the Carénage, Fort Royal harbour, Martinique, victualled for three months, and all ready for a start to sea. Although the suspicion that an attack might be made by a part of the blockading force had led to every commendable precaution to prevent sur-

_____

[1] Naval Chronicle, vol. xii., p. 206.　　　[2] So registered in the navy-lists.

prise; such as, loading the carriage-guns with grape, and the swivels (of which there were eight) and wall-pieces with musket-balls, spreading on the quarter-deck and in the arm-chest the muskets, sabres, pistols, tomahawks, and pikes, filling the cartouch-boxes, placing, as sentries, one marine at each gang-way-ladder, one at each bow, and two at the stern, tracing up the boarding-nettings, and directing a sharp look-out to be kept by every officer and man of the watch (28 in number), yet was the Curieux, owing to the vigour of the onset and the hour chosen for making the attack, unapprised of her enemy's approach until too late to offer a successful resistance.

At about three-quarters of an hour past midnight, after a hard pull of 20 miles, and just as the moon was peeping from be-hind a cloud, the Centaur's boats were hailed by the Curieux, and then fired into by the sentries, by two of the starboard 6-pounders, a swivel, and a wall-piece. The 12 marines returned the fire with their muskets, and the boats pulled rapidly on In the midst of a scuffle alongside, the barge pushed for the brig's stern. Here hung a rope-ladder, to which two boats were fast. Lieutenant Reynolds, and a seaman named Richard Templeton, ascended by it to the taffrail, and, in defiance of the swivels and wall-pieces mounted at this end of the vessel, were quickly followed by the rest of the barge's crew. In his way up the ladder, Lieutenant Reynolds, with admirable coolness, cut away one of the tracing-lines with his sword, whereby the corner of the netting fell, and thus enabled the three remaining boats to board on the brig's quarter.

Since the first alarm had been given, all the Curieux's officers and men, headed by their brave commander, had been at their quarters; and a sanguinary combat now ensued, in which the French officers took a much more active part than a portion of their men. The French, however, were soon overpowered: some were killed or badly wounded; others thrown down the hatchway; and the remainder, finding themselves abandoned, retreated to the forecastle. Here a line of pikes stood opposed to the British; but all was unavailable. Handspikes and the butt-ends of muskets became formidable weapons in the hands of the latter, and soon laid the captain and most of the officers near him prostrate on the deck. The majority of the surviving crew having by this time fled below, all further resistance pre-sently ceased. The British were not long in cutting the cables of their prize, nor in unfurling her sails; and, in a very few minutes, the Curieux, in the hands of her new masters, stood out

of Fort Royal harbour. A smart fire was successively opened
from Fort Edouard, a battery on Pointe Negro, and another at
Pointe Soloman, but the brig passed clear, and, long before
break of day, was at anchor by the side of the Centaur.

It was an additional cause of congratulation to the British,
that their loss of men, considering the magnitude of the enterprise, was small, consisting of only nine wounded. Three of
the number, it is true, were officers; Lieutenant Reynolds, the
gallant leader of the party, his able second, Lieutenant George
Edmund Byron Bettesworth, and Mr. John Tracy, a midshipman. The two latter were not badly wounded; but the first-
named officer had received no fewer than five severe, and, as
they eventually proved, mortal wounds: one of the seamen, also,
died of his wounds. The loss on the part of the French was
very serious. The Curieux had one midshipman and nine petty
officers, seamen, and marines killed, and 30, including all her
commissioned officers but one midshipman, wounded, many of
them severely, and some mortally. The French captain had a
singular escape: after having been knocked down and stunned,
he was thrown overboard, but fell on the fluke of the anchor,
whence he dropped into one of the Curieux's boats which was
alongside, full of water-casks. The only man in the boat immediately cut her adrift, and pulled for the shore; and Captain
Cordelier, on recovering his senses, was as much chagrined as
surprised at the novelty of his situation.

The Curieux had long been at sea, and was considered to be
one of the best-manned and best-disciplined brigs in the French
navy. Some of her crew were undoubtedly panic-struck; but
the time, and the suddenness of the attack, coupled with its
resistless impetuosity, may serve in part for their excuse. The
determined behaviour of the French officers excited the admiration of their opponents; and Lieutenant Louis-Ange Cheminant,
and Enseigne de vaisseau Jean-Joseph-Maurice Joly (both
wounded), as likewise was their brave commander, particularly
distinguished themselves. The conduct of the British upon the
occasion speaks for itself.

Commodore Hood, very considerately, despatched the Curieux
to Fort Royal as a flag of truce with the wounded Frenchmen;
and Vice-admiral Villaret-Joyeuse, the governor-general of the
island, with a proper sense of the act, sent back his acknow-
ledgments. Upon her return, the Curieux, under her French
name, became a British sloop of war, and was given to the
officer who had headed the party that captured her; but Cap-

tain Reynolds's wounds were of too severe a nature to admit of his taking the immediate charge of his new command. This gallant young officer, indeed, breathed his last in the early part of the ensuing September.

The following passage occurs in a translated copy (all, we believe, that has been published) of Lieutenant Cheminant's letter to Governor Villaret: "I render justice to the English ; they not only afforded the last military honours to the midshipman Bourgonnière, but they afforded the most particular assistance to the wounded, and not the value of a handkerchief was taken from the crew."

On the 5th of February, at 3 P.M., the British 12-gun schooner Eclair (18-pounder carronades), Lieutenant William Carr, while cruising about 68 leagues to the northward of the island of Tortola, saw and immediately chased a strange sail to the southward. In about half an hour the stranger was discovered to be a ship standing towards the Eclair. At 4 P.M., having by the usual mode of signalling ascertained that the vessel approaching her was an enemy, the schooner shortened sail and cleared for action. At 4 h. 30 m. the ship, which from subsequent information was the celebrated French privateer Grand-Décidé, Captain Mathieu Goy, of 22 long 8-pounders, and a complement including 80 soldiers, of about 220 men, being within musket-shot on the larboard and weather bow of the Eclair, hauled up her courses, hove to, and hoisted French colours. When within pistol-shot, the Grand-Décidé commenced the action, by discharging her larboard broadside and a heavy fire of musketry, and received in return the larboard broadside of the schooner. The Eclair then wore round and fired her starboard broadside. In this manner the action continued, without intermission on either side, until 5 h. 15 m. P.M. ; when the French ship slackened her fire, filled, and bore up, as if intending to rake the schooner; but, instead of doing so, the privateer ceased firing, and made all sail to the northward. The Eclair instantly filled, and made sail in chase. At 7 P.M. the Grand-Décidé was getting away fast, and by 8 h. 30 m. had run entirely out of sight.

In this truly gallant exploit, the Eclair, out of her 60 men and boys, lost one marine killed and four seamen wounded, and had her standing and running rigging cut to pieces, and her barricade, masts, and yards much damaged. That a ship so powerful in guns and men as the Grand-Décidé, should, in a 45 minutes' engagement, have done no more execution in personnel, is as extraordinary as that she should have ultimately fled from a vessel so much her inferior in guns, complement, and size. It was, however, established, to the entire satisfaction of Commodore Hood, that the privateer was the Grand-Décidé from Guadaloupe, and that she was so armed and manned. The gallantry of Lieutenant Carr in attacking such a vessel, and the ability and determination displayed by him, his officers, and crew, throughout a contest which, in spite of the inequality of force, terminated so creditably to the Eclair, merited all the praise called forth upon the occasion.

On the 5th of March, at 2 p.m., the Eclair, still commanded by Lieutenant Carr, while passing Englishman's Head, Guadaloupe, discovered a schooner, which shortly afterwards hoisted a red pendant, stood into the Hayes, and anchored close under some batteries on the shore. Upon a nearer approach, Lieutenant Carr ascertained that the vessel was a French privateer, filled with men : and he would then have sent in the cutter to attack her, had not the wind from the westward blown fresh on the shore. At 7 p.m. it fell calm; and the cutter, commanded by Mr. John Salmon, the master, having under him Mr. John B. Douglas, the surgeon (also a volunteer), and 10 seamen, quitted the Eclair, and proceeded towards the harbour in which the privateer lay.

Notwithstanding a smart fire from the battery at the entrance of the harbour, and from the vessel herself, the master persevered, and after a stout resistance of 10 minutes, boarded and carried the French privateer-schooner Rose, of one long brass-8-pounder on a pivot, and 49 men, well armed and fully prepared. Of these the privateer had five men killed, and 10, including the captain and four that jumped overboard, wounded. Of the 12 officers and men, who had in so gallant a manner effected this capture not one was hurt. The master's next difficulty was, in a dead calm, to carry off his prize. This he and his men at length did, by dint of towing and sweeping; and, although exposed to a fire of great guns and musketry from the shore, reached their vessel without the slightest accident. The Rose was well found, and victualled complete for a three months' cruise, upon which she was just going to sail, when the Eclair's boat so gallantly intercepted her.

On the 31st of January, Commodore Nathaniel Dance, of the honourable East India Company's service, sailed from Canton for Europe with the following 16 regular Indiamen, all of which are denominated " 1200-ton ships," the registered tonnage of most, however, exceeds 1300, and in some cases amounts to 1500 tons :—

Earl Camden . . .	Nathaniel Dance,
Warley	Henry Wilson,
Alfred	James Farquharson,
Royal George . . .	John Fam Timmins
Coutts	Robert Torin,
Wexford.	William Stanley Clarke,
Ganges	William Moffat,
Exeter	Henry Meriton,
Earl of Abergavenny .	John Wordsworth,
Henry Addington . .	John Kirkpatrick,
Bombay Castle . . .	Arch. Hamilton,
Cumberland . . .	William Ward Farrer,
Hope	James Pendergrass,
Dorsetshire	Rob. Hunter Brown,
Warren Hastings . .	Thomas Larkins,
Ocean	John Christ. Lochner,

also 11 country-ships, one Botany-bay and one Portuguese ship, and a fast-sailing armed brig, the Ganges, in the company's service ; total, 39 ships and one brig.

On the 14th of February, at 8 A.M., Pulo-Auro, in sight and bearing west-south-west, the Royal George made the signal for seeing four strange sail in the south-west. Commodore Dance immediately signalled the Alfred, Royal George, Bombay Castle, and Hope, to go down and examine the strangers : and Lieutenant Robert Fowler, late commander of the British armed store-ship Porpoise (wrecked in the preceding August), and at this time a passenger on board the Earl Camden, volunteered to go in the Ganges brig on the same service. The signals of the look-out ships soon apprised the commodore that the strange vessels were a French squadron, consisting of a line-of-battle ship, three frigates, and a brig. They were, in fact, the 74-gun ship Marengo, Captain Joseph-Marie Vrignaud, 40-gun frigate Belle-Poule, Captain Alain-Adélaïde-Marie Bruilhac, 36-gun frigate Sémillante, Captain Léonard-Bernard Motard, 22-gun corvette Berceau, Captain Emmanuel Halgan, and the Batavian 16-gun brig-corvette Aventurier, which Rear-admiral Linois, whose flag was on board the Marengo, had borrowed from the colonial government at Batavia and commissioned by one of his lieutenants. On the 10th of the preceding December, it will be remembered the Marengo and her three consorts anchored in the road of Batavia.[1] Thence they sailed on the 28th, accompanied by the Aventurier, and stored with six months' provisions, on

---

[1] See p. 211.

purpose to look after the China fleet, of whose strength and time of departure Rear-admiral Linois had, as he declares, been duly informed.

At 1 P.M. the British commodore recalled the look-out ships, and formed the line of battle in close order. Admiral Linois, as soon as he could fetch in the wake of the British fleet, which he knew to be that expected from China, put about. The ships of the latter continued their course under easy sail ; and, as the French were now close astern, Commodore Dance expected his rear to be attacked, and prepared to support it ; but, at night-fall, the French ships, preferring a daylight action, hauled close to the wind. The Ganges brig was sent to station the country-ships on the lee bow of the armed Indiamen, and, having done so, returned with some volunteers for the latter.

The British ships lay-to all night, the men at their quarters. At daybreak on the 15th the French, having made a proper use of the intermediate time, were about three miles to windward, also lying-to. M. Linois in his letters says: " If the bold front put on by the enemy in the daytime had been intended as a ruse to conceal his weakness, he would have profited by the darkness of the night to endeavour to conceal his escape ; and in that case I should have taken advantage of his manœuvres. But I soon became convinced that this security was not feigned ; three of his ships constantly kept their lights up, and the fleet con-tinued to lie-to, in order of battle, throughout the night. This position facilitated my gaining the wind, and enabled me to ob-serve the enemy closely."[1]

Both parties now hoisted their colours. Three of Commodore Dance's principal ships and the armed brig hoisted blue ensigns ; the remainder of the fleet, red; and the whole of the China ships, having been recently painted, cut rather an imposing figure. This circumstance, coupled with the information that only 23 ships and a brig had quitted Canton, led, as he states, M. Linois to believe, that the three supernumerary ships formed the escort to the fleet. Admitting this to have been the fact, the French admiral was justified in making his advance with caution. At 9 A.M., observing that the enemy's men of war did not come down, the Indiamen formed in order of sailing, and continued their course under an easy sail upon the starboard tack ; whereupon the three French ships and Batavian brig filled on the opposite tack, and edged away towards the mer-chant fleet.

[1] See Appendix, No. 20

At 1 P.M., finding that M. Linois intended to cut off his rear, Commodore Dance made the signal to tack in succession, bear down in line ahead, and engage on arriving abreast of the enemy. The manœuvre was correctly executed, the Royal George leading, followed successively, in close order, by the Ganges, Earl Camden, Warley, Alfred, and others. Thus formed, and carrying topgallantsails, the British ships stood towards the French ships ; and these, carrying royals, and some of them topgallant studding-sails, were keeping more away to facilitate the junction.

At about 1 h. 15 m. P.M. the French admiral opened his fire upon the Royal George and the ships next astern of her. The Royal George returned the fire in a very spirited manner, and was ably seconded, as they came up, by the Ganges and Earl Camden. The Warley and Alfred were the next ships that got into action. The Royal George was engaged about 40 minutes, and fired about eight or nine broadsides ; the Ganges, about 35 minutes, and fired seven or eight ; the Earl Camden, about 25 minutes, and may have fired five broadsides ; and the Warley and Alfred, who came into action nearly together, were engaged about 15 minutes. After the mutual cannonade had lasted in this way just 43 minutes, the Marengo and her consorts ceased firing, hauled their wind, and stood away under all sail to the eastward.

At 2 P.M. the Earl Camden made the signal for a general chase, and the Indiamen pursued the French admiral until 4 P.M. ; when, considering the immense property at stake, and fearing that his charge might be carried too far from the mouth of the Straits of Malacca, Commodore Dance made the signal to tack, which was immediately obeyed. At 8 A.M. the British ships anchored in a situation to enter the Straits in the morning, and soon lost sight of the squadron of M. Linois. The following is the French admiral's account of the defeat which he acknowledges to have experienced :—" The headmost enemy's ship, having sustained some damage, bore away ; but, supported by those astern, again brought her broadside to bear, and, as well as the others, kept up a very spirited fire. The ships which had tacked rejoined those which were engaging us, and three of the first engaged ships manœuvred to double our rear, while the remainder of the fleet, crowding sail and bearing up, evinced an intention to surround us.[1] By this manœuvre the enemy would

---

[1] We do not understand what is meant by this, and yet the account clearly so states, thus : " Trois de ceux qui avaient des premiers pris part à l'action, manœuv- raient pour nous doubler à l'arrière, tandis que le reste de la flotte, se couvrant de voile, et laissant arriver, annonçait le projet de nous envelopper."

have rendered my situation very dangerous. The superiority of his force was ascertained, and I had no longer to deliberate upon the part I should take to avoid the consequences of an unequal engagement : profiting by the smoke, I hauled up to port, and steering east-north-east, I increased my distance from the enemy, who continued the pursuit of the squadron for three hours, discharging at it several ineffective broadsides."[1]

The Royal George had one man killed and one wounded, and received several shot in the hull, and more in her sails; comparatively trifling casualties, considering that she bore the brunt of the action, and was so long engaged. Few shot touched either the Ganges or the Earl Camden; and no other loss or damage appears to have been sustained by the British during this three-quarters of an hour's partial cannonade. The fire of the Royal George, and the three or four ships in her wake, being chiefly directed at the rigging of the French ships, did not, according to M. Linois, injure a person on board of them.

With respect to the armament of the 16 Indiamen thus drawn up in line of battle, they carried from 30 to 36 guns each; but the strongest of them was not a match for the Sémillante, and some of them would have found it difficult to avoid yielding to the Berceau. Some of the ships carried upon the main deck 26 medium 18-pounders, or "cannonades," weighing about 28 cwt. and of very little use : guns of this description, indeed, have long since been exploded. Ten 18-pounder carronades on the quarter-deck made up the 36 guns. Others of the ships, and those among the largest, mounted long 12 and 6 pounders. No one of the crews, we believe, exceeded 140 men, and that number included Chinese, Lascars, &c. Mereover, in fitting the ships, so much more attention had been paid to stowage than to the means of attack and defence, that one and sometimes two butts of water were lashed between the guns, and the decks in general greatly lumbered. Of the force of the French ships it will be sufficient to say that the Marengo, Belle Poule, and Sémillante were armed as Nos. 4, 5, and 7 in the small Table at p. 59 of the first volume. The force of the Berceau has already appeared,[2] and that of the brig is too insignificant to notice.

.The promptitude and firmness of Commodore Dance and his brave associates undoubtedly saved from capture a rich and valuable fleet. The slightest indecision in him or them would have encouraged the French admiral to persevere in his attack; and, had he done so, no efforts, however gallant and judicious,

[1] See Appendix, No. 21.   [2] See p. 32.

could have prevented a part of the fleet at least from falling into his hands. It would be uncharitable to call in question the courage of Rear-admiral Linois: one must therefore suppose that it was, as he has stated, the warlike appearance of those 16 ships, the regularity of their manœuvres, and the boldness of their advance, that led the French admiral to doubt whether a part of them were not national cruisers; more especially as it was an uncommon occurrence, during a war, for an East-India fleet to be without the protection of one or more powerful king's ships.

The commanders, officers, and crews of their respective ships that had thus distinguished themselves were liberally rewarded by the East-India Company, as well as by the committee for managing the Patriotic Fund.[1] Commodore Dance, also, as he well merited, received from his late majesty the honour of knighthood. Among the sums of money voted to Sir Nathaniel were 5000*l.* by the Bombay Insurance Society; and the answer of thanks returned by the commodore contains the following passage :—" Placed, by the adventitious circumstances of seniority of service and absence of convoy, in the chief command of the fleet intrusted to my care, it has been my good fortune to have been enabled, by the firmness of those by whom I was supported, to perform my trust not only with fidelity, but without loss to my employers. Public opinion and public rewards have already far outrun my deserts ; and I cannot but be sensible that the liberal spirit of my generous countrymen has measured what they are pleased to term their grateful sense of my conduct, rather by the particular utility of the exploit than by any individual merit I can claim." Here is an instance of modesty and candour as exemplary as it is rare, and which sheds an additional lustre upon the character of Sir Nathaniel Dance.

On the 19th of February the British 14-gun brig-sloop Drake, under the temporary command of Lieutenant William King of the Centaur, while cruising off the port of Trinité on the north side of the island of Martinique, discovered in the harbour,

---

[1] This truly named " Patriotic Fund," originated at a meeting of the subscribers to Lloyd's Coffee-house, held on the 20th of July, 1803, Brook Watson, Esq., in the chair. The object is explained in the third resolution :—" That, to animate the efforts of our defenders by sea and land, it is expedient to raise by the patriotism of the community at large, a suitable fund for their comfort and relief—for the purpose of assuaging the anguish of their wounds, or palliating in some degree the more weighty misfortune of the loss of limbs—of alleviating the distresses of the widow and orphan — of smoothing the brow of sorrow for the fall of dearest relatives, the props of unhappy indigence or helpless age—and of granting pecuniary rewards, or honourable badges of distinction, for successful exertions of valour of merit."

taking in cargoes in defiance of the blockade, two American brigs and a schooner, moored within pistol-shot of a fort mounting three French 24-pounders. Being determined to make an attempt to cut out these vessels, Lieutenant King despatched the boats of the Drake, under the orders of Lieutenant William Cumpston, assisted by Mr. William Robson, the master, upon that service. The three American vessels were gallantly boarded and taken possession of, in the face of a heavy fire from the fort, and from two field-pieces: but, having no wind, Lieutenant Cumpston and his party could only succeed in bringing out the schooner, which was accomplished without loss.

On the night of the 24th Lieutenant King himself, with 21 seamen and nine marines, landed and spiked the guns at the fort and the two field-pieces, with the loss of one seaman killed, and Lieutenant Cumpston and one seaman slightly wounded.

On the night of the 4th of March the barge and pinnace of the 74-gun ship Blenheim, Captain William Ferris, having on board 50 officers and men under the orders of Lieutenant Thomas Furber, made a most gallant but unsuccessful attempt to cut out the French national schooner Curieuse, lying chain-moored close under a fort at the town of St. Pierre. The schooner had made very formidable preparations, having rigged out her sweeps, on each side, traced her boarding-nettings to her lower mast-heads, and there fastened them in the securest manner. Notwithstanding all this, and a heavy fire of great guns and musketry, as well from the schooner herself as from a party of soldiers drawn up on the beach, from the neighbouring forts, and from an armed sloop and several smaller vessels, Lieutenant Furber and those under him gallantly boarded and carried the Curieuse ; but, no sooner were her cables cut than the schooner, held fast by the chain, swang round and grounded upon the beach. The severe loss now sustained obliged Lieutenant Furber to desist from any further attempts ; and the two boats got back to the Blenheim, with one seaman, and two marines killed, five officers (names not reported), 11 seamen, and three marines wounded, and three seamen missing.

On the morning of the 13th of March the British 18-pounder 36-gun frigate Emerald, Captain James O'Brien, observed a French privateer-schooner, on account of inability to work up to St. Pierre's, run in and anchor close under a battery at Seron, just within the Pearl rock at the western extremity of Martinique. As the frigate herself, being considerably to leeward, was unable to reach the spot in time, Captain O'Brien de-spatched the armed sloop Fort Diamond, with Lieutenant Thomas Forrest and 30 volunteers, to attempt the service; and, in order to take off the attention of the battery from the move-ments of the sloop, he sent in a different direction the frigate's boats, joined by two from the 44-gun ship Pandour, which had just hove in sight.

Having reached the anchorage, Lieutenant Forrest dashed in, and laid the French schooner on board, the crew of which, amounting to about 60 whites and blacks, after discharging her broadside and a volley of musketry, fled over the side to the shore. By the force with which the Fort-Diamond struck the schooner, the chain by which the latter had fastened herself to the shore was broken, and about 20 feet of it remained hanging at her bows. The prize proved to be the privateer Mosambique, armed with ten 18-pounder carronades, commanded by Captain Vallentes, and fitted for a three months' cruise. This very gallant exploit was performed with so trifling a loss as one master's mate (Mr. Hall) and one seaman wounded.

On the 14th of March, in the morning, the British brig-sloop Drake, still commanded by Lieutenant William King, cruising off Englishman's Head, island of Guadaloupe, fell in with a French privateer-schooner, and a large ship in company, appa-rently her prize, but was unable to overtake either until the ship ran herself on shore near the batteries of the Hayes. The Drake now endeavoured to cut off the schooner; but, having had her maintopmast shot away and her rigging much damaged, was unable to effect her object. About this time another ship hove in sight in the offing, and appeared to be steering as if also with the intention to run on shore. Despatching two boats, under the orders of Mr. Robson the master, to watch the first ship, now observed to be again afloat, with directions to attack her should she endeavour to escape, Lieutenant King made sail after and recaptured the sail in the offing, an English merchantman, valuably laden.

The Drake's two boats, meanwhile, pulled in towards the ship in-shore, the crew of which, except one man who had not time to effect his escape, abandoned her as the former approached. Possession of the ship, which had 18 guns mounted and was very large, was thus easily obtained; but in half an hour she blew up, killing one master's mate, three seamen, and one marine, and mortally wounding Mr. Robson, who expired a few hours afterwards, and badly wounding several of the small party belonging to the two boats. In all cases, where a vessel is abandoned in this way, treachery should be suspected, and the magazine be quickly examined. There can be little doubt that the fellow who was behind his comrades, had laid the train which produced the fatal explosion.

On the 17th of March the British 16-gun brig-sloop Penguin, Captain George Morris, cruising off Sénégal bar, chased and drove upon it the French privateer-schooner Renommée of 12 long 6-pounders and 87 men, belonging to Sénégal. Owing to the continuance of the surf, no opportunity occurred of making an attempt to destroy her until the morning of the 24th. At this time the Renommée had shifted her position, from the efforts apparently of two armed schooners, which, since the preceding evening, had dropped down to the mouth of the river, and now lay within 200 yards of her.

Standing as close in as the shoalness of the water would admit, the Penguin opened a fire upon the three vessels; but, although shot were exchanged for an hour and a half, the brig could not get near enough to force the two schooners to retire up the river. At 10 P.M., therefore, Captain Morris despatched the jolly-boat, under the command of Lieutenant Charles Williams, with directions to endeavour to destroy the grounded schooner; a service which was executed in the ablest manner before 1 A.M. on the 25th, and that without any loss on the part of the British.

On the 23rd of March, the British 18-gun ship-sloop Osprey, Captain George Younghusband, cruising on the Windward-island station, discovered in the south-west quarter, and immediately chased, the French frigate-built privateer Egyptienne, of 36 guns, Captain Placiard, with three merchant-ships under her convoy. As soon as the Osprey had arrived within hail, the Egyptienne hoisted her colours and fired a broadside. This was instantly returned, and the two ships continued in close action for one hour and 20 minutes: at the end of which time the Egyptienne ceased firing, and began to make off, and her convoy to separate on different courses. To the regret of the British officers and crew, it was soon found that the French ship, even with her topsails on the cap, outsailed their vessel. The Osprey, however, continued the chase, until the Egyptienne disappeared in the dark.

The force of the Osprey consisted of 16 carronades, 32-pounders and two sixes, with a complement of 120 men and boys: that of the Egyptienne was 36 guns, French 12 and 6 pounders, with a crew on board of 248 men. The one ship measured, 386,[1] and the other, which was formerly the national frigate Railleuse,[2] since given or sold to some merchants at Bordeaux, 857 tons. The Osprey sustained a loss of one man killed and 16 wounded, and was a good deal damaged in her sails and rigging. The loss on board the Egyptienne, as afterwards ascertained, amounted, out of a crew of 248 men and boys, to eight men killed and 19 wounded; and the ship herself was very much cut by shot in hull, masts, sails, and rigging: a proof that the Osprey's carronades had been discharged with quickness and precision.

It is exploits like these that afford examples of gallantry in the true import of the word. Had Captain Younghusband, on discovering the size and strength of the Egyptienne, forborne to attack her, no imputation would have rested on his professional character. But he had a higher sense of the duties of a British naval commander: he chose to wrestle with his powerful antagonist; and so vigorous and effective was his attack, that nothing but lightness of heel saved the Egyptienne from becoming his prize. In such a creditable encounter we must not omit to state, that Lieutenant Francis Augustus Collier was second in command of the Osprey.

On the 25th, in the forenoon, this same Egyptienne fell in with the British 14-gun ship-sloop Hippomenes (ten long 12, and 2 long 8 pounders, and two 24-pounder carronades, all Dutch caliber), Captain Conway Shipley, and mistaking her probably for the ship she had been so beaten by two days before, crowded sail to get off. The Hippomenes pursued, and, after an arduous chase of 54 hours, and a running fight of three hours and 20 minutes more, came up with and captured the French ship. The Egyptienne struck the moment the sloop got fairly alongside; and, owing to her feeble resistance, inflicted no greater loss on the Hippomenes than slightly wounding one person, Mr. John Lloyd, a master's mate.

The bold front and rational confidence of the Egyptienne in the beginning of the one action, and her panic-struck behaviour and hasty flight in that of the other, occasion the principal difference in the merits of the two. The conduct of Captain Shipley was much enhanced by his readiness to do justice to the performance of his brother-commander of the Osprey, "whose gallantry," he says, "astonished them." It is probable that M. Placiard found a difficulty in persuading the merchants of

---

[1] See vol. ii., p. 482, note Y*   [2] See vol. i., p. 427.

Bordeaux again to place him in the command of one of their privateers.

Being 30 years old and much broken in her sheer, the Egyptienne was purchased into the British service merely as a prison-ship. Her name was changed to Antigua ; and she was stationed at English harbour, in the island of that name.

On the 24th of March the British ship-sloop Wolverine, of 13 guns,[1] Captain Henry Gordon, being in latitude 48° 15′ north, and longitude 23° 15′ west, on her way to Newfoundland with eight merchant-vessels under her protection, discovered to the eastward, which was directly to windward, two large sail bearing down for the convoy. At 2 h. 30 m. P.M. the strangers were made out to be vessels of force, and soon afterwards to be enemies. Finding it to be their intention to cut off the rear of the convoy, the Wolverine tacked ; and, as she stood on between the latter and them, signalled the merchantmen to make the best of their way into port.

At 4 P.M., having arrived within half gun-shot of the larger vessel, which was the French frigate-privateer Blonde, Captain Aregnaudeau, of 30 guns, including 24 long 8-pounders on the main deck, the Wolverine hove-to on the starboard tack ; whereupon the Blonde hauled her wind, and, after firing her broadside, wore, with the intention of raking the Wolverine. To frustrate this manœuvre, and to maintain her leeward position, which, on account of the extreme lowness of her ports and the consequent necessity of using her weather-battery, was more advantageous to her, the Wolverine, before she discharged a gun, wore also. The Blonde then hove-to on the Wolverine's larboard beam, within pistol-shot distance, and commenced a heavy and well-directed fire with great guns and small arms ; which was returned by the British vessel with considerable spirit, although one of her two long 18-pounders, in being shifted from the starboard to the larboard side, got jammed in the groove, and remained utterly useless. In this way the action continued for 50 minutes ; when, having had her rigging and sails cut to pieces, her wheel shot away, and her hull low down, so pierced with shot as to fill the hold with water, the Wolverine hauled down her colours.

Out of her complement of 76 men and boys, the Wolverine had one midshipman, one boatswain's mate, one quartermaster, and two seamen killed, and 10 seamen wounded, one of them mortally. The Blonde, formerly, it is believed, a French

1 For the extraordinary manner in which this sloop was fitted, see vol. ii., p. 353.

national "24-gun corvette" of 580 or 600 tons, out of a complement of 240 men and boys, did not, according to the admission of her officers, sustain any greater loss than her first-lieutenant mortally, and five of her men slightly, wounded. The damage done to the Blonde was confined to her rigging and sails, and that comparatively trifling.

In less than a quarter of an hour after the last boat with the prisoners had quitted her, the Wolverine gave a heel and went down; thereby affording an irrefragable proof that the ship had been defended to the last extremity, and that her officers and crew were barely saved, by their surrender, from perishing in the deep. The long duration of the action was not without its effect. The second privateer, either from bad sailing or bad management, could not overtake one of the eight merchant-vessels; nor could the Blonde withdraw herself in time to do more than capture two of the number: the remainder effected their escape.

A 50 minutes' close engagement between two ships so decidedly unequal in force entitled the weaker, although the vanquished party to at least as much praise as is usually bestowed upon the victor in a well-matched contest. Had the Blonde been a national ship, and even worse armed, worse manned, and worse fought than she was, Captain Gordon and his first-lieutenant would have been promoted for their gallantry, and the conduct of all on board the Wolverine been held up as an example of the devotedness of British seamen in upholding the honour of their flag, and in protecting the commercial interests of their country. But, as it was a privateer, a "paltry privateer," in the words of the Annual Register, which had captured the king's ship, the action of the Wolverine and Blonde was considered to be discreditable to the former, and therefore not worthy to be recorded in the annals of the British navy. To make success the sole criterion of merit is as unjust as it is discouraging: where, then, is the stimulus to persevere in an almost hopeless, or even in a barely doubtful cause; and what more can a seaman do, than stand to his gun until his vessel sinks under him?

This is as the account stands in our first edition; and, although not a line of the details here given is to be found in any other publication, we may usefully add the following from the work of a contemporary, published since; and to whom, we believe, that information on the subject was granted which was refused to us. " Captain Gordon, though many years a prisoner, was promoted to the rank of post-captain, and, on his return to England, most honourably acquitted by the sentence of a court-martial."[1] The admiralty list informs us, that Captain Gordon was made post on the 8th of April, 1805: it was this lapse of nearly 13 months, and our unacquaintance, for the reason already stated, with the requested particulars of his case, which occasioned us to suppose that Captain Gordon had not been rewarded in the manner he deserved.

On the 26th of March the British 36-gun frigate Apollo, Captain John William Taylor Dixon, and 28-gun frigate Carysfort, Captain Robert Fanshawe, sailed from the Cove of Cork with 69 merchant-vessels under convoy, bound to the West Indies. On the 2nd of April, at 3 A.M., while steering south-south-east with a strong south-west gale, to the astonishment of every person on board, the Apollo struck the ground. The ship continued striking very heavily, and making much water: in about 10 minutes, however, the Apollo beat over the shoal, and having lost her rudder, could not be steered. The ship then put before the wind, but, from the quantity of water she had made, and was still making, with every probability of soon foundering. In about five minutes, the Apollo struck the ground again, and continued striking with such tremendous shocks, that it was feared the ship would instantly go to pieces. The three masts were then cut away, and the ship fell on the starboard side with her gunwale under water. The violence with which the ship struck the ground, and the weight of the guns, those on the quarter-deck tearing away the bulwarks, soon made the frigate a perfect wreck abaft: only four or five guns, therefore, could be fired to alarm the convoy and give notice of danger.

Most of the officers and men were entirely naked, the captain among the rest; and who stood upon the cabin skylight grating, holding fast by the stump of the mizenmast, and making use of every soothing expression which could have been suggested to encourage men in so perilous a situation. Daylight, which appeared at about 4 h. 30 m., discovered the land, at the distance of about 200 yards, a long sandy beach reaching to Cape Mondego, three leagues to the southward. At the same time the melancholy sight presented itself of between 20 and 30 sail of the convoy on shore both to the northward and southward, and several of them perfect wrecks. An appearance of the ship's

---

[1] Brenton, vol. iii., p. 391. The complement of the Blonde is here reduced to "180 men;" but, in confirmation of the accuracy of our account, we may state that the ship was captured by the British a few months afterwards with 240 men on board.

parting occasioned the crew, or the 220 that remained (about 20 having perished between decks and otherwise), by the captain's orders to remove to the forepart of the ship; and, soon afterwards, the Apollo parted at the gangways. Several officers and men, who attempted to swim on shore, were drowned. About 30, however, succeeded in reaching the shore upon planks and spars: among them were Lieutenant Edward Harvey, and Mr. Callam, master's mate. The succeeding night was a dreadful one, many old men and boys, including two young midshipmen, dying through hunger and fatigue. During the whole of it Captain Dixon remained upon the bowsprit.

We shall give the remainder of the melancholy details in the words of one of the officers of the ship: "Tuesday morning presented us no better prospect of being relieved from the jaws of death, the wind blowing stronger, and the sea much more turbulent. About noon, this day, our drooping spirits were somewhat raised by seeing Lieutenant Harvey and Mr. Callam hoisting out a boat from one of the merchant-ships to come to the assistance of their distressed shipmates. They several times attempted to launch her through the surf, but being a very heavy boat, and the sea on the beach acting so powerfully against them, they could not possibly effect it, though assisted by nearly 100 of the merchant-sailors and Portuguese peasants. Several men went upon rafts this day, made from pieces of the wreck, but not one soul reached the shore; the wind having shifted, and the current setting out, they were all driven to sea; among whom was our captain, who, about three in the afternoon, went on the jib-boom with three seamen; anxious to save the remainder of the ship's company, and too sanguine of getting safe on shore, he ventured upon the spar, saying, on jumping into the sea, 'My lads, I'll save you all.' In a few seconds he lost his hold of the spar, which he could not regain: he drifted to sea, and perished. Such was also the fate of the three brave volunteers who followed his fortune. The loss of our captain, who, until now, had animated the almost lifeless crews; as well as the noble exertions of Lieutenant Harvey and Mr. Callam, to launch the boat, not succeeding, every gleam of hope vanished, and we looked forward for certain death the ensuing night, not only from cold, hunger, and fatigue, but the expectation of the remaining part of the wreck going to pieces every moment. Had not the Apollo been a new and well-built ship, that small portion of her could never have resisted the waves and stuck so well together, particularly as all the after-part from the chess-trees was gone, the starboard bow under water, the forecastle deck nearly perpendicular, the weight of the guns hanging to the larboard bulwark on the inside, and the bower and spare anchors on the outside, which it was not prudent to cut away, as they afforded resting places to a considerable number of men, there being only the fore channels and cathead, where it was possible to live in, and about which were stowed upwards of 150 men : it being impracticable to continue any longer in the head, or upon the bowsprit, by reason of the breakers washing completely over those places. The night drawing on, the wind increasing, frequent showers of rain, the sea washing over us, and looking every instant for the forecastle giving way, when we must all have perished together, afforded a spectacle truly deplorable, the bare recollection of which even now makes me shudder. The piercing cries of the people this dismal night, at every sea coming over them, which happened every two minutes, were pitiful in the extreme ; the water running from the head down all over the body, keeping us continually wet. This shocking night, the remaining strength of every person was exerted for his individual safety. From the crowding so close together in so narrow a compass, and the want of something to moisten their mouths, several poor wretches were suffocated, which frequently reminded me of the black hole, with this only difference, that these poor sufferers were confined by strong walls, we by water ; the least movement without clinging fast would have launched us into eternity. Some unfortunate wretches drank salt water, several their own urine, some chewed leather, myself and many more chewed lead, from which we conceived we found considerable relief, by reason of its drawing the saliva, which we swallowed. In less than an hour after the ship first struck the ground, all the provisions were under water, and the ship a wreck, so that it was impossible to procure any part. After the most painful night that it is possible to conceive, on daylight appearing, we observed Lieutenant Harvey and Mr. Callam again endeavouring to launch the boat. Several attempts were made without success, a number of men belonging to the merchant-ships being much bruised and hurt in assisting; alternate hopes and fears now pervaded our wretched minds; fifteen men got safe on shore this morning, on pieces of the wreck. About three in the afternoon of Wednesday the 4th, we had the inexpressible happiness of seeing the boat launched through the surf, by the indefatigable exertion of the above officers, assisted by the masters of the merchant-ships, with a number of Portuguese peasants, who were encouraged by Mr. Whitney, the British consul from Figuiera. All the crew then remaining on the wreck were brought safe on shore, praising God for a happy deliverance from a shipwreck which has never had its parallel. As soon as I stept out of the boat, I found several persons whose humanity prompted them to offer me sustenance, though improperly, in spirits, which I avoided as much as possible. Our weak state may be conceived, when it is considered that we received no nourishment from Sunday to Wednesday afternoon, and continually exposed to the fury of the watery elements. After eating and drinking a little, I found myself weaker than before, occasioned, I apprehend, from having been so long without either. Some men died soon after getting on shore, from imprudently drinking too large a quantity of spirits. All the crew were in a very weak and exhausted state, the greater part being badly bruised and wounded. About 40 sail of merchant-ships were wrecked at the same time on this dreadful beach. Some ships sunk with all their crew, and almost every ship lost from two to twelve men each; yet the situation of the remainder was not equal to that of the frigate's ship's company, as the merchant-ships drawing a less draught of water, were mostly driven close on the shore, and no person remained on board them after the first morning. The masters of the merchant-ships had tents upon the beach, and some provisions they had saved from the wrecks, which they very generously distributed, and gave every assistance to the Apollo's ship's company."

Fortunately for the remainder of the convoy, Captain Fanshawe, without signal, wore just as it grew dark; and, with all the ships who were near enough to see and adopt her change of course, the Carysfort arrived in safety at Barbadoes. Of the Apollo's crew, 61 officers and men were lost; but the number that perished from the merchant-vessels was comparatively insignificant, for the reason already given.

On the 28th of March the British 18-gun brig-sloop Scorpion, Captain George Nicholas Hardinge, having been detached by Rear-admiral Thornborough to reconnoitre the Vlie passage into the Texel, discovered two Dutch brig-corvettes at anchor in the road. At the outermost, which was the Atalante, of 16 long 12-pounders, Captain Hardinge resolved to make a dash with his boats; an attack by the Scorpion herself being impracticable, owing to the numerous shoals that surround the entrance. On the 31st, just as a favourable opportunity occurred,

and the men were about to embark, the British 14-gun ship-
sloop Beaver, Captain Charles Pelly, joined company. The
latter, at his urgent request, was permitted to serve under
Captain Hardinge; and at 9 h. 30 m. P.M., three boats from
the Scorpion, and two from the Beaver, containing between
them about 60 officers and men, pushed off from the first-named
sloop.

Having the flood-tide in their favour, the boats, in two hours,
arrived alongside of the Atalante, who had her boarding-nettings
traced up, and was fully prepared to resist the attack. Captain
Hardinge was the first man that leaped on board. His boat
was promptly supported by the others; and such was the impetuosity of the assault, that many of the Dutchmen quitted
their quarters and ran below "leaving to us," says Captain
Hardinge, in a private letter, "the painful duty of combating
those whom we respected the most." These, the remainder of
a crew on board of 76, after a short but severe conflict, in which
they had their commander and three seamen killed, their first-
lieutenant, two other officers, and eight seamen badly wounded,
were overpowered. The British then set about securing the
hatches, which the party below, headed by a lieutenant, repeatedly attempted to force. The Dutch officer, however, receiving a desperate wound, his men relaxed their efforts, and
at length surrendered. Of the five boats employed, those of
the Scorpion only sustained any loss; and that was comparatively trifling, amounting to only one lieutenant (Buckland
Stirling Bluett), the sloop's master (Woodward Williams), one
midshipman (Edmund Jones), and two seamen wounded.

The above private letter from Captain Hardinge contains
some interesting particulars, not less illustrative of the writer's
gallantry than of his goodness of heart. "The decks," he says,
"were slippery in consequence of rain; so that, grappling with
my first opponent, a mate of the watch, I fell, but recovering
my position, fought him upon equal terms, and killed him. I
then engaged the captain, as brave a man as any service ever
boasted: he had almost killed one of my seamen. To my
shame be it spoken, he disarmed me, and was on the point of
killing me, when a seaman of mine," as Captain H. thought at
the time, but it was Mr. Williams, the master of the Scorpion,
"came up, rescued me at the peril of his own life, and enabled
me to recover my sword. At this time all the men were come
from the boats, and were in possession of the deck. Two were
going to fall upon the captain at once. I ran up, held them

back, and then adjured him to accept quarter. With inflexible heroism he disdained the gift, kept us at bay, and compelled us to kill him. He fell, covered with honourable wounds."

Having, in the manner related, possessed themselves of the Atalante, the British had another enemy to combat: a sudden gale from an adverse quarter frustrated all their attempts to put to sea from the road. Captain Hardinge now secured his prisoners, stationed his men at the Atalante's guns, got the powder on deck, and made every arrangement to attack the other Dutch brig. The dawn of day, however, showed the latter at too great a distance to be approached, especially as the gale had not in the least abated. In this perilous state the British remained for 48 hours; during which, two of their boats had broken adrift, and two others had swamped alongside of the Atalante. At length, the wind again shifting, the Atalante made a push to get out; but the two captains found the navigation so difficult, that it was three days ere they could accomplish their object.

This, in all its bearings, was an exploit worthy of British seamen; and every admirer of meritorious conduct will be pleased to learn, that the officer who had so judiciously planned, and so gallantly led on to, the attack, together with his brave and able second, was immediately promoted. Lieutenant Bluett, also, as he well merited, was made a commander. A step to post-rank is frequently not without its alloy: Captain Hardinge, no longer qualified to command a sloop, was obliged to quit the Scorpion, a fine brig of 384 tons, just launched, to be the captain of a dull, convoy-keeping "post-ship," the Proselyte, of 404 tons, late a Newcastle collier; a cruiser, which any privateer could have run from, and any well-manned 18-gun brig, the Scorpion herself, for instance, have captured.

The following postscript to the private letter referred to at a previous page affords a fine specimen of a British officer's magnanimity: "In two days after the captain's death," says Captain Hardinge, "he was buried with all the naval honours in my power to bestow upon him. During the ceremony of his interment the English colours disappeared, and the Dutch were hoisted in their place. All the Dutch prisoners were liberated; one of them delivered an *éloge* upon the hero they had lost, and we fired three volleys over him as he descended into the deep." To give to this affair, so honourable to those engaged in it, the proper finish, Rear-admiral Thornborough sent a flag of truce to the Batavian Admiral Killkert inside, with the late Captain Carp's servant, and the effects of the deceased, in order that they might be delivered to his relations.

On the 3rd of April the British hired cutter Swift, of 77 tons, eight 4-pounders, and 23 men and boys, commanded by Lieutenant William Martin Leake, was fallen in with, engaged, boarded, and after a stout struggle, and the loss of her commander and many others of her small crew carried, by the French xebec-privateer Espérance, of 150 tons, 10 guns (represented, by the ship that afterwards captured her, as "24 and 12 pounders," probably carronades), and a crew of 54 men, commanded by Captain Escoffier. The Swift, it appears, was carrying despatches to Vice-admiral Lord Nelson off Toulon; but which, we rather think (for very few, if any particulars have been published), were thrown overboard previously to the cutter's capture. It does certainly seem strange, that, in a navy such as that of England, despatches to a commander-in-chief, upon an important foreign station, should be forwarded by a vessel not equal in force to a frigate's launch, when armed with her carronade and proper complement of men.

On the 9th of April, at daylight, in latitude 7° 44' north, and longitude 84° 30' east, the British armed en flûte late 12-pounder 32-gun frigate Wilhelmina, Captain Henry Lambert, steering west-north-west, with the wind at north by east, and accompanied by the country-ship William-Petrie, laden with government stores for Trincomalé, and which ship the frigate, being bound to Madras, had been ordered to protect as far as the courses of the two remained the same, discovered a sail in the east-south-east steering to the eastward. Shortly afterwards the stranger wore and stood after the British vessels. Towards noon it fell calm, and the afternoon and night passed with very little wind, the stranger, until dark, still in sight. At daylight on the 10th, the wind then a light breeze from the north-east, and the course of the frigate and her charge about west half-north, the stranger was seen in the east by north, steering to the south-west. In a little time the latter hauled to the wind on the starboard tack, and steered directly after the former. Observing that the vessel was a ship of force, and suspecting her to be an enemy's cruiser, Captain Lambert directed the master of the William-Petrie, who had already arrived at the point for parting company, to alter his course after dark, and make the best of his way to the port of his destination.

The jury-rig alone of an armed en flûte ship-of-war is a great deception, and it is generally in the power of the captain to give a mercantile appearance to the hull of his vessel. This was particularly the case in regard to the Wilhelmina, she being a ship of Dutch construction. It was the disguised appearance of the Wilhelmina that induced the stranger, who we may now introduce as the French frigate privateer Psyché, of 36 guns, Captain Trogoff, after reconnoitring as she had done, boldly to approach, with the determination of attacking the supposed Indiaman. At 6 P.M. came on a squall with rain ; through which, in her eagerness to close with the latter, the Psyché carried all sail. At 6 h. 45 m., it being dark and cloudy, the Wilhelmina, who to allow her opponent to come up had previously shortened sail, hove-to. At 9 P.M. the Wilhelmina filled, and, lowering her topgallant-sails and driver, continued under easy sail, discovering the Psyché at intervals through the flashes of lightning, which were extremely vivid.

On the 11th, at 3 h. 30 m. A.M., a heavy squall from the north-north-west obliged the Wilhelmina to hand her topgallant-sails and lower her topsails, and for the present shut out the Psyché from her view. At daylight, however, the latter re-appeared, still in the north-east ; and the British frigate immediately tacked, and with colours flying, stood toward her. The gallantry of this step will be better appreciated when it is known, that the Wilhelmina mounted only 14 long 9-pounders, and one 12 pounder carronade fitted upon trucks and used as a shifting gun, on her main-deck, and four long 9-pounders (which had been left by the Victorious at Madras) and two sixes on her quarter-deck and forecastle, with a complement of 134 men and boys, 10 of the men received out of the 50-gun ship Grampus, to work the four extra nines ;[1] whereas the Psyché, formerly a French national frigate, of the class and size of the Railleuse, or Egyptienne as subsequently named, mounted 24 long French 12-pounders on the main deck, and 10 (English, we believe) 18-pounder carronades and two French sixes on the quarter-deck and forecastle, with a crew of 250 men and boys.

At 5 h. 30 m. A.M., being on the larboard tack, with the wind still from the north-north-west, but moderate, the Wilhelmina

[1] A letter from Captain Lambert to Vice-admiral Rainier, giving a short account of this action, and copied into all the London papers, contains, in the manner of a postscript, the following paragraph:—" N.B. His Majesty's ship Wilhelmina carries eighteen 6-pounders and 100 men." It is probable that this " N.B." was added by the copyist or first publisher, and not by the writer, of the letter ; for the account in the text is not only taken from one of the officers who was present in the action, but, with the exception of the four supernumerary guns, agrees with the navy-office establishment upon all frigate-flûtes of the Wilhelmina's class.

passed about 50 yards to windward of the Psyché, then, with French colours flying, close hauled on the opposite tack. After a mutual broadside, accompanied on the part of the French ship by a hail to surrender, the Psyché tacked, and the Wilhelmina wore; each ship continuing to fire as her guns could be brought to bear. The plan adopted by the Psyché, of pointing every alternate gun upon the broadside at her opponent's rigging, occasioned the Wilhelmina, from the loss of bowlines and braces, to come to the wind on the starboard tack with every sail aback. While the British ship lay in this unmanageable state, the French ship passed under her stern; and, raking the Wilhelmina, knocked away the maintopmast, badly wounded the main-yard, and did considerable damage to her rigging and sails.

Having at length paid off and got before the wind, the Wilhelmina brought her larboard broadside to bear; and presently the Psyché evinced an intention to board the British frigate upon the quarter; but, on seeing that the latter was prepared to repel the attempt, the Psyché put her helm a-starboard and sheered off. A furious cannonade was now maintained on both sides, the yard-arms nearly locking, until the Psyché, ranging ahead, crossed her opponent's bows. In practising this manœuvre, the Psyché brought herself in the wind; but by throwing her headsails aback, and keeping her after-yards square or shivering, the French ship paid off: not, however, until the Wilhelmina, with her starboard guns, had poured in a raking fire astern. After this the two ships again got parallel to each other, and again engaged so closely, that the yards were over-hanging; when, at 7 A.M., profiting by her more perfect state aloft, and her very superior powers of sailing, the Psyché ceased firing, crowded all the canvas she could spread, and stood away to the south-east.

This being an action during the progress of which the combatants frequently changed positions, the details of it will be better understood by a reference to the diagram in the next page.

Ill calculated, indeed, was the Wilhelmina for a chase, either from or towards an enemy. Her maintopmast was down; her bowsprit wounded in two, and her foremast in 10 places; her fore and main yards, and her main and mizen masts were also wounded, and her lower rigging and all her boats more or less damaged. Her aftermost forecastle bits were shot away, and her hull was pierced with shot in several places. A Captain Wright, of the India-service, was on board the Psyché during the engagement, and subsequently mentioned, that the Wilhelmina's shot, comparatively small as they were, had reduced the privateer to nearly a sinking state; the latter, at the close of the action, having seven feet water in her hold, a circumstance that sufficiently explains the manner of its termination.

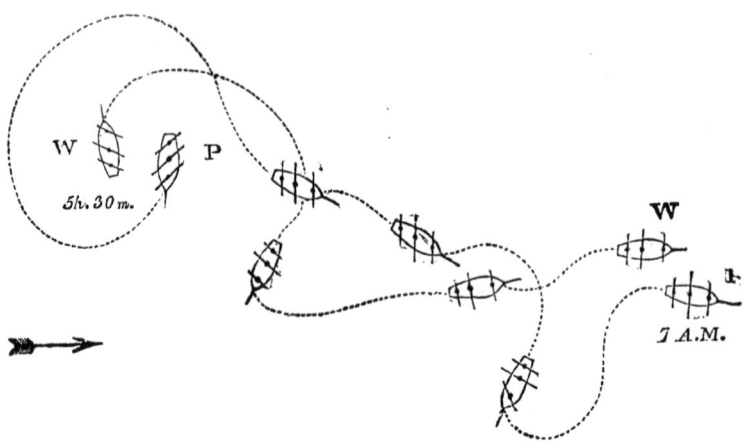

Of her 134 men and boys, the Wilhelmina had her boatswain and three seamen mortally, and six seamen slightly, wounded. It may here be remarked, that the additional height given to the trucks of the Wilhelmina's main-deck carriages, to suit them to ports constructed for 12-pounders, was found to increase the facility of working the nines; a circumstance which occasioned her inferiority in number of men to be less sensibly felt. With respect to the loss on board the Psyché, that ship, according to the statement of Captain Wright, had her second captain and 10 men killed, and her commander (dangerously) and 32 men wounded, 13 of them mortally.

With such a disparity of force as evidently existed against the Wilhelmina, this was an action highly honourable to the British ship. It is true that the Wilhelmina's opponent was a privateer; but the Psyché, by all accounts, was a better appointed, better manned, and better disciplined ship, than many frigates of the same force in the French navy. Commanded by no less a man than Captain Jacques Bergeret, already known to us as the Virginie's gallant captain, the Pysché had sailed from Madras in the beginning of February, bound to Pondicherry on commercial pursuits. Thence she proceeded to the

Isle of France, and arrived there in May. In June or July news of the war reached the island. The Psyché was immediately armed and equipped as a ship-of-war; but Captain Bergeret, preferring employment in the national navy, sent out his ship to cruise, under the command of Captain Trogoff, either the son or nephew of the French admiral who commanded the ships at Toulon when Lord Hood entered that port in August, 1793; Captain Trogoff was considered, in the eastern hemisphere, the chief scene of his exploits, to be a brave, skilful, and enterprising officer.

On the other hand, it was Captain Lambert's good fortune to have been preceded in the command of the Wilhelmina by an officer who knew how to appreciate (and how few do) the art of naval gunnery. Captain James Lind had been indefatigable in teaching his men to fire with precision; and the effect of the skill attained by the latter was visible in the execution they did to an antagonist, that otherwise, notwithstanding they continued to display, as no doubt they would, the characteristic bravery of British seamen, might, by her decided superiority of force, have ultimately compelled the Wilhelmina to surrender.

After quitting the latter, the Psyché proceeded, with all haste, pumping day and night, to the Isle of France. There she arrived in almost a sinking state; and, judging from the storm of shot with which their late opponent had assailed them, her officers publicly declared that the Psyché had "beaten off" (a very commodious, and therefore a very frequent expression in all similar cases) an English "44-gun frigate." As soon as she had repaired the most important of her damages, the Wilhelmina pursued her route to the road of Madras, where she safely arrived; and, as an additional proof of the discomfited state of the Psyché, the William-Petrie, whose cargo was valued at 40,000l. sterling, although not wholly out of sight at the commencement of the action, also arrived in safety at Trincomalé.

Captain Lambert's gallantry was rewarded, as it well merited, by immediate promotion to post-rank; and he was appointed to the command of the 12-pounder 32-gun frigate Terpsichore, one of the British cruisers upon the eastern station. In so creditable an action we are pleased in being able to state, that the two lieutenants of the Wilhelmina were George Tippet and George Phillimore, and her master Thomas Curtis.

From the details already given, it is evident that the character of this action mainly depends upon the actual, in contradistinction to the nominal, force of the combatants. For instance, call the Wilhelmina a British 12-pounder 32-gun frigate, or a frigate " of 32 guns," and you arm her, according to the admiralty-order fixing her establishment, with 38 guns, including six 24-pounder carronades, and with a crew of 215 men and boys. Call the Psyché even " a large," or a " frigate-built " privateer, and you will scarcely raise her, in the reader's estimation, above the Bellone, beaten off by the Milbrook, or the Blonde that captured the Wolverine. Even suppose the reader to rank the "large French frigate-built privateer" with the Egyptienne, beaten off by the Osprey, and afterwards captured by the Hippomenes, you have already made the implied full-armed Wilhelmina more than a match for her, and have therefore reduced the exploit of a British frigate far beneath that confessedly performed by a British sloop. Omit the name of the privateer, lengthen the duration of the action, and misstate the mode of its termination, and you convert that which, if not a conquest, was decidedly a victory, into a censurable defeat. It is with us an invariable rule not to state, without showing, that an action is gallant, or an officer a " hero." Above all things, we avoid making such an assertion when our own details, few as they may be, prove directly the reverse. These remarks premised, we subjoin the account of the Wilhelmina's action, as it stands in the work of a contemporary.

" Captain Henry Lambert commanded the Wilhelmina, of 32 guns, an old Dutch-built frigate, without one quality to recommend her as a ship-of-war, unless it were that of looking so unlike one in every respect that the enemy fearlessly approached her, and by that means were sometimes captured when a chase would have ended in disappointment. This ship, in the month of April, 1804, fell in, off the east side of Ceylon, with a large French frigate-built privateer, which she engaged with great obstinacy and fury for three hours, when the Frenchman being much disabled, and the British frigate still more so, they separated, nor was it in the power of our young hero to renew the action, the enemy having so much the advantage of him in point of sailing."[1]

On the 21st of June, at noon, the British ship-sloop Hippomenes,[2] now commanded by Captain Kenneth Mackenzie, cruising to windward of Antigua, in latitude 18° north, and longitude 58° west, with the wind at east, and her head to the northward, observed in the north-east a brig, which afterwards proved to be the French privateer Buonaparte, Captain Paim-

---

[1] Brenton, vol. iii., p. 344.   [2] See p. 258.

péni, of 18 long 8-pounders and 146 men. The peculiar construction of the Hippomenes, a Dutch-built corvette, had been
taken advantage of in so disguising her appearance, that the
privateer, believing the ship to be an African trader, bore down
under English colours, to take possession of her. At 1 h. 30 m.
P.M. the Buonaparte shortened sail, and the Hippomenes hauled
close to the wind to expedite the meeting. At 1 h. 50 m. P.M.
the Hippomenes opened her fire at the privateer, who had now
changed her colours to French. The latter instantly returned
the fire, and a spirited action ensued. In the course of 10 or
12 minutes the Buonaparte ranged up on the weather-quarter of
the Hippomenes, and in a little time, becoming unmanageable,
fell on board her opponent, dropping stem-on a little abaft the
latter's fore-chains. The guns of the Hippomenes, particularly two carronades on the upper deck, a Dutch 24-pounder
and an English 12, in a very few minutes did serious injury to
the Buonaparte; while the latter, from her tops, threw stink-pots
upon the decks of the former, thereby setting her on fire abaft.

It was at this crisis that, having to prevent the privateer's
escape caused her bowsprit to be lashed to his ship's mainmast,
Captain Mackenzie called to his crew to follow him in boarding,
and secure the victory. He then, followed by his officers, and,
as he thought by at least 50 or 60 of his men, rushed upon the
Buonaparte's forecastle. The onset was encouraging; for the
brig's crew, with scarcely a show of resistance, retreated abaft
the mainmast. Here the privateer's men rallied; and well they
might rally, for they now saw what a mere handful of enemies
stood upon their deck. The fact is, no more men had followed
Captain Mackenzie and his officers than made a total of 18
British; opposed to whom, allowing an ample deduction for
previous loss, were 100 French. The catastrophe may be
summed up in a few words. Captain Mackenzie, his officers,
and the few gallant fellows in company, defended themselves
until five of the party were killed and eight wounded, including
a master's mate severely, and the captain in as many as 14
places; and who, in endeavouring to regain his ship, fell senseless into her main chains, just a minute or two before the lashing
gave way and the vessels parted. Nine, including the captain
and master, got back to the Hippomenes. The first-lieutenant,
Mr. William Pierce, and the purser, Mr. William Collman, along
with two seamen, were taken prisoners; and the remaining five
lay dead upon the privateer's deck.

The Hippomenes had been but recently commissioned at the

Dutch port in which she had surrendered to the British ;[1] and
her complement had been made up, partly of draughts from other
ships-of-war, that is, by freeing each of them of a certain number
of skulkers, raw hands, and incorrigible rogues, and partly of
foreign renegadoes, who, tired of the restraints of a prison-ship
life, gladly " volunteered " their services to an enemy, from whom
they meant to escape (and who can blame them ?) the first
opportunity.   Perhaps a portion of the crew consisted of pressed
men ; but pressed men were to be found on board of every ship
in the British navy.   Moreover pressed men have proved themselves, on several occasions, among the best men in the ship.
That they should be so will not appear strange, when it is
considered that an officer, where he can, presses seamen ; and,
if he has liberty to take three men out of ten on board a merchant-vessel, he does not choose the worst.   A pressed man or
a volunteer, if he has the heart of an Englishman, will not suffer
himself to be bearded by an enemy ; and it is far from impro
bable that the majority of the eight or ten seamen who accompanied Captain Mackenzie in boarding the privateer, and who
suffered so heavily owing to the pusillanimity of their shipmates,
were pressed men.   Had the dastards but shown themselves on
the brig's forecastle, the colours, in all probability, would have
been hauled down ; for it is known that, before the boarding
commenced, the privateer had lost five men killed and 15
wounded, besides being very considerably damaged in masts,
rigging, and hull.   It was on this account that the Buonaparte
felt no inclination to renew the combat ; and; in the disabled
state of the sloop-of-war's rigging, this truly fortunate privateer
soon effected her escape.

   It is very common for the captain of a ship, when writing the
account of any capture unexpectedly made without a contest, to
anticipate the prowess that would have been displayed by his
men, had the enemy possessed strength or courage enough to
put it to the test.   Not quite three months before the affair of
the Buonaparte, the Hippomenes, it will be recollected, had the
singular good fortune to capture, almost without a blow, a
French privateer of 36 guns.   Captain Shipley, who then commanded the Hippomenes, wrote thus in his official letter : " I
feel much pleasure in saying, the officers and men behaved with
that coolness and intrepidity inherent in Englishmen ; and, had
the enemy allowed them a trial alongside, I am convinced her
superior force would not have availed them much."   The officers

[1] See p. 203

of the Hippomenes afterwards proved how well they had merited their captain's eulogium ; but as to the men—of them, however, enough has been said. Captain Paimpéni himself must have despised the wretches, to whose faint-heartedness he owed the preservation of his ship ; while the mangled bodies of their late comrades, still reeking upon his deck, must have taught him to discriminate between the counterfeit and the genuine British seaman.

On the 11th of July, at 10 P.M., three boats of the British 18-pounder 32-gun frigate Narcissus, Captain Ross Donnelly, three of the 38-gun frigate Seahorse, Captain the Hon. Courtenay Boyle, and four of the 12-pounder 32-gun frigate Maidstone, Captain the Hon. George Elliott, under the orders of Lieutenant John Thompson, first of the Narcissus, assisted by Lieutenants John Richard Lumley, of the Seahorse, Ogle Moore, of the Maidstone, and Hyde Parker, of the Narcissus, put off from the last-named frigate, to make an attack upon 12 settees, chiefly with cargoes on board, lying at La Vandour, in the bay of Hyères, distant between four and five miles from the ships. The vessels were moored head and stern, close to the beach, to which also they were completely secured, and were covered by a battery of three guns.

In the face of a tremendous fire of grape-shot and musketry, as well from the settees as from the battery and the houses of the town, Lieutenant Thompson and his party, about midnight, succeeded in boarding and setting fire to most of the vessels. One only was brought off, and a most costly prize she was; the loss on the part of the British amounting to one midshipman (Thomas Owen Roche), one marine, and two seamen killed, and one lieutenant (John Richard Lumley), one master's mate (Robert Mansell), three midshipmen (Thomas William Bedingfield, Thomas Alexander Watt, and John George Victor), 15 seamen, and three marines wounded, many of them severely. The gallantry of attacks like these no one can dispute ; but who will say that, had all the 12 settees, instead of one of them, been brought off, they would have compensated for the valuable blood which had been spilt ? Lieutenant Lumley's was a dreadful wound, and one from which it was next to a miracle that he ever recovered. His right arm was amputated at the shoulder-joint, and a portion of the scapula removed with it.

On the 12th of July the British 18-pounder 36-gun frigate Aigle, Captain George Wolfe, standing in for the Cordouan lighthouse with a moderate breeze from the north-east, discovered a French ship and brig steering to the southward. These were the Charante, of 20 long 6-pounders, four swivels, and 104 men, commanded by Lieutenant Joseph Samson, and the Joie, of eight "12-pounders" (if not carronades, more likely 8-pounders), two swivels, and 75 men, commanded by Lieutenant Benjamin Gadobert; both vessels from Rochefort, but last from the Gironde, bound to Bayonne, the brig laden with cannon and ordnance stores.

At 5 P.M. the Aigle closed with the French ship and brig; and, from their not having altered their course, and their now exchanging signals and shortening sail, Captain Wolfe expected that they meant to engage. To the surprise, however, of the British, the Charente and Joie, after firing their starboard broadsides without effect, ran upon the strand about 10 leagues to the southward of Cordouan, and within a stone's throw of each other. The French crews then took to the boats; but, these becoming swamped in the surf, many of the men were drowned. The Aigle immediately anchored about a mile from the beach, for the purpose of endeavouring to get the two vessels afloat; but the immense surf thrown up in consequence of a recent westerly gale rendered fruitless every effort, although persevered in for a whole night and part of the next day. Captain Wolfe was therefore obliged to destroy the French ship and brig; a service which was effectually executed, under the personal directions of Mr. Furlonger the master, and Mr. Steel the gunner.

On the 15th of July, at 2 h. 30 m. A.M., Cape Roman in the United States of America in sight, the French ship-rigged privateer Dame-Ambert, Captain Charles Lamarque (represented as a reduced officer of the French navy), saw and chased a ship to leeward. The latter, which was the British 14-gun ship-sloop Lilly, Captain William Compton, being equally desirous of a meeting, the two ships by 9 h. 30 m. A.M. were near enough for the Dame-Ambert to open her fire. The British ship, however, was compelled to wait until her paltry 12-pounder carronades (not equal in effectiveness to 4-pounder long guns) could reach her antagonist. Having disabled the Lilly in sails and rigging, and considerably weakened her in crew, the Dame-Ambert closed, in order to finish the contest by boarding. To do this effectually, the Dame-Ambert, who from the entire state of her rigging possessed the facility of manœuvring as she pleased, stationed herself in a raking position; and, having swept the Lilly's deck by her guns, lashed the sloop's bowsprit to her taffrail. In this state the French privateer made eight successive attempts to board, and was gallantly repulsed in all. On the ninth time, having killed the Lilly's captain, first-lieutenant, and others of her principal officers, and killed or wounded the greater part of her remaining crew, the Dame-Ambert, just two hours and 10 minutes from the commencement of the action, carried the British vessel.

The Lilly had been a Bermudian trader, and in the year 1795 was purchased for the British navy. She measured 200 tons, was armed with 14 carronades, 12-pounders, and two long fours, and had a complement of 80 men and boys. Her exact loss in the action cannot now be ascertained. Her captain and first-lieutenant were among the killed, which, according to the French accounts, amounted to a great proportion of the crew; and her badly wounded, on the same authority, were 15 or 16, including all her remaining officers. The Dame-Ambert had been the British packet Marlborough, one of the largest in the service, recently captured. She was afterwards refitted at Guadaloupe, and armed with 16 long French 6-pounders, and a complement of 140 men. The French say, that their crew, when they fell in with the Lilly (but this wants confirmation), was reduced to 75 men, and that the Dame-Ambert lost in the action five men killed and 11 wounded.

Nothing but the accidental circumstance of the Lilly's having three masts instead of two occasioned her not to be classed as a gun-brig; and truly, if·she had been a gun-brig, she would have been one of the least effective in the service. They all carry carronades of an 18-pounder caliber: hers were 12-pounders, and those of the old construction, short and badly formed, the derision of the merest tyro in naval gunnery. Unfortunately, owing to the mortality among the British officers, and the stigma that attaches to the capture of a king's ship by a privateer, no account of this action has been published, except in the French papers. It is only to call things by their right names, and that which seems a disgrace becomes, in reality, an honour. A defeat like the Lilly's is more creditable than many a puffed-up victory, for which chaplets have been worn and rewards bestowed. The fact of her having been a sloop-of-war was not lost upon the captors; and "une corvette de l'état" occurs in more than one place in the French account of the action. The prize was afterwards fitted out as a privateer, and named, after the Governor of Guadeloupe, Général-Ernouf.

On the 31st of July, at daybreak, the British 18-pounder

32-gun frigate Tartar, Captain Keith Maxwell, standing in to leeward of the island of Saona, West Indies, discovered from her mast-head a small sail, to which she immediately gave chase; keeping as close as possible to leeward of the island, in order to prevent the latter's escape that way, and compel her to make the attempt through the passage between Saona and St. Domingo, a very narrow and intricate channel even for small vessels. At about 7 A.M. the chase was made out to be a schooner, full of men, using her sweeps to escape through the before-mentioned channel. By carrying all possible sail, the Tartar, at 8 A.M., got within range of shot; but, owing to the short tacks she was obliged to make, could use her guns to very little purpose without losing ground in the chase. The schooner, therefore, which was the French privateer Hirondelle, Captain La Place, of 10 long 4-pounders and 50 men, notwithstanding that several of the frigate's shot passed over her and through her sails, persisted in beating to windward until 10 A.M ; when, having advanced nearly half-way up the channel, she came to an anchor under a reef of rocks.

Finding the Tartar to be in six fathoms water, without the possibility of anchoring in safety, or of effectually cannonading the schooner, Captain Maxwell despatched three boats, under the command of Lieutenant Henry Mullah, assisted by Lieutenant Nicholas Lockyer and several midshipmen, all volunteers, to endeavour to bring out the privateer. The instant the boats put off, the Hirondelle hoisted her colours, fired a gun, and warped her broadside towards them. As the British advanced, the privateer opened a fire from her large guns, and, as the boats drew nearer, from her small arms also. In spite of this, and of a strong sea-breeze directly on the bows of the boats, Lieutenant Mullah intrepidly pulled up to the privateer; and, after a short but obstinate resistance, boarded and carried her, with the loss only of one seaman and one marine wounded. The Hirondelle had nine killed and six wounded, besides three missing, supposed to have been drowned in attempting to swim on shore. The number of British in the boats does not appear in the official letter; but, admitting they amounted to 50, or even to 60 officers and men, and that they had an 18-pounder carronade in the launch, still, against a vessel so well armed and prepared, and under circumstances of weather which, by retarding the progress of the boats, exposed them the longer to the privateer's fire, the capture of the Hirondelle was highly honourable to the parties engaged.

On the 12th of August, at 4 h. 30 m. P.M., the British 18-pounder 32-gun frigate Galatea, Captain Henry Heathcote, cruising in the neighbourhood of Guadaloupe, ran down the channel between that island and the Saintes islands, with the intention of attempting to cut out the late British sloop-of-war Lilly, which, it was understood, had gone into the Saintes, to repair and refit as a French privateer. At 6 h. 30 m. P.M., observing the Lilly at anchor in the road near the Anse à Mire, the Galatea hove to, hoisted out her boats, and sent them, in the evening, manned and armed, to execute the service. The boats returned soon after daylight on the 13th, without having been able to discover the Lilly ; but the Lilly, and all who were interested in defending her, had discovered them, and were making suitable preparations to resist an attack, should one again be attempted. An officer and 30 soldiers were added to the Lilly's crew, and a privateer schooner, which happened to be in port, was moored athwart the hawse of the ship, in such a manner as completely to enfilade the assailants in their approach. So confident were the French in the means they had taken to repulse the British, that the commanding officer on shore gave orders to the different outposts, and to those in command at the batteries, not to fire or do anything to excite a suspicion that they were aware of the enemy's approach.

Having hoisted in her boats, the Galatea, who had dropped to leeward during the night, made sail and beat up, to reconnoitre more fully the position of the Lilly. On nearing the road, the Galatea discovered the French privateer schooner lying close to the ship; and, as a proof that there were batteries to protect both ship and schooner, the frigate was repeatedly fired at with shot and shells, some of the latter bursting at no great distance. The Galatea continued turning to windward until about 10 P.M., by which time she had nearly weathered the Saintes. Having hove to, the frigate hoisted out four boats, embarked in them about 90 officers and men, armed the launch with an 18-pounder carronade, and then towed the boats within three miles north-west of the citadel. Casting themselves off, the four boats, under the command of Lieutenant Charles Hayman, first of the Galatea, assisted by several other officers, including Lieutenant Robert Hall, of the marines, and Mr. Michael Birbeck, the master, pulled towards the harbour, hoping, under cover of the night, to surprise the object of their attack.

To prevent the possibility of such an occurrence, the Lilly, or rather, the Général-Ernouf, for that was the ship's new name, had, just as it grew dark, sent one of her boats to row guard at the entrance of the road. By this, the ship, the schooner, the forts, and the town, became fully apprised of the approach of the British; who, finding no shot fired at them from the batteries, no signals of alarm made along the coast, naturally concluded that they were unseen. Eager to be the first at the post of danger, Lieutenant Hayman in the barge pushed ahead of his comrades, and, at a few minutes past 1 A.M. on the 14th, got nearly alongside of the Lilly. Then it was that the fire began. Heedless of it all, the barge, followed by the other boats, was soon in contact with the ship. A dreadful struggle ensued. Lieutenant Hayman fell, mortally wounded both by musketry and the bayonet; and, out of 26 or 27 officers and men in the barge, three only, it appears, were left free from dangerous wounds. The three remaining boats tried in vain to overcome the numerous and still-increasing force opposed to them. After sustaining nearly an hour's fire from great guns and musketry, they were compelled to turn their bows to the offing, leaving the barge to her fate. But the British were only quitting one set of foes to get within the clutches of another. The batteries now opened their fire, and a dreadful fire it was. The cannonade continued, gradually slackening as the boats receded from the shore, until 3 h. 30 m. A.M., when it entirely ceased.

Just as the day dawned, the miserable remnant of the expedition reached the frigate. Out of about 90 officers and men, who had quitted the Galatea on the preceding night, not more than 20 returned in an unwounded state. Among the killed, besides Lieutenant Hayman, was the master, and Mr. Wall, a midshipman; and among the wounded were several officers, including Lieutenant Hall of the marines, who lost an arm and was made prisoner. The number of killed and wounded together, as reported on the return of the boats, was 44, including Lieutenants Hayman and Hall, but not, as it would appear, the seven killed and 14 wounded out of the 24 seamen and marines belonging to the barge. The addition of these makes the loss of the Galatea, in attempting to cut out the Lilly, 65 in killed and wounded : whereas the French acknowledge a loss of only four men killed ; and, although they do not enumerate the wounded, name, as among them, Captain Lapointe, commanding the Général-Ernouf, and Lieutenant Mouret, commanding the detachment of troops put on board by the commandant of the garrison.

The object of the service, upon which the Galatea's boats had been despatched on the evening of the 12th, was laudable ; inasmuch as it was not only to recapture a ship that belonged to the British navy, but to cut short the cruise of a privateer likely to do a serious injury to British commerce. Nor was the number of men sent, admitting it to have been each time the same, inadequate apparently to the purpose in view, that of surprising (for there lay the gist of the enterprise) and capturing the Lilly at her anchors in the road. The boats returned without finding the vessel. Having hoisted them in, the Galatea should have made sail from, not towards, the spot where the privateer lay. Instead of this, the frigate hovered off the port all the day, observed a second privateer moored along with the first, witnessed, and, the French say, felt, the strength of the batteries, that protected both privateers : and yet, in the evening, Captain Heathcote, a second time, sends his boats to pass, and, having accomplished or failed in their main object, to repass, those batteries ; batteries, the fire from which the Galatea herself, much less her boats, would have been unable to withstand.

For an enterprise so doubtful in its expediency and so fatal in its result, a brief English account would suffice ; and none, indeed, appears to have been published. The French, on the other hand, made public every particular ; every particular, at least, which they thought would contribute to aggrandise the exploit performed by Lapointe and Lieutenant Mouret. But they tell us nothing of any aid afforded by the schooner privateer, or by the batteries ; whose united fire, nevertheless, powerfully co-operated in repulsing the assailants. That there were forts, the account admits, openly, when alluding to the supposed effect of some shells thrown at the frigate, and tacitly, when dwelling upon the accident, which, the French declare, befel three of the British boats, in their endeavours to retire. These, they state, and positively state, were sunk, with their crews. With equal truth the French add, that there was a fifth boat present, but which kept rather aloof during the boarding-attempt, and suffered the loss of half its crew ere it got clear. " Trois furent coulées, une quatrième prise, et le cinquième canot, qui avait un peu tenu le large, échappa avec la moitié de son monde hors de combat."[1]

Whatever were the faults of this enterprise, they existed in

----

[1] Moniteur, March 2, 1805.

the plan, not in the execution. The heavy loss sustained by the boats proves that the British had effected as much as flesh and blood could effect: they had lost, in killed, wounded, and prisoners, more than two-thirds of their number; and yet the remainder would not yield, but bravely fought their way back to their ship. Much do we regret our inability to give a fuller account of the various difficulties which Lieutenant Hayman and his party had to contend with, in order that we may do justice to the memories of the dead, and cheer the feelings of the living, among those who, although unsuccessful in their object, so nobly maintained the character of British seamen.

On the 17th of August, in latitude 49° 30' north, longitude 12° 20' west, the British 38-gun frigate Loire, Captain Frederick Lewis Maitland, fell in with the French ship privateer Blonde, of Bordeaux, mounting 30 guns, 8-pounders on the main deck, with a crew of 240 men; the same ship that, about five months previous, captured the Wolverine. After a 20 hours' chase, including a running fight of a quarter of an hour, during which the Loire had one midshipman (Ross Connor) and five men wounded, and the Blonde two men killed and five wounded, the latter hauled down her colours.

On the 15th of September, at 6 A.M., the British 50-gun ship Centurion, commanded by Lieutenant James Robert Phillips, in the absence of Captain James Lind upon service on shore (and who was also acting in the absence of the ship's proper commanding officer, Captain John Sprat Rainier, dangerously ill), while at anchor in Vizagapatam road, waiting until two Indiamen were loaded and ready to return with her to Madras, perceived under the land in the south-west, at a distance of about 12 miles, three ships coming down before the wind, with all sail set. At 9 h. 30 m. A.M. the strangers were made out to be a line-of-battle ship and two frigates, the former with a flag at her mizen-topgallantmast-head. At 9 h. 45 m. the French ships steered directly in for the road, two without any colours, and the third, the outermost frigate, with a St. George's ensign. The Centurion immediately opened a fire at the headmost frigate, to induce her to show her colours. Soon afterwards the 74 made signals, which were answered by the frigates. This at once pointed out that the ships were enemies, and a signal to that effect was made by the Centurion to the two Indiamen in company, followed by another, directing them to put into a port in view. The Barnaby promptly answered the signal, cut her cable, and ran on shore ;[1] but the Princess Charlotte, Captain John Logan, who lay in-shore of the Centurion, kept at her anchors.

The flag-ship was suspected to be what she really was, the Marengo, Rear-admiral Linois ; and her two consorts were the 40-gun frigate Atalante, Captain Camille-Charles-Alexis Gaudin-Beauchène, and 36-gun frigate Sémillante, commanded as before by Captain Motard. It is seven months to a day since we left Rear-admiral Linois, with a force a trifle greater than that which he now possessed, running from a fleet of unescorted Indiamen ; a fleet which he had weighed from Pulo-Auro purposely to capture, but which, under the able directions of Commodore Nathaniel Dance, put him and his squadron to flight.[2] The French admiral afterwards proceeded to Batavia ; where, or on the passage to it, he was joined by the Atalante. Taking in a supply of provisions, he steered for the Isle of France, and arrived there on the 2nd of April, followed a day or two afterwards by two of his frigates, with a valuable prize. Here his discomfiture by the India fleet gained him the ill-will of General Decaen, who wrote to his government on the subject, and we believe, sent his despatches to France by the Berceau. After waiting two months and a half at the Isle of France, M. Linois put to sea with the Marengo, Atalante, and Sémillante. He cruised, first, to the southward of Madagascar, anchoring a part of the time, on account of bad weather, in the bay of Saint Augustin : he then moved to a station near the island of Ceylon, where he took several rich prizes. M. Linois subsequently entered the bay of Bengal, passed Madras at about 20 leagues' distance, and visited the roads of Masulipatam and Cosanguay : thence he swept the coast of Golconda, and arrived on the 15th of September off Vizagapatam ; not without an object, for he had, the day previous, when off Masulipatam, received information from some country-boats, that the British frigate Wilhelmina had recently sailed from that road, with an Indiaman in company, bound to Vizagapatam. It so happened that Vice-admiral Rainier had substituted the Centurion for the Wilhelmina ; a difference which the French admiral, to his cost, very soon discovered.

At a few minutes past 10 A.M. the Atalante, which was the headmost ship of the three, was distant from the Centurion about half a mile, and all three ships now hoisted French colours. The Centurion immediately cut her cable, and sheeted home her topsails, which had been previously unfurled. This

---

[1] This ship afterwards got into the surf, and was totally lost.   [2] See p. 254.

brought her broadside to bear; and the whole of it was immediately poured into the Atalante, then within the distance of
200 yards: at this time the Marengo and Sémillante were
ranging up on the larboard quarter of the Centurion. At 10 h.
10 m. A.M. the Marengo and Sémillante opened their fire, which
the Centurion returned. After the action had continued about
a quarter of an hour, the Centurion's colours were shot away,
as also were those of the Marengo; but both ensigns were
promptly replaced. At 10 h. 45 m. A.M. the 74, whose rigging
appeared much damaged, hauled her wind and stood out
followed by the frigates. A battery of three guns at the town,
under the command of Colonel Campbell of the 74th regiment,
had co-operated with the Centurion in resisting the unequal
attack.

Abandoned for the present, the Centurion continued to stand
in-shore, and, in passing, hailed the Princess Charlotte, and
desired her to cut her cable, but without effect. About this time
Captain Lind joined his ship; and, finding her rigging and
sails too much cut to admit of her being worked to advantage,
anchored at the back of the surf, about a mile and a half to the
north-east of the town, in six fathoms water. Here the Centurion, now too distant to be supported by the battery at the
town, prepared herself for renewing an engagement, which she
had no means of avoiding, without resorting to an alternative
not yet in contemplation.

At 11 h. 15 m. A.M. the Marengo and frigates put about and
again stood in; and in another quarter of an hour the 74, after
having repeatedly tried the range of her guns, dropped anchor
abreast of and about a mile distant from, the Centurion. Having
clewed up her topsails and furled her courses, the Marengo
recommenced the cannonade, supported occasionally by the
Atalante, who kept under sail on the Centurion's larboard
quarter, and lay nearer than the Marengo, and in a much
more annoying position. The Sémillante, meanwhile, was
taking possession of the Princess Charlotte. Unambitious of
sharing glory with the Centurion, the latter had struck her
colours without firing a shot, although she mounted 24 long
12-pounders, with a crew of 71 men, and was a very formidable-
looking ship of 610 tons burden. Colonel Campbell had sent
to her assistance about 50 seapoys; but the boats saw the
shameful occurrence in time to save themselves by pulling back
to the shore.

The distance at which the Marengo, doubtless from ignorance

of the bay and dread of grounding, had anchored, was far more favourable to her than to the Centurion, the latter having, except a 6-pounder or two, no other long guns than the 24s on her first or lower-deck. In consequence, the Centurion's hull, masts, yards, and rigging, were severely cut by the fire of her two assailants : several shot struck her between wind and water, and one went through the gunner's store-room. At length, at about 1 h. 15 m. P.M., a shot from the Marengo cut the cable of the Centurion ; and, about the same time, the 74 cut or slipped her cable, hoisted her jib, and, accompanied by the two frigates and prize, stood away to sea. The Centurion also made some sail ; but, on getting a little further off-shore, brought up again with the sheet-anchor, and continued her fire on the Marengo until the latter was out of gun-shot. By 4 P.M. the Centurion was again ready for action ; but the French squadron still pursued its course off-shore, and at sunset was standing before the wind to the north-east.

The principal damages of the Centurion have already been enumerated. Her loss was by no means commensurate : it amounted to only one man mortally, and nine slightly, wounded. The Marengo suffered a good deal in her masts, yards, and rigging ; and one shot carried away her fore-cap. Her loss amounted to two seamen killed, and one enseigne de vaisseau badly wounded. The Atalante had also two men killed, besides six wounded, one of them mortally. The Sémillante, thanks to the forbearance of the Princess Charlotte, had no casualty to complain of.

It is difficult to understand what it was that induced M. Linois to abandon an enterprise of such apparant ease as the capture or destruction of a 50-gun ship by a 74 and two frigates. The rear-admiral's official letter, as published in the Moniteur, is a very lame performance. Such excuses as, the shoalness of the water—the great force of the battery on shore—the "extraordinary" armament of the Centurion—the distance from a port in which he could refit—and the rumour that two English line-of-battle ships had been seen or heard of in the neighbourhood, could only have suggested themselves to one who felt a little ashamed at the want of energy he had displayed. The Centurion, for instance, could not have drawn less water than a French frigate of the class of those with the Marengo ; and the two frigates, mounting between them upwards of 80 guns, and manned by at least 600 men, might have laid the Centurion on board, or compelled her to run on shore. " La première batterie du fort," gravely says the French account, "n'est que de 8 canons de 32 ou 24. On ignore le nombre de la seconde, 4 pièces de campagne avaient été transportées par les troupes sur le rivage." The latter were so, and were 12-pounders; but, as already related, could not reach the Marengo. Among other mistakes, M. Linois states the Centurion to have carried "26 canons de 32 à la seconde batterie;" which, as she mounted "24 (or rather 22) canons de 24 à la première batterie," would, indeed, have been arming her "d'une manière extraordinaire." Her second-deck guns were 32-pounder carronades; and from the distance at which the action was fought, Captain Lind would have greatly preferred the long 12-pounders for which they had been substituted.

A half-laden merchant prize, although an Indiaman, or rather, as was the case, a country ship, was a sorry recompense for the defeat, and a defeat it was, which the French admiral had sustained. On the other hand, the officers and crew of the British ship gave an honourable proof of what may be done by a judicious perseverance in resisting the attack of a superior force. By conduct so laudable and exemplary, they preserved their vessel, and exalted the character of their country; and the two navies must continue to view, with very different feelings, the defence of the Centurion in Vizagapatam road.

An action between the single ships of two nations at peace is rare. Still more rare is an action, under similar circumstances, between two squadrons. Should the occurrence happen, it is usually at night, when the ships find a difficulty in understanding each other's signals; but, the instant the mistake is discovered, the firing ceases, and no breach is made in the amicable relations of the two powers. Unfortunately the next action in order of date was fought between an English and a Spanish squadron, not amidst darkness, but in the open day; not through any accident, but under express orders from the government of one of the combatants; and, so far from the matter being afterwards made up, it led to an almost immediate declaration of war by the party who had to complain of the aggression.

Without entering into a consideration of the political connexion which at this time subsisted between France and Spain, it may suffice to state that, towards the latter end of the summer of 1804, the British government received intelligence, through the officer, Rear-admiral the Honourable Alexander Cochrane, in command of the squadron stationed off Ferrol, that an armament was fitting out in that port; that a considerable Spanish force was already collected there; and that French troops were then on their march thither, and near at hand. It is true that all this was afterwards disproved by the Spanish government; but such proof could have no retroactive effect. Immediately on the receipt of Rear-admiral Cochrane's information, the British admiralty despatched a squadron off Cadiz, to intercept and detain, by force or otherwise, the four Spanish frigates, known to be bound to that court with an immense quantity of specie, which they were bringing from Monte-Video, in South America.

On the 3rd of October the British squadron sent upon this important service, and which consisted of the 44-gun frigate Indefatigable, Captain Graham Moore, 18-pounder 32-gun frigates Medusa, Captain John Gore, and Amphion, Captain Samuel Sutton, and 38-gun frigate Lively, Captain Graham Eden Hamond, assembled off Cape Santa-Maria. On the 5th, at 6 A.M., that cape bearing north-east distant nine leagues, the Medusa made a signal for four large sail bearing west by south, the wind at this time being about east-north-east. The squadron immediately wore, and made sail in chase. At 8 A.M. the strangers, which were the Spanish 40-gun frigate Medea, Rear-admiral Don Joseph Bustamente, and 34-gun frigates Fama (with a broad pendant), Clara, and Mercedes, formed the line of battle ahead, in the following order: Fama, Medea, Mercedes, Clara. At 9 h. 5 m. A.M. the Medusa placed herself within half pistol-shot, on the weather-beam of the Fama. Presently the Indefatigable took a similar station by the side of the Medea; and the Amphion and Lively, as they came up, ranged alongside the Mercedes and Clara, the Amphion judiciously running to leeward of her opponent.

After ineffectually hailing the Medea to shorten sail, the Indefatigable fired a shot across her forefoot: on which the Spanish frigate did as she had been requested. Captain Moore then sent Lieutenant Thomas Arscott to inform the Spanish commanding officer, that his orders were to detain the squadron, and that it was his wish to execute those orders without bloodshed, but that the Spanish admiral's determination must be instantly made. The boat not returning so soon as expected, the Indefatigable made a signal for her, and, to enforce it, fired a shot ahead of the Medea. The officer having at length returned with an unsatisfactory answer, the Indefatigable, at about 9 h. 30 m. A.M., fired a second shot ahead of the Medea, and bore down close upon her weather-bow. Immediately the Mercedes fired into the Amphion, and in a few seconds afterwards the Medea opened her fire upon the Indefatigable. The latter then made the signal for close battle; and it instantly commenced with all the animation, on one side at least, which the prospect of such trophies could inspire.

At the end of about nine minutes the Mercedes blew up alongside of the Amphion with a tremendous explosion. In a minute or two afterwards the Fama struck her colours; but, on the Medusa's ceasing her fire, rehoisted them, and attempted to make off. The Medusa immediately bore up under the Spanish frigate's stern, and poured in a heavy fire, but the Fama continued her course to leeward. Having sustained, during 17 minutes, the Indefatigable's heavy broadsides, and finding a new opponent in the Amphion, who had advanced on her starboard quarter, the Medea surrendered. In another five minutes the Clara did the same, and the Lively was left at liberty to aid the Medusa in the pursuit of the Fama. At about 45 m. past noon the Lively, being an admirable sailer, got near enough to fire her bow-guns at the Fama; and at 1 h. 15 m. P.M. this, the only remaining Spanish frigate, struck to the two British frigates in chase of her.

The force of the Indefatigable has already more than once appeared; that of the Lively was the full establishment of a 38, numbering 46 guns, and the Amphion and Medusa each mounted 40 guns. The Lively had two men killed and four wounded; the Amphion, three men wounded, one or two of them by the splinters which fell upon her decks when her unfortunate antagonist blew up. No other loss, and but a very trifling damage, was sustained by the British ships.

The Medea was a fine frigate of 1046 tons, and mounted 42 guns, 18-pounders on the main deck, and eights on the quarter-deck and forecastle, with a complement of 300 men; of whom two were killed and 10 wounded. The three remaining frigates were each armed similar to the Mahonesa, except perhaps in having an additional pair of 6-pounders.[1] The Fama, out of her 280 men and boys, had 11 killed and 50 wounded; the Clara, out of her 300, seven killed and 20 wounded; and the Mercedes lost, by the fatal explosion, the whole of her 280 in crew and passengers, except the second captain and about 40 men, who were taken off the ship's forecastle after it had sepa-

---

' See vol. i., p. 399.

rated from the remainder of the hull, and except two passengers, who happened to be on board the Medea.

It is therefore quite clear, that the Indefatigable and any two of her three consorts would have been a match, even in a time of notorious war, for these four Spanish frigates. As it was, the latter defended themselves with the characteristic bravery of Spaniards, notwithstanding that they could have been in no state of preparation, and that the melancholy loss of one of their number so early in the action increased the odds against them.

Two more circumstances conspired to invest this transaction with more odium than perhaps would otherwise have attached to it. One of those circumstances was the miserable fate of so many poor souls at the explosion of the frigate, and the heart-rending misfortune it entailed upon one, in particular, who had been a passenger on board. This gentleman, a Captain Alvear, of the Spanish navy, with his wife, four amiable daughters, and five sons grown up to manhood, had embarked in the Mercedes, carrying with him a fortune, estimated at about 30,000*l.* sterling, the gradual savings of 30 years' industry as a merchant in South America. Not many minutes before the engagement began, the captain and his eldest son had gone on board the Medea; and there, in a very little while, did he witness the catastrophe that hurled his wife, his daughters, and his remaining sons to destruction, and sent that treasure, which was mere dross in the comparison, to the bottomless deep.

The second circumstance alluded to was the tempting nature of the lading on board these vessels. The cargoes of the three captured frigates consisted of Vidona wool, cascarilla, ratinia, seal-skins, seal-oil, bars of tin, pigs of copper, dollars, and ingots of gold, and netted very little short of a million sterling. Therefore, as the Mercedes was similarly freighted, the total value of what had been shipped on board the squadron probably amounted to nearly a third of a million more. We must not omit to state, that the British government restored to Captain Alvear, out of the proceeds of the three cargoes, the 30,000*l.* sterling which he had lost in the Mercedes.

Many persons, who concurred in the expediency, doubted the right of detaining these ships; and many, again, to whom the legality of the act appeared clear, were of opinion, that a more formidable force should have been sent to execute the service, in order to have justified the Spanish admiral in surrendering without an appeal to arms.

The affair naturally created a great stir at Madrid, and on the 27th of November an order issued to make reprisals on English property; but it was not until the 12th of the following month that the King of Spain issued his formal declaration of war, nor until the 11th of January, 1805, that Great Britain directed letters of marque to be granted against Spanish vessels and property.

Colonial Expeditions.— West Indies.

Viewing the success of Captain Watkins at Curaçoa in September, 1800,[1] without apparently taking into consideration, or attaching the proper weight to, the circumstances out of which it arose, namely, the occupation of the whole west part of the island by a French republican force of six or seven times the strength of the Dutch garrison, Rear-admiral Sir John Thomas Duckworth, the commander-in-chief at Jamaica, flattered himself that he had only to send up a line-of-battle ship or two, and the inhabitants would again surrender the island to the arms of his Britannic majesty.

Nor was the rear-admiral the only British officer who had taken such an idea into his head, grounded upon the same partial view of the previous surrender. When, in the middle of the year 1803, intelligence of the declaration of war against Holland reached Port Royal, Jamaica, the 10-gun schooner Gipsy, Acting-lieutenant Michael Fitton, was despatched to Curaçoa, to warn any British cruisers that might be lying there of what had taken place, in order that they might provide for their safety. Arriving in the harbour of St. Ann, the Gipsy found at anchor there the 18-gun ship-sloop Surinam, Captain Robert Tucker. To this officer, in as secret a manner as he could, Lieutenant Fitton communicated the intelligence, and advised him immediately to get under way. "No," says Captain Tucker, "I'll summon the fiscal to surrender the island to me." In vain did the lieutenant represent the folly of such a proceeding; in vain did he point to the numerous batteries around the harbour: Captain Tucker went on shore, and made his proposal in form. The Dutch authorities had received no official account of the war; but they took the captain's word, and not only his word, but his sword, and his ship, and all that were on board of her. Knowing well what would happen, Lieutenant Fitton, in the mean time, had weighed and stood out; and the Gipsy was soon chased off the port by two armed

[1] See p. 38.

vessels of superior force, which, in consequence of Captain Tucker's imprudence, had been despatched in pursuit of her.

In the early part of December, 1803, the 74-gun ship Theseus, Captain John Bligh, arrived at Port Royal, Jamaica, from the mole of St. Nicholas. On the 17th Captain Bligh received an order directing him to proceed on the ensuing day off the city of Santo-Domingo, and, in company with the 74-gun ship Vanguard, Captain James Walker, previously stationed there, to blockade the port. Should the French in possession of the town[1] propose capitulation, Captain Bligh was authorised to treat with them, and was at the same time verbally informed by Sir John Duckworth, in strict confidence, that he would receive an order by the 74-gun ship Hercule, Captain Richard Dalling Dunn, to attack the island of Curaçoa; but that it was not his, Sir John's, intention that the safety of the line-of-battle ships should be risked by attempting to force the harbour of St. Ann.

On the 19th the Theseus sailed from Port Royal, and before the end of the month arrived off the city of Santo-Domingo; but the Vanguard was not there, nor, in fact, did that ship join at all. On the 15th of January, 1804, Captain Bligh received his orders by the Hercule, and by them was directed, taking with him the three 74s, already named, also the 18-pounder 36-gun frigates Blanche, Captain Zachary Mudge, and Pique, Captain William Bayne Hodgson Ross, and the 10-gun schooner Gipsy, Acting-lieutenant Michael Fitton, to proceed without a moment's loss of time off the island of Curaçoa; "having," says Sir John, "received certain information that the garrison of Curaçoa has not been strengthened since the commencement of the war, and consists only of 160 troops, with a frigate in the port whose officers and crew are said nearly all to have fallen victims to the climate." Captain Bligh is then directed to summon the island to surrender to his majesty's arms upon liberal conditions. In case of a refusal, and that he should have no reason to believe there had been any augmentation of the garrison, Captain Bligh is to land a part of the crews of the ships. Then follows this nugatory salvo: "But it is my duty to caution you by no means to hazard more than the object is worth." Nugatory, indeed; for by what standard was the relative value of the object and the means to be measured?

With his two 74s, two frigates, and one schooner, and with no other knowledge of the state of Curaçoa than was contained in the paragraph already quoted from his orders, and with no

[1] See p. 206.

person on board the squadron who had ever seen the island, except Captain Ross and Mr. Fitton, Captain Bligh made sail for his destination. Owing to calms and variable winds, the squadron did not, until the 30th of January, arrive in sight of the island of Bonaire, which lies off the east end of Curaçoa. In the evening the ships bore up, and early on the next morning, the 31st, hove to about six miles to the eastward of the town and harbour of St. Ann. Captain Ross having embarked on board the Gipsy, was despatched with a flag of truce and a summons to the Dutch governor or fiscal, to surrender the island to the British. At 9 h. 30 m. A.M. the Gipsy stood out of the harbour, with the preconcerted signal flying, announcing that the terms had been refused.

The passage into the harbour is so narrow, that, even with a fair wind (and it now blew off the land), a line-of-battle ship can with difficulty enter; and the batteries that command the harbour and town including Fort République, against which from its situation an attack by storm is impracticable, mounted nearly 100 pieces of cannon. In the harbour were lying the Dutch 12-pounder 36-gun frigate Hatslaar and two French privateers. Under these circumstances, no alternative remained but to try the effect of a landing. Leaving, therefore, the two frigates, as well to blockade the harbour as to cause a diversion of the enemy's force, Captain Bligh, with the two 74s and schooner, bore up for a small cove, which had been pointed out by Mr. Fitton as the most eligible spot for effecting a disembarkation.

According to a previous arrangement the boats of the squadron, containing all the marines of the four ships, 199 in number, and a detachment of 406 seamen, had assembled on board the Hercule, and were commanded as follows: the seamen of the Theseus, by Lieutenants Edward Henry a'Court and Richard Henry Muddle, assisted by six midshipmen; and her marines by Lieutenants Earle Harwood and Bertrand Cahuac. The seamen of the Hercule, by Lieutenants John B. Hills and Nisbet Josiah Willoughby; and the marines by Lieutenant Samuel Perrot. The seamen of the Blanche, by Lieutenant Charles Woolsey, of the Hercule, in lieu of their proper commanding officer, Lieutenant William Braithwaite, who, to his disgrace as an officer and a gentleman, was incapacitated from filling his proper station by habitual drunkenness. The marines of the Blanche were commanded by Lieutenant Edward Nicolls, the senior marine-officer in the squadron. The seamen of the

Pique, on account of the sickness of two of her three lieutenants, were commanded by Captain Ross, and her marines by
Lieutenant William Henry Craig; and the whole detachment
of seamen and marines, numbering 605 officers and men, was
placed under the orders of Captain Dunn, of the Hercule.

In passing Fort Amsterdam, situated on the south-east side
of the entrance to St. Ann, the two 74s were fired at, but without effect, the shot falling short. At 11 h. 30 m. Fort Piscadero,
mounting 10 Dutch 12-pounders, and protecting the intended
point of disembarkation, opened a fire. This was immediately
returned by the Theseus, within half musket-shot, although the
ship was unable to remain alongside owing to a strong head-
wind and lee current. By making short tacks, however, the
Theseus brought her guns to bear with such effect that the fort
fired only an occasional gun when the ship was in stays. At
1 P.M. the first division of seamen and marines in the boats
stormed and carried the fort without loss, and struck the Dutch
colours, which the enemy, on retreating, had left flying. By a
rapid movement the British gained the heights, and, with the
loss of only four or five killed and wounded, drove the Dutch
soldiers from the position. This done, the remainder of the
seamen and marines were landed, and the Gipsy schooner
anchored in the cove. Captain Bligh also went on shore; and,
as there was no anchorage for them, the Theseus and Hercule
continued to stand off and on, but, owing to the wind and current, found a great difficulty in keeping their stations. During
the night several shot were fired at the ships from Fort
Amsterdam; but, although one or two went over the Theseus,
not one shot struck either ship.

On the morning of the 1st of February two 18-pounder
carronades and a light field-piece were landed from the
Theseus, and, with great difficulty and some danger, were
dragged four miles to the advanced post at the height. This post
was situated about 800 yards to the westward of the town of
St. Ann, which it in part overlooked, and was placed under the
command of Lieutenant Willoughby, while the post between
that and the point of disembarkation was commanded by
Lieutenant Hills. On the 2nd two long 18-pounders were landed,
and one or both were got to " Willoughby's battery;" as was
also one of the Dutch 12-pounders from Fort Piscadero. But
this was not accomplished without some loss from the heavy
fire kept up by Fort République. Four more 18-pounder
carronades and another field-piece or two were landed and

mounted at one or the other of the posts; and a constant interchange of firing was kept up between the British and Dutch batteries. In this firing a French battery, mounted by some of the guns, and manned by the crews of the privateers, also took a part.

On the evening of the 4th there was a smart skirmish between the British at the advanced post and the enemy's sharpshooters, in which the latter were repulsed; and on the morning of the 5th a more serious affair took place between.the marines under Lieutenant Nicolls and a force of Dutch and French estimated at 500 men. Notwithstanding his numerical inferiority, Lieutenant Nicolls, in the most gallant manner, repulsed the allied forces; but, pursuing the enemy too far, not without the loss of nearly 20 in killed and wounded, chiefly from the cannon of Fort République. On the next day, the 6th, the connonade between the forts was resumed; but Lieutenaut Willoughby, finding it in vain to present any of his pieces at Fort République, directed them at the town and at the shipping in the harbour. By this means the town was partially set on fire; and the Hatslaar would probably have been destroyed, had not the Dutch placed alongside of her, as a sort of *fend-off*, two large merchant-vessels, whose hulls received the greater part of the shot.

In this way passed a number of successive days, the force of the British gradually decreasing, not merely by loss from the cannon of the forts and in the different skirmishes, but from fatigue and sickness. At length not an officer was left at the advanced battery but Lieutenant Willoughby and Midshipman Eaton Travers; and 63 of the men had been obliged to be re-embarked owing to an attack of dysentery: a circumstance not to be wondered at considering that both officers and men lay upon the ground, without any of those conveniences deemed indispensable in the encampment of an army. The force of the Dutch, too, instead of amounting to only 160 regulars, consisted of 250 effective men, besides a body of local militia, and the crews of the vessels in the harbour. In addition to all this, the Dutch learnt by deserters, nine of whom quitted in one night, the weak state of the British force, and that the squadron must soon raise the blockade for the want of provisions.

In this state of things Captain Bligh, on the morning of the 23rd, despatched the Gipsy to apprise Sir John Duckworth of his intention, unless anything favourable should happen, to re-embark his people on the 4th of March. In the course of that same 23rd, the Dutch received a reinforcement; and in the evening the Pique was obliged to bear up for Jamaica, on account of having damaged her rudder.

Nearly one-half, or 30 out of 67, of the Hercule's marines were Poles, part of the prisoners taken at St. Domingo; and who, most inconsiderately, had been allowed to enter. On the 24th these "volunteers," very naturally, evinced so clear an intention of going over to the enemy, that they were obliged to be sent on board their ship with all haste. The re-embarkation of the whole remaining force could now no longer be delayed; and on the 25th, by 9 p.m., every person was on board an American schooner and one or two other vessels of a light draught, except Lieutenant Hills and a small party left to destroy Fort Piscadero. At 11 p.m. this was effectually done, and the lieutenant and his men soon joined their companions afloat.

The loss of the British, in the different skirmishes that had taken place, amounted to one midshipman (Joseph Palmer), eight seamen, two sergeants and seven privates of marines killed, and three lieutenants of marines (Messrs. Harwood, Cahuac, and Perrot, the latter with the loss of an arm), 16 seamen, two sergeants and 21 privates of marines wounded : total, 18 killed and 42 wounded. The whole of the guns that had been landed from the ships were also left behind, except, we believe, two 3-pounder field-pieces; but the abandoned guns were all rendered unserviceable, and the carriages, platforms, &c. destroyed.

The circumstances under which Lieutenant Perrot received his severe wound are so extraordinary as to be worthy a recital. During almost every day of the three weeks and upwards that the advanced battery was held, Lieutenant Willoughby, with a recklessness of his person that, as it appears to us, the occasion did not warrant, used to sit in a chair upon the ramparts or breastwork of his little battery, exposed to a daily, nay almost to an hourly, discharge of shot from one or two guns mounted upon the Dutch fort above. The earth was ploughed up all around, and one man, we believe, was killed close to the spot; but still the table and chair, and the daring young officer who sat there, remained untouched. On one afternoon Lieutenant Perrot was induced to seat himself in the chair. Scarcely had he done so when a shot came, took off his left arm, badly wounded the knee upon which it had been resting, and knocked the table to atoms.

Notwithstanding the ill success which had attended this, as

Sir John himself not inaptly termed it, " child of his own brain,"
the addition of the Vanguard's seamen and marines, and of a
heavy mortar or two, would have enabled Captain Bligh to cut
off the water from the Dutch garrison, and probably have compelled the French faction that ruled the island to accede to the
proposed capitulation.   The British officers and men behaved
most admirably : and the masterly manner in which, for so long
a time and under so many privations, Lieutenant Hills and
Willoughby, the latter in particular, maintained their respective
posts, elicited the strong praise of Captain Bligh ; who also, in
reference to another officer, says to Sir John Duckworth : " Mr.
Fitton has throughout shown so much zeal and judgment, that
I should feel most happy if you can consistently give him a commission appointing him lieutenant of the Gipsy."   This recom-
mendation was attended to ; and, in a few days after the Gipsy
anchored in Port Royal, her commander, although the bearer of
despatches announcing a defeat, received, what years of active
employment and of hard and responsible service, what more
than one successful case of acknowledged skill and gallantry as
a commanding officer,[1] had failed to procure him, his commission
as a lieutenant.

On the 25th of April the British 74-gun ship Centaur, Cap-
tain Murray Maxwell, bearing the broad pendant of Commodore Samuel Hood, accompanied by the three armées en flûte or
reduced 44-gun ships Pandour, Captain John Nash, and Serapis,
Captain Henry Waring, and reduced 28-gun frigate Alligator,
Captain Charles Richardson, also the ship-sloop Hippomenes,
Captain Conway Shipley, brig-sloop Drake, Captain William
Ferris, and armed schooner Unique, Lieutenant George R.
Brand, with a fleet of transports having on board nearly 2000
troops under Major-general Sir Charles Green, after a passage
of 22 days from Barbadoes, arrived off the island of Surinam ;
when immediate measures were taken to send a division of the
army, of about 700 men, under the command of Brigadier-
general Maitland, to land at Warapee creek.   The direction of
the disembarkation being left to Captain Conway Shipley of
the Hippomenes, the latter, with that sloop, a transport, and
three armed vessels, landed the troops on the night of the 30th,
assisted by Captain Kenneth M'Kenzie of the brig-sloop Gua-
chapin ; and who, with great zeal, had quitted his sloop 50
leagues to leeward, with all her boats, on finding, from baffling
winds and currents, that she could not get up.

[1] See p. 38.

That no time might be lost, Brigadier-general Hughes, who had arrived in the Pandour, was ordered to endeavour to gain possession, on the following night, of Braam's point; and instructions were sent to Captain James O'Brien, of the 36-gun frigate Emerald, then lying off the bar of Surinam river, to carry this service, in concert with the brigadier, into execution. The Emerald lost not a moment, but as the tide flowed, pushed over the bar, followed by the Pandour and Drake, and anchored, close to a battery of seven 18-pounders. The fort commenced a brisk fire upon the Emerald; but, after the ships had anchored, it was silenced by a few broadsides, without any loss on their side. In the fort were captured 43 officers and men, three of whom were wounded. Not being able to approach nearer to the island in the Centaur, on account of the water she drew, the general and commodore removed the next morning to the Emerald, lying at the entrance of the river. Having there summoned the colony, an answer was received containing a refusal of the terms. The moment, therefore, that the tide served, every effort was made to get up the river; which, from the shallowness of the water, was very difficult, the Emerald having passed through the mud in three feet less than she drew. Owing to the lowness of the tide, it was not until the night of the 5th of May that the frigate reached a station near to the fort.

The officers of engineers having explored the roads through the woods, close to the 12-gun battery of Frederici, which communicated with Leyden redoubt of the same force, an attack was made, on the morning of the 30th, by a detachment of troops under Brigadier-general Hughes, conducted in the boats by Captain Maxwell, of the Centaur, and Captains Ferris and Richardson, of the Drake and Alligator. The party landed at Plantation Resolution; and, after a tedious march through woods and swamps, the brigadier and his detachment, accompanied by Captains Maxwell and Ferris, some other officers, and about 30 seamen, carried the battery of Frederici; and, although the enemy blew up the magazine, by which many of the British suffered on entering the work, the troops and seamen, passing without delay a causeway of 700 yards, in the face of five pieces of cannon that bore upon it, carried in a few minutes more the redoubt of Leyden.

Brigadier-general Maitland had come down the river Commowina, and the ships had all got up near Frederici. By this time, too, the troops were advancing, and the enemy's communications nearly intercepted by the activity of the armed boats of the British; whose provisions, stores, and cannon were already prepared for attacking fort New Amsterdam, mounting upwards of 80 guns.   Aware of all this, the Batavian commandant, Lieutenant-colonel Batenburg, on the 5th of May, sent a flag of truce ; and shortly after the receipt of it a capitulation was signed.

Commodore Bloys-Van-Treslong, on the British claiming the surrender of the ships, entered into the terms proposed.   He had stationed the Proserpine of 32 guns, 18-pounders, near to fort New Amsterdam, and had extended a line of defence across the river, with the Pylades corvette, of 18 guns, at the other extremity, about a mile above the redoubt Purmurunt : he had also placed three merchantmen, of from eight to 12 guns, in the centre, and had employed a schooner of 10 guns to reconnoitre and cover the shore at Voorburg, should the British troops have attempted to advance by that side.   Besides this force, the Dutch commodore had seven gun-boats ready to act as occasion required.

This important colony was gained, fortunately, with a very inconsiderable loss on either side.   That of the British navy amounted to one lieutenant (James Edward Smith, first of the Centaur), one midshipman (William Shuldham), one boatswain, and two seamen killed, and three lieutenants (William King and Robert Henderson, both of the Centaur, and George R. Brand, of the Unique), and five seamen wounded; and that of the army, three privates killed, and 13 officers and privates wounded; total of the British loss, eight killed and 21 wounded; and the greater part owing to the explosion at Frederici.   The Dutch appear to have sustained no other loss than the three men already mentioned as wounded in the battery at Braam's point. The number of prisoners taken at Surinam, exclusively of staff and detachments, amounted to 2001 ; and the total number of pieces of iron and brass ordnance, about half of which were dismounted, was 282.

On the 17th of January, late in the evening, a French squadron commanded by Lieutenant Jean-Michel Mahé, consisting of the armed ship Oncle Thomas, of 20 guns, and the schooners Renommée of 14, Oiseau of 10 guns, and Rosalie, Vigie, and another of two each, fitted out at Cayenne, and having on board 565 officers, soldiers, and sailors, anchored off the British settlement of Gorée.   The officer commanding there, Colonel Fraser, had at his disposal only 54 white men including officers, and made the best dispositions in his power for resisting an attack. On the 18th, at 3 A.M., eight boats from the squadron disembarked 240 troops upon the rocks to the eastward of the town, where the surf happened to be unusually low. An engagement immediately ensued ; when, after a loss of 19 men killed and wounded on the part of the British (most of whom were in a sickly state), and 75 on the part of the French, Colonel Fraser surrendered on a capitulation, and the port was taken possession of by the troops and seamen of Lieutenant Mahé.

The French remained in quiet possession of their conquest, until the 7th of March, in the morning, when the British 18-pounder 36-gun frigate Inconstant, Captain Edward Stirling Dickson, accompanied by a store-ship and three transports, arrived off the settlement. The appearance of English colours on the citadel occasioned Captain Dickson to send Lieutenant Charles Pickford on shore in the cutter, to ascertain in whose possession the place was. Not having, by 10 P.M., received any information, Captain Dickson despatched three boats, manned and armed, under Mr. Runciman, midshipman, to cut out a ship in the harbour. The service was executed, under a heavy fire from the batteries, which sank one of the boats and wounded one of the men. The strength of the garrison having by this means been obtained, the Inconstant weighed and stood to the westward, to prevent any succours being thrown in from Sénégal. Having, on the following day, been joined by a fourth merchant-ship or transport, the three boats of the latter made the sufficient number to carry the allotted portion of troops ; and Captain Dickson commenced preparations to disembark the men on the following day ; when, at daybreak on the 8th, English colours were seen flying over French at the fort, the French garrison having the night previous capitulated with Lieutenant Pickford. Thus was the settlement of Gorée restored, without the loss of a man, to its former masters.

America and the Barbary States.

From some cause respecting which it would be profitless to inquire, these belligerents[1] remained comparatively inactive until the latter months of the year 1803, when an adjustment of some differences, which had arisen between the Emperor of Morocco and the United States, left Commodore Preble, who now com-

1 See p. 49,

manded the American squadron, at liberty to direct his whole
attention to Tripoli. Scarcely, however, had the American commodore put his squadron into motion, ere it met with a very
serious loss.

On the 31st of October, at 9 A.M., the 44-gun frigate Philadelphia, Captain William Bainbridge, being about five leagues to
the westward of Tripoli, discovered and immediately chased a
sail in shore, under Tripolitan colours, standing before the wind
to the eastward. The Philadelphia soon opened her fire, and
continued it until 11 h. 30 m. A.M.: when, being in seven
fathoms water, and finding that he could not prevent the vessel
entering Tripoli, Captain Bainbridge discontinued the pursuit.
In working off from the shore under her topsails, and when about
four miles and a half from the town of Tripoli, the Philadelphia
struck upon a rock not laid down in the charts. A boat was immediately lowered to sound: and, the greatest depth of water
appearing to be astern, the topgallantsails were set, and all the
sails thrown flat aback. Three anchors also were cut from the
bows, the water in the hold started, and the guns thrown overboard excepting a few abaft, to defend the ship against the
attacks of the Tripolitan gun-boats then firing at her. All this,
however, proved ineffectual; as did the attempt to lighten the
ship forward, by cutting away the foremast. About sunset, observing a reinforcement of gun-boats approaching from Tripoli,
and having no means of defence left, the Philadelphia hauled
down her colours. The Tripolitans immediately took possession
of the American frigate, and made prisoners of the officers and
men; whose number, fortunately, did not at this time exceed
300. About 48 hours afterwards, by great exertion and a strong
breeze in their favour, the Tripolitans got the Philadelphia
afloat, and towed her into the harbour.

Before we proceed to give an account of the performances of
American seamen, the introduction of a few lines, published
eight years ago, and not since, to our knowledge, impugned,
will render it probable, that we may yet be recording, in part,
the exploits of British seamen: "It is fresh in the recollection
of many officers of the British navy, how difficult it was, at this
period, to keep the seamen from deserting to the Americans.
The short peace of 1803 occasioned many of our ships to be paid
off; and the nature of the service upon which the Americans
were engaged, held forth a strong inducement to the manly feeling of the British tar. It was not to raise his arm against his
own countrymen, but against barbarians, whose foul deeds

excited indignation in every generous breast. The Americans cannot deny, that the complements of their ships in the Tripolitan war consisted chiefly of British seamen, supplied by a Scotch renegado at New York, and by numerous other crimps in the different seaport towns of the United States; and that those complements were afterwards filled up, by similar means, at Cadiz and other ports of the Mediterranean. Was, not Commodore Preble, on account of being detected in some transaction of this sort, obliged to shorten his stay at Gibraltar, and to fix Syracuse, instead of Malta, for his next rendezvous? To such as know the facility with which, either in the ships or on the shores, of the United States, a deserter, or an emigrant, can obtain his naturalization, the term " American" requires an epithet to render it intelligible. In recording the exploits of "Americans," it is but to lop off the qualifying adjunct "adopted," and every native reader feels a hero's blood flowing in his veins. On the other hand, should disgrace be attached to the deed, Mr. Clark (the American naval historian) and his brother writers, anticipating the reader's wishes, seldom fail to state, that the parties were not American, but British sailors."[1]

We must premise, also, that the only accounts we have to refer to are those written by the Americans. The Tripolitans have no annalist to compile, no State-historiographer to magnify and blazon, the feats performed by themselves; nor have they any acute and patriotic writer to expose the exaggerations, and disprove the misstatements, published by their enemies. With such a one-sided case before us we almost fear to proceed; and yet we should be sorry to omit recording, or, by doubting, to throw a slight upon, an act of genuine gallantry, achieved by Frenchman or American, Christian or Mahomedan.

Feeling a laudable desire to prevent the Tripolitans from making any use of the fine frigate which, by an accident so untoward, had fallen into their hands, Lieutenant Stephen Decatur, of the United States 44-gun frigate Constitution, submitted to Commodore Preble a plan for setting fire to and destroying the Philadelphia in the harbour of Tripoli. The commodore at first thought the enterprise too hazardous, but at length gave his consent. On the 3rd of February, having embarked with 70 volunteers, including Lieutenant James Lawrence and Midshipman Charles Morris, on board a Turkish prize ketch, newly named the Intrepid, Lieutenant Decatur sailed from Syracuse,

[1] James's Naval Occurrences between Great Britain and America, p. 73.

accompanied by the 18-gun brig Syren, Lieutenant Charles Stewart; whose boats, covered by the brig's fire, were to co-operate in the attack.

On the 18th, in the evening, the Intrepid and Syren arrived off the harbour of Tripoli; but it appears that the two vessels "by a change of wind" separated, and that at 8 P.M. the Intrepid entered the harbour alone. The Philadelphia lay within half gun-shot of the Bashaw's castle and principal battery, with two Tripolitan cruisers at the distance of about 200 yards on her starboard quarter, and on the same bow a number of gun-boats. "All her guns were mounted and loaded."[1] At about 11 P.M., just as the Intrepid had arrived within 200 yards of the larboard and outward side of the Philadelphia, the latter hailed and desired the ketch to anchor on peril of being fired into. The pilot of the Intrepid, as he had been instructed, and who, we imagine, was himself a mussulman, answered that they had lost all their anchors. Upon this the ketch was suffered to advance; and, so well was the deception kept up, that a rope was per-mitted to be made fast to the frigate's fore-chains, by which the Intrepid hauled herself alongside.

Lieutenant Decatur and his party now gallantly sprang on board, and, rushing upon the alarmed Tripolitans, killed about 20, and quickly subdued the remainder. Having thus, in a much easier manner than could have been anticipated, got pos-session of the Philadelphia, Lieutenant Decatur directed her to be set on fire; which was done so promptly and effectively, that the Intrepid herself was nearly involved in the flames. A fine wind from the land, however, at that moment sprang up; and the ketch profiting by it, soon ran out of the harbour with the gallant party who had so fully executed the bold and perilous service intrusted to them. Although, as soon as the Tripolitans on shore had ascertained that the Philadelphia was in their enemy's possession, the forts and surrounding vessels opened a fire upon her, the Americans were so fortunate as to escape with only four men wounded.

In the course of the summer, at two or three different periods, the American squadron, assisted by some Neapolitan gun-boats, and bomb-vessels, bombarded the town and batteries of Tripoli; and lieutenant, or rather captain (for he then had been de-servedly promoted), Decatur, who commanded a gun-boat, again greatly distinguished himself. "Captain Decatur," says Mr. Clark, "having grappled a Tripolitan boat and boarded her

[1] Clark's Naval History of the United States, vol. i., p. 153. This wants confirmation.

with only 15 Americans ; in 10 minutes her decks were cleared, and she was captured. · Three Americans were wounded. At this moment Captain Decatur was informed that the gun-boat, commanded by his brother (Lieutenant James Decatur), had captured a boat belonging to the enemy ; but that his brother, as he was stepping on board, was treacherously shot by the Tripolitan commander, who made off with his boat. Captain Decatur immediately pursued the murderer, who was retreating within the lines ; having succeeded in coming alongside, he boarded with only 11 men. A doubtful contest of 20 minutes ensued. Decatur immediately attacked the Tripolitan commander, who was armed with a spear and cutlass. In parrying the Turk's spear, Decatur broke his sword close to the hilt, and received a slight wound in the right arm and breast ; but, having seized the spear, he closed ; and after a violent struggle both fell, Decatur uppermost. The Turk then drew a dagger from his belt ; but Decatur caught hold of his arm, drew a pistol from his pocket, and shot him."

An exploit fully equal to this is recorded of another American officer :—" Lieutenant Trippe boarded one of the enemy's large boats, with only a midshipman, Mr. Jonathan Henley, and nine men, his boat falling off before any more could join him. He was thus left either to perish or to conquer 36 men with only 11. Though at first the victory seemed doubtful, yet, in a few minutes, the Tripolitans were subdued ; 14 of them were killed, and 22 taken prisoners. Seven of these last were severely wounded. Lieutenant Trippe received 11 sabre wounds, some of them dangerous. The blade of his sword bending, he closed with his antagonist. Both fell. In the struggle, Trippe wrested the Turk's sword from him, and with it stabbed him to the heart."[1]

The American archives contain the records of several more such desperate feats between the American and Tripolitan officers and men. At length, however, an end was put to all hostility between the United States and the regency of Tripoli, by a treaty of peace concluded in June 1805, but not, it appears, upon terms so advantageous as the Americans had anticipated.

[1] Clark's Naval History of the United States, vol. i., p. 157.

BRITISH AND FRENCH FLEETS.

THE most remarkable feature, in the Abstract[1] for the commencement of the present year, is the number of vessels that appear in the two "Built" columns. At no former or subsequent period have 87 British ships-of-war been launched within the year. All these ships, except the five principal ones, had been ordered to be built since the commencement of the war, and upwards of 50 of them since the commencement of the year in which they first took the water. Nothing can better demonstrate the exertions made by the new lord of the admiralty (the late Lord Melville) to recover the British navy from the low state into which it had previously fallen. Of 87 vessels so launched in the year 1804, 80 had been built in the merchants' yards, a number amounting to nearly two-thirds of all that had been similarly built during the whole nine years of the preceding war.

Of the 88 new vessels ordered in 1804, 48 were gun-brigs, and 10 belonged to the N, or middling class of 74. The utility of the latter cannot be disputed; but the former would probably have better answered the intended purpose of their construction had they been differently armed. Their light draught of water enabled them, certainly, to approach very near to an enemy's coast; but what effective opposition could 18-pounder carronades offer to the heavy long guns mounted by the French batteries and gun-boats? The new gun-brigs were of a size (180 tons) to carry with ease four 32-pounder carronades, fitted to throw shells, and two long 18-pounders on traversing carriages, one at the bow, the other at the stern. With this reduction in their nominal, but increase in their real strength, these brigs

[1] See Appendix, Annual Abstract, No. 13.

would have been better able to cope with the description of force which they were likely to encounter in the waters that were to be the scene of their services.

The prize and casualty lists for the year 1804 will furnish the names and other particulars of the ships respectively contained in the fourth column of the " Increase," and first of the "Decrease" compartments of the Abstract.[1]

The number of commissioned officers and masters belonging to the British navy at the commencement of the year 1805 was—

Admirals.	50
Vice-admirals	36
Rear-admirals	63
,, superannuated 22	
Captains	639
,, superannuated 25	
Commanders, or sloop-captains . . .	422
,, superannuated 45	
Lieutenants	2472
Masters	556

And the number of seamen and marines voted for the service of the same year was 120,000.[2]

Scarcely had Spain issued her declaration of war against England[3] than France began to put in requisition the fleets and armies of her new ally. On the 4th of January, three days actually before the Spanish declaration reached London, a secret treaty between the two courts was signed at Paris, by Vice-admiral Decrès, on the part of France, and Vice-admiral Don Frederico Gravina on the part of Spain. The first article contains a display of the force by sea and land at the French emperor's disposal. At the Texel are 30,000 men, with the necessary transports. At Ostende, Dunkerque, Calais, Boulogne, and Hâvre, respectively, are flotillas, capable of embarking altogether, 120,000 men and 25,000 horses ; at Brest, a fleet of 21 sail of the line,[4] besides frigates and transports, with 25,000 men ready for embarkation ; at Rochefort, a squadron of six sail of the line (including the Achille 74, nearly ready for launching) and four frigates, having on board 4000 men; and at Toulon, a fleet of 11 sail of the line, eight frigates, and sundry transports, having on board 9000 ; total, 188,000 men.

[1] See Appendix, Nos. 22, 23, and 24.
[2] Ibid., No. 25.
[3] It bore date at Madrid, December 12, 1804. See p. 290.
[4] The Océan three-decker is here meant to be excluded, and probably some other ship equally in an unseaworthy state. See p. 215, where 23 sail of the line are mentioned as in the port.

By the second, third, and fourth articles, the King of Spain engages to arm, and supply with six months' provisions and four months' water, from 25 to 29 sail of the line, and to have them ready, with from 4000 to 5000 Spanish troops (in conjunction with 20,000 French to embark from Cadiz), by the 20th, or at furthest, the 30th of March. Of those 25 or 29 sail of the line, Ferrol is to furnish from seven to eight, and which are to combine in their operations with the five French sail of the line in that port; Cadiz is to supply from 12 to 15, and Carthagena six. By the fifth article the two high contracting parties mutually engage to augment their fleets by all the ships of the line and frigates that may be subsequently constructed, repaired, and fitted in their respective ports. The sixth article contains an engagement on the part of Napoleon to guarantee to his catholic majesty, as well the integrity of his European dominions, as the restitution of all colonies that may be taken from him during the war; and that, should the fortune of arms, " in accordance with the justice of the cause which their majesties are defending," grant success to their armies and fleets, the emperor will employ his influence to get Trinidad restored, and also the treasure taken out of the four frigates. The seventh article contains a mutual undertaking not to make a separate peace; and the eighth provides that the ratifications shall be exchanged within a month.[1] To the treaty a note is appended, signed by the Spanish ambassador, Don Frederico Gravina, in which he expresses a doubt as to the possibility of collecting a sufficiency of sailors for the ships, and, above all, of having ready, by the time stated, so many as six millions of rations.[2]

If Napoleon, with his 40 or 45 sail of the line, had calculated to create such a diversion of the British fleets as should give him a clear channel for his flotilla to cross, how must his expectations have been raised now that he possessed the disposal of upwards of 70 sail of the line. It is true that the public lists and journals did show and insist, that the number of commissioned line-of-battle ships belonging to England at the time amounted to 105; but, as respects sea-going ships, the fact was not so: the British navy could send forth no more than 83 sail of the line, and scarcely the whole of them. Buonaparte had constantly a Steel's list before him, and with the aid of the information derived from his numerous spies, knew, better by far

---

[1] They were exchanged on the 18th of January.

[2] For a copy of this important treaty, see vol. xi., p. 215, of Précis des Evènemens, &c.

than many in England, how to analyze the accounts, and separate the non-combatant from the combatant ships. Let it then be kept in remembrance, that, at the commencement of the year 1805, the British and the Franco-Spanish navies (leaving the Batavian navy out of the question) were, as to number of effective line-of-battle ships, nearly upon a par. What changes took place in the relative numbers of these navies before the close of this eventful year we shall now proceed methodically to relate.

The commencement of the year found Admiral Cornwallis at his station off Ushant, with a force not exceeding 11 sail of the line; while the French fleet that lay in the road of Brest, ready for sea, numbered, as has on more than one occasion been shown, 21 sail. On the 3rd of February, when the blockading force, by successive arrivals, had been augmented to 16 sail, the departure of five, under Vice-admiral Sir Robert Calder, to the station off Ferrol and Corunna, left the admiral again, for a short time, with only 11 sail. The perseverance with which, during a period of 22 months, including two boisterous winters, Admiral Cornwallis had maintained the blockade of Brest, affected his health, and obliged him to suspend his arduous labours, and seek a few weeks' relaxation on shore. Accordingly, on the 20th of March, the Ville-de-Paris anchored at Spithead, and in the course of the day struck the flag at her main. The command of the Channel fleet devolved upon Admiral Lord Gardner, whose flag was flying on board the Trent frigate at Cork. In the mean time the fleet, cruising off Ushant, and numbering 17 sail of the line, had been left in charge of Vice-admiral Sir Charles Cotton, in the 12-gun ship San-Josef.

On the 3rd of April, Admiral Lord Gardner, in the new first-rate Hibernia, arrived off Ushant, and relieved Sir Charles Cotton in the command of the fleet, then consisting of 21 sail of the line. On the 11th a gale of wind drove the British fleet from the French coast. On the 13th, in the afternoon, Lord Gardner, with 17 sail, regained his station; and, the next morning, the 14th, in consequence of some intelligence received from his look-out frigates, he despatched the Warrior 74 to reconnoitre the harbour of Brest. At 5 h. 30 m. P.M. Captain William Bligh rejoined, with the signal flying, that the French ships were getting under way. Upon this the British ships formed in line-of-battle to be ready to receive them. On the following morning, the 15th, the French van-division, composed of nine sail of the line, appeared in sight off the Black Rocks, and was presently joined by the main body, forming a total, as counted, of 40 sail of vessels, including 21 of the line.   This formidable fleet had on board 2000 troops, and was provisioned for six months.   The British admiral, whose force in the course of the day amounted to 24 sail of the line, strove his utmost to bring the French fleet to action; but the latter, after manœuvring for a few hours between Bertheaume and Camaret bays, returned into port.

Unlike a few former shifts of position and manœuvres in Brest and Bertheaume roads—and which served the double purpose of exercising the crews and of enabling the Moniteur to insert a boastful paragraph, about offering battle to, and chasing away, the blockading force—this was a real attempt to put to sea.   Vice-admiral Villeneuve had sailed from Toulon, and Napoleon's object now was, that the two fleets should effect their junction in the West Indies, and, after ravaging the British possessions there, return to the Channel, augmented, by the Rochefort squadron on the route and by the combined squadron at Ferrol on appearing off that port, to 56 sail of the line.   It was then that the great blow was to be struck.   All Napoleon's letters written at this period betray his anxiety about M. Ganteaume's departure.   In one dated "Au château de Stupinis, le 21 Avril," he says to his minister of marine, "Le non départ de Ganteaume me contrarie beaucoup;" and, in another dated at the same place two days afterwards, wherein he informs M. Decrès that he has despatched a courier to Ganteaume, to inform him that Nelson had gone to Egypt in search of Villeneuve, Buonaparte emphatically adds: "Dieu veuille que mon courrier ne le trouve point à Brest."

After a vain endeavour, by forging news of disastrous events to the English in India, to weaken by detachments abroad the fleet off Ushant, Napoleon directs that, if Ganteaume cannot put to sea before the 20th of May, he is to remain quiet.[1]   The fact is, that M. Villeneuve's stock of provisions was expending fast, and a longer delay might throw serious obstacles in the way of the expedition.   The British blockading fleet still retaining its menacing posture, the next plan was, that Vice-admiral Ganteaume should remove with his fleet to a position outside the goulet, between Camaret bay and the east end of Bertheaume bay.   To prevent the British from paying the spot a visit, when thus temptingly occupied, directions were given to strengthen the defences along the coast in the neighbourhood.   This was so

[1] Précis des Evènemens, tome xi., pp. 228-239.

expeditiously as well as effectually done, that, by the first week
in May, upwards of 150 pieces of cannon were mounted on the
different batteries around Bertheaume and Camaret bays. The
object of ordering M. Ganteaume to this outer anchorage was
to facilitate his putting to sea, but, above all, to enable him to
effect his junction with Vice-admiral Villeneuve ; who, on the
probability that the former would not be able to quit Brest in
time to meet the latter in the West Indies, had been directed to
hasten to Ferrol. Having there augmented his force to 34 sail
of the line, Vice-admiral Villeneuve was to take his choice of
four routes for reaching Boulogne. The first two supposed a
junction with the Brest fleet, thus : to appear before Rochefort,
and, joining the five ships there and the one at Lorient, proceed
to Brest, and then, with 60 sail of the line, enter the Channel ;
or, as the Rochefort squadron occupied an equal number of
British ships, letting that remain, proceed straight to M. Ganteaume's anchorage, and thence to the Channel with 54 sail
of the line : in either of which cases, it appears, Napoleon designed that Vice-admiral Ganteaume, although junior to M.
Villeneuve, should assume the command. All this was to be
effected, if possible, without an action ; but, should one be unavoidable, it was to be fought, for obvious reasons, as near as
possible to Brest. The third and fourth routes were, either to
double Ireland, and, calling for the Texel squadron of seven,
arrive before Boulogne with 41 sail of the line, or to pass straight
up Channel, out of view of the coasts or of the blockading fleet
off Brest, and, with 34 sail only, appear off Boulogne, four or
five days before the Channel fleet could arrive there ; in which
four or five days the flotilla was to cross and the descent be
effected.[1] A fifth plan, left as an alternative to M. Villeneuve,
having reference exclusively to a distant service, is deferred to
the proper period for introducing it.

It was at about the date of these orders that some reflections
in the English newspapers, cast upon the Brest fleet for not
sailing out and engaging a much inferior force, gave disquietude
to Napoleon, and caused him to write thus to his minister of
marine : "Have inserted in the journals of Holland an article
against the system of blockade : let it be made appear that we
sail out of Brest when we choose ; that Bruix sailed out such a
day ; Morard de Galles such a day ; Ganteaume several times :
that in his last trip to Bertheaume, nothing prevented his
putting to sea, and that the English squadron did not so much

1 Précis des Evènemens, tome xi., p. 253.

as know of his being under sail : that it is therefore impossible to blockade the port of Brest, especially in the months of September and October. This article will show, that we have no desire to put to sea, but wish merely to keep the enemy in awe." Many of the London opposition journals, taking all this for truth, became very strenuous coadjutors in Buonaparte's plan of deception.

On the 6th of July accounts reached the Channel fleet of the arrival of the combined fleet of Martinique ; and on the same day Admiral Cornwallis, having recovered his health, arrived in the Ville-de-Paris off Ushant, and relieved Lord Gardner in the command of the former, now consisting of 18 sail of the line, and which, considering the force likely to assail it from different points, was rather critically situated. On the 11th, in-telligence that the combined fleet was on its return reached Admiral Cornwallis from the admiralty, with orders for Rear-admiral Sterling to quit his station off Rochefort, and, with his five sail of the line, join Vice-admiral Calder off Ferrol. The circumstances under which these orders had been despatched are deserving of attention. The British brig-sloop Curieux, Captain George Edmund Byron Bettesworth, with the intelli-gence, anchored at Plymouth on the 7th, in the morning; and at about 11 P.M. on the 8th the captain arrived at the admiralty. The first lord having retired to rest, the despatches were not communicated to him until early on the morning of the 9th. At this Lord Barham was very angry, saying that seven or eight hours had been lost. Without waiting to dress himself, he wrote orders for Admiral Cornwallis to detach Rear-admiral Sterling from off Rochefort to join Vice-admiral Calder, who was to take a station to the westward of Cape Finisterre, while Admiral Cornwallis himself, with the Channel fleet, was to cruise between Ushant and Finisterre. By 9 A.M. the admiralty messengers were on their way to Portsmouth and Plymouth, and on the 11th, as already mentioned, Admiral Cornwallis received his orders. Such promptitude on the part of the British admiralty could not be credited by Napoleon. "Ce ne que le 20 messi-dor" (July 8), says he, " que le brick le Curieux est arrivé en Angleterre. L'amirauté n'a pu se décider dans les vingt-quatre heures sur les mouvemens de ses escadres : dans ce cas, il n'est pas probable que l'ordre à l'escadre devant Rochefort soit arrivé en trois jours. Je mets donc en fait que cette escadre a levé

---

[1] See Appendix, No. 26.

sa croisière par des ordres antérieurs à l'arrivée du Curieux à Londres."[1]

On the 20th Vice-admiral Ganteaume received orders to put to sea, and endeavour to form a junction, first with the Rochefort squadron of five sail of the line, off the Lizard, and then with M. Villeneuve. On the 29th the news of the latter's action with Sir Robert Calder reached the Channel fleet, and on the 14th of August Sir Robert himself joined the fleet with eight sail of the line; as, on the following day, the 15th, did Lord Nelson from his long western cruise, with 11. The departure of his lordship on the 16th, with two or three ships, left the admiral with a force of 34 sail of the line. On the 17th, on intelligence arriving that the Franco-Spanish fleet, numbering 27 or 28 sail of the line, had been seen off Ferrol, Admiral Cornwallis detached to that station Sir Robert Calder, with 18.[2] On the 20th, the Captain 74, from Plymouth, joined the Channel fleet, which then amounted to 17 sail of the line.

The affair off Cape Finisterre being considered to have entailed an equal loss of ships upon the British and the combined fleets, was not allowed to interrupt the grand design, in which the latter had been allotted to take so important a part. On the 20th of August, a little before the time when, as it was conjectured, Vice-admiral Villeneuve would be off the port, Vice-admiral Ganteaume received orders to quit Brest road, where the fleet had recently been lying, and anchor in Bertheaume. On the same day, at about 6 h. 30 m. P.M., the French advanced squadron began to get under way, but not unseen by the British 44-gun frigate Indefatigable, Captain John Tremayne Rodd; who, accompanied by the 38-gun frigate Niobe, and two or three smaller vessels, was reconnoitring the harbour, and for that purpose had taken a station about four miles south by east of the Black Rocks. On the following morning, the 21st, at 6 A.M., the whole French fleet, consisting of the following 21 sail of the line, five frigates, one ship-corvette, and two avisos, under Vice-admiral Ganteaume in the Impérial (late Vengeur, a name that no one in France, considering the circumstance out of which it had arisen, could expect would so soon have been changed), stood out of the goulet,

---

[1] Précis des Evènemens, tome xii., p. 243.

[2] Napoleon either thought, or affected to think, this to be an egregious folly :—

"insigne bêtise" on the part of Admiral Cornwallis. Précis des Evènemens, tome xii., p. 258.

and, at about 10 h. 30 m. A.M., anchored in the new position between Camaret and Bertheaume :—

Gun-ship.		Gun-ship.		Gun-ship.	
120	Impérial,		Batave,		Jean-Bart,
110	Invincible,		Brave,		Jupiter,
	Républicain,[1]		Cassard,		Patriote,
80	Alexandre,	74	Conquérant,	74	Tourville,
	Foudroyant,		Diomède,		Ulysse,
74	Alliance,		Eole,		Vétéran,
	Aquilon,		Impétueux,		Wattigny.

Frigates, Cornète, Félicité, Indienne, Valeureuse, Volontaire.
Ship-corvette, Diligente, and *brig-corvettes* Espiégle and Vulcain.

On the first discovery of the ships in the morning, the Felix schooner had been sent with the intelligence to the admiral off Ushant: and, on their anchoring, the 36-gun frigate Aigle, Captain George Wolfe, who had joined about an hour before, was despatched upon the same errand.

At the time the news reached him, which was soon after noon on the 21st, Admiral Cornwallis lay with his fleet, numbering 17 sail of the line, one frigate (exclusive of two others and a brig-sloop on the look-out in-shore), two cutters, and one schooner, about three leagues south by west of the island of Ushant. The British fleet, the names of the whole of the ships of which, owing to the frequent departures and arrivals of the preceding 10 days, we are unable to give, hauled to the wind on the larboard tack, with a moderate breeze at north by east, and at about 2 h. 30 m. P.M. passed the west end of Ushant within less than three miles. At 3 h. 30 m., having made Pointe Saint-Mathieu, the fleet shortened sail, and soon discovered the French ships, some at an anchor and others under way. The admiral being desirous himself to reconnoitre the enemy, the Ville-de-Paris made the signal for the fleet to disregard her motions, and then stood in towards the Indefatigable and her two consorts. At 5 P.M. the Ville-de-Paris and in-shore squadron, having a fair view of the French fleet, shortened sail and counted the number of vessels ; which was found to correspond with the number already given, except in the omission of the corvette. At 5 h. 30 m. P.M. Pointe Saint-Mathieu bearing north only a mile and a half distant, the Ville-de-Paris wore to rejoin her fleet. Immediately several shot and shells were fired at her and the ships in company, both from Pointe Saint-Mathieu and from the west point of Bertheaume, but without effect. At 6 h. 30 m. P.M. Admiral Cornwallis rejoined the fleet; and, having made

[1] Late Révolutionnaire.

known his intention to attack the French fleet at its anchorage early the next morning, anchored at 7 P.M. for the night, a short distance to the southward of the outer Black rock; which then bore from the Ville-de-Paris north half-east, St. Mathieu's lighthouse east-north-east, and the Bec du Raz south half-east.

On the 22nd, at 4 h. 30 m. A.M., the British fleet weighed, and, with the weather hazy and the wind still at north by east, stood in on the larboard tack for Camaret bay, in close order of battle; the Ville-de-Paris leading, and next to her the 80-gun ship Cæsar, Captain Sir Richard John Strachan, and 74-gun ship Montagu, Captain Robert Waller Otway. At 6 h. 30 m. A.M., the Porquelle rock being close ahead, the ships of the fleet tacked in succession. On the haze clearing away a little, the French fleet was seen at anchor; but at 8 A.M. the ships of the latter began getting under way. In 20 minutes afterwards the British ships tacked in succession, and again stood in under easy sail. At 9 A.M. the Indefatigable, being ahead, stood towards the French 80-gun ship Alexandre, Rear-admiral Willaumez, who was leading the French fleet, then standing out in line of battle. At 9 h. 30 m. the Alexandre fired a broadside at the Indefatigable, but without effect, and was answered by the latter's main-deck guns, the distance being too great for the carronades. On this the Indefatigable tacked, and the Ville-de-Paris and ships in her train made sail towards the French fleet; but the latter presently tacked for the harbour's mouth, as if to avoid an engagement. At 10 h. 45 m. A.M. the Cæsar and Montagu hauled out of the line to attack the Alexandre, who, with the Foudroyant and Impétueux, formed the rear of the French line. This, at about 11 A.M., brought on a fire from the batteries, which the Ville-de-Paris, Cæsar, and Montagu returned, the three rearmost French ships already named, and the Valeureuse and Volontaire frigates also taking part in it. At 11 h. 30 m., the west point of Bertheaume bearing north half-east distant one mile and a half, the British fleet wore and stood out in order of battle, the batteries keeping up, until a quarter-past noon, a constant fire of shot and shells.

The damage done to the British van, principally by the batteries, proved how well the latter were calculated to protect the French fleet at its new anchorage. On board the Ville-de-Paris one shell struck the spare anchor, and burst into innumerable pieces, which flew in all directions. A piece, weighing about a pound and a half, struck Admiral Cornwallis on the breast, but, being entirely spent, did not hurt him. A second piece struck and slightly wounded one of the midshipmen. No other person, it is believed, was hurt; but the ship had her hull struck in several places, and her rigging and sails a great deal cut. The Cæsar and Montagu both suffered in their rigging and sails; the former, indeed, owing to the close position she took, lost three men killed and six wounded. The Montagu had the heel of her foretopmast shot away, but does not appear to have sustained any loss in men. Of the French ships, the whole of which by 2 P.M. had re-anchored, the Alexandre, who was the Cæsar's principal opponent, is represented to have had her mizentopmast shot away, and, with two or three of the other ships, to have sustained some damage in rigging and sails. With respect to loss, the French accounts give it in the gross, merely stating that about 20 men were placed hors-de-combat by the fire of the British ships.

Admitting that this was an affair in which the French advanced squadron alone had retired from the fire of the British, still the two fleets were wholly in sight of each other, and M. Ganteaume had but to stand from under the protection of his batteries to bring on a general action. Considering that he had 21 sail of the line to oppose to 17, we cannot suppose that the French admiral would have declined a battle, had he, from the nature of his orders, been permitted to engage. To know that he was so restrained, and yet be compelled to keep his orders secret, must, to a brave officer like Vice-admiral Ganteaume, have been a sorry compensation for the public obloquy of the transaction, glossed over even as it was, by imperial command, in the columns of the Moniteur.

On every succeeding day, from the 23rd to the 30th of August, some of the French ships got under way and manœuvred about, but the Brest fleet made no serious attempt to put to sea. Matters remained in this inactive state until the 13th of December; when, taking advantage of a brisk gale from the northeast and the absence of the blockading fleet, which had retired into port to victual and refit, a division of the French fleet, consisting of 11 sail of the line, four frigates, and a corvette, quitted the anchorage outside the goulet, and put to sea. A succession of gales of wind, during the few days that remained of the year, prevented Admiral Cornwallis from regaining his station off Ushant, and concealed from his knowledge any positive information of the sailing of so large a division of the Brest fleet.

As we have done on other occasions, so we shall here, give some account of the different actions of the year fought between the British cruisers stationed off the French coast and the invasion-flotilla. In the course of the spring the corps of Marshal Davoust, encamped in the neighbourhood of Ostende, proceeded to join the grand invading army, of which it formed the right wing. This occasioned a corresponding movement in the Gallo-Batavian flotilla; and accordingly the Port of Ambleteuse was fixed upon as the point of rendezvous for the different divisions stationed at Ostende, Dunkerque, and Calais. Admiral Ver-Huell, whom in the preceding spring we left at Ostende, whither he had been driven by the squadron of Sir Sidney Smith,[1] succeeded, at length, in reaching Dunkerque; where a great portion of the Gallo-Batavian flotilla had now assembled, and lay watching an opportunity to get to the westward, by departing, a division at a time, as the readiest mode to avoid discovery and molestation.

On the 23rd of April, at 9 P.M., favoured by the darkness and a fresh wind from north-east, the first division, consisting of 33 gun-vessels and 19 transports, laden with stores from the camp at Ostende, weighed from Dunkerque road. The division passed Gravelines and Calais undiscovered; when, just before daybreak on the 24th, the wind shifted to south-east, and then to south-south-east. Having a change of tide also against them, the vessels were thrown into disorder. The greater part of them now steered for an anchorage between the capes Blanez and Grinez, while eight schuyts, which had kept too long on the larboard tack, found themselves seven or eight miles from the shore. In this state the division was gained sight of by a British squadron, consisting of the 38-gun frigate Leda, Captain Robert Honyman, sloops Harpy and Railleur, Captains Edmund Heywood and Valentine Collard, bomb-vessel Fury, Captain John Yelland, and eight gun-brigs, the whole, except two of the latter which were sailing guard off Ambleteuse, at anchor off Boulogne.

The two gun-brigs off Ambleteuse, which were the Gallant and Watchful, Lieutenants Thomas Shirly and James Marshall, immediately chased north-east by signal, and the remainder of the squadron weighed and stood in the same direction. At 8 A.M. the above two gun-brigs closed with the eight armed schuyts, and a smart cannonade commenced between the latter, aided by the heavy batteries on shore, and the brigs. In a few minutes four large shot from the batteries struck the Gallant between wind and water, and compelled her to haul on the starboard tack in order to stop the leaks, which were gaining fast. One schuyt struck to the Watchful. The Railleur, and the gun-

[1] See p. 224.

brigs Locust and Starling, Lieutenants John Lake and Charles
Napier, coming up, compelled six others, before 10 A.M., also to
surrender, but not until after a spirited resistance on the part of
the schuyts.

Early on the morning of the 25th two other schuyts, which
had drifted off the land, were captured by the Archer gun-brig,
Lieutenant William Price, whose one seaman wounded was all
the loss sustained by the British.   The eight Gallo-Batavian
schuyts averaged about 75 tons, mounted three guns each,
chiefly long 24-pounders, and carried, altogether, 142 sailors
and soldiers.   The remainder of the division, assisted by several
armed launches, containing grapnels and hawsers, sent out from
Boulogne by Rear-admiral Lacrosse (since the death of Admiral
Bruix, on the 19th of March, the commander-in-chief of the
French flotilla) succeeded, after a while, in reaching Ambleteuse,
the port of its destination.

On the 10th of June, at 7 A.M., a division of the French flotilla,
consisting of the two " corvettes-canonnières " Foudre, Capitaine
de vaisseau Jacques-Felix-Emmanuel Hemelin, and Audacieuse,
Lieutenant Dominique Roquebert, each mounting 10 guns (four
or six long 18-pounders, the remainder brass 36-pounder carronades, with upwards of 80 men), four gun-vessels, of three
long 24-pounders, and an 8-inch mortar each, three others of
one 24-pounder and a field-piece each, eight others, of two 4 or
6 pounders, and 14 transports, in all 31 vessels, sailed from the
port of Hâvre bound to Fécamp.   By the time they had got
abreast of Brunevel, the French vessels were chased by the
British 12-pounder 36-gun frigate Chiffonne, Captain Charles
Adam, who, with the ship-sloop Falcon, Captain George Sanders,
gun-brig Clinker, Lieutenant Nisbet Glen, and the Frances hired
armed cutter, was cruising off the coast.

At 9 h. 30 m. A.M. the Chiffonne, then in 10 fathoms water,
considerably ahead of her companions, and close in with the
flotilla, opened her fire upon the van, where the Foudre had
stationed herself: but, in a quarter of an hour, shoaling her
water, the frigate was compelled to haul further off.   At 10 h.
30 m. A.M. the frigate, followed by the sloop and gun-brig, recommenced firing.   Shortly afterwards one of the French brigs
caught fire, but succeeded in extinguishing it, and some of the
other vessels ran on shore.   Towards noon the Chiffonne, who
had bore the brunt of this attack, again hauled out into deeper
water.   Shortly afterwards the van of the French flotilla ran
close under the batteries of Cap-de-Caiset, until joined by the

rearmost vessels, when they again bore up to proceed on their course. At 1 h. 30 m. P.M. the three British vessels again stood in, and at 2 P.M. recommenced firing. The Falcon presently became closely engaged with the two sternmost of the French brigs, one of which was the Audacieuse. As the British passed along the coast, the forts kept firing shells and shots at them without the smallest intermission : notwithstanding which the Chiffonne and Falcon continued the engagement, and at 3 h. 15 m. P.M. shot away a brig's foretopmast and then her mainmast. The Falcon and Clinker, not sailing by any means equal to the frigate, gradually dropped astern, and the flotilla sheltered themselves completely under Fécamp batteries; but the latter did not until 4 h. 30 m. P.M. cease firing at the Chiffonne.

Several shot struck the Chiffonne in the hull, one of which entered between wind and water; and her rigging was also much cut. Her loss amounted to two men killed and three wounded. The Falcon suffered in rigging and sails, and had four men wounded; the Clinker, one marine killed and one seaman wounded by the same shot. The French admit a loss of three men killed and 12 wounded, including among the latter the commander of one of the gun-brigs.

On the 15th of July the British gun-brigs Plumper, Lieutenant James Henry Garrety, and Teazer, Lieutenant George Lewis Ker, while cruising off the port of Granville, on the coast of France, found themselves becalmed, and likely to be carried into danger by the strength of the tide. They therefore anchored near the island of Chausey, but, owing to the exigency of the moment, at too great a distance apart to benefit by any mutual support, in the event of being attacked before a breeze sprang up. The critical situation of these brigs being plainly seen from Granville, which was not four leagues distant, Capitaine de vaisseau Louis-Léon Jacob, commanding the several divisions of the flotilla that were assembled between St. Malo and Cherbourg, resolved to send some gun-vessels to attempt the capture of the British vessels.

Accordingly, on that same evening, as soon as it grew dark, seven of the largest class of French gun-vessels, armed each with three long 24-pounders, and an 8-inch howitzer, and amply supplied with men and musketry, swept out of the port, under the command of Capitaine de frégate Joseph Collet. On the 16th, at 2 h. 30 m., they arrived within long range of the nearest brig, the Plumper, and opened a fire upon her from their heavy long guns; taking such a safe position, as they advanced, that

the brig's 18-pounder carronades could only at intervals be
brought to bear upon them. In the course of half an hour
Lieutenant Garrety, who, from the first, had conducted himself
in the bravest manner, had his arm shot away; but he continued,
for some time, to animate his men in repulsing the enemy. At
length, at the end of an hour's cannonade, from which she had
greatly suffered in hull and crew, the Plumper surrendered.

Having shifted their prisoners and manned the prize, the
French rested at an anchor, until the tide turned again in their
favour at 6 A.M.; when, accompanied by the Plumper, they
weighed, and stood for her late consort. At 8 h. 45 m. A.M. the
seven French gun-vessels and their prize commenced firing at
the Teazer; who, at 9 A.M., cut her cable, and, setting all sail,
tried to escape. But, the calm continuing, the brig made little
or no progress; and her opponents soon surrounded and captured her. The British loss on this occasion has been noticed
nowhere but in the French accounts. By these it appears that
the two brigs had, including Lieutenant Garrety, 17 men badly
wounded, the greater part on board the Plumper; but, with
respect to the killed, which probably amounted to four or five,
no intelligence was obtained. The loss on board the French gun-
vessels appears to have amounted to five men wounded, including Captain Collet; who, on the afternoon of the day on which
he had captured them, entered Granville with his two prizes.

The time approaching for concentrating near Boulogne the
invading-flotilla and the army it was to transport, Admiral Ver-
Huell, about the middle of May, became impatient to quit Dunkerque with the division of gun-vessels that lay at anchor in the
road and harbour. The majority of these he had himself, in the
latter part of April, conducted from Ostende,[1] and the remainder had since arrived, by three or four at a time, as opportunity offered. The right wing of the army, then encamped
between Ostende and Dunkerque, prepared to march; and
Marshal Davoust who commanded it, preferring a water-passage,
embarked with Admiral Ver-Huell. Unfavourable winds prevented the latter from weighing; nor did a change take place
until towards the middle of July: in the interim the marshal had
disembarked, and, with his corps, had marched for Ambleteuse.
On the 17th of the month, at 6 P.M., a light north-east wind
enabled the Dutch admiral to put to sea (if keeping close along
shore can be called so) with the four prames, Ville-d'Aix, Ville-
d'Anvers. Ville-de-Genève, and Ville-de-Mayence, and 32 first.

1 See p. 315.

class gun-vessels; the latter under the command of two captains
of the Batavian navy, the former of the French capitaine de
frégate Bernard-Isidore Lambour. The admiral, with great
judgment, formed his division into two lines, in such a manner
that all the vessels could fire together with ease: two of the
prames were placed in the centre of the outer line, where the
admiral himself commanded, and the other two at the extremities, which were the stations assigned to the two Dutch captains.
Several other gun-vessels were at Dunkerque, but they, being
of a smaller class, had retired into the harbour to escape the
fury of the north-west gales. Directions had been left by
Admiral Ver-Huell for these gun-vessels to follow, in two divisions, as soon as an engagement should be seen to take place
between his division and the enemy.

Owing to the numerous banks and shoals off Ostende and
Dunkerque, the British squadron in the vicinity, consisting of
the 20-gun ship Ariadne, Captain the Honourable Edward King,
three or four ship-sloops and bombs, and about as many gun-
brigs, was at anchor off Gravelines. Ships loom large in thick
weather. It must have been owing to this, that the French
mistook the Ariadne, a ship not above a third larger than either
of the French prames, for "un vaisseau rasé," and her companions (increased in number as well as size) for "deux frégates,
trois corvettes à trois mâts, et neuf bricks."[1] At 6 h. 30 m. P.M.
the Ariadne and squadron discovered the flotilla, then just under
way; but the lightness of the wind and the slow sailing of the
prames so retarded its progress, that its course was not clearly
ascertained until 7 h. 15 m. P.M.; when instantly, the British cut
their cables and made sail, to meet the Dutch admiral. At 9 h.
15 m. P.M. the Ariadne and one or two of her nearest companions
opened their fire upon the flotilla; and, notwithstanding the
shallowness of the water, the obscurity of the night, and the
incessant cannonade maintained, both by the prames and gun-
vessels, and by the heavy batteries on the coast, the Ariadne
and her consorts succeeded in driving three or four gun-vessels
on shore, and in cutting away the mainmast and damaging the
rigging of the Ville-de-Genève, the rearmost prame. With,
however, such powerful support from the shore, and the aid of
the long 24-pounders mounted by the prames, the bulk of the
flotilla, at 11 h. 30 m. P.M., came to anchor in the road of Calais.
The only British ship that appears to have sustained any injury
was the Ariadne herself: she had one sergeant of marines mor-

---

[1] Victoires et Conquêtes, tome xvi., p. 76.

tally, one lieutenant of marines dangerously, and two seamen slightly, wounded, and her rigging and sails a good deal cut. Some loss must undoubtedly have been incurred on the part of the flotilla, especially on board the Ville-de-Genève and stranded gun-vessels, but none has been recorded.

The noise of the firing had caused a great bustle among the shipping in the Downs; and, soon after midnight, the 50-gun ship Trusty, Captain George Argles, 28-gun frigate Vestal, Captain Stephen Thomas Digby, and three ship-sloops, weighed and stood across towards Calais. On the 18th, at 4 A.M., the Vestal, out-sailing the others, joined the Ariadne and squadron ; and in half an hour afterwards the British recommenced the action with the Dutch flotilla and the batteries in front of Calais. After a two hours' cannonade, in which the nines of the Vestal stood a very poor chance against the 36s and 24s of the forts and gun-vessels, the frigate, with a corporal of marines mortally wounded, made the signal to discontinue the action ; and, with her companions, bore away to the westward, where a spirited firing had just commenced, and whither the Trusty and sloops had already proceeded.

Will it be believed that the following passage refers to the Vestal and squadron? "Il y fut attaqué le matin, avec aussi peu d'effet que la veille, par dix-neuf bâtimens, dont deux vaisseaux de ligne, onze frégates, et six bricks.[1] So also it stands, merely substituting "cinq frégates, six grandes corvettes," for "onze frégates," in another French historical work.[2] These and other similar statements were no doubt originally framed to exalt the flotilla in the opinion of the country, or to serve some such temporary purpose. How careful, then, ought the historian to be in compiling his materials ; otherwise, he unknowingly assists in propagating a falsehood, not merely by the publicity of his work, but by the sanction of his name.

Informed of the approach of the Gallo-Batavian flotilla and of the attack made upon it, Admiral Lacrosse, on the 18th, at 4 A.M., ordered several divisions of gun-vessels to get under way from the road of Boulogne, in order, by feigning an attack upon the British vessels at their anchorage, to operate a diversion in favour of Admiral Ver-Huell. The Immortalité, still commanded by Captain Owen,[3] accompanied by the 12-pounder 32-gun frigate Hebe, Captain Macajah Malbon, 20-gun ship Arab, Captain Keith Maxwell, and the remainder of the detached squadron, immediately weighed from their station off

1 Précis des Evènemens, tome xii., p. 44.   2 Victoires et Conquêtes, tome xvi., p. 77.
3 See p. 230

the port, and stood to meet the flotilla, many of the brigs of which had worked up abreast of Vimereux. By the time the Immortalité and the leading ships had got within gun-shot, 49 brigs and 64 luggers were under way, and immediately the batteries and the horse-artillery along the shore opened a fire upon the British vessels; but these reserved their fire until they could bestow it with more effect. At 4 h. 30 m. A.M., having got within half a mile north-west of Vimereux, the Immortalité, Hebe, Arab, and a few other of the British vessels, commenced firing upon the nearest French brigs; which latter, in a few minutes, re-anchored in great confusion, close under the batteries. Without having incurred any loss, and no greater damage than a 9-pounder gun disabled on board the Arab, the British squadron shortly afterwards re-anchored also about five miles to the north-westward of Boulogne, Captain Owen having previously sent one or two gun-brigs to look out off Cape Grinez.

By way of insuring to Admiral Ver-Huell a safe passage during the remainder of his short but somewhat hazardous voyage, Marshal Davoust, who had long been waiting for him at Calais, had strengthened with men and ammunition all the batteries on the coast between Calais and Ambleteuse; one of which only, that on the promontory of Cape Grinez, mounted 55 pieces of heavy cannon, besides six immense mortars, placed on a high platform, and where, from its importance as a point of attack, the general of artillery, Lariboissière, commanded in person. This was not all. General Sorbier, commandant of artillery, had been ordered with a strong division of flying artillery and long-range howitzers, " des obusiers à longue-portée," to follow the flotilla along the coast, and afford to Admiral Ver-Huell the same protection as formerly, when Captain Hancock with the Cruiser and Rattler, gave so much annoyance to the latter in his voyage from Flushing to Dunkerque.[1]

On the 18th at 3 P.M., Admiral Ver-Huell, accompanied in his schooner by Marshal Davoust, weighed from the road of Calais, and, with his three remaining prames, and 21 out of his original 32 gun-vessels (a tolerable proof how many had been damaged or destroyed), steered straight for Cape Blanez; off which, at some distance, lay the Trusty, Vestal, Ariadne, and about a dozen sloops and other vessels, of a class the best adapted for these shallow waters. At 4 P.M. the gun and mortar batteries on Cape Blanez opened a tremendous fire upon the British; who

<hr>

¹ See p. 222.

immediately returned it, but to a great disadvantage, the Trusty having, besides losing the use of her main stay, received a large shot in her slop-room, which caused a great quantity of water to rush in, and obliged her to haul off and heave to, to try to stop the leak.   Meanwhile the flotilla proceeded without much further annoyance, until off Wissant; where, the shore offering less resistance, the cannonade recommenced on the part of the British vessels, among which, by this time, were the Immortalité and a part of the detached squadron from off Boulogne. Such was the ardour displayed by the Arab to close with the flotilla, that she found herself within musket-shot of the shore, in two fathoms water.   The brig-sloop Calypso, Captain Matthew Forster, La Fleche, Captain Thomas White, and two or three of the gun-brigs, strove to emulate the Arab, and, by their united exertions, drove on shore, before 7 P.M., six of the gun-vessels.   The bank off Cape Grinez, and the shot and shells from the right face of its powerful battery, soon compelled the Arab, Calypso, La Fleche, and gun-vessels to haul off from the shore.   The Calypso had her captain wounded; and the Arab had her maintopgallant-yard shot away, her rigging much cut, and the head of her mainmast splintered, and a part of the top and crosstrees carried away by a shell.   This ship also received several shot in the hull; one of which, or the fragment of a shell, set fire to her on the poop, but the flames were fortunately extinguished.   By some of the other shot that fell on board of her, the ship had seven men wounded, two of them dangerously. The Fleche was the closest in shore owing to her light draft of water, so much so indeed as to render it necessary for the French at Blanez to depress their guns; one shot took off the top of a man's hat, shattered a boat under the booms, and went through the water-way on the off side.   The Fleche had five men severely wounded and her running rigging much injured. The Arab and Calypso rendered themselves conspicuous objects from the shore, as appears by the following passage in one of the French accounts: "Une frégate et un brick, serrant la terre, s'engagèrent de très-près."[1]

The Immortalité, followed by the Hebe, had, since 5 P.M., lay to between the end of the Banc-à-laine and Cape Grinez; and even, when the former found herself in a quarter less four (scarcely half a fathom more water than she drew), her distance from the flotilla was too great to do execution.   The two frigates thereupon hauled off and threw all aback, to wait for

---
[1] Précis des Evènemens, tome xii., p. 45.

the prames; who were ahead of the French gun-vessels, and with
the latter warmly engaged, as just related, by the Arab, Calypso,
and gun-brigs. Soon after 6 P.M. the Immortalité and Hebe,
being within about half a mile of the shore, and a quarter of a
mile of the prames, opened a brisk fire upon the latter ; which
they and the batteries returned with equal spirit, and, as might
be expected, with decidedly more effect. Two schooners, however, were driven on shore : soon after which, or at about 7 P.M.,
the prames and the remainder of the gun-vessels ran in and
anchored under the protection of the batteries between the
towers of Endreselles and Ambleteuse. At about 7 h. 30 m. P.M.
the firing, in which the 12-pounder 36-gun frigate Renommée,
Captain Sir Thomas Livingstone, baronet, had latterly taken a
part, wholly ceased; and the British ships hauled off to repair
their damages.

The Immortalité had her foremast, maintopmast, and spanker-
boom shot through, also three of her boats: her rigging and
sails were much cut; her hull struck in several places, and the
muzzles of two carronades shot away. Her loss amounted to
four men killed and 12 wounded, several of them badly. The
Hebe had her maintopmast and mainyard wounded, her rigging
and sails much injured, and one carronade disabled : she also
received three bad shot through her hull, and had three men
wounded, one of them mortally. The Renommée escaped comparatively unhurt. Captain Owen had gained for the Immortalité a high character along this part of the French coast. " Le
Capitaine Owen, commandant la frégate l'Immortalité, fit
admirer son audace et sa persévérance sous le feu des batteries
de la rade."[1] By exaggerating tenfold the force of the British,
and by concealing the injuries done to the vessels of the flotilla,
it was declared, apparently with reason, that "l'Amiral Ver-
Huell s'acquit beaucoup de gloire dans cette journée." Of the
two French works usually quoted in these passages, one is written
by a military officer. The consequence is, that M. le Comte
Dumas has taken care not to overlook the assistance afforded to
Admiral Ver-Huell by the batteries on shore ; while his contemporary, in the " Victoires et Conquêtes," writes as if every shot
or shell directed at the British came from the flotilla. The
esprit-de-corps has been here of use in aiding the development
of truth.

Encouraged by the success of the flotilla to the eastward, and
favoured by foggy weather and a fine south-west wind, Captain

[1] Précis des Evènemens, tome xii., p. 47.

Hamelin, whom we left at Fécamp with his division of gun-vessels, resolved to attempt his passage to Boulogne. Accordingly, on the 23rd of July, at 5 h. 15 m. A.M., he put to sea with, according to the French accounts, the Audacieuse and Foudre brigs, six first-class gun-vessels, brig-rigged, 10 of the second class (two or three brigs, the remainder luggers), and eight armed pinnaces (luggers and schooners), total 26, or rather, according to the logs of the several British ships, 34 sail.

At this time the British 22-gun ship Champion, Captain Robert Howe Bromley, gun-brigs Clinker and Cracker, Lieutenants Nesbit Glen, and William Henry Douglas, and the Francis hired armed cutter, lay at anchor at the distance of little more than a league north-north-east from the jettees of the harbour. The British vessels were soon under way to attack the flotilla ; and at 7 A.M., the Champion commenced action with the two corvettes, and some of the heaviest of the gun-vessels. The latter presently run on shore under the batteries of Seuneville, and the remainder of the flotilla hugged the coast so closely, that the British vessels, in order to use their carronades with effect, were compelled to approach within range of the batteries. The consequence was, that they were soon cut up in their hulls, masts, and rigging; but in spite of all the obstacles they had to contend with, the Champion and the two brigs, particularly the Cracker, compelled the French captain, at about 10 h. 30 m. A.M., to shelter himself under the batteries of St. Valery en Caux.

What with the heavy long guns on board the flotilla, and those mounted on the shore, the British vessels were considerable sufferers. The Champion had all three masts, particularly her foremast, wounded, her rigging and sails much cut, and several large shot-holes in her hull, very low down. The Cracker received a large shot through her foremast, which left it in a tottering state, and had her shrouds and stays cut to pieces. The Clinker also received some damage and coming out of action, had three feet water in the hold. It appears, however, that the Champion was the only vessel that sustained any loss : she had two seamen killed, her boatswain (severely) and two seamen wounded. The French admit that several of their vessels were much damaged, and that they lost four men killed and 22 wounded, 11 of them dangerously. As soon as it was known that the Champion and her companions had stood away towards the Downs to refit, M. Hamelin, leaving his wounded men and the most damaged of his vessels. set sail with the remainder, and reached Boulogne without further interruption.

The French, as usual, when they came to fight this battle over again on paper, made it redound greatly to their advantage. They dignified the Champion and the two gun-brigs by calling them, "une frégate et deux corvettes;" and Captain Hamelin is represented to have considered the squadron as "la même croisière ennemie qu'il avait déjà combattue," although the latter consisted of two ships and a brig, and one of those ships double the size and force of the Champion. As in most of the other accounts, no allusion is made to the land-batteries, or to the difficulties that the British must have experienced in navigating so near to the shore. "Les cris à l'abordage! à l'abordage!" says the writer, "retentissaient dans la ligne française." This, if we are to credit the French accounts, is about the hundredth time that the same cry has been uttered; and yet the French sailors, for some reason or other, have not moved from their own decks.

If, by his perseverance in pushing on towards Ambleteuse, Admiral Ver-Huell had got his gun-vessels somewhat roughly handled by the British, he had brought down upon the latter such a storm of shot and shells from the French batteries, as compelled them to retire to repair damages, thereby leaving open a passage for the remaining divisions of the Gallo-Batavian flotilla at Dunkerque; some of which appear to have reached Ambleteuse in the course of the night succeeding the action. On the next day, the 20th, an account was taken of the different vessels of the flotilla, armed and unarmed, which then lay at the seven ports, Etaples, Boulogne, Vimereux, Ambleteuse, Calais, Dunkerque, and Ostende, whence the expedition was to depart. The number of prames and gun-vessels at Boulogne alone amounted to 578, and the number of transports to 526, together 1104 vessels; and the total of the flotilla amounted to 1339 armed and 954 unarmed vessels, making a grand total of 2293. These were destined to carry 163,645 men and 9059 horses, including among the former, 16,783 sailors.[1]

The flotilla was separated into six grand divisions. The first under the designation of the left wing, commanded by Rear-admiral Jean-François Courand, and stationed at the port of Etaples, was destined to carry the troops from the camp of Montreuil, commanded by Marshal Ney; the second and third, called the left and right wings of the centre of the flotilla, under

1 See Appendix, No. 27.

the respective commands of Rear-admiral Daniel Savary and Capitaine de vaisseau Julien Le Ray, occupied the port cf Boulogne, and were destined to carry the troops from the two camps to the right and left of the town, commanded by Marshal Soult ; the fourth, named the right wing of the flotilla, commanded by Capitaine de vaisseau François-Henri-Eugène Daugier, occupied the port of Vimereux, and was to carry the corps of Marshal Lannes, composed of sundry divisions of light infantry, among which were those of the grenadiers of the advance and of the reserve. The Gallo-Batavian flotilla, assembled at the port of Ambleteuse under the command of Vice-admiral Ver-Huell, formed the fifth grand division of the expedition, and was to carry the troops commanded by Marshal Davoust. The sixth or reserve division, lying in the port of Calais, under the command of Capitaine de frégate Charles L'Evêque, was destined to transport the division of Italian infantry, and several divisions of dragoons, mounted and dismounted.

The first four grand divisions only had a regular organization : each was separated into two portions, called " escadrilles ;" and each of the latter was to embark a division of the army, composed of four regiments of the line, and one of light infantry, with its cavalry, artillery, and baggage. It would be entering too much into detail, to explain all the regulations that contributed to perfect the system of this armament : suffice it that everything was adopted which ingenuity could devise and ability execute, without much regard to the labour or the expense.

Anxious to have ocular proof of the degree of celerity with which the army could be embarked, Napoleon, who arrived at Boulogne on the 3rd of August, ordered the operation to be executed twice in his presence. The result surpassed his belief. Although the troops had to march from camps, the extremities of which were more than two miles from the point of embarkation, one hour and a half after the beating of the *générale*, men and horses, all were on board.

This, as well it might, excited the admiration of the generals and other officers present, and all were elated at the prospect it held out; all, save the prime mover himself, and he, although he did not appear so, was filled with regret. His fleets were not in the Channel, and without them, he knew full well that his plan could not succeed. Could he, by any means, have drawn away England's ships from England's coast, he considered England's fate as depending upon his nod. " Je ne sais pas, en vérité," says the French emperor, in one of his letters, of date

June 9 in this year, to his minister of marine, " quelle espèce de précaution elle peut prendre pour la mettre à l'abri de la terrible chance qu'elle court. Une nation est bien folle, lorsqu'elle n'a point de fortifications, point d'armée de terre, de se mettre dans le cas de voir arriver dans son sein une armée de cent mille hommes d'élite et aguerris. Voilà le chef-d'œuvre de la flottille; elle coûte de l'argent, mais il ne faut être maître de la mer que six heures pour que l'Angleterre cesse d'exister."[1]

Even admitting that the Channel, Mediterranean, and North Sea fleets of England were away, were no other ships to check the course of the flotilla? Let but a breeze have blown from any point of the compass, and innumerable frigates, heavy frigates too, sloops, bombs, gun-brigs, and cutters, would soon have been on the spot. No shoals or shore-batteries would then have interposed to prevent the guns of the British from producing their full effect. The more numerous the French troops. the greater would have been the slaughter amongst them, the greater the difficulty for the sailors to manœuvre the vessels. Confusion would have ensued; and the destruction or flight of a part of the flotilla would, in the end, have compromised the safety of the remainder. Every hour's delay would have brought fresh British vessels to assist in the general overthrow. Admitting, however, that a considerable portion of the flotilla overcame all these obstacles, and approached the British shore, was there nothing further to dread? Were there really, as Napoleon fancied, " no fortifications, no army "?—The invaders would have made the discovery, to their cost, the moment they arrived within shell and shot range. As they advanced nearer they would have found the beach already occupied by the van of an army composed of soldiers, who, if they had not fought at " Lodi, at Zurich, at Héliopolis, at Hohenlinden, and at Marengo," were then fighting in England.

But, in the event of a calm, would he not succeed? was a question frequently asked, as well by those who wished, as those who dreaded, the invasion. Calms in the British Channel are very uncertain: they seldom continue more than 12 hours, and even then may prevail at one part of the coast and not at another. Admitting that a calm existed at Boulogne and the adjacent ports, some time would elapse ere, under the most favourable circumstances, the flotilla could make a start. It has done so, and the oars begin to move: by this time, a boat from every British ship that witnessed the preparation is half across

[1] Précis des Evènemens, tome xi., p. 270.

the Channel with the intelligence, and the vessel herself, if less
than a frigate, is sweeping with all her strength in the same
direction. A fleet of 1200 or 1300 vessels must be rather
awkward to manage; particularly when assembled together for
the first time, and possessed, as these variously constructed gun-
vessels necessarily were, of different powers of progression.
Against the prames sad complaints were raised; and yet, as
there were 17 of these vessels, armed each with 12 long
24-pounders, and carrying altogether about 2000 men and 840
horses, they must be waited for. All this would create confusion. Cross tides and partial currents would increase it.
Signals would be necessary: they would, it is more than probable, amidst the many repeaters required to transmit them, be
misunderstood. A part of the fleet stops, or pulls in a different
direction. Delay ensues. Presently up springs a breeze; and
which, in all likelihood, blows either up or down, and not across
the Channel. In this case the weather wing of the flotilla begins
first to spread its sails, and, without great care, presses upon the
centre; and that, in its turn, upon the lee wing. Meanwhile the
breeze has not travelled without company, as is evident from
the number of white patches that now skirt the windward
horizon, swelling and gathering at every moment. Of the operations likely to follow, a slight sketch has already been given.

But, in truth, no attempt would have been made by the flotilla
to cross over, even were the Channel clear of British fleets, and
a calm, even a two days' calm, to prevail; none whatever, unless
a powerful French fleet lay off Boulogne, ready to afford its
protection. In a note dictated by him at his return from Boulogne, on the 1st of September, the French officer thus unfolds
his plan: " Je voulais réunir," says he, " quarante ou cinquante
vaisseaux de guerre dans le port de la Martinique, par des opérations combinées de Toulon, de Cadix, de Ferrol et de Brest;
les faire revenir tout d'un coup sur Boulogne; me trouver pendant quinze jours maître de la mer; avoir cent cinquante mille
hommes et dix mille chevaux campés sur cette côte; trois ou
quatre mille bâtimens de flottille, et aussitôt le signal de l'arrivée
de mon escadre, débarquer en Angleterre, m'emparer de Londres
et de la Tamise.[1] The construction of the heavy prames, and
the arming of the flotilla generally, were intended for no other
purpose than to deceive the British into a belief, that Napoleon
did not contemplate the assistance of his fleet, and that, therefore, the object of sending M. Villeneuve to the West Indies had

[1] Précis des Evènemens, tome xii., p. 315.

really in view an attack upon some of the British colonies : hence, the use of the few troops embarked, especially when rumour had multiplied them fivefold, as Napoleon knew would be the case. His own words prove that, in arming the flotilla with cannon, he was only practising a *ruse de guerre* upon England. "Si cinquante vaisseaux de ligne," says he, in the same important document just quoted, "devaient venir protégér le passage de l'armée en Angleterre, il n'y avait besoin d'avoir à Boulogne que des bâtimens de transport ; et ce luxe de prames, de chaloupes canonnières, de bateaux plats, de péniches, etc ; tous bâtimens armés, était parfaitement inutile. Si j'eusse ainsi réuni quatre mille bâtimens de transport, nul doute que l'ennemi n'eût vu que j'attendais la présence de mon escadre pour tenter le passage ; mais, en construisant des prames et des bateaux canonniers, en armant tous ces bâtimens, c'étaient des canons opposés à des canons ; des bâtimens de guerre opposés à des bâtimens de guerre, et l'ennemi a été dupé. Il a cru que je me proposais de passer de vive force par la seule force militaire de le flottille. L'idée de mon véritable projet ne lui est point venue ; et lorsque les mouvemens de mes escadres ayant manqué, il s'est aperçu du danger qu'il avait couru, l'effroi a été dans les conseils de Londres, et tous les gens sensés ont avoué que jamais l'Angleterre n'avait été si près de sa perte."[1]

The French emperor had, therefore, some reason to be sorrowful, when he beheld so disciplined, so zealous, and so numerous an army, without the means of safe transport to the goal of his wishes. In his letter to M. Decrès of June 9 (see p. 327), Napoleon appeared sanguine that he should succeed with 100,000 men ; in his note upon the flotilla, written in September and already twice quoted, he states 150,000 as the number which he had assembled for the purpose ; and, according to his confessions of much later days, he did not intend to carry over fewer than 200,000 men.[2] It is remarkable, too, that an increase in the time, during which the channel was required to be clear of British ships, accompanies each increase of the army that was to conquer the country. Thus : the letter says, "six days," the note, "fifteen days," and O'Meara,[3] "two months." It is doubtful, however, if, at the time that the expedition (all except the fleet which was to cover it) was declared to be ready, there were as many even as 140,000 fighting men in a situation to embark.

[1] Précis des Evènemens, tome xii., p. 316.

[2] O'Meara's Napoleon in Exile, vol. i. p. 349.

[3] Ibid., vol. ii., p. 378.

Being in the constant habit of perusing, by the aid of inter-
preters, the contents of the London newspapers, Napoleon
must have seen, with a feeling of bitter disappointment, the
formidable preparations that were making to resist his army
on its landing: those to obstruct the passage of the flotilla,
he cared less about, having, as already has appeared, no intention to make the attempt unless his fleets were in the temporary possession of the Channel. Buonaparte was not the
first foreigner who had reckoned too much upon the grumbling
character of the English: he did not consider that, although
discontented with their government, they were extremely jealous
of foreigners. He ought to have known that, in such a case, a
third party would experience much the same treatment as pro-
verbially follows a similar interference in domestic disagree-
ments: the hitherto mutually opposed parties unite, heart and
hand, to expel the intruder. The treatment which, at a subsequent period of his life, Napoleon experienced from the English
populace, tended, owing to a misconception on his part, to
strengthen the opinion he had originally formed of the
"canaille" to aid him in conquering their country. There,
again, he mistook the character of the people. It was not
love for his person which collected the crowds that flocked
from far and near to gain a sight of him: it was curiosity,
endemial curiosity, to behold a man who had compelled most
monarchs but their own to succumb to him; who had governed,
if not conquered, all Europe, save the little insulated spot
in whose power he then was. If they forebore to upbraid or
taunt him, it was because he was their prisoner; if they treated
him with respect, and even with kindness, it was because they
felt some degree of awe in the presence of one who had been so
mighty a potentate, and commiserated his fallen greatness.

Intelligence of the battle between Sir Robert Calder and M.
Villeneuve reached the French emperor at Boulogne, between
the 3rd and 9th of August, probably about the 8th; and on the
11th he became acquainted with the arrival of the combined
fleet at Ferrol. Buonaparte's rage was most violent, but it was
of short duration. This extraordinary man soon carved out work
for his army. The intelligent author of a French work now well
known in England has exhibited, in a single act of Napoleon's,
arising out of the circumstances above stated, a most extraordinary instance of his transcendent genius. "At the time I
was writing this passage" (one in which M. Dupin has given it
as his opinion that, before anything could be effected against

England, the combined fleet must be in possession of the Channel), "I was unacquainted with a very remarkable fact, which deserves a place in history. I am indebted for the knowledge of it to the Count Daru, whose able *History of Venice* we have already cited. In 1805 M. Daru was at Boulogne, the intendant general of the army. One morning the emperor sent for him into his closet. Daru found him transported with rage, striding up and down his apartment, and only breaking a sullen silence by the abrupt and sudden exclamations—"What a navy!—what an admiral!—what sacrifices lost!—my hopes are frustrated!— this Villeneuve! Instead of being in the Channel he has put into Ferrol!—I see it clearly! he will be blockaded.—Daru, sit down there, listen and write. The emperor had, early that morning, received advices of the arrival of Villeneuve in a port of Spain; he saw at once that the conquest of England had miscarried; that the immense expense of the fleet and the flotilla was lost for a long time, perhaps for ever! Then, in the violence of a rage which would scarcely suffer another man to retain his senses, he adopted one of the boldest resolutions, traced one of the most admirable plans of a campaign, that any conqueror could have conceived, even when at leisure and perfectly composed. Without hesitating, without stopping, he dictated the whole plan of the campaign of Austerlitz, the departure of the different corps of the army, as well from Hanover and Holland, as from the western and southern boundaries of France. The order of the routes, their duration, the points of convergence and reunion of the columns; the attacks by surprise and by open force, the various movements of the enemy, the whole is provided for: victory is assured in every one of the hypotheses. Such was the accuracy of this plan, and the immense foresight it displayed, that upon a line of march of 200 leagues, lines of operations of 300 leagues in length were conducted according to the original design, day by day, and league by league, all the way to Munich. Beyond that capital the time alone underwent some alteration; but the points were reached, and the *ensemble* of the plan crowned with success. Such, then, was the military talent of this man, not less terrible to his enemies by the mightiness of his genius, than to his countrymen by the severity of his despotism."[1] The truth of this anecdote is corroborated by the author of the Précis des Evènemens, who states, that he himself also heard it related by the Comte Daru.[2]

[1] For the original passage, see Appendix, No. 28.

[2] Précis des Evènemens, tome xii., p. 118.

On the 31st of August Buonaparte became apprised of the departure of the combined fleet from Ferrol and Corunna, as he hoped, for Brest. This re-animated, in some degree, the hopes of the emperor; and on the 22nd Marshal Berthier, the minister of marine, by Napoleon's directions, writes thus to General Marmont, the commander-in-chief of the army of Holland : " Je vous préviens, général, que l'escadre de l'empereur est partie du Ferrol le 26 thermidor (14 août) avec l'escadre espagnole. Si ces escadres combinées arrivent dans la Manche, l'empereur fait de suite l'expédition d'Angleterre ; mais si, par des circonstances de vents contraires, ou enfin, par le peu d'audace de nos amiraux,[1] elles ne peuvent se rendre dans la Manche, l'empereur et roi ajournera l'expédition à une autre année, parcequ'elle n'est plus possible." The marshal then directs the general to be ready, at a moment's notice, to disembark his troops, estimated at 20,000, and proceed with them to Mayence, &c.[2] In about four days after the date of this letter the fatal news arrives that M. Villeneuve, having quitted Ferrol with 29 sail of the line, had steered for Cadiz instead of the Channel, where the emperor and his army had been so long anxiously expecting him.

Thus had the crisis arrived for adjourning the expedition against England to another year. By the end of August, the troops that had been encamped at Ostende, Ambleteuse, Boulogne, and Montreuil, were making forced marches to the banks of the Rhine. On the 4th of September the emperor quitted Boulogne for Paris, having left orders with Rear-admiral Lacrosse to send out occasionally a division of gun-boats to manœuvre, and to maintain the utmost discipline and good order among the officers and men. The greater part, if not the whole, of the gun-vessels at all the depôts but Boulogne, were, in a short time, dismantled and laid up. It was the intention of Napoleon to keep a body of troops encamped upon the heights of Boulogne, partly, in conjunction with the gun-vessels in the basin and road, to deceive the British, but chiefly, as it was a remarkably healthy spot, to have an army of 30,000 or 40,000 men ready to act on any emergency. The operations against the remnant of the flotilla were now confined to Boulogne; and,

---

[1] This reflection upon the admirals is only to be found in the quotation from the letter contained in the text of M. Dumas (tome xii., p. 122): it is wholly omitted in what purports to be the entire copy inserted among the " Pièces Justificatifs." We may conclude from this, that the author made his extract from the original, without reflecting upon the meaning or tendency of the passage alluded to, but that, when he, or another for him, came to transcribe the letters for the Appendix, the discovery was made, and the offensive words omitted.

[2] Précis des Evènemens, tome xii., p. 334.

although in September and November two attempts were made to destroy the line of gun-vessels at anchor in the road, the stormy state of the weather, in the last case in particular, rendered them both abortive.

British and Franco-Spanish Fleets.

The declaration of war by Spain, followed up so quickly as it was by the hurried equipment of ships at all her principal depôts in fulfilment of the secret treaty which she had concluded with France,[1] soon assembled a British naval force upon the coasts of the former. Off Ferrol, in which port lay, ready for sea, five French and seven Spanish sail of the line, exclusively of three of the latter fitting, cruised a British squadron of seven sail of the line, under Rear-admiral the Honourable Alexander Cochrane, in the Northumberland 74. In Cadiz one French and seven Spanish sail of the line were ready for sea, and four of the latter equipping; and in Carthagena, six Spanish sail of the line were ready for sea. Off Cadiz was stationed a British squadron of five, and occasionally six sail of the line, under Vice-admiral Sir John Orde, in the Glory 98; and who, in conjunction with Vice-admiral Lord Nelson, whom, with 10 sail of the line, we left on the 31st of December cruising off Cape San-Sebastian,[2] kept an occasional eye upon the ships in Carthagena.

The junction of the six French and 20 Spanish sail of the line, ready for sea in Ferrol, Cadiz, and Carthagena, with the 11 French sail of the line, also ready for sea in Toulon, was a preliminary step towards the final success of the grand design which reigned the master-thought in the mind of him, who, such was the mean subserviency of Spain, had the whole 37 ships as much under his command, as if the French flag waved at the peak of every one of them. What efforts were made by the one party to accomplish, and by the other to defeat, the important object in agitation, will appear as we proceed in the details upon which we are now about to enter.

Having detached the 38-gun frigates Active and Seahorse, Captains Richard Hussey Moubray and the Honourable Courtenay Boyle, to watch the port of Toulon, Lord Nelson, on the 3rd of January, made sail from his station off Cape San-Sebastian towards the Magdalena islands, and on the 11th came to at his old anchorage in Agincourt sound. On the 15th the Superb rejoined from Algiers; whither she had been sent to arrange some difference with the Dey.   The force of Lord Nelson now consisted of 11 sail of the line, with scarcely a frigate or sloop to detach for intelligence.

On the 17th of January, early in the afternoon, the French fleet, consisting of the following 11 sail of the line, seven frigates, and two brigs, commanded by Vice-admiral Villeneuve, and having on board a body of 3500 troops under General Lauriston, put to sea from the road of Toulon, with a strong wind from the north-north-west :—

Gun-ship.

80	{ Bucentaure · ·	{ Vice-admiral P.-C.-J.-Bapt.-Silv. Villeneuve. { Captain Jean-Jacques Magendie.
	{ Formidable · ·	{ Rear-admiral P.-R.-M.-E. Dumanoir-le-Pelley. { Captain Jean-Marie Letellier.
	Neptune · · · ·	. Commodore Esprit-Tranquille Maistral.
	Indomptable · ·	. Captain Jean-Joseph Hubert.
74	{ Annibal · · · ·	. Commodore Julien-Marie Cosmao-Kerjulien.
	Mont-Blanc · · ·	. Captain Guillaume-J.-Noël La Villegris.
	Swiftsure · · · ·	,, C.-E. L'Hospitalier-Villemadrin.
	Atlas · · · · ·	,, Pierre-Nicolas Rolland.
	Intrépide · · · ·	,, Léonore Deperonne.
	Scipion · · · ·	,, Charles Berrenger.
	Berwick · · · ·	,, Jean-Gilles Filhol-Camas.

Frigates, Cornélie, Hortense, Incorruptible, Rhin, Sirène, Thémis, and Uranie.

Brigs, Furet and Naïade.

By 5 P.M. the last French ship was outside Cape Sepet; and at 6 h. 30 m. the advanced or reconnoitring division, consisting of two sail of the line and a frigate, was descried by the British frigates Active and Seahorse.   On the 18th, at 9 h. 15 m., the French advanced ships, still in sight, hauled their wind to the northward, and the two British frigates did the same.   At 4 P.M. the island of Polacross bore from the latter north by west five leagues, and the wind now blew a strong gale from west-north-west.   At 9 h. 45 m. the Seahorse, who was to windward of her consort, saw nine sail of the French fleet in the north quarter, only three miles distant, and apparently steering south. The frigate showed a light, and immediately bore up; on which the enemy's advanced ship threw up two rockets.   The Active and Seahorse kept sight of the latter ship until 2 A.M. on the 19th; and, by carrying a press of sail, were, at 1 h. 50 m. P.M., sufficiently near to their friends in Agincourt sound to make the distant signal of the enemy's being at sea.

At 4 h. 30 m. P.M. Lord Nelson weighed with the following 11 sail of the line and two frigates :—

Gun-ship.		
100	Victory . . .	Vice-admiral (w.) Lord Nelson, K.B. Rear-admiral (b.) George Murray. Captain Thomas Masterman Hardy.
	Royal Sovereign .	Rear-admiral (r.) Sir R. H. Bickerton, Bart. Captain John Stuart.
80	Canopus . . . . . ,,	John Conn.
74	Superb . . . . . ,,	Richard Goodwin Keats.
	Spencer . . . . ,,	Hon. Robert Stopford.
	Swiftsure . . . . ,,	Mark Robinson.
	Belleisle . . . . ,,	William Hargood.
	Conqueror . . . ,,	Israel Pellew.
	Tigre . . . . , ,,	Benjamin Hallowell.
	Leviathan . . . ,,	Henry William Bayntun.
	Donegal . . . . ,,	Pulteney Malcolm.

Frigates, Active and Seahorse.[1]

The fleet made sail for the passage between the island of Biche and Sardinia; a passage so narrow that the ships had to proceed in line ahead, each, except the Victory who undertook to lead the fleet, being guided by the stern-lights of her second ahead. At 6 p.m. the Victory was clear, and at 7 p.m. every ship in her train. Lord Nelson then despatched the Seahorse round the southern extremity of Sardinia, to look into St. Pietro for the French fleet, and to return immediately. At 8 h. 30 m. p.m. the fleet, with now only one frigate attending it, bore away along the island of Sardinia. On the following day, the 20th, the vice-admiral appointed the Spencer and Leviathan, as the two fastest-sailing ships, to be a detached squadron; directing Captain Stopford to keep on the Victory's weather-beam, to be ready to act as occasion might require. During the latter part of this, and the whole of the succeeding day, the fleet encountered very hard gales from south-south-west to south-west; and, for a great part of the time, the ships were under their storm-staysails.

On the 22nd, at 10 a.m., the Seahorse rejoined, having, on the preceding afternoon, been chased by the French 40-gun frigate Cornélie, standing in for Pulla. The gale was so heavy and the weather so thick, that the Seahorse could not see the anchorage either in that bay or in Cagliari, and, from the same cause, lost sight of the French frigate in the night. The Seahorse, accompanied by the Active, was sent back to Cagliari, but no French ships were lying there; and a message to the viceroy and consul at that port, carried by the Active, and for a reply to which Lord Nelson waited off the island of Serpentina,

1 Lord Nelson was continually complaining to the admiralty of the small number of frigates attached to his command.

produced no better intelligence. The Seahorse was then sent with despatches to Naples, and the Active directed to cruise for three days to the eastward, about five or six leagues from Serpentina, to speak any British ship that might be in search of the British admiral.

On the 25th, at noon, Cape Carbonara, island of Sardinia, bore from the Victory north-north-east half-east distant three and a half leagues; and on the next day, the 26th, the 18-pounder 36-gun frigate Phœbe, Captain the Honourable Thomas Bladen Capel, joined company. On the 19th, at 4 P.M., when sailing down the west coast of Corsica with a strong west-north-west wind, the Phœbe discovered a disabled line-of-battle ship, the Indomptable, one of M. Villeneuve's fleet, standing in for the land, under courses only, having carried away her topmasts. The frigate immediately hauled up towards, and at 4 h. 45 m. passed within hail of, the Indomptable, who had previously hoisted French colours. Having ascertained that the dismasted ship was an enemy's two-decker, bound apparently for Ajaccio bay, the Phœbe did not, as it appears, make any attempt to molest her, but bore up for the Magdalen islands, where Captain Capel expected to find Lord Nelson. It was owing to this circuitous route that the frigate was so many days in joining the fleet.

Having sent in all directions to gain information, but without effect, Lord Nelson continued his course to the eastward, and at 3 A.M. on the 29th, rounded the island of Stromboli. As a proof that, in his anxiety to overtake the enemy, Lord Nelson had passed a sleepless night, the following memorandum appears in his diary: "Stromboli burnt very strongly throughout the night of the 28th." His own persuasion was that the French fleet had gone to Egypt; and thither his lordship hastened, still detaching his frigates, as fast as they joined, to gather what tidings they could.

On the 4th of February, the Canopus made the land of Egypt. On the 7th, the Tigre was sent into Alexandria; but the Turks had nothing to communicate, and on the following day, the 8th, Captain Hallowell rejoined the fleet. Lord Nelson, now half-distracted, steered for Malta; on the 14th, was within 100 leagues of it; and in a few days afterwards received from Naples intelligence of what had really become of the French fleet. It had, on the second day, after quitting Toulon, when crossing the gulf of Lyons, encountered a violent gale of wind, which damaged several of the ships in their masts and rigging, and drove them, on the 20th, with the exception of four, back to their port. The missing ships were the Indomptable and Cornélie already mentioned, and the frigates Hortense and Incorruptible. The Cornélie, after sheltering herself at Genoa, reached Toulon on the 22nd, as did the Indomptable in two days afterwards; but the Hortense and Incorruptible remained out for six or seven weeks.

It was on the 14th of February, when about 100 leagues to the eastward of Malta, on his return to Sardinia, that Lord Nelson wrote his celebrated letter to the first lord of the admiralty (Lord Melville), explaining why he had considered Egypt to be the destination of the French fleet. "Feeling as I do," he says, "that I am entirely responsible to my king and country for the whole of my conduct, I find no difficulty at this moment, when I am so unhappy at not finding the French fleet, nor having obtained the smallest information where they are, to lay before you the whole of the reasons which induced me to pursue the line of conduct I have done. I have consulted no man, therefore the whole blame of ignorance in forming my judgment must rest with me. I would allow no man to take from me an atom of my glory had I fallen in with the French fleet, nor do I desire any man to partake of any of the responsibility. All is mine, right or wrong: therefore I shall now state my reasons, after seeing that Sardinia, Naples, and Sicily were safe, for believing that Egypt was the destination of the French fleet; and at this moment of sorrow I still feel that I have acted right. Firstly, the wind had blown from north-east to south-east for 14 days before they sailed; therefore they might, without difficulty, have gone to the westward. Secondly, they came out with gentle breezes at north-west and north-north-west. Had they been bound to Naples, the most natural thing for them to have done would have been to run along their own shore to the eastward, where they would have ports every 20 leagues of coast to take shelter in. Thirdly, they bore away in the evening of the 18th, with a strong gale at north-west or north-north-west steering south or south by west. It blew so hard that the Seahorse went more than 13 knots an hour to get out of their way. Desirable as Sardinia is for them, they could get it without risking their fleet, although certainly not so quickly as by attacking Cagliari. However I left nothing to chance in that respect, and therefore went off Cagliari. Having afterwards gone to Sicily, both to Palermo and Messina, and thereby given encouragement for a defence, and knowing all was safe at Naples, I had only the Morea and

Egypt to look to. For, although I knew one of the French ships was crippled, yet I considered the character of Buonaparte; and that the orders given by him on the banks of the Seine would not take into consideration wind or weather. Nor, indeed, could the accident of even three or four ships alter, in my opinion, a destination of importance: therefore such an accident did not weigh in my mind, and I went first to Morea, and then to Egypt. The result of my inquiries at Coron and Alexandria confirms me in my former opinion; and therefore, my lord, if my obstinacy or ignorance is so gross, I should be the first to recommend your superseding me. But, on the contrary, if, as I flatter myself, it should be found that my ideas of the probable destination of the French fleet were well founded, in the opinion of his majesty's ministers, then I shall hope for the consolation of having my conduct approved by his majesty; who will, I am sure, weigh my whole proceedings in the scale of justice."[1]

On the 27th, in the evening, the British fleet, every ship of which, since the 21st of January, had remained prepared for battle, without a bulkhead up night or day, anchored in Pulla road, bay of Cagliaria, to water. On the 2nd of March Lord Nelson weighed, but, owing to the severity of the weather, was compelled to re-anchor. The wind shifting in the course of the night to north-north-east, the fleet reweighed at daylight on the 3rd, and stood to the westward; but before noon the wind returned to the north-west, and blew so strong, that the fleet had again to bear up for Pulla. The morning of the 4th brought a return of the north-east wind; but scarcely had the persevering admiral taken advantage of it, than it again shifted to the northwest. Blowing moderately this time, the fleet (some of the ships having anchored for a few hours in the bay of Rouze) succeeded in working to the westward of the gulf of Palma; but, the wind increasing to a heavy gale, the British were compelled, on the evening of the 8th, to run in there for shelter. On the 10th, in the morning, after one or two fruitless attempts to get out, the fleet weighed with a fine south-east wind, and passed between the island of Vache and the main; or, rather, the Victory and a few ships only went through this narrow channel, the remainder of the fleet passing on the outer side of Vache.

A continuance of fine weather brought into view, on the morning of the 12th, the high land over Toulon; and on the 15th, in the evening, Lord Nelson gained his old winter station, a few miles to the eastward of Cape San-Sebastian. After detaching

[1] Clarke and M'Arthur, vol. ii., p. 397.

the Leviathan off Barcelona, to induce a belief that he was
fixed on the coast of Spain, his lordship worked back to the
eastward, and on the evening of the 25th, arrived close off the
west end of the island of St. Pietro. On the following day, the
26th, the wind shifted from south-east to south-west, and
enabled the fleet, on the 27th, to anchor in the gulf of Palma,
where the victuallers and storeships were lying. On the preceding day, Rear-admiral Thomas Louis had joined in the 32-gun
frigate Ambuscade, Captain William Durban, and now shifted
his flag to the Canopus; taking on board of her, in the room of
Captain Conn, Captain William Francis Austen, who had accompanied the admiral from England. While Lord Nelson is pro-
visioning and refitting his ships, let us turn our attention to the
harbour of Toulon.

Vice-admiral Villeneuve used the utmost despatch in refitting
his ships. The Annibal (late British Hannibal), being found
unserviceable, was replaced by the new ship Pluton; to whom
at the same time the former transferred the whole of her officers
and men. A similar exchange took place between the frigates
Uraine and Hermione. As to the Incorruptible, she had suffered so much from her action with the Arrow, of which we shall
hereafter give an account, as to be for the present laid up. The
French fleet, therefore, consisted of 11 sail of the line, six frigates,
and two brigs,[1] and still retained on board the 3500 troops under
General Lauriston. The departure of Lord Nelson for the gulf
of Palma, enabled M. Villeneuve, on the evening of the 29th of
March, to sail from Toulon road with the whole of his fleet;
which, on clearing Cape Sepet, steered south-south-west, with a
moderate breeze from the north-east.

The wind on the following morning veered to north-north-
west, and, instead of increasing as had been expected, fell considerably. Owing to this the French fleet, during that and the
succeeding day, made very little progress, and on the afternoon
of the 31st, Cape Sicie bearing north distant 10 or 12 leagues,
was discovered, and recognised by the British frigates Active
and Phœbe. These ships kept in sight of it until evening; when
the Phœbe bore up for the gulf of Palma, with a fresh breeze at
west-north-west, and the Active, in order to keep company with
the French ships, stood upon a wind to the south-west, but,
after dark, saw no more of them. On the 1st of April, in the
morning, a Ragusian vessel informed M. Villeneuve that, five
days before, she had seen the British fleet to the southward of

[1] Their names will be seen at p. 334, omitting the Incorruptible, and substi-tuting the Pluton for the Annibal, and the Hermione for the Uranle.

Sardinia. In consequence of this intelligence, which was correct, the French admiral, who, from previous information that Lord Nelson was off Barcelona (a proof that the ruse with the Leviathan had begun to take effect), had intended to pass to the eastward of the Balaric islands, was induced to alter his course and pass to the westward of them. The fleet accordingly kept close to the coast of Spain, and on the 6th, in a calm, arrived off the port of Carthagena; where we will leave M. Villeneuve awhile, to show what effect his activity had produced upon the movements of him to avoid whom was so principal a point in the instructions given to the French admiral.

Wanting water for his ships, Lord Nelson had, on the 1st of April, removed from Palma to Pulla bay; whence he had again sailed on the morning of the 3rd, steering to the westward, with a moderate breeze at north-east. On the following morning, the 4th, when a few leagues to the westward of the island of Toro, the wind shifted to the north-north-west; and at 8 A.M., in the midst of hazy, unsettled weather and drizzling rain, the Phœbe made her appearance in the offing, with the exhilarating signal that the French admiral was at sea. Cruisers were instantly despatched in all directions; and, on the supposition that the French fleet had continued its course to the southward (as would have been the case, had the Ragusian vessel not crossed it), the British fleet lay to all night, and, on the morning of the 5th, was about midway between the coasts of Barbary and Sardinia.

After waiting in this narrow channel until the 7th, the fleet bore up for Palermo, in order to cover Sicily and the more eastern parts of the Mediterranean, should the French have passed to the northward of Corsica. Two more days having elapsed without the slightest intelligence, Lord Nelson, on the 9th, being then off the western end of Sicily, stood to the westward. Of this change of course to the westward, Napoleon was for a long time unapprised. Even so late as a fortnight afterwards he sent a courier to M. Villeneuve, with information that Lord Nelson was gone to Egypt; and, lest the latter should learn that the French fleet had passed the Straits, he ordered the insertion of a paragraph in the Dutch journals, to the effect, that a French fleet had landed 6000 men in Egypt; that the admiral had made a feint of passing the Straits, but, in the night, had returned unseen along the African coast, and thereby deceived Lord Nelson.[1]

---

[1] Précis des Evènemens, tome xi., p. 231.

The line-of-battle ships making but slow progress against the westerly and north-west winds, Lord Nelson despatched some light vessels in advance to Gibraltar and Lisbon. On the 16th, while the fleet was beating hard against a strong westerly wind, to get round the southern extremity of Sardinia, and obtain a glimpse of Toulon, a neutral vessel informed the Leviathan that the French fleet had been seen on the 7th off Cape de Gata. This was quickly followed by intelligence that M. Villeneuve had passed the Straits on the 8th. The prevalence of strong southerly and westerly winds made it the 30th ere Lord Nelson got sight of the rock of Gibraltar; and about this time he heard that M. Villeneuve had been reinforced by some ships from Cadiz. There being no possibility of passing the Straits with the prevailing wind, and the fleet standing in great need of water and provisions, Lord Nelson, on the 4th of May, anchored in Mazari bay, on the Barbary shore, to water, and sent the Superb to Tetuan for cattle, fruit, and vegetables.

We will now see what is become of the object of Lord Nelson's pursuit; of that which, as will clearly appear by the following letter from his lordship to Captain Ball, at Malta, dated April 19, when the fleet was buffeting with head winds, was the principal source of his uneasy frame of mind. "My good fortune, my dear Ball, seems flown away. I cannot get a fair wind, or even a side wind—dead foul! dead foul!—but my mind is fully made up what to do when I leave the Straits, supposing there is no certain information of the enemy's destination. I believe this ill-luck will go near to kill me; but, as these are times for exertion, I must not be cast down, whatever I may feel." In another letter, of the same date, to Lord Melville, this extraordinary man writes: "I am not made to despair; what man can do shall be done. I have marked out for myself a decided line of conduct, and I shall follow it well up, although I have now before me a letter from the physician of the fleet, enforcing my return to England before the hot months. Therefore, notwithstanding I shall pursue the enemy to the East or West Indies, if I know that to have been their destination, yet, if the Mediterranean fleet joins the Channel, I shall request, with that order, permission to go on shore." [1]

Returning to M. Villeneuve, while off Carthagena, he sent a boat on shore, to offer his services and the protection of his fleet to the six Spanish ships ready for sea in the port; but Rear-admiral Salzeco, having been ordered with his squadron on a

[1] Clarke and M'Arthur, vol. ii., p. 404,

different service, declined the junction. So says M. Villeneuve; but the Spanish ambassador at Paris asserted, that the refusal to join came from the French admiral. Napoleon denies this roundly; adding, in his usual energetic way: "Mais que l'amiral Villeneuve, passant par le détroit et ayant des craintes, eût refusé le secours de six vaisseaux, un ambassadeur, un homme sensé ne se laisse pas dire de pareilles nigauderies." [1]

On the evening of the 7th a fresh breeze sprang up from the eastward (and yet at this very time Lord Nelson was plagued with gales from the westward), and the French admiral continued his course towards the Straits. On the 8th, at daylight, Gibraltar appeared in sight; and at noon the French fleet, formed in two columns, with the frigates ahead, entered the gut, causing alarm-guns to be fired from all points of the rock. At 4 P.M. the French stood into the bay of Cadiz, driving away Vice-admiral Sir John Orde and his five sail of the line. Finding the wind to blow strong off shore, M. Villeneuve anchored his ships, having previously despatched the Hortense. frigate into the harbour, to apprise the Spaniards of his arrival and quicken their movements. In consequence of this, the French 74-gun ship Aigle, Captain Pierre-Paul Gourrège, ship-corvette Torche, and brig-corvette Argus, accompanied by five out of the following six Spanish sail of the line and one frigate, having 1600 troops on board, sailed out of the harbour and anchored in company with the Toulon fleet:—

Gun-ship.

80	{	Argonauta	. .	{	Admiral don Frederico Gravina.
					Rear-admiral don Antonio Escano.
		San-Rafaël	. .		. Commodore don Francisco Montez.
78	{	Firme	. . .	. Captain don Rafaël Villavicencio.
		Terrible	. . . .	,, don Francisco Mondragon.
64	{	America	. . . .	,, don —— Darrac.
		Espana	. . . .	,, don —— Monios.

On the 9th, at 2 A.M., the combined French and Spanish fleet, consisting of 17 sail of the line (12 French and five Spanish), one Spanish, and six French frigates, one ship-corvette, and three brig-corvettes, got under way, and steered a westerly course; leaving the San-Rafaël, which had run on shore in coming out, to follow to the rendezvous at Martinique, as soon as she could be got off.

The discreditable practice, adopted by the French emperor's

[1] Précis des Evènemens, tome xi., p. 236.

orders, of altering official despatches for the purposes of deception, is nowhere more apparent than in the published correspondence connected with this expedition. M. Villeneuve is made to say that he was joined by eight Spanish sail of the line from Cadiz, thus: "Peu d'instans après, un officier espagnol vint à mon bord, et m'annonça que huit vaisseaux de S. M. C. et une frégate, sous les ordres de S. E. l'amiral Gravina, allaient mettre sous voiles; et avant minuit je les vis sortir successivement du port, et mouiller en dehors." [1] On the other hand, the Madrid Gazette, of April 13, gives the correct number of ships, both French and Spanish, that joined M. Villeneuve; and so does Napoleon himself, when writing confidentially to his minister of marine: "Il paraît que cinq vaisseaux et une frégate ont rallié l'amiral Villeneuve; qu'un sixième avait touché, mais allait partir." [2] And yet no French writer, such is the permanent injury of distorting historical facts, has been able to give a consistent account of this transaction.

Scarcely had daylight on the 9th made its appearance, than the French admiral was constrained to shorten sail for his Spanish friends; and to the additional regret of M. Villeneuve, the wind, before the close of the day, shifted to the westward. An alternation of contrary winds and calms, coupled with the indifferent sailing of one of the French (the Atlas) and two or three of the Spanish ships, made it the 12th of May before the fleet arrived in sight of the island of Martinique. In the course of the following day, the 13th, the five Spanish, and 11 of the 12 French sail of the line, accompanied by the seven frigates (one of them Spanish), one ship-corvette, and three brig-corvettes, also by a large storeship, and the late British ship-sloop Cyane, a prize, anchored in the harbour of Fort Royal, or, as named at the commencement of the republican dynasty, Fort-de-France, but not without having sustained, in passing, a smart cannonade from the Diamond rock.[3]

In the course of the same night, it is believed, the twelfth French line-of-battle ship (probably, from her acknowledged badness of sailing, the Atlas) anchored with her companions; and on the 16th, early in the morning, the Spanish 80-gun ship San-Rafaël, which had sailed from Cadiz on the 10th of April, rounded Pointe-Saline. At 8 A.M. she hoisted a Spanish ensign and pendant; whereupon, by way of decoy, French colours were displayed at the flag-staff of the Diamond. At 9 A.M. the

[1] Mon. July 14, 1805.   [2] Précis des Evènemens, tome xi., p. 228   [3] See p. 245.

Spanish ship, having unsuspiciously approached close under the lee of the rock, on which English colours had just been substituted for French, received a fire as unexpected as it proved annoying. The San-Rafaël quickly put her helm up, and, returning one ineffectual shot as she wore, hastened out of range, as fast as the little wind would permit her ; anchoring, the same afternoon, in company with M. Villeneuve's fleet.

A very different story from all this is told in the publication which the Moniteur was compelled to insert in the shape of a letter from M. Villeneuve, and a translation of which, as of a document of undoubted authenticity, went the rounds of the English newspapers. "Le 19 floréal," says this arrant piece of forgery, "me trouvant à la hauteur prescrite par mes instructions, j'ai, conformement à leur contenu, remis à l'amiral Gravina ses dépêches, et, sur le signal qui en a été fait, six vaisseaux de S. M. C., deux frégates et deux bricks de S. M. I., se sont rangés sous son pavillon; nous avons été en vue le reste de la soirée, mais le lendemain je n'en ai plus de connaissance, et j'ai lieu de le croire rendre à sa destination. Le 24, au point du jour, j'ai donné dans le canal de Sainte-Lucie, et dans la journée le mouillai à la Martinique, avec l'escadre que m'a confiée S.M. et deux vaisseaux et une frégate espagnols." The number of French and Spanish ships that entered Martinique, as counted both from the Diamond rock, and the Triton West-Indiaman which lay in Basse-Terre road, Sainte-Lucie, agrees exactly with the statement as we have given it. But, it being P.M. when the ships passed, the two accounts are dated, according to log-time, on the 14th instead of on the 13th of May. That the last is the correct date appears, not only from the above letter (there being no interest to deceive in that particular), but from an entry in the rôle d'équipage of the French ship Formidable, to which we have had reference.

Even French historians were led into error by the Moniteur's forgeries : " L'Amiral Gravina," says M. Dumas, "ne se sépara point de lui (Villeneuve) pour remplir une mission particulière, et c'est encore un fait que nous devions rétablir; il mouilla à la Martinique avec le reste de la flotte combinée et ne la quitta point : ceci doit servir d'erratum au premier paragraphe de la page 131, où, trompés par divers rapports officiels, nous avions dit que l'amiral Gravina, après s'être détaché de la flotte combinée pour porter des secours à Porto Rico et à la Havane, était venu la rejoindre à sa station aux îles du Vent."[1] The object

---

[1] Précis des Evènemens, tome xii., p. 417.

of all this fraud was evidently to induce the British government to weaken still more the force in the Channel, by detaching a greater number of ships to the West Indies: and that object, we believe, was partly accomplished.

Lord Nelson, whom on the 4th of May we left refitting his fleet in Mazari bay,[1] was enabled, early on the 5th, by the emulation and activity of those he commanded, and by a sudden change of wind to the eastward, to weigh and make sail to the westward. Such, indeed, was Lord Nelson's haste to get away, that the Superb was recalled from Tetuan, just as the cattle and other refreshments for the fleet were being brought down to the beach ; and which, in consequence, the ship was obliged to leave behind. On the 7th, at 2 P.M., a failure of the breeze obliged the Victory and some of the other ships to anchor in Rozia bay, Gibraltar. In the course of the afternoon Rear-admiral Sir Richard Bickerton, who was to be left as the commanding officer in the Mediterranean, shifted his flag from the Royal Sovereign to the Amfitrite (late Spanish) frigate ; and, a fine easterly wind now again springing up, Lord Nelson, at 6 P.M., weighed and stood through the Straits.

It had been his lordship's intention, on the supposition that the French were bound to Ireland, to have proceeded to a spot about 50 leagues to the westward of Scilly ; but some intelligence, of an undoubted character, pointing to the West Indies as the real destination of the combined fleet, Lord Nelson resolved, at every risk of professional censure, to follow it thither. That information was derived from Rear-admiral Donald Campbell (by birth a Scotchman), of the Portuguese navy, well known to Lord Nelson, from having previously served under him, and from having, on a former occasion, rendered some essential service to the British. For his visit to the Victory, Rear-admiral Campbell appears to have suffered most severely. Notwithstanding the rigid secrecy observed by Lord Nelson, the Spanish naval commander-in-chief at Algeziras got hold of the circumstance, and made a formal complaint against the rear-admiral. This brought down the vengeance of the French ambassador at the court of Portugal, and Rear-admiral Campbell was laid upon the shelf.[2]

On the 10th, in the evening, the fleet anchored in Lagos bay, to clear some transports which had been left there by Sir John Orde, when the latter retreated from before M. Villeneuve. Having, in the course of the night, by extraordinary exertions,

[1] See p. 341.   [2] Clarke and M'Arthur, vol. ii., p. 406.

completed his ships to five months' provisions, Lord Nelson, at 9 A.M. on the 11th, weighed and sailed out of the bay. The expected arrival from England of a fleet of transports, with 5000 troops on board under General Sir James Craig, induced his lordship to remain a short time off Cape St. Vincent; and on the 12th, in the afternoon, the Queen 98, Rear-admiral Knight, and Dragon 74, Captain Edward Griffiths, with their valuable charge, joined company. In order to afford to the convoy an additional protection in its passage through the Straits, Lord Nelson detached the Royal Sovereign; and, with his remaining 10 ships of the line and three frigates, namely, the Victory, Canopus, Superb, Spencer, Swiftsure, Belleisle, Conqueror,[1] Tigre, and Leviathan, and Amazon, Décade, and Amphion, crowded sail to the westward, in chase of an enemy's fleet which he knew consisted of 18 ships of the line, and at least treble his number of frigates. One of the British ships, too, the Superb, not having been in a home port since the 16th of January, 1801, was in a very crazy state; and it was only upon the urgent solicitations of Captain Keats, that the Superb was allowed to make one in the pursuing fleet.

Lord Nelson has been accused of rashness, in being so eager to engage a force nearly double his own; but it should be re-collected, that he fully expected to be joined, on reaching Barbadoes, by six sail of the line. During his passage to the West Indies, Lord Nelson prepared a plan of attack, to be adopted in case he should overtake the enemy's fleet. The plan met the general approval of his officers; but we cannot discover by it whether the vice-admiral contemplated a meeting before or after the expected reinforcement.[2]

On the 15th of May the British fleet made Madeira: and on the 29th the Amazon was sent on to Barbadoes, to enable Rear-admiral Cochrane to have his ships ready for the expected junction. On the 3rd of June Lord Nelson gained, for the first time, certain intelligence that the combined fleet was in the West Indies; and on the 4th he anchored with his squadron in Carlisle bay. Here he found Rear-admiral Cochrane, with only the Northumberland and Spartiate 74s, his remaining four ships having been detained by Rear-admiral Dacrès at Jamaica. An unfounded report, circulated, no doubt, on purpose to mislead,

[1] For this ship a contemporary has substituted the Excellent, Captain Frank Sotheron, left by Lord Nelson in Naples bay. See Brenton, vol. iii., p. 429.

[2] That plan, being the work of an acknowledged proficient, may with propriety be transcribed into these pages. It will therefore be found at No. 29 of the Appendix.

that the enemy was bound to Tobago and Trinidad, induced the vice-admiral to receive on board his ships 2000 troops under General Myers, and to proceed with them, on the morning of the 5th, towards those two islands. On the 7th, when in the gulf of Paria, the British discovered that they had been misled ; and, although so far to leeward, the fleet arrived, on the 9th, off Grenada. Here Lord Nelson received accounts that the enemy had passed the island of Dominique on the 6th, steering to the northward. Having, on the morning of the 13th, reached Antigua, the British fleet there disembarked the troops ; and at noon the same day, taking with him the Spartiate, Captain Francis Laforey, but leaving the Northumberland to remain as Rear-admiral Cochrane's flag-ship on the station, Lord Nelson, with 11 sail of the line, stood to the northward ; not absolutely in pursuit of an enemy, whose force he knew to consist of at least 18 sail of the line, but in the hope, by a superior knowledge of tactics, to reach the shores of Europe before him.

In one of those unreserved conversations which he occasionally held with his captains when visiting him on board the Victory, Lord Nelson is represented to have said, in reference to the object which had drawn him so far from his station : " I am thankful that the enemy has been driven from the West India islands with so little loss to our country " (alluding to the capture of the Antigua convoy) ; " I had made up my mind to great sacrifices, for I had determined, notwithstanding his vast superiority, to stop his career, and to put it out of his power to do any further mischief. Yet do not imagine I am one of those hot-brained people who fight at immense disadvantage, without any adequate object. My object is partly gained. If we meet them we shall find them not less than 18, I rather think 20, sail of the line ; and therefore do not be surprised if I should not fall on them immediately. We won't part without a battle. I think they will be glad to let me alone, if I will let them alone ; which I will do either till we approach the shores of Europe, or they give me an advantage too tempting to be resisted."[1]   And yet the two writers from whose work this extract is taken, seldom indulge in their own remarks without making a perfect braggadocio of their hero. Mr. Southey is nearly as bad as Messrs. Clarke and M'Arthur. Much, indeed, has the memory of this great man suffered by the overweening zeal of his biographers

On the very day, June 9th, on which Lord Nelson arrived off the island of Grenada, Napoleon, writing from Milan, says : " Je

[1] Clarke and M'Arthur, vol. ii., p. 413.

suis d'opinion, cependant, que Nelson est encore dans les mers
d'Europe. Le sentiment le plus naturel est qu'il devrait être
rentré en Angleterre pour se ravitailler et verser ses équipages
sur d'autres bâtimens ; car ses vaisseaux ont besoin d'entrer dans
le bassin, et son escadre peut être considérée comme étant en
très-mauvaix état."[1] The latter part of this statement was true
enough, but Napoleon did not seemingly reflect what might be
done by such a man as Nelson. The velocity, as well as the
direction, of the British admiral's movements had quite out-
stripped the French emperor's calculations.

That M. Villeneuve was not, in reality, with 18 sail of the
line running from 11, is natural to suppose ; and yet many
persons, both in France and England, have thought otherwise.
Nor, indeed, could the French admiral's departure from Martinique have had any possible reference to the arrival of the
British admiral at Barbadoes, owing to the simple fact, that the
two occurrences took place on the same day. M. Villeneuve's
instructions, as well as we can collect what they were from the
mass of orders and counter-orders which issued on the subject,
may afford us some clue to the French admiral's proceedings.

In the published correspondence between the Emperor Napoleon and his minister of marine, a break occurs of nearly seven
months, from September 29, 1804, to April 14, 1805. As, in
the interim, the Toulon fleet had twice sailed, and the last time
had got fairly to sea, this hiatus happens rather inopportunely.
Coupling the April and September instructions, however, we
may gather, that M. Villeneuve was neither to detach ships to
take St. Helena, nor, with the aid of the Rochefort squadron,
himself to capture Surinam and the other Dutch colonies in the
Antilles ;[2] but that, on being joined by the Spaniards, he was
to proceed straight to Martinique, and, with the 5100 men on
board the combined fleet, capture Sainte-Lucie, if not already
taken by the Rochefort squadron; leave a garrison there, and,
if necessary, strengthen the garrisons of Dominique, Martinique,
and Guadaloupe, the two latter of which had already, the one
1500, the other 1600 troops. He was then to wait a month in
the Antilles, in order to afford Vice-admiral Ganteaume an opportunity of joining with his 21 sail of the line; and, to make
the intervening time pass profitably as well as pleasantly, he
was to do all possible injury to the enemy, "faire tout le mal
possible à l'ennemi." The governor-generals of Martinique and
of Guadaloupe, Vice-admiral Villaret Joyeuse and General

[1] Précis des Evènemens, tome xi., p. 267.   [2] See p. 242.

Enouf, were to lend their aid, and, if necessary, a portion of their respective garrisons, towards the fulfilment of this object. The want of provisions in the fleet, or of unanimity in the council, or some other unexplained cause, kept M. Villeneuve's ships in the harbour of Fort Royal until the latter end of May; when two of the 74s moved out to attack the Diamond rock, which, with its sloop's company of officers and men, still persisted to fire at and annoy every French vessel that passed within range of its heavy cannon.

The expedition destined to retake this very harassing and not informidable "king's ship," consisting of the Pluton and Berwick 74s, 36-gun frigate Sirène, 16-gun brig-corvette Argus, Fine armed schooner, and 11 gun-boats, under the orders of Commodore Cosmao of the Pluton, having on board from 300 to 400 troops of the line commanded by chef d'escadron Boyer. On the 29th of May, at 5 h. 30 m. P.M., the expedition sailed from Fort Royal. By the morning of the 30th the ships had not made much progress; but on the 31st, at daybreak, they were far to windward of the rock, and at 7 A.M. bore down towards it. The Diamond had been blockaded ever since the arrival of the combined fleet at Martinique: therefore Captain Maurice, when he saw Commodore Cosmao's squadron sail out, anticipated its destination, and prepared accordingly.

Considering it impossible to defend the lower works against such a force as was approaching, Captain Maurice abandoned them, spiking the two guns, drowning the powder, and cutting away the launch from the landing-place. At 8 A.M. the ships opened their fire; which was returned by Hood's battery and Fort Diamond, the one being the 24-pounder about midway up the rock, the other the two 18-pounders on its summit. The ships bombarded the rock during the 31st of May and 1st of June, and until 4 h. 30 m. P.M. on the 2nd; when Captain Maurice, having, as he states, "but little powder left, and not a sufficient quantity of ball-cartridges to last until dark," threw out a flag of truce. At 5 P.M. the Fine schooner hoisted a similar flag; and terms honourable to the garrison, which consisted of 107 officers and men, were agreed to the same evening.

In their defence of this extraordinary post, the British sustained a loss of only two men killed and one man wounded. The chef d'escadron Boyer enumerates the loss of the French troops, "from a hasty calculation," at about 50 in killed and wounded. Captain Maurice considers the loss of the French,

who landed at the foot of the rock, to have amounted to at least
30 men killed and 40 wounded, exclusively of the loss sustained
on board the ships and boats. Three gun-boats and two rowing-
boats are stated to have been entirely lost. On his subsequent
trial by court-martial, Captain Maurice was not only most
honourably acquitted for the loss of the Diamond rock, but
highly complimented for his firm and determined behaviour.

On the 1st of June, while the governor-general, General
Lauriston, Admirals Villeneuve and Gravina, and a number of
other officers, were inspecting the Diamond rock from the con-
tiguous shore, the French 40-gun frigate Didon, Captain Pierre-
Bernard Milius, arrived from Guadaloupe; bringing fresh instructions from Napoleon, and likewise intelligence that two
French 74s had arrived at that island as a reinforcement to the
combined fleet. The Didon had sailed from Lorient on the 2nd
of May, with duplicates of the instructions, with which, on the
day previous, Rear-admiral Magon, with the two new 74-gun
ships Algésiras, Captain Gabriel-Auguste Brouard, and Achille,
Captain Gabriel Denieport, had sailed from Rochefort. In
those instructions Napoleon directs that Vice-admiral Villeneuve, and General Lauriston, having now with the 2100 troops
composing (see p. 348) the united garrison of Martinique and
Guadaloupe, the 3400 carried out by Rear-admiral Missiessy,
the 5100, including Spaniards in the combined fleet, and the 840
on board Rear-admiral Magon's two ships, upwards of 11,400
men to take St. Vincent, Antigua, Grenada; "et pourquoi ne
prendrait-on pas la Barbade?" Certainly, there was no reason
why, among the "ten Windward islands, including Tobago and
Trinidad," Barbadoes alone should escape free. Tobago having
been a French island, was not to be ill-treated, but such of the
other English colonies as it might not be convenient to retain,
were to be stripped and pillaged thus: "Il ne faudrait point
maltraiter l'île de Tobago, parcequ'elle est française; mais pour
les autres colonies anglaises qu'on jugerait devoir abandonner
après les avoir occupées, on pourrait en tirer la moitié des noirs,
lever une contribution sur les habitans, en ôter l'artillerie, et
vendre les noirs à la Martinique et à la Guadaloupe."[1]

Having done all this, and waited in the Antilles for the Brest
fleet 35 days from the day of receiving his despatches, Vice-
admiral Villeneuve was to proceed straight to Ferrol, to carry
into effect, in the way already explained,[2] the ultimate object of
the expedition; and, compared to which, in the eyes of Napo-

[1] Précis des Evènemens, tome xi., p. 477.   [2] See p. 309.

Icon, the capture and pillage of the British West India islands was mere child's play.

On the 4th of June the combined fleet composed of the same vessels with which it had anchored, except the Santa Madalena Torche, Naïade, and Cyane, and having on board, in addition to the troops it had brought out, a portion of the garrison of Martinique, set sail from the harbour of Fort Royal, steering a northerly course. On the same or following day the two 74s, Algésiras and Achille, which had arrived at Guadaloupe on the 29th of the preceding month, and had sailed on the 2nd of June in search of the admiral, effected their junction. On the 6th M. Villeneuve lay to off the road of Basse-Terre, and received on board his fleet a portion of the garrison of Guadaloupe.

Thus reinforced, the French admiral, with his 20 sail of the line, seven frigates, and two brigs, passed to windward of Montserrat and Redundo, and to leeward of Antigua, with what precise object in view has never been satisfactorily explained. However concealment or a distortion of facts might suit the policy of Napoleon, it was aiming a deadly blow at the reputation of his officers to make their public letters the channel of his falsehoods. In M. Villeneuve's letter of 8 thermidor (26th of July), published in the Moniteur of August 11, a void occurs between the day of his departure from Martinique, "le 16 prairial," or 4th of June, and that on which he made Cape Finisterre, "le 21 messidor," or 9th of July. Not a word is there about the junction of the two 74s, or the abstraction of the colonial garrisons; a tolerable proof that one or more important paragraphs had been suppressed.

On the 8th, having doubled Antigua, as if with the real intention of operating among the British islands, M. Villeneuve received intelligence from an American schooner, that in the north-north-east he would find a British homeward-bound convoy, which had sailed the day previous from that island. Chase was immediately given; and before night the Franco-Spanish fleet overtook 15 sail of merchant-vessels, under the protection of the British 28-gun frigate Barbadoes, Captain Joseph Nourse, and 14-gun schooner Netley, Lieutenant Richard Harward. The two men-of-war effected their escape; but the merchantmen, valued with their cargoes at five millions of francs, were captured. The prizes were given in charge to the Sirène frigate, with orders to escort them to Guadaloupe, and rejoin the fleet off the Western Islands.

Scarcely had the frigate and her rich convoy parted company

than a rumour reached Admiral Villeneuve, derived, no doubt, from some of the prisoners, that Lord Nelson had arrived in the West Indies in search of him. Smarting under their heavy losses, and suspecting from the troops on board that the combined fleet, even yet, was destined to act against some of the British colonies (nearly the whole of which, according to a French writer, had drawn up the capitulations they meant to propose to M. Villeneuve, and counted out the sums of money they could afford to pay him for their ransom[1]), the merchant-masters did, most probably, exaggerate the British force under Lord Nelson, in the hope to drive the French admiral back to Europe. If so, the plan produced its effect; for, on the 9th or 10th, all the troops which had been withdrawn from Martinique and Guadaloupe were precipitately embarked on board the Hortense, Didon, Hermione, and Thémis frigates, with orders to Captain La-Marre-la-Meillerie, of the Hortense, the senior officer, to disembark them at the last-named island, and then to rejoin the fleet at the appointed rendezvous.

That, in acting thus, the French admiral was but obeying his orders, is to be inferred from the fact, that Napoleon anticipated that M. Villeneuve would return straight to Europe on learning that he was pursued. " Je hâterai mon arrivée (à Boulogne) de quelques jours, parce que je pense, que l'arrivée de Nelson " (whose force he in another place states at " dix seuls vaisseaux"), " en Amérique pourrait pousser Villeneuve à partir pour le Ferrol."[2] The only act for which Napoleon blamed M. Villeneuve, was for not leaving at Martinique and Guadaloupe the troops which the fleet had carried out. In his anger, at the partial failure of his projects, the French emperor did certainly attribute this omission on the part of M. Villeneuve to fright, "épouvante," at the rumour of his being pursued; but, at a subsequent day, when the thoughts of invading England had long ceased to agitate his breast, Buonaparte frankly admitted that Villeneuve was a brave man.[3]

On the 26th of June, when, having executed their mission, they were returning to the fleet, the Didon, Hermione, Hortense, and Thémis fell in with the Sirène and her valuable charge; and that but a short distance to windward of the spot whence the latter had made sail 17 days before. Coupling the time already lost with the time it would still take to get a fleet of dull-sailing merchantmen so far to windward as Guadaloupe, Captain La-

---

[1] Victoires et Conquêtes, tome xvi., p. 121.   [2] Précis des Evènemens, tome xi., p. 282.
[3] See O'Meara's Napoleon in Exile, vol. i., p. 57.

Marre-la-Meillerie determined to bear up with them for Porto-Rico. On the following day, the 27th, when about 180 miles to north-east of Barbuda, the British 18-gun ship-sloops, Kingfisher, Captain Richard William Cribb, and Osprey, Captain Timothy Clinch, appeared in sight to windward, and were chased by the French frigates. In making sail to escape, the two sloops hoisted signals and fired guns, as if to a fleet ahead. This had the desired effect. The chasing ships immediately bore up; and, in a very little time, the whole 15 merchant-vessels, with all the rum and sugar and coffee on board, were in flames. A French writer confirms the fact; calling by mistake the two sloops "frigates," and seeming to be unapprised of the ruse that was practised.[1]

On the 30th of June, when about 20 leagues to the north-east of the island of Corvo, the northernmost of the Azores, M. Villeneuve was rejoined by his five frigates. On the same day the Didon captured and burnt an English privateer, of 14 guns and 49 men. On the 3rd of July the fleet recaptured the late Spanish galleon Matilda, with treasure on board to the estimated value of from 14 to 15 millions of francs; and at the same time captured the privateer, the Mars, of Liverpool, who had made prize of the galleon, and was conducting her to an English port. The privateer was set on fire, and the galleon taken in tow by the Sirène frigate. Nothing further of consequence happened to the combined fleet until it arrived off Cape Finisterre on the 9th of July; on which day a violent gale of wind from the north-east carried away the maintopmast of the Indomptable, and otherwise slightly damaged some of the ships. The wind moderated, but continued to blow from the same adverse quarter, until a day or two before the 22nd; when, with a favourable change of wind, occurred an event the account of which had best be deferred till we have brought up the proceedings of the chasing fleet.

After quitting Antigua on the 13th of June,[2] Lord Nelson, still with no more than his own discretion for a guide, hastened towards Europe, and on the 17th of July came in sight of Cape St. Vincent; "making," observes the admiral in his diary, " our whole run from Barbuda, day by day, 3459 miles. Our run from Cape St. Vincent to Barbadoes," he adds, "was 3227 miles; so that our run back was only 232 miles more than our run out, allowance being made for the difference of the latitudes and longitudes of Barbadoes and Barbuda; average per day 34 leagues wanting nine miles." On the following day, the 18th,

[1] Victoires et Conquêtes, tome xvi., p. 128.   [2] See p. 347.

being on his way to Gibraltar for provisions for his fleet, Lord Nelson fell in with Vice-admiral Collingwood, with the Dread-nought 98 and two other sail of the line; but who had not the slightest information to communicate beyond what his own sagacity—and that was of no common kind—suggested. Vice-admiral Collingwood considered the voyage to the West Indies in the right point of view, merely as a means of drawing off the British force from the Channel, to admit of an attack upon Ireland; and, it will be recollected, a disembarkation on Ireland was one of the preliminary steps in Napoleon's plan.[1]

On the 19th of July the British fleet anchored in Gibraltar bay; and " on the 20th," says Lord Nelson in his diary, " I went on shore for the first time since June 16, 1803, and from having my foot out of the Victory, two years wanting 10 days." On the 22nd the fleet weighed and stood across to Tetuan to water, anchoring at 8 P.M. in Mazari bay. On the 24th, at noon, the fleet again got under way and steered for Ceuta, and remained during the night in the gut, with variable winds and a thick fog. On the 25th the 18-gun ship-sloop Termagant, Captain Robert Pettet, from England, joined, with information that the brig-sloop Curieux, on her way home with Lord Nelson's despatches, had, on the 19th of June,[2] in latitude 33° 12′ north, longitude 58° west, fallen in with the combined fleet, steering, at first, north by west, but afterwards north-north-west. This intelli-gence, stale as it was in being communicated five weeks after it bore date, was the earliest of a positive nature which the vice-admiral had received.

After passing the Straits, Lord Nelson bore away to the west-ward, and then proceeded off Cape St. Vincent, to be ready to steer more northerly as circumstances might direct. On the 3rd of August the fleet was in latitude 39° north, longitude 16° west, with light northerly airs. By his acuteness, Lord Nelson, about this time, extracted from a log-book, found by an American merchant-ship on board a vessel which had been set on fire and abandoned, but not destroyed, some far from unimportant infor-mation. The circumstances, as related by each of Lord Nelson's biographers, are as follows: " A log-book and a few seamen's jackets were found in the cabin, and these were brought to Nelson. The log-book closed with these words: 'Two large vessels in the W.N.W.;' and this led him to conclude that the

<hr>

[1] See p. 216; also a letter from Vice-admiral Collingwood to Lord Nelson on this subject, Appendix, No. 30.

[2] Both Southey in his, and Clarke and M'Arthur in their, "Life of Nelson," make this the 19th of July; a serious mistake. See p. 310.

vessel had been a Liverpool privateer cruising off the Western Islands. But there was in this book a scrap of dirty paper, filled with figures. Nelson, immediately upon seeing it, observed that the figures were written by a Frenchman ; and, after studying this for a while, said : ' I can explain the whole. The jackets are of French manufacture, and prove that the privateer was in possession of the enemy. She had been chased and taken by the two ships that were seen in the W.N.W. The prize-master, going on board in a hurry, forgot to take with him his reckoning : there is none in the log-book, and the dirty paper contains her work for the number of days since the privateer left Corvo, with an unaccounted-for run, which I take to have been the chase, in his endeavour to find out her situation by back-reckoning. By some mismanagement I conclude she was run on board by one of the enemy's ships and dismasted. Not liking delay (for I am satisfied that those two ships were the advanced ones of the French squadron), and fancying we were close at their heels, they set fire to the vessel, and abandoned her in a hurry.' " The compilers of the anecdote, unfortunately, have omitted the dates, both of the last entry in the log-book, and of the day on which the wreck was fallen in with. We might otherwise have been able to show, that it was the late Liverpool privateer Mars herself, which had given rise to Lord Nelson's speculations. If so, the jackets had probably belonged to some of the Matilda's crew, and the scrap of paper been written upon by a Spaniard. Whichever way it was, the inference remained just as the vice-admiral had drawn it, that the capturing fleet had steered to the northward.

A northerly course thus appearing to have been taken by M. Villeneuve, a northerly course was taken by his ardent pursuer, but, to the latter's regret, against northerly winds and hazy weather. On the 8th of August the wind became more favourable. On the 12th the Niobe frigate joined from the Channel fleet, but, strange to say, still without intelligence. On the 15th Lord Nelson himself joined Admiral Cornwallis off Ushant, from whom he heard all that had happened, and, on the same evening, proceeded with the Victory and Superb to Portsmouth ; leaving the remainder of his fleet (except the Belleisle, who steered for Plymouth) as a reinforcement to the Channel fleet.[1] On the 18th the Victory and Superb anchored at Spithead ; and Lord Nelson shortly afterwards struck his flag and went on shore.

[1] See p. 311.

BRITISH AND FRANCO-SPANISH FLEETS.

On the 19th of February, in the afternoon, Vice-admiral Sir Robert Calder, in the Prince of Wales 98, was detached from the Channel fleet to take the command of the blockading squadron off Ferrol, in the room of Rear-admiral the Hon. Alexander Cochrane, who with five sail of the line and a frigate had quitted the station since the 24th of February for the West Indies, in pursuit of the Rochefort squadron, also of five sail of the line, and of the proceedings, of which we shall hereafter give some account. On the 1st of March, in the evening, the Prince of Wales arrived off Cape Prior, and joined six sail of the line under the command of Captain the Hon. Arthur Kaye Legge, in the Repulse 74, the senior officer at the departure of Rear-admiral Cochrane. The Franco-Spanish fleet in Ferrol at this time amounted to 10 sail of the line ready for sea, and two or three others fitting. Between the 22nd of April and the 31st of May Sir Robert, at no one time, had with him a greater force than nine sail of the line, and for days together not so many.

On the 15th of July the vice-admiral was reinforced by five sail of the line under Rear-admiral Stirling in the Glory 98, from off Rochefort.[1] This made Sir Robert Calder's force consist of the following 15 sail of the line and smaller vessels:

Gun-ship.

98	Prince of Wales .	Vice-admiral (b.) Sir Robert Calder. Captain William Cuming.
	Glory	Rear-admiral (b.) Charles Stirling. Captain Samuel Warren.
	Barfleur . . .	,, George Martin.
	Windsor Castle . .	,, Charles Boyles.

[1] See p. 310.

Gun-ship.

80	Malta . . . . . . Captain Edward Buller.	
74	⎧ Thunderer . . . ,, William Letchmere.	
	⎪ Hero . . . . . ,, Hon. Alan Hyde Gardner.	
	⎪ Repulse . . . . ,, Hon. Arthur Kaye Legge.	
	⎨ Defiance . . . . ,, Philip Charles Durham.	
	⎪ Ajax . . . . . ,, William Brown.	
	⎪ Warrior . . . . ,, Samuel Hood Linzee.	
	⎪ Dragon . . . . ,, Edward Griffiths.	
	⎩ Triumph . . . . ,, Henry Inman.	
64	⎰ Agamemnon . . . ,, John Harvey.	
	⎱ Raisonable . . . ,, Josias Rowley.	

Frigates, Egyptienne, Captain the Hon. Charles Elphinstone, Fleming, and Sirius, Captain William Prowse.

Lugger Nile, Lieutenant John Fennell, and *cutter* Frisk, Lieutenant James Nicholson.

With this force the vice-admiral was directed to proceed 30 or 40 leagues to the westward of Cape Finisterre, and there endeavour to intercept the combined fleet from the West Indies, represented, upon the authority of the Diamond-rock account, to consist of only 16 sail of the line.[1] Thus had the blockade of two ports been raised, in which, at the time, were about as many ships of the line ready for sea as, by all accounts, composed the fleet which the blockading squadrons, when united, were ordered to intercept. The policy of this measure does not seem very clear. If the Ferrol squadron did not, as the Rochefort had done, take advantage of the circumstance and sail out, it was merely because it had received no orders from France.

On the 19th Sir Robert received a copy of Lord Nelson's despatch, of date the 15th of June, addressed to the British commanding officer off the Tagus, stating that the combined fleet, of what force not mentioned, had passed Antigua on the 8th of June, and was probably on its way to Europe. On the 22nd of July, in the forenoon, that same combined fleet, composed of 20 sail of the line, seven frigates, and two brigs,[2] besides the recaptured galleon Matilda, made its appearance to windward, in the manner we shall proceed to relate.

On the morning of the 22nd, in latitude 43° 34' north, and longitude 16° 13' west, from Paris, the combined fleet, formed in three divisions, and having a light breeze from west-north-west, was steering in a thick fog, east-south-east, a direct course for Ferrol, when, at about 11 A.M., on a sudden clearing up of the weather, the French leading-ship, the Indomptable, disco-

---

[1] See p. 343.   [2] See p. 353.

vered and signalled 10 sail in the north-north-east, approaching on the starboard tack. The frigates sent ahead to reconnoitre presently augmented the number to 21 sail; namely, 17 British ships, the lugger and cutter, and two Danish merchant-brigs, one brought to by the Dragon, the other by the Egyptienne. In the mean time the Defiance, the British look-out ship, and which then lay about three leagues to windward of her fleet, discovered and signalled a strange fleet in the south-west.

At noon, latitude 43° 54' north, longitude (from Greenwich) 11° 38' west, Ferrol east-south-east distant 49, and Cape Finisterre south-east distant 39 leagues, the Prince of Wales made the signal to prepare for battle, and in a few minutes afterwards to form the order of sailing in two columns. This was followed by a signal to form the line; and at 1 h. 15 m. P.M., to keep in close order. At 2 h. 15 m. P.M. the latter signal was repeated; and at 3 P.M. the Defiance having stood on until within less than two miles of the enemy, joined and took her station in the line, the ships of which, when in their places, ranked as follows: Hero, Ajax, Triumph, Barfleur, Agamemnon, Windsor Castle, Defiance, Prince of Wales, Repulse, Raison-able, Dragon (then under a press of sail to leeward, as soon as she should join), Glory, Warrior, Thunderer, Malta; most of the ships with their topgallantsails set, and all, except the Dragon, with their courses up, standing, as before, on the starboard tack.

At about the same time the ships of the combined fleet formed themselves in line of battle, in the following order: Argonauta, Terrible, America, Espana, San-Rafaël, Firme, Pluton, Mont Blanc, Atlas, Berwick, Neptune, Bucentaure, Formidable, Intrépide, Scipion, Swiftsure, Indomptable, Aigle, Achille, Algésiras.[1] At 3 h. 30 m. P.M., after having hove to some time, the combined fleet filled, and under topsails, stood on upon the larboard tack, rather off the wind, in a close well-formed line; one frigate ahead, another, the Sirène, who had just taken the galleon in tow, astern, and the remaining five frigates, in a second line, to windward of the centre and rear. The British fleet was at this time nearly abeam, and about seven miles distant; but, owing to the fog, neither fleet was more than partially in sight of the other.

Since 1 P.M. the Egyptienne and Sirius, then a short distance to windward of the Defiance, had been ordered, by signal, to keep sight of the enemy. The frigates accordingly made sail to

---

[1] For the names of their several commanders see pp. 334, 339, and 342.

get nearer to the latter; and the Sirius, the weathermost frigate, as she passed from van to rear of the combined fleet, made the signal of the exact number of line-of-battle ships and smaller vessels composing it. At 3 h. 20 m. P.M. Sir Robert made the signal to engage the enemy; and at 3 h. 22 m., to tack together. At 3 h. 26 m. the same signal was repeated and annulled. At 3 h. 27 m. a signal was made for the starboard division to make all possible sail, and steer south-south-west.

At 3 h. 30 m. the same signal was made to the Hero, who probably had commenced tacking in obedience to the signal at 3 h. 22 m. At 3 h. 31 m. the signal was made to form the line of battle in open order; at 3 h. 53 m., to alter course one point to starboard; and at 4 h. 21 m., to tack in succession.

The signal to tack in succession appears to have been made by each commander-in-chief about the same time; but, in the foggy state of the weather, neither fleet saw the commencement of the other's manœuvre. The British tacked, to prevent their opponents escaping them on the opposite tack; but the Franco-Spaniards, who had hauled close to the wind on getting within about three miles of the British fleet, wore, in consequence of the Sirène, which had the galleon in tow, making signals, by guns fired in quick succession, that the rear was in danger of being cut off.

This was occasioned by the bold approach of the Sirius, who, as soon as she had got sufficiently to windward to fetch into the wake of the combined line, had tacked, with the intention of attempting to carry, by boarding, the great object of the enemy's solicitude. While making the necessary preparation to effect his object, Captain Prowse discovered, through the haze on his lée-bow, the enemy's van-ship, the Argonauta, approaching with the wind nearly abeam. The Sirius herself being now in jeopardy, Captain Prowse abandoned his design upon the galleon, and bore up to pass to leeward of the Franco-Spanish line. With a forbearance highly honourable to Admiral Gravina, the Argonauta passed the British frigate without firing; and so did the Terrible and America. By the time, however, that the Sirius had got abreast of the Espana, which was at about 5 h. 15 m. P.M., the Hero, the British van-ship, then with royals set, hove in stays. Instantly the Spanish ships, all of whom had royals and courses set, hoisted their colours and commenced the action; the Argonauta firing her larboard guns at the Hero, and the Espana hers at the Sirius, which ship, in consequence, had two men killed and three wounded

At 4 h. 30 m. P.M. the Prince of Wales had made the signal
to engage the enemy's centre; at 4 h. 45 m., to keep in close
order; and, at 5 h. 9 m., to engage the enemy as closely as
possible. At 5 h. 20 m. P.M., which was about five minutes
after she had tacked, the Hero opened a fire from her starboard
guns. The reason of the Hero's having tacked without a signal
was, that her advanced station had enabled her to see, what the
fog concealed from the ships in her wake, that the enemy had
come round on the starboard-tack. Precisely as the Hero tacked
to starboard, the Windsor Castle, the sixth British ship from the
van (the majority of the ships now with royals and courses set),
tacked to port. We have chosen this moment for representing
in a diagram the position of the two fleets; or rather of the van
and rear of the combined, and of the ten leading ships of the
British fleet.

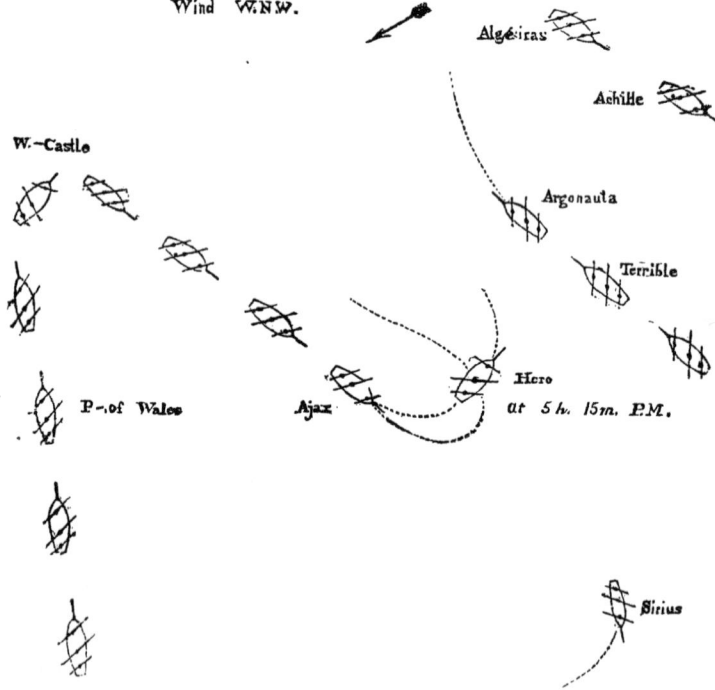

At 5 h. 45 m. P.M., the Ajax tacked astern of the Hero; but,
unfortunately for the success of Captain Gardner's gallant

manœuvre, the Ajax put her helm up, and bore away to speak the admiral. On passing within hail of the Prince of Wales, Captain Brown informed Sir Robert Calder of the change of position in the two vans. The Ajax then wore, and fell into the line astern of the Glory; thus making herself, instead of the second, the twelfth ship from the van. At 5 h. 50 m. P.M., by which time the five ships in line between the Ajax and Prince of Wales had successively tacked, the latter, as she probably would have done, had the Ajax followed her gallant leader into the thick of the enemy's fire, hoisting the signal to tack in succession, tacked also, and, in a quarter of an hour or 20 minutes, joined in the cannonade, now becoming general and furious. By 6 P.M. all the ships in the British line, except the Dragon, which was still to leeward working up, had got round on the starboard tack, and the greater part had found opponents in the opposite line ; but, what with the fog and the smoke, no ship could see much beyond her own length.

Owing to the disorder to which this gave rise, some of the ships in both fleets had several opponents upon them at once. On the British side, the Windsor Castle was a principal sufferer ; and the Ajax, Prince of Wales, Thunderer, and Malta, the last especially, participated in this unequal warfare. On the part of the combined fleet, the San-Rafaël, Firme, and Espana, having dropped to leeward, became greatly exposed to the fire of the British. Seeing the situation of the Firme, the latter's second astern, the Pluton, gallantly bore up out of the line, and, for a while, covered the Spanish ship from the destructive effects of their enemy's fire ; but the Firme was too powerfully opposed to profit by the aid afforded her, and the Pluton herself with difficulty regained her station.

The critical situation of the Espana induced Captain Cosmao-Kerjulien, a second time, to interpose himself between one of his Spanish allies and the British line. In this instance, being assisted by the Mont Blanc and Atlas, the Pluton succeeded, and the Espana was rescued. Amidst the derangement of the Franco-Spanish line, the Atlas suffered most severely, and, but for the support of her friends, among whom the Neptune was foremost, would certainly have been captured.

Soon after 8 P.M. the Firme, with the loss of her main and mizen masts, and subsequently of all her masts, struck ; and the San-Rafaël, with the loss of her maintopmast, and subsequently of all her masts also, did not hold out many minutes longer. At 8 h. 25 m., at which time the British ships were dis-

united and scattered, the body of the combined fleet barely
within gun-shot to windward, and the shades of night combining
with the fog and smoke to render objects still more indistinct,
Sir Robert made the night private signal to discontinue the
action.   At about 9 P.M. the Windsor Castle, with her foretopmast gone, passed close to windward of the Prince of Wales,
and then bore up and was taken in tow by the Dragon; who,
with all her efforts, had not got up in time to take more than a
very slight part in the action; indeed, it was nearly 8 P.M. when
the Dragon fell into line ahead of the Barfleur, who herself had
been unable to get very close to the enemy.   The signal to discontinue the action being seen but by few ships, the general
firing did not cease until 9 h. 30 m. P.M.   The British ships soon
afterwards brought too upon the starboard tack, with their heads
about south-west by west, and lay by for the night, repairing
their damages, in order to be ready to renew the contest on the
morrow.

The loss in gross sustained by the British fleet, amounted
to 39 officers and men killed and 159 wounded; and, as Sir
Robert Calder, in his official return, has, contrary to what is
customary, omitted to specify the names or qualities of the
officers killed and wounded, we are constrained to do the same.
One ship, the Warrior, escaped with entire impunity; and the
Hero, Agamemnon, Repulse, Raisonable, Glory, and Dragon,
lost between them but three men killed and 14 wounded; nor
were the Dragon's four men wounded by the enemy's shot, but
by an accidental explosion.   No ship had a mast shot away but
the Windsor Castle and Agamemnon, nor a yard except the
Ajax.[1] The loss on board the two prizes was stated to consist of
about 600 in killed and wounded; but a careful comparison of
the number of wounded and unwounded prisoners, with the
number of men deposed to have been on board each ship at the
commencement of the action, has reduced the number considerably.   In this amended state, the gross loss sustained by
the combined fleet amounts to 476 officers and men killed and
wounded.[2] With respect to damages, the French and Spanish
ships did not exhibit many marks in their masts and rigging;
but some of them, undoubtedly, were much hit in the hull.   One
ship, we believe the Atlas, had the head of her bowsprit shot
away; another, her fore-yard and foretopgallantmast; and a
third, a topsailyard.   Had a court-martial on the French, as was
the case with the British, commander-in-chief, called for a specific

[1] See Appendix, No. 31.   [2] See Appendix, No. 32.

statement of each ship's damage, every wounded topgallantmast and spritsail-yard, every cut rope and shot-graze would have been formally set forth; and then, and then only, would a fair opportunity have been afforded of comparing the relative damage on board the two fleets.

It was extremely natural for the French writers to make the most of the minute statement of damages published along with the proceedings of the court-martial which sat upon Sir Robert Calder; but they evinced very little candour, when they confronted the whole loss on the British side with a part only of the loss on their side, and then drew from it the inference that their fleet had suffered the least in the action. To have acted impartially, they should have struck out of the British returns the two ships that had sustained the heaviest loss, as a set-off against the two prizes, whose united loss, although the French were unable to enumerate it, they knew amounted to much more than that of any other two, or any four ships in the combined fleet. This would have made the numbers stand thus : British loss in killed and wounded, except of Windsor Castle and Malta. 108 ; Franco-Spanish loss in killed and wounded, except of San-Rafaël and Firme, 171. But, if we add the loss of the two omitted ships on each side, as given (with respect to the Spanish ships for the first time) in the preceding page, the relative quantum of loss will be more than two to one in favour of the British.

Daybreak on the 23rd found the two fleets about 17 miles apart, reckoning from their respective centres; but, owing to the hazy state of the morning, neither fleet had of the other more than a partial view. The ships of each were lying to, or making very little way, with the wind as on the preceding day, a moderate breeze from the north-west by west. The British fleet had just come to the wind on the larboard tack, but the combined fleet still remained on the starboard. The British advanced squadron, consisting of the Barfleur, Hero, Triumph, and Agamemnon, lay about five miles to windward of the main body ; and, at the distance of about six miles to windward of the former lay M. Villeneuve's advanced squadron, consisting also of four sail of the line, besides a few frigates. To windward of these again, at the distance of other five or six miles, lay the body of the Franco-Spanish fleet. To leeward of the British main body, about five miles, lay the crippled Windsor Castle, with the Dragon approaching to take her in tow; and still further to leeward, at about an equal distance, lay the Malta,

Thunderer, two frigates. and prizes, all of whom were out of sight of the admiral.

At 6 h. 30 m. A.M. the Prince of Wales, and the ships with her, filled their maintopsails ; and at 8 A.M. the van-division, by signal, bore up to close the former, which had then wore, and, under their topsails, were running to leeward to join the prizes and the ships with them. At 9 A.M., having concentrated his fleet, the British admiral hauled up on the larboard tack, and steered about north-east ; keeping between the Franco-Spanish fleet and his three disabled ships. Of these the Windsor Castle was in tow by the Dragon, the Firme, by the Sirius, and the San-Rafaël, at present by the Egyptienne, who had recently taken charge of her from the Malta.

No sooner had the weathermost British ship bore up to join the prizes than, imagining that the former, although under top-sails only, were flying in disorder, "fuyant en désordre," the French admiral went with his staff on board the Hortense frigate, and calling to him all the other frigates except the Didon, which latter had been sent ahead to reconnoitre, ordered them to inform his captains that he meant to bring on a decisive action, and that they were to lay their ships as close as possible alongside of the enemy.[1] While the five frigates were hailing the line-of-battle ships successively, to acquaint them, "au porte-voix," with their chief's intention, the Didon, confiding in her superior sailing, had approached very near to the British fleet ; so near, that the Triumph, at 11 A.M., for the want of a frigate to perform the office, tacked and chased her away.

Towards noon the wind veered more to the northward and got very light, and a heavy swell came on from the same quarter. At a few minutes past noon the combined fleet, formed in order of battle, bore up towards the British fleet, then about four leagues off in the east-south-east ; but, owing to the distance, and to the extreme lightness of the breeze, it was not until 3 h. 10 m. P.M. that the advance of the French and Spaniards was noticed by the British. Immediately the ships of the latter hoisted their colours, and hauled closer to the wind, awaiting the expected attack. At 4 P.M., however, the ships of the com-bined fleet, with colours also hoisted, and then distant about three leagues from their opponents, hauled to the wind on the same tack as the British ships ; thus evidently declining, for the present, a renewal of the engagement. For a fact so important, and so utterly at variance with the statement at first given out

---

[1] Victoires et Conquêtes, tome xvi., p. 142.

by the French, some authority may be requisite. "A midi, toute la flotte prit chasse sur l'ennemi, qu'on estimait à trois lieues et demie : le vent était faible. A quatre heures, on n'avait encore gagné qu'une lieue à l'escadre anglaise ; il n'y avait par conséquent pas d'espoir de l'atteindre avant la nuit, mais on pouvait au moins l'approcher davantage ; cependant Villeneuve fit signal à la flotte de serrer le vent, son intention étant de n'attaquer l'ennemi que le lendemain ; ce signal étonna autant qu'il affligea les officiers et les marins ; on prévit dès lors qu'on ne parviendrait plus à joindre l'ennemi." [1]

The British admiral resumed his course to the north-east, but was soon driven from it by a change of wind; which, commencing about midnight at north, became, by 8 A.M. on the 24th, north-north-east, and occasionally north-west, but it was very moderate, amounting almost to a calm. This brought the combined fleet nearly astern of the British fleet; which was now to windward, and might, in all probability, have renewed the action. No attempt of the kind was made. Sir Robert, for reasons that will appear presently, continued with his prizes, under easy sail, working towards a British port, steering about south-east by east. The combined fleet had steered the same course as the British fleet until 8 A.M.: the ships then edged away and steered south-east by south. At 4 P.M. one ship only of the Franco-Spanish fleet was in sight of the British fleet, and by 6 P.M. the two fleets had wholly disappeared from each other.

In examining the merits of the affair between Sir Robert Calder and M. Villeneuve, we shall take each day's proceeding by itself. The battle was fought, as has already been shown, between 14, or, gratuitously adding the Dragon (for she was not engaged till at the very close), 15 British, and 20 French and Spanish sail of the line. Cases have occurred where the French have enumerated frigates as a part of the force opposed to them. Here, be it observed, there were seven on one side, and two only on the other : those seven frigates had also been ordered, as will hereafter be made manifest, to take a part in the action, and one frigate did, for a short time, with other ships, engage the Windsor Castle. If, between the four 80-gun ships in the combined fleet, and the four 98-gun ships in the British, any allowance is expected for the nominal (for it is not real [2]) superiority of the latter, let four of the five surplusage frigates be added to the

---

[1] Victoires et Conquêtes, tome xvi., p. 143.   [2] See vol. ii., p. 208.

former; which will be leaving three opposed to the British two, because one of the latter, the Egyptienne, mounted 24-pounders on her main deck. When, also, it is considered, that, from the weight of metal, and number of men she carries, a French 74 is of greater force than a British 74, no objection on the part of the French or Spaniards can be urged against an estimate which, grounded on the numerical line-of-battle strength on each side, fixes the ratio of force in their favour as four is to three.

With, then, the inferiority of one-fourth in point of force, the British succeeded in capturing two ships out of the adverse line. If these were slow sailers and bad workers, how many slow sailers and bad workers did the British fleet contain? If the density of the fog obstructed the French and Spaniards in their manœuvres, what effect must it have had upon the British, to whom, in spite of all that had been urged to the contrary, so many signals were made and so few seen or understood; and who actually performed the evolution, which brought on the close action, without a signal at all? The tacking of the Hero, for instance. Certainly, too, the fog, combined with the smoke, incommoded the British, who were to leeward, more than the French and Spaniards, who were to windward. A victory, therefore, it was that Sir Robert Calder had gained, but not a "decisive," nor a "brilliant" victory. To have made the action decisive, one way or the other, was exclusively in the power of M. Villeneuve; but he kept his wind, and the firing ceased, owing principally, if not wholly, to his having hauled out of gunshot.

It may throw some light upon the proceedings of M. Villeneuve, both in this action and generally since he last quitted Toulon, if we transcribe a portion of the instructions which, on the eve of his departure, he addressed to the captains of his fleet. "I do not," he says, "intend to go in search of the enemy: I would even avoid him in order to get to my destination; but, should we meet him, let there be no discreditable evolution: it would dishearten our men and insure our defeat. If the enemy be to leeward of us, having the power to adopt what evolution we please, we will form our order of battle, and bear down upon him in line abreast; each ship to close with her natural opponent in the enemy's line, and to board him should a favourable opportunity present itself."—"Every captain, who is not closely engaged, is not in his station; and a signal to recall him to his duty will be a stain upon his character. The frigates must equally take part in the action.[1] no signals to that effect will be necessary; they must proceed to the point where their co-operation may be most advantageous, whether to hasten the surrender of an enemy's ship, or to cover a French ship too closely pressed, and to take her in tow or otherwise assist her."[2] No shyness betrays itself here; an additional proof that, in his apparent disinclination to close with an inferior force, Vice-admiral Villeneuve was acting a compulsory part.

On the 23rd of July the parties, in point of relative force, stood nearly the same. The combined fleet had been reduced from 20 to 18 ships, and the British from 15 to 14. But the one had its seven frigates ready to act upon any service; while the other had its two frigates employed in towing the prizes of the preceding day; and which prizes, in the attention they otherwise claimed, impeded the British fleet in its progress, and prevented it from attempting any manœuvre whereby an advantage might be gained. Considering the little value of the vessels, the San-Rafaël, a ship of 34, and the Firme, a ship of 51 years old, and both battered to pieces, their destruction would have been not only a justifiable measure, but, under circumstances, the most eligible that could have been devised.

With respect to the power of commencing the action, a continuance of the same wind kept it where it had been on the day previous; yet, with the exception of an hour's demonstration or show-off, as it may be termed, the party possessing that power declined to use it. On the 24th a change of wind, to nearly an opposite point of the compass, produced a corresponding change in the position of the two fleets; but still they did not approach nearer each other. The truth is, that since the close of the first day's proceedings, Sir Robert Calder, unless some unlooked-for advantage should offer itself, did not intend to be a second time the assailant: he would neither attack nor retreat; nor would he deviate one point from the course necessary to convoy his crippled ship and his two worthless prizes beyond the reach of danger. Each fleet, therefore, on the afternoon of the 24th, pursued its route, as if the other were not present, or that no hostility existed between them.

"Notre intention est que vous fassiez votre jonction en évitant le combat," says Napoleon, in his instructions to M. Villeneuve; and, in another place, "Si vous prenez le parti de faire votre réunion avec l'escadre de Brest, vous devez tenter de le faire sans combat." Buonaparte, also, when writing to M. Decrès,

---

[1] See p. 366.   [2] For the original of this curious production, see Appendix, No. 33.

asks, "A quoi aboutissait une bataille?" and immediately answers the questions himself,—"A rien."[1] If one admiral, therefore, had the misfortune to act under orders that forbade him to fight unless with such odds in his favour as would insure success, the other was also controlled, in some degree, by extraneous circumstances ; sufficient, if not to excuse him for declining to assail an equal force, to justify him in acting a peculiarly cautious part, when himself assailed by a force decidedly superior. Sir Robert Calder knew that the very ships composing his fleet had been abstracted from watching as many enemy's ships as had composed the combined fleet on his first meeting it; he himself, with 10, had been ordered from off a port in which lay 15, waiting, as he had every reason to believe, solely for his departure, to slip out and join M. Villeneuve. Rear-admiral Stirling, also, with five ships, had been called from off another port, out of which he knew, and informed Sir Robert, that five French ships had been seen getting under way just as the blockading squadron was disappearing from the coast;[2] and which five ships, since known to have sailed on the 16th, were endeavouring to effect their junction, either with M. Villeneuve at sea, or with Rear-admiral Gourdon at Ferrol. So well grounded were Sir Robert Calder's apprehensions on this head, that, on the 23rd of July, Rear-admiral Allemand, with his squadron, was on the very spot on which the battle of the preceding day had been fought. Moreover, Sir Robert had been ordered by the admiralty, and by the commanders-in-chief of the Channel and of the Mediterranean fleets, to be on his guard in case of a junction between the fleet of M. Villeneuve and the squadron from Ferrol; whose united force would have been at least 35, and, if the Rochefort squadron had joined, 40 sail of the line.

Matters would have passed off, and Sir Robert Calder's success, in having, with a fleet of 15 sail of the line, captured two out of an enemy's fleet of 20 sail of the line, been taken as an earnest of how much more would have been effected had the parties met on fairer terms. But the accounts on shore marred all. The British admiralty suppressed an important paragraph in Sir Robert's letter to Admiral Cornwallis; taking care that the published extract (to confirm the delusion, stated to be a "copy" of the official letter) should end where hopes were held

[1] Précis des Evènemens, tome xi., pp. 248, 252, and 276.

[2] See Minutes of the court-martial upon Sir Robert Calder: Rear-admiral Stirling's evidence

out of a renewal of the engagement; thus: "They are now in sight to windward; and, when I have secured the captured ships and put the squadron to rights, I shall endeavour to avail myself of any opportunity that may offer to give you a further account of these combined squadrons." The suppressed paragraph was this: "At the same time it will behove me to be on my guard against the combined squadrons in Ferrol, as I am led to believe they have sent off one or two of their crippled ships last night for that port;[1] therefore, possibly I may find it necessary to make a junction with you immediately off Ushant, with the whole squadron." The admiralty, it is true, may have acted thus upon the oral information of the officer bearing the despatches; and which, in every version of it, conveys an absolute intention on the part of Sir Robert Calder to renew the action. Several of the British captains also understood that to be the nature of the message delivered to them by Lieutenant Nicholson, just as he was quitting the fleet for England.

The French official accounts, really dictated by the French emperor, but purporting to be the statement of the French commander-in-chief, claimed the victory as theirs, and boasted that the combined fleet had repeatedly chased the British fleet, and at length compelled it to fly. These accounts, translated into English, and published in all the newspapers of the country, rivetted the effect produced by the admiralty bulletin, and spread far and wide that spirit of discontent which finally compelled Sir Robert Calder to demand a court-martial upon his conduct. That court-martial, which sat on board the Prince of Wales, in Portsmouth harbour, from the 23rd to the 26th of December, "severely reprimanded" the British admiral, for not having done his utmost to renew the engagement on the 23rd and 24th of July; but the sentence admitted, that his conduct had not been actuated either by cowardice or disaffection. The preceding details, now for the first time so fully given to the public, will enable even a landman to form some opinion of the justice of the sentence pronounced upon Sir Robert Calder.

The following remarks of an eminent French writer will show what he thought, as well of that sentence as of the "victory" which M. Villeneuve, by his master's arts, had been made to say that he had gained over the British. "Admiral Calder," says M. Dupin, "with an inferior force, meets the Franco-

[1] This may have arisen from the Defiance's signal of the preceding day at noon having been for 22 "sail of the line," when on the morning of the 23rd 18 only were counted.

Spanish fleet; in the chase of it, he brings on a partial engagement, and captures two ships. He is tried and reprimanded,
because it is believed that, had he renewed the action, he would
have obtained a more decisive victory. What would they have
done with Calder, in England, if he had commanded the superior
fleet, and had lost two ships, in avoiding an engagement which
presented so favourable a chance to skill and valour ? What
would they have done with the captains ?"[1]

We stated, a page or two back, that the French official accounts of the meeting between M. Villeneuve and Sir Robert
Calder were dictated by the French emperor. As this is a very
serious charge, we shall endeavour to substantiate it. The
Moniteur published two letters, as from Admiral Villeneuve,
giving an account of the action ; one dated July 27, in the
paper of August 11; the other dated July 29, in the paper of
August 14. Both letters, of course, make a good story ; and
both commend (the last, in set terms) the noble behaviour of
Admiral Gravina and the Spanish ships. And yet a letter from
Napoleon to his minister of marine, dated on the 13th of August,
contains these sentences: "De quoi donc se plaint Villeneuve
de la part des Espagnols ? Ils se sont battus comme des lions."[2]
Hence, the commendations in the published letters were not the
sentiments of the nominal writer ; nor, by a fair inference, could
any of the misstatements in those letters be laid to the charge of
M. Villeneuve. But the Moniteur of August 13 contained, with
a translation of Sir Robert Calder's letter, very copious remarks
upon every part of it. And Napoleon, in his letter to M. Decrès
of August 11, after observing upon the statements in the British
official account, proceeds thus : "L'arrivée de Villeneuve à la
Corogne fera tomber ces gasconnades, et, aux yeux de l'Europe,
nous donnera l'air de la victoire : cela est beaucoup. *Faites
sur-le-champ une relation, et envoyez-la à M. Maret : voici comme je
la conçois.*"[3] All that follows M. le Comte Dumas has left
blank. Enough, however, remains to show who penned the
remarks in the Moniteur ; and yet these very remarks, without,
apparently, their real origin being suspected, were translated
into most of the London journals.

On the 31st of July, after having been escorted by the fleet
beyond the probable reach of the Rochefort squadron, the two
prizes anchored in Plymouth Sound. The San-Rafaël was
built at Havana in the year 1771, measured 2130 tons English,

[1] For the original, see Appendix, No. 34. [2] Précis des Evènemens, tome xii., p. 251.
[3] Ibid., p. 248,

and mounted on her first and second decks the same nominal
force as the French 80, No. 3, in the small Table at p. 59 of
the first volume, upon her quarter-deck and forecastle 10 long
8-pounders (two of them brass) and 10 carronades, 36-pounders,
and upon her poop six 24-pounder carronades, total 88 guns;
with a complement, on the morning of the action, of 800 men
and boys, and 104 soldier-passengers. The Firme was built at
Cadiz in the year 1754, and measured 1805 tons. Neither the
San-Rafaël nor the Firme, as a proof how little their destruction
would have been felt, was ever employed in the British service
except as a prison-ship.

When, at 8 P.M. on the 26th, he had seen his prizes to the
prescribed latitude, Sir Robert Calder, with his 14 sail of the
line, wore and stood back to the rendezvous off Cape Finisterre,
in the expectation of there being joined by the fleet under Lord
Nelson. On the 27th, at a little before noon, the wind changed
to the north-west, and the vice-admiral shortly afterwards
reached the rendezvous. Not finding Lord Nelson there, Sir
Robert, with the wind at west, steered for Ferrol; and, arriving
off that port on the 29th, sent in the Dragon to reconnoitre. On
a report from the latter, that the combined fleet had not entered
Ferrol, Sir Robert concluded that M. Villeneuve had proceeded
to the southward, and he resumed the blockade of the port.

On the 31st the vice-admiral sent the Malta to England to
get refitted. Taking due advantage of this circumstance, one of
the French writers gravely asserts, that almost every ship of
Admiral Calder's fleet was obliged to return to an English port
to get repaired;[1] and Napoleon, as soon as he learnt that the
Windsor Castle and Malta had been ordered home, directed his
minister of marine, in his letter of condolence to the Prince of
Peace on the loss of the San-Rafaël and Firme, to acquaint the
latter, " que deux vaisseaux ennemis sont arrivés coulant bas à
Plymouth."[2] Respecting these two " sinking " ships, the
Windsor Castle did not enter the harbour of Plymouth, but
refitted herself in Cawsand bay, and in three weeks was again
at sea; and the Malta would have been only half that time in
port, had she not required to be newly coppered.

On the 1st of August, in the forenoon, Sir Robert Calder was
driven by a strong south-westerly wind far to the north-east of
his port. On the 2nd, at noon, agreeably to his orders from
Admiral Cornwallis, the vice-admiral detached, to resume the

---

[1] Victoires et Conquêtes, tome xvi., p.
144.
[2] Précis des Evènemens, tome xii., p.

blockade of the now vacant port of Rochefort, Rear-admiral
Stirling, with four sail of the line; and, on the same evening,
with his remaining nine sail, regained his station off Ferrol. On
the 9th, at 3 P.M., the Dragon reconnoitred, in a very gallant
and effectual manner, the neighbouring ports of Ferrol and
Corunna, and found M. Villeneuve's fleet lying at the entrance
of the latter harbour; making, with the ships at anchor in the
harbour of Ferrol, 29 French and Spanish sail of the line, ready
for sea. In this state of things, Sir Robert, with his nine sail of
the line, abandoned the blockade, and on the 14th joined
Admiral Cornwallis off Ushant.

It has already on more than one occasion appeared, that
M. Villeneuve's primary destination, after quitting the West
Indies, was the harbour of Ferrol, there to effect a junction
with the Rear-admirals Grandallana and Gourdon and their
respective squadrons. Accordingly, after losing sight of the
British fleet on the evening of the 24th, the combined fleet
steered as direct a course for Ferrol as the prevailing north-
east wind would permit. M. Villeneuve, no doubt, soon found
that the masts and yards of many of his ships were not in a
state to withstand a strong head or beating wind and a heavy
sea : moreover, it became necessary that the sick and wounded
should be landed as early as possible. Under these circumstances, the French admiral acted wisely in bearing up for the
bay of Vigo; where, on the evening of the 26th, he came to an
anchor with his fleet.

In Napoleon's instructions to Vice-admiral Villeneuve, of
May 8, was contained an alternative that, if by events in
America, or in the course of his homeward voyage, the latter
should find himself in a situation not immediately to appear
before Brest or enter the Channel, he was to order away upon a
cruise Rear-admiral Gourdon's squadron, accompanied by three
or four of the fastest sailing ships out of the squadron of Vice-
admiral Grandallana; and that then, joining himself to the
remainder of the latter's ships, and to the Rochefort squadron,
he was to proceed off Cadiz, and enable the squadron from
Carthagena to enter that port. With his powerful fleet,
M. Villeneuve was next to occupy the Straits of Gibraltar, strip
the road of its shipping, and (a feasible plan, indeed!) the town
of its stores and provisions. Having effected all this, he was to
steer for the Channel, and endeavour to perform the last, and,
in Napoleon's estimation, the only important, article in his instructions.[1]

[1] Precis des Evènemens, tome xi., p. 254.

The first step taken by M. Villeneuve on reaching Vigo, was to despatch a courier to Ferrol, as well to apprise the two rear-admirals of his arrival, as to be put in possession of any fresh instructions which they might have to communicate. Meanwhile the French admiral proceeded to disembark his sick and wounded, also the prisoners made on the voyage. M. Villeneuve then took on board a supply of water, and, as may be supposed (for it is not acknowledged), commenced refitting his ships. The French, indeed, were sedulous in concealing the state of their ships; but the Spaniards on shore gave out, that the Terrible, America, and Espana, the two last especially, were considerably damaged; and a neutral merchant-master, who rowed round the ships in the harbour, declared that the larboard or engaged side of the Atlas was like a riddle, and that, in the hulls of the two last-named Spanish ships, innumerable shot-holes were visible.

On the 29th or 30th the courier returned, if not with any additional instructions, with the important intelligence, that on the 28th, the day of his departure, no British ships were in sight from Ferrol or Corunna. No time was to be lost. Accordingly, on the 30th of July, leaving behind him the America, Espana, and Atlas, not because they or any one of them had been so battered in the action of the 22nd as to render them for the present ineffective ships, but simply because they were "slow sailers" and might "delay the progress of the fleet," M. Villeneuve, with 13 French and two Spanish sail of the line, seven frigates, and two brigs, got under way, and steered for Corunna; with a wind blowing from west-south-west, so fair, and at the same time so strong, that even a slow-sailing merchantman, much more a slow-sailing man-of-war, would have found no difficulty in keeping company. On the evening of the very day, the 1st of August, on the morning of which the British fleet, which had so recently arrived off the port, was driven from its station, the combined fleet entered Corunna.

Learning, while at this anchorage, that the Rochefort squadron was at sea in search of him, M. Villeneuve, on the 5th, despatched the Didon frigate to endeavour to find M. Allemand, and enable him to join. On the 9th, in the evening, the combined fleet, the French part of which consisted, besides the whole of the ships named at page 358, except the Atlas, of the 74s Argonaute, Duguay-Trouin, Fougueux, Héros, and Redoutable, and the Spanish part, of the Principe-de-Asturias, three-decker, 80s

Argonauta and Neptuno, 74s Terrible, Monarca, Montanez, San-Augustin, San-Francisco de Asis, San-Ildefonso, and San-Juan-Nepomuceno, and 64 San-Fulgencio, making altogether 29 ships of the line, exclusive of frigates and corvettes, weighed and made sail from Ferrol and Corunna; but, the wind being scant, M. Villeneuve, on the 10th, anchored at Zerez, a small port near Ferrol. On the following day, the 11th, the fleet again weighed, and, with a fine easterly wind, got out to sea.

With respect to M. Villeneuve's real destination after quitting Ferrol, not a word, beyond conjecture, appears in any French naval history. The course steered by the combined fleet, when, on the afternoon of the 13th, the British 12-pounder 32-gun frigate Iris, Captain Edward Brace, fell in with it abreast of Cape Ortugal, was about west-north-west; which, with the wind at east, evinced an intention on the part of the French admiral, as soon as he had joined M. Allemand's squadron, then supposed to be (and really) hovering about the coast, to carry his 34 sail of the line straight to the British Channel. On the 14th the wind shifted to north-east; and at 2 P.M. the advanced French ship, which had been chasing the Iris since 6 P.M. on the preceding day, quitted her and bore up for the combined fleet. At 4 h. 30 m. P.M. not a ship of that fleet was to be seen from the Iris, then in company with the 38-gun frigate Naïad, Captain Thomas Dundas. On this very day, the 14th, the Rochefort squadron was spoken by an American ship, within two degrees north-east of Cape Ortugal, namely, in latitude 46° 18′ north, and longitude 9° west from Greenwich. In two days afterwards M. Allemand anchored in Vigo bay, but did not, it appears, find any instructions left there by M. Villeneuve for his future guidance.

About half an hour before the combined fleet lost sight of the British frigates Naïad and Iris to windward, the British 74-gun ship Dragon, accompanied by the 36-gun frigate Phœnix, Captain Thomas Baker, having in tow her prize the late French frigate Didon, both much disabled, hove in sight to leeward. One of the French advanced frigates was then speaking a Danish ship, from Lisbon to the Baltic, which had that morning been boarded by the Dragon, and by the latter been informed, that 25 British sail of the line were near her. On gaining this important information from the Dane, the effect of which the Dragon took care to strengthen by firing guns and hoisting signals, the French frigate made several signals, and then tacked towards her fleet; which, when last seen by the Dragon, at about sunset, was steering north-west. Shortly after this, it is believed, M. Villeneuve altered his course and steered to the southward. That M. Villeneuve first steered a north-west, and then a south course, is indeed admitted by a French writer. "Il mit à la voile le 13 par un bon vent d'est, n'ayant en vue aucune force ennemie; il fit d'abord route au nord-ouest, et changeant tout à coup de direction, il mit le cap au sud, longea hors de vue la côte de Portugal, attéra six jours après sur le Cap St. Vincent, où il s'empara de quelques bâtimens marchands, et entra à Cadix le 21 août, le jour même qu'il était attendu à Brest."[1] The dates in this account are wrong: those given by us have their correctness proved by the roles d'équipage of several of the ships belonging to M. Villeneuve's fleet.

Keeping out of sight of the Portuguese coast, the combined fleet, on the 18th, arrived off Cape St. Vincent, and there captured and burnt three merchantmen, bound from Gibraltar to Lisbon, under convoy of the British 16-gun brig-sloop Halcyon, which vessel, however, managed to effect her escape. On the 20th, at 10 A.M., Cadiz bearing north-east distant about nine leagues, the combined fleet, steering south-east, with the wind at west-south-west, discovered three British sail of the line right ahead. At 1 P.M. the latter, which were the 98-gun ship Dreadnought, Vice-admiral Cuthbert Collingwood, Captain Edward Rotheram, and 74s Colossus and Achille, Captains James Nicholl Morris and Richard King, tacked to reconnoitre. On this, the advanced ships of the combined fleet, which had shortened sail, chased away the British to the southward; and at 3 P.M. M. Villeneuve and his whole fleet bore up for the harbour of Cadiz. At midnight, having been joined by the 74-gun ship Mars, Captain George Duff, from Tangier bay, Vice-admiral Collingwood, with his four sail of the line, tacked inshore, and, before daylight on the 21st, gallantly resumed his station off an enemy's port, in which lay, ready for sea, including six Spanish ships previously at anchor in the harbour, 35 French and Spanish sail of the line. A seventh Spanish ship, the Glorioso 74, had formed part of Rear-admiral Alava's squadron; but, on the 31st of the preceding May, this ship, finding that a frigate and two brigs were the only British force off Cadiz, put to sea, and, after exchanging a few ineffectual broadsides with the frigate, which was the Lively, Captain Graham Eden Hamond, effected her escape into Carthagena.

As soon as he was apprised of the battle between Sir Robert

[1] Précis des Evénemens, tome xii., p. 71.

Calder and M. Villeneuve, Napoleon directed his minister of marine to impress upon the latter, how highly dishonourable it would be to the imperial fleets, that a three hours' skirmish, and an action with 14 (a singular admission for Buonaparte to make) sail of the line, "qu'une échauffourée de trois heures et un engagement avec quatorze vaisseaux," should defeat the grand plan. For some days after M. Villeneuve had sailed from Ferrol, Napoleon, ignorant of the circumstance, betrayed the utmost impatience for his departure. He asks if, with 28 or 30 French and Spanish sail of the line, the French admiral would allow himself to be blockaded by 13, or even by 20, English sail of the line. The emperor directs that, if less than 23 of the latter are before Ferrol, M. Villeneuve is to sail out and attack them; and that, if Allemand joins with his five, making "35 sail of the line," he is not to be stopped by less than 29 English sail of the line.

M. Villeneuve, in short, is always to attack, when he is superior in numbers, counting two Spanish ships for one, "ne comptant deux vaisseaux espagnols que pour un," and making some allowance for the three-deckers in the British fleet. This was paying a sorry compliment to the Spaniards, and is hardly reconcilable with Napoleon's declaration, made in another letter of the same date (August 13), and equally meant to be private, that the Spaniards had "fought like lions."[1] Finally, the French admiral is to save the imperial flag from the shame of being blockaded at Ferrol by an inferior force; that is, he is to save 18 French, and "12" Spanish sail of the line, 30 in all, from the shame of being blockaded by less than 24 British sail of the line, the number which, in Napoleon's estimation, equalizes the two forces.[2] The same letter authorizes M. Villeneuve, if he should think fit, to man the frigates Guerrière and Revanche, lying at Corunna, with the officers and crew of the Atlas, left at Vigo. He is also at liberty to disembark all his troops, except as many as he thinks will be serviceable on board the fleet.

On some day between the 22nd of August and the 4th of September, Napoleon first became apprised of the Franco-Spanish fleet's arrival at Cadiz. If he had previously condemned M. Villeneuve because, in spite of wind and weather, he did not sail from Ferrol, what must he have thought of the latter, now that, instead of going straight to Brest, he had suddenly changed his route and sailed for Cadiz? Some of Napoleon's expressions are very severe. "Villeneuve," he says, "est un de ces hommes

---

[1] See p. 370.   [2] Précis des Evènemens, tome xii., pp. 246, 249, 250, 254.

qui ont plutôt besoin d'éperon que de bride." Again, he asks, "Ne sera-t-il donc pas possible de trouver dans la marine un homme entreprenant, qui voit de sang froid, et comme il faut voir, soit dans le combat, soit dans les différentes combinaisons des escadres?"[1]

The French emperor's sentiments will be found fully developed in the following set of charges which he is represented to have drawn up with his own hand: "First; he (Villeneuve) did not disembark at Martinique and Guadaloupe the 67th regiment and the troops that Admiral Magon had on board. Secondly; he placed these colonies in jeopardy by sending back to them, by four frigates, 1200 men only of the pick of the garrisons. Thirdly; he conducted himself ill in the battle of the 23rd of July, in not re-engaging a disabled fleet which had two ships in tow. Fourthly; that, having arrived at Ferrol, he left the sea to Admiral Calder, while he waited to be joined by five sail of the line, and did not cruise off Ferrol until that squadron arrived. Fifthly; he (Villeneuve) was informed that the fleet saw some enemy's ships having the Didon frigate in tow, but he did not chase those ships and oblige them to cast off the frigate. Sixthly; he departed from Ferrol the 14th of August,[2] and, instead of going to Brest, proceeded to Cadiz, thereby violating his positive instructions. Seventhly and finally; he knew that the squadron of M. Allemand was to go to Vigo for orders, and yet he sailed from Ferrol without giving that officer any new orders, having, on the contrary, sent him (by the Didon, it is probable) instructions quite opposite, and such as endangered the squadron, which received orders to repair to Brest, while Villeneuve himself steered for Cadiz."[3] In these charges two important facts disclose themselves: one, that M. Villeneuve, in spite of all the nonsense published in the Moniteur, did not, on the 23rd of July, attempt to bring to action Sir Robert Calder's fleet; the other, that something unexpected, and which, by a fair inference, was the false intelligence received through the Danish ship from the Dragon 74, caused the Franco-Spanish fleet to run from an English ship of the line and two disabled frigates, and subsequently to change its destination from Brest to Cadiz.

A part of Napoleon's vexation with M. Villeneuve arose, no doubt, from the dissatisfaction with which the Spaniards viewed the loss of their two ships. This was augmented by the apparent

[1] Précis des Evènemens, tome xii., p. 253.

[2] As to this and other dates, see p. 375.

[3] This extract is of too important a character not to be given in the original: it will therefore be found in the Appendix, at No. 35.

unwillingness of the French admiral, even though he had under him so powerful a fleet, to sail out, in the face of 11 English sail of the line cruising off Cadiz, and enable the Carthagena squadron to form a junction with Admiral Gravina. In a letter of September 17, Napoleon complains of M. Villeneuve for this, and directs his minister of marine to order out the latter, with the French ships alone ("mon escadre," not "les escadres franco-espagnols," or "la flotte combinée"), upon a new expedition. M. Villeneuve is to proceed off Naples, and disembark, at some point on the coast, all the troops on board the French ships, in order that they may join the army under General Saint-Cyr. He is then to capture the English ship of the line (Excellent 74) and Russian frigate cruising in the bay of Naples; to do all possible injury to the English; to intercept an expedition (Sir James Craig's) which Napoleon supposes to be destined for Malta, and then to enter Toulon; where M. Villeneuve was to find everything necessary for repairing and revictualling his ships. Part of the plan, if not previously accomplished, was to call at Genoa for the new 74 Génois; and then, with the Borée (launched at Toulon, June 26) and Annibal 74s, there would be a fleet of 21 sail of the line in Toulon. The emperor's brother Jérôme, who had been appointed to the 40-gun frigate Pomone, was also, with the assistance of the Borée, and of the Annibal, if the latter could be made serviceable, to do all possible mischief to the British in the Mediterranean.

But the most extraordinary part of this letter is Napoleon's apparent persuasion, that the "excessive pusillanimity" of M. Villeneuve would prevent him from undertaking the expedition. He therefore directs, that Vice-admiral Rosily be despatched to supersede M. Villeneuve in the command; and who is to carry out orders to the latter to return immediately to France, to render an account of his conduct. "J'estime donc," says Napoleon, "qu'il faut faire deux choses: 1°. Envoyer un courrier extraordinaire à l'amiral Villeneuve, pour lui prescrire de faire cette manœuvre; 2°. Comme son excessive pusillanimité l'empêchera de l'entreprendre, vous enverrez, pour le remplacer, l'amiral Rosilly, qui sera porteur de lettres qui enjoindront à l'amiral Villeneuve de se rendre en France pour rendre compte de sa conduite." [1]

Harsh and very unmerited was this treatment of M. Villeneuve. The main point in the French admiral's instructions had always been, to avoid an engagement, and to bring his fleet

[1] Précis des Evènemens, tome xii., p. 261.

fresh and entire into the English Channel.   Doubtless M. Villeneuve had, from the first, been much retarded in his proceedings
by the natural supineness of his Spanish friends ; and who, now
that they knew the object of all this voyaging to and fro, must
have felt less inclined than ever to co-operate with the French
admiral.

On the 22nd of August Vice-admiral Collingwood was reinforced by four sail of the line under Rear-admiral Sir Richard
Bickerton ; but who subsequently shifted his flag from the
Queen 98 to the Décade frigate, and proceeded to England for
the recovery of his health.   On the 30th Sir Robert Calder, last
from off Ferrol, where he had learnt that the combined fleet,
nine days previous, had made sail for Cadiz, joined with 18
line-of-battle ships.[1]   Some of these were occasionally detached
to Gibraltar for water and provisions ; and with the remainder
Vice-admiral Collingwood continued to cruise before Cadiz,
until the evening of the 28th of September, when Vice-admiral
Lord Nelson arrived, to take the chief command of the Mediterranean fleet.   His lordship had sailed from Portsmouth in
his old ship the Victory, on the morning of the 15th, accompanied by the Euryalus frigate.   On the 18th, when the two ships
were off Plymouth, the Ajax and Thunderer joined.   On the
26th Lord Nelson despatched the Euryalus ahead, to acquaint
Vice admiral Lord Collingwood with his approach, and to direct
that, on his assuming the command, no salute should be fired
nor colours hoisted, in order that the enemy might be unapprised of the arrival of a reinforcement.

The force now under Lord Nelson consisted of 27 sail of the
line, 22 of which cruised about 15 miles off Cadiz, while the
remaining five, under Rear-admiral Louis in the Canopus, were
stationed close off the harbour, to watch the motions of the
combined fleet.   Considering that, if he kept the main body of
his fleet out of sight of land, the French admiral, being ignorant
of the exact amount of the British force, might feel disposed to
put to sea, Lord Nelson retired to a distance of 16 to 18 leagues
west of Cadiz.   The force close off the harbour was now reduced to two frigates, the Euryalus and Hydra ; and it may here
be remarked that Lord Nelson was continually complaining, as
he had done in the preceding war, of the few frigates attached
to his command.   Beyond these two frigates, at convenient
intervals for distinguishing signals, were three or four sail of the
line, the westernmost of which could communicate directly with

[1] See p. 311.

the easternmost ship of the main body. The new station taken by the fleet possessed the additional advantage, that, in case the usually strong westerly gales should prevail, the danger was lessened of being forced into the Mediterranean; in which event the Franco-Spanish fleet, on the first change of wind, might easily effect its escape.

On the 1st of October the Euryalus frigate, Captain the Honourable Henry Blackwood, reconnoitred the port of Cadiz, and plainly discovered, at anchor in the outer harbour, and apparently ready for sea, 18 French and 16 Spanish sail of the line, four frigates, and two brigs. On the 2nd Lord Nelson detached Rear-admiral Louis, with the Canopus, Queen, Spencer, Tigre, and Zealous, of the line, to Gibraltar, for provisions and water. On the same day a Swedish ship from Cadiz, bound to Alicant, informed the Euryalus, that the combined fleet had re-embarked the troops on the 30th of September, and intended to put to sea the first easterly wind. This intelligence, meeting the rear-admiral on his way to the eastward, induced him, on the 3rd, to return with his squadron to the fleet; but Lord Nelson, conceiving the whole to be a stratagem to draw him nearer to Cadiz for the purpose of obtaining a more accurate knowledge of his force, ordered the rear-admiral to proceed in the execution of his orders.

On the 4th, twice in the course of the day, several Spanish gun-boats, taking advantage of the calm state of the weather, pulled out from Cadiz and attacked the Euryalus and Hydra; but, after the exchange of a few ineffectual shot, the former retired to the harbour's mouth. On the 7th the Defiance joined from England, and on the 8th the Leviathan from Gibraltar. On the same day, with the aid of a fine south-east wind and clear weather, the Euryalus was again enabled to count 34 sail of the line in Cadiz harbour. The proximity of the Euryalus to the entrance of the harbour may be judged by the frigate's bearings at the time she tacked to stand out. They were, Rota point north half-west, San-Sebastian south half-west distant two miles and a quarter.

The possibility that the Cadiz, Carthagena, and Rochefort ships might effect a junction, and thereby present a force of 46 sail of the line (a rumour indeed prevailed, that the Brest fleet was out, which, without the junction of the Carthagena and Rochefort squadrons, would have made the combined fleet 54 or 55 sail), induced Lord Nelson, on the 10th, to draw up and transmit to the flag-officers and captains of his fleet, a plan of

attack, in which, hourly expecting to be reinforced, particularly
by a squadron of fast-sailing two-deckers under Vice-admiral
Thornborough, he calculates, by anticipation, the strength of
his fleet at 40 sail of the line. As this plan, or "General
Memorandum," of which a translation appears in several French
historical works, is universally considered to be a complete
masterpiece of the kind; and particularly as it agrees in principle with that adopted in the great battle presently to be
detailed, we shall offer no apology for inserting it entire in these
pages.

"Thinking it almost impossible," says the noble chief, "to
form a fleet of 40 sail of the line into a line of battle, in variable
winds, thick weather, and other circumstances which must occur,
without such a loss of time, that the opportunity would probably
be lost of bringing the enemy to battle in such a manner as to
make the business decisive; I have therefore made up my mind
to keep the fleet in that position of sailing (with the exception
of the first and second in command), that the order of sailing is
to be the order of battle; placing the fleet in two lines of 16
ships each, with an advanced squadron of eight of the fastest
sailing two-decked ships: which will always make, if wanted,
a line of 24 sail, on whichever line the commander-in-chief may
direct. The second in command will, after my intentions are
made known to him, have the entire direction of his line, to make
the attack upon the enemy, and to follow up the blow until they
are captured or destroyed.

" If the enemy's fleet should be seen to windward in line of
battle, and that the two lines and the advancing squadron could
fetch them, they will probably be so extended that their van
could not succour their rear. I should therefore probably make
the second in command's signal, to lead through about the
twelfth ship from their rear, or wherever he could fetch, if not
able to get so far advanced. My line would lead through about
their centre; and the advanced squadron to cut two (cut
through?), three, or four ships ahead of their centre; so as to
insure getting at their commander-in-chief, whom every effort
must be made to capture. The whole impression of the British
fleet must be, to overpower two or three ships ahead of their
commander-in-chief (supposed to be in the centre) to the rear
of their fleet. I will suppose 20 sail of the enemy's line to be
untouched: it must be some time before they could perform a
manœuvre to bring their force compact to attack any part of the
British fleet engaged, or to succour their own ships; which

indeed would be impossible without mixing with the ships engaged. The enemy's fleet is supposed to consist of 46 sail of the line: British 40: if either is less, only a proportionate number of enemy's ships are to be cut off. British to be one-fourth superior to the enemy cut off. Something must be left to chance. Nothing is sure in a sea-fight: beyond all others, shot will carry away the masts and yards of friends as well as of foes; but I look with confidence to a victory before the van of the enemy could succour their rear; and then that the British fleet would, most of them, be ready to receive their 20 sail of the line, or to pursue them should they endeavour to make off. If the van of the enemy tack, the captured ships must run to leeward of the British fleet; if the enemy wear, the British must place themselves between the enemy and the captured, and disabled British ships; and should the enemy close, I have no fear for the result.

"The second in command will, in all possible things, direct the movements of his line, by keeping them as compact as the nature of the circumstances will admit. Captains are to look to their particular line, as their rallying point; but, in case signals cannot be seen or clearly understood, *no captain can do very wrong if he places his ship alongside that of an enemy.*

"Of the intended attack from to-windward, the enemy in the line of battle ready to receive an attack:

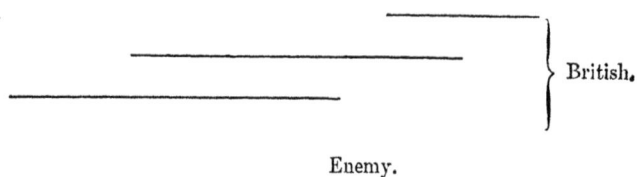

British.

Enemy.

"The divisions of the British fleet will be brought nearly within gun-shot of the enemy's centre. The signal will most probably then be made, for the lee line (three lines?) to bear up together; to set all their sails, even their steering-sails, in order to get as quickly as possible to the enemy's line, and to cut through, beginning at the twelfth ship from the enemy's rear. Some ships may not get through their exact place, but they will always be at hand to assist their friends. If any are thrown round the rear of the enemy, they will effectually complete the business of 12 sail of the enemy. Should the enemy wear together, or bear up and sail large, still the 12 ships, composing, in the first position, the enemy's rear, are to be the object of attack of the lee line, unless otherwise directed by the commander-in-chief: which is scarcely to be expected; as the entire management of the lee line, after the intentions of the commander-in-chief are signified, is intended to be left to the judgment of the admiral commanding that line. The remainder of the enemy's fleet, 34 sail of the line, are to be left to the management of the commander-in-chief, who will endeavour to take care that the movements of the second in command are as little interrupted as possible."

With the crews of so many ships to victual, Cadiz had become much straitened for provisions. To remedy the evil in part, especially as regarded his own fleet, the French emperor had ordered shipments to be made at Nantes, Bordeaux, and other ports in the bay of Biscay. The carriers were nominally Danish vessels, that landed their cargoes at Ayamonte, Conil, Algeziras, and at some other little harbours between the latter port and Santa-Maria, whence they were conveyed in coasting-boats to Cadiz without any interruption. As some check to this, a vigorous blockade had been adopted by Vice-admiral Collingwood, and was still maintained by his successor; who considered it a more likely mode to drive the combined fleet to sea than a bombardment by Congreve rockets, as had been contemplated by the British admiralty. The arrival of the Naïad, Phœbe, Sirius, Juno, and Niger frigates, with one or two smaller vessels, enabled Lord Nelson to detach a part of them; and the interruption thereby given to the coasting-trade was of increased annoyance to Cadiz and the shipping within it.

Between the 9th and 13th of October the Royal Sovereign, Belleisle, Africa, and Agamemnon joined the fleet. The British force off Cadiz was now at its greatest height, 29 sail of the line; and the whole force under Lord Nelson's command, including the five ships recently gone to Gibratar, amounted to 33 sail of the line. Since the 10th the Franco-Spanish fleet had moved to the entrance of the harbour, and evinced every disposition to put to sea the first opportunity. On the 14th Lord Nelson, as he had been directed, detached to England Sir Robert Calder, in the Prince of Wales, and on the 17th was obliged to send the Donegal to Gibraltar, to get a ground tier of casks. This done, the fleet under his lordship's immediate command consisted of the following 27 sail of the line, four frigates, one schooner, and one cutter :—

Gun-ship.

100	Victory . . .	{ Vice-admiral (w.) Lord Nelson, K.B. { Captain Thomas Masterman Hardy.
	Royal Sovereign .	{ Vice-admiral (b.) Cuthbert Collingwood. { Captain Edward Rotheram.
	Britannia . . .	{ Rear-admiral (w.) the Earl of Northesk. { Captain Charles Bullen.
98	Téméraire . . .	,, Eliab Harvey.
	Prince	,, Richard Grindall.
	Neptune	,, Thomas Francis Fremantle.
	Dreadnought . . .	,, John Conn.
80	Tonnant	,, Charles Tyler.
74	Belleisle	,, William Hargood.
	Revenge	,, Robert Moorsom.
	Mars	,, George Duff.
	Spartiate	,, Sir Francis Laforey, Bart.
	Defiance	,, Philip Charles Durham.
	Conqueror . . .	,, Israel Pellew.
	Defence	,, George Hope.
	Colossus	,, James Nicoll Morris.
	Leviathan	,, Henry William Bayntun.
	Achille	,, Richard King.
	Bellerophon . . .	,, John Cooke.
	Minotaur	,, Charles John Moore Mansfield.
	Orion	,, Edward Codrington.
	Swiftsure	,, William George Rutherford.
	Ajax	. Lieutenant John Pilfold, } acting.[1]
	Thunderer . . .	. ,, John Stockham, }
64	Polyphemus . .	. Captain Robert Redmill.
	Africa	,, Henry Digby.
	Agamemnon . . .	,, Sir Edward Berry.

Frigates, Euryalus, Naïad, Phœbe, and Sirius ; Captains the Hon. Henry Blackwood, Thomas Dundas, the Hon. Thomas Bladen Capel, and William Prowse.

Schooner, Pickle, Lieutenant John Richards Lapenotiere, and *cutter* Entreprenante, Lieutenant John Puver.

On the very day on which Lord Nelson arrived to take command of the Mediterranean fleet, arrived at Cadiz a courier, with the French emperor's orders for M. Villeneuve to put to sea. These orders, it may be recollected, had issued since the 17th of the preceding month, and required that the fleet should pass the Straits, land the troops on the Neapolitan coast, sweep the Mediterranean of all British commerce and cruisers, and enter the port of Toulon to refit and revictual.[2] Although in M. Villeneuve's instructions no mention is made of the Spanish fleet, it may naturally be supposed that the latter would desire

[1] For Captains William Brown and William Lechmere, gone to England to attend as witnesses on Sir Robert Calder's court-martial.
[2] See p. 378.

ADMIRAL VISCOUNT NELSON.

to take advantage of the exit of a formidable French fleet, to effect its junction with the seven sail of the line hitherto so closely blocked up in the port of Carthagena. That, indeed, would be but the return of a similar favour, granted nine years before to the French Rear-admiral Richery.[1] Every exertion was therefore made to fill up the complements of the six ships, which, in all other respects, had been ready for sea ever since Vice-admiral Villeneuve's arrival. Of the two that had been present in Sir Robert Calder's action, one, the Argonauta, had since been repaired and refitted; but the damage done to the other, the Terrible, proved of so serious a nature that she was disarmed, and her crew divided among the short-manned ships.

On the 9th or 10th of October, the French troops having re-embarked,[2] the Franco-Spanish fleet, with the exception of one ship, the San-Fulgencio 64 (for some unknown reason detained), moved to the entrance of the harbour, to be ready for a start at a moment's warning. From the 10th to the 17th hard gales from the westward continued to blow, with very slight inter-missions. On the 17th, at midnight, the wind shifted to the eastward; and on the 18th Admiral Villeneuve informed Admiral Gravina of his intention to put to sea on the following day. On the same evening, as a preparatory measure, a strong force of gun-boats drew up in line across the entrance of the harbour; and on the 19th, at 7 A.M., the Franco-Spanish fleet, by signal from the commander-in-chief, began getting under way, with a light breeze at north by east.

This and every other movement of the Franco-Spanish fleet was seen and reported by the British reconnoitring frigates. Owing to the lightness of the wind, 12 ships only succeeded in getting out, and these lay becalmed till early in the afternoon; when, a breeze springing from the west-north-west, the whole 12 stood to the northward on the larboard tack, accompanied, at the distance of not more than two or three miles to windward, by the British frigates Euryalus and Sirius. At 8 A.M. the wind, still very light, shifted to south-west, and the course of the ships became north-west by west: the point of San-Sebastian at this time bearing from the Euryalus east half-south distant about four miles. At daylight on the morning of the 20th the remainder of the combined fleet in Cadiz harbour, consisting, with the ships already outside, of 33 sail of the line, five frigates, and two brigs, weighed and put to sea with a light breeze at south-east while the ships in the offing, as was fre-

---

[1] See vol. i., p. 345.　　　　　[2] See p. 380.

quently the case on this coast, had the wind from the south-south-west. The French and Spanish ships composing this fleet were as follows :—

French.

Gun-ship.		
80	Bucentaure . .	{ Vice-admiral P.-Ch.-J.-B.-S. Villeneuve. { Captain Jean-Jacques Magendie.
	Formidable . .	{ Rear-admiral P.-R.-M.-E. Dumanoir-le-Pelley. { Captain Jean-Marie Letellier.
	Neptune . . .	. Commodore Esprit-Tranquille Maistral.
	Indomptable . .	. ,, Jean-Joseph Hubert.
74	Algésiras . . .	{ Rear-admiral Charles Magon. { Captain Gabriel-Auguste Brouard.
	Pluton . . .	. Commodore Julian-Marie Cosmao-Kerjulien.
	Mont-Blanc . .	. ,, Guill.-Jean-Noël La Villegris.
	Intrépide . . .	. ,, Louis-Antoine-Cyprien Infernet.
	Swiftsure . . .	. Captain C.-E.-L'Hospitalier-Villemadrin.
	Aigle	. ,, Pierre-Paul Gourrège.
	Scipion . . .	. ,, Charles Berenger.
	Duguay-Trouin .	. ,, Claude Touffet.
	Berwick . . .	. ,, Jean-Gilles Filhol-Camas.
	Argonaute. . .	. ,, Jacques Epron.
	Achille . . .	. ,, Gabriel Denieport.
	Redoutable . .	. ,, Jean-Jacques-Etienne Lucas.
	Fougueux . . .	. ,, Louis-Alexis Beaudouin.
	Héros	. ,, Jean-Bap.-Jos.-Remi Poulain.

Spanish.

Gun-ship.		
130	Santisima-Trinidad	{ Rear-admiral Don B. Hidalgo Cisneros. { Commodore Don Francisco de Uriarte.
112	Principe-de-Asturias	{ Admiral Don Frederico Gravina. { Rear-admiral Don Antonio Escano.
	Santa-Ana . .	{ Vice-admiral Don Ign. Maria de Alava. { Captain Don Josef Gardoqui.
100	Rayo	. Commodore Don Enrique Macdonel.
80	Neptuno . . .	. ,, Don Cayetano Valdés.
	Argonauta . .	. ,, Don Antonio Parejas.
74	Bahama . . .	. Captain Don Dionisio Galiano.
	Montanes . . .	. ,, Don Josef Salzedo.
	San-Augustin . .	. ,, Don Felipe Xado Cagigal.
	San-Ildefonso . .	. ,, Don Josef Bargas.
	S.-Juan-Nepomuceno .	,, Don Cosme Churruca.
	Monarca . . .	. ,, Don Teodoro Argumosa.
	S.-Francisco-de-Asis .	,, Don Luis de Flores.
	San-Justo . . .	. ,, Don Miguel Gaston.
64	San-Leandro . .	. ,, Don Josef Quevedo.

Frigates (all French), Cornélie, Hermione, Hortense, Rhin, Thémis; *brigs* Argus and Furet.

Scarcely had the Franco-Spanish fleet cleared the harbour, than the south-south-west wind, attended by thick weather,

began to baffle the ships in their progress. Meanwhile the
Euryalus and Sirius kept their stations, watching every manœuvre. At 8 h. 30 m. A.M. the Agamemnon with a heavy
merchant-brig in tow, was unconsciously running into the midst
of the enemy's ships; when, at length, after repeated signals,
enforced by guns from the Euryalus, the British 64 (but still
without casting off her deeply-laden prize) hauled to the wind
on the starboard tack and got clear. Although ordered by telegraph from the Euryalus, whose captain was senior to Sir
Edward Berry, to hasten to the British fleet, then to the southward of the former, with intelligence of the number and position of the enemy, the Agamemnon continued standing to the
north-west with her prize in tow. This seemed an unaccountable remissness on the part of Lord Nelson's favourite ship.

The Sirius was also in some danger. She had waited so long
for the return of her boat from an American vessel, that the
enemy's advanced ships found themselves near enough to chase
and fire at her; but the frigate, crowding sail, effected her
escape. Between 2 and 3 P.M. the horizon cleared, and the
wind shifted to west-north-west. Whereupon Vice-admiral
Villeneuve ordered his fleet to form in five columns, agreeably to
a plan which he had previously communicated to his flag-officers
and captains. The fleet accordingly divided itself into two
parts. The first part, consisting of 21 sail of the line, and
denominated the line of battle, then subdivided itself into three
squadrons of seven ships each; of which the centre was commanded by M. Villeneuve himself, the van by Vice-admiral Alava,
and the rear by Rear-admiral Dumanoir. The second part, or
corps de réserve, divided itself into two squadrons of six ships
each; the first was under the orders of Admiral Gravina, and
the second of Rear-admiral Magon.

At the time of communicating the foregoing plan of formation,
Admiral Villeneuve reminded his officers of the instructions he
had given to them previously to his quitting Toulon at the
commencement of the year.[1] In case of being to windward,
M. Villeneuve's directions then were, for the line to bear down
together, and each ship to take her opponent in the enemy's
line, whom she was to engage closely even to boarding. If, on
the contrary, the opposite fleet lay to windward, his fleet was to
wait the attack in close line of battle. "The enemy," says the
French admiral, "will not confine himself to forming a line of
battle parallel to ours, and engaging us with his cannon, where

1 See p. 366.

success often attends the most skilful, and always the most fortunate : he will endeavour to turn our rear, to pass through our
line, and, such of our ships as he may succeed in cutting off,
will endeavour to surround and reduce with clusters (pelotons)
of his own. In this case a captain would do better to trust to
his courage and ardour for glory, than to the signals of the
commander-in-chief; who, himself engaged and covered with
smoke, would perhaps be unable to make them."[1] " There is
nothing to alarm us," adds M. Villeneuve, " in the sight of an
English fleet; their 74-gun ships have not 500 men on board;
the seamen are harassed by a two years' cruise " (alluding to the
state of Lord Nelson's ships in January, 1805); " they are not
more brave than we are, they have infinitely fewer motives to
fight well, and possess less love of country. They are skilful at
manœuvring. In a month, we shall be as much so as they are.
In fine, everything unites to inspire us with hopes of the most
glorious success and of a new era for the imperial marine."[2]
The most remarkable feature in this plan is, that it persists in
ordering the movements to be conducted in close line of battle,
even while it admits that the enemy, in all likelihood, will adopt
a different mode of attack, that of cutting off the rear of the
line and making of it an easy conquest. Such, however, were
the ancient rules of naval tactics; and France did not yet
possess a Rodney or a Nelson to be the first to break through
them.

Shortly after the Franco-Spanish fleet had formed, as already
mentioned, in five columns, one of the advanced frigates made
the signal of 18 sail of British ships in sight. On this the combined fleet, still on the larboard tack, cleared for action, and at
about 5 P.M. tacked and stood towards the mouth of the Straits.
Shortly afterwards the four British frigates approached, and
were chased by the Argonauta, Achille, and a few other ships;
to which, as a reinforcement, and to serve also as a squadron
of observation, were added the Principe-de-Asturias, Aigle,
Algésiras, and San-Juan-Nepomuceno, under the command of
Admiral Gravina, with orders to reunite with the main body
before nightfall. At 7 h. 30 m. P.M. the Aigle made the signal
of 18 British ships in line of battle to the southward; and
shortly afterwards the combined fleet wore and stood to the
north-west.

A little before daybreak on the morning of the 21st, finding

[1] Victoires et Conquêtes, tome xvi., p.
109.   [2] For the original passages, see Appendix, No. 36.

that the British were to windward instead of to leeward, and that their force, instead of being only 21 sail of the line, was nearly equal to his own, the French admiral abandoned his plan of restricting his line of battle to 21 ships, and ordered the three columns composed of the latter, without regard to priority of rank among the ships, to form in close line of battle on the starboard tack, upon the leewardmost division, consisting of the 12 ships in advance under Admiral Gravina and Rear-admiral Magon, and to steer south-west.

The order in which the French and Spanish ships (the latter we have distinguished by italics) ranged themselves, beginning at the van, or south-east extremity of the line, was, according to a credible French account,[2] as follows :—*Principe-de-Asturias*, Achille, *San-Ildefonso*, *San-Juan-Nepomuceno*, Berwick, *Argonauta*, *Montanez*, Argonaute, Swiftsure, Aigle, *Bahama*, Algésiras, Pluton, *Monarca*, Fougueux, *Santa-Ana*, Indomptable, *San-Justo*, Redoubtable, *San-Leandro*, Neptune, Bucentaure, *Santisima-Trinidad*, Héros, *San-Augustin*, *San-Francisco-de-Asis*, Mont-Blanc, Duguay-Trouin, Formidable, *Rayo*, Intrepide, Scipion, *Neptuno;* extending over a space, admitting a cable's length, or 200 yards, to be betwixt each ship, of nearly five miles.

This manœuvre executed, daylight found the two hostile fleets at the distance apart of not more than 10 or 12 miles, and therefore fairly in each other's sight. The centre of the Franco-Spanish fleet at this time bore about east by south of the centre of the British fleet, and the wind was a light breeze from west-north-west, accompanied by a heavy westerly swell.

It was on the 19th, at 9 h. 30 m. A.M., while the British fleet was lying to about 16 leagues west-south-west from Cadiz, that the Mars, who, with the Defence and Agamemnon, then formed the cordon of communication between the Euryalus and Victory, repeated the signal, that the enemy was coming out of port. Lord Nelson immediately made sail in chase to the south-east, with light and partial breezes, mostly from the south-south-west. At 3 P.M. the Colossus repeated the signal, that the enemy was at sea. Towards evening Lord Nelson directed that the fleet should observe the motions of the Victory during the night ; that the Britannia, Dreadnought, and Prince, being heavy sailers, should take their stations as most convenient to them ; and that the Mars, Orion, Belleisle, Leviathan, Bellerophon, and Polyphemus should proceed ahead, carry a light, and steer for the Straits' mouth.

1 See preceding page.   2 See Précis des Evènemens, tome xiii., p. 187

On the 20th, at daybreak, the British found themselves near the entrance of the Straits, but saw nothing of the enemy. The fleet thereupon wore, and made sail to the north-west, with a fresh breeze at south-south-west. At 7 A.M. the Phœbe made the signal that the enemy bore north; and by noon the Victory and fleet were to the south-west of Cadiz, and within eight or nine leagues of it, standing to the west-north-west on the larboard tack. At 2 P.M. the fleet was taken aback by a breeze from the west-north-west, and at 4 P.M. wore and again came to on the larboard tack, steering north. At 5 P.M., just after the Euryalus had telegraphed that the enemy appeared determined to go to the westward, the Victory telegraphed, that Lord Nelson relied upon Captain Blackwood's keeping sight of the enemy during the night; and the Naïad, shortly afterwards, made the signal of 31 sail of the enemy, bearing north-north-east. At 8 h. 40 m. P.M. the British fleet wore and stood to the south-west; and at 4 A.M. on the 21st the fleet wore again, and steered, under easy sail, north by east. At 6 A.M., Cape Trafalgar bearing east by south distant about seven leagues, the Victory and ships with her obtained a sight of the combined fleet, also bearing about east by south, and distant, as already mentioned, 10 or 12 miles.

At 6 h. 40 m. A.M. the Victory made the signals (Nos. 72 and 13), to form the order of sailing in two columns, and to prepare for battle; and in 10 minutes afterwards, the signal No. 76, to bear up. The two columns of the British fleet accordingly bore up to the eastward under all sail. This prompt mode of attack was that which Lord Nelson had previously directed,[1] in order to avoid the inconvenience and delay of forming a line of battle in the usual manner.

The near approach of the British fleet rendering an action unavoidable, the French admiral, at 8 h. 30 m. A.M., made the signal for his ships to wear together, and form the line in close order upon the larboard tack; thereby to bring Cadiz on his lee bow, and to facilitate, if necessary, his escape to that port. It was near 10 A.M. before the manœuvre was completed; and then owing to the lightness of the wind, the partial flaws from off the land, the heavy ground-swell, and the incapacity or inexperience of some of the captains, the Franco-Spanish line was very irregularly formed: so much so that, instead of being straight, it was curved or crescent-like; and, instead of the ships being in line ahead, some were to leeward, others to windward, of

[1] See p. 380

their proper stations. For the most part, indeed, the ships were two, and in a few cases three, deep ; thus accidentally presenting more obstacles to the success of the plan of attack decided upon by the British admiral, than if each French and Spanish ship had been in the wake of her leader. The ships, generally, were under topsails and topgallant-sails, with the main topsail shivering, and lay a point, or rather more, off the wind.

Owing to the lightness of the breeze, the British fleet, after bearing up, made very slow progress, scarcely going, with studding-sails set, three knots an hour. While thus gradually nearing the enemy's line, Lord Nelson, dressed in the same threadbare frock uniform-coat which was his constant wear, having for its appendages, sewed amidst the folds of the left breast, the same four weather-tarnished and lack-lustre stars always to be seen there, visited the different decks of the Victory ; and addressing the men at their quarters, cautioned them not to fire a single shot without being sure of their object.

Considering that the Victory, both as being the van-ship of a column and as bearing the flag of the commander-in-chief, would draw upon himself the whole weight of the enemy's fire, and thereby doubly endanger the life of him to whom all looked up for the success of the day, the principal officers present expressed among themselves a hope that Lord Nelson might be persuaded to allow the Téméraire, then close astern, to go ahead. Captain Blackwood undertook the delicate task of broaching the matter to the admiral. He did so ; and Lord Nelson smiling significantly at Captain Hardy, replied, " Oh! yes, let her go ahead ;" meaning, if she could. At about 9 h. 40 m. A.M. the Téméraire was accordingly hailed,[1] to take her station ahead of the Victory. At about the same time Lieutenant John Yule, who then commanded upon the forecastle, observing that the lee or starboard lower studding-sail was improperly set, caused it to be taken in for the purpose of setting it afresh. The instant this was done, Lord Nelson ran forward, and rated the lieutenant severely for having, as he supposed, begun to shorten sail without the captain's orders. The studding-sail was quickly replaced ; and the Victory, as the gallant chief intended, continued to lead the column.[2]

[1] But not, it is believed, as stated in a popular little work, "by his lordship." See Authentic Narrative of the Death of Lord Nelson, by William Beatty, M.D., &c., p. 89.

[2] When the Tréméraire ranged up on the Victory's quarter in order to pass her and lead, Lord Nelson hailed her; and speaking, as he always did, with a slight nasal intonation, said, "I'll thank you, Captain Harvey, to keep in your proper station, which is *astern* of the Victory."—ED.

Shortly after this fruitless attempt to induce Lord Nelson to yield the post of danger, the captains of frigates were ordered back to their ships; and Captain Blackwood, in his way to the Euryalus, called on board the Téméraire, and explained, what appears to have been but indistinctly heard, the object of the previous hail. Some time after quitting the Téméraire, Captain Blackwood boarded the Leviathan, then the fifth ship of the weather-column, and acquainted her captain, that it was the commander-in-chief's wish, that the Leviathan, as a previous signal had signified, should fall into the line between the Téméraire and Victory. From the known zeal of Captains Harvey and Bayntun, no doubt can exist as to the earnestness of their endeavours to reach the honourable stations assigned them; but the Téméraire was unable to do so from the causes already assigned, and the Leviathan did not receive the message by Captain Blackwood until the head of the column was too near the enemy to render any change proper or even practicable.

The direction in which the combined fleet now lay, with a home-port scarcely seven leagues off on the lee-bow, and the evident forging ahead of the ships, whereby that distance was every minute diminishing, induced Lord Nelson to steer a trifle more to the northward, and to telegraph his second in command, "I intend to pass through the van of the enemy's line, to prevent him from getting into Cadiz." The reversed order of that line, in the prevailing state of the wind, had produced another danger to be guarded against : it had brought the shoals of San-Pedro and Trafalgar under the lee of both fleets. Accordingly, at 11 h. 30 m. A.M., the Victory made the signal (No. 63, with the preparative), for the British fleet to prepare to anchor at the close of day.

This done, no other signal seemed wanting, when Lord Nelson remarked, that he must give the fleet something by way of a fillip. After musing awhile, he said, "Suppose we telegraph that 'Nelson expects every man to do his duty.'" The officer, whom he was then addressing, suggested whether it would not be better, "England expects," &c. Lord Nelson rapturously exclaimed, "Certainly, certainly!" and, at about 11 h. 40 m. A.M., up went to the Victory's mizen topgallantmast-head, the first flag of the celebrated telegraphic message, "ENGLAND EXPECTS THAT EVERY MAN WILL DO HIS DUTY;"[1] a signal which,

[1] There is not, that we are aware of, a single publication which gives this message precisely as it was delivered. The following is a minute of the several flags, as noted down on board of more than one ship in the fleet :—

the instant its signification became fully known, was greeted with three cheers on board of every ship in the fleet, and excited among both officers and men the most lively enthusiasm.

The general formation of the Franco-Spanish line, and the manner in which the British fleet, by its two columns, bore down to the attack, will appear with sufficient and, we believe, all attainable accuracy, by the following diagram. As the ships

of the combined fleet were constantly varying their positions, we shall not attempt to point out the stations of any others than the ships of the four principal flag-officers. The commander-in-chief in the Bucentaure, with the Santisima-Trinidad as his second ahead, was directly in front of the Victory, the leader of the weather-column; and the Santa-Ana, the flag-ship of Vice-

---

253   269   863   261   471 958 220 370 4 21 19 24
"England expects that every man will do his d u t y."
The French translation, as given in one   and expressive:—"L'Angleterre compte
or two historical works, is equally short   que chacun fera son devoir."

admiral Alava, was in the same direction from the Royal
Sovereign, the leader of the lee column. The Spanish commander-in-chief, Admiral Gravina, in the Principe-de-Asturias,
was the rearmost ship of the fleet. Of the frigates it may
suffice to state, that they were ranged in an inner line considerably to leeward of the fighting line. One, however, in the
centre, believed to have been the Rhin, was so near as to be
seen by the Royal Sovereign repeating signals ; a circumstance
that induced Vice-admiral Collingwood, a few minutes before
the action commenced, to telegraph Lord Nelson, that the
enemy's commander-in-chief was on board a frigate.

According to the average time noted down on board the different ships of the British fleet, it was just at noon, the wind
very light, the sea smooth with a great ground-swell setting
from the westward, and the sun shining, in a beautiful manner,
upon the fresh-painted sides of the long line of French and
Spanish ships, that the Fougueux, the second astern of the
Santa-Ana, whose station was a little abaft the centre of the
combined line, opened by signal a fire upon the Royal Sovereign,
then bearing on the French ship's larboard bow, and considerably within gun-shot ; also bearing from the Victory south-
east, distant about two miles, and from her own second astern,
the Belleisle, about west by south three-quarters of a mile.
Immediately the three British admirals hoisted their respective
flags, and the ships of both divisions of the fleet, the white
or St. George's ensign ; a measure adopted to prevent any confusion in the heat of battle, from a variety of national flags.
As an additional mark of distinction, each British ship carried,
or was ordered to carry, a union-jack at her maintopmast-stay,
and another at her foretopgallant-stay. At the Victory's maintopgallantmast-head, also, was fast belayed Lord Nelson's
customary signal on going into action, No. 16, " Engage the
enemy more closely ;" consisting of two flags, quarter red and
white over blue, white, and red, or the Dutch republican ensign
reversed. At about the same time that the firing commenced,
the ships of the combined fleet hoisted their ensigns, and the
admirals (with the exception, to which we shall presently
advert, of the French commander-in-chief) their flags. In
addition to her ensign, every Spanish ship also hung to the end
of the spanker-boom a large wooden cross.

At about 10 minutes past noon, having reached a position
close astern of the Santa-Ana, the Royal Sovereign fired into
her, with guns double-shotted ; and with such precision as, by

the subsequent acknowledgment of the Spanish officers, to kill or wound (incredible as it may appear) nearly 400 of her crew, and to disable 14 of her guns. With her starboard broadside, similarly charged, the Royal Sovereign raked the Fougueux, but, owing to the distance and the smoke, with little if any effect. It was just as the Royal Sovereign was passing between these two enemy's ships, that Vice-admiral Collingwood called out to his captain: " Rotherham, what would Nelson give to be here !" And, by a singular coincidence, Lord Nelson, the moment he saw his friend in his enviable position, exclaimed : " See how that noble fellow Cóllingwood carries his ship into action."

Having, in the most gallant manner, passed under the stern of and saluted the Santa-Ana in the way already mentioned, the Royal Sovereign put her helm a-starboard, and, without any difficulty, ranged close alongside of her ; so close that the guns were nearly muzzle to muzzle. Between the two three-deckers a tremendous cannonade ensued. But the Royal Sovereign soon found that she had more than one opponent to contend with. The Fougueux, having bore up, raked her astern ; and, ahead of the English ship, at the distance of about 400 yards, lay the San-Leandro, who, wearing, raked her in that direction ; while, upon the Royal Sovereign's starboard bow and quarter, within less than 300 yards, were the San-Justo and Indomptable ; as will better appear by the following diagram :—

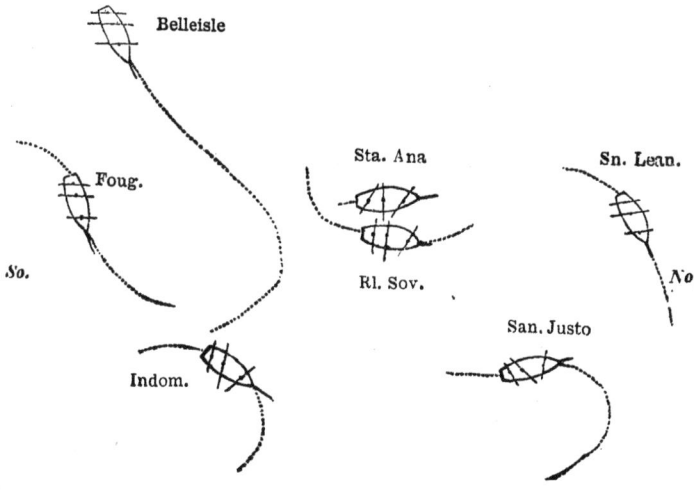

So incessant was the fire kept up by all these ships, that the people of the Royal Sovereign frequently saw the shots come in contact with each other. Aware, at length, of the injury which they were thus sustaining by their own cross fire, and observing that three or four British ships were fast approaching to the support of their gallant leader, the four two-deckers, one by one, drew off from the Royal Sovereign, and left her to combat solely with the Santa-Ana; who, although in force rather more than a match for her antagonist, began already to exhibit proofs that, in practical gunnery, she was decidedly her inferior.

For upwards of 15 minutes the Royal Sovereign was the only British ship in close action. At the end of that time, when the former had taken a position upon her opponent's lee bow, and was making the best possible use of it, the Belleisle, hauling up, fired a broadside into the lee quarter of the Santa-Ana, and then bore away towards the Indomptable. Owing to some of the ships astern of the Fougueux pressing forward to support the centre, while others remained with their sails aback or shivering, the Franco-Spanish line (if line we must call it) was becoming even more irregular than it had been. The slanting direction in which, on account of this movement, the British lee column was obliged to advance, enabled the ships to discharge their starboard guns at the enemy's rear; and an interchange of animated firing ensued, the smoke from which, for the want of a breeze to carry it off, spread its murky mantle over the combatants, and increased the confusion into which the rear of the combined fleet had already been thrown by the crash at its centre.

Lord Nelson had already, in a two-decker, evinced how little he dreaded coming in contact with a Spanish first-rate; and even the towering and formidable-looking four-decker at present in front of him had, on that very occasion, been driven from her purpose by his well-known prowess. But, although he directed the Victory to be steered towards the bow of his old opponent, it was not with the intention of attacking her: a Spanish rear-admiral, whatever the force of his ship, was considered an unworthy object while a French vice-admiral commanded the fleet. Lord Nelson did not feel a doubt, and the sequel proved he was correct, that M. Villeneuve was in one of the two or three ships next astern of the four-decker; and, knowing that to fetch a ship lying to at a distance ahead, he must keep her on his lee bow, he ordered the Victory to be steered in the manner just related.

Although every glass on board the Victory was put in requisition to discover the flag of the French commander-in-chief, all the answers to the repeated questions of Lord Nelson on the subject ended in disappointment. The four-decker's flag at the mizen could be made out, and some signals were occasionally seen at the main of two or three of the ships, but no French flag at the fore.[1] Often did the little man himself, with his remaining eye, cast an anxious glance towards the Franco-Spanish line in search of the ship which he meant the Victory first to grapple with; and so lightly did Lord Nelson value personal risk, that, although urged more than once on the subject, he would not suffer those barriers from the enemy's grape and musketry, the hammocks, to be placed one inch higher than—to facilitate his view of objects around him—they were accustomed to be stowed. The Victory, meanwhile, was slowly advancing to a gun-shot distance from the enemy's line.

At 20 minutes past noon, which was about 20 minutes after the Fougueux had opened her fire upon the Royal Sovereign, and about 10 after the latter had passed under the stern of the Santa-Ana, the Bucentaure fired a shot at the Victory, then, with studding-sails set on both sides, steering about east and going scarcely a knot and a half through the water. The shot fell short. Two or three minutes elapsed, and a second shot was fired; which, the Victory then about a mile and a quarter distant, fell alongside. A third shot almost immediately followed, and that went over the ship. One or two others did the same, until, at length, a shot went through the Victory's maintop-gallant-sail; affording to the enemy the first visible proof that his shot would reach. A minute or two of awful silence ensued; and then, as if by signal from the French admiral, the whole van, or at least seven or eight of the weathermost ships, opened a fire upon the Victory, such a fire as had scarcely before been directed at a single ship. In a few minutes a round shot killed Mr. John Scott, Lord Nelson's public secretary, while he was conversing with Captain Hardy.

Since the commencement of the firing the wind had gradually died away to a mere breath. Still the Victory, driven onward by the swell and the remains of her previous impetus, was going slowly ahead in the direction now of the interval between the Santisima-Trinidad and Bucentaure; both of which ships, aided

[1] It was probably signals, made when the Victory was much closer, that gave rise to the following entry in the log of the Spartiate:—"Observed her bearing down between a Spanish four-decker and a French two-decker, with admiral's flags at the main."

occasionally by the Redoutable astern of the latter, continued upon her a very heavy and destructive fire. To this heavy and unremitting cannonade the Victory neither did, nor from her position could, bestow any return. In a very few minutes, however, after the firing had opened upon her, one of the foremost guns on the starboard side went off by accident. In a private ship this would scarcely have been noticed; but, as happening on board the ship of the commander-in-chief, it excited the attention of the fleet, and was minuted down in the log of one ship, the Polyphemus, as a real commencement of the action by the Victory; thus: " About 20 m. past 12, Victory fired upon by the enemy's van, which was returned with a few of her foremost guns on the starboard side."

Seeing, by the direction of her course, that the Victory was about to follow the example of the Royal Sovereign, the French and Spanish ships ahead of the British weather-column closed like a forest. This movement, headed by the stoppage in the headway of the Santa-Ana, and by the bearing up of the two Spanish ships ahead of her in the manner already related, divided the combined line nearly in the centre, leaving, including the Redoutable from her station astern of the San-Leandro, 14 ships in the van, and 19 in the rear, with an interval between them of at least three-quarters of a mile.

Just as she had got within about 500 yards of the larboard-beam of the Bucentaure the Victory's mizentopmast was shot away about two-thirds up. A shot also struck and knocked to pieces the wheel; and the ship was obliged to be steered in the gun-room, the first-lieutenant (John Quilliam) and master (Thomas Atkinson) relieving each other at this duty. Scarcely had two minutes elapsed before a double-headed shot killed eight marines on the poop, and wounded several others; on which the admiral ordered Captain Adair to disperse his men round the ship, that they might not suffer so much from being together. Presently a shot, that had come through a thickness of four hammocks near the larboard chess-tree, and had carried away a part of the larboard-quarter of the launch as she lay on the booms, struck the fore-brace bits on the quarter-deck, and passed between Lord Nelson and Captain Hardy; a splinter from the bits bruising the left foot of the latter, and tearing the buckle from his shoe. "They both," says Doctor Beatty, "instantly stopped, and were observed by the officers on deck to survey each other with inquiring looks, each supposing the other to be wounded. His lordship then smiled and said,

'This is too warm work, Hardy, to last long;' and declared that, through all the battles he had been in, he had never witnessed more cool courage than was displayed by the Victory's crew on this occasion."[1]

In a few seconds afterwards, as the Bucentaure slowly forged ahead, a large French ship was seen upon her lee-quarter, and another ship astern of the former, in the act of ranging up, as if with the intention of completely closing the interval. Now it was that Captain Hardy represented to Lord Nelson the impracticablity of passing through the line without running on board one of the ships. His lordship quickly replied, "I cannot help it: it does not signify which we run on board of. Go on board which you please : take your choice."[2] At this moment, such had been the effect of the heavy and unremitting fire to which she had so long been exposed, the loss on board the Victory amounted to 20 officers and men killed, and 30 wounded ; a loss that would have been still more severe had not the enemy's guns been pointed at the rigging and sails, rather than at the hull of the ship. In consequence of this, every studding-sail boom on the foremast (the Victory, unlike other ships, had no booms rigged out upon her mainmast) had been shot off close to the yard arm, and every sail, especially on the foremast, was like a riddle : her almost new foresail, indeed, had from 80 to 100 yards of it stripped from the yard. This clearly shows what an advantage the centre and rear had lost in not having opened an earlier fire upon the Royal Sovereign. "Quel but avantageux," says a French writer, " offraient aux canonniers ces deux groupes de vaisseaux, dont chacun présentait une quantité de mâts et de vergues et une masse de cordages et de voiles, où pas un boulet ne devait être perdu."[3]

At 1 P.M.[4] the 68-pounder carronade on the larboard side of the Victory's forecastle, containing its customary charge of one round shot and a keg filled with 500 musket-balls, was fired right into the cabin windows of the Bucentaure. As the Victory slowly moved ahead, every gun of the remaining 50 upon her broadside, all double, and some of them treble shotted, was

---

[1] Beatty's Narrative, p. 27.
[2] Ibid., p. 30.
[3] Victoires et Conquêtes, tome xvi., p. 170.
[4] According to the Victory's log, at four minutes past noon; but that would allow fourteen minutes only for the Victory, with scarcely a breath of wind, to go a distance of at least a mile and a half. We know also that, owing to the death early in the action of the two persons whose places (in succession) it was to take minutes, the log entries were written the next day. Moreover, the log of the Spartiate, one of the best kept in the fleet, says: — "At 12 h. 59 m. Victory commenced firing."

deliberately discharged in the same raking manner. So close were the ships, that the larboard main yard-arm of the British three-decker, as she rolled, touched the vangs of her opponent's gaff: so close, indeed, that had there been wind enough to blow it out, the large French ensign trailing at the Bucertaure's peak might, even at this early period of the action, have been a trophy

Eng.   Nept.

I P.M.   *I h.* [10] *m. P.M.*

S².

Tém.

Vict.

Bucent.   Tém.   Bu.

Red.   Trin   V   R.

Fr. Nept.   Fr. Nept.

in the hands of the Victory's crew. While listening, with characteristic avidity, to the deafening crash made by their shot in the French ship's hull, the British crew were nearly suffocated with the clouds of black smoke that entered the Victory's portholes; and Lord Nelson, Captain Hardy, and others that were walking the quarter-deck, had their clothes covered with the dust which issued from the crumbled wood-work of the Bucentaure's stern. The position of the Victory just as, while receiving into her bows the foremost guns of a French 74 and the

whole broadside of a French 80, she is about to pour her broadside into the stern of a second French 80, we have endeavoured
to illustrate by the first set of figures in the preceding diagram.

Although the work of scarcely two minutes, and although not
a mast or yard of the Bucentaure was seen to come down, the
effects of the British three-decker's broadside upon the personnel
of the French ship, as acknowledged a day or two afterwards by
Vice-admiral Villeneuve, and long subsequently by his flag-
captain M. Magendie, was of the same destructive character as
the broadside poured by the Royal Sovereign into the stern of
the Santa-Ana. The amount which the Bucentaure's officers
gave, as the extent of their loss in killed and wounded by the
Victory's fire, was " nearly 400 men." They represented, also,
that 20 of their guns were dismounted by it, and that the Bucentaure was reduced to a comparatively defenceless state.

Prevented by position, even had she not been incapacitated
by loss, from returning the Victory's tremendous salute, the
Bucentaure found an able second in the Neptune. This fine
French 80, the moment the Victory's bows opened clear of the
Bucentaure's stern, poured into them a most destructive fire.
Among other damages occasioned by it, the flying jib-boom and
sprit and sprittopsail-yards were cut away; also the starboard
cathead was shot completely off, notwithstanding its immense
stoutness. The bower-anchor, and a sheet-anchor stowed near
it, were also quite disabled; and a third anchor on that side was
much injured. Several shot also entered the Victory's bows
between wind and water, and the foremast and bowsprit were
badly wounded.

The Neptune, fearing, as the Victory advanced, that she
intended to run on board of her, set her jib, and keeping away a
little, ranged ahead; but, Captain Hardy having decided to run
on board the ship on his starboard hand, and into which a
broadside had been poured the instant it would bear with effect,
the Victory put her helm hard a-port. This quickly brought
her head in the direction of the Redoutable; who, with her
foremost guns continued to aid the Neptune in raking the
Victory, and with her aftermost ones fired occasionally at the
Téméraire, as the latter drew out from the wake of her leader.
Just, however, as the Victory was coming in contact with her,
the Redoubtable shut most of her lower-deck ports, and fired
from them no more. In about a minute after she had shifted her
helm, the Victory ran foul of the Redoutable; the sheet-anchor
of the one striking the spare anchor of the other.

Very soon afterwards, or at about 1 h. 10 m. P.M., the two ships dropped alongside of each other. This account corresponds with that given by the French. "Nelson," says M. Parisot, "voyant qu'il (the Redoutable's captain) n'était pas disposé à plier, fit venir le Victory au vent tout d'un coup, et le laissant tomber en travers, il aborda de long en long le Redoutable."[1] Owing to the slight impetus in the Victory, caused by the want of wind, the concussion of the firing would probably have separated her from the Redoutable, had not the Victory's starboard foretopmast studdingsail boom-iron, as the ships were in the act of rebounding off, hooked into the leech of the Redoutable's foretopsail. This held the ships together; and, with the lower deck guns of the Victory touching the side of the Redoutable, and the latter's mainmast in a line about midway between the former's fore and main masts, the two ships fell off a few points from the wind.[2]

Almost immediately after the Victory had got hooked alongside the Redoutable, Mr. William Willmet, the boatswain of the former, found a ready means of clearing the French ship's gangways by firing the starboard 68-pounder carronade, loaded as the larboard one had been, right upon the Redoutable's decks. The guns of the middle and lower decks were also occasionally fired into the Redoutable, but very few of the 12-pounders, on account chiefly of the heavy loss among those who had been stationed at them. The Redoutable, on her part, fired her main-deck guns into the Victory, and used musketry, as well through her ports into those of the Victory, as from her three tops down upon the latter's deck. In her fore and main tops, also, the Redoutable had some brass cohorns, which, loaded with langridge, were frequently fired with destructive effect upon the Victory's forecastle. The larboard guns of the Victory were fired occasionally at the Bucentaure; but it was with little or no effect, the latter ship continuing to move to the northward, while the Victory and Redoutable kept inclining their heads to the eastward. The Santisima-Trinidad also received into her starboard or lee quarter and stern a portion of the Victory's fire.

Never allowing mere personal comfort to interfere with what he considered to be the good of the service, Lord Nelson, when the Victory was fitting to receive his flag, ordered the large skylight over his cabin to be removed, and the space planked

---

[1] Victoires et Conquêtes, tome xvi., p. 171.   [2] See second position in diagram at p. 400.

up, so as to afford him a walk amidships, clear of the guns and ropes. Here, along an extent of deck of about 21 feet in length, bounded abaft by the stancheon of the wheel and forward by the combings of the cabin ladder-way, were the admiral and Captain Hardy, during the whole of the operations we have just detailed, taking their customary promenade. At about 1 h. 25 m. P.M., just as the two had arrived within one pace of the regular turning spot at the cabin ladder-way, Lord Nelson, who, regardless of quarter-deck etiquette, was walking on the larboard side,[1] suddenly faced left about. Captain Hardy, as soon as he had taken the other step, turned also, and saw the admiral in the act of falling. He was then on his knees with his left hand just touching the deck. The arm giving way, Lord Nelson fell on his left side, exactly upon the spot where his secretary, Mr. Scott, had breathed his last, and with whose blood his lordship's clothes were soiled.

On Captain Hardy's expressing a hope that he was not severely wounded, Lord Nelson replied: "They have done for me at last, Hardy." "I hope not," answered Captain Hardy. "Yes," replied his lordship, "my backbone is shot through."[2] The wound was by a musket-ball, which had entered the left shoulder through the fore part of the epaulet, and, descending, had lodged in the spine. That the wound had been given by some one stationed in the Redoutable's mizentop was rendered certain, not only from the nearness (about 15 yards) and situation of the mizentop in reference to the course of the ball, but from the circumstance that the French ship's maintop was screened by a portion of the Victory's mainsail as it hung when clewed up. That the ball was intended for Lord Nelson is doubtful, because, when the aim must have been taken, he was walking on the outer side, concealed in a great measure from view by a much taller and stouter man. Admitting, also (which is very doubtful), that the French seaman or marine, whose shot had proved so fatal, had selected for his object, as the British commander-in-chief, the best dressed officer of the two, he would most probably have fixed upon Captain Hardy, or, indeed, such, in spite of Dr. Beatty's print, was Lord Nelson's habitual carelessness, upon any one of the Victory's lieutenants who might have been walking by the side of him. Sergeant Secker

---

[1] This may be relied upon as correct, although completely at variance with the account published by the Victory's surgeon (Beatty, p. 32), and which, owing to its apparent authenticity, has been made the ground-work of every other published account, including that in the first edition of this work.

[2] Beatty's Narrative, p. 33.

of the marines, and two seamen, who had come up on seeing the admiral fall, now, by Captain Hardy's direction, bore their revered and much-lamented chief to the cockpit; where we will for the present leave him.   The position of the Victory and of the ships near to her at the time Lord Nelson received his wound, drawn up with as much accuracy as the case admits, will be found in the following diagram :—

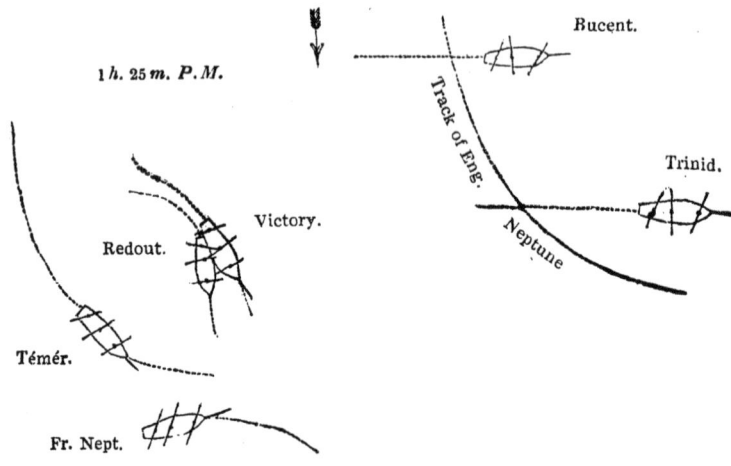

Previously to our entering upon the account of each ship's proceedings, we will endeavour to present a general view of the engagement, and of its immediate result.   Soon after the first four ships of the British lee division had cut through between the centre and rear of the Franco-Spanish line, the remainder successively as they came up, pierced the mass (for it could no longer be called line) of enemy's ships, in various directions, and found opponents as they could.   Meanwhile the leading ships of the weather-division had begun to engage in a similar manner, a little ahead of the centre.   The action, which had commenced, as we have elsewhere shown, at noon, arrived at its height about 1 h. 30 m. P.M.   At 3 P.M. the firing began to slacken, and, at about 5 P.M., wholly ceased.   Of the 14 van-ships of the combined line, reckoning to the Redoubtable inclusive, three only were captured in their places.   The remaining 11 wore out of the line.   Of these 11, three were captured, and eight escaped; four, by hauling to windward, and four by running for Cadiz.   Of the 19 rear-ships, 12, including one burnt, were taken, and seven escaped into Cadiz; making, as the result of the first day's proceedings, nine French (including one burnt), and nine Spanish sail of the line captured, total 18, and nine French, and six Spanish sail of the line escaped, total 15: of which latter number four French ships got away to the southward, and 11, five of them French and six Spanish, and most of the ships much shattered, with all the frigates and brigs, reached the bay of Cadiz.

So far as to the collective operations of the two fleets in the Trafalgar battle. Our attention is now due to the individual exertions of the ships on each side ; and we shall proceed to give the most accurate account that our researches, far and near, have enabled us to obtain, taking the British ships of each division in the order in which, according to the best judgment to be formed from the variety of times noted down in their logs, they successively got into action.

The Royal Sovereign we left just as, after 15 minutes of close action with three or four ships, the Belleisle had come to her relief. The latter, passing on to the eastward, left the Royal Sovereign upon the Santa-Ana's starboard bow. In a short time the Spanish three-decker lost her mizentopmast ; and, at the end of about an hour and a quarter from the commencement of the combat, her three masts fell over the side. At about 2 h. 15 m. P.M., after a hot, and with the exception of the Belleisle's broadside, an uninterrupted engagement between the two ships from 10 minutes past noon, the Santa-Ana struck to the Royal Sovereign.

This occurrence took place just as the mizenmast of the Royal Sovereign came down, and when her fore and main masts from their shattered condition, were ready to follow it. No sooner, indeed, did the Royal Sovereign, in order to put herself a little to rights, move a short distance ahead of her prize, than her mainmast fell over on the starboard side, tearing off two of the lower-deck ports. The foremast, having been shot through in several places, and stripped of nearly the whole of its rigging, was left in a tottering state. Hence the English three-decker was reduced to almost, if not quite, as unmanageable a state as the Spanish three-decker, which she had so gallantly fought and captured.

The French accounts say : " Le vaisseau la Santa-Ana, vaillamment attaqué par l'amiral Collingwood, fut non moins vaillamment défendu par le vice-amiral Alava ; mais, accablé par le nombre, il dut céder."[1] And yet out of the 26 remaining

[1] Victoires et Conquêtes, tome **xvi.**, p. 179.

406 BRITISH AND FRANCO-SPANISH FLEETS. [1805

British ships, no ship except the Belleisle, and that with merely a broadside in passing, asserts that she fired into the Santa-Ana. Here is the proper place to notice the modesty with which Vice-admiral Collingwood, in his official despatch, refers to the part taken by his own ship. "The commander-in-chief in the Victory," he says, "led the weather column, and the Royal Sovereign, which bore my flag, the lee. The action began at 12 o'clock by the leading ships of the columns breaking through the enemy's line, the commander-in-chief about the tenth ship from the van, the second in command about the twelfth from the rear, &c." The Royal Sovereign is not again mentioned, except in reference to matters that occurred subsequently to the battle.

The loss sustained by the Royal Sovereign was tolerably severe: she had one lieutenant (Brice Gilliland), her master (William Chalmers), one lieutenant of marines (Robert Green), two midshipmen (John Aikenhead and Thomas Braund), 29 seamen, and 13 marines killed, two lieutenants (John Clavell and James Bashford), one lieutenant of marines (James le Vesconte), one master's mate (William Watson), four midshipmen (Gilbert Kennicott, Grenville Thompson, John Farrant, and John Campbell), her boatswain (Isaac Wilkinson), 69 seamen, and 16 marines wounded.

Respecting the Santa-Ana's loss in killed and wounded, nothing is known beyond the amount already specified as the alleged effect of her opponent's raking fire. That the Spanish ship's loss must have been uncommonly severe may be inferred, as well from the length and closeness of the action, as from the fact, that her starboard side was nearly beaten in by the Royal Sovereign's shot. Among the Santa-Ana's dangerously, if not mortally wounded, was Vice-admiral Alava; and it was understood that her killed and wounded comprised a great proportion of officers.

After having, for the space of 20 minutes, sustained the tremendous fire opened by the rear of the combined line, and after having suffered, in consequence, a loss of between 50 and 60 men in killed and wounded, the Belleisle, at about a quarter past noon, exchanged a few shot with the Monarca, and passed through the line abreast of the Fougueux, then distantly raking the Royal Sovereign. In hauling up on the larboard tack, the Belleisle was enabled, owing to the advanced position of the latter, to pour a full broadside into the lee quarter of the Santa-Ana. Bearing away a little, the Belleisle then passed close astern of the Indomptable ; who, quickly wearing, exchanged a few broadsides with her, and then bore up to the south-east. In the mean time the Belleisle was engaged with a Spanish ship, the San-Juan-Nepomuceno, at some distance on her starboard beam. At about 45 minutes past noon the Belleisle's maintopmast was shot away ; and, as the enemy's rear ships were now pressing forward to support the centre, her situation became extremely critical.

At 1 P.M. the Fougueux ranged up in the smoke on the Belleisle's starboard beam, and struck her at the gangway with her larboard bow, rolling at the same time with her fore yard over the British ship's quarter-deck. The Fougueux immediately began engaging the Belleisle, and in 10 minutes shot away her mizenmast about six feet above the deck, the wreck falling over the larboard quarter. In about 10 minutes more, on the Mars beginning to engage her, the Fougueux, who had received a smart fire from the Belleisle's aftmost guns, dropped astern and hauled to the northward. At 1 h. 30 m. P.M. the French Achille came ranging past the stern of the Belleisle, then with her head a little to the southward of east, and stationed herself on the latter's larboard quarter. In this position, the Achille kept up a steady fire, with comparative impunity, on account of the wreck of the Belleisle's mizenmast masking her aftermost guns. Meanwhile the Aiglo, having replaced the San-Juan, was distantly cannonading the British ship on the starboard side ; and the San-Justo and San-Leandro, as they stood athwart the bows of the Belleisle to join Admiral Gravina in the rear, opened a passing fire.

Thus in a manner surrounded, the Belleisle soon had her rigging and sails cut to pieces, and at 2 h. 10 m. P.M. lost her mainmast about four feet above the deck ; the wreck of which fell upon the break of the poop, while the topmast, with the yards, sails, and shrouds, hung over upon the larboard side, where already lay the wreck of the mizenmast. Her larboard guns thus completely covered by wreck, the Belleisle was prevented from returning by a single shot the Achille's animated and destructive fire. At 2 h. 30 m. P.M., driven from her capital station upon the bows of the Victory and Téméraire, by the approach of the Leviathan, the French Neptune placed herself across the starboard bow cf the Belleisle ; and at 2 h. 45 m. the foremast and bowsprit of the latter, still engaged by two other ships, were shot away by the board.

At 3 h. 15 m. P.M. the Polyphemus interposed herself between

the Belleisle and Neptune. In five minutes more the Defiance
took off the fire of the Aigle ; and at 3 h. 25 m. P.M. the Swiftsure, passing astern of the Belleisle, commenced engaging the
Achille, who about this time lost her main and mizen topmasts.
As the Swiftsure passed close under the Belleisle's stern the two
ships cheered each other ; and to signify that, notwithstanding
her dismasted and shattered state, the Belleisle still remained
unconquered, a union-jack was suspended at the end of a pike
and held up to view, while an ensign was being made fast to the
stump of her mizenmast. Thus, by the timely arrival of her
friends, saved from being crushed by the overwhelming force
around her, the Belleisle ceased firing. Observing soon afterwards on his larboard beam a Spanish two-decker that had
already surrendered, Captain Hargood sent the master, Mr.
William Hudson, and Lieutenant Owen of the marines (who
volunteered although wounded), in the only remaining boat, the
pinnace, and took possession of the 80-gun ship Argonauta. The
position of the Belleisle, at the time she was so fortunately
relieved, we have endeavoured to illustrate by the following
diagram :—

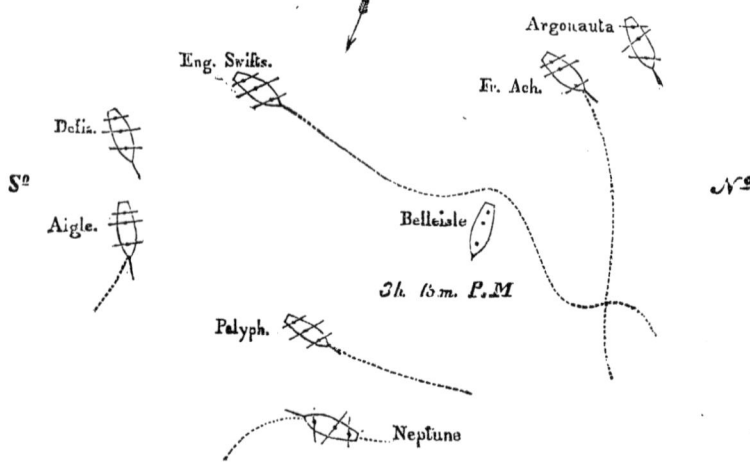

The Belleisle's hull was knocked almost to pieces : both sides
of it were about equally damaged. Ports, port-timbers, channels,
chain-plates, all exhibited unequivocal marks of the terrible maul-
ing she had received. Her three masts and bowsprit, as we have
seen, were shot away, and so was her figure-head. Her boats

and anchors shared the same fate. If the Belleisle s damages were severe, her loss of men was not less so: she had two lieutenants (Ebenezer Geall and John Woodin), one midshipman (George Nind), 22 seamen, and eight marines killed, one lieutenant (William Ferrie), one lieutenant of marines (John Owen), her boatswain (Andrew Gibson), two master's mates (William Henry Pearson and William Cutfield), one midshipman (Samuel Jago), one first-class volunteer (J. T. Hodge), 67 seamen, and 19 marines wounded.

In her way down astern of the Belleisle, the Mars suffered severely from the heavy raking fire of the ships ahead of her, the San-Juan-Nepomuceno, Pluton, Monarca, and Algésiras. As the Mars was directing her course to cut the line between the first two of these ships, the Pluton, who was to windward of the San-Juan, ranged ahead: whereupon, to avoid being raked by so close an opponent, the Mars hauled up, with the intention to pass on and cut the line ahead of the San-Juan. In attempting this manœuvre, the Mars was followed and engaged by the Pluton. Having by that time had her rigging and sails greatly damaged, the Mars was obliged to come head to wind in order to avoid running on board the Santa-Ana; whereby the Mars lay with her stern exposed to the Monarca and Algésiras. At this moment, however, the Tonnant came up, and soon found full employment for both of those ships. Meanwhile, as she paid off in her completely unmanageable state, the Mars became also exposed to a heavy fire from the Fougueux, then with her larboard guns engaging the Belleisle, and presently received into her stern a most destructive fire from the Pluton; a fire that almost cleared the poop and quarter-deck of both officers and men. It was at about 1 h. 15 m. P.M., while Captain Duff was standing at the break of the quarter-deck looking over the side, that a cannon-shot from the Pluton struck him on the breast, knocked off his head, and cast his body on the gangway. The same shot killed two seamen, who were standing close behind their captain. The command now devolved upon Lieutenant William Hennah. By this time succour was at hand; and, while the Fougueux made off to the northward in the direction of the Téméraire, the Pluton stood away to the southeast to join Admiral Gravina.[1]

The Mars had her maintopmast and spankerboom shot away, and her three lower masts, fore and main yards, and foretopmast, very badly wounded: her foremast, indeed, was left in so

----

[1] See second set of figures in diagram at p. 411.

shattered a state that it subsequently fell overboard. The main piece of her rudder was badly wounded, her stern and quarters much cut, and nine of the poop-beams, besides sundry knees, &c., shot to pieces. The ship had also some guns disabled, and had received several shot between wind and water. The loss on board the Mars was proportionably severe : she had her captain, one master's mate (Alexander Duff), two midshipmen (Edward Corbyn and Henry Morgan), 17 seamen, and eight marines killed, and two lieutenants (Edward William Garrett and James Black), her master (Thomas Cook), one captain of marines (Thomas Norman), five midshipmen (John Young, George Guiren, William John Cook, John Jenkins, and Alfred Luckraft), 44 seamen, and sixteen marines wounded.

With respect to the injuries sustained by the Pluton, the ship is represented to have been unable, after the action, to muster more than 400 effective men out of a complement of about 700 : consequently, her loss must have been severe. It appears, also, that the Pluton made three feet water an hour from the shot she had received in the hull.

Having, as already stated, fired at the ships that were pressing upon the Mars, the Tonnant steered straight for the larboard bow of the Algésiras, then moving slowly onwards the same as her companions in the line, and very near to her present leader, the Monarca. As the Tonnant advanced, the Algésiras, having already her maintopsail to the mast, backed her mizentopsail, and thus enabled the former, at about 45 minutes past noon, to run close under the Spanish ship's stern. Pouring in a raking fire, the Tonnant hauled up, and engaged the Monarca alongside ; but, dreading to encounter so large and powerful a ship, the latter fired a few ineffective shot, dropped astern, and struck her colours, although she afterwards rehoisted them. The Tonnant's people believed, although they were not certain, that the Monarca struck ; but the Spartiate, who, not being engaged until late, had leisure for observation, saw the flag hauled down and in her log says accordingly : " At 1 h. 7 m. a Spanish two-decker struck to the Tonnant."

Filling her main and mizentopsails, the Algésiras now evinced an intention to cross the stern of the Tonnant, who, by this time, had had her foretopmast and mainyard shot away ; but the Tonnant, putting her helm hard-a-port, ran the Algésiras on board, and defeated the manœuvre. The bowsprit and anchors of the Algésiras getting entangled with the main rigging of the Tonnant, the two ships were held fast together, greatly, on account of their relative positions, to the advantage of the Tonnant. It was, doubtless, while the Tonnant's attention was thus occupied that the Monarca, being left to herself, and having suffered comparatively little in the action, re-hoisted her colours.

While thus fast to the Algésiras on her starboard side, the Tonnant fired her larboard aftermost guns athwart the hawse of the Mars at the Pluton lying upon the latter's larboard bow, and her larboard foremost guns at the San Juan Nepomuceno lying upon her own bow. Meanwhile the Mars, until she and the Pluton dropped astern, fired several well-directed shot into the larboard quarter of the Algésiras. The position of the Tonnant and ships around her at this time, which was about 1 h. 35 m p.m., we have endeavoured to illustrate by the following diagram.

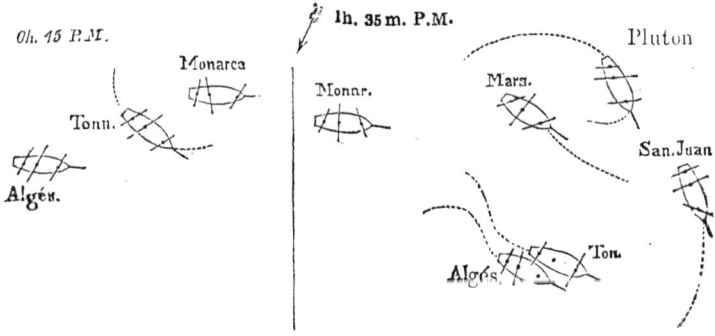

At about 1 h. 40 m. p.m., Captain Tyler received a severe wound, and was obliged to be taken below. The command of the Tonnant thereupon devolved upon Lieutenant John Bedford. In the mean time an animated cannonade was kept up between the two ships ; by which the Algésiras soon lost her foremast, and the Tonnant her main and mizen topmast. The Algésiras made a serious attempt to board ; but the marines of the Tonnant maintained so steady and well-directed a fire, that the French crew did not succeed, except in the case of one man, who contrived to enter one of the Tonnant's maindeck ports, and whose life, to the credit of those who took him, was spared. At about 2 h. 15 m. p.m., just as her main and mizen masts were about to share the fate of her foremast, the Algésiras, after a very gallant defence, struck her colours ; and Lieutenant Charles Bennett, with Lieutenant of marines Arthur Ball, and about 48 men, stepped on board and took possession of her. In another quarter of an hour the San Juan hailed that she surrendered ;

and Lieutenant Benjamin Clement was sent in the jolly-boat with two hands to take possession. The boat being damaged by shot, swamped, before she reached a quarter of the way. The two men could swim, but not the lieutenant. While the latter was clinging to the boat, a shot struck her and knocked off her quarter. The boat then turned bottom upwards ; and Lieutenant Clement held fast by the boat's fall until one of his two companions, a black man, Macnamara by name, swam to the Tonnant, and returned with a rope that lead out of the ship's stern port. By this means a brave young officer, who had been in two or three of the general actions of the preceding war, was saved to his country.

Among the damages sustained by the Tonnant in the hull, was a bad wound in the rudder, a portion of the head of which was shot away ; and a great part of her starboard quarter-piece, with the rails and gallery, was carried away by the Algésiras when the vessels got foul. The loss on board the Tonnant amounted to one midshipman (William Brown,) 16 seamen, and nine marines killed, her captain (severely), boatswain (Richard Little), the captain's clerk (William Allen), one master's mate (Henry Ready), 30 seamen, and 16 marines wounded. The Algésiras had upwards of 200 men killed and wounded, including several officers, and among the mortally wounded, the brave and highly-respected Rear-admiral Magon, who had previously been wounded in two places, but would not quit the deck.

After having captured the Algésiras and disengaged herself from her prize, the Tonnant fired several shot at the squadron of M. Dumanoir passing to windward ; but, having no boat left, could not send again to take possession of the San Juan. That Spanish ship, however, was shortly afterwards engaged and secured by the Dreadnought.

In consequence of the novel mode of attack adopted by the commander-in-chief, each British ship, as she bore up in line ahead, was obliged to follow in the wake of her leader until close upon the enemy's line ; her commander, then, acting up to Lord Nelson's instructions, as contained in the memorandum at a previous page, that no captain could do very wrong who placed his ship alongside that of an enemy, attached himself to the first Frenchman or Spaniard that crossed his path. Most of the captains had also received, on the morning of the action, Lord Nelson's verbal directions, transmitted through the captains of the frigates, that they were to break the enemy's line wherever they conveniently could. This, in effect, discretionary power was particularly beneficial towards the height of the battle, when the enemy's ships, by an irregular movement from the rear to the centre, and, in some instances, from the centre and van to the rear, were every instant shifting their positions, and giving to their line, if line it could be called, a new face.

It was not until full 15 minutes after the Tonnant had cut the line, that her second astern, the Bellerophon, owing to her distance from the former and the lightness of the wind was enabled to do the same. This she accomplished by passing under the stern of the Monarca, as the latter, with colours re-hoisted, was dropping away from the Tonnant. In luffing up to lay the Monarca alongside to leeward, the Bellerophon, at about 50 minutes past noon, ran foul of the Aigle, the latter's main yard locking with her fore yard. The British ship now fired from both sides, having the Monarca on the larboard, and the Aigle on the opposite bow. In a short time three other enemy's ships opened a cannonade upon her, the Montanez (we believe), with her aftermost guns on the larboard quarter, the French Swiftsure on the starboard quarter, and the Bahama, with some of her foremost guns, athwart her stern. The first set of figures in the following diagram will perhaps assist in showing the situation of the British ship at this period of the battle :—

At about 1 P.M. the Bellerophon's main and mizentopmasts fell over on the starboard side, and the maintopsail and topgallantsail immediately caught fire with the flash of the guns, assisted by the hand-grenades which the Aigle's people kept throwing from her tops. At 1 h. 5 m. P.M. the master was killed ; and at 1 h. 11 m. Captain Cooke. The command now devolved

upon Lieutenant William Pryce Cumby. Shortly afterwards the
Montanez dropped out of gun-shot astern, and the Bahama and
French Swiftsure became engaged with the Colossus. The
musketry from the Aigle had by this time played sad havoc upon
the Bellerophon's quarter-deck, forecastle, and poop. At 1 h.
40 m. P.M. the Aigle, who had once or twice vainly attempted to
board her opponent, dropped astern, exposed as she fell off to a
raking fire, first from the Bellerophon herself, and then from the
Revenge. The Bellerophon, now quite in an unmanageable state,
fired a few shot at the Monarca, who instantly hauled down her
colours for the last time, and was taken possession of by the
former; as, nearly at the same time, was the Bahama, who had
previously struck, to relieve herself from the destructive fire of
the Colossus.

The Bellerophon had her main and mizen topmasts shot away,
her foretopmast, all three lower masts, and most of her yards,
badly wounded, and her standing and running rigging nearly
cut to pieces. In hull also she was much injured, having had
several knees and riders shot away, and part of her lower deck
ripped up, besides other damage. Her loss consisted of her
captain, master (Edward Overton), one midshipman (John Sim-
mons), 20 seamen, and four marines killed, one captain of marines
(James Wemyss), her boatswain (Thomas Robinson), one
master's mate (Edward Hartley), four midshipmen (William N.
Jewell, James Stone, Thomas Bant, and George Pearson), 96
seamen, and 20 marines wounded. A great proportion of this
heavy loss unfortunately arose from the explosion of a quantity
of loose powder spilt about the decks from the cartridges; and
which, but for the water that lay around the entrance of the
magazine, must have destroyed the ship and all on board of her.

Although no particular account can be given of the damage or
loss sustained by the Aigle, it may with certainty be stated, that
she suffered greatly in masts, rigging, and hull, and lost in
killed and wounded, from the successive fire of the Bellerophon,
Revenge, and Defiance, nearly two-thirds of her crew, including
among the killed her captain and first-lieutenant, and among
the wounded several of her officers. The loss on board the
Monarca does not appear to have been recorded; but it must
have been severe, from her first action with the Tonnant, and
from the length of time she was exposed to the close and uninterrupted fire of the Bellerophon, one of the best manned,
although one of the smallest 74s, in the British fleet.

At 1 P.M., or thereabouts, after having, during 10 minutes or so, in her efforts to close, received the fire of two or three enemy's ships, the Colossus ran past the starboard side of the French Swiftsure;[1] who had just before bore up, as well to avoid being raked by the Colossus, as to bring her larboard guns to bear upon the Bellerophon. The density of the smoke on the starboard side hid from view all the enemy's ships in that direction, until, having run a short distance to leeward, the Colossus found herself close alongside of the Argonaute, whose larboard yard-arms locked into her starboard ones. A spirited cannonade now ensued between the two ships, and lasted for about 10 minutes, when the Argonaute's fire became nearly silenced, except from a few of her aftermost guns; a shot from one of which, just as the ships, driven apart by the concussion of the guns, began to settle broadside off, struck Captain Morris a little above the knee. As soon as, by this lateral movement, she had cleared her yards, the Argonaute paid off, and went away, receiving into her stern the parting fire of the Colossus. The latter, in the meanwhile, was firmly engaged on her larboard quarter, with the French Swiftsure, and also with the Bahama, who lay close on that ship's larboard bow, and fired at the Colossus across the Swiftsure's fore-foot.

At a few minutes before 3 P.M., having forged ahead, the Swiftsure got between the Bahama and Colossus, and being thus more fully exposed to the latter's well-directed broadsides, soon slackened her fire and dropped astern. The Colossus was now enabled to devote her sole attention to the Bahama; who, on her mainmast falling, as it presently did, over her engaged side, showed an English jack from the hen-coops on her poop, to denote that she had struck. Meanwhile the French Swiftsure endeavoured to bear up under the stern of the Colossus; but the latter, wearing more quickly, received a few only of the former's larboard guns, before she poured in her starboard broadside. This brought down the French Swiftsure's mizenmast. At the same time the Orion, in passing, gave the French ship a broadside, which brought down her tottering mainmast; whereupon the Swiftsure made signs to the Colossus of having surrendered. In hauling up to take possession of her two prizes, the latter lost her wounded mizenmast over the starboard side.

The mainmast of the Colossus was so badly wounded, that she was compelled, during the ensuing night, to cut it away; and her damages altogether were extremely severe. Her only remaining stick, the foremast, had been shot through in several

1 See the diagram at p. 413.

places; two of her anchors and three of her boats had been destroyed, and some of her guns disabled. Four of her starboard lower-deck ports had also been knocked away by running on board the Argonaute, and her hull in every part of it was much shattered. The Colossus lost in the action her master (Thomas Scriven), 31 seamen, and eight marines killed, her captain,[1] two lieutenants (George Bully and William Forster), one lieutenant of marines (John Benson), her boatswain (William Adamson), one master's mate (Henry Milbanke), eight midshipmen (William Herringham, Frederick Thistlewayte, Thomas G. Reece, Henry Snellgrove, Rawden M'Lean, George Wharrie, Timothy Renou, and George Denton), 115 seamen, and 31 marines wounded.

The Argonaute, the first broadside-opponent of the Colossus, although she lost none of her masts, must have suffered severely in the hull, having had, according to the French accounts, nearly 160 of her crew killed and wounded: she, nevertheless, effected her escape. Some of the French writers are very severe in their strictures upon the conduct of the French Argonaute. It appears that the Hermione frigate, in compliance with the practice of the French navy, hoisted the signal, for ships unengaged to engage, and, finding no attention paid to it, added the number of the Argonaute, and kept both signal and pendant flying for one hour.[2] The Bahama and French Swiftsure, reduced to the state of wrecks, suffered a proportionate loss of men; the first having had nearly 400 killed and wounded, including among the former, her captain, and the second very little short of that number.

Being close astern of the Colossus and sailing well, the English Achille became, in a few minutes after the former, warmly engaged. Having passed close astern of the Montanez, the Achille luffed up and engaged that ship to leeward. In less than a quarter of an hour the Montanez sheered off, and the Achille made sail to succour the Belleisle, then lying to leeward totally dismasted, with three enemy's ships upon her. While on her way to perform this duty, the Achille found herself obstructed by the Argonaute. The British 74 immediately brought to on the Spanish 80's larboard beam, and a close

[1] With a truly gallant spirit, Captain Morris would not go below, but, applying a tourniquet to his thigh, remained at his post near the head of the poop-ladder until, to avoid the fall of the mizenmast, he descended to the quarter-deck. After the battle was over, and the Agamemnon had come down to take the Colossus in tow, Captain Morris, having become faint from loss of blood, was carried below, and was landed in his cot some days afterwards at Gibraltar.

[2] Victoires et Conquêtes, tome xvi., p. 178.

action ensued, which lasted an hour. The Argonauta now attempted to set her mainsail to shoot ahead, but, failing in that, ceased firing, shut her lower-deck ports, and, as it appeared on board the Achille, threw an English jack or ensign over her larboard quarter.

At this moment two French ships came up, and one of them soon found other employment for the English Achille than taking possession of the Argonauta. The French Achille edged down on her English namesake's larboard quarter, and engaged her in passing to windward; and the Berwick, who had been distantly engaged with the Defence, ranged up on the English Achille's starboard side, between the latter and the Argonauta. The French Achille passing on in the direction of the Belleisle, and the Argonauta dropping to leeward, the English Achille and Berwick were left in fair single combat. The action continued for upwards of an hour, when the Berwick hauled down her colours, and was taken possession of by the Achille.

The masts of the latter, although all standing, were badly wounded, and so was her bowsprit: her hull had also received considerable damage. The loss on board the English Achille amounted to one midshipman (Francis John Mugg), six seamen, and six marines killed, and two lieutenants (Parkins Prynn and Josias Bray), one captain and one lieutenant of marines (Palms Westropp and William Leddon), one master's mate (George Pegge), three midshipmen (William H. Staines, William J. Snow, and William Smith Warren), 37 seamen, and 14 marines wounded.

The Argonauta, the English Achille's first steady, opponent appears to have suffered greatly in rigging, hull, and crew, but to have had no spars of any consequence shot away: her loss is represented to have amounted to nearly 400 in killed and wounded, including among the dangerously wounded her captain. It is doubtful if the whole of this damage and loss was inflicted by the English Achille: the Argonauta must have exchanged some broadsides in passing with other British ships. The Berwick was dreadfully cut up in her hull, and her three masts were left in a tottering state. The Achille's officer, who took possession of the ship, counted, upon her decks and in her cockpit and tiers, 51 dead bodies, including that of her gallant captain, M. Camas; and the wounded of the Berwick, according to the report of her few surviving officers, amounted to nearly 200: her loss in officers was very severe, the quarter-deck having been twice cleared. Nearly the whole of this loss was attributable to the close and unremitting cannonade kept up, for more than an hour, by the English Achille. On the other hand, the principal part of the latter's damage and loss was caused by the steady fire and determined opposition of the Berwick.

We quitted the Victory at about 1 h. 30 m. P.M., or just as Lord Nelson had been carried to the cockpit, mortally wounded from the mizentop of the Redoutable.[1] So destructive to the Victory was the fire kept up from the Redoutable's tops, as well as from her second deck guns, occasionally pointed upwards, that, within a few minutes of Lord Nelson's fall, several officers and about 40 men, nearly the whole of them upon the third or upper deck, were killed or wounded. A single 18-pounder carronade on the poop, mounted upon an elevating carriage, might very soon have destroyed the Redoutable's mizentop and all that were in it; but the Victory had no guns whatever mounted on her poop. The same effect might have been produced upon the fore and main tops by one of the 68-pounder carronades; but their carriages would not give the required elevation. Nor, we believe, could the 68-pounder on the starboard side be even fired a second time upon the decks of the Redoutable,[2] owing to some accident that had since befallen it.

Although, from the loss of the men stationed at them, the 12-pounders of the Victory were for the most part abandoned, the larboard guns, her 24 and 32 pounders upon the decks below continued to fire, for a few minutes (until the English Neptune and ships astern of her intervened), distantly at the starboard quarters of the Bucentaure and Santisima-Trinidad, and the starboard guns, with much more certain effect, right into the hull of the Redoutable. "The starboard guns of the lower and middle decks," says Dr. Beatty, "were depressed, and fired with a diminished charge of powder, and three shot each, into the Redoutable. This mode of firing was adopted by Lieutenants Williams, King, Yule, and Brown, to obviate the danger of the Téméraire's suffering from the Victory's shot passing through the Redoutable; which must have been the case if the usual quantity of powder, and the common elevation, had been given to the guns. A circumstance occurred in this situation, which showed in a most striking manner the cool intrepidity of the officers and men stationed on the lower-deck of the Victory. When the guns on this deck were run out, their

1 See p. 403.   2 See p. 402.

muzzles came into contact with the Redoutable's side ; and consequently at every discharge there was reason to fear that the enemy would take fire, and both the Victory and the Témé-raire be involved in her flames. Here then was seen the asto-nishing spectacle of the fireman of each gun standing ready with a bucket full of water, which, as soon as his gun was dis-charged, he dashed into the enemy through the holes made in her side by the shot."[1]

The respectability of the authority has induced us to give this quotation entire, yet we positively deny that the Victory's guns were fired in the manner there stated. Not only have our in-quiries fully satisfied us respecting this fact ; but we doubt even if the Téméraire had come in contact with the Redoutable at the period to which the statement refers. When, too, the Téméraire did lash herself to the Redoutable, all effective opposition on the part of the latter had ceased, to the Victory at least ; and, after firing a few shot, and ascertaining that the Téméraire was foul on the Redoutable's starboard side, the Victory began to busy herself in getting clear, to seek a more worthy antagonist. This hitherto disputed fact, the details of the Téméraire's proceed-ings, into which we are now about to enter, will more clearly establish.

Being an extraordinarily fast sailing line-of-battle ship, the Victory, urged as she was, would probably have been, like the Royal Sovereign, far ahead of the ships in her wake ; but that the Téméraire, having on board very little water or provisions, was, what the sailors call, " flying light." After the Téméraire, having closed the Victory, had, instead of leading the column as at first proposed, been directed to take her station astern of the Victory,[2] the dismantled state of the latter from the enemy's shot, rendered it very difficult for the Téméraire to avoid going ahead of her leader ; and to keep astern she was obliged, besides cutting away her studding-sails, occasionally to yaw or make a traverse in her course. Hence the Téméraire shared with the Victory, although by no means to so great an extent, the damage and loss sustained by the head of the weather column from the enemy's heavy and incessant raking fire. Shortly after the Victory had poured her larboard broadside into the Bucentaure's stern, the Téméraire opened her fire at the Neptune and Re-doutable. When the Victory put her helm a-port to steer towards the Redoutable, the Téméraire, to keep clear of her leader, was compelled to do the same ; receiving, as she passed

[1] Beatty's Narrative, p. 31.   [2] See Note, p. 391.

the Redoutable, a fire that carried away the head of her mizen-topmast. When, after striking the Redoutable, the Victory again brought her head to the northward, the Téméraire stood slowly on a short distance to the south-east; and then hauled up to pass through the enemy's line. Meanwhile the Victory had, as already stated, dropped alongside the Redoutable, and the two ships were paying off to the eastward.

Scarcely had she begun to haul up, so as to avoid being raked by the French Neptune, ere the Téméraire discovered, through the smoke, the Redoutable driving towards and almost on board of her. Even had the breeze, now barely sufficient to fill the sails, permitted the Téméraire to manœuvre to clear herself from the Redoutable, the Neptune, who, to avoid getting foul of the Redoutable and Victory, had wore and come to again on the same tack, and at this time lay with her larboard broadside bearing upon the starboard bow of the Téméraire, opened so heavy a raking fire, that in a few minutes the latter's fore-yard and main topmast were shot away, and her foremast and bow-sprit, particularly the latter, greatly damaged. In this un-manageable state, the Téméraire could do no more than continue to cannonade the Redoutable with her larboard guns. This the former did until, having, as she had done those on the opposite side, shut down her lower-deck ports, the Redoutable, at about 1 h. 40 m. P.M., fell on board the Téméraire, the French ship's bowsprit passing over the British ship's gangway a little before the main rigging; and where, in order to have the benefit of bestowing a raking fire, the crew of the Téméraire immediately lashed it. The raking fire was poured in, and very destructive, as we shall soon show, did it prove.

Most of the few effective men, left upon the Victory's upper deck after the Redoutable's destructive fire formerly noticed,[1] being employed in carrying their wounded comrades to the cockpit, Captain Hardy, Captain Adair of the marines, and one or two other officers, were nearly all that remained upon the quarter-deck and poop. The men in the Redoutable's mizen-top soon made this known to their officers below; and a con-siderable portion of the French crew quickly assembled in the chains and along the gangway of their ship, in order to board the British three-decker, whose defenceless state they inferred, not merely from her abandoned upper deck, but from the tem-porary silence of her guns on the decks below, occasioned by a supposition that the Redoutable, having discontinued her fire,

was on the eve of surrendering. A party of the Victory's officers
and men quickly ascended from the middle and lower decks; and,
after an interchange of musketry, the French crew, who, in
addition to the unexpected opposition they experienced, found
that the curve in the hulls of the two ships prevented their stepping from one to the other, retired within-board.

The repulse of this very gallant assault cost the Victory
dearly. Captain Adair and 18 men were killed, and one lieutenant (William Ram, mortally), one midshipman (George
Augustus Westphal), and 20 men wounded. Captain Adair met
his death by a musket-ball received at the back of the neck,
while standing upon the Victory's gangway encouraging his
men, and several seamen and marines were also killed by the
French musketry; but the lieutenant and midshipman, and four
or five seamen standing near them, were struck by a round shot,
or the splinters it occasioned, which shot had come obliquely
through the quarter-deck, and must have been fired from one of
the Redoutable's maindeck guns pointed upwards in the manner
already described.

The account which the French give of the origin of this
boarding attempt, and of the cause that led to its failure, is as
follows: " In the twinkling of an eye " (alluding to the time
when Lord Nelson was carried below), "the quarterdeck of this
ship (the Victory) was deserted: the gallant fellows of the Redoutable wanted to rush upon it; but the *rentrée* of the two
vessels presented an obstacle. In order to obviate this, Captain
Lucas directed the main yard of his ship to be lowered, meaning to make of it a bridge whereon to pass on board the Victory.
At that moment the three-decker Téméraire ran foul of the Redoutable on the side opposite to that on which the Victory lay,
pouring in at the same time the whole of her broadside. The
effect of this fire was terrible upon the crew of the Redoutable,
the whole of whom were then assembled upon the forecastle,
gangway, and quarter-deck. Nearly 200 were placed hors de
combat. The brave Captain Lucas, although wounded, remained
on deck. The junction of the Téméraire giving fresh courage
to the crew of the Victory, the latter recommenced firing, but
soon afterwards ceased in order to disengage herself from the
French ship."[1]

Is it likely that a French 74 would attempt to board a British
three-decker fast to her on one side, while a second British
three-decker was foul of her on the other? We have not a

[1] For the original, see Appendix, No. 37.

doubt, therefore, that the French account is in this respect correct. In fixing the relative time of these occurrences, we should say that, in about five minutes after Lord Nelson was carried off the deck, or at 1 h. 35 m. P.M., the boarding indication commenced. Admitting the contest, when the Téméraire put an end to it, by lashing the Redoutable's bowsprit to the fore part of her main rigging, and pouring in her destructive raking fire, to have continued five minutes, that would fix the time of the Téméraire's getting foul, as we have already stated it, at 1 h. 40 m. P.M.; and another five minutes may be allowed for the ship to drop early alongside.

Less considerate than either of her antagonists about fire, although in equal if not greater danger from its effects, the Redoutable continued throwing hand-grenades from her tops and yard-arms ("les grenades pleuvent des hunes du Redoutable"[1]), some of which, falling on board herself, set fire to her larboard fore-chains and starboard fore-shrouds. The fire from the fore-shrouds presently communicated to the foresail of the Téméraire; but, by the active exertions of her forecastle-men, led by the boatswain, the flames on board both ships were presently extinguished. The Victory's crew, after having put out a fire that had spread itself among some ropes and canvas on the booms, also lent their assistance in extinguishing the flames on board the Redoutable, by throwing buckets of water from the gangway upon her chains and forecastle.

All further hostility having, as well as it might, ceased on board the Redoutable, Captain Hardy ordered two midshipmen, Messrs. David Ogilvie and Francis E. Collingwood, with the sergeant-major of marines and eight or ten hands, to go on board the French ship, and (not to "take possession,"[2] for, had that been deemed of any importance, a lieutenant would have been sent, but) to assist in putting out a fire which had just broken out afresh. This party, not being able to step on board for the reason already given, embarked from one of the Victory's stern-ports in the only remaining boat of the two that had been towing astern, and got to the Redoutable through one of her stern-ports. As a proof, too, that all hostility had then ceased on board the French ship, the Victory's people were well received. Their boat, we believe, was soon afterwards knocked to pieces by a shot. The other boat had been cut adrift by a shot just as the Victory was about to open her fire, and was afterwards picked up with her oars and tackle as complete as

[1] Victoires et Conquêtes, tome xvi., p. 174.   [2] Beatty's Narrative, p. 55.

when, early in the forenoon, she had been lowered down from the quarter.

Very soon after these young midshipmen had been despatched, a lieutenant of the Victory, looking out of one of her aftermost ports on the starboard side, saw a second French two-decker lying close upon the Téméraire's starboard side; and, as the Victory, a few minutes afterwards, was in the act of booming her bows off·from the Redoutable, the same officer read the name upon the stern of each French ship. The circumstances under which the second French ship came in contact with the Téméraire, we shall now proceed to relate.

In our account of the proceedings of the Belleisle and Mars, we noticed the hauling off from the former of the French ship Fougueux. After quitting the Belleisle, the Fougueux stood slowly across the wide space between the Santa-Ana and Redoutable, steering a course directly for the starboard beam of the Téméraire, then with her head nearly east. The object of the Fougueux was probably to pass to windward of the Téméraire and rake her: or it might have been (and the French crew were actually assembled on the forecastle in apparent readiness) to board the British three-decker, the appearance of the latter indicating that she was much disabled, and her colours being at this time down, owing to the fall of her gaff. Indeed, as the number of men with which the Téméraire had begun the action was only about 660, and as, of the number at this time fit for duty, not perhaps exceeding 550, nearly the whole were below, whither they had been sent by Captain Harvey, that they might not be injured by the hand-grenades constantly thrown from the Redoutable's tops, the Fougueux, with her 700, or, allowing for a slight loss, 680 men, might have made a serious impression upon the Téméraire's decks.

While Captain Harvey devoted his attention to the Redoubtable on the larboard side, the first-lieutenant, Thomas Fortescue Kennedy, assembled a portion of the crew on the opposite side, to receive the Fougueux. Not having yet discharged her starboard broadside, the Téméraire was in perfect readiness there, but delayed firing until the Fougueux arrived so close that she could not well escape. At length the latter got within 100 yards. Instantly the Téméraire's broadside opened, and a terrible crash was heard on board the Fougueux. Crippled and confused, the French ship, at about 2 h. P.M., ran foul of the Téméraire, and was immediately lashed, by her fore-rigging, to the latter ship's spare anchor. Lieutenant Kennedy, accompanied by Mr. James

Arscott, master's mate, and Mr. Robert Holgate, midshipman. and 20 seamen and six marines, then boarded the Fougueux in her larboard main rigging. On the French ship's quarter-deck lay Captain Beaudoin, mortally wounded; and the second captain and other officers were encouraging the men to repel the boarders. In the onset, however, the second captain became severely wounded; whereupon the French crew suffered themselves to be driven off the quarter-deck by the British, few as they were; and, in 10 minutes from the time of her being boarded by Lieutenant Kennedy and his 28 followers, the Fougueux was completely in the possession of the Téméraire.

This occurrence took place at about 2 h. 10 m. P.M.; and it was within five minutes afterwards, or at 2 h. 15 m. P.M., that the Victory, by fire-booms and the slight assistance which her helm and sails could afford, disengaged herself from the Redoutable. While the Victory gradually got her head to the northward, the three fast-locked ships from which she had just parted, the Redoutable, Téméraire, and Fougueux, swang with their heads to the southward.

Scarcely had the Victory broken away from the group, ere the main and mizen masts of the Redoutable came down. The mainmast, falling on board the Téméraire, carried away the stump of the latter's mizen topmast, broke down the poop-rail, and with its wreck encumbered the whole after-part of the ship. This accident put an entire stop to the Redoutable's hitherto formidable musketry (even admitting it to have continued till this time, which we doubt), and her only remaining antagonist prepared to take possession. The mainmast of the Redoutable, as it lay upon the Téméraire's poop, forming a bridge of easy descent, this was soon accomplished; and, at about 2 h. 20 m. P.M., a portion of the British crew, headed by Lieutenant John Wallace, second of the Téméraire, stepped on board, and took quiet possession of the gallantly-fought Redoutable. About the time that this occurrence happened, having got her head well to the southward, the Téméraire was enabled to fire a few of her foremost guns on the larboard side, clear of the Redoutable's bows, at the French Neptune; whereupon the latter, who also observed the Leviathan approaching, ceased her annoyance and bore away.

Before we enter upon the proceedings of any other ship, we will give a brief description of the damage and loss sustained by the Victory and Téméraire and the two French 74s on board of them. The Victory's mizentopmast, as already stated, was shot away ; and her fore and main masts and their yards, bow-sprit, jib-boom, maintopmast, and cap, and fore and main tops, were badly wounded. All her rigging was cut to pieces, and her spare spars were rendered unfit for use : hull much damaged, particularly in the wales, clamps, and waterways ; and some shot had been received between wind and water. Several beams, knees, and riders were injured, and ports and port-timbers knocked off. The starboard cathead was also shot away, and the starboard bower and spare anchor totally disabled.

The loss on board the Victory will show, that the top-cohorns and musketry of the Redoutable had made ample amends for the comparative silence of her great guns. Besides Lord Nelson and his secretary, the Victory had one captain of marines, (Charles W. Adair), one lieutenant (William Ram), two mid-shipmen (Robert Smith and Alexander Palmer), the captain's clerk (Thomas Whipple[1]), 32 seamen, and 18 marines killed, two lieutenants (John Pasco and George Miller Bligh), two lieu-tenants of marines (Lewis Buckle Reeves and J. G. Peake), three midshipmen (William Rivers, George Augustus Westphal, and Richard Bulkeley), 59 seamen, and nine marines wounded. This was according to the official account ; but 27 additional wounded men reported themselves to the surgeon after the returns had been drawn up.[2] Among this number was included the boat-swain, William Willmet ; who, although painfully wounded in the thigh, did not quit his quarters.

The damages of the Téméraire were scarcely less than those of the Victory. The former had her maintopmast, the head of her mizenmast, her fore-yard, and her fore and main topsail-yards shot away, her fore and main masts so wounded as to render them unfit to carry sail, and her bowsprit shot through in several places. Her rigging of every sort was cut to pieces, and her starboard cathead and bumpkin were shot away ; also the head of her rudder at the water's edge, by the fire of the Redoutable, while rounding the latter's stern. Eight feet of the starboard side of the lower deck abreast of the mainmast was also stove in, and the whole of her quarter-galleries on both sides were carried away by the two ships that had run foul of her.

The Téméraire's loss amounted to one captain and one lieute-

---

[1] This gentleman was killed by the wind of a round shot, whilst speaking to Mr. (now Sir) George Westphale. He had no wound or scratch on any part of his body, and is, perhaps, the only in-stance on record of such an event.

[2] Beatty's Narrative, p. 61.

nant of marines (Simeon Busigny and John Kingston), her carpenter (Lewis Oades), one midshipman (William Pitts), 35
seamen, and eight marines killed, and one lieutenant (James
Mould), one lieutenant of marines (Samuel J. Payne), her boatswain (John Brooks), one master's mate (Francis S. Price), one
midshipman (John Eastman), 59 seamen, and 12 marines
wounded. A part of this heavy loss in killed and wounded
arose from the following accident :—A stinkpot thrown from
the Redoutable entered the powder-screen on the quarter-deck,
and caused a destructive explosion upon the main deck. Had
it not, indeed, been for the presence of mind of the master-at-
arms, John Toohig, who was quartered in the light-room, the
fire would have communicated to the after-magazine, and probably have occasioned the loss not only of the Téméraire, but of
the ships lashed to her.

The damages and loss of the Redoutable, jammed as she had
been betwixt two such formidable antagonists, might well be
severe. The fall of her main and mizen masts has already been
stated : her foretopmast and bowsprit shared th same fate.
Her rudder was destroyed, and her hull shot through in every
direction, above and below water. An 18-pounder gun, and a
36-pounder carronade near the stern, had burst, and 20 of her
guns, including nine lower-deckers on the side opposite to the
Victory, lay dismounted. Out of a crew of 643, the Redoutable
had, according to the French official returns, 300 killed and 222
wounded, including nearly the whole of her officers. Neither
the damage nor the loss of the Fougueux was by any means so
severe as that incurred by the generality of the captured ships.
None of her masts had, at this time, actually fallen, although
one or more of them had been badly struck, and her loss could
not have well exceeded its reputed amount, 40 in killed and
wounded, including among the latter her first-lieutenant, and
among the former her captain.

We formerly mentioned that Captain Blackwood went on
board the Téméraire with the commander-in-chief's instructions
to Captain Harvey.[1] After quitting the latter, Captain Blackwood proceeded to the Leviathan, and informed Captain
Bayntun that Lord Nelson had consented that his ship should
precede the Victory in going into action. From her station
astern of the Conqueror, the Leviathan immediately crowded
all sail to reach the enviable post assigned her : but, owing to
the late hour (about 11 h. 30 m.) at which the message was

[1] See p. 392.

delivered, the Leviathan did not get further ahead than just abreast of the Conqueror, before the Victory was beginning to suffer from the enemy's fire.

The necessity of shortening sail for awhile, to facilitate the endeavours of the Leviathan to pass ahead to her newly-allotted station, and the almost calm state of the weather after the firing had lasted a short time, made it 1 h. 45 m. P.M. before the English Neptune became closely engaged. At this time, having with all her endeavours been unable to go ahead, the Leviathan had resumed her station in the line, and was close in the wake of the Neptune, and a short distance ahead of the Conqueror. Hauling up towards the nearest ship, the English Neptune soon found herself close under the stern of the Bucentaure. The broadside of the Neptune, as she passed on in this direction, shot away the Bucentaure's main and mizen masts nearly by the board, and doubtless killed or wounded a great many of her crew. The Leviathan poured in her fire within 30 yards of the French ship's stern, and the Conqueror soon afterwards did the same.

The Conqueror then hauled up on the lee quarter and beam of the Bucentaure, and shot away her foremast. In a few minutes afterwards the ship of the commander-in-chief of the combined fleet, whose fate had been previously sealed by the Victory's tremendous broadside, hauled down her colours, and was taken possession of by the Conqueror. The officer in charge of the boat was Captain James Atcherley, of the marines, who had with him but five hands, a corporal and two privates of his corps, and two seamen. On the captain's stepping upon the Bucentaure's quarter-deck, M. Villeneuve and his two captains presented their swords, but conceiving that it more properly belonged to Captain Pellew to disarm officers of their rank, Captain Atcherley declined the honour of receiving them. Having secured the magazine and put the key in his pocket, and placed two of his men as sentries, one at each cabin-door, Captain Atcherley, accompanied by the French admiral and his two captains, pulled off, with his three remaining hands, and at length boarded, not the Conqueror, who had proceeded in chase, but the Mars, her sister-ship ; where on account of some mistake about the nature of the message sent by Lieutenant Hennah, the acting commander of the Mars, to Captain Hardy, the French officers were ordered to remain.

Hauling up, after having raked the Bucentaure,[1] the Neptune

---

[1] See diagram at p. 404.

soon found herself in a similar position astern of the Santisima-Trinidad, whose main and mizen masts came down with a tremendous crash, just as the Leviathan was in the act of seconding a fire which her leader had so successfully opened. The English Neptune then luffed up alongside the Santisima-Trinidad to leeward, while the Conqueror, with her starboard guns, kept up a distant fire upon her to windward. At about 2 h. 30 m. P.M. the foremast of the Spanish four-decker shared the fate of her main and mizen masts, and she lay an unmanageable wreck upon the water. At this moment the Neptune had her attention suddenly called off by the movement that was making in the combined van, some of the ships of which, on bearing up, raked her, and caused the principal part of the damage and loss which she sustained in the action.

The Africa 64, having had the misfortune to lose sight of her fleet in the night, was, when the firing commenced, broad upon the Victory's larboard beam, and nearly abreast of the van-ship of the combined line. Seeing her danger, Lord Nelson ordered the Africa's signal to be thrown out, to make all possible sail. The intention of this signal appears to have been misunderstood ; and, instead of using means to run his ship out of danger, Captain Digby set every sail he could spread to hasten her into it. Passing along, and exchanging broadsides in succession with the ships of the combined van, the Africa, with much less injury done to her than might have been expected, bore down ahead of the Santisima-Trinidad.

Meeting no return to her fire, and seeing no colours hoisted on board the latter, Captain Digby concluded that the four-decker had surrendered, and sent Lieutenant John Smith in a boat to take possession. Upon the lieutenant's reaching the quarter-deck, and asking an officer who advanced to meet him, whether or not the Santisima-Trinidad had surrendered, the Spaniard replied, "Non, non," pointing at the same time to one Spanish and four French sail-of-the-line then passing to windward. As, for the want of masts, the Santisima-Trinidad was settling fast to windward of the two fleets, and he had only a boat's crew with him, Lieutenant Smith quitted the Spanish ship (the crew of which, singularly enough, permitted him to do so), and returned on board the Africa.

The Santisima-Trinidad remained without a prize-crew until 5 h. 30 m. P.M.; when the Prince, by signal, boarded and took her in tow. The Trinidad's loss, although we are unable to particularize it, is described to have been, and no doubt was, extremely severe: she had been exposed to the raking fire, in succession, of four ships, the Victory (distantly and partially), Neptune, Leviathan, and Conqueror; and her hull, in consequence, had been dreadfully shattered, especially about the stern and quarters.

Before we proceed in our relation of the further part which the Leviathan took in the action, we will briefly state what damages and loss were sustained by the Neptune, Conqueror, and Bucentaure. The Neptune's masts were all more or less wounded, but not dangerously so, and her standing and running rigging somewhat damaged: she had received nine shot between wind and water, and had incurred a loss of 10 seamen killed, her captain's clerk, 30 seamen, and three marines wounded.

The Conqueror had her mizen topmast and maintopgallantmast shot away, her fore and main masts badly wounded, and her rigging of every sort much cut; several shot had also struck her on the larboard side between wind and water. The loss on the part of the Conqueror, up to the period of the Bucentaure's surrender (her further loss will be shown presently), was comparatively trifling: she had one seaman killed, and one lieutenant of marines (Thomas Wearing), one lieutenant of the Russian navy (Philip Mendel), and seven seamen wounded. The damages of the Bucentaure in her masts have already been described: her hull also was much cut up; and her loss in killed and wounded, according to the verbal report of her few surviving officers, amounted to upwards of 400 officers and men, including among the slightly wounded Admiral Villeneuve and his captain.

Leaving the Santisima-Trinidad to the care of the English Neptune, the Leviathan stood on towards the French Neptune, then amusing herself in the manner we have related,[1] with now a second French ship, the Fougueux, joined to the Téméraire. As the Leviathan approached, and before she was in a position to fire a shot, the Neptune, at whom the Téméraire had just brought some of her foremost guns to bear, wore round, and, in going off before the wind, at least enabled the former to identify, by the name on her stern, the French ship that chose to fly, the moment an antagonist appeared, who was in a condition to oppose her, although, evidently, not of force enough to maintain the combat with any prospect of success.

Disappointed here, Captain Bayntun hauled up on the lar-

[1] See p. 424.

board tack, and presently observed that all the ships of the combined van ahead of the Santisima-Trinidad were tacking or wearing, as if to double upon the headmost ships of the British weather column, and place them betwixt two fires. Sure of finding an opponent among those—and, such is the confidence inspired among the ships of a British fleet, as sure that, if likely to be overmatched, some friend or other would hasten to her rescue—the Leviathan stood on to the north-east.

A Spanish 74, the San-Augustin, who was steering south-east, appeared to be desirous to measure her strength with the British 74; and at about 3 P.M., when within 100 yards, put her helm hard a-starboard, in the hope to be able to rake the Leviathan ahead. To frustrate a manoeuvre so likely to be serious in its effects, the Leviathan put her helm hard a-port, and, having fresher way than the San-Augustin, felt its influence more quickly. The consequence was, that the guns of the British ship were brought to bear before those of her antagonist : and, loaded with three shot each, were discharged, with admirable precision, and at the distance of less than 50 yards, into the starboard quarter of the San-Augustin. Down went, in an instant, the Spanish ship's mizenmast, and with it her colours, and feeble was the return she bestowed.

The probability now was, that, as the Leviathan kept forging ahead, and could not, on account of the previously damaged state of her rigging, back her sails, the San-Augustin would be able to wear under her stern. To prevent this, the Leviathan, putting her helm a-starboard, ran on board the San-Augustin, in such a way, that the latter's jib-boom entangled itself in the former's larboard main rigging, thereby exposing the San-Augustin's upper-deck to the poop carronades and marines of the Leviathan. A smart and well-directed fire soon drove the Spaniards below ; and Lieutenant John Baldwin, third of the Leviathan, at the head of a party of seamen and marines, leaped on board the San-Augustin, and carried her without further opposition. The British 74, with her stream-cable, then lashed the prize to herself. Scarcely had the Leviathan effected this, ere the Intrépide, another fresh ship from the combined van, came crowding up, and, after raking the Leviathan ahead, ranged along the starboard side; but waited only to exchange a passing fire, as the Africa and one or two other British ships were fast approaching to the assistance of their friend. The first two set of figures in the following diagram will assist in explaining the manoeuvres of the Leviathan and her Spanish opponent :

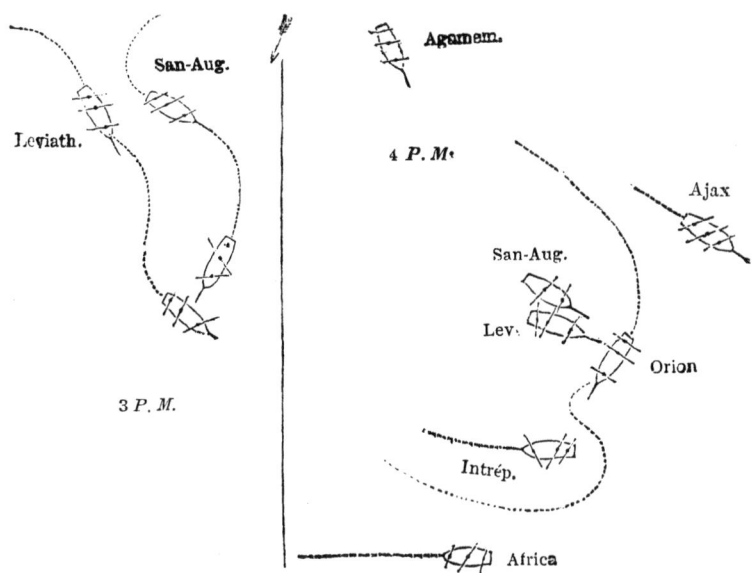

In this spirited, and, for its undisturbed occurrence in a
general action, rather singular combat, the Leviathan's damages
and loss, although we are not enabled to exhibit them sepa-
rately, were, it is certain, of trifling amount. Including what
she had previously sustained, the Leviathan had the main piece
of her head shot through, all three masts and bowsprit, and
most of her lower and topsail yards wounded, her mizentopsail
yard shot away, and a great part of her rigging cut to pieces.
She received eight shot between wind and water, and had one
long 32 and one long 18 pounder, and one 18-pounder carronade, completely disabled. Her loss amounted to two seamen
and two marines killed, one midshipman (J. W. Watson), 17
seamen, and four marines wounded. Besides the loss of her
mizenmast, the San-Augustin had her remaining masts injured,
and her hull struck in several places, particularly near the starboard quarter: her loss was represented by her officers to have
amounted to 160 in killed and wounded, including among the
latter her captain, Don Felipe Xado Cagigal.

Being, except the Leviathan, the nearest British ship to the
Intrépide, the Africa was the first that brought the latter to
action. This, at about 3 h. 30 m. P.M., the Africa most gallantly
did, and, in spite of her decided inferiority of force, maintained

the contest for nearly three quarters of an hour; when the Orion came up, and opened a fire upon the Intrépide's starboard quarter. The Orion then wore round the French ship's stern, and, bringing to on the lee bow of the latter between her and the Africa, whose fire, without any disparagement to her, was nearly silenced, maintained so heavy and well-directed a cannonade, that in less than a quarter of an hour the main and mizen masts of the Intrépide, already injured by the Africa's fire, fell over her side. The proximity of the Conqueror, and the approach of the Ajax and Agamemnon, left to the Intrépide no alternative but to strike her colours. This the French ship did at 5 P.M., having been greatly damaged in hull as well as masts, and incurred a loss, according to the representation of her officers, of nearly 200 in killed and wounded. The second set of figures in the last diagram will show the track of the Orion in her way towards, and during the time she engaged, the Intrépide.

The Africa had her maintopsail-yard shot away, and her bowsprit and three lower masts so badly wounded that none of the latter could afterwards stand. Her remaining masts and yards were also more or less injured; her rigging and sails cut to pieces; and her hull, besides its other serious damage, had received several shot between wind and water. Her loss amounted to 12 seamen and six marines killed, one lieutenant (Matthew Hay), one captain of marines (James Tynmore), two master's mates (Henry West and Abraham Turner), three midshipmen (Frederick White, Philip J. Elmhurst, and John P. Bailey), 30 seamen, and seven marines wounded; a loss which, considering that her complement was only 490 men and boys, and that Captain Digby had voluntarily engaged so superior a force, proves that, although but a 64, the Africa had performed as gallant a part as any ship in the British line. The Orion, who came so opportunely to the aid of the Africa, had her foremast wounded, and her maintopsail-yard and maintopgallantmast shot away. The loss on board the Orion, however, amounted to only one seaman killed, and two midshipmen (Charles Tause and Charles P. Cable, both slightly), 17 seamen, and four marines wounded.

It was at about 2 h. 30 m. P.M. that the whole of the Franco-Spanish van, except the Santisima Trinidad, who lay dismasted abreast and to leeward of the Bucentaure, equally a wreck and either a prize or in the act of becoming one, began to put about, some by staying, others by wearing, in obedience to a signal made by the commander-in-chief at 1 h. 50 m. P.M. to the follow-ing purport : " The French fleet, engaging to windward or to leeward, orders the ships which, from their present position, are not engaging, to take such a position as will bring them the most quickly into action." " L'armée navale Française, combattant au vent ou sous le vent, ordre aux vaisseaux qui, par leur position actuelle, ne combattant pas, d'en prendre une quelconque, qui les reporte le plus promptement possible au feu."[1] It appears that, five minutes before, Rear-admiral Dumanoir had signalled the commander-in-chief that the van had no enemy to contend with.

According to the admiral's previous instructions to his cap-tains, the above signal was to be considered as casting a stigma upon those to whom it was addressed.[2] At all events no imme-diate attempt was made by the generality of the ships to comply with the signal, and those that were the most prompt in obeying it were baffled by the calm state of the weather. The Formi-dable, and one or two of the other ships, had to employ their boats to tow themselves round. Hence the manœuvre was slow, partial, and imperfect. When the 10 ships did at length get on the starboard tack, five (four French and one Spanish), under Rear-admiral Dumanoir, hauled their wind, and the remaining five kept away, as if to join Admiral Gravina, then to leeward of the rear, in the act of making off.

It was in the height of all this confusion in the combined van, that the Britannia, Agamemnon, Orion, and Ajax got inter-mingled among the French and Spanish ships, which had wore and edged away in the manner related. The Britannia appears to have been engaged, a short time, with the San-Francisco-de-Asis, and subsequently with the Rayo three-decker. It was con-sidered on board the Britannia, that the ship she engaged, after the San-Francisco-de-Asis, was the French Neptune, with " a tier of guns on her gangway." Owing to the obscurity occa-sioned by the smoke, and to the want of wind to blow out the flags, a mistake respecting the colours might easily be made ; and certainly the Neptune had no guns on her gangway, but was a regular 80, similar to the Bucentaure.

The Agamemnon and Ajax also exchanged a few broadsides with some of the ships that had bore up ; and the Orion, as already stated, was the first, after the Africa, that became closely engaged with the Intrépide. The latter and the San-Augustin were the only ships of the five, that seemed to have

1 Victoires et Conquêtes, tome xvi., p. 173.   2 See p. 366.

any other object in view than a retreat. The San-Francisco-de-Asis might reasonably have declined closing with the Britannia; but the Héros appears to have had no three-decker opposed to her, although she probably was one of the ships that raked the British Neptune, after the latter had silenced the Santisima-Trinidad. The Héros had her captain killed, but sustained no other loss of consequence, and very slight damage. What loss the Rayo suffered is not known; but she did undoubtedly incur a loss, and had her masts and rigging tolerably wounded and cut up.

The Britannia, with some slight damage to her masts and still less to her hull, had one lieutenant (Francis Roskruge), eight seamen, and one marine killed, her master (Stephen Trounce), one midshipman (William Grant), 33 seamen, and seven marines wounded. The Ajax was very slightly damaged, and had only two seamen killed and nine wounded. The principal damage sustained by the Agememnon was a large hole below the quarter, probably from a shot fired by one of M. Dumanoir's ships. In consequence of this the ship made four feet water an hour: her loss consisted of only two seamen killed and eight wounded.[1]

The five French and Spanish ships which hauled to the wind, after wearing in the manner already stated, were the Formidable, commanded by Rear-admiral Dumanoir, Duguay-Trouin, Mont-Blanc, Scipion, and Neptuno. The very British ships that, from their disabled state, were calculated to offer the least opposition, having little or no sail to force them to leeward, lay nearest to the track of M. Dumanoir's squadron. Among those the Victory, Téméraire, and Royal Sovereign were the most exposed. The Victory, with her mizen topmast gone, lay with her head to the northward, having the Bucentaure, a mere hulk, a point or two on her weather bow, two or three ships' lengths off, and the Santisima-Trinidad, another hulk, at a somewhat greater distance on her lee bow. At about three-quarters of a mile astern of the Victory, or rather upon her weather-quarter, lay the Téméraire with her two prizes. The head of the Téméraire, and of the Redoutable also, whose mainmast still held her fast to the former, was pointed to the southward; and her crew were busied in booming off the Fougueux from her starboard side, to be ready to salute the French ships as they passed. The Royal Sovereign, with only her foremast standing, lay a short distance astern and to leeward of the Téméraire, in

---

[1] The Agamemnon expended 6781 lbs. of powder, and fired 1145 shot.

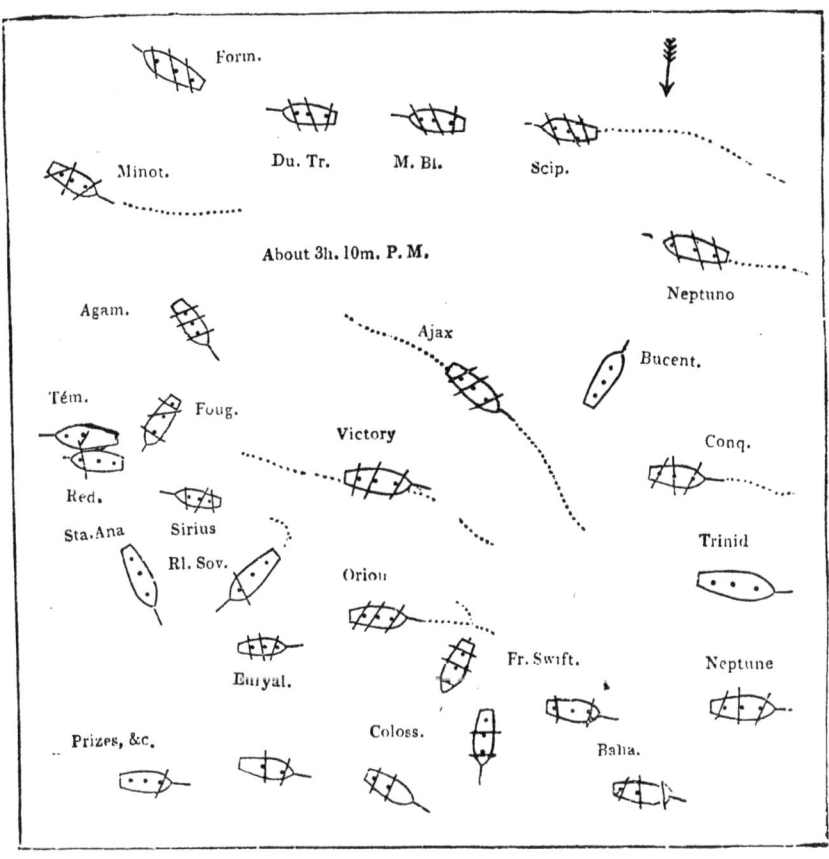

the act of being towed clear of her dismasted prize, the Santa-
Ana, by the Euryalus frigate. The relative position of all
these ships will perhaps be better understood by the above
diagram; which, however, as respects some of its details, is
not given with quite so much confidence as the generality of
the others.

Among the first shots fired by M. Dumanoir's ships, after
they had put about, was one that killed two of the Conqueror's
lieutenants. The manner in which this fatal accident happened
is as extraordinary as it was distressing. Lieutenant William
M. St. George, third of the ship, while passing Lieutenant
Robert Lloyd, who was first, good-humouredly tapped him on
the shoulder, and gave him joy of his approaching epaulet as a

commander. Just as Lieutenant St. George, having moved on a step or two had turned his face round, was in the act of smiling on his friend, a cannon-shot took off the head of the latter, and struck the former senseless on the deck.

In passing the Victory, M. Dumanoir's squadron, having kept away a little for the purpose, exchanged a few distant and ineffectual shot with her. By the time the van-ship, the Formidable, had arrived abreast of the Téméraire, the latter had succeeded in clearing her starboard broadside of the Fougueux, who now lay athwart the Téméraire's stern, with her head to the eastward, and consequently with her stern exposed to the raking fire of the enemy. One or two broadsides were exchanged between the Téméraire and the ships to windward; and the fire from the latter cut away the main and mizen masts of the Fougueux, and killed and wounded some of her people. One shot also shattered the leg of a midshipman belonging to the Téméraire, who had been sent on board the Redoutable to assist Lieutenant Wallace, and who died the same evening, after having undergone amputation by the French surgeon.

A great deal of odium has been cast by the English journals and even by grave historical works, upon Rear-admiral Dumanoir, for having fired upon the French and Spanish prizes in his passage to windward of the fleets. Admitting the inutility of the act to be an argument (its " barbarity " is none, because the prisoners ought to have been stationed below) against the propriety of its adoption, it surely was the duty of the French admiral to fire at, and injure as much as he could, the different British ships within the reach of his guns. In his letter to the editor of the Gibraltar Chronicle, whose gross inaccuracy on another point we shall soon have to expose, M. Dumanoir positively denies that he intentionally fired at the prizes; but how, let us ask, was it possible for the shot to pass clear of them, when, in some instances, they lay within less than their own length of, and, in others, absolutely masked, the ships that had captured them?

The hauling to windward of M. Dumanoir afforded to the Minotaur and Spartiate an opportunity which, as the two rearmost ships of the weather column, they would otherwise have sought in vain. At about 3 h. 10 m. P.M., having hauled close on the larboard tack, the Minotaur and Spartiate lay to with their main topsails to the masts, and exchanged broadsides in passing with the Formidable, Duguay-Trouin, Mont-Blanc, and

Scipion, and, as the Neptuno was considerably astern, succeeded in cutting her off. At 4 P.M. the two British 74s wore, and got close alongside of the Spanish 80; who, after defending herself in the most gallant manner, surrendered at about 5 h. 10 m. P.M. with the loss of her mizenmast and fore and main topmasts, and with, no doubt, a serious loss in men, although it has not been recorded. Having been captured directly to windward of the Téméraire and her two prizes, the Neptuno drifted upon and fell on board the former. This gave rise to the extraordinary mistake contained in Lord Collingwood's official despatch, representing that the Téméraire had been boarded by a French ship on one side and a Spaniard on the other.

The Minotaur had her foretopsail-yard shot away; and both she and the Spartiate had their masts, yards, and rigging in general a good deal damaged. The Minotaur had three seamen killed, her boatswain (James Robinson), one midshipman (John Samuel Smith), 17 seamen, and three marines wounded; and the Spartiate had also three seamen killed, and her boatswain (John Clarke), two midshipmen (Henry Bellairs and Edward Knapman), 16 seamen, and one marine wounded. A great proportion of the loss suffered by these two ships was no doubt inflicted by the Neptuno; who, as the Intrépide was the last French, was herself the last Spanish, ship that struck to the British on this eventful day. We have still some arrears to bring up in the lee column, a task we shall hasten to execute.

It was about 2 P.M. when the Dreadnought got into action with the San-Juan Nepomuceno, then surrounded by the Principe-de-Asturias, San-Justo, and a French 80-gun ship, the Indomptable. In about 15 minutes the Dreadnought ran on board of and captured the San-Juan; who had previously been engaged by the Tonnant, Bellerophon, Defiance, and some other ships, and was nearly in a defenceless state. Without, as it would appear, staying to take possession of the Spanish 74, the Dreadnought pursued and fired at the Spanish three-decker; but, after the exchange of two or three broadsides, a shot from one of which struck off the left arm of Admiral Gravina, the Principe-de-Asturias made sail and effected her escape.

The Dreadnought had her masts cut with shot, but none carried away: her loss amounted to six seamen and one marine killed, and one lieutenant (James L. Lloyd), two midshipmen (Andrew M'Culloch and James Sabbin), 19 seamen, and four marines wounded. Besides being dismasted, the San-Juan Nepomuceno was much shattered in her hull, and sustained a

loss, as represented, of nearly 300 in killed and wounded, including among the mortally wounded her gallant commander.

Having yawed to starboard to allow the Dreadnought to pass
on to the Spanish three-decker, then the rearmost enemy's ship
by two, the Polyphemus attempted to haul up again; but,
finding the English Swiftsure close upon her larboard quarter,
she was obliged to wait until the latter passed ahead. It was at
about 3 h. 25 m. P.M. that the English Swiftsure, having passed
the Belleisle's stern, opened her fire upon the French Achille;
who, passing along the larboard beam of the Belleisle, edged
away to the south-east, followed and engaged by the former.
The Swiftsure presently succeeded in crossing her opponent's
stern and in getting to leeward of her;[1] when the Polyphemus,
who had received a heavy fire from the French Neptune, in
passing between the latter and the Belleisle, advanced on the
French Achille's weather-quarter. In about 40 minutes after
the Swiftsure had commenced the action with the Achille, the
latter, having had her mizenmast and fore-yard shot away, and
having also caught fire in the fore-top, ceased engaging, and, as
it appeared to the Polyphemus, waved a union-jack at her starboard cathead. The Polyphemus then stood away to assist the
Defence in engaging the San-Ildefonso, but who struck before
the Polyphemus got up; and the Prince three-decker bore down
between the French Achille and English Swiftsure, just as the
latter, considering the Achille a beaten ship, was hauling off
to seek a more worthy opponent. But the business of the day,
at this end of the line at least, was now nearly over.

The Swiftsure had her mizentopmast shot away, and mizenmast badly wounded, and lost seven seamen and two marines
killed, and one midshipman (Alexander Bell Handcock), six
seamen, and one marine wounded. The Polyphemus had her
main and maintop masts badly wounded, her spanker-boom cut
through, and one lower-deck gun disabled, but escaped with the
slight loss of two men killed and four wounded.

While the Revenge was attempting to pass through the
enemy's line, and just as she had put her helm a-port, to place
herself athwart the hawse of the Aigle,[2] the latter's jib-boom
caught the mizentop-sail of the former; and, before the two
ships got clear, the Revenge was enabled to pour into the Aigle's
bows two deliberate broadsides. The Revenge then stood on,
and, while hauling up on the larboard tack, received a tre-

[1] See diagram at p. 408, where the tracks
cross.

[2] See second set of figures in diagram a·
p. 413.

mendous fire into her lee quarter from the Principe-de-Asturias; who, in conjunction with three two-deckers, probably the Neptune, Indomptable, and San-Justo, nearly fresh ships from the centre, continued cannonading the Revenge, until the Dreadnought and Thunderer came up and engaged the Spanish three-decker. The latter, who, it appears, would suffer no British ship to get to leeward of her, soon afterwards bore away, along with the most efficient of the ships in her company.

The exposed situation of the Revenge had occasioned her damages and loss of men to be very severe. Her bowsprit, three lower masts, maintopmast, and gaff were badly wounded : she had received nine shot below the copper ; her stern, transoms, and timbers, and several beams, knees, riders, and iron standards, were very much wounded, and so was her hull generally. She had several chain-plates shot away, several of her lower-deck ports destroyed, and three of her guns dismounted. With respect to the loss, the Revenge had two midshipmen (Thomas Grier and Edward F. Brooks), 18 seamen, and eight marines killed, and her captain, master (Luke Brokenshaw), one lieutenant (John Berry), one captain of marines (Peter Lily), 38 seamen, and nine marines wounded.

At about 2 h. 30 m. P.M. the Defence commenced firing at the Berwick; who, in less than half an hour, hauled off and was engaged, as already stated, by the Achille.[1] The Defence, shortly afterwards, began engaging the San-Ildefonso, and, at the end of an hour's action, compelled the Spanish ship to strike. The Defence had her mainmast shot through and wounded in several places, her gaff cut in two, and her lower and topmast rigging much injured : she had, also, several hanging knees and chain-plates carried away, one shot-hole through the knee of the head, and five between wind and water. Her loss amounted to four seamen and three marines killed, and 23 seamen and six marines wounded. The San-Ildefonso, having been engaged by one or two other British ships before the Defence arrived up, had suffered greatly in masts, rigging, and hull, and lost a full third of her crew in killed and wounded.

It was about 3 P.M. when, having bore up to assist the Revenge, the Thunderer wore athwart the hawse of the Principe-de-Asturias, and having raked her distantly, brought to on the starboard tack. In about five minutes the French Neptune came to the assistance of the Spanish three-decker (into whom the Dreadnought was now firing), and engaged the Thunderer

[1] See p. 416.

for a short time; when these two ships, with most of the others near them, bore up and made off. The Thunderer's main and mizen masts and bowsprit had a shot in each, but otherwise her damages were not material. Her loss amounted to two seamen and two marines killed, and one master's mate (John Snell), one midshipman (Alexander Galloway), nine seamen, and one marine wounded. The Principe-de-Asturias, at the time she bore up to escape, had been partially engaged by the Revenge and Defiance, and had received two broadsides from the Prince, in addition to the contest she had previously maintained with the Dreadnought and other British ships: hence her damages and loss were comparatively severe. None of the Spanish three-decker's masts appear to have been shot away, but that all were more or less damaged may be inferred from the fact, that her main and mizen masts were unable to withstand the gale that ensued. The loss sustained by the Principe-de-Asturias amounted to a lieutenant and 40 men killed, and 107 men badly wounded, including Admiral Gravina himself, as already mentioned, in the left arm (which was afterwards amputated, but too late to save his life), and some other officers.

Finding her rigging and sails too much cut to enable her to follow the Principe-de-Asturias, the Defiance stood for the Aigle, whose crippled state had prevented her from making sail. At about 3 P.M. the Defiance ran alongside of the Aigle, lashed the latter to herself, boarded her with little resistance, got possession of the poop and quarter-deck, hauled down the French colours, and hoisted the English in their stead; when, suddenly, so destructive a fire of musketry was opened upon the boarders from the forecastle, waist, and tops of the Aigle, that the British, before they had been well five minutes in possession of their prize, were glad to quit her and escape back to their ship.

As soon as the lashings were cut loose, the Defiance sheered off to a half-pistol-shot distance, and there kept up so well-directed a cannonade that, in less than 25 minutes, the Aigle, the fire from whose great guns had also been nobly maintained, called for quarter, and was presently taken quiet possession of. The Defiance afterwards took possession of the San-Juan Nepomuceno; which ship, besides her crippled state from the previous attacks she had sustained, had already surrendered to the Dreadnought. On the coming up, therefore, of the latter ship, Captain Durham sent the San-Juan's captain and officers to her.

The Defiance had her bowsprit and fore and main masts shot

through in the centre of each, also her mizenmast, three top-masts, jib and driver-booms, and gaff wounded: her rigging and sails were likewise much cut, and her hull struck with shot in several places. She had one lieutenant (Thomas Simens), her boatswain (William Forster), one midshipman (James Williamson), eight seamen, and six marines killed, and her captain (slightly), two master's mates (James Spratt and Robert Browne), two midshipmen (John Hodge and Edmund Andrew Chapman), 39 seamen, and nine marines wounded. The Aigle, although her principal masts do not appear to have been shot away, had received several shot through them, and was otherwise much disabled. Her hull was pierced in every direction, and her starboard-quarter nearly beaten in. The Aigle had been successively engaged by six or seven British ships, and had conducted herself in the most gallant manner. Her loss amounted to about 270 in killed and wounded, including several of her officers.

Of the 19 ships composing the combined rear, 11 have been captured, and seven have quitted the line and run to leeward; thus leaving one ship only, the French Achille, whose fate remains to be shown. This ship, in her successive encounters with the English Achille, Belleisle, Swiftsure, and Polyphemus, had lost her mizenmast, maintopmast, and foreyard, and having since, owing, in all probability, to her swivels or musketry there, caught fire in her fore-top, was without the means of extinguishing the flames on account of the destruction of her engine by the enemy's shot. The only alternative left was to cut away the mast. At 4 h. 30 m. P.M., while the crew were preparing to do this, so that it might fall clear of the ship, a broadside from the Prince cut the mast in two about its centre; and the wreck, with its flaming top, fell directly upon the boats in the waist. These soon caught fire, and so in succession did the decks below.

After the discharge of one or two broadsides, the Prince discovered the accident that had befallen her antagonist, and, wearing, hove to, and in company with the Swiftsure, sent her boats to save as many as possible of the French Achille's crew: in which laudable attempt, soon afterwards, the Pickle schooner and Entreprenante cutter zealously employed themselves. This was a dangerous service, on account of the French ship's guns, when heated discharging their contents. The Swiftsure's boats had two or three men killed and wounded in consequence. The Achille had already suffered a heavy loss in killed and wounded, including among the latter her captain and the principal part of her officers; leaving not a doubt, that the ship had most gallantly conducted herself throughout the engagement.

It was at about 5 h. 45 m. P.M. that the Achille exploded, and with her perished her then commanding-officer, Enseigne de vaisseau Charles-Alexandre Cauchard, and a great portion of her crew. It may be, as the French say, that the Achille at this time had her colours flying; but the ship certainly had, two hours before, made signs of submission, and was, in consequence, spared by the British ship (Polyphemus) then in action with her. The damages of the Prince consisted of a shot in her bowsprit, three shots in her foremast, and the same in her mizen-mast; but she experienced the singular good fortune, as a ship of this fleet, not to have a man of her crew injured.

We have now, according to the best information in our power, gone through the details of each British ship's preceedings in the battle of Trafalgar. Should justice not have been done to the exertions of any particular ship on this glorious occasion, we hope it will be attributed, rather to the confused manner in which the attack, the latter part of it especially, was carried on, than to any deficiency of research in us. How far the published accounts on either side are calculated to guide the historian, has already in part appeared, and will be more fully shown when some of those accounts pass under review. As to the accounts furnished exclusively for this work by individuals present in the battle, much as we, and through us the public, owe to them, they are, in many instances, imperfect, obscure, and even contradictory. Nor can it be wondered at, considering how each officer's attention must have been absorbed in the immediate duties of his station; and how few yards, beyond the side of his own ship, the smoke of so many combatants would permit him to see.

According to the official returns the aggregate loss in killed and wounded on the part of the British amounted to 1690;[1] of which amount about six-sevenths, or 1452, fell to the share of 14 out of the 27 ships in the fleet. With a few exceptions,

---

[1] The following is a recapitulation of the loss of men and masts sustained by the British fleet, the ships of each column being ranged in the order in which they appear to have bore down to the attack. The masts "left tottering," actually fell, or were taken down a day or two after the action. Besides these, many bowsprits, masts, yards, and topmasts, were badly wounded, and subsequently replaced by new ones. A column has been added, with the names, as accurately as we have been able to get them, of the officers acting as first, second, third, and fourth lieutenants of the Victory, first and second of the Royal Sovereign, and first of the ships remaining, at the close of the battle.

the ships so suffering were in the van of their respective columns. This was a consequence of the peculiar mode of attack adopted by Lord Nelson, coupled with the fall of the breeze after the firing had begun. For instance, the leading ships of each column, as they approached within gun-shot of the combined fleet, were exposed to the deliberate and uninterrupted fire of seven or eight ships drawn up in line ahead, without being able, until nearly on board of them to bring a gun to bear in return. The moment the former did begin to engage, the French and

Ships.	Loss.			Bowsprit, lower and top masts and their yards.		First Lieutenants.
	Kill.	Wd.	Tot.	Shot away.	Left tottering.	
Weather column.						
Victory . . .	57	102	159	Mizentopmast . .	Mizenmast . . {	John Quilliam. Edward Williams. Andrew King. John Yule.
Téméraire . .	47	76	123	{ Main and head of mizenmasts, foretopsail & fore-yds. }	. .	Thomas Kennedy.
Neptune . .	10	34	44	. .	. .	George Acklom.
Leviathan . .	4	22	26	Mizentopsail-yard .	. .	Eyles Mounsher.
Britannia . .	10	42	52	. .	. .	Arthur Atchison.
Conqueror . .	3	9	12	Mizentopmast . .	. .	James Couch.
Africa . . .	18	44	62	Maintopsail-yard .	{ All three lower masts . . . }	John Smith.
Agamemnon .	2	8	10	. .	. .	Hugh Cook.
Ajax	2	9	11	. .	. .	Jerem. Brown.
Orion	1	23	24	Maintopsail-yard .	. .	Richard Croft.
Minotaur . .	3	22	25	Foretopsail-yard .	. .	James Stuart.
Spartiate . .	3	20	23	. .	Maintopmast .	John M'Kerlie.
Lee column.						
Royal Sovereign	47	94	141	{ Main and mizen masts and foretopsail-yard . . }	Foremast . . {	John Ellis. William Stephens.
Belleisle . . .	33	93	126	{ All three masts and bowsprit . . . }	. .	Thomas Fife.
Mars	29	69	98	{ Maintopmast and spanker-boom. . }	Foremast . .	Benjamin Patey.
Tonnant . . .	26	50	76	{ Three topmasts and mainyard . . . }	. .	John Bedford.
Bellerophon .	27	123	150	Main & miz. topmasts	Foretopmast .	Edw. F. Thomas.
Colossus . . .	40	160	200	Mizenmast . . .	Fore & mainmasts	Thos. Rd. Toker. Wm. W. Daniel.
Achille . . .	13	59	72	. .	. .	John Clavell.
Dreadnought .	7	26	33	Maintopsail-yard .	. .	George Mowbray.
Polyphemus .	2	4	6	. .	. .	Lewis Hole.
Revenge . . .	28	51	79	. .	. .	James Lilburne.
Swiftsure . .	9	8	17	Mizentopmast . .	. .	William Hellard.
Defiance . . .	17	53	70	. .	. .	John Clark.
Thunderer . .	4	12	16	. .	. .	James Green.
Defence . . .	7	29	36	. .	. .	William Godfrey.
Prince . . .	..	..	..	.	. .	
Total . .	449	1241	1690			

Spanish ships closed for mutual support; whereby the latter not only prevented each other from firing at such of the British ships as were still bearing down, but became too seriously occupied with close antagonists, to bestow much attention upon distant ones.

We regret our inability to particularize, as usual, the loss sustained by the ships of the Franco-Spanish fleet. Of the many that were captured, not one has her loss stated in the British official account; and neither the French nor the Spaniards, except in the case of the Redoutable and of one or two Spanish ships, have published any returns. It is therefore impossible for us to do more than point to the effects of the British shot upon the majority of the French and Spanish ships, deducible from the state of their masts and rigging already so fully described; leaving it to be inferred, that the antagonist of a British ship seldom has her masts shot away, until her hull has been greatly shattered, and a large proportion of her crew killed or disabled.

While the British ships are securing their prizes, and getting the latter and themselves into a state to keep the sea; and while the more fortunate of the French and Spanish ships are profiting by the occasion to effect their escape from the scene of so much disaster, we will conduct the reader to the cockpit of the Victory, where lay the chief hero of this triumphant day eking out the last remnant of that life's blood which he had so often before lavishly shed in the cause of his country. The manner in which Lord Nelson received his wound has already been described. "The ball," emphatically adds Doctor Beatty, and who states that he has it still in his possession, "was not fired from a rifle piece:" and yet Messrs. Clarke and M'Arthur, and after them Mr. Southey, have since declared, that the Redoutable and all the French ships had riflemen in their tops, and that it was one of these who aimed at and wounded Lord Nelson.[1] With marked illiberality, too, the gentlemen exult over the supposed death of "the fellow;"[2] who at least did his duty on the occasion, and none sooner than the noble victim would have been ready to acknowledge it. A French writer, well known in England for his general accuracy and candour, says. "Dans la *Vie de Nelson,* écrite par Southey, panégyriste salarié de la cour de l'Angleterre, sous le nom de poëte lauréat, il est dit qu'au combat de Trafalgar Nelson fut tué par un des arquebusiers tyroliens, apostés pour tirer sur lui. C'est une grossière imposture: il n'y avait

[1] Clarke and M'Arthur, vol. ii., pp. 445, 449.   [2] Southey, vol. ii., p 264

pas un seul Tyrolien sur notre flotte; il n'y avait pas même
d'armes carabinées."[1]

"While the men," says Doctor Beatty, "were carrying him
(Lord Nelson) down the ladder from the middle deck, his lordship observed that the tiller-ropes were not yet replaced: and
desired one of the midshipmen stationed there to go upon the
quarter-deck and remind Captain Hardy of that circumstance,
and request that new ones should be immediately rove. Having
delivered this order, he'took his handkerchief from his pocket
and covered his face with it, that he might be conveyed to the
cockpit at this crisis unnoticed by the crew."[2]

Although the very unlikely circumstance, that a practised
seaman, like Lord Nelson, would expect the tiller-ropes to have
been rove when the wheel was shot away and the ship foul of
another, coupled with the fact that no orders to that effect
reached the second in command, renders it doubtful if any
remark was made by his lordship about the tiller-ropes, or even
about the relieving tackles, the usual substitutes when the wheel
is gone, the covering of his face and stars with his handkerchief
(of which there is no doubt), lest the crew of the Victory should
be disheartened at the sight of the bleeding body of him upon,
whom they justly reckoned so much, proved that even the pangs
of death could not weaken the interest which the hero felt in
the final success of the day.

"It must occur to the reader," says Doctor Beatty, "that
from the nature of the scene passing in the cockpit, and the
noise of the guns, the whole of his lordship's expressions could
not be borne in mind, nor even distinctly heard, by the different
persons attending him."[3] Doctor Beatty has not, however,
scrupled to give to the world every disjointed sentence, every
half-uttered word, which he or his relaters could catch from the
lips of a dying, and at times, such was the intensity of his sufferings, irrational man. Our strictures upon the conduct of Lord
Nelson in the bay of Naples show, that we would blink nothing
which we considered to be the fair subject of historical observation; but we should have rejected as matters irrelevant to the
subject, the rhapsodies of a disordered mind: more especially,
when the subject to which they related was wholly of a private, and, compared with passing events, of an uninteresting
nature.

Doctor Beatty's narrative having gone through two editions

[1] Dupin's Voyage dans la Grande Bretagne, tome iv., p. 10.

[2] Beatty's Narrative, p. 35
[3] Ibid., p. 52.

and having been considered authentic, the objectionable circu-
lation of private remarks has been much increased by other
authors having transferred them to their pages, and under
which the press, in reference especially to Messrs. Clarke and
M'Arthur's two ponderous volumes, may be said to have
groaned. To our increased regret, a slight mistake, which we
made, but hastened to correct and apologize for, has been the
ostensible cause of the appearance, very recently, of a third
edition of Doctor Beatty's doubtless well-intended, but much
misnamed, "tribute of respect to the memory of the departed
hero." The discrepancy that exists between our present and
our former account of the Victory's proceedings in the battle of
Trafalgar, shows how much we erred, in relying upon the
accuracy of statements which, as emanating from an officer of
the ship, we took to be authentic. In justice to ourselves we
must observe, that it was owing to causes over which we had no
control, and not to any lack of exertion in collecting facts, that
the whole of the amended statements now given did not appear
in the first edition of this work.

After Lord Nelson had been laid upon a purser's bed on the
deck of the cockpit, he was stripped of his clothes, for the purpose of having the wound examined and the course of the ball
probed. The surgeon soon ascertained that the wound was
mortal; and Lord Nelson himself appears, from the first, to have
entertained a similar opinion. His sufferings from pain and
thirst were manifestly great. "He frequently called for drink,
and to be fanned with paper, making use of these words : 'Fan,
fan,' and 'Drink, drink.'" He kept constantly pushing away
the sheet, the sole covering upon him; and one attendant was as
constantly employed in drawing it up again over his slender
limbs and emaciated body. This recklessness about exposing
his person afforded a strong proof of the injury done to his
intellect; and well would it have been for Lord Nelson's
memory, had the listeners around his dying couch possessed
discernment enough to distinguish, and friendship enough (as
writers) to separate, the irrelevant utterings of a mind in a
paroxysm of delirium, from the patriotic effusions of the same
mind, when lit up, for a moment or so, by a ray of returning
reason.

In about an hour and 10 minutes after Lord Nelson had
received his wound, or at about 2 h. 35 m. P.M. Captain Hardy
found a moment's leisure from his anxious duty on deck to
comply with the frequently repeated request of the admiral,

conveyed through the surgeon, to visit him in the cockpit, "They shook hands affectionately, and Lord Nelson said: 'Well, Hardy, how goes the battle? How goes the day with us?'—'Very well, my lord,' replied Captain Hardy: 'we have got 12 or 14 of the enemy's ships in our possession; but five of their van have tacked, and show an intention of bearing down upon the Victory. I have therefore called two or three of our fresh ships round us, and have no doubt of giving them a drubbing.'—'I hope,' said his lordship, 'none of our ships have struck, Hardy.'—'No, my lord,' replied Captain Hardy; 'there is no fear of that.' Lord Nelson then said: 'I am a dead man Hardy. I am going fast: it will be all over with me soon.'"[1]

. Captain Hardy, in a minute or two, returned to the deck. Soon afterwards the Victory opened her larboard guns upon Rear-admiral Dumanoir's squadron passing to windward, and fired a few of her foremost starboard guns at the Swiftsure, then preparing to rake the Colossus.[2] The concussion of the firing so affected Lord Nelson, that, apostrophizing his ship, he called out: "Oh, Victory, Victory, how you distract my poor brain!" Then adding, after a short pause, "How dear is life to all men!" M. Dumanoir's ships passing on to the southward, and the Orion ranging up athwart the Swiftsure's stern, the Victory ceased her fire; and, after an interval of about 50 minutes from the conclusion of his former visit, Captain Hardy descended a second time to the cockpit. "Lord Nelson and Captain Hardy shook hands again; and while the captain retained his lordship's hand, he congratulated him, even in the arms of death, on his brilliant victory; which, he said, was complete, though he did not know how many of the enemy were captured, as it was impossible to perceive every ship distinctly. He was certain, however, of 14 or 15 having surrendered. His lordship answered, 'That is well, but I bargained for 20;' and then emphatically exclaimed, 'Anchor, Hardy, anchor!'—'I suppose, my lord, Admiral Collingwood will now take upon himself the direction of affairs.'—'Not while I live, I hope, Hardy,' cried the dying chief; and at that moment endeavoured ineffectually to raise himself from the bed. 'No,' added he, 'do you anchor, Hardy.' Captain Hardy then said, 'Shall we make the signal, sir?'—'Yes,' answered his lordship, 'for, if I live, I'll anchor;' meaning," adds the doctor in a note, "that in case of his lordship's surviving till all resistance on the part of the enemy had ceased, Captain Hardy was then to anchor the British fleet and prizes, if it should be found prac-

1 Beatty's Narrative, p. 42.   2 See diagram at p. 435.

ticable."[1] Captain Hardy remained with the dying chief in all about three (not " eight "[2]) minutes. In about a quarter of an hour after the captain had quitted the cockpit, Lord Nelson became speechless; and, great as must have been his previous sufferings, he expired without a struggle or a groan at, by the Victory's time, 4 h. 30 m. P.M., or, according to the time we have thought it preferable to use, about ten minutes or a quarter of an hour later.[3]

The moment it was announced to him that Lord Nelson was no more, and not previously as stated by Doctor Beatty,[4] Captain Hardy directed Lieutenant Alexander Hills to take the punt, the only remaining boat, proceed in her to the Royal Sovereign, and acquaint Vice-admiral Collingwood, not that Lord Nelson was actually dead, but, to save the feelings of a dear friend of the deceased, that he was mortally or dangerously wounded. Shortly afterwards Captain Blackwood came on board the Victory, to inquire after the safety of his friend and patron, and then learnt the first tidings of Lord Nelson's wound and death. Captain Hardy, soon afterwards, embarking with Captain Blackwood in the Euryalus's boat, went himself to acquaint Vice-admiral Collingwood with what had really happened, as well as to deliver to the new commander-in-chief Lord Nelson's dying request, that, for their preservation in reference to the shore and the prospect of a gale, the fleet and prizes, as soon as was practicable, might be brought to an anchor. Bosom friends as they always had been, Nelson and Collingwood were diametrically opposed in their plans of proceeding; as was most evident when the latter exclaimed : " Anchor the fleet ? Why, it is the last thing I should have thought of." Accordingly it was not done, and the consequences followed, which we shall presently have to relate.

To die in the arms of victory is, of all deaths, that which a true warrior most covets. What, then, was there so particularly to deplore in the death of Lord Nelson? Had he survived the battle, he would perhaps have passed some 15 or 20 years in in-

---

[1] Beatty's Narrative, p. 47.
[2] Ibid., p. 49.
[3] Doctor Beatty's official report of the course and site of the ball, as ascertained since death, will be found in the Appendix, No. 38.
The editor of this new edition differs greatly in opinion with Mr. James, relative to the suppression of *all* the conversation related by Beatty. Surely there was no wandering of thought when Nelson requested " that his carcass might be sent to England, and not thrown overboard." And when after the ejaculation of " Oh, Victory, Victory !" he added, " How dear is life to all men." That his last wish was for his country is beyond a doubt; but the human heart may retain feelings of affection for those it loved, and who loved it, and find a relief in its expression, although dying on a bed of glory, wrapped in the arms of victory.
[4] Beatty's Narrative, p. 46.

BATTLE OF TRAFALGAR. 449

glorious inactivity ; for nothing more, and certainly nothing greater, was left for him to do. His time come, he would have died, not on a midshipman's pallet in the cockpit of the Victory, but on a down bed in a chamber of his seat at Merton. What a contrast! Lord Nelson's friends, strictly such, did probably wish a slight modification in the manner of his death—that he had died on the spot where he had fallen, and where he wished he had remained, the Victory's quarter-deck, and that the only words heard from his lips had been the last which he actually uttered :—" I have done my duty ; I praise God for it."

As, in bestowing our humble tribute of praise upon the professional character of Lord Nelson, we may not, after all that has been written upon the subject, be able to steer clear of plagiarism, we shall be contented with transcribing three, as they appear to us, not less eloquently than justly drawn opinions. The first, penned by an Englishman and a friend to the deceased ; the second, either by, or for, the author of a contemporary work ; and the third, by a Frenchman who, if not personally an enemy of the British admiral, belonged to a nation whose brightest hopes had been humbled by repeated acts of his skill and valour, by the last act in particular.

" Thus," says Doctor Beatty, " died this matchless hero, after performing in a short but brilliant and well-filled life, a series of naval exploits, unexampled in any age of the world. None of the sons of fame ever possessed greater zeal to promote the honour and interest of his king and country ; none ever served them with more devotedness and glory, or with more successful and important results. His character will for ever cast a lustre over the annals of this nation, to whose enemies his very name was a terror. In the battle off Cape St. Vincent, though then in the subordinate station of a captain, his unprecedented personal prowess will long be recorded with admiration among his profession. The shores of Aboukir and Copenhagen subsequently witnessed those stupendous achievements which struck the whole civilized world with astonishment. Still these were only preludes to the battle of Trafalgar ; in which he shone with a majesty of dignity as far surpassing even his own former renown, as that renown had already exceeded everything else to be found in the pages of naval history ; the transcendently brightest star in a galaxy of heroes. His splendid example will operate as an everlasting impulse to the enterprising genius of the British navy."[1]

" Thus," says Captain Brenton, " fell the greatest sea-officer

[1] Beatty's Narrative, p. 53.

VOL. III. 2 G

of this or any other nation, recorded in history; his talents, his
courage, his fidelity, his zeal, his love for his king and country,
were exceeded by none. Never had any man the happy intuitive
faculty, of seizing the moment of propitious fortune, equal to
Nelson. His whole career, from his earliest entrance into the
service, offers to the youth of the British navy the most illustrious examples of every manly virtue; whether we view him as
a midshipman, a lieutenant, as the captain of a frigate, or a commander-in-chief. We have seen him, as captain of the Agamemnon, in Larma bay, writing his despatches while his ship
lay aground in an enemy's port; we have seen him as captain of
a 74-gun ship, on the 14th of February, lay a Spanish first-rate
and an 84-gun ship on board, and with his little band of heroes
rush from ship to ship, and take them both. Equally great in
the hour of defeat as of victory, see him at Teneriffe with his
shattered arm going to the rescue of his companions and saving
their lives, while every moment of delay increased the peril of
his own by hemorrhage and exhaustion: see him walk up the
ship's side—hear him command the surgeon to proceed to amputation; and see the fortitude with which he bore the agonizing
pain. Follow him to the Nile, and contemplate the destruction
of the fleet of France, and the consequent loss of her vast army
led by Buonaparte. How great was his professional knowledge
and decision at Copenhagen, when, despising death, he refused
to obey the signal of recal; because he knew that by such
obedience his country would have been disgraced, the great
object of the expedition frustrated, and Britain, overpowered by
the increased energy of the northern confederacy, might have
sunk under the multiplied force of her enemies. See him on the
same occasion sit down in the midst of carnage, and address a
letter to the Crown Prince of Denmark, which, while it gave a
victory to his country, added to her glory by stopping the useless effusion of human blood. We have seen him the patient,
watchful, and anxious guardian of our honour, in the Mediterranean, where, for two years, he sought an opportunity to engage
an enemy of superior force. Three times we have seen him
pursue the foes of his country to Egypt, and once to the West
Indies. And these great steps he took entirely on his own responsibility, disregarding any personal consideration, any calculation of force, or any allurement of gain. Coming at last to
the termination of his glorious career, the end of his life was
worthy of all his other deeds; the battle of Trafalgar will
stand, without the aid of sculpture or painting, the greatest

memorial of British naval valour ever exhibited ; no pen can do justice, no description can convey an adequate idea of the glories of that day ; and the event, which deprived us of our favourite chief, consummated his earthly fame, and rendered his name for ever dear to his country. Had not his transcendent virtues been shaded by a fault, we might have been accused of flattery. No human being was ever perfect, and however we may regret the blemish in the affair of Caraciolli, we must ever acknowledge, that the character of Nelson, as a public servant, is not exceeded in the history of the world."[1]

" Nelson," says M. Dupin, " ought to be held up as a pattern for admirals, by the extreme pains he took to impress upon his flag-officers and captains the spirit of the enterprises which he resolved to undertake. He unfolded to them his general plan of operations, and the modifications with which the weather or the manœuvres of the enemy might force him to qualify his original design. When once he had explained his system to the flag and superior officers of his fleet, he confided to them the charge of acting according to circumstances, so as to lead, in the most favourable manner, to the consummation of the enterprise thus planned. And Nelson, who was allowed to choose the companions of his glory, possessed the talent and the happiness to find men worthy of his instruction and confidence ; they learnt, in action, to supply what had escaped his forethought, and in success, to surpass even his hopes."[2]

Just as the battle with the combined fleet had terminated, Cape Trafalgar was seen from the Royal Sovereign, bearing south-east by east distant eight miles. Hence the name given to this battle ; of which the immediate result, as a French writer, not always so liberally disposed, has been brought to admit, was 17 French and Spanish ships captured, and one French ship burnt, if not after the flag which she had so long and so gallantly supported had been struck, at least when, an enemy's three-decker having attacked her, she had ceased to make resistance, and when 200 of her officers and men (unfortunately all that could be saved out of a crew, as deposed by her officers, originally numbering 700) were being received on board the tenders of the British fleet. Four other ships, as we have seen, had hauled to the southward ; and, no four British ships being sufficiently to windward, and at the same time sufficiently perfect in their rigging and sails, for an immediate pursuit, they effected their escape. Meanwhile Admiral Gravina, with 11

[1] Brenton, vol. iii., p. 463.   [2] For the original, see Appendix, No. 39.

French and Spanish ships of the line, and all the smaller vessels, was running to the north-east. Several of these ships, the Indomptable, Héros, San-Francisco-de-Asis, and Montanez, in particular, having scarcely a hole in their sails, were in excellent order for flight. Others were in tow by the frigates; and the whole in the course of the night anchored about a mile and a half from Rota, not being able to enter the bay or harbour of Cadiz on account of the strong south-south-east wind then blowing in shore. In the offing, however, the wind was still from the west-south-west.

At 6 P.M. Vice-admiral Collingwood, now the commander-in-chief of the British fleet, shifted his flag to the Euryalus frigate; and at 6 h. 15 m. P.M. the latter, taking the Royal Sovereign in tow, stood off-shore with her. At this time several of the British ships were more or less dismasted, and very few in a condition to carry sail; and out of the 27 in the fleet, 14 were tolerably damaged in hull. Of the 17 prizes, eight were wholly, and the remainder partially, dismasted. Some of these ships, too, were nearly in a sinking state, and none were without shattered hulls. To add to the perilous condition of the British fleet and prizes, the ships were then in 13 fathoms water, with the shoals of Trafalgar but a few miles to leeward. Fortunately the wind, which was at west-south-west, and therefore dead on the shore, blew moderately; but there was a very uneasy swell, highly distressing to the ships, particularly the dismasted ones. At 9 P.M., which was about four hours too late, the vice-admiral made the signal for the fleet to prepare to anchor. It is stated, that few of the ships had an anchor to let go, their cables having been cut by shot. Towards midnight the wind veered to south-south-west, and freshened considerably. Taking immediate advantage of this favourable change, the vice-admiral made the signal for the ships to wear with their heads to the westward. Four of the dismasted prizes, in proof that their cables would hold, had previously anchored off Cape Trafalgar. The remaining ships wore, as directed, and drifted to seaward.

On the 22nd, at 8 A.M., the Euryalus cast off the Royal Sovereign, and signalled the Neptune to take the latter in tow. In the course of the forenoon the vice-admiral issued a general order of thanks to the officers and men of the fleet for their valour and skill in the action; and he also ordered a day to be appointed for returning thanks to God for the success which had attended the British arms. During the whole of this day, the 22nd, the wind blew fresh from the southward, with repeated squalls; but, through the skill and activity of British seamen, the whole 13 prizes, that remained under way, were got hold of, and towed towards the appointed rendezvous in the west, round the Neptune and Royal Sovereign.

At 5 P.M. the Redoutable, in tow by the Swiftsure, being actually sinking, hoisted a signal of distress. The latter ship immediately sent her boats, and brought off part of the prize-crew, and about 120 Frenchmen, which were as many as the boats would contain. At 10 h. 30 m. P.M. the Redoutable being with her stern entirely under water, the Swiftsure cut herself clear. At about midnight the wind shifted to north-west, and still blew a gale. At 3 h. 30 m. A.M. on the 23rd, attracted by the cries of the people, the Swiftsure, who had wore to the southward, again sent her boats, and, from three rafts which the French crew, amidst a dreadful night of wind, rain, and lightning had constructed from the spars of their sunken ship, saved 50 more of the sufferers: making a total of about 170, including 70 out of the 222 described as wounded.[1] Captain Lucas had been previously removed to the Téméraire. The remaining survivors of the Redoutable's late officers and crew, and 13 of the Téméraire's, and five of the Swiftsure's men, perished in her.

Other casualties were the consequence of this night's gale. The Fougueux, having on board, besides a great portion of her late crew, 30 men belonging to the Téméraire, drifted on the rocks between Torre-Bermeja, and the river Sancti-Petri, and was totally wrecked, with the loss of all on board, except about 25 persons.

When the Algésiras parted from the Tonnant,[2] the situation of Lieutenant Bennett and his small party was critical in the extreme. The ship had lost all three masts nearly by the board. Her hull had been much battered by shot; but, so far fortunately, no holes were below the water-line. Of her anchors the two at the bows were all that remained: one of these was broken in the shank, and the stock of the other shot nearly away. On board the Algésiras at this time, including 40 or 50 wounded, were about 600 Frenchmen; and the whole of these were to be kept in subjection by 50 British. The prisoners were sent below, and the gratings secured over them. It was then found that not a man could be spared from guarding the hatch-ways, to rig jurymasts and endeavour to work the ship off a lee-shore; nor was there any chance of being taken in tow, the few

[1] See p. 427.   [2] See p. 411.

British ships near at hand being almost in as dismasted a state as the prize.

In this state was passed the whole of the blowing night of the 21st; and the morning of the 22nd found the Algésiras separated from the British fleet, and drifting bodily towards the rocky shore to the northward of Cape Trafalgar. On the evening of that day, being three miles only to windward of the spot where the Fougueux was then beating to pieces, Lieutenant Bennett ordered the hatches to be taken off, to afford to the French crew an opportunity of saving the lives of the 650 beings whose existence was now at stake. The French crew rushed on deck, and, after confining Lieutenant Bennett and his party in the after-cabin, began to rig jurymasts. Three topgallantmasts were soon stepped, and some small sails set upon them. With the aid of these, the Algésiras bent her head to the northward, and presently brought the port of Cadiz about two points on her lee bow. The ship, however, still continued in so unmanageable a state, owing to the strength of the wind, and the frequent blowing away of the sails, that she barely trailed along the shore clear of the rocks. At length the Algésiras reached Cadiz; and, to the credit of those whose prisoners they then were, Lieutenant Bennett and his 49 companions were allowed to return to their friends outside in one of the two French frigates, which, by Vice-admiral Collingwood's permission gratuitously conveyed to the governor of Andalusia, the Marquess of Solano, went with a flag of truce to receive, upon the usual conditions of not serving again till exchanged, the wounded Spaniards found on board the captured ships. In return for this courtesy, the Spanish governor offered the use of the Cadiz hospitals for the British wounded, and pledged the honour of Spain that they should be carefully attended.

The Bucentaure, another hull, having on board Lieutenant Richard Spear and a party of men from the Conqueror, by whom, amidst the severity of the gale, a vain attempt had been made to take her in tow, drifted towards the shore, and was compelled for safety to anchor near the castle of San-Sebastian. On the following day, the 22nd, the Bucentaure was wrecked on the Puerques; but her crew were all, or the greater part, saved, including the British. These were taken out of the wreck by the boats of one of the French frigates ; and, nothwithstanding that the Gibraltar Chronicle, of November 9, in this year, contains a long paragraph, filled with abuse of the " dastardly French," the " infamous and cowardly crew of the frigate," for alleged ill-treatment of the British taken out of the Bucentaure, the latter, by their own acknowledgment, were treated with humanity and kindness. Unfortunately, the co-authors of the "Life of Nelson," with reckless haste, have copied into their pages[1] the atrocious falsehood ; and, to give additional currency to a statement so accordant with their repeatedly expressed sentiments towards the French, Messrs. Clarke and M'Arthur have omitted to add, that they took the paragraph from the columns of a newspaper.

The north-westerly wind, that blew on the morning of the 23rd, being fair for quitting his anchorage at the bay or entrance of the outer harbour of Cadiz, Captain Cosmao-Kerjulien, the senior French officer in the port, weighed and made sail, with the Pluton, inefficient as she was, Indomptable, Neptune, Rayo, and San-Francisco-de-Asis, the five frigates, and the two brigs, hoping to be able to recapture some of the remaining prize-hulls, then driving about the coast. It is doubtful if any of the remaining six French and Spanish ships in Cadiz, unless it was the Héros and Montanez, were in a state to put to sea. At all events the Principe-de-Asturias and San-Leandro had each rolled away her main and mizen masts soon after anchoring on the night of the 21st. Nor could Admiral Gravina, as Vice-admiral Collingwood supposed, have commanded the squadron, as he was then suffering the pains of a mortal wound.

Soon after the above five sail of the line, five frigates, and two brigs had sailed out, the wind shifted to the west-south-west, and blew with extreme violence, raising such a sea, that most of the prizes broke their tow-ropes, and drifting far to leeward, were in part only again secured. The Franco-Spanish squadron making its appearance about noon, the most efficient of the British line-of-battle ships cast off the hulls of which they had with so much difficulty recovered possession, and by 3 P.M. were formed in line, to the number of 10 sail, between the greater part of those prizes and the ships of M. Cosmao. The odds were far too great for the French commodore, even had the wind been in his favour, to venture within gun-shot ; but his frigates soon effected the principal object for which he had sailed out: they recaptured the Santa-Ana and Neptuno, and carried both safe into port. The recapture of the two Spanish prizes was not, however, without its alloy. On the 24th the fine French 80-gun ship Indomptable was wrecked off the

---

[1] Clarke and M'Arthur, vol. ii., p. 456.

town of Rota, situated on the north-west point of the bay of Cadiz. Unfortunately the Indomptable had on board, in addition to her own, the survivors of the Bucentaure's crew, amounting to nearly 500 men ; making in all 1100 or 1200 souls, of whom not more than 100 are represented to have been saved. The San-Francisco-de-Asis parted her cables, and went on shore in Cadiz bay, near Fort Santa-Catalina : her crew, except a small portion, were saved. The Rayo, three-decker, another of M. Cosmao's squadron, not being able to enter Cadiz bay, anchored off San-Lucar, a town at the mouth of the river Guadalquivir, a few leagues to the north-west of Rota. There the Rayo soon rolled away her masts, which had been previously wounded by shot.

Observing that some of the leewardmost of the prizes were running for, and had already approached very near to, the Spanish coast, the Leviathan obtained leave of the commander-in-chief to endeavour to bring them to anchor. On the 24th, at daylight, when standing after the Monarca, the Leviathan discovered the Rayo, with Spanish colours flying, still at an anchor off the shoals of San-Lucar. At this time the 74-gun ship Donegal, Captain Pulteney Malcolm, from Gibraltar,[1] was stretching in from the southward, on the larboard tack, with a moderate breeze from north-west by north, and steering direct for the Spanish three-decker. At about 10 A.M., just as the Monarca had got within little more than a mile of the Rayo, who was at about an equal distance from the Donegal and Leviathan, the latter fired a shot wide of the Monarca, in order to oblige her to drop anchor. The shot falling about midway between the Monarca and the Rayo, the latter, conceiving probably that it was intended for her, hauled down her colours, and was taken possession of by the Donegal ; who presently anchored alongside and took out the prisoners. Meanwhile the Leviathan kept standing on towards the Monarca, and on boarding her, found that she was in a sinking state. Captain Bayntun, as quickly as possible, removed all the Englishmen, and nearly the whole of the Spaniards. It was well the Leviathan did so, for, in the gale of the ensuing night, the Monarca parted her cable and went on shore. A similar fate, a day or two afterwards, attended the Rayo ; and, of the 107 officers and men put on board by the Donegal, 25 were drowned : the remainder were made prisoners by the Spaniards.

The supposition that the Franco-Spanish squadron, which

[1] See p. 383.

had sailed out of Cadiz on the 22nd, consisted of 10, instead of five sail of the line, was doubtless the reason that as many as 10 sail of British line-of-battle ships had been ordered to cut adrift their prizes, and form in order of battle. This untoward circumstance, and the continuance of bad weather, determined Vice-admiral Collingwood to destroy all the leewardmost of the captured ships. Accordingly the Santisima-Trinidad was cleared, scuttled, and sunk by the Neptune and Prince; but, in spite of every pains to remove the wounded by lowering them down in cots from the stern and quarter-gallery windows, 28 of them perished in the ship. The south-west gale increasing to a most violent degree, it took several days to collect and anchor the remaining hulls preparatory to their destruction. Notwith-standing every exertion was used on the part of the Defiance, the Aigle drifted into Cadiz bay on the night of the 25th, and was stranded on the bar off Port Santà-Maria.

The few remaining prizes were at length anchored between Cadiz and about six leagues to the westward of San-Lucar; and on the 28th the body of the British fleet lay also at anchor to the north-west of Lucar, the Royal Sovereign without any masts except jury main and mizen ones, and the Mars with main and mizen masts only, each ship having lost her foremast in the last severe gale. Between the 28th and 30th the Intrépide was burnt by the Britannia, and the San-Augustin by the Leviathan and Orion; and the Argonauta was scuttled and sunk by the Ajax. Another of the hulls, the Berwick, after having anchored in apparent safety, was wrecked off San-Lucar, entirely owing to the frenzied behaviour of a portion of the prisoners who cut the cables. The Donegal, being at anchor near, cut her cables, and, standing towards the drifting ship, sent her boats to save the people on board. This noble proceeding of Captain Malcolm was only partially successful, when the Berwick struck upon the shoals; and in her perished about 200 persons.

As a practical proof of the benefit that might have been derived to the fleet and prizes by attending to Lord Nelson's dying injunctions, the Defence, accompanied by her prize, the San-Ildefonso, anchored on the evening of the action, and weathered the gale in safety. The example of these ships was followed by two other of the prizes, the Swiftsure and Bahama; and, with the assistance rendered by the Donegal and Phœbe, these also were saved. The fourth and only remaining prize, the San-Juan-Nepomuceno, being less disabled, had not been in such imminent danger, and was already safe in the offing.

On the 30th, in the afternoon, Vice-admiral Collingwood was joined by Rear-admiral Louis, with the 80-gun ship Canopus, Captain Francis William Austin, 98-gun ship Queen, Captain Francis Pender, and 74-gun ships Spencer, Captain the Honourable Robert Stopford, and Tigre, Captain Benjamin Hallowell; which squadron, as already stated, had been detached to Gibraltar for water, and to escort a convoy up the Mediterranean.[1] While reconnoitring Cadiz, just before the squadron joined, the Queen had a slight brush with the batteries and with the Argonaute, who, with only her foremast standing, lay at anchor at the entrance of the bay. On the 31st, in the morning, Vice-admiral Collingwood shifted his flag from the Euryalus to the Queen.

To sum up the result of the battle of Trafalgar, the French, out of 18 sail of the line, preserved only nine, and the Spaniards, out of 15 sail of the line, lost all except six. Of the 19 French and Spanish ships, including the Rayo, which the British captured, one, the Achille, was accidentally burnt, and 14 were recaptured, wrecked, foundered, or destroyed; leaving but four ships, one French and three Spanish 74s, as trophies in the hands of the conquerors. The following recapitulatory Table may here be usefully introduced:

	French.		Spanish.						Total.
	Gun-ships.		Gun-ships.						
	80	74	130	112	100	80	74	64	
	No.	No.	No.	No.	No.	No.	No.	No.	No.
Combined fleet. On the day of battle: present	4	14	1	2	1	2	8	1	33
captured	1	8	1	1	..	2	5	..	18
escaped	3	6	..	1	1	..	3	1	15
Recaptured on the 23rd	1	1	..	1	..	1	..	..	4
	4	7	..	2	1	1	3	1	19
Wrecked and captured on the 24th	2	..	..	..	1	..	1	..	4
	2	7	..	2	..	1	2	1	15
Remaining to France and Spain: at sea	1	3	..	..	..	..	..	..	4
in Cadiz	1	4	..	2	..	1	2	1	11
Brit. prizes. Accidentally burnt	..	1	..	..	..	..	..	..	1
Recaptured on the 23rd	1	1	..	1	..	1	..	..	4
Wrecked or foundered	..	4	..	..	1	..	1	..	6
Destroyed	..	1	1	..	..	1	1	..	4
Sent to Gibraltar	..	1	..	..	..	..	3	..	4
Total captured on 21st and 24th	1	8	1	1	1	2	5	..	19

[1] See p. 380.

In reviewing the merits of the battle of Trafalgar, we shall take the number of ships in each line, 27 and 33, as a fair criterion of the relative force of the two fleets. It is singular that the aggregate of the rated number of guns on each side, 2148 and 2626, affords about the same result, a full sixth part in favour of the French and Spaniards. The real number of guns on each side would very slightly reduce the disparity. A few examples will establish this. The Victory and Téméraire mounted, the one two, the other four, guns only more than the numbers of their respective classes, or 102 guns each. Those of the Victory consisted, in equal divisions upon her first, second, and third decks, of 90 long 32, 24, and 12 pounders, and of 10 long 12-pounders and two 68-pounder carronades on her quarter-deck and forecastle. The guns upon the three principal decks of the Téméraire were 86 long 32 and 18-pounders (30 of the latter on the third or upper deck), and those upon the quarter-deck and forecastle were four long 18-pounders and twelve 32-pounder carronades. These two ships, therefore, although of different rates (first and second), mounted the same number of guns; and the 98 was actually 50 lbs. heavier in her broadside than the 100.

As the Victory and Téméraire were the two ships of the British fleet whose rated and real number of guns approximated the nearest, so were the Tonnant and Belleisle, the latter in particular, the two in which there was in that respect the greatest difference. The Tonnant, for instance, whose rate was 80, mounted 90 guns; and the same number were mounted by the Belleisle, although she was only a 74. The latter was even the heavier ship in broadside force, the age and weakness of the former having required the substitution of 18 for 24 pounders on the main deck; while the Belleisle was enabled to carry on her main deck a whole tier of the larger of those calibers. No other 74-gun ship, however, in the British fleet, to our knowledge, mounted more than 82 guns; and that number would of course include six light poop-carronades.

With respect to the gun force of the ships in the Franco-Spanish fleet, our previous statements upon the subject have left little to add. The force, in long guns, of the Santisima-Trinidad, and of a Spanish first-rate of the class of the Santa-Ana and Principe-de-Asturias, has already appeared; and so has the force of a Spanish 80 and 74 gun ship of the old or small construction.[1] For an 80 of a more recent build and equipment,

<hr>

[1] See vol. ii., p. 75.

the San-Rafaël, taken by Sir Robert Calder, may be referred
to :[1] and, for a 74, the San-Ildefonso, captured on the present
occasion. The guns of the latter consisted of 58 long 24-pound-
ers on the first and second decks, four long 8s and 10 iron
36-pounder carronades on the quarter-deck and forecastle, and
six iron 24-pounder carronades on the poop; total 78. The
presence of these carronades renders it probable, that most if
not all of the other Spanish ships in the fleet carried a proportion of them, thereby adding four at least to their rated
number of guns.

The force of that fine and powerful ship of war, a French 80,
has already appeared in the statement of the guns found on
board the Franklin.[2] It is doubtful, however, if either of the
French 80s in the combined fleet carried any brass long guns :
if not, their guns, instead of being 92, would be 86, as formerly
mentioned to be the establishment of the class,[3] and as subsequently ascertained to have been the armament of the Formidable, and of the ships in this fleet. All the French 74s captured
out of this fleet were found to mount, upon their first and second
decks, the 58 guns already so frequently specified, except the
Berwick and Swiftsure, which, having been English ships,
carried 28 instead of 30 guns on the second deck. Upon the
quarter-deck many of the ships appear to have mounted, by
filling the cabin ports, 20 instead of 16 long eights : thus
making their total force, including four, and in some instances
six, brass carronades on the poop, 82, and in the latter case 84
guns. These were exclusive of brass cohorns in the tops, the
fire from which, at close quarters, had in this very engagement
proved extremely destructive. Most of the captured French
ships were also found to have on board one field-piece (in some
instances two), with carriage and apparatus complete.

No deduction need be made for inexperience in the Franco-
Spanish crews ; for the whole of the 18 French, and nine out of
the 15 Spanish, ships had been some time at sea, and 13 of the
former had, as recently as the 22nd of the preceding July,
gained over the British what the French considered, a victory.
The British and the Franco-Spanish fleets, therefore, which met
and fought off Cape Trafalgar on the 21st of October, 1805,
with the exception of a difference in force of say a sixth in
favour of the latter, were fairly opposed.

The French and Spaniards, in general, fought bravely : some
individual ships, indeed, of both nations behaved most heroic-

[1] See p. 370.   [2] See vol. ii., p. 208.   [3] See vol. i., p. 59.

ally. Those who, writing when Spain was at peace and France still at war with England, declared, that "the Spaniards, throughout the battle, showed a more uniform firmness and spirit than the French,"[1] did but prove how completely their judgment was held in thraldom by their politics. Thinking to compliment Spain at the expense of France, the same writers wished their readers to infer, that there was a want of unanimity between the ships of the two nations. That a native of France or of Spain, as some excuse for his country's share of the defeat, should have alleged a want of co-operation in her ally, might be expected ; but is it not singular that Englishmen should resort to such a method to enhance the victory which Englishmen gained at the battle of Trafalgar ? Not only does no French or Spanish writer, as far as we can discover, make any complaint of the kind, but it was obvious to many of the British ships engaged, that the French and Spanish ships came indiscriminately to each other's aid when attacked ; and that, as they had been stationed in the line, so they mingled in the battle, without the slightest national prejudice.

All Europe must recollect how, the instant Sir Robert Calder's action became known in France, the Moniteur filled its columns with the details. For weeks together, long accounts were published, and great pains taken, in several successive numbers, to refute the British statements, and to prove that the engagement terminated in a victory to the combined fleet. Far otherwise was it when the news of the battle of Trafalgar reached Paris. A grave-like silence was imposed: not a word, not a whisper transpired. Not, at least, until towards the end of the year, when the captain and principal surviving officers of the Redoutable had the honour to figure in public as heroes, the single prowess of whose ship, even in Napoleon's opinion, shed a lustre upon the events of a day in other respects so disastrous to the French. The French emperor appears to have believed every tittle of the account transmitted to him by Captain Lucas, and a great deal more than even that account contained : for, at a subsequent day (March 2, 1806), in his address to the legislative body, his imperial majesty had the effrontery to use these words, and these words only, in reference to the fate of his fleet at the battle of Trafalgar : "The storm has occasioned to us the loss of a few ships, after a battle imprudently fought." "Les tempêtes nous ont fait perdre quelques vaisseaux après un combat imprudemment engagé." The writer of the French work, from

---

[1] Clarke and M'Arthur, vol. ii., p. 455. Mr. Southey indulges in the same strain.

which we quote the passage, adds in a note, " That of Trafalgar.
We have already shown that the storm was not the sole cause
of these losses. Was it not committing an outrage upon the
French nation thus to misstate the result of this *imprudently
fought battle ?*" " Celui de Trafalgar. Nous avons fait voir
plus haut que les tempêtes ne furent pas les seules causes de
ces pertes. N'était-ce pas outrager la nation française, que
de dénaturer ainsi les résultats de ce *combat imprudemment
engagé ?*"[1]

The account, given in the French work from which this
extract is taken, of the proceedings of the generality of French
and Spanish ships engaged at Trafalgar, is tolerably fair, but, to
our regret, very brief; partly, no doubt, in consequence of the
sad havoc caused by the gale that so quickly succeeded the
battle. In one point the French writer, who is evidently a
naval officer, is quite wrong. He states, that the Bucentaure,
Santisima-Trinidad, and Redoutable, sustained, for some time,
nearly the whole united efforts of the 12 ships in Lord Nelson's
column.[2] The ample details given in these pages afford the
most complete refutation of that statement. The fact is, that
the leading ship of the lee column, the Royal Sovereign, was in
hot action, after having cut through the combined line, for upwards of a quarter of an hour before any ship did or could come
to her assistance. The Victory and Téméraire were also closely
engaged for even a longer period, before the three or four ships
astern of them could get to their support. The nature of the
attack, combined with the lightness of the breeze, was such,
indeed, that the whole business was done by 12 or 14 ships of
the 27; and that without the slightest disparagement to the
conduct of the remainder.

On the 28th the Victory, towed by the Neptune, arrived at
Gibraltar; where she found, among other ships, the Belleisle,
who, having been taken in tow by the Naïad, sent to her assistance by Captain Hardy, had anchored in the bay on the third
day after the termination of the battle in which she had performed so distinguished a part. On the 3rd of November, having
been partially refitted, the Victory sailed for England, passed
the Straits on the 4th, and on the 4th of the following month,
anchored at St. Helen's, having on board, preserved in spirits,
the body of the lamented hero, whose flag she had so long
borne, and which was then flying on board of her, but in a
melancholy position, at half-mast. On the 10th of December

---

[1] Victoires et Conquêtes, tome xvi., p. 217.   [2] Ibid., p. 182.

the Victory again sailed, and on the 22nd, when crossing the flats from Margate, was boarded by Commissioner Grey's yacht, the Chatham, which had been despatched by the Board of Admiralty to receive Lord Nelson's body, and convey it to Greenwich. The body was removed into the coffin made from a part of the wreck of the Orient, burnt at the battle of the Nile, and which had been presented to Lord Nelson by Captain Hallowell, of the Swiftsure, in 1799. This coffin with its contents was placed within a leaden coffin. The latter was then soldered, and never afterwards opened. On the coffin's being lowered into the yacht, the Victory struck, for the last time, Lord Nelson's flag at the fore, and the same was hoisted half-mast high on board the yacht.

On the 24th, at 2 P.M., the yacht, having in the passage up had military honours paid to her illustrious charge on both sides of the river, anchored off Greenwich; and at 7 P.M. the body was landed at the centre gate of the royal hospital, amidst an immense crowd of spectators. The awful and imposing ceremony which subsequently took place having been minutely described by other publications, we shall content ourselves with stating, that on the 9th of January, 1806, this first of naval captains was buried at St. Paul's cathedral, with all the pomp and solemnity befitting the occasion.[1]

The honours paid by a grateful country to the memory of Lord Nelson were commensurate with his worth, and with the importance of the achievement which he had died in consummating. His brother William was made an earl, with a grant of 6000l. per annum; 10,000l. were voted for each of his sisters, and 100,000l. for the purchase of an estate. Two ships, a first and a second rate, were ordered to be built, one of 120 guns, named Nelson, the other of 98 (afterwards increased to 120) guns, named Trafalgar.

The living participators in the great and glorious victory received also their share of the national honours and rewards. A unanimous vote of thanks of both houses of parliament was a matter of course. Vice-admiral Collingwood was made a baron of the united kingdom, under the title of Baron Collingwood, of Caldburne and Hethpoole, in the county of Northumberland, with a grant of 2000l. per annum. Rear-admiral the Earl of Northesk was honoured with the insignia of the order of the

---

[1] See Clarke and M'Arthur, vol. ii., p. 460, et seq. See also the Annual Register for the year 1806, the January Number of the Gentleman's Magazine and the Naval Chronicle, vol. xv., p. 45.

Bath, and Captain Hardy was made a baronet. It was probably owing to a paucity of vacant ribands of the Bath, and the intention of the British government to institute a new military order of merit, that the remaining captains of the Trafalgar fleet received no honorary distinctions. Medals were of course granted in the customary way. The first-lieutenant of the Victory, the lieutenants acting as captains of the Ajax and Thunderer, and the first-lieutenants of the Mars and Bellerophon, whose captains had been killed in the action, were promoted to post-captains ; and the first, second, third, and fourth lieutenants of the Victory, the first and second lieutenants of the Royal Sovereign, and the first lieutenants of all the other ships engaged, were made commanders. Four midshipmen of the Victory, three of the Royal Sovereign, two of the Britannia, and one belonging to every other ship of the line and frigate present in the action, were also promoted to lieutenants.

Passing over as unworthy of notice a ludicrous account of the state of the British fleet after the action, inserted by some wag in the Journal de Paris of the 7th of December, we shall bestow a few words upon the accounts of the battle published in England. The letter of Vice-admiral Collingwood to the secretary of the admiralty claims our first attention. This letter has been praised for its style : we wish we could say as much of its accuracy. The accidental irregularity of the enemy's line is represented as the result of design. " They formed their line of battle," says the admiral, " with great closeness and correctness." " The structure of their line was new : it formed a crescent convexing to leeward." " Before the fire opened every alternate ship was about a cable's length to windward of her second ahead and astern, forming a kind of double line." With such authority for a guide, no wonder that tacticians should set about investigating M. Villeneuve's new line of battle, " the double crescent convexing to leeward."[1]

" A circumstance occurred during the action," observes Vice-admiral Collingwood, " which so strongly marks the invincible spirit of British seamen when engaging the enemies of their country, that I cannot resist the pleasure in making it known to their lordships. The Téméraire was boarded, by accident or design, by a French ship on one side, and a Spaniard on the other : the contest was vigorous, but in the end the combined ensigns were torn from the poop, and the British hoisted in their

---

[1] For the representation of this line, see Ekins's Naval Battles, part 2, plate xxix.
(51) Fig. 4.

places.'' Unfortunately for the fame of those concerned, this soul-inspiring passage contains not a word of truth. The mistake arose thus :—The Spanish ship Neptuno, after having, with the loss of her mizenmast and other damage, surrendered to the Minotaur and Spartiate, drifted on board the Téméraire, while the latter had still foul of her, on the lee or larboard side, the late French ship Redoutable, and scarcely clear of her astern, the Fougueux.[1]

Long before Captain Harvey and his officers landed in England, a spirited representation of this their valorous exploit was exhibited in the London printshops; and many persons to this day have not the most remote idea that the fact was ever questioned : especially as, although the London Gazette contained two or three supplementary letters from Vice-admiral Collingwood, not a hint was given that the first contained a misstatement. For even the letter, showing that the admiral had overrated by one (20 for 19) the number of prizes made on the 21st and 24th, was written by Captain Blackwood at the office of the admiralty. That the various periodical publications of the day should place full confidence in an uncontradicted official statement was to be expected; but it will hardly be credited that, nearly 20 years afterwards, an historical writer, who, at the period of the battle, had attained the rank of commander in the British navy, and who boasts, and may well boast, of the "great opportunities he enjoys of obtaining the most correct information,"[2] should first declare that the "real facts" of the Trafalgar battle are detailed "in the admirable letters of Vice-admiral Collingwood,"[3] and then do no more than cast a reluctant doubt upon the passage in question, by the following note: "Subsequent information has proved this statement wanted confirmation:"[4]—a note that, we verily believe, would not have been added, but for our positive denial in the first edition of this work, of the statement to which it refers.

"I have not only," says Vice-admiral Collingwood, "to lament, in common with the British navy and the British nation, in the fall of the commander-in-chief, the loss of a hero whose name will be immortal, and his memory ever dear to his country, but my heart is rent with the most poignant grief for the death of a friend, to whom, by many years' intimacy, and a perfect knowledge of the virtues of his mind, which inspired ideas

---

[1] For the position of these three ships just before the Neptuno surrendered, see diagram at p. 435.

[2] Brenton, vol. iii., Preface, p. 1.
[3] Ibid., p. 472.
[4] Ibid., p. 475.

superior to the common race of men, I was bound by the
strongest ties of affection ; a grief to which even the glorious occasion in which he fell does not bring the consolation which
perhaps it ought. His lordship received a musket ball in his
left breast about the middle of the action, and sent an officer to
me immediately with his last farewell, and soon after expired."

Admiring, as we must, the feeling and impressive manner in
which the death of Lord Nelson is here adverted to, we are
obliged to refer to a previous page of this work for a satisfactory
proof that the statement with which the extract concludes is incorrect.[1] The death of Lord Nelson in the moment of victory,
and the delay until then of any announcement to the second in
command that the first was incapable of acting, show that the
following passage in Vice-admiral Collingwood's letter, as far as
regards the inference meant to be drawn from it, rests upon no
better foundation. " The Royal Sovereign having lost her masts,
except her tottering foremast, I called the Euryalus to me while
the action continued, which ship, lying within hail, made my
signals ; a service which Captain Blackwood performed with
great attention."

The few signals, made by the Euryalus for the dismasted
Royal Sovereign, while the action continued, must have been
such only as the second in command of the fleet had been
directed to make, if necessary, to his own division or column.
How, indeed, could it be otherwise, when Lord Nelson flatly
refused to give up the command of the fleet, and did not breathe
his last until the action had virtually terminated ? Even then,
agreeably to the rules of the service, the Victory's flag remained
flying.

Among the numerous omissions and misstatements that per-
vade the official accounts of this celebrated battle, the most
extraordinary, as well as the most unjust, is the neglect to notice
the services, or even to mention the name, of the Victory's captain ; of the officer who, from a few minutes before the action
was at its height to the moment of its successful termination, a
period of three hours, acted in the capacity, and held the responsibility, of the commander-in-chief. Unfortunately the
mere omission of Captain Hardy's name in the public letter of
Vice-admiral Collingwood is not all the injury done to him.
That might have arisen from unintentional neglect, and have
been atoned for, in part, by a subsequent explanation and apology. But nothing short of the most humiliating acknowledg-

[1] See p. 448.

ment could nullify the statement, that Lord Nelson sent to inform Vice-admiral Collingwood of his mortal wound " immediately " after he had received it; and that the latter thereupon took upon himself the direction of the fleet, and ordered the Euryalus, " while the action continued," to make his signals. Truth, however, will ultimately prevail; and Captain Hardy became rewarded, not only in a baronetcy, but in the marked approbation of the board of admiralty, who have never lost sight of him when a service was to be performed that required the exercise of a large proportion of those qualities which characterize the good officer.

Two published accounts of this battle, one historical, the other tactical, come next under consideration. In the first few details are given, except in reference to the proceedings of the Victory; and, as the relation of the occurrences, on board that ship, including the manner of Lord Nelson's death, is little more than a transcript from the works of Doctor Beatty, Messrs. Clarke and M'Arthur, and Mr. Southey, the value of that part of the account may be appreciated by what has already appeared in these pages. Nor have the other authorities, upon which our contemporary has relied for information, benefited him a whit more. Where, for instance, did he learn that the captain of the Redoutable was " mortally wounded ?"[1] or that the Tonnant, and not the Bellisle, came to the assistance of the Royal Sovereign ?[2] or that the San-Augustin, and not the Neptuno, struck to the Spartiate and Minotaur ?[3]

But, for these errors of the pen, the pencil is to atone, in the shape of " a rough sketch of the action taken after the firing had ceased in the rear, and the enemy's van had wore to recover the prizes." This is the description given by the draftsman in his " Key to the plate;" but, according to the statement of Captain Brenton himself (p. 458), the " very moment" referred to is two hours afterwards, or just as Lord Nelson had expired in the cockpit of the Victory. As is often the case in much more elaborate performances of the kind, one time will answer as well as another. For instance, the Formidable and the four ships in her train are seen just hauled up on the starboard tack, almost ready to begin firing at the nethermost British ship, the Neptune. Let us suppose this to have been at about 2 h. 30 m. P.M. But then the Minotaur and Spartiate are also represented on the starboard tack; whereas they were not so until about 4 h. 30 m. P.M., after M. Dumanoir and his four countrymen

---

[1] Brenton, vol. iii., p. 455.   Ibid p. 466.   [3] Ibid., p. 467.

had passed on to the southward, and left the Spanish Neptuno to her fate. Another division of the sketch would answer for three hours later in the day. The Victory, for example, appears with her mizenmast and maintopmast gone; whereas that ship did not lose her mizenmast until 7 P.M., nor strike her maintopmast (at which time her fore one also was struck) until within a few minutes of the same period. Of the remaining ships scattered over this much-vaunted plate, few that are named are correct either in their positions or the state of their masts. The Téméraire lies with her head directly where her stern ought to be, and, instead of having her three lower masts and their yards (the fore-yard broken in two), and her foretop and topgallant-masts, standing, is represented as bare as a hulk.

An attempt to sketch the state, positions, and relative bearings of nearly 50 vessels, spread over an extent of at least five miles, was not very likely to succeed; especially when the draftsman was on board a ship situated at one extremity of the line. If it was a degree of presumption in " a young gentleman, a midshipman of the Neptune," to attempt a sketch of so complicated, so numerous, and so expanded a group of figures, as must have been spread over the field of Trafalgar, what was it in a post-captain of 16 years' standing, quite away from the spot, to entitle Mr. Herbert's "rough sketch," " a view of the British and combined fleets at the conclusion of the battle of Trafalgar," and to recommend it to the British public as " an invaluable memorandum of the battle ?"[1]

For an unprofessional writer to arraign the merits of a work on naval tactics, would seem to be a presumption equal to the highest degree of that which we have just been condemning. But tactical reasoning, like all other reasoning, must be built upon facts, or upon what are assumed as facts. Surely, then, to inquire into the reality of those alleged facts, is within the province of a writer, whose avowed purpose, to the extent of his subject, and of his ability, is to separate truth from fiction.

Bold as is the assertion, yet do we confidently make it,— Admiral Ekins has entirely misunderstood the principle upon which the battle of Trafalgar was fought. After describing the plan of attack, as set forth in Vice-admiral Collingwood's letter, and illustrated by a diagram taken from one in the possession of the board of admiralty, the writer says: " Whatever degree of credit the above plan may be entitled to, backed as it is by the vice-admiral's letter, it is well known to all the captains of

[1] Brenton, vol. iii., p. 459.

that fleet, that the plan of attack from the windward was, by previous concert, to have been of a different and still more formidable nature; for, as the order of sailing was the order of battle, and the enemy seen to leeward, the commander-in-chief in that case would 'bring the British fleet nearly within gunshot of the enemy's centre, and the signal, most probably, then be made up for the lee division to *bear up together*, to set all sails, even steering-sails, &c.' The secret memorandum at the end of these remarks, will best explain his lordship's intention and remove the doubt. We therefore venture to give the approach as in fig. 1, Plate XXVIII. The lee division bearing up together, followed soon after by the centre; the fleet originally formed in the order of sailing upon a wind on the larboard tack: the enemy formed in close line convexing to leeward, heads to the northward. This must be considered as the preconcerted plan of attack; but that it may have deviated from the exact design, from circumstances to which events of this nature are always liable, it is easy to believe; and it will be particularly apparent to sea-officers: for, supposing a line, like that of Lord Collingwood's of 15 ships, all in their station when the signal to bear up together should be made; and supposing the signal to be obeyed with equal alacrity by all; yet the different rates of sailing in them will soon be conspicuous; and the advantages of some over others, neither to be reckoned upon nor accounted for, they will consequently be found to tail away as in the fig. 2. Be it as it may, it will be readily admitted that, both from the design and the execution, no mode of attack could have been formed better calculated for effecting the purpose of the determined chief; the capture or destruction of the centre and rear of the enemy."[1]

In his interpretation of Lord Nelson's plan of attack from to-windward, the writer of this passage is certainly borne out by the literal meaning of the words, "the lee line to bear up together;" but the context ought to have convinced him, that this could not have been the mode of attack contemplated by Lord Nelson. If the ships of the lee line were to "bear up together," so must those of the weather and the advanced lines; and then see how the ships would have been arranged:—

---

[1] Ekins's Naval Battles, p. 268.

The confidential friends of Lord Nelson, many of whom are now living, can testify, that he had the strongest objection to the plan of bearing up in line abreast, and that he attributed the partial success of Lord Howe on the 1st of June to his having adopted that mode of attack. His own plan appears to have been, to bring his force, in the most effective state, into contact with the force of the enemy, and, for that purpose, to present while advancing to close, the smallest possible front to the enemy's fire. As the leading ship of the attacking line or column would of necessity receive the whole weight of that fire, Lord Nelson very naturally chose the post himself. If more lines or columns than one, the commanding officer of each would of course follow the example of the chief.

In order to make quick, as well as decisive work of it, Lord Nelson purposed, in the first instance, cutting off a portion of the enemy's line: he then left everything to the valour and address of his captains; well observing, that no captain could do very wrong who placed his ship alongside that of an enemy. The greater the confusion, the greater were his hopes of success, because he knew that the British, besides being better prepared for fighting their guns on either side, or in any direction, were better skilled in working their ships than the French or Spaniards. A gale of wind, or a dark night, was accordingly considered as a ship or two in his favour. The reason that Lord Nelson gave, for placing so little dependence upon evolutions, was, that he generally found the inconvenience, which resulted from the mistakes too frequently made, to outweigh the benefit expected to be derived from the most correct performance of the manœuvre. Hence the sum of Lord Nelson's tactics was, to close his enemy, and to overpower and annihilate him as quickly as possible.

There are, we believe, very few of the captains present in the Trafalgar battle, with whom we have not conversed or corresponded ; and yet no one of them has ever raised a doubt as to the meaning of Lord Nelson's instructions, or the manner in which he purposed to bear down upon the enemy's line. That the expression used in the memorandum is at variance with what we still contend was the meaning of the gallant chief, we have already admitted; but would not so simple an alteration as the change of one word to another of similar sound, and of another word from the singular to the plural number (an interpolation we have ventured to make in our transcript of the memorandum[1]), reconcile the difference? That a mistake of the

[1] See p. 382.

kind may easily have happened, we can see no difficulty in supposing. For instance, Lord Nelson, when he drew up his instructions, was almost certain that the combined fleet would
sail with an easterly wind, and therefore be found to windward.
Hence the principal part of the memorandum is filled with the
plan of atack from to-leeward. The attack from to-windward,
being a very doubtful contingency, occupied much less of his
lordship's attention. Nor did he, of course, write a line of the
memorandum. The secretary, or the clerk, wrote it by his
lordship's dictation. How easy, then, for either of the former
to have mistaken, " The signal will be made for the *three lines*
to bear up together," for " The signal will be made for the *lee
line* to bear up together?" The two words once miswritten
would scarcely be looked at again; especially as all the principal officers of the fleet had heard Lord Nelson repeatedly
describe, in his own clear and energetic manner, the plan which
he meant to adopt.

But, after all, what was the signal by which the British fleet
actually steered towards the fleet of the enemy? Was it No. 81,
with the east compass signal, " Alter the course *together* to
east "? Or, rather, was it not No. 76, " Bear up *in succession* " [1]
to that point? That No. 76 was the signal hoisted, the author
of " Naval Battles " must have been satisfied, because it is so
stated in the quotation which he himself makes from the log of
the Bellerophon.[2] The argument about the British ships " tail-
ing away " because of their inequality of sailing, can hold good
only until it is known that, with the exception perhaps of the
Royal Sovereign, Belleisle, Victory, and Téméraire, the ships
in the two principal divisions sailed nearly alike. And with
respect to the Britannia, Prince, and Dreadnought, whose slow-
ness was far more conspicuous than the velocity of the ships just
named, they were allowed to depart from the prescribed order
of sailing in line ahead, that they might steer obliquely between
the two columns, and by that means get more of their sails to
draw.

Having thus, as we conceive, shown the fallacy of the pre-
mises, by which a tactical writer of the present day has hoped
to throw a new light upon a celebrated naval battle fought 20
years ago,[3] we shall merely observe, that his remaining state-

---

[1] The signal merely expresses, " Bear
up and sail large, on the course steered by
the admiral, or that pointed out by signal;" but the 14th article of the printed
" Sailing Instructions " refers to this signal, as that to be used " when the fleet is
to bear up in succession."

[2] Ekins's Naval Battles, p. 284.

[3] Mr. James's new edition was published in 1826.

ments are, for the most part, equally ill-founded. As to the
" six plans of the battle, delineated by the same hand, to the
accuracy of which, many who were engaged have borne testimony,"[1] if the three plans not published tends as little to
"illustrate" this great victory, as the three which the writer
has selected for his work, a great deal of pains and expense has
been bestowed to a very little purpose. The three plans selected
are the fourth, fifth, and sixth, representing different periods of
the action, from the moment the combined van began wearing,
to the termination of the battle by the capture of the Neptuno.
In every one of these plans, the Victory is represented clear of
the Redoutable, but upon the starboard tack, with her head to
the southward. The Agamemnon is shifted from the weather,
to the lee column : and equally misplaced in their relative positions are the Orion, Africa, and their gallant opponent, the Intrépide. In short, there is scarcely a ship, among those of the
British especially, that seems to be in her proper situation. Nor
are these plans little unpretending sketches, but large and costly
copper-plate engravings, by their imposing size, numerous
figures, and laboured appearance, calculated to enthral the
judgment, and to divert, if not to defy, the efforts of criticism.

If a printed misstatement upon an important point of history
may be justifiably set right, have we not an equal privilege over
a painted misstatement of the same nature ; especially when
produced under circumstances the most likely of any to inspire
a confidence in its accuracy ? Previously to our submitting any
remarks upon the merits of the painting of the Victory going
into, or (for, as we shall presently see, it is doubtful which is
meant) coming out of, the battle of Trafalgar, we will endeavour
to relate how it happened that that distinguished artist, Mr.
J. M. W. Turner, of the Royal Academy, became engaged to
trace with his powerful pencil so interesting an epocha in
British naval history ; a subject which, well executed, would,
we conceive, have done that gentleman as much honour as any
of his previous performances.

Soon after the battle of the 1st of June the justly-celebrated
marine painter, P. J. de Loutherbourg, was employed by some
enterprising individual to represent the Queen Charlotte engaging
the Montagne. In about four years the picture, which measured
12 feet by eight and a half, and cost, we believe, 500l., was
completed, and soon afterwards exhibited to the public. Without descending to minutiæ, the grand mistake in it was, that the

Queen Charlotte was placed where Lord Howe wanted to get, but never could get, a little before the lee beam of his antagonist. Among others, the officer, whose duty it was (and who would have succeeded, but for the hasty flight of the Montagne and the loss of the Queen Charlotte's foretopmast[3]) to place the British ship in the desired position, went to see the picture. At the first glance the gallant seaman pronounced the picture a libel upon the Queen Charlotte; inasmuch as, had she been in the position represented, it would have been her fault for letting the Montagne escape. Whether it was owing to this capital blemish, or to the half a dozen minor offences against truth in different parts of it, we cannot say, but the picture gradually sank into disrepute, and eventually became, we believe, lodged with an eminent printseller for some debt amounting to less than a third of its prime cost. After lying rolled up in a corner of one of his rooms, encased in dust, for a number of years, the printseller was fortunate enough, as we have understood, to find a purchaser in his late majesty's surveyor-general of the Board of Works.

The painting, thus restored to credit and the light, was intended to be hung up, as a national memento of the naval victory to which it relates, in the council-room of St. James's palace. As a companion to it, a picture was required, representing the Victory engaged in the battle of Trafalgar. The first marine painter of the day undertook the task; and, in due time, the large area of canvas, which, to correspond with the other picture, became necessary for this, was covered with all the varied tints which Mr. Turner knows so well how to mingle and combine, to give effect to his pictures and excite the admiration of the beholder.

Unfortunately for the subject which this splendid picture is meant to represent, scarcely a line of truth, beyond perhaps the broadside view of the Victory's hull, is to be seen upon it. To say what time of the day, or what particular incident in the Victory's proceedings, is meant to be referred to, we do not pretend; for the telegraphic message is going up, which was hoisted at about 11 h. 40 m. A.M., the mizentopmast is falling, which went about 1 P.M., a strong light is reflected upon the Victory's bow and sides from the burning Achille, which ship did not catch fire until 4 h. 30 m., nor explode until 5 h. 45 m. P.M., the foretopmast, or rather, if our memory is correct, the foremast, of the British three-decker is falling, which never fell

1 See vol. i., p. 165.

at all, and the Redoutable is sinking under the bows of the
Victory, although the French ship did not sink until the night
of the 22nd, and then under the stern of the Swiftsure.

We are sorry to be obliged to add that, with all these glaring
falsehoods and palpable inconsistencies upon it, the picture
stands, or until very lately did stand, in that room of the king's
palace, for which it was originally designed. The principal
reason urged for giving to this very costly and highly honoured
performance so preposterous a character, is that an adherence to
truth would have destroyed the pictorial effect. Here is a ship,
shattered in her hull, and stripped of the best part of her sails,
pushing into a cluster of enemy's ships without a grazed plank
or a torn piece of canvas to fire her first gun. Here is sym-
bolized the first of naval heroes, with chivalric valour, devoting
himself to his country's cause ; and yet, says an artist of high
repute, "there is a lack of pictorial materials." We hope some
public-spirited individual, if not the State itself, will show whether
this is really the case ; for it is almost a national disgrace that
there should yet be wanted a picture which, in accuracy of representation, no less than in strength and brilliancy of execution,
is calculated to illustrate, and to stand as a lasting memorial of
one of the greatest sea-battles that ever has been, or that perhaps ever will be fought : a battle to the success of which
England at this time owes, if not her political existence, her
prosperity, happiness, and exalted station.

To any artist, who may consider it worth his while, or within
his powers, to attempt such a picture, the following remarks, in
addition to those he will find a few pages back,[1] may not be un-
useful. Let his point of view be the small cross in the diagram
at p. 400. He will then have, for his two principal figures, the
Victory on the right, and the Bucentaure on the left. Behind
these will be the Neptune and Redoutable ; both firing, the
latter her foremost guns, the former her whole broadside, right
into the bows of the Victory. On the extreme right of the
picture will be the bows of the Téméraire, and on the extreme
left, the stern and quarter-galleries of the Santisima-Trinidad.
Quite in the foreground may be represented the boat, which a
shot had cut adrift a few minutes before. With this hint to
the painter, we end our long, but, we hope, not uninteresting
account of the battle of Trafalgar.

[1] See pp. 394, 395, 400, 401, and 422.

APPENDIX.

No. 1.—See p. 40.

A List of Ships of the Line and Frigates, late belonging to the French Navy, Captured, Destroyed, Wrecked, Foundered, or Accidentally Burnt during the year 1800.

Name.	How, when, and where Lost.
Gun-ship.	
80 (K) Guillaume-Tell	Captured, March 30, by a British squadron off Malta.
74 (M) Généreux	Captured, February 18, by a British squadron in the Mediterranean.
64 { (P) Athénien .. Dégo	Captured, September 4, at the surrender off Malta.
Gun-frig.	
.. Concorde	Captured, August 5, by the British 64, Belliqueux, near Rio-Janeiro, South America.
40 { (Z) Diane	Captured, August 24, by a British squadron off Malta.
,, Vengeance	Captured, August 25, by the British 38-gun frigate Seine, in the Mona Passage.
(B') Désirée	Captured, July 8, by the British 28-gun sloop Dart, in Dunkerque roads.
38 { ,, Pallas	Captured, February 6, by the Loire, British frigate and other vessels near the Seven Islands, coast of France.
.. Carthagénoise	Captured, with the Athénien and Dégo.
36 { .. Médée	Captured, August 5, by the Bombay Castle, and Exeter Indiaman, in sight of the Belliqueux 64, and convoy.
28 .. Vénus	Captured, October 22, by the British frigates Indefatigable and Fisgard, off Lisbon.

No Dutch ship-of-war as high as a 24-gun corvette, captured, &c. during the year 1800.

No. 1.—*continued*.

A List of Ships of the Line and Frigates, late belonging to the Spanish Navy, Captured, Destroyed, Wrecked, Foundered, or Accidentally Burnt, during the year 1800.

Name.	Commander.	How, when, and where Lost.
Gun-frig. 34 { (D) Del-Carmen { ,, Florentina	{ Don Fraquin { Porcel. { Don Manuel { Norates.	Captured, April 7, by the Leviathan 74, and Emerald 36, near Cadiz. The prizes were laden with 3000 quintals of quicksilver.

An Abstract of French, and Spanish Ships and Vessels of War, Captured, &c. during the year 1800.

		Lost through the Enemy.		Lost through Accident.			Total lost to the French and Spanish Navies.	Total added to the British Navy.
		Capt.	Dest.	Wrecked.	Foundered.	Burnt.		
Ships of the line.	Fr.	4	..	..	..	..	4	3
Frigates.	Fr.	8	..	..	..	..	8	4
	Sp.	2	..	..	..	..	2	2
Total . .		14	..	..	..	..	14	9

No. 2.—See p. 40.

A List of Ships and Vessels, late belonging to the British Navy, Captured, Destroyed, Wrecked, Foundered, or Accidentally Burnt, during the year 1800.

Name.	Commander.	How, when, and where Lost.
Gun-ship. 100 (D) Queen Charlotte	{ Lord Keith { (V.-Admi 1). { Andrew Todd	Accidentally burnt and blown up, March 17, off Leghorn: crew, except 167, perished.
74 (O) Marlborough .	Thomas Sotheby .	Wrecked, November 4, on a sunken rock near Belleisle: crew saved.
64 (P) Repulse .	James Alms .	Wrecked, March 10, on a sunken rock 25 leagues south-east of Ushant: crew, except 10, saved on the Glenan islands, but made prisoners.
Gun-frig. 32 (F) Stag .	. Robert Winthrop	Wrecked, September 6, in Vigo Bay: crew saved.

No. 2.—*continued.*

Name.	Commander.	How, when, and where Lost.
Gun p. ship. 20 { (*O*) *Danaé*	. Lord Proby .	Captured, March 17, by her crew mutinying and carrying her into Brest.
(*P*) *Cormorant*	Courtney Boyle	Wrecked, exact date unknown, on the coast of Egypt: crew saved, but made prisoners by the French.
G. sh. slp. (*S*) *Brazen*	. James Hanson .	Wrecked, January 26, near Brighton : crew, except one man, perished.
18 { ,, *Chance*	. George S. Stovin	Foundered, October 9, after upsetting on her beam-ends : crew, except 25, perished.
,, *Trompeuse*	Parker Robinson	Foundered, May 16 or 17, as is supposed, having parted company in a gale in the Channel : crew perished.
16 { (*T*) *Havick*	Phil. Bartholomew	Wrecked, November 9, in St. Alban's Bay, Jersey : crew saved.
(*U*) *Martin*	Hon. Mat. St.-Clair	Foundered, in October, in the North Sea, as is supposed : crew perished.
14 (*X*) *Railleur*	. John Raynor .	Foundered, at the same time as the *Trompeuse.*
G. bg. slp. 18 { (*Z*) Diligence	C.B.Hodgson Ross	Wrecked, in September, on a small island near Havana : crew saved.
,, Hound	. W. Jas. Turquand	Wrecked, September 26, near Shetland : crew perished.
14 (b) *Albanaise*	Fran. Newcombe	Captured, November 23, by her crew mutinying and carrying her into Malaga.
F.S. { (e) Comet	. Thomas Leef .	Destroyed, July 7, in Dunkerque roads, in attempting to burn some French frigates.
,, Falcon	. H. Samuel Butt	
,, *Rosario*	. James Carthew	
,, Wasp .	. John Edwards .	
Gun-brig 12 (g) Mastiff	. James Watson .	Wrecked, January 5, on Yarmouth sands : crew, except eight, saved.
T.S. { (r.) Weymouth	Ambrose Crofton	Wrecked, January 21, on the Bar of Lisbon : crew saved.
(s.) Dromedary	Benj. W. Taylor	Wrecked, August 10, in the Bocca, near the island of Trinidad : crew saved.

ABSTRACT.

	Lost through the Enemy.		Lost through. Accident.			
	Capt.	Dest.	Wrecked.	Foundered.	Burnt.	Total.
Ships of the line .	..	..	2	..	1	3
,, under the line .	2	4	9	4	..	19
Total . .	2	4	11	4	1	22

No. 3.—See p. 41.

	£	s.	d.
For the pay and maintenance of 97,304 seamen and 22,696 marines for three lunar months, and of 105,000 seamen and 30,000 marines, for the remaining ten lunar months	6,412,500	0	0
„ the wear and tear of ships, &c.	5,850,000	0	0
„ the ordinary expenses of the navy, including the half-pay to sea and marine officers; also the expense of sea-ordnance	1,269,918	5	8
„ the extraordinaries; including the building and repairing of ships, and other extra work	933,900	0	0
„ the expense of the transport-service	1,920,718	14	6
„ the care and maintenance of prisoners of war . .	190,000	0	0
Total supplies granted for the sea-service . . .	£16,577,037	0	2

No. 4.—See p. 96.

Je proposai de conduire l'armée navale de la république à Lisbonne, de mouiller l'armée devant cette capitale, à une portée de fusil de la ville et du palais du roi; de la faire précéder par une frégate parlementaire, qui annoncerait que l'armée de la république ne vient pas pour nuire aux Portugais, quoiqu'alliés et esclaves de l'Angleterre; mais qu'elle vient pour exiger que tous les magasins et vaisseaux anglais lui soient livrés sur-le-champ, sous peine de raser la ville de la fond en comble. Cette opération procurait à la France 200 millions en numéraire ou en marchandises anglaises; l'Angleterre recevait un échec terrible, qui y causait·et des banqueroutes et une désolation générale. Notre armée, sans être fatiguée de la mer, revenait à Brest, comblée de richesses, couverte de gloire, et la France étonnait encore l'Europe par un nouveau triomphe.—*Relation des Combats, &c.*, par Kerguelen, p. 373.

No. 5.—See p. 118.

No. 5.—See p. 118.

A quatre heures du matin, il aperçut dans ses eaux quatre bâtimens, qu'il reconnut pour ennemis c'était en effet une partie de l'escadre anglaise : le César, monté par l'amiral Saumarez, le Vénérable, le Superbe et la frégate la Tamise. Le brave Troude se disposa au combat et renforça ses batteries par les hommes des gaillards. Il fut joint d'abord par le Vénérable et la Tamise : le premier envoya sa volée par la hanche de babord, et le Formidable arriva pour serrer cet adversaire au feu : le combat le plus vif s'engagea vergue à vergue, et souvent à longueur d'écouvillon. Le capitaine français ordonna de mettre jusqu'à trois boulets dans chaque canon. La Tamise le battait en poupe ; mais ses canons de retraite ripostaient à ce feu. Les deux autres vaisseaux ennemis arrivèrent successivement, et, ne pouvant doubler le Formidable au vent, ils prirent position par sa hanche de babord. Les premières volées du vaisseau française démâtèrent le Vénérable de son perroquet de fougue, et bientôt après de son grand mât : l'anglais laissa arriver ; mais Troude le suivit dans ce mouvement pour le battre en poupe, en même temps qu'il faisait canonner le César, qui, se trouvant de l'avant du Vénérable, ne pouvait riposter : pas un boulet français n'était perdu. Dans cette position, le Vénérable perdit encore son mât de misaine. Troude fit diriger ensuite tout son feu sur le César, le serrant le plus près possible ; après demi-heure d'engagement, quoique l'anglais, qui avait toutes ses voiles, dépassât le Formidable, et forçât celui-ci à manœuvrer pour le tenir par son travers, le César abandonna la partie, arriva en désordre, prit les amures à babord, et rejoignit le Vénérable, auquel la Tamise portait des secours. Il restait encore à combattre le Superbe, qui était par la joue de babord du vaisseau français ; mais l'anglais laissa arriver, passa sous le vent au Formidable, hors de portée, et rejoignit les autres bâtimens. A sept heures du matin, le capitaine Troude etait maître du champ de bataille. Il fit monter dans les batteries le reste des boulets, qui pouvaient lui faire tenir encore une heure de combat, rafraîchir le vaillant équipage qui l'avait si bien secondé, et réparer son gréement ; ses voiles étaient en lambeaux ; la brise de terre avait cessé, et il se trouvait en calme, à portée de canon de l'escadre ennemie, dont les embarcations étaient alors occupées à secourir le Vénérable. Ce vaisseau avait encore démâté de son mât d'artimon, et les courans le portaient à la côte. A dix heures, le vent ayant fraîchi, la Tamise essaya de prendre ce même vaisseau à la remorque ; mais, ne pouvant se relever, il fut s'échouer entre l'île de Léon et la pointe Saint-Roch, à deux ou trois lieues de Cadix.—*Victoires et Conquétes,* tome xiv., p. 168.

No. 6.—See p. 154.

A List of Ships of the Line and Frigates, late belonging to the French Navy, Captured, Destroyed, Wrecked, Foundered, or Accidentally Burnt during the year 1801.

Name.	How, when, and where Lost.
Gun-ship.	
74 (N) Saint-Antoine	Captured, July 12, by squadron of Sir James Saumarez, Straits of Gibraltar.
64 .. Causse	Captured, September 2, by combined British and Turkish force at the capitulation of Alexandria.
Gun-frig.	
44 (W) Egyptienne	
40 { (Z) Africaine	Captured, February 19, by the British frigate Phœbe, Mediterranean.
.. Justice	Captured, with Egyptienne, and transferred to the Turks.
38 (B) Carrère	Captured, August 3, by a squadron of British frigates, Mediterranean.
.. Bravoure	Destroyed by being driven on shore, September 2, by a squadron of British frigates off Vado.
36 { (D) Chiffonne	Captured, August 19, by the British frigate Sibylle, at the Seychelles.
„ Dédaigneuse	Captured, February 5, by a squadron of British frigates, off the coast of Portugal.
„ Régénérée	Captured with the Egyptienne.
32 { (H) Succès	Captured, September 2, by a squadron of British frigates, Mediterranean.
.. Name unknown	}Captured with Egyptienne.
.. Ditto	

No. 7. See p. 154.

A List of Ships of the Line and Frigates, lately belonging to the Spanish Navy, Captured, Destroyed, Wrecked, Foundered, or Accidentally Burnt, during the year 1801.

Name.	How, when, and where Lost.
Gun-ship.	
112 { .. Real-Carlos	Destroyed, July 12, by being set on fire in an engagement with a British squadron in the Straits of Gibraltar; and the greater part of the two crews perished.
.. San-Hermenegildo . . .	
Gun-frig.	
34 .. Perla	Destroyed, by sinking off the Barbary coast, from damage received in the same engagement.
Gun-xebec	
30 .. Gamo	Captured, May 6, by the British 14-gun brig Speedy, near Barcelona.

No. 8.—See p. 154.

A List of Ships of the Line, late belonging to the Danish Navy, Captured, Destroyed, Wrecked, Foundered, or Accidentally Burnt, during the year 1801.

Name.	How, when, and where Lost.
Gun-ship.	Captured, April 2, by Admiral Parker's fleet, off Copenhagen. The Zealand was afterwards destroyed.
74 .. Zealand	
64 (P) Holstein	

These are the only vessels of the 13 taken, sunk, and destroyed off Copenhagen that can be considered as ships of war: the remainder were merely floating batteries.

An Abstract of French, Spanish, and Danish Ships of the Line and Frigates, Captured, &c., during the year 1801.

	Lost through the Enemy.		Lost through Accident.			Total loss to the F. S. & D. Navies.	Total added to the British Navy.
	Capt.	Dest.	Wrecked.	Foundered.	Burnt.		
Ships of the line { Fr.	2	..	..	..	..	2	1
Sp.	..	2	..	..	..	2	..
Da.	2	..	..	..	..	2	1
Frigates . . { Fr.	10	1	..	..	..	11	7
Sp.	1	1	..	..	..	2	..
Total . .	15	4	..	..	..	19	9

No. 9.—See p. 154.

A List of Ships and Vessels late belonging to the British Navy, Captured, Destroyed, Wrecked, Foundered, or Accidentally Burnt, during the year 1801.

Name.	Commander.	How, when, and where Lost.
Gun-ship.		
(O) Hannibal .	Solomon Ferris .	Captured, July 5, by a French squadron, under the batteries of Algesiras, Gibraltar bay.
74 { „ Invincible	Tho. Totty (R.-ad.) John Rennie, Capt.	Wrecked, March 16, on Hasborough Sand, near Yarmouth: crew, except about 126, perished.
„ Swiftsure,	Benjamin Hallowell	Captured, June 24, by a French squadron, under Rear-admiral Ganteaume, Mediterranean.
Gun-frig.		
44 (W) *Forte* . .	Lucius Hardyman	Wrecked, in June, in Jedda harbour Red Sea: crew saved.

No. 9—*continued.*

Name.	Commander.	How, when, and where Lost
Gun-frig.		
36　(*B*) Jason . Hon. James Murray		Wrecked, July 21, by striking on a sunken rock in the bay of St. Malo: crew saved, but made prisoners.
(*G*) *Prosélyte* . George Fowke .		Wrecked, September 4, by striking on a sunken rock off the island of St. Martin, West Indies: crew saved.
(*H*) Lowestoffe　Robert Plampin		Wrecked, August 11, on the island of Heneäga, West Indies: crew saved.
32 {　„　Meleager Hon. T. Bladen Capel		Wrecked, June 9, on the Triangles in the Gulf of Mexico: crew saved.
„　Success　. Shuldham Peard		Captured, February 13, by a French squadron under Rear-admiral Ganteaume, Mediterranean.
G. p. ship 20　(*O*) *Babet* . Jemmett Mainwaring		Foundered, as is supposed, exact date unknown, in the West Indies: crew perished.
G. sh. slp. (*R*) *Légere* . Cornelius Quinton		Wrecked, exact date unknown, near Carthagena, South America: crew saved, but made prisoners.
18 {　(*S*) *Bonetta* . Thomas New .		Wrecked, October 25, on the Jardines, Cuba: crew saved.
„　*Scout* . Henry Duncan .		Wrecked, March 25, on the Shingles, west end of the Isle of Wight: crew saved.
G. bg. slp. 16　(a) *Utile* . . Edw. Jekyl Canes		Foundered, in November, by upsetting in a gale on passage from Gibraltar to Malta: crew perished.
13　(b) Speedy . Lord Cochrane .		Captured, in June, by a French squadron under Rear-admiral Linois.
Bb.　(d) Bulldog . Barrington Dacres		Captured, February 27, at Ancona, having entered unapprised of its being in the possession of the French.
F.S.　(e) Incendiary, Rich. Dalling Dunn		Captured, January 29, by Rear-admiral Ganteaume, Mediterranean.
Gun-brig. 12　(g) Blazer . John Tiller .		Captured, March 23, under the Swedish fort of Warberg, Baltic; but afterwards restored.
0　(h) *Requin* . Samuel Forvell		Wrecked, January 1, on the French coast near Quiberon: crew saved, but about 20 were made prisoners.

No. 9—*continued.*

Name.	Commander.	How, when, and where Lost.
G. cut. 12 (k) Sprightly . Robert Jump .		Captured, February 10, by Rear-admiral Ganteaume, Mediterranean.
T.S. (t) Iphigenia . Hassard Stackpole		Accidentally burnt, in July, at Alexandria, Mediterranean: crew saved.

ABSTRACT.

	Lost through the Enemy.		Lost through Accident.			
	Capt.	Dest.	Wrecked.	Foundered.	Burnt.	Total.
Ships of the line. .	2	..	1	..	..	3
„ under the line.	6	..	9	2	1	18
Total . . .	8	...	10	2	1	21

No. 10.—See p. 155.

	£	s.	d.
For the pay and maintenance of 100,000 seamen and 30,000 marines, for five lunar months, of 70,000 seamen, and 18,000 marines, for one lunar month, and of 56,000 seamen, and 14,000 marines, for the remaining seven lunar months	4,601,000	0	0
„ the wear and tear of ships, &c.	3,684,000	0	0
„ the ordinary expenses of the navy, including the half-pay to sea and marine officers; also the expense of sea-ordnance	1,365,524	17	5
„ the extraordinaries; including the building and repairing of ships, and other extra work	773,500	0	0
„ the expense of the transport-service, and maintenance of prisoners of war in health	1,321,545	15	1
„ the care and maintenance of sick prisoners of war .	58,000	0	0
„ an increase of half-pay to the commissioned, and of additional pay to the warrant officers of the navy, for six months, commencing 1st July	30,000	0	0
Total supplies granted for the sea-service	£11,833,570	12	6

No. 10 *bis.*—See p. 156.

RECAPITULATORY ABSTRACT.

Showing the Number of French, Dutch, Spanish, and Danish Ships of the Line and Frigates, Captured, Destroyed, Wrecked, Foundered, and Accidentally Burnt, during the War commencing in February, 1793, and ending in 1801; also the Number of Captured Ships added to the British Navy during the same period.

		Lost through the Enemy.		Lost through Accident.			Total lost to the F. D. S. & Da. Navies.	Total added to the British Navy.
		Capt.	Dest.	Wrecked.	Foundered.	Burnt.		
Ships of the line . .	Fr.	34	11	5	4	1	55	28
	Du.	18	..	..	..	..	18	17
	Sp.	5	5	..	..	..	10	4
	Da.	2	..	..	..	..	2	1
Total . .		58	16	5	4	1	84	50
Frigates .	Fr.	82	14	4	2	..	102	62
	Du.	33	..	..	..	..	33	25
	Sp.	11	4	..	..	..	15	7
Grand Total.		184	34	9	6	1	234	144

No. 11.—See p. 157.

RECAPITULATORY ABSTRACT.

Showing the Number of British Ships and Vessels of War Captured, Destroyed, Wrecked, Foundered, or Accidentally Burnt, during the War commencing in February, 1793, and ending in October, 1801; with the Foundered Vessels divided into British and Foreign Built.

	Lost through the Enemy.		Lost through Accident.				Total.
	Capt.	Dest.	Wrecked.	Foundered.		Burnt.	
				Br.-built.	For.-built.		
Ships of the line . .	5	..	9	..	..	6	20
„ under the line .	37	9	73	8	14	4	145
Total . .	42	9	82	8	14	10	165

Of the eight foundered British-built vessels, one, the Malabar, had been an East Indiaman. Seven of the others were sloops, the largest of which did not exceed 324 tons; and it is even doubtful whether three of those were not *wrecked.* The remaining vessel was the Leda frigate; which vessel, according to one account, struck on a sunken rock, and, according to a third, filled in consequence of having her side stove by some of her guns that had broken loose in a severe gale of wind: in fact, the fate of the Leda is still involved in mystery.

No. 12.—See p. 166.

A List of Ships and Vessels late belonging to the British Navy, Wrecked, Foundered, or Accidentally Burnt, during the year 1802.

Name.	Commander.	How, when, and where Lost.
Gun-ship.		
50 (T) Assistance .	Richard Lee .	Wrecked, March 29, between Dunkerque and Gravelines: crew saved.
G. sh. slp.		
18 (S) Scout . .	Henry Duncan .	Foundered, exact date unknown, off coast of Newfoundland: crews perished.
14 (W) Fly .	Thomas Duval .	
T.S. (t) Sensible. .	Robert Sauce .	Wrecked, March 2, on a quicksand off Ceylon: crew saved.

ABSTRACT.

	Wrecked.	Foundered.	Burnt.	Total.
Ships under the line . . .	2	2	..	4

No. 13.—See p. 167.

	£.	s.	d.
For the pay and maintenance of 38,000 seamen and 12,000 marines, for two lunar months, commencing January 1, of 45,600 seamen, and 14,400 marines, for four lunar months, commencing February 26, and of 77,600 seamen, and 22,400 marines, for seven lunar months, commencing June 12	3,900,000	0	0
„ the wear and tear of ships, &c.	3,120,000	0	0
„ the ordinary expenses of the navy, including half-pay to sea and marine officers : also the expense of sea-ordnance	1,488,238	13	1
„ the extraordinaries, including the building and repairing of ships and other extra work	901,140	0	0
„ the expense of the transport-service, and maintenance of prisoners of war, in health and sickness .	802,000	0	0
Total supplies granted for the sea-service .	£10,211,378	13	1

No. 14.—See p. 168.

French Line-of-Battle Force in March, 1803.

		No.	No.
Ordered to be built from Dutch models at {	FLUSHING, and shores of the Scheldt . .}	5	
	NANTES	2	
	BORDEAUX . . .	1	
	MARSEILLES . . .	1	
	OSTENDE . . .	1	
		—	10
BREST,	{ afloat, repaired or repairing	18	
	{ building and nearly ready	3	
		—	21
LORIENT, building,	{ nearly ready	3	
	{ ordered	2	
		—	5
SAINT-MALO, ordered			1
ROCHEFORT, building,	{ nearly ready	3	
	{ ordered	3	
		—	6
TOULON,	{ afloat	8	
	{ building { nearly ready	2	
	{ ordered.	2	
		—	12
GENOA, ordered			1
AT SEA			10
		—	
	Total . . .		66

No. 15.—See p. 169.

Instruction particulière du premier Consul au général de division Decaen, capitaine-général des établissemens français au delà du cap de Bonne-Espérance.

Paris, février 1803.

Indépendamment des instructions générales que le ministre donnera au capitaine-général des possessions françaises dans les Indes, et à l'amiral, l'un et l'autre auront des instructions d'un ordre supérieur, lesquelles seront signees par le premier consul.

Il faudra donc ôter des deux instructions ci-jointes tout ce qui a rapport à la haute politique et à la direction des forces militaires ; ce qui se réduit à retrancher quelques paragraphes. Les instructions particulières seraient rédigées ainsi :—" Le ministre de la marine a dû remettre au capitaine-général des instructions sur l'administration et les différens droits et prérogatives dont nos établissemens et notre commerce doivent jouir aux Indes ; mais le premier consul a cru devoir signer lui-même toutes les instructions servant de base à la direction politique et militaire. Le capitaine-général arrivera dans un pays où nos rivaux dominent, mais où ils pèsent aussi sur tous les peuples de ces vastes contrées. Il doit donc s'attacher à ne leur donner aucun sujet d'alarme, aucun sujet de querelle, et à dissimuler le plus possible. Il doit s'en tenir aux relations indispensables pour la sûreté et l'approvisionnement de nos établissemens, et dans les relations qu'il aura avec les peuples ou les princes qui supportent le plus impatiemment le joug anglais, il s'étudiera à ne mettre aucune affectation, à ne leur donner aucune inquiétude. Ils sont les tyrans des Indes ; ils y sont inquiets et jaloux, il faut s'y comporter avec douceur, dissimulation et simplicité.

" Six mois après son arrivée aux Indes, le capitaine-général expédiera en France, porteur de ses dépêches, un des officiers ayant le plus sa confiance, pour faire connaître en grand détail tout ce qu'il a connu de la force, situation et disposition d'esprit des différens peuples des Indes, ainsi que de la force et de la situation des différens établissemens anglais. Il fera connaître ses vues et les espérances qu'il aurait de trouver de l'appui en cas de guerre, pour pouvoir se maintenir dans le presqu'île, en faisant connaître la quantité et qualité de troupes, d'armemens et d'approvisionnemens dont il aurait besoin pour nourrir la guerre pendant plusieurs campagnes au centre des Indes. Il doit porter la plus grande attention dans toutes les phrases de son Mémoire, parce que toutes seront pesées et pourront servir à décider, dans des circonstances imprévues, la marche et la politique du gouvernement. Pour nourrir la guerre aux Indes plusieurs campagnes, il faut raisonner dans l'hypothese que nous ne serions pas maîtres des mers, et que nous aurions à espérer peu de secours considérables. Il paraîtrait difficile qu'avec un corps d'armée on pût long-temps résister aux forces considérables que peuvent opposer les Anglais, sans alliances et sans une place servant de point d'appui, où dans un cas extrême on pût capituler et se trouver encore maître de se faire transporter en

France ou à l'Ile-de-France avec armes et bagages, sans être prisonniers, et sans compromettre l'honneur et un corps considérable de Français.

Un point d'appui doit avoir le caractère d'être fortifié, et d'avoir une rade ou un port où des frégates ou des vaisseaux de commerce soient à l'abri d'une force supérieure. Quelle que soit la nation à laquelle appartienne cette place, portugaise, hollandaise, ou anglaise, le premier projet paraît devoir tendre à s'en emparer dès les premiers mois, en calculant sur l'effet de l'arrivée d'une force européenne inattendue et incalculée. Après avoir fait un plan d'alliance et de guerre avec une force demandée, il faudrait établir ce que croirait devoir faire le capitaine-général, si, au lieu de cette force, on ne lui en envoyait que la moitié. Après avoir pensé aux alliances et à un point d'appui, les objets qui intéressent le plus une armée dans une campagne, sont les vivres et les munitions de guerre, objets que le capitaine-général traitera également dans le plus grand detail. Six mois après cet envoi, le capitaine-général, dans un nouveau Mémoire, traitera les mêmes questions, en y ajoutant les nouvelles connaissances qu'il aura pu acquérir.

"Ainsi, il sera établi que tous les six mois le capitaine-général enverra en France des officiers sûrs, des Mémoires traitant toujours les mêmes questions, et confirmant, modifiant ou contre-disant les idées des Mémoires précédens. Si la guerre venait à se déclarer entre la France et l'Angleterre avant le 1er vendémiaire an XIII, et que le capitaine-général en fût prévenu avant de recevoir les ordres gouvernement, il a carte blanche, est autorisé à se reployer sur l'Ile-de-France et le Cap, ou à rester dans la presqu'île, selon les circonstances où il se trouvera, et les espérances qu'il pourrait concevoir, sans cependant exposer notre corps de troupes à une capitulation honteuse, et nos armes à jouer un rôle qui ajouterait à notre discrédit aux Indes, et sans diminuer, par l'anéantissement de nos forces, la résistance que peut présenter l'Ile-de-France en s'y reployant. On ne conçoit pas aujourd'hui que nous puissions avoir la guerre avec l'Angleterre, sans y entraîner la Hollande. Un des premiers soins du capitaine-général sera de s'assurer de la situation des établissemens hollandais, portugais, espagnols, et des ressources qu'ils pourraient offrir,

"La mission du capitaine-général est d'abord une mission d'observation sous les rapports politique et militaire, avec le peu de forces qu'il mène et une occupation de comptoirs pour notre commerce ; mais le premier consul, bien instruit par lui et par l'exécution ponctuelle des instructions qui précèdent, pourra peut-être le mettre à même d'acquérir un jour la grande gloire qui prolonge la mémoire des hommes au-delà de la durée des siècles."—*Précis des Evènemens*, tome xi., p. 189.

No. 16,—See p. 212.

A List of Ships of the Line and Frigates, late belonging to the French Navy, Captured, Destroyed, Wrecked, Foundered, or Accidentally Burnt, during the year 1803.

Name.	How, when, and where Lost.
Gun-ship.	
74 (M) Duquesne	Captured, July 25, by the Bellerophon and Vanguard 74s, and others, off St. Domingo.
Gun-frig.	
(Z) Créole	Captured, July 1, by a British squadron, under Captain Henry W. Bayntum, off St. Domingo.
40 ,, Clorinde	Captured, November 30, by a British squadron, under Captain John
,, Surveillante	Loring, at the surrender of Cape
,, Vertu	Français, St. Domingo.
36 (D) Franchise	Captured, May 28, by a British squadron in the Channel.
32 (H) Embuscade	Captured, May 28, by the 100-gun ship Victory, on passage to Gibraltar.
28 ,, Baïonnaise	Destroyed, November 27, by her own crew, after having been chased on shore near Cape Finisterre by the Ardent 64.

No Dutch ship-of-war above an 18-gun corvette captured, &c. in 1803.

An Abstract of French Ships of the Line and Frigates Captured, &c., during the year 1803.

	Lost through the Enemy.		Lost through Accident.			Total Loss to the French Navy.	Total added to the British Navy.
	Capt.	Dest.	Wrecked.	Foundered.	Burnt.		
Ships of the line	1	..	..	..	..	1	1
Frigates	6	1	..	..	..	7	6
Total	7	1	..	..	..	8	7

No. 17.—See p. 212.

A List of Ships and Vessels, late belonging to the British Navy, Captured, Destroyed, Wrecked, Foundered, or Accidentally Burnt, during the year 1803.

Name.	Commander.	How, when, and where Lost.
Gun-frig.		
38 { (Z) *Minerve*	Jahleel Brenton	Captured, July 2, after having run aground near Cherbourg: crew saved, but made prisoners.
,, *Seine*	David Milne	Wrecked, in the night of June 5, on a sand-bank near the Texel: crew saved.
36 { (C) Resistence	Hon. P. Wodehouse	Wrecked, May 31, on Cape St. Vincent: crew saved.
,, Shannon,	Ed. Leveson Gower	Wrecked in a gale, December 10, under the batteries near Cape la Hogue: crew saved, but made prisoners. Hull of the ship destroyed by the Merlin's boats.
28 (I) Circe	Charles Fielding	Wrecked, November 16, on the Lemon and Ower, North Sea, in chase of an enemy: crew saved.
Gun p. ship.		
22 { (N) *Garland*	Frederick Cottrell	Wrecked, November, off Cape Français, St. Domingo: crew saved.
,, *Déterminée,*	Alexander Becher	Wrecked, March 26, on a sunken rock off the island of Jersey: crew and passengers (soldiers) saved, except 19.
G.-sh. slp.		
18 (S) *Surinam*	Robert Tucker	Captured by the Dutch, at the island of Curaçoa.
16 (T) Calypso	William Venour	Foundered, August, by being run down in a gale, by one of a convoy coming from Jamaica: crew perished.
14 (X) Avenger	Frs. Jackson Snell	Foundered, December, off the Weser: crew saved.
G. b. slp.		
16 (a) *Suffisante*	George Heathcote	Wrecked, December 15, in a gale off Spike island, Cork harbour: crew saved.
Gun-brig.		
12 (g) Grappler,	A.Wantner Thomas	Wrecked, December 31, on the isles de Chosey, and hull destroyed by the French: crew saved, but made prisoners.
Gun-sch.		
12 (k) Redbridge	George Lempriere	Captured, August, by a squadron of French frigates, near Toulon.
SS. (r.) Porpoise	Robert Fowler	Wrecked, August 17, on a reef of coral in the Pacific Ocean: crew saved.

No. 17—*continued.*

ABSTRACT.

	Lost through the Enemy		Lost through Accident.			
	Capt.	Dest.	Wrecked.	Foundered.	Burnt.	Total.
Ships of the line . .	..	..	..	..	..	..
„ under the line .	3	..	9	2	..	14
Total . .	3	..	9	2	..	14

No. 18.—See p. 213.

	£	s.	d.
For the pay and maintenance of 78,000 seamen and 22,000 marines	4,875,000	0	0
„ the wear and tear of ships, &c.	3,900,000	0	0
„ the ordinary expenses of the navy, including the half-pay to sea and marine officers; also the expense of sea-ordnance	1,345,670	9	9
„ the extraordinaries; including the building and repairing of ships, and other extra work	948,520	0	0
„ the expense of the transport service, and the maintenance of prisoners of war, in health and sickness . .	971,415	17	9
„ increasing the naval defence of the country . . .	310,000	0	0
Total supplies granted for the sea-service .	£12,350,606	7	6

No. 19.—See p. 239.

Abord du Bucentaure en rade du Toulon,
le 26 prairial, an 12.

Général,

J'ai l'honneur de vous rendre compte de la sortie de toute l'escadre à mes ordres. Sur l'avis que j'avais reçu que plusieurs corsairs anglais infestaient la côte et les îles d'Hières, je donnai l'ordre, il y a trois jours, aux frégates l'Incorruptible et la Syrène, et le brick le Furet, de ce rendre dans la baie d'Hières. Le vents d'est les ayant contrariées, elles mouillèrent sous le château de Porqueroles. Hier matin, les ennemis en eurent connaissance. Vers midi, ils détachèrent deux frégates et un vaisseau, qui entrèrent par la grande passe, dans l'intention de couper la retraite à nos frégates. Du moment où je m'aperçus de sa manœuvre, je fis signal d'appareiller à toute l'escadre; ce qui fut exécuté. En 14 minutes, tout était sous voiles, et je fis porter sur l'ennemi pour lui couper le chemin de la petite passe, et dans le dessein de l'y suivre s'il avait tenté d'y passer; mais l'amiral anglais ne tarda pas à renoncer à son projet, rappela son vaisseau et ses deux frégates engagés dans l'îles, et prit chasse. Je l'ai poursuivi jusqu'à la nuit : il courait au sud-est. Le matin, au jour, je n'en ai eu aucune connaissance.

Je vous salue avec respect,

LA TOUCHE-TREVILLE.

No. 20.—See p. 251.

" Si la contenance des ennemis pendant le jour n'avait été qu'une ruse ayant pour but de nous en imposer, pour cacher leur faiblesse, ils auraient pu profiter de l'obscurité de la nuit pour tenter de nous dérober leur marche, et dans cette occasion je pus profiter avec avantage de leur manœuvres. Mais je pus bientôt me convaincre que cette sécurité n'avait point été simulée ; trois de leurs vaisseaux eurent constamment leurs feux allumées, et la flotte conserva la panne tout la nuit, en se tenant bien ralliée. Cette position me facilita les moyens de lui gagner le vent et de l'observer de près."

No. 21.—See p. 253.

" Le vaisseau ennemi le plus avance (the Royal George) ayant éprouvé quelques avaries, laissa arriver ; mais, soutenu par ceux qui la suivaient, il prêta de nouveau côté, et fit, ainsi que les autres bâtimens, un feu très-nourri. Les vaisseaux qui avaient viré se réunirent à ceux qui nous combattaient, e trois de ceux qui avaient des premiers pris part à l'action, manœuvraient pour nous doubler à l'arrière, tandis que le reste de la flotte, se couvrant de voile, et laissant arriver, annonçait le projet de nous envelopper. Les ennemis, pa. cette manœuvre, auraient rendu ma position très-dangereuse ; la supériorite de leurs forces était reconnue, et je n'avais plus à délibérer sur le parti que je devais prendre pour éviter les suites funestes d'un engagement inégal ; profitant de la fumée qui m'enveloppait, je virai lof-pour-lof pour venir sur babord, et courant à l'est-nord-est, je m'éloignai de l'ennemi, qui continua à poursuivre la division jusqu'à trois heures, en lui envoyant plusieurs bordées sans effet."

No. 22.—See p. 305.

A List of Ships of the Line and Frigates, late belonging to the Dutch Navy, Captured, Destroyed, Wrecked, Foundered, or Accidentally Burnt, during the year 1804.

	Name.	How, when, and where Lost.
Gun-frig.		
32 (*G*)	Proserpine	Captured, May 4, at the surrender of Surinam to the British.

No French ship of the line or frigate captured, &c. in 1804.

No. 23.—See p. 305.

A List of Ships of the Line and Frigates, late belonging to the Spanish Navy, Captured, Destroyed, Wrecked, Foundered, or Accidentally Burnt, during the year 1804.

Name.	How, when, and where Lost.
Gun-frig. 40 { (A) Amfitrite	Captured, November 25, by the British 74 gun-ship Donegal, off Cadiz.
,, Medea	Captured, October 5, by a squadron of four British frigates under Captain Graham Moore.
,, Fama	
(D) Clara	
34 { .. Mercedes	Destroyed, by being blown up on the same occasion: crew and passengers, except 41 persons, perished.
(G) Sta.-Gertruyda	Captured, December 7, by the Polyphemus 64 and Lively frigate, off Cape Santa-Maria.

An Abstract of Dutch and Spanish Ships of the Line and Frigates, Captured, &c., during the year 1804.

	Lost through the Enemy.		Lost through Accident.			Total loss to the D. & S. Navies.	Total added to the British Navy.
	Capt.	Dest.	Wrecked.	Foundered.	Burnt.		
Ships of the Line	..	..	..	..	..	..	..
Frigates { Du.	5	..	..	..	..	1	1
{ Sp.	1	1	..	..	..	6	5
Total	6	1	..	..	..	7	6

No. 24.—See p. 305.

A List of Ships and Vessels, late belonging to the British Navy, Captured, Destroyed, Wrecked, Foundered, or Accidentally Burnt, during the year 1804.

Name.	Commander.	How, when, and where Lost.
Gun-ship. 74 { (O) Magnificent	Wm. Hen. Jervis	Wrecked, March 25, near the Pierres Noires, in the environs of Brest: crew saved, but 86 made prisoners.
,, Venerable	John Hunter.	Wrecked, November 24, on sunken rocks in Torbay: crew saved.
Gun-brig. 64 (P) York	Henry Mitford	Foundered, as is supposed, in January, in the North Sea: crew perished.
50 (T) Romney	Hon. John Colville	Wrecked, November 19, on the Haaks, near the Texel: crew saved.

No. 24—*continued.*

Name.	Commander.	How, when, and where Lost.
Gun-frig.		
38 { (Z) *Créole* . Austen Bissell		Foundered, January 2, on passage from Jamaica: crew saved.
(A) Hussar . Philip Wilkinson .		Wrecked, February, on the Saintes, in the Bay of Biscay: crew saved.
36 (C) Apollo . J. W. Taylor Dixon		Wrecked, April 1, on the coast of Portugal: captain and many of the crew perished.
G.-sh.-slp.		
14 (X) Lilly. . William Compton		Captured, July 14, by the Dame-Ambert Fr. privateer, off the Coast of Georgia.
G.-br.-slp.		
18 (Y) *Raven* . Spelman Swaine .		Wrecked, July 6, on the coast of Sicily, Mediterranean: crew saved.
16 (a) *Vincejo* . Jas. Wesley Wright		Captured, May 20, in a calm, by a flotilla of Fr. gun-boats, in Quiberon bay.
(b) *Drake* . William Ferris .		Wrecked, September, on a shoal off the island of Nevis: crew saved.
14 { ,, Weazle . William Layman		Wrecked, March 1, on Cabareta Point, Gibraltar bay: crew, except one man, saved.
,, Wolverine, Henry Gordon .		Captured, March 24, by a French privateer, on passage to New-foundland.
bb. (d) Tartarus . Thomas Withers .		Wrecked, December 20, on Margate sands: crew saved.
Gun-brig.		
(g) Conflict . Charles C. Ormsby		Wrecked, October 24, in chase of the enemy, near Nieuport, Isle of Wight: crew saved.
,, Fearless . George Williams		Wrecked, February, off Redding Point, Cawsand bay: crew saved.
12 { ,, Mallard . Thomas Reed . .		Captured, December 25, after running on shore near Calais: crew saved, but made prisoners.
,, Sterling . George Skottowe		Wrecked, December 18, near Calais: crew saved.
10 (h) *Cerbère*. . Joseph Patey		Wrecked, February 19, on the Berry Head: crew saved.
G.-sch.		
6 { (n) *Morne-Fortunée,* John L. Dale		Wrecked, in December, on Crooked Island, West Indies: crew saved.
,, *Demerara* . Thomas Dutton		Captured, July 14, by the Fr. priv. Grand-Décidé, West Indies.
TS. (q) Severn . . Prince of Bouillon		Wrecked, December 21, in Grouville bay, Jersey: crew saved.
SS. (r) Hindostan . John Le Gros .		Burnt, April 2, having caught fire in the hold, Mediterranean: crew, except five men, saved.
RS. (a) *De-Ruyter* . J. Beckett . .		Wrecked, September 3, in the hurricane at Antigua: crew saved.

ABSTRACT.

	Lost through the Enemy.		Lost through Accident.			
	Capt.	Dest.	Wrecked.	Foundered.	Burnt.	Total.
Ships of the Line . .	..	..	2	1	..	3
,, under the Line	5	..	14	1	1	21
Total . . .	5	..	16	2	1	24

No. 25.—See p. 305.

	£.	s.	d.
For the pay and maintenance of 90,000 seamen and 30,000 marines	5,850,000	0	0
,, the wear and tear of ships, &c.	4,680,000	0	0
,, the ordinary expenses of the navy, including half-pay to sea and marine officers; also the extra of sea-ordnance	1,394,940	6	9
,, the extraordinaries, including the building and re-pairing of ships, and other extra work	1,553,690	0	0
,, the expenses of the transport-service, and the main-tenance of prisoners of war, in health and sickness .	1,557,000	0	0
Total supplies granted for the sea-service . .	£15,035,630	6	9

No. 26.—See p. 310.

Faites mettre dans les journaux de Hollande un article contre le système de blocus; faites-y-sentir que nous sommes sortis de Brest quand nous l'avons voulu; que Bruix est sorti tel jour, Morard de Galles tel jour, Gantheaume tant de fois; que dans sa dernière sortie à Bertheaume, rien ne l'empêchait de sortir, et que l'escadre le savait tellement qu'elle mit à la voile; qu'il est donc impossible de bloquer le port de Brest, surtout aux mois de septembre et d'octobre. Cet article fera sentir que nous ne voulons pas sortir, mais tenir l'ennemi en échec.—*Précis des Evènemens*, tome xi., p. 271.

No. 27.—See p. 325.

The following Table will show the state of the flotilla at the different ports, on July 20, 1805, with the number of men and horses it was destined to carry.

FLOTILLA.	Étaples.	Boulogne.	Vimereux.	Ambleteuse.	Calais.	Dunkerque.	Ostende.	Total of Vessels.	Men.	Horses.
	PORTS.								**TOTAL.**	
Prames	..	13	..	3	1	..	..	17	1,920	840
Bombardes, Paquebots, and Avisos . . . . }	1	11	..	..	..	..	..	12	480	56
Gun-vessels { French . .	217	530	144	1	2	...	30	924	89,885	676
{ Dutch . .	..	..	..	135	14	131	..	280	28,038	404
Caïques, corvettes de pêche and péniches . }	1	22	..	..	81	..	..	88	9,315	233
Vessels of war	219	578*	144	139	98	131	30	1,339	130,638	2,219*
Transports	146	526	92	34	105	26	25	954	30,577	6,840
Grand Total . . .	365	1104	236	173	203	157	55	2,293	161,215	9,059
Crews of Transports . .	..	..	..	..	..	..	..	..	2,430	
									163,645	

The two totals marked * do not quite agree with the items; but, as it is impossible, without the originals, to discover where the error lies, and as the difference is not at all material, the figures have been left as they appear in the work that contains the Table whence this has been extracted.—See Précis des Evènemens, tome xii., p. 304.

No. 28.—See p. 331.

" A l'époque où j'écrivais ce passage, j'ignorais un fait bien remarquable, et qui mérite de prendre place dans l'histoire. J'en dois la connaissance à M. le comte Daru, dont nous avons déjà cité la savante Histoire de Venise. En 1805, M. Daru était à Boulogne, intendant général de l'armée. Un matin l'empereur le fait appeler dans son cabinet. Daru l'y trouve transporté de colère, parcourant à grands pas son appartement, et ne rompant un morne silence que par des exclamations brusques et courtes. . . . Quelle marine ! . . . Quel amiral ! . . . Quels sacrifices perdus ! . . . Mon espoir et déçu ! . . . Ce Villeneuve; Au lieu d'être dans la Manche, il vient d'entrer au Férol . . . C'en est fait ! Il y sera bloqué.—Daru, mettez-vous là, écoutez et écrivez. L'empereur avait reçu de grand matin la nouvelle de l'arrivée de Villeneuve dans un port d'Espagne; il avait vu sur-le-champ la conquête de l'Angleterre avortée; les immenses dépenses de la flotte et de la flottille perdues pour long-temps, pour toujours peut-être ! Alors, dans l'emportement d'une fureur qui ne permet pas même aux autres hommes de conserver leur jugement, il avait pris l'une des résolutions les plus hardies, et tracé l'un des plans de campagne les plus admirables qu'aucun conquérant ait pu concevoir à loisir et de sang-froid. Sans hésiter, sans s'arrêter, il dicte en entier le plan de la campagne d'Austerlitz, le départ de tous les corps d'armée, depuis le Hanovre et la Hollande jusqu'aux confins de l'ouest et du sud de la France. L'ordre des marches, leur durée, les lieux de convergence et de réunion des colonnes; les enlèvemens par surprise et les attaques de vive force, les mouvemens divers de l'ennemi, tout est prévu: la victoire est assurée dans toutes les hypothèses. Telle était la justesse et la vaste prévoyance de ce plan, que, sur une ligne de départ de deux cents lieues, des lignes d'opérations de trois cents lieues de longueur furent suivies d'après les indications primitives, jour par jour, et lieu par lieu, jusqu'à Munich. Au-delà de cette capitale, les époques seules éprouvèrent quelques altérations; mais les lieux furent atteints et l'ensemble du plan fut couronné d'un succès complet. Tel était donc le talent militaire de cet homme, aussi redoutable à ses ennemis par la puissance de son génie, qu'à ses concitoyens par la force de son despotisme!"—*Voyages dans la Grande Bretagne, Force Navale*, tome i., p. 244.

No. 29.—See p. 346.

LORD NELSON'S PLAN OF ATTACK.

"The business of an English commander-in-chief," says his lordship, "being first to bring an enemy's fleet to battle, on the most advantageous terms to himself (I mean, that of laying his ships close on board those of the enemy as expeditiously as possible, and secondly, to continue them there without separating until the business is decided), I am sensible, beyond this object, it is not necessary I should say a word, being fully assured, that the admirals and captains of the fleet I have the honour to command will, knowing my precise object, that of a close and decisive battle, supply any deficiency in my not making signals; which may, if extended beyond these objects, either be misunderstood, or, if waited for, very probably, from various causes, be impossible for the commander-in-chief to make. Therefore it will only be requisite for me to state, in as few words as possible, the various modes by which it may be necessary for me to obtain my object, on which depends not only the honour and glory of our country, but possibly its safety, and, with it, that of all Europe, from French tyranny and oppression.

"If the two fleets are both willing to fight, but little manœuvring is necessary. The less the better; a day is soon lost in that business. Therefore I will only suppose that the enemy's fleet being to leeward, standing close upon a wind on the starboard tack, and that I am nearly ahead of them, standing on the larboard tack; of course I should weather them. The weather must be supposed to be moderate; for, if it be a gale of wind, the manœuvring of both fleets is but of little avail, and probably no decisive action would take place with the whole fleet. Two modes present themselves; one, to stand on just out of gun-shot until the van-ship of my line would be abreast of the centre ship of the enemy, then make the signal to wear together, then bear up, engage with all our force the six or five van-ships of the enemy, passing certainly, if opportunity offered, through their line. This would prevent their bearing up, and the action, from the known bravery and conduct of the admirals and captains, would certainly be decisive; the second or third rear-ships of the enemy would act as they pleased, and our ships would give a good account of them, should they persist in mixing with our ships. The other mode would be, to stand under an easy but commanding sail, directly for their headmost ship, so as to prevent the enemy from knowing whether I should pass to leeward or to windward of him. In that situation, I would make the signal to engage the enemy to leeward, and to cut through their fleet about the sixth ship from the van, passing very close; they being on a wind, you, going large, could cut their line when you please. The van-ships of the enemy would, by the time our rear came abreast of the van-ship, be severely cut up, and our van could not expect to escape damage. I would then have our rear-ship, and every ship in succession, wear, continue the action with either the van-ship or second ship, as it might appear most eligible from her crippled state; and, this mode pursued, I see nothing to prevent the capture of the five or six ships of the enemy's van. The two or three ships of the enemy's rear must either bear up or wear; and, in either case, although they would be in a better plight probably than our two van-ships (now the rear), yet they would be separated and at a distance to leeward, so as to give our ships time to refit; and by that time, I believe, the battle would, from the judgment of the admirals and captains, be over with the rest of them. Signals from these moments are useless, when every man is disposed to do his duty. The great object is, for us to support each other, and to keep close to the enemy and to leeward of him. If the enemy are running away, then the only signals necessary will be, to engage the enemy as arriving up with them, and the other ships to pass on for the second, third, &c.; giving, if possible, a close fire into the enemy in passing, taking care to give our ships engaged notice of your intention."—*Clarke and M'Arthur's Life of Nelson*, vol. ii., p. 427.

No. 30.—See p. 354.

VICE-ADMIRAL COLLINGWOOD TO LORD NELSON.

"We approached, my dear lord, with caution, not knowing whether we were to expect you or the Frenchmen first. I have always had an idea that Ire-land alone was the object they have in view, and still believe that to be their ultimate destination. They will now liberate the Ferrol squadron from Calder, make the round of the Bay, and, taking the Rochefort people with them, will appear off Ushant, perhaps with thirty-four sail, there to be joined by twenty more. This appears a probable plan; for, unless it be to bring their powerful fleets and armies to some great point of service, some rash attempt at conquest, they have only been subjecting them to chance of loss, which I do not believe the Corsican would do, without the hope of an adequate reward.   *   *   *   *   *   *

The French government never aim at little things, while great objects are in view. I have considered the invasion of Ireland as the real mark and butt of all their operations. Their flight to the West Indies was to take off the naval force, which proved the great impediment to their undertaking."—*Clarke and M'Arthur's Life of Nelson*, vol. ii., p. 416.

No. 31.—See p. 362.

The following short Table will show the numerical loss sustained by each Ship, also her principal damages in Rigging, Masts, and Yards, or Hull.

SHIPS.	Loss K.	Loss W.	Rigging, &c.	Masts and Yards. Shot away.	Masts and Yards. Wounded.	Hull, &c.
Hero	1	4	Much cut	None reported	Fore and main masts and top-masts, badly.	Several shots between wind & water.
Ajax	2	16	,,	Mainyard & driver-boom	None reported	One lower-deck gun disabled, starboard bumpkin shot away. Two lower-deck guns disabled.
Triumph	5	6		Driver-boom	Bowsprit and mainmast.	
Barfleur	3	7	No damage reported	None reported	Foremast and foreyard.	
Agamemnon	0	3	,,	Foretopsail-yard & mizen-topmast.	Fore and main yards and main-topmast.	No damage reported.
Windsor Castle	10	35	Much cut	Foretopmast, and a great part of foretop.	Head of foremast, fore and main yards and bowsprit.	
Defiance	1	7	,,	Mizentopsail-yard	Mainmast, foreyard, and driver-boom.	
Prince of Wales	3	23	,,	Foretopsail-yard	Mizentopmast and main yard badly.	Rudder shot through two feet above water's edge. Knee of the head damaged. Some shots struck, &c.
Repulse	0	4	No damage reported	None reported	Bowsprit badly	
Raisonable	1	1			Cross-jack yard	
Dragon	0	4		,,	None reported.	
Glory	1	1	Much cut	,,	Fore-yard	
Warrior	0	0	,,	,,	Spritsail-yard, foretopgallant-yard, and driver-boom.	No damage reported.
Thunderer	7	11	,,	,,	Mizenmast, fore-yard, and main-topsail-yard.	Upper cheek of knee of head shot through, &c.
Malta	5	40		Mizentopsail-yard	Mizenmast and topmast, and fore-topmast, also main-yard badly.	No damage reported.
Egyptienne	0	0	No damage reported			
Sirius	2	3		None reported	None reported.	

No. 32.—See p. 362.

The following statement will show the exact loss sustained by each ship of the combined fleet, in killed and wounded.

SHIPS.	K.	W.	Total.	SHIPS.	K.	W.	Total.
				Brought forward	131	305	436
Argonauta . . .	4	3	7	Neptune	1	7	8
Terrible	1	4	5	Bucentaure . . .	3	3	6
America	3	8	11	Formidable . . .	4	6	10†
Espana	3	6	9	Intrépide	5	5	10
San Rafaël . . .	53	114	167	Scipion	..	..	..
Firme	41	97	138	Swiftsure	..	..	..
Pluton	8	22	30	Indomptable . .	1	1	2
Mont-Blanc . . .	6	11	17	Aigle	4	..	4
Atlas	10	32	42*	Achille	..	..	..
Berwick	2	8	10	Algésiras	..	..	..
Carried forward	131	305	436	Total . . .	149	327	476

* Including captain and two lieutenants among the killed.
† Including captain among the killed.

No. 33.—See p. 367.

" Je ne me propose point d'aller chercher l'ennemi, je veux même l'éviter pour me rendre à ma destination ; mais, si nous le rencontrions, point de manœuvre honteuse ; elle découragerait nos équipages et entraînerait notre défaite. Si l'ennemi est sous le vent à nous, maîtres de notre manœuvre, nous formerons notre ordre de bataille et nous arriverons sur lui tous à la fois : chacun de nos vaisseaux combat celui qui lui correspond dans la ligne ennemie et ne doit pas hésiter à l'aborder si la circonstance lui est favorable.—Tout capitaine qui ne serait pas dans le feu, ne serait pas à son poste, et un signal pour l'y rappeler serait une tâche déshonorante pour lui. Les frégates doivent également prendre part à l'action ; je n'en ai pas besoin pour les signaux ; elles doivent choisir le point où leur co-opération peut être avantageuse, pour décider la défaite d'un vaisseau ennemi, ou pour soutenir un vaisseau français trop vivement pressé, et lui donner le secours de la remorque ou tout autre qui lui serait nécessaire."—*Victoires et Conquêtes*, tome xvi., p. 109.

No. 34.—See p. 370.

" L'amiral Calder, avec des forces inférieures, rencontre les flottes espagnole et française combinées ; il engage, en les poursuivant, une affaire d'avant-garde et prend deux vaisseaux. Il est mit en jugement et censuré ; parce qu'on suppose qu'en renouvelant le combat, il pouvait obtenir un succès plus décisif. Qu'aurait-on fait de Calder, en Angleterre, s'il eût commandé la flotte la plus nombreuse, et perdu deux vaisseaux, en fuyant une affaire qui devait présenter une si belle chance au savoir et à la vaillance ? Qu'aurait-on fait des capitaines ?"—*Voyages dans la Grande Bretagne*, par Dupin. Deuxième partie, tome ii., p. 17.

No. 35.—See p. 377.

" 1°. Il n'a pas débarqué à la Martinique et à la Gaudeloupe le 67° régiment, et les troupes que l'amiral Magon avait à bord. 2°. Il a exposé ces colonies en ne renvoyant que par quatre frégates douze cents hommes de l'élite des garnisons. 3°. Il s'est mal comporté dans le combat du 23 juillet, en ne réattaquant pas une escadre dégrée qui avait deux vaisseaux à la traine. 4°. Arrivé au Ferrol, il a laissé la mer à l'amiral Calder, quand il attendait une escadre de cinq vaisseaux, et n'a point croisé devant le Ferrol jusqu'à l'arrivée de cette escadre. 5°. Il a été instruit que l'escadre voyait des vaisseaux ennemis mener la frégate la Didon à la rémorque, et il n'a point fait chasser ces vaisseaux pour dégager la frégate. 6°. Il est parti du Ferrol le 14 août, et au lieu de venir sur Brest, il s'est dirigé sur Cadiz, violant ainsi ses instructions positives. 7°. Enfin il a su que l'escadre de Lallemand devait venir à Vigo prendre des ordres et il a appareillé du Ferrol sans donner de nouveaux ordres à cet officier, lui ayant au contraire fait remettre des instructions toutes opposées qui compromettaient cette escadre, puisqu'elle avait ordre de se rendre à Brest, tandis que lui Villeneuve allait à Cadix."—*Précis des Evènemens*, tome xii., p. 84.

No. 36.—See p. 388.

" L'ennemi ne se bornera pas à se former sur une ligne de bataille parallèle à la nôtre, et à venir nous livrer un combat d'artillerie, dont le succès appartient souvent au plus habile, mais toujours au plus heureux; il cherchera à entourer notre arrière-garde, à nous traverser, et à porter sur ceux de nos vaisseaux qu'il aurait désunis des pelotons des siens pour les envelopper et les réduire. Dans ce cas, c'est bien plus de son courage et de son amour de la gloire qu'un capitaine-commandant doit prendre conseil que des signeaux de l'amiral qui, engage lui-même dans le combat, et enveloppé dans la fumée, n'a peut être plus la facilité d'en faire. Rien ne doit nous étonner dans la vue d'une escadre anglaise : leurs vaisseaux de 74 n'ont pas cinq cents hommes à bord ; ils sont harassés par une croisière de deux ans ; ils ne sont pas plus brave que nous, et ont infiniment moins de motifs pour se bien battre, moins d'amour de la patrie. Ils sont habiles à la manœuvre. Dans un mois, nous le serons autant qu'eux. Enfin, tout se réunit pour nous donner la confiance des succès les plus glorieux et d'une nouvelle ère pour la marine impériale."— *Victoires et Conquêtes*, tome xvi., p. 110.

No. 37.—See p. 421.

" En un clin d'œil, les gaillards de ce vaisseau furent déserts ; es braves du Redoutable voulurent s'y précipiter ; mais la rentrée de deux vaisseaux y mit obstacle. Afin d'y remédier, le capitaine Lucas donna l'ordre d'amener la grande vergue de son vaisseau, et d'en faire un pont pour passer à bord du vaisseau ennemi. Dans ce moment, le vaisseau à trois ponts le Téméraire aborda le Redoutable du côté opposé au Victory, en lui lâchant toute sa bordée. L'effet de cette bordée fut terrible sur l'équipage du Redoutable, rassemblé alors tout entier sur les gaillards et les passavans: près de 200 hommes furent mis hors de combat; le brave capitaine Lucas, quoique blessé, demeura sur le pont. L'arrivée du Téméraire ranimant le courage de l'équipage du Victory, le feu recommença à bord de ce vaisseau, qui le cessa ensuite presque entièrement pour se dégager d'avec le vaisseau français."—*Victoires et Conquêtes*, tome xvi., p. 174.

No. 38.—See p. 448.

Course and site of the Ball as ascertained since Death.

" The ball struck the fore part of his lordship's epaulette; and entered the left shoulder immediately before the processus acromion scapulæ, which it slightly fractured. It then descended obliquely into the thorax, fracturing the second and third ribs; and after penetrating the left lobe of the lungs, and dividing in its passage a large branch of the pulmonary artery, it entered the left side of the spine between the sixth and seventh dorsal vertebræ, fractured the left transverse process of the sixth dorsal vertebra, wounded the medulla spinalis, and fracturing the right transverse process of the seventh vertebra, made its way from the right side of the spine, directing its course through the muscles of the back; and lodged therein, about two inches below the inferior angle of the right scapula. On removing the ball, a portion of the gold lace and pad of the epaulette, together with a small piece of his lordship's coat, was found firmly attached to it.

" W. BEATTY."

No. 39.—See p. 451.

" Nelson doit être cité comme le modèle des amiraux, par le soin extrême, qu'il apportait à pénétrer tous ses généraux et tous ses capitaines, de l'esprit des attaques qu'il se proposait d'entreprendre. Il leur développait son plan général d'opérations, les modifications que le temps ou les manœuvres de l'ennemi pourraient le forcer d'apporter à sa détermination primitive. Dès qu'une fois il avait bien expliqué son système aux commandans généraux et supérieurs de son armée, il se reposait sur eux du soin d'agir suivant les circonstances, pour se porter au point le plus favorable à l'exécution de l'enterprise ainsi concertée. Or, Nelson, qui put choisir les compagnons de sa gloire, et eut le talent et le bonheur de trouver des hommes dignes de ses leçons et de sa confiance; ils apprirent dans l'action, à suppléer ce que n'avait pu deviner sa prévoyance, et dans le succès, à surpasser jusqu'à son espérance."— Dupin's *Voyages, &c.*, tome iv., p. 66.

An ABSTRACT of the Ships and Vessels belonging to the British Navy at the commencement of the Year 1801.

Letters of Reference	RATE	CLASS	CRUISERS In Commission No.	Tons	In Ordinary, under or for Repair No.	Tons	TOTAL No.	Tons	No. British Built	No. Foreign Built	Stationary Harbour-ships In Commission No.	Tons	Not in Commission No.	Tons	No. British Built	No. Foreign Built
		Three-deckers.														
A	First.	120-gun ship	1	2351	–	–	1	2351	1	–	1	2747	–	–	–	1
B	,,	112 ,, 18-pounder	1	2457	–	–	1	2457	1	–	–	–	–	–	–	–
C	,,	120 ,, 12 ,,	1	2286	–	–	1	2286	1	1	–	–	1	2398	–	1
D	,,	,, 18 ,,	1	2175	2	4253	3	6428	3	–	–	–	–	–	–	–
E	Second.	98 ,, 18 ,, – large	–	–	–	–	–	–	–	–	–	–	–	–	–	–
F	,,	,, 18 ,, – small	2	4240	–	–	2	4240	2	–	–	–	–	–	–	–
G	,,	,, 12 ,,	12	23420	1	1827	13	25247	13	–	1	1869	–	–	1	–
H	,,	90 ,,	–	–	1	1814	1	1814	1	–	2	3699	–	–	2	–
		Two-deckers.														
K	Third.	80 ,,	5	10635	3	6803	8	17438	2	6	–	–	1	1942	–	1
L	,,	74 ,, 24-pounder	8	15259	–	–	8	15259	6	2	–	–	–	–	–	–
M	,,	,, 18 ,, – large	9	16961	3	5661	12	22622	6	6	3	5447	1	1869	–	4
N	,,	,, ,, – middl.	4	6917	–	–	4	6917	4	–	–	–	1	1778	–	1
O	,,	,, ,, – small	35	57219	11	17952	46	75171	45	1	8	12740	4	6538	11	1
P	,,	64 ,,	21	29092	6	8138	27	37230	21	6	5	6869	11	15112	8	8
Q	Fourth.	60 ,,	–	–	–	–	–	–	–	–	1	1226	3	3718	3	1
		Line –	100	173012	27	46448	127	219460	105	22	21	34597	22	33355	25	18
R	,,	56 ,, flush	2	2682	–	–	2	2682	2	–	1	1182	–	–	1	–
S	,,	54 ,, ,,	1	1249	–	–	1	1249	1	–	–	–	1	–	–	–
T	,,	50 ,,	9	9604	1	1052	10	10656	9	1	2	2101	6	6335	4	4
V	Fifth.	44 ,,	3	2687	–	–	3	2687	3	–	1	882	3	2564	2	2
		One-deckers.														
W	,,	44-gun frigate	4	5530	–	–	4	5530	3	1	–	–	1	1357	–	1
X	,,	40 ,, 24-pounder	2	2516	1	1183	3	3699	1	2	–	–	–	–	–	–
Y	,,	,, 18 ,,	2	2302	–	–	2	2302	2	–	–	–	–	–	–	–
Z	,,	38 ,, – large	13	14317	–	–	13	14317	3	10	–	–	2	2245	–	2
A	,,	,, – small	15	15028	–	–	15	15028	13	2	–	–	–	–	–	–
B	,,	36 ,, 18-pounder – large	9	9313	–	–	9	9313	4	5	–	–	1	1011	–	1
C	,,	,, ,, – small	14	12891	1	881	15	13772	15	–	–	–	1	882	1	–
D	,,	32 ,, 18 ,, – large	14	12959	–	–	14	12959	–	14	4	3600	6	5358	–	10
E	,,	,, ,, – small	1	914	–	–	1	914	1	–	–	–	–	–	–	–
F	,,	,, 12 ,, – large	4	3218	–	–	4	3218	4	–	–	–	1	770	–	1
G	,,	,, ,, – small	5	3993	–	–	5	3993	3	2	–	–	1	770	–	1
H	Sixth.	28 ,,	24	16507	1	724	25	17231	25	–	–	–	1	704	–	1
I	,,	24-gun post-ship quarter-decked	10	6002	1	586	11	6588	8	3	3	1793	4	2387	4	3
K	,,	,, flush	5	2646	–	–	5	2646	4	1	–	–	3	1653	3	–
L	,,	22 ,,	1	625	–	–	1	625	–	1	–	–	–	–	–	–
N	,,	20 ,, quarter-decked	6	3249	–	–	6	3249	1	5	–	–	–	–	–	–
O	,,	,, flush	6	2818	1	498	7	3316	3	4	1	481	2	903	2	1
P	Sloops.	Arrow & Dart, mounting 28 carronades	3	1530	1	513	4	2043	–	4	–	–	–	–	–	–
Q	,,	18-gun ship-sloop, quarter decked	2	772	–	–	2	772	2	–	–	–	–	–	–	–
R	,,	,, flush	11	4706	–	–	11	4706	10	1	–	–	1	486	1	–
S	,,	16 ,, quarter-decked, large	18	6700	1	425	19	7125	12	7	–	–	4	1447	–	4
T	,,	,, ,, small	13	4941	–	–	13	4941	11	2	–	–	3	1020	2	1
U	,,	,, flush	4	1292	–	–	4	1292	4	–	–	–	3	319	1	–
V	,,	14 ,, quarter-decked	1	275	2	605	3	880	–	3	–	–	4	1147	–	4
W	,,	,, flush	6	1780	–	–	6	1780	6	–	1	304	2	601	3	–
X	,,	18-gun brig-sloop – large	1	200	–	–	1	200	1	–	–	–	–	–	–	–
Y	,,	,, – small	8	2988	–	–	8	2988	7	1	–	–	–	–	–	–
Z	,,	16 ,,	8	2622	–	–	8	2622	6	2	–	–	1	346	–	1
a	,,	14 ,,	14	3896	–	–	14	3896	1	13	–	–	4	1056	1	3
b		Bombs, of 8 guns and 2 mortars	15	3505	–	–	15	3505	3	12	–	–	1	202	1	–
d		Fireships, 12 ,,	14	4687	–	–	14	4687	14	–	–	–	–	–	–	–
e		Gun-brigs, 12 ,,	3	1050	–	–	3	1050	3	–	1	423	–	–	1	–
f		,, 10 ,,	6	1175	1	258	7	1433	3	4	–	–	1	202	–	1
g		,, 14 ,,	57	9006	–	–	57	9006	55	2	–	–	–	–	–	–
h		Cutters, &c. 14 ,,	6	952	1	137	7	1089	–	7	–	–	1	170	–	1
i		,, 12 ,,	4	734	–	–	4	734	–	4	–	–	1	181	1	–
k		,, 10 ,,	9	1311	–	–	9	1311	7	2	–	–	–	–	–	–
l		,, 8 ,,	7	817	–	–	7	817	–	7	–	–	–	–	–	–
m		,, 6 ,,	3	315	–	–	3	315	–	3	–	–	–	–	–	–
n		,, 4 ,,	2	185	–	–	2	185	–	2	–	–	–	–	–	–
o		,,	7	493	–	–	7	493	3	4	–	–	–	–	–	–
q		Third-rate, 36 ,,	–	–	–	–	–	–	–	–	9	12197	–	–	4	5
r		Fourth ,, 26 ,,	–	–	–	–	–	–	–	–	6	6732	–	–	4	2
s		Fifth ,, 24 ,,	–	–	–	–	–	–	–	–	20	18156	2	1808	20	2
t		,, 18 ,,	–	–	–	–	–	–	–	–	24	17089	1	804	17	8
u		Float. Batt. 46 ,,	–	–	–	–	–	–	–	–	1	1373	–	–	1	–
v		,, ,, 20 ,, and under	–	–	–	–	–	–	–	–	4	1489	–	–	4	–
w		Gun-vessels, from 1 to 4 guns	–	–	–	–	–	–	–	–	15	1339	7	470	–	22
z		Armed Transports	–	–	–	–	–	–	–	–	14	4818	–	–	9	5
a		Temporary Prison-ships	–	–	–	–	–	–	–	–	–	–	–	–	–	–
b		Yachts – royal, or large	–	–	–	–	–	–	–	–	3	513	1	232	4	–
c		,, – small	–	–	–	–	–	–	–	–	3	264	2	135	5	–
		*Grand Total –	472	359994	39	53310	511	413304	358	153	134	109333	90	70170	118	106

Increase and Decrease in the Classes since the date of the last Year's Abstract.

Grand Total	Launched — King's Yards		Launched — Merchants' Yards		Purchased		Captured		Converted from other Classes		Ordered to be Built		Total of Increase		Loss by Capture, &c.		Converted to other Classes		Sold, or taken to Pieces		Total of Decrease	
Tons.	No.	Tons.	No.	Tons.	No.	Tons.	No.	Tons.	No.	Tons.	No.	Tons.	No	Tons.	No.	Tons.	No.	Tons.	No.	Tons.	No.	Tons.
7871																						
2351																						
4855																						
2286	—	—	—	—	—	—	—	—	—	—	—	—	—	—	1	2286	—	—	—	—	1	2286
6428																						
4554																						
6363																						
27116																						
5513																						
19380	—	—	—	—	—	—	1	2265	—	—	—	—	1	2265								
26672																						
29938	—	—	1	1917	—	—	1	1926	—	—	—	—	2	3843	—	—	—	—	1	1799	1	1799
24332	1	1772	—	—	—	—	—	—	—	—	7	12115	8	13887	—	—	—	—	—	—		
94449	—	—	—	—	—	—	—	—	—	—	—	—	—	—	1	1642	—	—	1	1685	2	3327
59211	—	—	—	—	—	—	1	1404	2	2795	—	—	3	4199	1	1387	—	—	—	—	1	1387
4944																						
326263	1	1772	1	1917	—	—	3	5595	2	2795	7	12115	14	24194	3	5315	—	—	2	3484	5	8799
2682																						
2431																						
21333																						
6133	—	—	—	—	—	—	—	—	—	—	—	—	—	—	—	—	1	904	—	—	1	904
6887																						
3699																						
3474																						
17638	1	1071	—	—	—	—	2	2322	—	—	—	—	3	3393								
15028																						
10324	—	—	1	1053	—	—	2	2043	—	—	—	—	3	3096								
18542	—	—	2	1872	—	—	—	—	—	—	2	1921	4	3793								
21917	—	—	—	—	—	—	2	1810	—	—	—	—	2	1810	—	—	1	923	—	—	1	923
4542	—	—	—	—	—	—	—	—	—	—	3	2734	3	2734								
3218	—	—	—	—	—	—	—	—	—	—	—	—	—	—	1	792	—	—	—	—	1	792
4763	—	—	—	—	—	—	—	—	—	—	—	—	—	—	—	—	2	1606	—	—	2	1606
17935	—	—	—	—	—	—	—	—	—	—	—	—	—	—	—	—	2	1425	1	704	3	2129
10768																						
4299																						
625																						
3249	—	—	—	—	—	—	2	1127	—	—	—	—	2	1127								
4700	—	—	—	—	—	—	—	—	—	—	—	—	—	—	1	508	1	505	—	—	2	1013
2043	—	—	—	—	—	—	1	513	—	—	—	—	1	513	1	564	—	—	—	—	1	564
772																						
5614																						
9015	—	—	—	—	—	—	2	831	—	—	—	—	2	831	3	1096	—	—	—	—	3	1096
5961	—	—	—	—	—	—	—	—	—	—	—	—	—	—	1	365	—	—	—	—	1	365
1611	—	—	—	—	—	—	—	—	—	—	—	—	—	—	1	329	—	—	—	—	1	329
2027																						
2685																						
200	—	—	—	—	—	—	—	—	—	—	—	—	—	—	1	261	—	—	—	—	1	261
2988																						
2968	—	—	—	—	—	—	—	—	—	—	—	—	—	—	2	633	—	—	—	—	2	633
4952	—	—	—	—	1	289	3	802	—	—	—	—	4	1091	1	238	—	—	1	223	2	461
3707	—	—	—	—	—	—	3	659	—	—	—	—	3	659	—	—	—	—	1	230	1	230
4687	—	—	—	—	—	—	—	—	—	—	—	—	—	—	4	1044	—	—	—	—	4	1044
1473																						
1635																						
9006	—	—	—	—	—	—	—	—	—	—	—	—	—	—	1	163	—	—	—	—	1	163
1259	—	—	—	—	—	—	4	664	—	—	—	—	4	664	—	—	—	—	1	192	1	192
915	—	—	—	—	—	—	1	162	—	—	—	—	1	162								
1311																						
817	—	—	—	—	—	—	2	248	—	—	—	—	2	248								
315																						
185																						
493	—	—	—	—	1	93	—	—	—	—	—	—	1	93								
12197																						
6732	—	—	—	—	—	—	—	—	—	—	—	—	—	—	1	1434	—	—	—	—	1	1434
19964	—	—	—	—	—	—	—	—	1	904	—	—	1	904	1	884	—	—	—	—	1	884
17893	—	—	—	—	—	—	—	—	5	3954	—	—	5	3954								
1373																						
1489																						
1809	—	—	—	—	—	—	1	167	1	505	—	—	2	672								
4818	—	—	—	—	—	—	—	—	—	—	—	—	—	—	—	—	2	2795	—	—	2	2795
1222	—	—	—	—	—	—	—	—	—	—	2	477	2	477	—	—	—	—	2	338	2	338
399																						
644985	2	2843	4	4442	2	382	28	16943	9	8158	14	17247	59	50415	22	13626	9	8158	8	5171	39	26955

An ABSTRACT of the Ships and Vessels belonging to the British Navy at the commencement of the Year 1802.

Letters of Reference	RATE.	CLASS.	CRUISERS — In Commission No.	Tons.	In Ordinary, under or for Repair No.	Tons.	TOTAL No.	Tons.	No. British Built	No. Foreign Built	Harbour-ships In Commission No.	Tons.	Not in Commission No.	Tons.	No. British Built	No. Foreign Built
		Three-deckers.														
A	First.	120-gun ship	1	2351	—	—	1	2351	1	—	1	2747	—	—	—	1
B	,,	112 ,, 18-pounder	1	2457	—	—	1	2457	1	—	—	—	1	2398	—	1
C	,,	100 ,, 12 ,,	1	2286	—	—	1	2286	1	—	—	—	—	—	—	—
D	,,	100 ,, 18 ,,	1	2175	2	4253	3	6428	3	—	—	—	—	—	—	—
E	Second.	98 ,, 12 ,, — large	3	6363	—	—	3	6363	3	—	—	—	—	—	—	—
F	,,	,, ,, 18 ,, — small	11	21544	1	1876	12	23420	12	—	1	1869	—	—	1	—
G	,,	,, ,, 12 ,,	—	—	—	—	—	—	—	—	1	1781	1	1918	2	—
H	,,	90 ,,	1	1814	—	—	1	1814	1	—	—	—	—	—	—	—
		Two-deckers.														
I	Third.	80 ,,	7	15181	1	2257	8	17438	2	6	—	—	1	1942	—	1
K	,,	74 ,, 24-pounder	8	15259	1	1854	9	17113	7	2	—	—	—	—	—	—
L	,,	,, ,, 18 ,, — large	12	22500	1	1949	13	24449	7	6	2	3648	1	1869	—	3
M	,,	,, ,, ,, ,, — middl.	4	6917	2	3477	6	10394	5	1	—	—	1	1778	—	1
N	,,	,, ,, ,, ,, — small	34	55403	9	14831	43	70234	42	1	7	11126	5	8152	11	1
O	,,	64 ,,	20	27671	5	6900	25	34571	19	6	5	6831	12	16470	8	9
P	Fourth.	60 ,,	—	—	—	—	—	—	—	—	—	—	4	4944	3	1
		Line — —	104	181921	22	37397	126	219318	103	23	17	28002	26	39471	25	18
R	,,	56 ,, flush	2	2682	—	—	2	2682	2	—	—	—	—	—	1	—
S	,,	54 ,, ,,	1	1249	—	—	1	1249	1	—	1	1182	—	—	1	—
T	,,	50 ,,	8	8544	2	2112	10	10656	9	1	4	4201	4	4255	4	4
V	Fifth.	44 ,,	3	2687	—	—	3	2687	3	—	1	882	3	2564	2	2
		One-deckers.														
W*	,,	44-gun frigate	5	6897	—	—	5	6897	4	1	1	1357	—	—	—	1
X	,,	40 ,, 24-pounder	2	2516	1	1183	3	3699	1	2	—	—	—	—	—	—
Y	,,	40 ,, 18 ,,	2	2302	—	—	2	2302	2	··	—	—	—	—	—	—
Z	,,	38 ,, — large	14	15402	—	—	14	15402	3	11	—	—	2	2245	—	2
A	,,	38 ,, — small	14	14008	1	1020	15	15028	13	2	—	—	1	1011	—	1
B	,,	36 ,, ,, — large	9	9273	—	—	9	9273	4	5	—	—	1	882	1	—
C	,,	,, ,, 12 ,, — small	15	13878	1	971	16	14849	16	—	—	—	6	5358	—	10
D	,,	32 ,, 18 ,, — large	16	14735	1	968	17	15703	—	17	4	3600	6	5358	—	10
E	,,	,, ,, ,, ,, — small	5	4542	—	—	5	4542	5	··	—	—	—	—	—	—
F	,,	,, ,, 12 ,, — large	4	3218	—	—	4	3218	4	··	—	—	1	770	—	1
G	,,	,, ,, ,, ,, — small	21	14434	2	1407	23	15841	23	—	—	—	1	704	—	1
H	Sixth.	28 ,,	8	4779	1	594	9	5373	7	2	2	1167	6	3623	3	5
I	,,	24-gun post-ship, quarter-decked	4	2083	1	563	5	2646	4	1	—	—	2	1147	—	2
K	,,	22 ,, flush	1	625	—	—	1	625	1	—	—	—	—	—	—	—
L	,,	22 ,,	5	2727	—	—	5	2727	—	5	—	—	1	522	1	—
M	,,	20 ,, quarter-decked	3	1369	1	498	4	1867	2	2	—	—	5	2322	3	2
N	,,	20 ,, flush	3	1530	1	513	4	2043	—	4	—	—	—	—	—	—
		Sloops.														
O	,,	Arrow & Dart, mounting 28 carronades	2	722	—	—	2	772	—	2	—	—	—	—	—	—
P	,,	18-gun ship-sloop, quarter-decked	10	4253	—	—	10	4253	10	—	—	—	—	—	—	—
Q	,,	16 ,, flush	16	6066	3	1143	19	7209	9	10	—	—	5	1817	1	4
R	,,	16 ,, quarter-decked, large	12	4575	—	—	12	4575	10	2	—	—	2	680	1	1
S	,,	,, ,, ,, small	3	659	1	322	4	981	3	—	—	—	1	311	1	—
T	,,	14 ,, flush	5	1787	2	605	7	2392	4	3	—	—	—	—	—	—
U	,,	14 ,, quarter-decked	4	1170	—	—	4	1170	4	—	1	304	3	910	4	—
V	,,	18-gun brig-sloop — large	6	2249	—	—	6	2249	5	1	—	—	1	370	1	—
W	,,	,, ,, — small	8	2613	—	—	8	2613	6	2	—	—	1	318	1	—
X	,,	16 ,,	13	3617	—	—	13	3617	13	—	—	—	—	—	—	—
Y	,,	14 ,,	11	2595	—	—	11	2595	1	10	—	—	—	—	—	—
Z	Bombs, of	8 guns and 2 mortars	8	2655	6	2032	14	4687	14	—	—	—	2	447	1	1
a	Fireships,	14 guns	1	425	1	243	2	668	2	··	—	—	1	423	1	—
b	Gun-brigs,	14 ,,	7	1433	—	—	7	1433	3	4	—	—	—	—	—	—
d	,,	12 ,,	52	8652	6	1034	58	9686	56	2	—	—	19	2971	19	—
e	,,	10 ,,	6	924	—	—	6	924	6	—	—	—	—	—	—	—
		Cutters, &c.														
f	,,	14 ,,	4	734	—	—	4	734	4	—	—	—	1	181	1	—
g	,,	12 ,,	7	1012	1	148	8	1160	6	2	—	—	—	—	—	—
h	,,	10 ,,	10	1210	—	—	10	1210	—	10	—	—	—	—	—	—
i	,,	8 ,,	2	220	—	—	2	220	—	2	—	—	—	—	—	—
k	,,	6 ,,	2	185	—	—	2	185	—	2	—	—	—	—	—	—
l	,,	4 ,,	7	493	—	—	7	493	3	4	—	—	—	—	—	—
m	Third-rate,	36 ,,	—	—	—	—	—	—	—	—	7	9400	2	2797	4	5
n	Fourth ,,	26 ,,	—	—	—	—	—	—	—	—	6	6732	—	—	4	2
o	Fifth ,,	24 ,,	—	—	—	—	—	—	—	—	22	19964	—	—	20	2
q	,,	18 ,,	—	—	—	—	—	—	—	—	25	18081	—	—	17	8
r	Float. Batt.	46 ,,	—	—	—	—	—	—	—	—	1	1373	—	—	1	—
s	,,	20 ,, and under	—	—	—	—	—	—	—	—	4	1489	—	—	4	—
t	Gun-vessels, from 1 to 4 guns		—	—	—	—	—	—	—	—	13	1198	9	611	—	22
u	Advice-boats		—	—	—	—	—	—	—	—	2	358	—	—	2	—
v	Sloop on Discovery		—	—	—	—	—	—	—	—	1	334	—	—	1	—
w	Armed Transports		—	—	—	—	—	—	—	—	14	4818	—	—	9	5
x	Yachts — royal, or large		—	—	—	—	—	—	—	—	2	328	2	417	4	—
c	,, — small		—	—	—	—	—	—	—	—	—	—	5	399	4	—
		*Grand Total — — — —	451	363813	54	52753	505	416566	351	154	128	104770	113	77526	142	99

Increase and Decrease in the Classes since the date of the last Year's Abstract.

Grand Total	Launched				Purchased		Captured		Converted from other Classes		Ordered to be Built		Total of Increase		Loss by Capture, &c.		Converted to other Classes		Sold, or taken to Pieces		Total of Decrease	
Tons.	King's Yards No.	Tons.	Merchants' Yards No.	Tons.	No.	Tons.	No.	Tons.	No.	Tons.	No.	Tons.	No.	Tons.	No.	Tons.	No.	Tons.	No.	Tons.	No.	Tons.
7871																						
2351																						
4855																						
4575											1	2289	1	2289								
10732											2	4304	2	4304								
4554																						
6363	1	2123											1	2123								
25289																	1	1827			1	1827
5513																						
19380																						
29672			1	1854									1	1854								
29966									1	1827			1	1827					1	1799	1	1799
26032	1	1777					1	1700					2	3477								
89512															3	4937					3	4937
57872							1	1395					1	1395					2	2734	2	2734
4944																						
326481	2	3900	1	1854			2	3095	1	1827	3	6593	9	17269	3	4937	1	1827	3	4533	7	11297
2682																						
2431																						
21333																						
6133																						
8254					1	1338	1	1430					2	2768	1	1401					1	1401
3699																						
3474																						
19878							1	1085			1	1155	2	2240								
15028																						
10284							1	1013					1	1013	1	1053					1	1053
21189			2	1946							4	3516	6	5462			1	869			1	869
24661							3	2744					3	2744								
4542																						
3218															1	748					1	748
4015							1	683					1	683	3	2073					3	2073
16545																			1	605	1	605
10163																			1	506	1	506
3793																						
625																						
3249																						
4189															1	511					1	511
2043																						
772															1	453			1	486	2	939
4675							5	1871					5	1871	2	754	1	334	1	329	4	1477
9469																			2	706	2	706
5255																			1	319	1	319
1292																			5	1422	5	1422
2392					4	1467	1	320					5	1787					1	301	1	301
2384																						
868					2	668							2	668					1	369	1	369
2619																			1	346	1	346
2931					1	309							1	309	1	279			4	1056	5	1335
3617							1	245					1	245	1	208	1	243	2	459	4	910
3042							1	317					1	317	1	317					1	317
4687									1	243			1	243	1	422			1	203	2	625
1091																			1	202	1	202
1433																						
12657			20	3651			1	161					21	3812	1	161					1	161
924															1	165			1	170	2	335
915															1	151					1	151
1160																						
1210							3	393					3	393								
220																			1	95	1	95
185																						
493																						
12197																						
6732																						
19964																						
18061									1	869			1	869	1	681					1	681
1373																						
1489																						
1809																						
358	2	358											2	358								
334									1	334			1	334								
4818																						
1222																						
399																						
650976	4	4258	23	7451	8	3782	21	13357	4	3273	8	11264	68	43385	21	14314	4	3273	28	12107	53	29694

Letters of Reference.	RATE.	CLASS.	For Sea-service. (a) In Commission. No.	Tons.	In Ordinary. No.	Tons.	TOTAL. No.	Tons.	No. British Built.	No. Foreign Built.	For Harbour-service, &c. (b) In Commission. No.	Tons.	In Ordinary. No.	Tons.	No. British Built.	No. Foreign Built.
	Three-deckers. First.	120-gun ship	–	–	–	–	–	–	–	–	–	–	–	–	–	–
A	,,	112 ,, 18-pounder	–	–	1	2351	1	2351	1	–	–	–	–	–	–	–
B	,,	100 ,, 12 ,,	–	–	1	2457	1	2457	–	1	–	–	–	–	–	–
C	,,	100 ,, 18 ,,	–	–	1	2286	1	2286	1	–	–	–	1	2398	–	1
D	Second.	98 ,, 12 ,,	–	–	3	6428	3	6428	3	–	–	–	–	–	–	–
E	,,	98 ,, 18 ,, – large	–	–	–	–	–	–	3	–	–	–	–	–	–	–
F	,,	98 ,, 18 ,, – small	1	2119	2	4244	3	6363	3	–	–	–	–	–	–	–
G	,,	98 ,, 12 ,,	–	–	11	21470	11	21470	11	–	–	–	–	–	–	–
H	,,	90 ,,	–	–	1	1814	1	1814	1	–	–	–	–	–	–	–
I	Two-deckers. Third.	80 ,,	1	2185	5	10868	6	13053	2	4	–	–	3	6327	–	3
K	,,	74 ,, 24-pounder	4	7622	5	9491	9	17113	7	2	–	–	–	–	–	–
L	,,	74 ,, 18 ,, – large	5	9244	8	15229	13	24473	8	5	–	–	2	3738	–	2
M	,,	74 ,, 18 ,, – middl.	3	5222	2	3495	5	8717	5	–	–	–	3	5198	1	2
N	,,	74 ,, 18 ,, – small	13	21365	24	39094	37	60459	36	1	–	–	12	19342	9	3
O	,,	64 ,,	5	7043	15	20912	20	27955	18	2	–	–	16	21851	6	10
P	Fourth.	60 ,,	–	–	–	–	–	–	–	–	–	–	2	2511	1	1
Q		Line – –	32	54800	79	140139	111	194939	96	15	–	–	39	61365	17	22
R	,,	56 ,, flush	1	1426	–	–	1	1426	1	–	–	–	–	–	–	–
S	,,	50 ,, common or quar.-decked	6	6387	4	4327	10	10714	10	–	1	1110	6	6308	3	4
T	Fifth.	44 ,,	2	1798	–	–	2	1798	2	–	–	–	1	882	1	–
V	One-deckers.	44-gun frigate	1	1375	4	5572	5	6947	4	1	–	–	1	1357	–	1
W	,,	40 ,, 24-pounder	–	–	2	2460	2	2460	1	1	–	–	–	–	–	–
X	,,	40 ,, 18 ,,	2	2302	–	–	2	2302	2	–	–	–	–	–	–	–
Y	,,	38 ,, – large	9	9780	5	5622	14	15402	3	11	–	–	1	1065	–	1
Z	,,	38 ,, – small	8	8141	5	4848	13	12989	12	1	–	–	1	999	1	–
A	,,	36 ,, 18-pounder large	8	8260	1	1040	9	9300	3	6	–	–	2	2024	–	2
B	,,	36 ,, 12 ,, small	13	12200	3	2719	16	14919	16	–	–	–	2	1808	2	–
C	,,	32 ,, 18 ,,	6	5546	4	3713	10	9259	–	10	–	–	5	4594	–	5
D	,,	32 ,, 12 ,, large	3	4542	–	–	5	4542	5	–	–	–	–	–	–	–
E	,,	32 ,, 12 ,, small	2	1619	2	1599	4	3218	4	–	–	–	2	1626	1	1
F	,,	32 ,, 12 ,, large	2	1631	1	782	3	2413	1	2	–	–	2	2413	1	1
G	,,	32 ,, 12 ,, small	8	5502	9	6212	17	11714	17	–	–	–	7	4831	6	1
H	Sixth.	28 ,, 24-gun post-ship, quarter-decked	4	2378	4	2396	8	4774	8	–	–	–	3	1761	2	1
I	,,	28 ,, flush	2	1043	2	1082	4	2125	3	1	–	–	2	1049	2	1
K	,,	22 ,,	–	–	–	–	–	–	–	–	–	–	1	625	–	1
L	,,	20 ,, quarter-decked	4	2204	–	–	4	2204	–	4	–	–	1	523	–	1
M	,,	20 ,, flush	1	433	2	930	3	1363	2	1	–	–	3	1421	2	1
N	Sloops.	Arrow & Dart, mounting 28 carronades	–	–	3	1529	3	1529	–	3	–	–	1	514	–	–
O	,,	18-gun ship-sloop, quarter-decked	1	386	1	386	2	772	2	–	–	–	–	–	–	–
P	,,	18 ,, flush	7	2979	3	1274	10	4253	10	–	–	–	–	–	–	–
Q	,,	16 ,, quarter-decked, large	10	3924	5	1766	15'	5690	6	9	–	–	1	312	–	1
R	,,	16 ,, small	8	3064	1	370	9	3434	6	–	1	371	1	425	2	–
S	,,	16 ,, flush	1	326	1	322	2	648	2	–	–	–	1	333	1	–
T	,,	14 ,, quarter-decked	1	1467	2	605	6	2072	4	2	–	–	–	–	–	–
U	,,	14 ,, flush	3	868	–	–	3	868	3	–	1	304	1	302	2	–
V	,,	18-gun brig-sloop large	6	2249	–	–	6	2249	5	1	–	–	–	–	–	–
W	,,	16 ,, small	7	2264	–	–	7	2264	6	1	–	–	1	349	–	1
X	,,	16 ,,	6	1772	3	806	9	2578	1	8	–	–	2	584	–	2
Y	,,	14 ,,	4	968	2	488	6	1456	4	2	–	–	3	676	3	–
Z	Bombs, or Fireships.	8 guns and 2 mortars	–	–	10	3407	10	3407	10	–	–	–	3	960	3	–
a	Gun-brigs.	14 guns	–	–	2	668	2	668	2	–	–	–	–	–	–	–
b	,,	12 ,,	1	258	3	588	4	846	3	1	–	–	2	395	1	1
d	,,	10 ,,	22	3955	11	1776	33	5731	33	–	–	–	6	984	6	–
e	,,	14 ,,	–	–	2	313	2	314	2	–	–	–	–	–	–	–
f	Cutters, &c.	12 ,,	3	577	–	–	3	577	2	1	–	–	–	–	–	–
g	,,	10 ,,	5	762	–	–	5	762	4	1	–	–	3	398	3	–
h	,,	8 ,,	4	516	–	–	4	516	4	4	–	–	–	–	–	–
i	,,	6 ,,	–	–	–	–	–	–	–	–	–	–	–	–	–	–
k	,,	4 ,,	1	86	–	–	1	86	1	–	–	–	–	–	–	–
		Cruisers –	210	158090	178	198310	388	356400	300	88	3	1785	162	98470	54	51
q	Troop-ship, (g) (forming "Third-rates," &c.) –		17	14900	19	17820	36	32720	29	7	–	–	15	14673	11	4
r	Storeships, (forming "Fourth-rates," &c.) –		2	1774	9	6005	11	7779	9	2	–	–	4	1937	2	2
s	Fifth-rates –		–	–	–	–	–	–	–	–	–	–	–	–	–	–
t	Float. Batts. 46 guns		–	–	–	–	–	–	–	–	–	–	–	–	–	–
u	20 ,, and under		–	–	–	–	–	–	–	–	–	–	–	–	–	–
v	Gun-vessels, from 1 to 4 guns		–	–	–	–	–	–	–	–	–	–	12	815	–	12
w	Advice-boats and Tenders – – –		2	358	4	606	6	9r4	6	–	–	–	–	–	–	–
x	Sloop on Discovery – – –		1	334	–	–	1	334	1	–	–	–	–	–	–	–
y	Armed Transports – –		–	–	–	–	–	–	–	–	–	–	–	–	–	–
z	Hospital, Prison, Receiving-ships, (i) &c.		–	–	–	–	–	–	–	–	2	3045	23	29062	14	11
b	Yachts – – – royal, or large		–	–	–	–	–	–	–	–	2	871	–	–	–	–
c	,, – – small (k)		–	–	–	–	–	–	–	–	–	–	5	–	–	–
		Troop-ships, &c. –	22	17366	32	24431	54	41797	45	9	7	3856	54	46487	32	29
		GRAND TOTAL (l) – – –	232	175456	210	222741	442	398197	345	97	10	5641	156	144957	86	80

Increase and Decrease in the Classes since the date of the last Year's Abstract.

| GRAND TOTAL | | Built. (c) | | | | Purchased. | | Converted from other Classes. | | Ordered to be Built. | | TOTAL of Increase. | | Wrecked, Foundered, &c. | | Converted to other Classes. | | Sold, or taken to Pieces, &c. (d) | | TOTAL of Decrease. | |
| | | King's Yards. | | Merchants' Yards. | | | | | | | | | | | | | | | | | |
No.	Tons.	No.	Tons.	No.	Tons.	No.	Tons.	No.	Tons.	No.	Tons.	No.	Tons.	No.	Tons.	No.	Tons.	No.	Tons.	No.	Tons.
	5124	–	–	–	–	–	–	–	–	–	–	–	–	–	–	–	–	1	2747	1	2747
	2351																				
	4855																				
	4575																				
	10732																				
	4554																				
	6363																				
	21470	–	–	–	–	–	–	–	–	–	–	–	–	–	–	2	3819	–	–	2	3819
	1814															2	3699	–	–	2	3699
	19380																				
	26672																				
	28211	–	–	–	–	–	–	1	1950	–	–	1	1950	–	–	1	1836	1	1869	2	3705
	29457	–	–	1	1743	–	–	–	–	2	3425	2	3425	–	–	4	6487	2	3224	6	9711
	81475	–	–	–	–	–	–	–	–	1	1674	1	1674	–	–	6	8066	–	–	6	8066
	49806	–	–	–	–	–	–	–	–	–	–	–	–	–	–	2	2433	–	–	2	2433
	2511																				
	299350	–	–	1	1743	–	–	1	1950	3	5099	4	7049	–	–	17	26340	4	7840	21	34180
	1426	–	–	–	–	–	–	–	–	–	–	–	–	–	–	1	1256	–	–	1	1256
																1	1249	1	1182	2	2431
	18132	2	2221	–	–	–	–	–	–	–	–	–	–	1	1053	–	–	2	2148	3	3201
	2680	–	–	–	–	–	–	–	–	–	–	–	–	–	–	2	1760	2	1693	4	3453
	8304																				
	2460																				
	3474	–	–	–	–	–	–	–	–	–	–	–	–	–	–	–	–	1	1239	1	1239
	19774	–	–	–	–	–	–	–	–	1	1076	1	1076	–	–	1	1180	–	–	1	1180
	13988	–	–	–	–	–	–	–	–	–	–	–	–	–	–	1	1040	–	–	1	1040
	11324	–	–	–	–	–	–	1	1040	–	–	1	1040	–	–	–	–	–	–		
	21189																				
	13853	–	–	–	–	–	–	–	–	–	–	–	–	–	–	3	2696	9	8112	12	10808
	4542																				
	3218																				
	4039	–	–	–	–	–	–	1	827	–	–	1	827	–	–	–	–	1	803	1	803
	6545																				
	6535																				
	3174	–	–	–	–	–	–	–	–	–	–	–	–	–	–	1	619	6	3628	6	3628
	625																	1	610	1	610
	2727																				
	2784	–	–	–	–	–	–	–	–	–	–	–	–	–	–	–	–	1	522	1	522
	2043	–	–	–	–	–	–	–	–	–	–	–	–	–	–	–	–	3	1405	3	1405
	772																				
	4675																				
	6445	–	–	–	–	–	–	–	–	–	–	–	–	1	448	1	374	6	2202	8	3024
	9395	–	–	–	–	–	–	–	–	14	5165	14	5165	–	–	–	–	3	1025	3	1025
	981	–	–	–	–	–	–	–	–	–	–	–	–	–	–	–	–	1	311	1	311
	2072	–	–	–	–	–	–	–	–	–	–	–	–	–	–	–	–	1	320	1	320
	1478	–	–	–	–	–	–	–	–	–	–	–	–	1	202	–	–	2	604	3	906
	868																				
	4555	–	–	–	–	–	–	–	–	6	2306	6	2306	–	–	–	–	1	370	1	370
	2613	–	–	–	–	–	–	–	–	–	–	–	–	–	–	–	–	1	318	1	318
	3162	–	–	–	–	1	286	–	–	–	–	1	286	–	–	–	–	3	741	3	741
	2132	–	–	–	–	–	–	–	–	–	–	–	–	–	–	–	–	4	910	4	910
	4367	–	–	–	–	–	–	–	–	–	–	–	–	–	–	–	–	1	320	1	320
	668	–	–	–	–	–	–	–	–	–	–	–	–	–	–	–	–	1	423	1	423
	1241	–	–	–	–	–	–	–	–	–	–	–	–	–	–	–	–	1	192	1	192
	6715	–	–	–	–	–	–	–	–	–	–	–	–	–	–	–	–	38	5942	38	5942
	314	–	–	–	–	–	–	–	–	–	–	–	–	–	–	–	–	4	610	4	610
	577	–	–	–	–	–	–	–	–	–	–	–	–	–	–	–	–	2	338	2	338
	1160																				
	516	–	–	–	–	–	–	–	–	–	–	–	–	–	–	–	–	6	694	6	694
	–	–	–	–	–	–	–	–	–	–	–	–	–	–	–	–	–	2	220	2	220
	–	–	–	–	–	–	–	–	–	–	–	–	–	–	–	–	–	2	185	2	185
	86	–	–	–	–	–	–	–	–	–	–	–	–	–	–	–	–	6	407	6	407
46	516978	2	2221	1	1743	1	286	3	3817	24	13646	28	17749	3	1803	28	36514	115	44704	146	83021
51	47393	–	–	–	–	–	–	44	37820	–	–	44	37820	–	–	1	1264	1	1360	2	2624
15	9716	–	–	–	–	1	463	14	9253	–	–	15	9716	–	–	6	6732	–	–	6	6732
	–	–	–	–	–	–	–	–	–	–	–	–	–	–	–	21	19077	1	887	22	19964
	–	–	–	–	–	–	–	–	–	–	–	–	–	1	946	22	15490	2	1646	25	18082(h)
	–	–	–	–	–	–	–	–	–	–	–	–	–	–	–	–	–	1	1373	1	1373
12	815	–	–	–	–	–	–	–	–	–	–	–	–	–	–	–	–	4	1489	4	1489
6	964	–	–	–	–	–	–	4	606	–	–	4	606	–	–	–	–	10	994	10	994
1	334																				
25	32107	–	–	–	–	–	–	25	32107	–	–	25	32107	–	–	12	4526	2	292	14	4818
7	1288	–	–	–	–	–	–	1	66	–	–	1	66	–	–	–	–				
	–	–	–	–	–	–	–	–	–	–	–	–	–	–	–	1	66	4	333	5	399
17	92617	–	–	–	–	1	463	88	79852	–	–	89	80315	1	946	63	47155	25	8374	89	56475
63	609595	2	2221	1	1743	2	749	91	83669	24	13646	117	98064	4	2749	91	83669	140	53078	335	139490

2 o

An ABSTRACT of the Ships and Vessels belonging to the British Navy at the commencement of the Year 1804.

Letters of Reference.	RATE.	CLASS.	For Sea-service. In Commission. No.	Tons.	In Ordinary. No.	Tons.	TOTAL. No.	Tons.	British Built.	Foreign Built.	For Harbour-service, &c. In Commission. No.	Tons.	In Ordinary. No.	Tons.	British Built.	Foreign Built.
		Three-deckers.														
A	First.	120-gun ship	1	2351	–	–	1	2351	1	–	–	–	–	–	–	–
B	,,	112 ,, 18-pounder	1	2457	–	–	1	2457	1	–	1	2398	–	–	–	1
C	,,	100 ,, 12 ,,	–	–	1	2286	1	2286	1	–	–	–	–	–	–	–
D	,,	,, 18 ,,	3	6428	–	–	3	6428	3	–	–	–	–	–	–	–
E	Second.	98 ,, 12 ,, – large	3	6363	–	–	3	6363	3	–	–	–	–	–	–	–
F	,,	98 ,, 18 ,, – small	5	9914	6	11556	11	21470	11	–	–	–	–	–	–	–
G	,,	90 ,,	–	–	1	1814	1	1814	1	–	–	–	–	–	–	–
		Two-deckers.														
K	Third.	80 ,,	5	11050	1	2003	6	13053	2	4	1	1942	2	4385	–	3
L	,,	74 ,, 24-pounder	8	15208	2	3854	10	19062	7	3	–	–	–	–	–	–
M	,,	18 ,, – large	11	20635	3	5673	14	26308	8	6	–	–	2	3738	–	2
N	,,	,, ,, – middl.	9	15663	–	–	9	15663	9	–	1	1778	2	3420	1	2
O	,,	,, ,, – small	21	34370	14	22784	35	57154	34	1	–	–	11	17667	9	2
P	,,	64 ,,	8	11227	12	16728	20	27955	18	2	6	7952	10	13899	6	10
Q	Fourth.	60 ,,	–	–	–	–	–	–	–	–	–	–	2	2511	2	1
		Line	75	135666	40	66698	115	202364	98	17	9	14070	29	45620	17	21
R	,,	56 ,, flush	7	7549	3	3165	10	10714	10	–	1	1426	–	–	1	–
T	,,	50 ,, common or quarter-decked	–	–	–	–	–	–	–	–	4	4273	3	3145	3	4
V	Fifth.	44 ,,	2	1798	–	–	2	1798	2	–	1	882	–	–	1	–
		One-deckers.														
W	,,	44-gun frigate	5	6947	–	–	5	6947	4	1	1	1357	–	–	–	1
X	,,	40 ,, 24-pounder	2	2460	–	–	2	2460	1	1	–	–	–	–	–	–
Y	,,	18 ,,	2	2302	–	–	2	2302	2	–	–	–	–	–	–	–
Z	,,	38 ,, – large	13	14227	2	2252	15	16479	3	12	–	–	2	2138	–	2
A	,,	,, – small	10	10077	3	2912	13	12989	12	1	–	–	2	999	1	–
B	,,	36 ,, 18-pounder – large	8	8271	1	1029	9	9300	3	6	–	–	2	2024	–	2
C	,,	,, – small	15	13967	1	881	16	14848	16	–	1	926	2	1808	3	–
D	,,	,, 12 ,,	9	8327	2	1830	11	10157	–	11	–	–	5	4594	–	5
E	,,	32 ,, 18 ,, – large	5	4542	–	–	5	4542	5	–	–	–	–	–	–	–
F	,,	,, – small	4	3218	–	–	4	3218	4	–	–	–	–	–	–	–
G	,,	12 ,, – large	3	2413	–	–	3	2413	1	2	2	1626	–	–	1	1
H	,,	,, – small	10	6910	9	6210	19	13120	19	–	1	683	5	3492	2	1
I	Sixth.	28 ,, 24-gun post-ship quarter-decked	6	3772	1	1178	7	4950	7	1	2	1167	1	594	2	1
K	,,	flush	4	2125	–	–	4	2125	3	1	–	–	1	1049	1	1
L	,,	22 ,,	2	1130	–	–	2	1130	2	–	–	–	1	625	1	1
N	,,	20 ,, quarter-decked	4	1844	–	–	4	1844	2	2	1	481	1	523	2	1
O	,,	flush	3	1660	1	511	4	2171	–	4	–	–	1	940	2	1
P	Sloops.	Arrow & Dart, mounting 28 carronades	2	772	–	–	2	772	2	–	–	–	1	514	1	1
Q	,,	18-gun ship-sloop, quarter-decked	9	3830	1	423	10	4253	10	–	–	–	–	–	–	1
R	,,	flush	17	6466	–	–	17	6466	6	11	1	312	–	–	–	–
S	,,	16 ,, quarter-decked, large	7	2682	–	–	7	2682	7	–	1	425	1	410	2	–
T	,,	,, small	2	648	–	–	2	648	2	–	–	–	–	–	–	–
U	,,	flush	12	4265	–	–	12	4265	10	2	–	–	–	–	–	–
V	,,	14 ,, quarter-decked	1	248	1	322	2	570	2	–	–	–	2	604	2	–
W	,,	flush	6	1605	–	–	6	1605	6	–	–	–	–	–	–	–
X	,,	18-gun brig-sloop – large	8	3036	–	–	8	3036	6	2	–	–	–	–	–	–
Y	,,	,, – small	7	2264	–	–	7	2264	6	1	1	349	–	–	1	–
Z	,,	16 ,,	12	3597	–	–	12	3597	1	11	1	260	–	–	1	–
a	,,	14 ,,	6	1456	–	–	6	1456	4	2	2	456	–	–	2	–
b	Bombs, or Fireships,	8 guns and 2 mortars	17	6088	–	–	17	6088	17	–	1	307	2	653	3	–
d		14 guns	1	425	1	243	2	668	2	–	–	–	–	–	–	–
e	Gun-brigs	12 ,,	6	1201	–	–	6	1201	3	3	–	–	–	–	–	–
f	,,	12 ,,	32	5561	–	–	32	5561	32	–	–	–	–	–	–	–
g	,,	10 ,,	3	459	–	–	3	459	–	3	–	–	–	–	–	–
h	Cutters, &c.	14 ,,	4	774	–	–	4	774	2	2	–	–	–	–	–	–
i	,,	12 ,,	7	1079	–	–	7	1079	3	4	1	123	2	275	3	–
k	,,	10 ,,	5	629	–	–	5	629	–	5	–	–	–	–	–	–
l	,,	8 ,,	1	98	–	–	1	98	1	–	–	–	–	–	–	–
m	,,	6 ,,	1	81	–	–	1	81	–	1	–	–	–	–	–	–
n	,,	4 ,,	1	86	–	–	1	86	1	–	–	–	–	–	–	–
		Cruisers	356	286555	67	87654	423	374209	314	109	27	28058	68	71072	47	48
q	Troop-ships		23	21164	11	9923	34	31087	27	7	3	2257	12	12386	11	4
r	Storeships		9	6564	1	907	10	7471	9	2	–	–	12	1432	2	1
w	Gun-vessels, from 1 to 4 guns		–	–	–	–	–	–	–	–	–	–	5	329	–	5
x	Advice-boats and Tenders		6	964	–	–	6	964	6	–	–	–	–	–	–	–
y	Sloop on Discovery		1	334	–	–	1	334	1	–	–	–	–	–	–	–
a	Hospital, Prison, Receiving-ships, &c.		–	–	–	–	–	–	–	–	10	13909	15	17322	15	10
b	Royal Yachts (g)		–	–	–	–	–	–	–	–	5	811	–	–	5	–
		Troop-ships, &c.	39	29026	12	10830	51	39856	43	9	18	16977	35	31469	33	20
		GRAND TOTAL (g)	395	315581	79	98484	474	414065	357	118	45	45035	103	102541	80	68

Increase and Decrease in the Classes since the date of the last Year's Abstract.

Grand Total Tons.	Built — King's Yards No.	Tons.	Merchants' Yards No.	Tons.	Purchased (a) — British Vessels or Enemy's Privateers No.	Tons.	Enemy's National Vessels No.	Tons.	Converted from other Classes No.	Tons.	Ordered to be Built No.	Tons.	Total of Increase No.	Tons.	Captured, Destroyed, Wrecked, &c. No.	Tons.	Converted to other Classes No.	Tons.	Sold, or taken to Pieces No.	Tons.	Total of Decrease No.	Tons.
5124																						
2351																						
4855																						
4575																						
10732																						
4554																						
6363																						
21470																						
1814																						
19380																						
26740	1	1881							1	1949			1	1949			1	1881			1	1881
30046			4	6946			1	1903	1	1881			2	3784			1	1949			1	1949
32902											2	3445	2	3445					3	4980	3	4980
76495																						
49806																						
2511																						
299718	1	1881	4	6946			1	1903	2	3830	2	3445	5	9178			2	3830	3	4980	5	8810
1426																						
18132																						
2680																						
(f)																						
8304																						
2460																						
3474																						
27319							4	4398			5	5395	9	9793	2	2248					2	2248
13988																						
11324																						
21187			3	2711							2	1854	2	1854	2	1856					2	1856
14751							1	898					1	898								
4542																						
3218																						
4059																						
17295									1	684	1	722	2	1406					1	656	1	656
6711					1	775b							1	775	1	599					1	599
3174																						
625																						
1653															2	1074					2	1074
3265							1	481					1	481								
2685							1	642					1	642								
772																						
4675																						
8019							3	1189			2	798	5	1987	1	413					1	413
8682															1	342			1	371	2	713
648					6	2193c							6	2193			1	304			1	304
4265																						
1174					4	1001d							4	1001	1	264					1	264
1605																						
9201			1	384e			1	403			11	4243	12	4646								
2613																						
3857							4	1305					4	1305	1	286			1	324	2	610
1912																			1	220	1	220
7048					7	2681f							7	2681								
668																						
1201							2	355					2	355					2	395	2	395
5561															1	170			6	984	7	1154
459							1	145					1	145								
774							1	197					1	197								
1477							3	465					3	465	1	148					1	148
629							1	113					1	113								
98					1	98							1	98								
81					1	81							1	81								
1022											12	936	12	936								
538411	1	1881	8	10041	20	6829	25	13178	3	4552	34	16671	82	41230	13	7400	3	4134	16	8263	32	19797
45730																	1	722	1	941	2	1663
8903															1	308			1	505	2	813
329																			7	486	7	486
964																						
334																						
31231									1	304			1	304					1	1180	1	1180
1288																						
88779									1	304			1	304	1	308	1	722	10	3112	12	4142
627190	1	1881	8	10041	20	6829	25	13178	4	4856	34	16671	83	41534	14	7708	4	4856	26	11375	44	23939

Letters of Reference.	RATE.	CLASS.	For Sea-service.							For Harbour-service, &c.					
			In Commission.		In Ordinary.		TOTAL.		No.		In Commission.		In Ordinary.		No.	
			No.	Tons.	.	Tons.	No.	Tons.	British Built.	Foreign Built.	No.	Tons.	No.	Tons.	British Built.	Foreign Built.	N
	Three-deckers.																
A	First.	120-gun ship — — — — —	1	2508	—	— —	1	2508	1	—	—	— —	—	— —	—	—	
B	,,	112 ,, 18-pounder — — —	1	2351	—	— —	1	2351	1	—	—	— —	—	— —	—	—	
C	,,	,, 12 ,, — — —	1	2457	—	— —	1	2457	—	1	1	2398	—	— —	—	1	
D	,,	100 ,, 18 ,, — — —	—	— —	1	2286	1	2286	1	—	—	— —	—	— —	—	—	
E	,,	,, 12 ,, — — —	3	6428	—	— —	3	6428	3	—	—	— —	—	— —	—	—	
F	Second.	98 ,, 18 ,, — large	—	— —	—	— —	—	— —	—	—	—	— —	—	— —	—	—	
G	,,	,, ,, — small	3	6363	—	— —	3	6363	3	—	—	— —	—	— —	—	—	
H	,,	,, 12 ,, — —	8	15681	3	5789	11	21470	11	—	—	— —	—	— —	—	—	
I	,,	90 ,, — — —	—	— —	—	— —	—	— —	—	—	—	— —	—	— —	—	—	
	Two-deckers.																
K	Third.	80 ,, — — — ~ —	4	8865	2	4188	6	13053	2	4	1	1942	2	4385	—	3	
L	,,	74 ,, 24-pounder — — —	8	15197	2	3865	10	19062	7	3	—	— —	—	— —	—	—	
M	,,	,, 18 ,, — large	11	20655	3	5564	14	26219	9	5	—	— —	3	5641	—	3	
N	,,	,, ,, — middl.	11	19110	—	— —	11	19110	11	—	1	1778	3	3420	1	2	1
O	,,	,, ,, ,, — small	19	31117	13	21144	32	52261	31	—	—	— —	12	19279	10	2	
P	,,	64 ,, — — —	13	18197	9	12468	22	30665	20	2	8	10692	7	9795	5	10	
Q	Fourth.	60 ,, — — —	—	— —	—	— —	—	— —	—	—	—	— —	2	2511	1	1	
		Line — — —	83	148929	33	55304	116	204233	100	16	11	16810	28	45031	17	22	2
R	,,	56 ,, flush — — —	—	— —	—	— —	—	— —	—	—	1	1426	—	— —	1	—	
S	,,	54 ,, ,, — — —	1	1176	—	— —	1	1176	1	—	—	— —	—	— —	—	—	
T	,,	50 ,, com. or quarter-decked	9	9695	1	1061	10	10756	10	—	1	1063	6	6355	3	4	
U	,,	,, flush — — —	2	1823	—	— —	2	1823	2	—	—	— —	—	— —	—	—	
V	Fifth.	44 ,, — — —	1	906	1	892	2	1798	2	—	1	882	—	— —	1	—	
	One deckers.																
W	,,	44-gun frigate — — —	4	5577	—	— —	4	5577	3	1	—	— —	2	2727	1	1	
X	,,	40 ,, 24-pounder — —	1	1277	—	— —	1	1277	1	—	—	— —	—	— —	—	—	
Y	,,	,, 18 ,, — —	4	4657	—	— —	4	4657	3	1	—	— —	—	— —	—	—	
Z	,,	38 ,, — — — large	13	14328	2	2157	15	16485	4	11	—	— —	2	2138	—	2	
A	,,	,, ,, — — — small	10	9996	3	3030	13	13026	10	3	—	— —	2	1978	1	1	
B	,,	36 ,, 18-pounder — large	6	6185	3	3115	9	9300	3	6	—	— —	2	2024	—	2	
C	,,	,, ,, ,, — small	14	13011	1	881	15	13892	15	—	1	926	2	1808	3	—	
D	,,	,, 12 ,, — —	10	9195	4	3741	14	12936	1	13	—	— —	5	4650	—	5	
E	,,	32 ,, 18 ,, — large	5	4542	—	— —	5	4542	5	—	—	— —	—	— —	—	—	
F	,,	,, ,, ,, — small	6	4733	—	— —	6	4733	6	—	—	— —	—	— —	—	—	
G	,,	,, 12 ,, — large	3	2458	—	— —	3	2458	—	3	2	1626	2	1570	2	2	
H	,,	,, ,, ,, — small	18	12342	5	3469	23	15811	23	—	1	683	6	4175	6	1	
I	Sixth.	28 ,, 24-gun post-ship, quarter-decked —	7	4454	3	1776	10	6230	9	1	2	1167	1	594	2	1	
K	,,	,, ,, flush —	5	2644	—	— —	5	2644	4	1	—	— —	2	1049	1	1	
L	,,	22 ,, — — —	—	— —	1	532	2	1130	—	2	—	— —	—	— —	—	—	
M	,,	20 ,, quarter-decked — —	3	1305	1	481	4	1786	2	2	1	481	2	940	2	1	
N	,,	,, flush — —	3	1660	1	511	4	2171	—	4	—	— —	1	514	1	—	
O	Sloops.	Arrow & Dart, mounting 28 carronades —	2	772	—	— —	2	772	2	—	—	— —	—	— —	—	—	
P	,,	18-gun ship-sloop, quarter-decked —	10	4267	1	429	11	4696	11	—	—	— —	—	— —	—	—	
Q	,,	,, flush — —	19	7271	—	— —	19	4271	9	10	1	312	—	— —	—	1	2
R	,,	16 ,, quarter-decked, large	14	5207	1	422	15	5629	15	—	1	425	1	410	2	—	7
S	,,	,, ,, small	3	975	—	— —	3	975	3	—	—	— —	—	— —	—	—	
T	,,	,, ,, flush ,, —	14	5048	—	— —	14	5048	12	2	—	— —	—	— —	—	—	
U	,,	14 ,, quarter-decked — —	2	570	—	— —	2	570	2	—	—	— —	2	604	2	—	
V	,,	,, flush — —	13	3788	—	— —	13	3788	13	—	—	— —	—	— —	—	—	
W	,,	18-gun brig-sloop — — — large	20	7744	—	— —	20	7644	19	1	—	— —	—	— —	—	—	9
X	,,	,, — — — — small	7	2264	—	— —	7	2264	6	1	—	— —	1	349	—	1	
Y	,,	14 ,, — — — —	12	3650	—	— —	12	3650	1	11	—	— —	—	— —	—	—	
Z	,,	14 ,, — — — —	3	744	—	— —	3	744	2	1	—	— —	2	456	—	2	
a	Bombs, of	8 guns and 2 mortars — —	17	6148	—	— —	17	6148	17	—	1	307	2	653	3	—	
b	Fireships,	14 guns — — —	1	243	—	— —	1	243	1	—	1	425	—	— —	1	—	
d	Gun-brigs,	12 ,, — — —	8	1626	—	— —	8	1626	3	5	—	— —	—	— —	—	—	7
e	,,	12 ,, — — —	73	12835	—	— —	73	12835	73	—	—	— —	—	— —	—	—	
f	,,	10 ,, — — —	2	321	—	— —	2	321	—	2	—	— —	—	— —	—	—	
g	Cutters, &c.	14 ,, — — —	4	774	—	— —	4	774	2	2	—	— —	—	— —	—	—	1
h	,,	12 ,, — — —	8	1237	—	— —	8	1237	3	5	1	123	2	275	3	—	
i	,,	10 ,, — — —	13	1624	—	— —	13	1624	—	13	—	— —	—	— —	—	—	12
k	,,	8 ,, — — —	1	98	—	— —	1	98	1	1	—	— —	—	— —	—	—	
m	,,	6 ,, — — —	2	184	—	— —	2	184	1	1	—	— —	—	— —	—	—	
n	,,	4 ,, — — —	16	1232	—	— —	16	1232	15	1	—	— —	—	— —	—	—	
o		Cruisers — — —	473	330013	61	77801	534	407814	414	120	26	26656	73	78300	51	48	80
q	Troop-ships — — — —			14	11665	7	6723	21	18388	15	6	3	2257	14	13953	13	4	—
r	Storeships — — — —			10	5890	1	907	11	6797	10	1	—	— —	2	782	2	—	—
w	Gun-vessels, from 1 to 4 guns — —			5	655	—	— —	5	655	5	—	—	— —	—	— —	—	—	—
x	Advice-boats and Tenders — —			6	964	—	— —	6	964	6	—	—	— —	—	— —	—	—	—
y	Sloop on Discovery — — —			—	— —	—	— —	—	— —	—	—	—	— —	—	— —	—	—	—
a	Hospital, Prison, Receiving-ships, &c. —			—	— —	—	— —	—	— —	—	—	10	13502	15	16255	15	10	—
b	Royal Yachts — — — —			—	— —	—	— —	—	— —	—	—	6	1089	—	— —	6	—	1
		Troop-ships, &c. — —	35	19174	8	7630	43	26804	36	7	19	16848	31	30990	36	14	1
	GRAND TOTAL (k) — — —		508	349187	69	85431	577	434618	450	127	45	43504	104	109298	87	62	81

Increase and Decrease in the Classes since the date of the last Year's Abstract.

GRAND TOTAL. Tons.	Built. King's Yards No.	Tons.	Merchants' Yards No.	Tons	Purchased. British Vessels or Enemy's Privateers No.	Tons.	Enemy's National Vessels No.	Tons.	Converted from other Classes No.	Tons.	Ordered to be Built No.	Tons.	TOTAL of Increase No.	Tons.	Captured, Destroyed, Wrecked, &c. No.	Tons.	Converted to other Classes No.	Tons.	Sold, or taken to Pieces No.	Tons.	TOTAL of Decrease No.	Tons.
5124	1	2508a																				
2351																						
4855																						
4575																						
10732																						
4554																						
6363																						
21470	–	–	–	–	–	–	–	–	–	–	–	–	–	–	–	–	1	1814	–	–	1	1814
19380																						
26740																						
31860	–	–	–	–	–	–	–	–	1	1814b	–	–	1	1814								
50266	–	–	2	3447	–	–	–	–	–	–	10	17364	10	17364								
73214	–	–	–	–	–	–	–	–	–	–	–	–	–	–	2	3281					2	3281
51152	·	–	–	–	–	–	–	–	3	4153	–	–	3	4153	1	1443	–	–	1	1364	2	2807
2511																						
315147	1	2508	2	3447	–	–	–	–	4	5967	10	17364	14	23331	3	4724	1	1814	1	1364	5	7902
1426																						
1176	–	–	–	–	–	–	–	–	1	1176	–	–	1	1176								
18174	–	–	–	–	–	–	–	–	1	1088	–	–	1	1088	1	1046	–	–	–	–	1	1046
1823	–	–	–	–	2	1823c	–	–	–	–	–	–	2	1823								
2630																						
8304																						
1277	–	–	–	–	–	–	–	–	–	–	–	–	–	–	–	–	1	1183	–	–	1	1183
4657	–	–	1	1172	–	–	–	–	1	1183	–	–	1	1183								
26249	1	1076	–	–	–	–	–	–	–	–	–	–	–	–	1	1070	–	–	–	–	1	1070
15995	–	–	–	–	–	–	3	3061	–	–	1	991	4	4052	1	1043	–	–	1	1002	2	2045
11324															1	956	–	–	–	–	1	956
20231	–	–	–	–	–	–	2	1924	2	1813	–	–	4	3737	–	–	–	–	1	902	1	902
17586																						
4542																						
4733	–	–	–	–	2	1515d	–	–	–	–	–	–	2	1515								
5654	–	–	–	–	–	–	2	1015	–	–	–	–	2	1615								
22651	4	2656e	–	–	–	–	–	–	1	718	7	4638	8	5356								
7991	–	–	–	–	–	–	–	–	2	1280	–	–	2	1280								
3693	–	–	–	–	1	519f	–	–	–	–	–	–	1	519	–	–	–	–	1	625	1	625
– –	–	–	–	–	–	–	–	–	–	–	–	–	–	–	–	–	–	–	1	523	1	523
1130	–	–	–	–	–	–	–	–	–	–	–	–	–	–	–	–	–	–	1	498	1	498
3207	–	–	–	–	–	–	1	440	–	–	–	–	1	440								
2685																						
772																						
5118	–	–	–	–	–	–	–	–	1	443	–	–	1	443	–	–	1	443	1	462	2	905
8381	–	–	4	1710	–	–	–	–	–	–	3	1267	3	1267								
9053	–	–	7	2576	1	371	–	–	–	–	–	–	1	371								
975	–	··	–	–	1	327	–	–	–	–	–	–	1	327								
5048	–	–	–	–	2	783	–	–	–	–	–	–	2	783								
1174																						
3788	–	–	–	–	–	–	8	2383	–	–	–	–	8	2383	1	200	–	–	–	–	1	200
11114	–	–	13	4998	–	–	–	–	–	–	6	2303	6	2303	1	390	–	–	–	–	1	390
2613	–	–	–	–	–	–	1	330	–	–	–	–	1	330	1	277	–	–	1	260	2	537
3650	–	–	–	–	–	–	–	–	–	–	–	–	–	–	3	712	–	–	–	–	3	712
1200																						
7108	–	–	–	–	1	404	–	–	–	–	–	–	1	404	1	344	–	–	–	–	1	344
668																						
1626	–	–	–	–	–	–	–	–	2	425	–	–	2	425								
14090	–	–	41	7317g	4	652	–	–	–	–	48	8572h	52	9224	4	695	–	–	–	–	4	695
321	–	–	–	–	–	–	–	–	–	–	–	–	–	–	1	138	–	–	–	–	1	138
926	–	–	–	–	–	–	–	–	–	–	1	152	1	152								
1635	–	–	–	–	1	158	–	–	–	–	–	–	1	158								
2956	–	–	–	–	7	876	1	119	–	–	12	1332	20	2327								
98																						
184	–	–	–	–	–	–	–	–	–	–	–	–	–	–	2	212	–	–	–	–	2	212
1232	–	–	12	936	3	210	–	–	–	–	–	–	3	210								
586065	6	6240	80	22156	36	10336	12	7914	13	13668	88	36619	149	68537	21	11807	3	3440	8	5636	32	20883
34598	–	–	–	–	–	··	–	–	–	–	–	–	–	–	1	904	10	10228	–	–	11	11132
7579	–	–	–	–	2	575	–	–	–	–	–	–	2	575	1	1249	–	–	1	650	2	1899
655	–	–	–	–	5	655	–	–	–	–	–	–	5	655	–	–	–	–	5	329	5	329
964	–	–	–	–	–	–	–	–	–	–	–	–	–	–			1	334	–	–	1	334
29757	–	–	–	–	1	857	–	–	1	334	–	–	2	1191	1	1264	–	–	1	1401	2	2665
1288	1	278																				
74841	1	278	–	–	8	2087	–	–	1	334	–	–	9	2421	3	3417	11	10562	7	2380	21	16359
660906	7	6518	80	22156	44	12423	12	7914	14	14002	88	36619	158	70958	24	15224	14	14002	15	8016	53	37242

NOTES TO ANNUAL ABSTRACTS.

NOTE TO ABSTRACT, No. 9.

* THE hired vessels numbered about 104. In consequence of the mistake of a unit in the "Tons," of class t, not discovered until after Abstract No. 9 was printed, this total exceeds by 1 the corresponding total in Abstract No. 8.

NOTES TO ABSTRACT, No. 10.

W*. THE purchased ship of this class was the Cornwallis, late a teak-built Indiaman.

x*. A very ancient class revived. "Advice boats, so called officially, are said to have been employed, for the first time, in 1692, before the battle off Cape La Hogue, in order to gain intelligence of what was passing at Brest." See Derrick, p. 113, note *.

* As the hired vessels had begun to be discharged, they now numbered only about 62. This Abstract, having been put to press along with the one which precedes it, contains the same deficiency of a unit in the "Tons," that is remarked upon in the single note of Abstract No. 9.

Owing to an inadvertency on our part, two 74s, one of the N, the other of the O class, that were, late in the year 1801, ordered to be built, have been left out of the "Ordered" column. The addition of them will make the line numerical grand total 191, and the general numerical grand total 783.

NOTES TO ABSTRACT, No. 11.

(a) WITH the view to render the remaining Abstracts more perspicuous and useful, a partial alteration has been made in the manner of heading them. Instead of being confined to "Cruisers," this compartment now extends to every ship fitted or about to be fitted for sea-service; and lines are drawn to show the totals, as well of the former, as of the less material portion of the navy.

(b) This head has also been slightly altered; and in particular the "&c." has a different signification from that assigned to it in note ‡ to No. 1 Abstract. See vol. i., p. 450. It signifies that all the ships and vessels of this, as we shall call it, the second compartment, which are not commissioned for harbour-service, remain in ordinary until sold or taken to pieces, a period which is sometimes extended to several years.

(c) The term "Built" has been substituted for "Launched," as being more explicit, and contrasting better with "Purchased." In the preceding Abstracts every ship down this pair of columns formed part of the "Total of Increase," and having, in the generality of cases, been included among the "Ordered to be built" of an antecedent year, became reckoned twice over. To obviate this, a double line now excludes the built ships from the increase; and the increase-total, without any other deduction than the decrease-total may require, proves the grand total. For instance, the grand total of N, by the former method, must have been produced thus: 15 | 26032 (the corresponding total in No. 10 Abstract) +3 | 5168 = 18 | 31200—1 | 1743 = 17 | 29457, instead of by simply adding the 2 | 3425.

(d) The " &c." includes ships converted to sheer-hulks, breakwaters, and similar uses.

(e) The correction of a mistake of 50 tons in one ship (the Cornwallis, see note W* in the preceding page), occasions this total to exceed by that amount the corresponding total in the preceding Abstract.

(f) See last note.

(g) This division of the *armées en flûte* into "Troop-ships" and "Store-ships" tends to simplify the arrangement, but it was not adopted in the official register until a much later period. There, as elsewhere observed, the reduced ships, with few exceptions, ranked, until very recently, along with their full-armed classmates. The lower columns of the first compartment are now no longer in blank, the substituted term at the top admitting all ships fitted or about to be fitted " for sea-service."

(h) The addition of the deficient unit remarked upon in notes * to Nos. 9 and 10 Abstracts, appears in the excess of this total over its corresponding one in the latter.

(i) This is merely a separation from various other classes of such stationary ships as are so registered in the official list, and might have been made a class from the first. In strictness, the three commissioned harbour-service ships at T, T, and W, and all others, which may appear in that column throughout the series, ought to belong to it: but, as the official list continues them in their original classes, we have done the same.

(k) The "Small Yachts," with the exception of the Medina, not being commanded by naval officers, this class has been reduced; and the one next above it, now including the Medina, will henceforward be denominated "Royal Yachts."

(l) This being a year of peace, no hired vessels were attached to the navy. As to the grand total of " Tons," see notes e, f, and h.

NOTES TO ABSTRACT, No. 12.

(a) It was remarked in note ‡ to No. 2 Abstract, that "captured vessels are also purchased from the captors before they can enter the service." The union of these two columns under the head of "Purchased," subject to the distinction pointed out, claims a preference, therefore, over the plan adopted in the preceding Abstracts. The names of the ships in the second column will, without the exception formerly requisite, be found in the proper list in the work; and where, among the vessels in the first column, a purchased British merchantman rates above a gun-brig, the circumstance will be adverted to in a note.

(*b*) Late the Brave, French privateer; presented by the merchants of Barbadoes to the British government, and on that account named Barbadoes.

(*c*) These had been British merchant-vessels.

(*d*) Also these.

(*e*) The Scorpion; built from the draught of the Cruiser. See vol. ii., p. 482, note *Y**. The four British-built vessels, exclusive of these, in the "Sea-service" total, are the remnant of eight, built of fir in 1795, measuring about 369 tons each, and now nearly worn out. Considering the fine qualities of the Cruiser, it is rather surprising that, during six years, three vessels only should have been built from her draught. These were launched in 1798, and were not brig, but ship rigged: consequently they belong to class *S*. The Osprey, Snake, and Victor, were, however, found fault with as ships; and all others from the same draught were thenceforward constructed as brigs. As a man-of-war, a ship has a decided advantage, in action, over a brig. A ship will lie to more closely, and, if she loses her mizenmast or spanker, has still a trysail on the mainmast; whereas, the moment a brig has her gaff or main-boom shot away, she loses the use of her boom mainsail, and is no longer manageable. It may, however, be said on the behalf of brig-rigged vessels, that many of their apparent faults arise from an improper mode of handling them.

(*f*) These, also, had been British merchant-vessels.

(*g*) The hired vessels numbered about 34

NOTES TO ABSTRACT, No. 13.

(*a*) THE Hibernia; ordered in 1790, and intended to be of the same tonnage as the Ville-de-Paris, but afterwards lengthened eleven feet. Began building November, 1792; launched November 17, 1804.

(*b*) The Namur; reduced from a 90 to a 74 gun ship, under the direction of Mr. Robert Seppings, the master builder at Chatham. It having occurred to the philosophic mind of this ingenious architect, that, by not removing the solid bow in the wake of the second deck, in order to substitute the usual flimsy fabric, called the beak-head, the ship would acquire additional strength in that part of her frame, as well as afford some protection to her crew when going end-on upon an enemy, the circular bow of the Namur was allowed to remain. The advantages of this important alteration struck every one who saw the ship when finished; and subsequently, as we shall hereafter have occasion more fully to relate, every ship in the British navy was ordered to be constructed with a solid circular bow instead of a beak-head.

(*c*) Had been Indiamen, and were built of teak.

(*d*) The same.

(*e*) The two latest-built frigates of this class were launched in 1786, the Aquilon of 724, and the Thames of 656 tons. As the ships in general were a full third smaller than those of any French frigate class, the class was considered not worth keeping up until the year 1804, when some newly-discovered properties in the Thames at her breaking up caused seven frigates to be laid down from her draught, one of old oak and named after herself, the remainder of fir. This was at a time, too, when scarcely a single 12-pounder frigate belonged to the French or any foreign navy. Frigates carrying 18-pounders were justly preferred, and, with the French in particular, were rapidly increasing in number.

(*f*) Had been a British merchant-vessel; and so had every one of the 13 ships next below her in the same column.

(*g*) This will exemplify the exception to the generality of cases adverted to in note *c* to No. 11 Abstract. According to the method adopted previously to the date of the latter, 41 built or launched gun-brigs would have been separated from the 48 at *b*, and the difference, 7, have become the apparent number that had been ordered to be built. No deduction would here have been requisite towards proving the grand total: at the same time the true number ordered could only be obtained by noticing that none had been left as building in the preceding Abstract. For a case in point a reference may be made to the same class in Abstracts No. 10 and 9. Now, the "Ordered" column shows, at one view, and without any operation of figures, the precise number of ships ordered to be built within the year.

(*h*) See last note.

(*i*) These vessels were a disgrace to the British navy. They were built at Bermuda, of the pencil-cedar, measured about 78 tons, mounted four 12-pounder carronades, and were manned with 20 men and boys. In point of force, three of them united were not more than a match for a single gun-boat, as usually armed. Their very appearance as "men-of-war" raised a laugh at the expense of the projector. Many officers refused to take the command of them. Others gave a decided preference to some vessels built at the same yard, to be employed as water-tanks at Jamaica. Moreover, when sent forth to cruise against the enemies of England, to "burn, sink, and destroy" all they met, these "king's schooners" were found to sail wretchedly, and proved so crank and unseaworthy, that almost every one of them that escaped capture went to the bottom with the unfortunate men on board.

(*k*) Number of hired vessels about 140.

END OF VOL. III.

PRINTED BY WILLIAM CLOWES AND SONS, LIMITED, LONDON AND BECCLES.

Milton Keynes UK
Ingram Content Group UK Ltd.
UKHW021839020924
447784UK00006B/106